Two week loan

Please return on or before the last
date stamped below.
Charges are made for late return.

UNIVERSITY OF WALES, CARDIFF, PO BOX 430, CARDIFF CF1 3XT

LF 114/0895

European Community and International Media Law

European Business Law & Practice Series

European Community and International Media Law

David B. Winn

LLB (Exon) Solicitor of the Supreme Court

Graham & Trotman/Martinus Nijhoff
Members of the Kluwer Academic Publishers Group
LONDON/DORDRECHT/BOSTON

Graham & Trotman Limited
Sterling House
66 Wilton Road
London SW1V 1DE
UK

Kluwer Academic Publishers Group
101 Philip Drive
Assinippi Park
Norwell, MA 02061
USA

ISBN: 1-85333-760-9
Series ISBN: 1 85333 714 5

© David B. Winn 1994
First published 1994

British Library Cataloguing in Publication Data is available

Library of Congress Cataloging-in-Publication Data

Winn, David B. (David Benjamin)
    European Community and international media law/David B. Winn. p. cm.
        —(European business law & practice series)
    Includes index.
    ISBN 1-85333-760-9
    1. Mass media—Law and legislation—European Economic Community countries.
    I. Title. II. Series: European law library. European business law & practice series.
    KJE6946.W56 1994
    343.409'9—dc20
    [344.0399]   93-36978
                                                                                CIP

Typeset in 10/11 Goudy by Concept Typesetting Ltd., Salisbury, Wiltshire
Printed and bound in Great Britain by Hartnolls Ltd., Bodmin, Cornwall

Contents

Chapter Three: Distinction Between Media Goods and Media Services

Chapter Four: Competition Law

Chapter Five: Fundamental Human Rights and Community Law

Chapter Seven: International Conventions

Chapter Eight: Enforcing Rights in Broadcast and Cable Transmissions

Appendix 3: Treaty Tables   533

Preface

This book seeks to set out the rights of the cultural community—both individuals and industry—a body whose work is perhaps more capable than any other of melting away the barriers forced between people by frontiers. It is for this reason that their role in the establishment of Europe's common trading area has been pre-eminent and their appearance in the jurisprudence frequent.

It is not surprising that, in a Community whose focus has been the creation of a 'Common Market', it is the economic aspects of copyright—in particular the right of remuneration conferred upon the author or other right holder—which has featured in the case law. However, recently, in the *Magill* cases, the Court of First Instance has recognised that the protection of moral rights—rights which safeguard the integrity of a work—is just as essential a function of copyright as is the securing of economic rights. This acknowledgement is not before time. The derogatory treatment of a work, or its misattribution, can be as wounding to the author as the failure to remunerate him properly for his endeavour is unjust. There is still much work to be done at Community level in enshrining these vital rights.

In this reference work I have attempted to combine, on the one hand, an explanation of the concepts for those new to European Community law and the jurisprudence of the European Convention for the Protection of Human Rights and Fundamental Freedoms, with, on the other, a detailed synthesis of principles for the use of practitioners. I hope, however, that this work is also beneficial to those practitioners outside of Europe who need recourse both to the law governing international copyright (and neighbouring rights), and the principles involved in the acquisition of broadcasting rights.

At the time of writing, the Treaty on European Union—under which the Treaty of Rome (the EEC Treaty) has been amended and becomes the EC Treaty—had not yet been ratified. Accordingly, this work retains references to the EEC Treaty and reproduces articles from that Treaty as amended by the Single European Act of 1986. One part of the Treaty needs particular mention. Because of their close connection, the provisions on freedom of establishment and freedom to provide services are often analysed in tandem. Whilst there is inevitably some overlap—individual cases can straddle the two freedoms and subsidiary legislation in the form of Directives often deals with both freedoms in a single instrument—their scope, as defined by the European Court of Justice, differs. Thus, for the sake of clarity and despite the risk of some repetition, they are treated separately within this work. Since it is principally the provisions on services which affect the media industry, and of that industry, broadcasting in particular, a thorough analysis of the scope of Article 59 of the EEC Treaty is given.

I have attempted to state the law as at 1 January 1993, although it has been possible to include some later material. Tables in Appendix 3 are correct as at 1 July 1993.

Use of the masculine pronoun throughout this book should be read as including the feminine.

There are a number of people who have helped bring this work to fruition and who I would like to thank. Fergal Martin of Graham & Trotman has given much kind support assisted by Stephen Honey and Patrizia Signorini. Mark Brierley offered constant encouragement and read and commented upon chapters one to four. Any errors that remain are entirely my own. I am particularly grateful to my parents for their support. Finally, special thanks are due to Martine who always spurred me on.

DBW
London, 1993

Acknowledgments

I am grateful to the following bodies for their permission to reproduce legislation or conventions published or administered by them: the Council of Europe in respect of (i) the European Agreement for the Exchange of Television Films, (ii) the European Agreement on the Protection of Television Broadcasts and (iii) the European Convention on Transfrontier Television; the European Community in respect of EEC legislation; the United Nations Educational, Scientific and Cultural Organisation in respect of the Universal Copyright Convention as revised on 24 July 1971 and the World Intellectual Property Organisation in respect of (i) the Berne Convention for the Protection of Literary and Artistic Works (Paris Act), (ii) the International Convention for the Protection of Performers, Producers of Phonograms and Broadcasting Organisations, (iii) the Convention for the Protection of Producers of Phonograms Against Unauthorised Duplication of Their Phonograms and (iv) the Convention relating to the Distribution of Programme-carrying Signals Transmitted by Satellite.

Table of Cases and Decisions

EUROPEAN COMMUNITY

European Court of Justice

European Court of First Instance

Commission Decisions

COUNCIL OF EUROPE—EUROPEAN CONVENTION
FOR THE PROTECTION OF HUMAN RIGHTS AND
FUNDAMENTAL FREEDOMS

European Court of Human Rights

European Commission of Human Rights

CHAPTER ONE

Relationship Between Community Freedoms and National Laws

I. Intellectual Property Laws

1. Introduction

1.001. Creation of the European Economic Community. The signing and subsequent ratification of the Treaty of Rome (the 'Treaty') brought the European Economic Community (the 'EEC') into being,[1] and the evolution of the 'Common Market' had begun. Scarred by the ravages of war, the founding Member States sought to 'lay the foundations of an ever closer union amongst the peoples of Europe' and to this end constructed a trading block.[2] The framers of the Treaty wished to create a vast area, comprising their combined territories, within whose boundaries goods, persons, services and capital could move freely.[3]

Barriers on the trading of goods were perhaps the most visible obstacles to be dismantled and the early part of the Treaty is devoted to that task. Specifically,

---

[1] The EEC Treaty (now the EC Treaty) entered into force on 1 January 1958. The European Community (which the European Economic Community has become since the passage of the Treaty on European Union) is only one of three communities which compose the European Communities, the two others being the European Coal and Steel Community and the European Atomic Energy Community. On the concept of the European Communities, see D Lasok and J W Bridge, *Law and Institutions of the European Communities,* (5th Edn, 1991), Chapter 2.

[2] EEC Treaty, Preamble.

[3] P J G Kapteyn and P VerLoren van Themaat, Ed. Gormley, *Introduction to the Law of the European Communities,* (2nd Edn, 1989), Chapter 3, 3.4, define a Common Market as '. . . a market in which every participant within the Community in question is free to invest, produce, work, buy and sell, to supply or obtain services under conditions of competition which have not been artificially distorted wherever economic conditions are most favourable'. By 1986, the Common Market had still not been fully fashioned and the Member States entered into the Single European Act in which they agreed to progressively establish the so called 'internal market' over a period expiring on 31 December 1992. (See Article 8A of the EEC Treaty as amended by the 1986 Single European Act).

Article 9 et seq. is concerned with the setting up of a customs union. However, customs were only one barrier and all obstacles had to be shattered. Articles 30 to 37 of the Treaty[4] were framed to break down those other barriers. These are what the Treaty terms 'quantitative restrictions' and 'measures having equivalent effect'. Article 30 states:

> Quantitative restrictions on imports and all measures having equivalent effect shall, without prejudice to the following provisions, be prohibited between Member States.[5]

1.002. Preservation of intellectual property. All Member States have evolved laws which bestow on society's creators and inventors certain monopoly rights.[6] The conception of these laws—known generically either as 'intellectual' or 'industrial' property laws—happened during an era long before the EEC and the concept of a Common Market came into being. Consequently, their frame of reference is the national territory and they usually confer upon their beneficiaries, be they creators or inventors, the exclusive right to reproduce and market their works within the boundaries of the national territory.

Whilst many laws were to be abolished in pursuit of the Common Market, the Member States did not, in general, want to undermine their property laws. They stated so clearly in Article 222:

> This Treaty shall in no way prejudice the rules in Member States governing the system of property ownership.

But more specifically, the framers of the Treaty sought to protect their intellectual property laws. For they incorporated Article 36 into the Treaty. That article permits a derogation from the rules guaranteeing the free movement of goods, if necessary for the 'protection of industrial and commercial property.[7]

2. The Distinction between the Existence and Exercise of Rights

1.003. The balancing exercise—Article 30 versus Articles 36 and 222. If an owner of intellectual property rights could assert Articles 36 and 222 and invoke national intellectual property laws granting him the exclusive right to exploit his work, he could achieve absolute control over the marketing of his products in the Community. He might, for example grant an exclusive licence in one Member State and forbid the exporting of licensed products into another Member State greeting any infraction with an infringement action. And in such circumstances, the trade barriers

---

[4] Part Two, Title I, Chapter 2.

[5] Article 34 prohibits quantitative restrictions on exports and any measures having equivalent effect. For an analysis of measures which are in breach of Article 30, see §1.063 below.

[6] On the intellectual property laws of the United Kingdom, see generally W Cornish, *Intellectual Property*, (2nd Edn, 1989).

[7] Article 36 states: 'The provisions of Arts. 30 to 34 shall not preclude prohibitions or restrictions on imports, exports or goods in transit justified on grounds of public morality, public policy or public security; the protection of health and life of humans, animals or plants; the protection of national treasures possessing artistic, historic or archaeological value; or the protection of industrial and commercial property. Such prohibitions or restrictions shall not, however, constitute a means of arbitrary discrimination or a disguised restriction on trade between Member States.'

which the Treaty seeks to melt away would not disappear, but would, on the contrary, be strengthened.[8] Indeed, many rights owners have tried this tactic.

In principle, there is a simple, legislative means of foiling such behaviour: all national intellectual property laws could be replaced with a unified system covering the entire Community thus treating the Common Market as a single territory.[9] But that is an ambitious solution which would require many years, if not decades, to fulfil. In its absence, the Court has deftly circumvented attempts to sabotage the Treaty's goal of creating a 'Common Market', by fashioning a fundamental principle, namely, the distinction between the 'existence' and the 'exercise' of intellectual property rights.

1.004. The meaning of the distinction between the existence and exercise of intellectual property rights. The Court states that it does not govern the 'existence' of intellectual property laws but only the 'exercise' of those laws.[10] In plain words, this might be put in the following way: the mere ownership or grant of intellectual property is permitted, but how it is exploited may be condemned or controlled. When the Court proclaims that it does not govern the 'existence' of intellectual property, it means that it leaves untouched rights which it considers reflect the essence or fundamental purpose of intellectual property laws.[11] The Court employs more arcane language. It describes these elements as rights which constitute the 'specific subject matter' of intellectual property.[12] So, if an owner exploits non-essential rights, this constitutes an unlawful 'exercise' of that particular form of intellectual property. The main advantage of the 'specific subject matter' formula is that it allows subtle distinctions to be made depending on the type of intellectual property in issue.[13]

1.005. Article 36—general principles. Generally, Article 36 is interpreted in the light of the ideals expressed by Articles 2 and 3 of the Treaty.[14] Because Article 36 is an exception to the fundamental provisions of the Treaty it is interpreted strictly by the Court.[15] Thus the Court has refused to include within it the safeguarding of consumers' interests or the protection of creativity and cultural diversity.[16] Furthermore, it may only fulfil temporary role: if the Community has taken measures to harmonize the particular national laws which the Court of Justice has hitherto

---

[8] See e.g. the Court of Justice's appraisal of this problem in Case 24/67 Parke, Davis & Co Probel [1968] ECR 55, [1968] CMLR 47 and the Opinion of Advocate General Jacobs in Case C—10/89 CNL-Sucal NV SA v. Hag GF AG [1990] ECR 3711, [1990] 2 CMLR 571.

[9] See the Court of Justice's remarks in Case 24/67 Parke, Davis & Co v. Probel [1968] ECR 55, [1968] CMLR 47.

[10] Joined Cases 56, 58/64, Établissements Consten SARL and Grundig-Verkaufs-GmbH v. EEC Commission [1966] ECR 299, [1966] CMLR 418 and Case 78/70 Deutsche Grammophon Gesellschaft mbH v. Metro-SB-Grossmärkte GmbH & Co KG [1971] ECR 487, [1971] CMLR 631.

[11] Whether they are copyright, trademark, design or patent laws. See Case 78/70 Deutsche Grammophon Gesellschaft mbH v. Metro-SB-Grossmärkte GmbH & Co KG [1971] ECR 487, [1971] CMLR 631, per Advocate General Roemer and Case 270/80 Polydor Ltd v. Harlequin Record Shops Ltd [1982] ECR 329, [1982] 1 CMLR 677, per Advocate General Rozès.

[12] Case 78/70 Deutsche Grammophon Gesellschaft mbH v. Metro-SB-Grossmärkte GmbH & Co KG [1971] ECR 487, [1971] CMLR 631.

[13] Case C—10/89 CNL-Sucal NV SA v. Hag GF AG [1990] ECR 3711, [1990] 3 CMLR 571, per Advocate General Jacobs.

[14] Case 270/80 Polydor Ltd v. Harlequin Record Shops Ltd [1982] ECR 329, [1982] 1 CMLR 677.

[15] Case 229/83 Association des Centres Distributeurs Edouard Leclerc v. Au Blé Vert Sàrl [1985] ECR 1, [1985] 2 CMLR 286.

[16] Ibid. and Case 95/84 Boriello v. Darras [1986] ECR 2253 ie as opposed to intellectual property rights falling within the term 'industrial and commercial property'.

recognised as deserving of its protection, Article 36 must yield to those new laws.[17] Finally, Article 36 is subject to the express proviso that any prohibitions or restrictions shielded behind it 'cannot constitute a means of arbitrary discrimination or a disguised restriction on trade between Member States'.[18] Thus any law (and the conduct it sanctions) seeking protection by Article 36 must satisfy a proportionality test.[19]

3. Exhaustion of Intellectual Property Rights

1.006. To determine whether intellectual property laws are being 'exercised' in contravention of Article 30 to impede the free movement of goods through the Community, the Court has evolved a doctrine of 'exhaustion' of rights. According to this doctrine, the owner of intellectual property has the exclusive right to put his product on the Community's market for the first time or determine who else may do so, so as to allow him to obtain the reward for his creative labour: this constitutes the 'specific subject matter' of those rights.[20] But with that single payment the proprietor's right to a reward becomes exhausted. And he may not rely upon national legislation to prevent that product being imported into another Member State, for this would amount to 'exercising' his intellectual property unlawfully.[21]

---

[17] Case 35/76 *Simmenthal SpA v. Italian Minister for Finance* [1976] ECR 1871, [1977] 2 CMLR 1; Case 144/81 *Keurkoop BV v. Nancy Kean Gifts BV* [1982] ECR 2853, [1983] 2 CMLR 47; Case 341/87 *EMI Electrola GmbH v. Patricia Im- und Export* [1989] ECR 79, [1989] 2 CMLR 413; Case T—69/89 *Radio Telefís Eireann v. EC Commission* [1991] 4 CMLR 586; Case T—70/89 *The British Broadcasting Corporation and BBC Enterprises Ltd v. EC Commission* [1991] 4 CMLR 669; Case T—76/89 *Independent Television Publications Ltd v. EC Commission* [1991] 4 CMLR 745. Harmonisation Directives are issued pursuant to Article 100 of the Treaty. See §1.056 et seq which sets out those laws which have been harmonised. As for the extent to which Article 100A(4) of the Treaty (introduced by the Single European Act) may allow Member States to justify under Article 36, a derogation from a Harmonising Directive, see Kapteyn and VerLoren van Themaat, *op. cit.*, Chapter 7, 3.3.

[18] Article 36, second sentence. For an example of the operation of this proviso, see §1.026 below.

[19] Case 144/81 *Keurkoop BV v. Nancy Kean Gifts BV* [1982] ECR 2853, [1983] 2 CMLR 47; Case 341/87 *EMI Electrola v. Patricia Im. Und Export* [1989] ECR 79, [1989] 2 CMLR 413; Case T—69/89 *Radio Telefís Eireann v. EC Commission* [1991] 4 CMLR 586; Case T—70/89 *The British Broadcasting Corporation and BBC Enterprises Ltd v. EC Commission* [1991] 4 CMLR 669; Case T—76/89 *Independent Television Publications Ltd v. EC Commission* [1991] 4 CMLR 745.

[20] Case 78/70 *Deutsche Grammophon Gesellschaft mbH v. Metro-SB-Grossmärkte GmbH & Co KG* [1971] ECR 487, [1971] CMLR 631, per Advocate General Roemer; Case 270/80 *Polydor Ltd v. Harlequin Record Shops Ltd* [1982] ECR 329, [1982] 1 CMLR 677, per Advocate General Rozés and Case 341/87 *EMI Electrola v. Patricia Im- Und Export* [1989] ECR 79, [1989] 2 CMLR 413, per Advocate General Darmon. This principle is firmly rooted in the Court's jurisprudence finding its application to all forms of intellectual property. See e.g. in the case of patents Case 15/74 *Centrafarm BV v. Sterling Drug Inc* [1974] ECR 1147, [1974] 2 CMLR 480. In Case 27/87 *Louis Erauw-Jacquery Sprl v. La Hesbignonne Société Coopérative* [1988] ECR 1919 [1988] 4 CMLR 576, a case concerning plant breeder's rights, the Court of Justice sanctioned an absolute ban on the licensee exporting so called 'basic seeds'. A basic seed is to a plant breeder, what copyright is to an author or a patent is to an inventor. Therefore, the Court gave the plant breeder the right to put his product on the Community's market for the first time or determine who else could do so.

[21] Case 78/70 *Deutsche Grammophon Gesellschaft mbH v. Metro-SB-Grossmärkte GmbH & Co KG* [1971] ECR 487, [1971] CMLR 631; Joined Cases 55, 57/80 *Musik-Vertrieb membran GmbH v. GEMA* [1981] ECR 147, [1981] 2 CMLR 44; Case 270/80 *Polydor Ltd v. Harlequin Record Shops Ltd* [1982] ECR 329, [1982] 1 CMLR 677; Case 341/87 *EMI Electrola v. Patricia Im- und Export* [1989] ECR 79, [1989] 2 CMLR 413, per Advocate General Darmon; Case 395/87 *Ministère Public v. Tournier* [1989] ECR 2521, [1991] 4 CMLR 248.

Thus, the Court employs a mélange of the 'existence/exercise' and the 'exhaustion' principle to decide if Article 36 can be invoked.

4. Copyright and the EEC Treaty

1.007. Distinction between authors' rights and neighbouring rights. In the media industry, intellectual property laws are usually copyright, although certain legal regimes, namely the droit d'auteur systems, have distinguished copyright from so called 'neighbouring rights'.[22] Copyright proper attaches to the work of authors ie to their literary, musical and artistic works. Neighbouring rights are, as their name suggests, one step removed from copyright. They belong to persons who exploit (and interpret) copyright works. Thus a performer or phonogram producer are owners of rights neighbouring copyright in their performances and phonograms respectively. Terminology apart, copyright and neighbouring rights resemble each other because they usually confer exclusive rights on their owners ie the legal regimes of most Member States grant to the author the exclusive right to reproduce his work[23] or give to the phonogram manufacturer the exclusive right to reproduce copies of his phonograms.

1.008. Copyright as 'industrial and commercial property'. The term 'industrial... property', contained in Article 36 of the Treaty, clearly has a technological connotation: it was probably designed to cover patents and trademarks. So it is not surprising that the Court of Justice, in *Deutsche Grammophon Gesellschaft mbH v. Metro-SB Grossmärkte GmbH & Co KG*,[24] found little difficulty in holding that a phonogram manufacturer's right of reproduction[25]— a right of an organisation to authorise a technical process—was encompassed by the term. However, it is not certain that the framers of the Treaty had personal rights, such as those of authors, in the forefront of their minds when they drafted Article 36.[26] Be that as it may, any speculation must now be consigned to the history books, for the Court of Justice has recognised that the preservation of copyright under Article 36 is vital if the Community's culture is to be nurtured. For it is both a just recompense and a spur to creativity.[27] Thus in *Musik-Vertrieb membran GmbH v. GEMA*,[28] the Court of Justice rejected an argument that copyright was entirely personal and outside of the

---

[22] On the evolution of neighbouring rights, see H Cohen Jehoram, 'The Relationship between Copyright and Neighbouring Rights' RIDA [1990] 144, 80.

[23] For a comparative study on European Community copyright laws, see Dietz, *Copyright Law in the European Community* (1978).

[24] Case 78/70 [1971] ECR 487, [1971] CMLR 631.

[25] ie a neighbouring right in the sense in which it is used in the droit d'auteur systems.

[26] The provisions which seek to preserve property laws. See, in particular the discussion in, H Johannes, *Industrial Property and Copyright in European Community Law*, (1976), Part VI, 3.b, citing Gotzen Jnr, *Artistieke Eigendom en Mededingingsregels van de Europese Economische Gemeenschap*, (1971).

[27] Historically, the droit d'auteur systems have seen the droit d'auteur as an author's natural right flowing from the mere creation of a work. For the common law systems copyright is perceived as a necessary reward, without which an author might be less inclined to invest his labour either in the act of creation or the exploitation of his work. This distinction has become blurred with the passage of time. See §7.102 fn 300 below.

[28] Joined Cases 55, 57/80 [1981] ECR 147, [1981] 2 CMLR 44, para. 12.

scope of 'industrial and commercial property' simply because it protected, amongst other things, the moral rights of an author. The Court held:

> It is true that copyright comprises moral rights . . . However, it also comprises other rights, notably the right to exploit commercially the marketing of the protected work, particularly in the form of licences granted in return for payment of royalties. It is this economic aspect of copyright which is the subject of the question submitted by the national court, and, in this regard, in the application of Article 36 of the Treaty there is no reason to make a distinction between copyright and other industrial and commercial property rights.[29]

The Court of Justice tends now to assimilate neighbouring rights to authors' rights under the single term 'copyright' and for the purposes of this chapter, they are generally so treated.

1.009. The specific subject matter of copyright. The Court has defined the specific subject matter of copyright to include:

(1) the exclusive right of the proprietor to authorise the reproduction and initial distribution of his work;[30]

(2) the exclusive right of the proprietor to authorise performances of his work;[31]

(3) the right of the proprietor of copyright in a film to prevent a television broadcast of the film until it has been exhibited in cinemas for a certain period of time;[32]

(4) the exclusive right of the proprietor to authorise the hiring out of his work to the public;[33]

---

[29] See also Case 262/81 *Coditel SA v. Ciné Vog Films SA* [1982] ECR 3381, [1983] 1 CMLR 49, para. 10 where the Court of Justice stated that Article 36 covers 'literary and artistic property including copyright' and Case 341/87 *EMI Electrola GmbH v. Patricia Im- und Export* [1989] ECR 79, [1989] 2 CMLR 413, para. 8 where the Court of Justice stated that Article 36 'covers literary and artistic property including copyright, to the extent in particular that it is commercially exploited. Consequently, it includes the protection of exclusive reproduction and distribution rights in sound recordings, which, under the applicable national legislation, is assimilated to copyright protection'. In fact, the Court of Justice has acknowledged that moral rights may be protected by Article 36, see §1.009 fn 36 below.

[30] Case 78/70 *Deutsche Grammophon Gesellschaft mbH v. Metro-SB-Grossmärkte GmbH & Co KG* [1971] ECR 487, [1971] CMLR 631 (phonogram producer—sound recordings on vinyl disc); Joined Cases 55, 57/80 *Musik-Vertrieb membran GmbH v. GEMA* [1981] ECR 147, [1981] 2 CMLR 44 (collecting society—sound recordings on vinyl disc); Case 270/80 *Polydor Ltd v. Harlequin Record Shops Ltd* [1982] ECR 329, [1982] 1 CMLR 677 (phonogram producer—sound recordings on vinyl disc); Case 158/86 *Warner Brothers Inc v. Christiansen* [1988] ECR 2605, [1990] 3 CMLR 684, (film producer—recordings of cinematographic works ie video-recordings); Case 341/87 *EMI Electrola v. Patricia Im- und Export* [1989] ECR 79, [1989] 2 CMLR 413 (phonogram producer—sound recordings on vinyl disc).

[31] Case 62/79 *Compagnie Générale pour la Diffusion de la Télévision, Coditel SA v. Ciné Vog Films SA* [1980] ECR 881, [1981] 2 CMLR 362 (broadcasting organisation—film broadcast on television); Case 262/81 *Coditel SA v. Ciné Vog Films SA* [1982] ECR 3381, [1983] 1 CMLR 49 (broadcasting organisation—film broadcast on television): Case 402/85 *Basset v. SACEM* [1987] ECR 1747, [1987] 3 CMLR 173 (collecting society—sound recordings on vinyl disc); Case 158/86 *Warner Brothers Inc v. Christiansen* [1988] ECR 2605, [1990] 3 CMLR 684 (film producer—cinematographic work); Case 395/87 *Ministère Public v. Tournier* [1989] ECR 2521, [1991] 4 CMLR 248 (collecting society—sound recordings on vinyl disc).

[32] Case 62/79 *Compagnie Générale pour la Diffusion de la Télévision, Coditel SA v. Ciné Vog Films SA* [1980] ECR 881, [1981] 2 CMLR 362 affirmed in Case 262/81 *Coditel SA v. Ciné Vog Films SA* [1982] ECR 3381, [1983] 1 CMLR 49.

[33] Case 158/86 *Warner Brothers Inc v. Christiansen* [1988] ECR 2605, [1990] 3 CMLR 684, (film producer—recordings of cinematographic works ie video-recordings).

(5) conditions, detailed rules and procedures under which protection is granted;[34]
(6) the duration of protection;[35]
(7) moral rights.[36]

5. Free Movement of Goods and Services

(1) Copyright Goods in Circulation in the Community's Market

(i) Musical Recordings

1.010. Reserving an exclusive territory. Often an undertaking will reserve for itself or confer upon another undertaking in a territory within the Community, the exclusive right to manufacture and distribute a product protected by copyright. The question arises whether that undertaking (or its assignee) has the right to prevent goods protected by the same copyright and marketed elsewhere in the Community by another licensee, being imported into its territory.

The first case to consider the effect of copyright on the free movement of goods was *Deutsche Grammophon GmbH v. Metro-SB Grossmärkte & Co KG*.[37] Deutsche Grammophon operated a wholly owned subsidiary company in France to which it sold records for distribution to the French retail trade. A German chain of retail shops called Metro obtained, via a wholesaler, the records put on the market in France by Deutsche Grammophon. Metro then sold those records in the Federal Republic of Germany. Deutsche Grammophon had reserved the German territory for itself and pointing to Article 36 of the Treaty, asserted its copyright in the recordings. It said that Article 36 gave it exclusive distribution rights and therefore permission to impede Metro's imports. The Court of Justice defeated the argument by applying the 'exhaustion' doctrine. It held that the words 'industrial property' contained in Article 36 did not embrace all national intellectual property rights, merely the essence of those laws; in its language 'rights which constituted the specific subject matter of those laws'.

It understood that copyright was a vital form of intellectual property, so the Court would offer Deutsche Grammophon certain protection: the right to exclusively

---

[34] Case 341/87 *EMI Electrola GmbH v. Patricia Im- und Export* [1989] ECR 79, [1989] 2 CMLR 413 (phonogram producer—sound recordings on vinyl disc, duration of copyright); Case T—69/89 *Radio Telefis Eireann v. EC Commission* [1991] 4 CMLR 586 (broadcasting organisation—copyright in programme details); Case T—70/89 *The British Broadcasting and BBC Enterprises Ltd v. EC Commission* [1991] 4 CMLR 745 (broadcasting company—copyright in programme details); Case T—76/89 *Independent Television Publications Ltd v. EC Commission* [1991] 4 CMLR 745 (broadcasting company—copyright in programme details).

[35] Case 341/87 *EMI Electrola GmbH v. Patricia Im- und Export* [1989] ECR 79, [1989] 2 CMLR 413 (phonogram producer—sound recordings on vinyl disc).

[36] Case T—69/89 *Radio Telefis Eireann v. EC Commission* [1991] 4 CMLR 586, (broadcasting organisation—copyright in programme details); Case T—70/89 *The British Broadcasting and BBC Enterprises Ltd v. EC Commission* [1991] 4 CMLR 745 (broadcasting company—copyright in programme details); Case T—76/89 *Independent Television Publications Ltd v. EC Commission* [1991] 4 CMLR 745 (broadcasting company—copyright in programme details).

[37] Case 78/70 [1971] ECR 487, [1971] CMLR 631.

determine who could manufacture the records and put them on the market for the first time 'since it ensures for the holder the benefit to which he is entitled'.[38] But Deutsche Grammophon could not then assert its copyright to prevent the movement of those records as they were resold throughout the Community. This was because the benefit conferred by Article 36 had been 'exhausted': 'the objective of the industrial property right was attained when the goods were first placed on the market, since it was possible to use the monopolistic opportunity for gain'.[39] The Court affirmed the now well rehearsed concept of the distinction between the 'existence' and the 'exercise' of intellectual property rights. The Court respects the 'existence' of national intellectual property laws but it will strike them down if they are being 'exercised' in a manner offensive to the Treaty. The Court ruled that:

> It is in conflict with the provisions prescribing the free movement of products within the common market for a manufacturer of sound recordings to exercise the exclusive right to distribute the protected articles, conferred upon him by the legislation of a Member State, [ie copyright] in such a way as to prohibit the sale in that State of products placed on the market by him or with his consent in another Member State solely because such distribution did not occur within the territory of the first Member State.

1.011. Claiming additional royalties on importation. In *Musik-Vertrieb membran GmbH v. GEMA*,[40] the Court of Justice ruled that claims for royalties are exhausted once a product is put on the Community's market with the rightholder's consent.[41] GEMA, a German collecting society sued two undertakings who had imported into the Federal Republic of Germany sound recordings on record and cassette protected by copyright there. It was accepted that those recordings had been manufactured and marketed elsewhere in the Community with the consent of the copyright owners through licenses and that the appropriate royalties (calculated on the basis of distribution in the country of manufacture) had been paid. However these royalty rates were less than the copyright owners would have been entitled to in the Federal Republic of Germany and when the products were resold in Germany, GEMA sued for the balance. The Court of Justice rejected the claim stating that the copyright owner's rights had been exhausted and that the exercise of such rights in this manner constituted a breach of Article 30 unprotected by Article 36. It held that:

> It should further be observed that in a common market distinguished by free movement of goods and freedom to provide services, an author, acting directly or through his publisher, is free to choose the place, in any of the Member States, in which to put his work into circulation. He may make that choice according to his best interests, which involve not only the level of the remuneration provided in the Member State in question but other factors such as, for example, the opportunities for distributing his work and the marketing facilities which are further enhanced by virtue of the free movement of goods within the Community. In those circumstances, a copyright management society may not be permitted to claim, on the importation of sound

---

[38] Per Advocate General Roemer.
[39] *Ibid.*
[40] Joined Cases 55, 57/80 [1981] ECR 147, [1981] 2 CMLR 44.
[41] Note, however, that 'performance' royalties are never exhausted. See §1.035 et seq. below.

recordings into another Member State, payment of additional fees based on the difference in the rates of remuneration existing in the various Member States.[42]

(ii) Literary Works

1.012. The preceding cases concerned copyright in recordings but it is most likely that the same principles will be applied by the Court to literary works (ie books) protected by copyright. In fact, the Commission has taken this approach. Thus it required Ernest Benn Ltd, a United Kingdom publisher, to delete a note in its catalogue describing a particular book as not for export to the Federal Republic of Germany. The company had entrusted distribution of that same title in Germany to a separate firm. The Commission stated:

> ... the Commission's general view is that once a copy of a book has been sold by or with the consent of the copyright owner in one Member State, that copy must be free to move throughout the EEC in the same way as patented or trademarked goods.[43]

(2) Trademark Goods in circulation in the Community's Market

(i) General Principles

1.013. Specific subject matter of a trademark. Looked at from the point of view of the consumer, the function of a trademark is to guarantee the origin of the product to which it is attached. In other words, it confers a pedigree on that product. From the manufacturer's vantage point, the trademark's function is to win purchasers by its guarantee of pedigree and a manufacturer may have spent substantial sums of money carving out the image of his product.[44]

With these notions in mind, the Court of Justice has spelled out the 'specific subject matter' of a trademark thus:

> ... the specific subject-matter of trade marks, is in particular to guarantee to the proprietor of the trade mark that he has the right to use that trade mark for the purpose of putting a product into circulation for the first time and therefore to protect him against competitors wishing to take advantage of the status and reputation of the trade mark by selling products illegally bearing that mark. In order to determine the exact scope of this right exclusively conferred on the owner of the trade mark regard must be had to the essential function of the trade mark, which is to guarantee the identity of the origin of the marked product to the consumer or ultimate user by enabling him without any possibility of confusion to distinguish that product from products which have another origin.[45]

1.014. Reserving an exclusive territory. *Dansk Supermarked A/S v. Imerco A/S*[46] demonstrates the free movement rules as they apply to a product protected by a

---

[42] [1981] ECR 147, [1981] 2 CMLR 44, para. 25, affirmed in Case 395/87 *Ministère Public v. Tournier* [1989] ECR 2521, [1991] 4 CMLR 248.

[43] Commission, Ninth Report on Competition Policy (1979), point 118.

[44] Case 58/80 [1981] ECR 181, [1981] 3 CMLR 590.

[45] *Ibid.*

[46] See, in particular, the Opinion of Advocate General Mayras in Case 119/75 *Terrapin (Overseas) Ltd v. Terranova Industrie CA Kapferer & Co* [1976] ECR 1039, [1976] 2 CMLR 482.

trademark (as well as copyright). The facts were as follows. The Respondents had commissioned a British undertaking to manufacture china bearing their tradename as well as several designs, for exclusive distribution by the Respondent's group of companies. A proportion of the final product was substandard and it was agreed that these could be marketed by the manufacturer in the UK. However, under no circumstance were these 'seconds' to be distributed in Denmark. The Appellants purchased substantial quantities of the 'seconds' in the United Kingdom which they then imported into Denmark and sold at a lower price than the china sold by the Respondents. The respondents issued proceedings to prevent the Applicant distributing the 'seconds', asserting their copyright and trademark rights. On a reference from the Danish Appeal Court, the Court of Justice stated that the Respondent's actions had been unlawful because their intellectual property rights had been exhausted. It held:

> Articles 30 and 36 of the EEC Treaty must be interpreted to mean that the judicial authorities of a Member State may not prohibit, on the basis of a copyright or of a trademark, the marketing on the territory of that State of a product to which one of those rights applies if that product has been lawfully marketed on the territory of another Member State by the proprietor of such rights or with his consent.[47]

(ii) Where there are Confusingly Similar Trademarks Registered in different Member States

1.015. *Dansk Supermarked A/S v. Imerco A/S,* the aforementioned case, is concerned with the traditional scenario in which the proprietor of a trademark owns rights in his trademark in both the exporting and importing Member State. But often manufacturers of goods in separate Member States will independently develop a business and trademark which are similar to each other. Each has registered the trademark in their respective State but may wish to market their goods in the other's territory. Are they entitled to do so?

Terrapin (Overseas) Ltd v. Terranova Industrie CA Kapferer and Co,[48] concerned two confusingly similar marks. The Appellant's request for registration of its mark in the Federal Republic of Germany had been refused because the registrar considered it to be confusingly similar to the Respondent's mark, already registered. Nevertheless, the Appellant marketed its goods in the German territory and the Respondent took action to prevent it doing so. On an Article 177 reference, the Court of Justice ruled—bearing in mind the 'specific subject matter' of the right— that Article 36 gave the owner of the trademark the absolute right to market products bearing his mark in the Member State in which it was registered:

> It is compatible with the provisions of the EEC Treaty relating to the free movement of goods for an undertaking established in a Member State, by virtue of a right to a trademark and a right to a commercial name which are protected by the legislation of that state, to prevent the importation of products of an undertaking established in another Member State and bearing by virtue of the legislation of that State a name giving rise

---

[47] Case C—10/89 *CNL-Sucal NV SA v. Hag GF AG* [1990] ECR 3711, [1990] 3 CMLR 571. See also Case 3/78 *Centrafarm BV v. American Home Products Corp* [1978] ECR 1823, [1979] 1 CMLR 326 and Case 102/77 *Hoffmann-La Roche & Co AG v. Centrafarm Vertriebsgesellschaft Pharmazeutischer Erzeugnisse mbH* [1978] ECR 1139, [1978] 3 CMLR 217.

[48] Case 119/75 [1976] ECR 1039, [1976] 2 CMLR 482.

to confusion with the trade-mark and commercial name of the first undertaking provided that there are no agreements restricting competition and no legal or economic ties between the undertakings. . . [49]

In cases where a single undertaking has registered similar marks in different Member States with the intention of partitioning the Common Market, the Court of Justice has sanctioned the 'repackaging' (by third parties) of goods to which those marks have been affixed.[50]

(3) Direct Sales into a Licensee's Territory

1.016. Introduction. The exhaustion doctrine holds that once a product is lawfully marketed with the rightholder's consent in a Member State, its importation into other Member States cannot be impeded.[51] But a licensee in one territory might try to penetrate another licensed territory by directly selling the licensed product there. The question arises whether the exhaustion doctrine prevents him doing so.

1.017. Goods protected by copyright. The Commission has interpreted the concept of 'previous lawful marketing' tendentiously by deciding that it was unlawful for a collecting society to oppose cross-frontier deliveries of recordings between companies belonging to the same group. The Commission held that the records were in free circulation and hence the distribution rights had been exhausted, by the mere supply of the recordings by the manufacturers to the retailers.[52] The Court has not yet ruled on this issue but the Commission's reasoning has been doubted.[53]

1.018. Goods protected by a trademark. There are no Commission Decisions or Court cases concerning trademarks. The comments made above,[54] however, are equally applicable to trademarks.

---

[49] See also the principles which the Court of Justice has developed in respect of design rights (deemed to be included within the concept of Article 36) in Case 144/81 *Keurkoop BV v. Nancy Kean Gifts BV* [1982] ECR 2853, [1983] 2 CMLR 47. On the registration of trademarks, see First Council Directive 89/104/EEC of 21 December 1988 to approximate the laws of the Member States relating to trademarks, OJ No L 40, 11.2.89, p.1.

[50] Case 102/77 *Hoffmann-La Roche & Co AG v. Centrafarm Vertriebsgesellschaft Pharmazeutischer Erzeugnisse mbH* [1978] ECR 1139, [1978] 3 CMLR 217 and Case 3/78 *Centrafarm BV v. American Home Products Corp* [1978] ECR 1823, [1979] 1 CMLR 326. On repackaging of trademark goods, see generally, C W Bellamy and G D Child, *Common Market Law of Competition* (3rd Edn, 1987), 7-030.

[51] Joined Cases 55, 57/80 *Musik-Vertrieb membran GmbH v. GEMA* [1981] ECR 147, [1981] 2 CMLR 44 and Case 395/87 *Ministère public v. Tournier* [1989] ECR 2521, [1991] 4 CMLR 248. See §1.011 above.

[52] Commission Statement of 9 January 1984, Re Performing Rights Societies [1984] 1 CMLR 308.

[53] See Bellamy and Child, *op. cit.*, 7-021 (n. 79) who have stated that 'The Commission's view must be based on some concept other than "exhaustion of rights" since in the case of direct sales there has been no "previous marketing" to give rise to the requisite "exhaustion" .'

[54] See §1.017 above.

(4) The Importance of 'Consent' to the Doctrine of Exhaustion of Rights

(i) Goods produced under compulsory or statutory licences

1.019. Many Member States, as permitted under international treaties, impose licensing regimes on owners of intellectual property. The free movement issue which typically evolves from such licences, is, whether a copyright owner or assignee in one Member State can impede the importation into that State of products manufactured under an imposed (compulsory or statutory) licence in another Member State.

The case law has hitherto drawn a distinction between two types of imposed licensing regime. The first type is that permitted by the Berne Convention for the Protection of Literary and Artistic Works. It allows member countries to award compulsory licences for the manufacture of musical recordings of works which have already been reproduced with the author's consent.[55] This was the form of licence in issue in *Musik-Vertrieb membran GmbH v. GEMA*.[56] Section 8 of the United Kingdom Copyright Act of 1956 (no longer in force) provided that a manufacturer could manufacture sound recordings of a musical work protected by copyright without infringing the copyright, if the work had already been reproduced in the United Kingdom on a sound recording for the purpose of retail sale by the author himself or with his consent and if, in addition, the manufacturer notified the copyright owner of his intention to make the recording of the work for the purpose of sale and paid him a royalty of 6.25% of the retail selling price of the sound recording. The practical result of this system was that 6.25% was the maximum that any copyright owner could demand for the reproduction of his work, for if he refused, the applicant would be entitled to receive a compulsory licence set at that amount.

The Appellant duly demanded and received consent from the United Kingdom copyright management society to manufacture recordings all of which had been previously released in the United Kingdom by the owners of the copyright. The records were imported into Germany where a higher statutory licence royalty rate was in force and the German copyright management society (the Respondent) tried to claim the difference. The Court of Justice held that the right to put the product on the market for the first time, once vested in that copyright, had been exhausted. The element which proved fatal for the Respondents was that the compulsory licence mechanism was set in motion only after the copyright owner had consented to his recordings being marketed in the United Kingdom.[57]

The scenario explored in *Musik-Vertrieb membran GmbH v. GEMA* must be distinguished from the case where national legislation imposes licences regardless of whether or not the owner of the rights has consented to goods protected by those rights being marketed there prior to the institution of the licence. There is no copyright case which turns upon this particular issue. However, in a case concerning patented goods, *Pharmon BV v. Hoechst AG*,[58] the Court of Justice enshrined principles of general application. It stated that:

---

[55] See Article 13(1) of the Berne Convention for the Protection of Literary and Artistic Works (Paris Act of July 24, 1971, as amended on 2 October 1979). See §7.058 et seq. below.

[56] Joined Cases 55, 57/80 [1981] ECR 147, [1981] 2 CMLR 44.

[57] Although, in fact consent had been granted for the manufacture of the records in dispute, it is clear that the legislation would have flattened any obstruction placed by the copyright owner in the path of an applicant and it is equally clear that the Court made its ruling on this basis.

[58] Case 19/84 *Pharmon BV v. Hoechst AG* [1985] ECR 2281, [1985] 3 CMLR 775, para. 25.

... when the competent authorities in a Member State. . . grant a compulsory licence to a third party which allows him to carry out manufacturing and marketing operations which the patentee would normally have the power to prohibit, the patentee cannot be regarded as having consented to the actions of the third party. In fact, the holder of the patent is deprived by such an official act of his right to decide freely on the conditions under which he will place his product on the market.

The Court thus ruled that:

Articles 30 and 36 of the Treaty do not preclude the application of a law of a Member State which gives the proprietor of a patent the right to prevent the marketing in that State of a product which has been manufactured in another Member State by the holder of a compulsory licence granted under a parallel patent held by the same proprietor.

In that respect, it makes no difference whether a prohibition on exportation is attached to the compulsory licence, whether that licence fixes royalties payable to the patentee or whether the patentee has accepted or refused such royalties.

These principles are encapsulated in Advocate General Mancini's maxim that 'The licensees consent is the key which opens the door of the common market to patented goods.'[59]

The same principles must, it is submitted, apply by analogy to the marketing of copyright goods. In fact, in *EMI Electrola v. Patricia Im- und Export*,[60] a case concerning copyright goods, the Court of Justice[61] approved of the reasoning in *Pharmon BV v. Hoechst AG* and endorsed Advocate General Mancini's dictum.

(ii) Goods Marketed after Expiry of Copyright in a Member State

1.020. In *EMI Electrola v. Patricia Im- und Export*,[62] the Court of Justice emphasised that the element of consent which brings the exhaustion doctrine into operation, is absent where products protected by copyright are released on to the market after the expiry of the term of protection. The facts were as follows.

The Plaintiff owned copyright in recordings by the artist Cliff Richard in the Federal Republic of Germany. The Plaintiff had also owned the copyright in the same recordings in Denmark until 1985 when the recordings fell into the public domain there. The Defendants, two German undertakings, pressed vinyl discs of the Cliff Richard recordings at the request of a Danish undertaking and delivered them to this undertaking in Denmark. The discs were then reimported into the Federal Republic of Germany by the Defendants. The Plaintiffs sued to prevent the distribution of the Danish pressings on the ground that their rights were not exhausted because the Defendants had not sought their consent for the manufacture of the records. The Court of Justice held for the Plaintiffs stating that since the recordings had not been put on the market with their consent, their rights had not been exhausted. It stated:

In so far as the disparity between national laws may give rise to restrictions on intra-Community trade in sound recordings, such restrictions are justified under Article 36 of the Treaty if they are the result of differences between the rule governing the period of protection and this is inseparably linked to the very existence of the exclusive rights.

---

[59] Case 19/84 *Pharmon BV v. Hoechst AG* [1985] ECR 2281, [1985] 3 CMLR 775.
[60] Case 341/87 [1989] ECR 79, [1989] 2 CMLR 413.
[61] Per Advocate General Darmon.
[62] Case 341/87 [1989] ECR 79, [1989] 2 CMLR 413.

The Court therefore ruled that:

Articles 30 and 36 of the EEC Treaty must be interpreted as not precluding the application of a Member State's legislation which allows a producer of sound recordings in that Member State to rely on the exclusive rights to reproduce and distribute certain musical works of which he is the owner in order to prohibit the sale, in the territory of that Member State, of sound recordings of the same musical works when those recordings are imported from another Member State in which they were lawfully marketed without the consent of the aforesaid owner or his licensee and in which the producer of those recordings had enjoyed protection which has in the meantime expired.

1.021. Comment on EMI Electrola GmbH v. Patricia. This case is good example of the subtle interplay between the existence/exercise doctrine, the exhaustion doctrine and the notion of the 'specific subject' of intellectual property rights. The Court states that the duration of copyright is a fundamental element of copyright. In other words, it forms the 'specific subject matter' of copyright and hence relates to the 'existence' of copyright. If it produces barriers to trade, that does not amount to an unlawful 'exercise' of copyright. The exhaustion doctrine gives to the copyright owner, the power to grant or withhold consent to the putting of his product on the market. The expiry of protection in one Member State means that the crucial element of consent is absent, and so rights are not exhausted. In this case, the principles are merged.

(iii) The Doctrine of 'Common Origin'

1.022. Introduction. Intellectual property rights which were once in common ownership may become fragmented in the Community, perhaps for historic reasons outside of the control of the rightholders or on the contrary as a result of an intentional act. Two independent parties may thus end up owning exclusive rights in identical goods in two separate Member States. Both have the right to market their goods in their own Member States but does either have the right to prohibit the import of the other's goods? The Court of Justice has courted a doctrine of 'common origin' which it has now rejected.

1.023. Goods protected by a trademark— historical account. The Court of Justice had ruled in *Van Zuylen Frères v. Hag AG*[63] that where trademarks have a 'common origin', that is, where the right to market the particular goods in issue, originated in a single party but ended up in the ownership of different parties in different Member States, the exhaustion rule applied to goods put on the market by either party. The Defendants, a German company had been the owners of the trademark 'Café Hag' associated with a decaffeinated coffee they had developed. Long before the Second World War they had assigned their mark to a Belgian subsidiary which satisfied the production requirements of the Benelux countries. After the War, the Belgian authorities confiscated the subsidiary on its territory thus taking it out of German hands and placing it in the ownership of a Belgium family, who later transferred it to the Plaintiff. In 1972, the Defendant attempted to penetrate the Belgium market once again by selling coffee bearing the 'Café Hag' mark and proceedings were issued against it. On a reference, the Court of Justice held that the Plaintiff's initial exclusive right to market, in the Community,

---

[63] Case 192/73 [1974] ECR 731, [1974] 2 CMLR 127.

products bearing their mark, had been extinguished. In a terse but revolutionary judgment, the Court of Justice stated that:

> The exercise of a trademark right tends to contribute to the partitioning off of the markets and thus to affect the free movement of goods between Member States, all the more so since—unlike other rights of industrial and commercial property—it is not subject to limitations in point of time.
>
> Accordingly, one cannot allow the holder of a trademark to rely upon the exclusiveness of a trademark right—which may be the consequence of the territorial limitation of national legislations—with a view to prohibiting the marketing in a Member State of goods legally produced in another Member State under an identical trademark having the same origin.
>
> Such a prohibition, which would legitimize the isolation of national markets, would collide with one of the essential objects of the Treaty, which is to unite national markets into a single market.
>
> Whilst in such a market the indication of origin of a product covered by a trademark is useful, information to consumers on this point may be ensured by means other than such as would affect the free movement of goods.

The Court of Justice attempted to cast more light on this somewhat evasive judgment in the later case of *Terrapin (Overseas) Ltd v. Terranova Industrie CA Kapferer and Co.*[64] It justified the Hag ruling thus. It pointed out that basic function of the trademark is to guarantee to the consumer that a product has a particular origin. This purpose, it said, is fatally undermined by the subdivision of the original right. The consumer may no longer take it for granted that this is the quality product he thought it to be. But as Advocate General Jacobs underscored in *CNL-Sucal SA v. Hag GF AG*,[65] the second 'Hag' case, the Court of Justice seemed to have been harbouring a mistrust of trademarks which surfaced each time it came into contact with a trademark owner trying to assert his rights. In one case, the Court of Justice had made these disparaging remarks:

> . . . From the human point of view, the debt which society owes to the 'inventor' of the name 'Prep Good Morning' [a brand of shaving cream] is certainly not of the same nature, to say the least, as that which humanity owes to the discoverer of penicillin.[66]
>
> . . . a trademark right is distinguishable in this context from other rights of industrial and commercial property, inasmuch as the interests protected by the latter are usually more important, and merit a higher degree of protection, than the interests protected by an ordinary trademark.[67]

1.024. Current law applying to trademarks. In *CNL-Sucal SA v. Hag GF AG*,[68] which has come to be known as the 'Hag 2' case, the Court of Justice reversed its judgment in the 'Hag 1' case and allowed the 'ordinary' trademark to be treated just like any other form of intellectual property. The history of the case is identical to its predecessor, the Hag 1 case, save that this time it was the Plaintiff attempting to penetrate the Defendant's territory. The Court held:

---

[64] Case 119/75 [1976] ECR 1039, [1976] 2 CMLR 482.

[65] Case C—10/89 [1990] ECR 3711, [1990] 3 CMLR 571.

[66] Case 40/70 *Sirena Srl v. Eda Srl* [1971] ECR 69, [1971] CMLR 260, per Advocate General Dutheillet de Lamothe.

[67] Case 40/70 *Sirena Srl v. Eda Srl* [1971] ECR 69, [1971] CMLR 260, para. 7.

[68] Case C—10/89 [1990] ECR 3711, [1990] 3 CMLR 571.

Trade mark rights are, it should be noted, an essential element in the system of undistorted competition which the Treaty seeks to establish and maintain. Under such a system, an undertaking must be in a position to keep its customers by virtue of the quality of its products and services, something which is possible only if there are distinctive marks which enable customers to identify those products and services. For the trade mark to be able to fulfil this role, it must offer a guarantee that all goods bearing it have been produced under the control of a single undertaking which is accountable for their quality.

Consequently, as the Court has ruled on numerous occasions, the specific subject matter of trademarks, is in particular to guarantee to the proprietor of the trademark that he has the right to use that trademark for the purpose of putting a product into circulation for the first time and therefore to protect him against competitors wishing to take advantage of the status and reputation of the trade- mark by selling products illegally bearing that mark. In order to determine the exact scope of this right exclusively conferred on the owner of the trademark regard must be had to the essential function of the trademark, which is to guarantee the identity of the origin of the marked product to the consumer or ultimate user by enabling him without any possibility of confusion to distinguish that product from products which have another origin (see in particular, the judgments in Case 102/77 *Hoffmann-La Roche v. Centrafarm* [1978] ECR 1139, para. 7 and Case 3/78 *Centrafarm v. American Home Products Corporation* [1978] ECR 1823, paras. 11 and 12).

For the purpose of evaluating a situation such as that described by the national court in the light of the foregoing considerations, the determinant factor is the absence of any consent on the part of the proprietor of the trademark protected by national legislation to the putting into circulation in another Member State of similar products bearing an identical trademark or one liable to lead to confusion, which are manufactured and marketed by an undertaking which is economically and legally independent of the aforesaid trademark proprietor.

In such circumstances, the essential function of the trademark would be jeopardized if the proprietor of the trademark could not exercise the right conferred on him by national legislation to oppose the importation of similar goods bearing a designation liable to be confused with his own trademark, because, in such a situation, consumers would no longer be able to identify for certain the origin of the marked goods and the proprietor of the trademark could be held responsible for the poor quality of goods for which he was in no way accountable.[69]

It made no difference that the marks had a common origin, since as the Court went on to explain, in spite of their common origin, each of the marks had independently fulfilled, within its own territorial limits, its function of guaranteeing that the marked products came from a single source. As the Advocate General pointed out, the Hag 1 ruling seemed to be based on the erroneous assumption that consumers are only interested in the historical origin of a mark. But consumers do not care how a particular mark came into being. They only wish to be reassured that the product which they have bought was manufactured by the specific manufacturer they have come to recognise as associated with the mark.

1.025. Goods protected by copyright. The Court has not yet had the opportunity to consider the question of 'common origin' in relation to copyright goods. It is most unlikely that the Court would have applied Hag 1 principles bearing in mind

---

[69] Case C—10/89 *CNL-Sucal NV SA v. Hag GF AG* [1990] ECR 3711, [1990] 3 CMLR 571, paras. 13 to 16.

that copyright does not serve to indicate the origin of a product. It is suggested that the owner's exclusive right to market products would be upheld.

(5) Rightholders' Remedies Limited by the Terms of Legislation in the Member State of Importation

1.026. The proviso contained in Article 36 of the Treaty, namely that restrictions cannot 'constitute a means of arbitrary discrimination or a disguised restriction on trade between Member States' is an important factor in determining whether legislation may be invoked by a rightholder to assert exclusive rights. For example, consider a scenario in which copyright goods marketed in a Member State without the owners consent, are then imported into a Member State whose legislation denies owner's of copyright exclusive rights, or grants exclusive rights which discriminate against imported goods and are liable to be struck down by the Court. What are the owners' remedies?

The fundamental point to emphasise is that the remedies available to any owner or assignee of intellectual property rights in a particular Member State are limited by the constraints imposed upon him by national legislation in force there. This was graphically illustrated by the Court of Justice's decision in *Allen and Hanburys Ltd v. Generics (UK) Limited.*[70] The case concerned patents, but its principles are equally applicable to copyright. The Plaintiffs were owners in the United Kingdom of a patent for a particular drug. They had been unable to register any patent protection in Italy (due to the non-existence of a patent regime there) and the Defendants produced the drug in Italy and imported it into the United Kingdom in infringement of the Plaintiff's patent rights. United Kingdom law provided that a person who produced and marketed a patented product in the United Kingdom in infringement of existing patent rights would not be injuncted but awarded a 'licence of right' if he undertook to take such a licence and paid damages to the patent holder. However, the legislation would not grant this privilege to importers of infringing products.

The Court of Justice noted that the 'specific subject matter' of patent rights includes the exclusive right of the owner of those rights to put his product on the Community's market for the first time. This was guaranteed by Article 36. (The same would apply to copyright.) However, the United Kingdom legislation was discriminatory. It would perfect the act of a domestic undertaking but would not do so with that of an importer. It thus offended against the second limb of Article 36 which states that '. . . prohibitions or restrictions shall not, however, constitute a means of arbitrary discrimination or a disguised restriction on trade between Member States'.

The Court would not deprive the owner of rights in the United Kingdom of all protection and would protect the Plaintiff's right to equitable remuneration but it would cut away the offensive provisions of national law. It held:

> Articles 30 and 36 of the Treaty must be interpreted as precluding the courts of a Member State from issuing an injunction prohibiting the importation from another Member State of a product which infringes a patent endorsed 'licences of right' against

---

[70] Case 434/85 [1988] ECR 1245.

an importer who has undertaken to take a licence on the terms prescribed by law where no such injunction may be issued in the same circumstances against an infringer who manufactures the product in the national territory.

Furthermore, the Court ruled that:

Articles 30 and 36 of the Treaty must be interpreted as prohibiting the competent administrative authorities from imposing on a licensee terms impeding the importation from other Member States of a product covered by a patent endorsed 'licences of right' where those authorities may not refuse to grant a licence to an undertaking which would manufacture the product in the national territory and market it there.

(6) Free Movement of Goods Originating in Third Countries

(i) Where no Trade Agreement Exists

1.027. Goods protected by a trademark. Article 30 prohibits restrictions on the free movement of goods 'between' Member States. It follows, that restrictions on goods entering the Community through a border with a third country, are not caught because they do not 'affect trade between Member States'. This has always been the case even where the trademarks have had a common origin, as is well illustrated by the judgments in *EMI Records Ltd v. CBS United Kingdom Ltd*,[71] *EMI Records Ltd v. CBS Grammofon A/S*[72] and *EMI Records Ltd v. CBS Schallplatten GmbH*.[73] The cases concerned the trademark 'Columbia'. It had originally belonged to an American company but in 1917 that company transferred its interest in various Community countries in that mark to an English subsidiary. The American company however retained its interest in the mark in the United States and certain third countries. Through a series of transactions, the mark wound up belonging to the Plaintiff companies who exploited it in Community countries. The Defendants, the proprietors of the mark in the third countries had imported records into the Community but usually obliterated the work 'Columbia'. On occasion they neglected to do so and the Plaintiffs sued for infringement of their mark. The Court held that Article 30 presented no bar to their action:

Article 36, in particular, after stipulating that Articles 30 to 34 shall not preclude restrictions on imports, exports or goods in transmit justified inter alia on grounds of the protection of industrial and commercial property, states that such restrictions shall in no instance constitute a means of arbitrary discrimination or disguised restriction on trade 'between Member States'.

Consequently the exercise of a trademark right in order to prevent the marketing of products coming from a third country under an identical mark even if this constitutes a measure having an affect equivalent to a quantitative restriction, does not affect the free movement of goods between Member States and thus does not come under the prohibitions set out in Article 30 et seq. of the Treaty.

In such circumstance the exercise of a trademark right does not in fact jeopardize the unity of the common market which Article 30 et seq. are intended to ensure.

---

[71] Case 51/75 [1976] ECR 811, [1976] 2 CMLR 235.
[72] Case 86/75 [1976] ECR 871, [1976] 2 CMLR 235.
[73] Case 96/75 [1976] ECR 913, [1976] 2 CMLR 235.

1.028. Goods protected by copyright. There has not yet been a case concerning copyright goods dealing with this point. However, the principles fashioned by the Court of Justice in *EMI Records Ltd v. CBS United Kingdom Ltd*,[74] *EMI Records Ltd v. CBS Grammofon A/S*[75] and *EMI Records Ltd v. CBS Schallplatten GmbH*,[76] must, it is submitted, apply by analogy to copyright goods.

(ii) Where a Trade Agreement Exists

1.029. Treaty-making powers and their significance. The EEC Treaty permits the Community to enter into two types of agreement with third countries.[77] Article 113 provides for the conclusion of trade and tariff agreements in the pursuit of the common commercial policy. It states that:

> After the transitional period has ended, the common commercial policy shall be based on uniform principles, particularly in regard to changes in tariff rates, the conclusion of tariff and trade agreements, the achievement of uniformity in measures of liberalisation, export policy and measures to protect trade such as those to be taken in case of dumping or subsidies.

In addition, Article 238 enables the conclusion of association agreements. It provides that:

> The Community may conclude with a third State, a union of States or an international organisation agreements establishing an association involving reciprocal rights and obligations, common action and special procedures.

The Community regularly enters into agreements in pursuance of its powers.[78] And often the terms of such agreements reflect the Treaty of Rome ie they have provisions such as Articles 30 and 36 of the EEC Treaty. The question arises whether these third countries are to be assimilated to the Community as far as the application of the exhaustion doctrine is concerned. Or in other words, must a product placed in such a third country with the rightholder's consent, be allowed to travel freely between that third country and any Community Member State because the Article 36 concept applies and intellectual property rights have been exhausted?

1.030. Goods protected by copyright and by a trademark. In *Polydor Ltd v. Harlequin Record Shops Ltd*,[79] the Court of Justice addressed this matter in respect of goods protected by copyright. The facts were as follows. Portugal had entered into a trade agreement with the Community with the purpose of consolidating and extending economic relations. To that end the parties decided to eliminate progressively obstacles to substantially all their trade in accordance with the General Agreement on Tariffs and Trade (GATT). Articles 14(2) and 23 of the Portuguese Agreement mirrored exactly Articles 30 and 36 respectively of the Treaty of Rome.

---

[74] Case 51/75 [1976] ECR 811, [1976] 2 CMLR 235.
[75] Case 86/75 [1976] ECR 871, [1976] 2 CMLR 235.
[76] Case 96/75 [1976] ECR 913, [1976] 2 CMLR 235.
[77] See, generally, *Halsbury's Laws of England* (4th Edn, 1986), Vol 51, 4.31 et seq; Kapteyn and VerLoren van Themaat, *op. cit.* Chapter 11 and T C Hartley, *The Foundations of European Community Law*, (2nd Edn, 1988), Chapter 6.
[78] The agreements are negotiated by the Commission in accordance with Article 228 of the Treaty.
[79] Case 270/80 [1982] ECR 329, [1982] 1 CMLR 677.

RSO Records Inc, owners of copyright in recordings of 'The Bee Gees' granted an affiliated company, Polydor Limited (the Plaintiff), an exclusive licence to manufacture and distribute records and cassettes of those recordings in the United Kingdom. RSO Records Inc also licensed two companies in Portugal to manufacture and market the same recordings there. Simons Records Limited purchased the records marketed in Portugal in order to import them into the United Kingdom and sold a number to Harlequin Record Shops Limited (the Defendant) for retail sale.

The Plaintiff established copyright infringement in accordance with English law. The defendant argued that the Plaintiff could not rely upon its copyright to restrain the importation of a product into a Member State, if the product had been lawfully placed on the market in Portugal by him or with his consent because Article 23 of the trade agreement had to be interpreted like Article 36 of the Treaty of Rome. The Court, however, held that the Plaintiff could block the import on the basis of Article 23 of the trade Agreement ie on the grounds of protecting industrial property. It acknowledged the similarities between Article 23 and Article 36 of the Treaty of Rome, but said that this was not a sufficient reason for transposing Community case law exhaustion principles to the interpretation of the trade agreement. It stated that:

> The considerations which led to that interpretation of Articles 30 and 36 of the Treaty do not apply in the context of the relations between the Community and Portugal as defined by the Agreement. It is apparent from an examination of the Agreement that although it makes provision for the unconditional abolition of certain restrictions on trade between the Community and Portugal, such as quantitative restrictions and measures having equivalent effect, it does not have the same purpose as the EEC Treaty, inasmuch as the latter, as has been stated above, seeks to create a single market reproducing as closely as possible the conditions of a domestic market.[80]

The Court said that it was all the more necessary to make the distinction because the instruments which the Community has at its disposal to apply Community law uniformly and achieve the progressive abolition of legislative disparities within the Common Market had no equivalent in the context of the relations between the Community and Portugal.

In Joined Cases *EMI Records Ltd v. CBS United Kingdom Ltd*,[81] *EMI Records Ltd v. CBS Grammofon A/S*[82] and *EMI Records Ltd v. CBS Schallplatten GmbH*,[83] an earlier set of cases than *Polydor Ltd v. Harlequin Record Shops Ltd*,[84] but dealing with the same issue save in the context of a trademark action,[85] the Court of Justice held that:

> . . . the provisions of the Treaty on commercial policy do not, in Article 110 et seq., lay down any obligation on the part of the Member States to extend to trade with third countries the binding principles governing the free movement of goods between Member States and in particular the prohibition of measures having an effect equivalent to quantitative restrictions. . .

---

[80] [1982] ECR 329, [1982] 1 CMLR 677, para. 18. Advocate General Rozès noted that the trade Agreement did not strive to achieve the freedom of movement of persons, services and capital, which are essential for the establishment of the 'Common Market'.
[81] Case 51/75 [1976] ECR 811, [1976] 2 CMLR 235, paras. 17 and 18.
[82] Case 86/75 [1976] ECR 871, [1976] 2 CMLR 235, paras. 17 and 19.
[83] Case 96/75 [1976] ECR 913, [1976] 2 CMLR 235, paras. 10 and 11.
[84] Case 270/80 [1982] ECR 329, [1982] 1 CMLR 677.
[85] See §1.027 above.

The binding effect of commitments undertaken by the Community with regard to certain countries cannot be extended to others.

The Court thus held that[86] the Plaintiff who owned exclusive trademark rights in all Member States could lawfully block the import into the Community of goods bearing an identical trademark and which had been lawfully placed on the market in a third country.

1.031. Specific agreements with third countries. The Court of Justice has often judged the status of trade agreements. It has declared the following conventions incapable of creating the same obligations as are established by the Treaty of Rome: the General Agreement on Tariffs and Trade;[87] the ACP-EEC Convention of Lomé of 28 February 1975;[88] the agreement with Sweden and Switzerland of 22 July 1972;[89] the agreement between the Community and Morocco of 31 March 1969,[90] and the European Free Trade Association Convention ('EFTA' Convention).[91] In an Opinion, the Court of Justice has declared that the Treaty creating the European Economic Area, that is, the agreement binding the Community and the EFTA countries, does not create a 'homogeneity' of laws throughout the European Economic Area and also therefore does not create rights identical to those brought into existence by the EEC Treaty. Although the EEC and EEA Treaty contain equivalent rules on free trade (and competition), the EEC Treaty has higher goals, namely economic integration leading to the establishment of an internal market and economic and monetary union amongst the Member States. The EEC Treaty thus sets in place a constitutional framework to which the Member States have subjugated their sovereign rights and (unlike the EEA Treaty) a whole range of its provisions are absorbed into the constitutional laws of the Member States.[92] One agreement which may have created rights equivalent to those of the Treaty of Rome, and thus concerning which doubts have been expressed, is the Yaoundé Convention of 1963.[93]

(7) Supremacy of Article 36 over EEC Customs Laws

1.032. Treaty terms. Article 30 concerns the abolition of what are called 'quantitative restrictions' and 'measures having equivalent effect'. But as well as

---

[86] apart from any injunction based on infringement of the Plaintiff's mark, which would have been a sufficient ground in itself to block the import.

[87] Case 51/75 *EMI Records Ltd v. CBS United Kingdom Ltd* [1976] ECR 811, [1976] 2 CMLR 235; Case 86/75 *EMI Records Ltd v. CBS Grammofon A/S* [1976] ECR 871, [1976] 2 CMLR 235; Case 96/75 *EMI Records Ltd v. CBS Schallplatten GmbH* [1976] ECR 913, [1976] 2 CMLR 235, per Advocate General Warner.

[88] *Ibid.*

[89] *Ibid.*

[90] *Ibid.*

[91] Case 270/80 *Polydor Ltd v. Harlequin Record Shops Ltd* [1982] ECR 329, [1982] 1 CMLR 677, per Advocate General Rozès.

[92] Opinion 1/91 Re The Draft Treaty on a European Economic Area [1992] 1 CMLR 245, paras. 15 to 22.

[93] Case 270/80 *Polydor Ltd v. Harlequin Record Shops Ltd* [1982] ECR 329, [1982] 1 CMLR 677, per Advocate General Rozès. See also Case 87/75 *Bresciani v. Ammininstrazione Italiana delle Finanze* [1976] ECR 129, [1976] 2 CMLR 62.

those restrictions, the Treaty provides specifically for the abolition of customs duties. Article 10(1) of the Treaty states the following:

> Products coming from a third country shall be considered to be in free circulation in a Member State if the import formalities have been complied with and any customs duties or charges having equivalent effect which are payable have been levied in that Member State, and if they have not benefited from a total or partial drawback of such duties or charges.

Article 9(2) of the Treaty states:

> The provisions of Chapter 1, Section 1, and of Chapter 2 of this Title shall apply to products originating in Member States and to products coming from third countries which are in free circulation in Member States.

1.033. Goods protected by a trademark. In Joined Cases *EMI Records Ltd v. CBS United Kingdom Ltd*,[94] *EMI Records Ltd v. CBS Grammofon A/S*[95] and *EMI Records Ltd v. CBS Schallplatten GmbH*,[96] the Defendants argued that since the records they had put in circulation on the Community's market had complied with all customs formalities, Articles 9(2) and 10(1) of the Treaty eclipsed any arguments that the Plaintiffs might assert under Article 36. The Court of Justice held that:

> Since those provisions only refer to the effects of compliance with customs formalities and paying customs duties and charges having equivalent effect, they cannot be interpreted as meaning that it would be sufficient for products bearing a mark applied in a third country and imported into the Community to comply with the customs formalities in the first Member State where they were imported in order to be able then to be marketed in the common market as a whole in contravention of the rules relating to the protection of the mark.

1.034. Goods protected by copyright. The principles annunciated by the Court of Justice in Joined Cases *EMI Records Ltd v. CBS United Kingdom Ltd*,[97] *EMI Records Ltd v. CBS Grammofon A/S*[98] and *EMI Records Ltd v. CBS Schallplatten GmbH*,[99] must, it is submitted, apply by analogy to products protected by copyright.

(8) The Exhaustion Doctrine and Works Exploited by Public Performance

1.035. The practical problem. The exploitation of a book or record, is inextricably linked with its distribution on the market in material form. So it would be possible, at least in principle, to identify each article floating around the Community and confirm that it is there with the copyright owner's consent. The same cannot, however, be said of a television signal where a viewer watches a screen. For it does not matter whether there are ten, ten thousand or even ten million viewers, the copyright owner need only have supplied a single copy of the copyright medium to the exhibitor. So determining what rights constitute the 'specific subject matter'

---

[94] Case 51/75 [1976] ECR 811, [1976] 2 CMLR 235.
[95] Case 86/75 [1976] ECR 871, [1976] 2 CMLR 235.
[96] Case 96/75 [1976] ECR 913, [1976] 2 CMLR 235.
[97] Case 51/75 [1976] ECR 811, [1976] 2 CMLR 235.
[98] Case 86/75 [1976] ECR 871, [1976] 2 CMLR 235.
[99] Case 96/75 [1976] ECR 913, [1976] 2 CMLR 235.

of copyright in a film broadcast on television is not as straightforward as a similar consideration in the case of goods. But as with any other form of intellectual property the Court has recognised that it is the legitimate right of the creator to be remunerated for his endeavour and this is now explained.

1.036.   Relevant Treaty provision. The broadcasting of a film constitutes the provision of a service.[100] Article 30 of the Treaty which governs the free movement of goods is not applicable in cases involving services. The relevant provision is an analogous provision, namely, Article 59 of the Treaty.[101]

1.037. Compagnie Générale pour la Diffusion de la Télévision, Coditel SA v. Ciné Vog Films SA. In *Compagnie Générale pour la Diffusion de la Télévision, Coditel SA v. Ciné Vog Films SA*[102] the Court of Justice had to consider whether the exhaustion doctrine applied to a film broadcast on television. The facts were as follows.

On 8 July 1969 a French company, the SA 'Les Films la Boétie' ('La Boétie'), a film producer, granted to a Belgium company the SA 'Ciné Vog Films', the exclusive right to broadcast on television and distribute in the cinema in both Belgium and Luxembourg, a film called 'Le Boucher' for a period of seven years. The agreement provided that the film was not to be shown on television in Belgium until the expiry of forty months after its first showing in a cinema there, nor was it to be shown on television in Luxembourg until the seventh year after its first cinema exhibition there. The right to distribute 'Le Boucher' in Germany was granted by La Boétie to a French company called 'Filmedis'. Filmedis was entitled to exploit the German television rights in the film immediately and it was shown on German television on 5 January 1971. The programme was picked up in Belgium by Coditel, a cable operator and relayed to its subscribers. Consequently, Coditel's subscribers saw the film only seven months after it had been first released to cinemas in Belgium and before Ciné Vog had the right to exhibit it themselves on television.

In defending a claim for copyright infringement Coditel asserted Article 59 of the Treaty and the exhaustion doctrine. Coditel argued that once the copyright work ie the television signal carrying the film, had been put on the market by the copyright owner or by someone else with his consent, it could freely circulate throughout the Community because the copyright owner's right to remuneration had been 'exhausted'. It said that the programme broadcast in Germany was thus freed from the reigns of national copyright laws. The Court however rejected this rationale holding that the exhaustion theory did not apply to non-material copyright works. It reasoned in the following way. It underscored the unique problem in identifying the rights flowing from copyright in a film:

> A cinematographic film belongs to the category of literary and artistic works made available to the public by performances which may be infinitely repeated. In this respect the problems involved in the observance of copyright in relation to the requirements of the Treaty are not the same as those which arise in connection with literary and artistic works the placing of which at the disposal of the public is inseparable from the circulation of the material form of the works, as in the case of books or records.

---

[100]   See §§2.029 and 3.008 below.
[101]   For the terms of Article 59 et seq. of the Treaty, see §2.009 below.
[102]   Case 62/79 [1980] ECR 881, [1981] 2 CMLR 362.

1.038. Specific subject matter of copyright in a film. The Court affirmed that the essential function of copyright is to ensure that the author is properly remunerated for his endeavour. Because a film is exploited in non-material form to an audience who pay a fee, the copyright owner can be properly rewarded only if he knows how many performances there have been or are likely to be and how many people are viewing his work. Thus, stated the Court:

> . . . the owner of the copyright in a film and his assigns have a legitimate interest in calculating the fees due in respect of the authorization to exhibit the film on the basis of the actual or probable number of performances. . .
>
> . . . the right of a copyright owner and his assigns to require fees for any showing of a film is part of the essential function of copyright in this type of literary and artistic work. . . [103]

The Court therefore held that Article 59 had to yield to action which safeguarded this right:

> Whilst Article 59 of the Treaty prohibits restrictions upon freedom to provide services, it does not thereby encompass limits upon the exercise of certain economic activities which have their origin in the application of national legislation for the protection of intellectual property, save where such application constitutes a means of arbitrary discrimination or a disguised restriction on trade between Member States. Such would be the case if that application enabled parties to an assignment of copyright to create artificial barriers to trade between Member States.

1.039. Absolute exclusivity permitted. The decision that the owner of copyright in a film has the right to receive fees for the exploitation of his work by performance still poses the question in which precise way is he going to guarantee that he receives those fees? One way he could do this is to limit the exhibition of his film to a confined area. If the film is to be exhibited on television, it is likely that the area defined by the Licensor would coincide with territorial boundaries because television broadcasting is usually a monopoly in Member States.[104] The Court accepted that this was a valid means of ensuring that the copyright owner was properly remunerated. It thus held that as long as the boundaries so defined are not an 'arbitrary means of discrimination or a disguised restriction on trade between Member States'[105] it would permit a derogation from the terms of Article 59 of the Treaty:[106]

> The effect of this is that, whilst copyright entails the right to demand fees for any showing or performance, the rules of the Treaty cannot in principle constitute an obstacle to the geographical limits which the parties to a contract of assignment have agreed upon in order to protect the author and his assigns in this regard. The mere fact that those geographical limits may coincide with national frontiers does not point to a different solution in a situation where television is organised in the Member States

---

[103] [1980] ECR 881, [1981] 2 CMLR 362, paras. 13 to 15., affirmed by the Court of Justice in Case 262/81 *Coditel SA v. Ciné Vog Films SA* [1982] ECR 3381, [1983] 1 CMLR 49.

[104] Permitted by competition law. See §4.175 and §4.179 below.

[105] Article 36, second sentence.

[106] Because Articles 59 to 66 do not contain a provision equivalent to Article 36, the derogation is by way of analogy with that permitted by Article 36 in the context of the free movement of goods: see Joined Cases 52, 62/79 *Compagnie Générale pour la Diffusion de la Télévision, Coditel SA v. Ciné Vog Films SA* [1980] ECR 881, [1981] 2 CMLR 362, per Advocate General Warner who noted that '. . . the omission from Articles 59 to 66 of the Treaty of any provision for the protection of industrial and commercial property is much more likely to have been due to an oversight than to deliberate intention.'

largely on the basis of legal broadcasting monopolies, which indicates that a limitation other than the geographical field of application of an assignment is often impracticable.[107]

The Respondents were therefore within their rights when they sued Coditel for infringement of copyright.

1.040. Practical consequences of the Coditel case. The consequence of this judgment is that the provisions of Articles 59 to 66 must yield to a performance right in a film or programme. Or in other words, an undertaking is permitted to partition the Community by asserting a performance right. The exhaustion principle simply does not apply and cannot be invoked by infringement actions.[108]

1.041. Different works to which principle applies. The principle that an author is entitled to receive fees for a performance of his work applies to films, whether the means whereby they are shown to the public is the cinema or television.[109] The Court of Justice has held it equally applicable to sound recordings exploited by performance:

> The problems, in relation to the requirements of the Treaty, involved in the observance of copyright in musical works made available to the public through their performance are not the same as those which arise where the act of making a work available to the public is inseparable from the circulation of the physical medium on which it is recorded. In the former case the copyright owner and the persons claiming through him have a legitimate interest in calculating the fees due in respect of the authorization to present the work on the basis of the actual or probable number of performances . . .[110]

(9) Use of a Product in Free Circulation in the Community for a Public Performance

1.042. The divisible nature of a copyright. A copyright product, such as a vinyl or compact disc which has been marketed and on which a royalty has been paid to

---

[107] [1980] ECR 881, [1981] 2 CMLR 362, para. 16. In Case 262/81 *Coditel SA v. Ciné Vog Films SA* [1982] ECR 3381, [1983] 1 CMLR 49, Advocate General Reischl questioned the notion that in order to calculate the fees due to the rightholder for the performance of his work in the cinema, (as opposed to being broadcast on television), it is necessary to license the exhibition on an exclusive basis. He said that '. . . such a calculation is feasible even when a number of licensees are competing within a single territory, since each of several film distributors to whom performance rights are assigned . . .is dealing with certain particular cinemas so that the number of performances may serve to measure his remuneration upon which, in its turn, the percentage share accruing to the original owner of the right may be calculated.'

[108] As Advocate General Warner noted in Joined Cases 55, 57/80 *Musik-Vertrieb membran GmbH v. GEMA* [1981] ECR 147, [1981] 2 CMLR 44, the specific subject matter of a performing right '. . . imports that the owner of it is entitled to authorise or forbid each and every performance of the work to which it relates, from which it follows that one cannot apply in the domain of performing rights the doctrine of "exhaustion of rights" as it applies in the domain of the marketing of goods.'

[109] Case 262/81 *Coditel SA v. Ciné Vog Films SA* [1982] ECR 3381, [1983] 1 CMLR 49. See §1.038 et seq. above.

[110] Case 395/87 *Ministère Public v. Tournier* [1989] ECR 2521, [1991] 4 CMLR 248, para. 12 (collecting society — sound recordings on vinyl disc), affirming the Court of Justice's decision in Case 402/85 *Basset v. SACEM* [1987] ECR 1747, [1987] 3 CMLR 173 (collecting society — sound recordings on vinyl disc).

the rightholder, might subsequently be played to the public. The distribution rights have been exhausted but does this mean that the copyright owner has lost all claim to remuneration for the exploitation of his work through what essentially amounts to a performance? In *Ministère Public v. Tournier*[111] the Court of Justice considered this question. The French collecting society Société des auteurs, compositeurs et éditeurs de musique ('SACEM') charged the owners of discotheques a performance royalty each time they played a record. M. Tournier contested this on the basis that as the discs he played had been imported from another Member State and a royalty paid to the copyright owner when they were first put on the market, all intellectual property rights were exhausted. The Court stated that reproduction rights and performance rights are quite separate from each other:

> It is true that the present case raises the specific question of the distinction between the conditions applicable to those two situations, in so far as sound-recordings are products covered by the provisions on the free movement of goods contained in Article 30 et seq. of the Treaty but are also capable of being used for public performance of the musical work in question. In such circumstances, the requirements relating to the free movement of goods and the freedom to provide services and those deriving from the observance of copyright must be reconciled in such a way that the copyright owners, or the societies empowered to act as their agents, may invoke their exclusive rights in order to require the payment of royalties for music played in public by means of a sound-recording, even though the marketing of that recording cannot give rise to the charging of any royalty in the country where the music is played in public.

It thus held that:

> Articles 30 and 59 of the Treaty must be interpreted as not preventing the application of national legislation which treats as an infringement of copyright the public performance of a protected musical work by means of sound recordings without payment of royalties, where royalties have already been paid to the author, for the reproduction of the work, in another Member State.

The significance of this judgment is that although the copyright owner is entitled to receive a royalty on the sale of his product only once (that is, when it is first marketed in the Community), he will be entitled to receive performance royalties each time that same product is exploited for a public performance. As far as the abusive or discriminatory nature of the rate of royalty is concerned, the Court stated that this 'must be appraised in relation to the competition rules contained in Articles 85 and 86. The rate of royalty is not a matter to be taken into account in considering the compatibility of the national legislation in question with Articles 30 and 59 of the Treaty.'[112]

1.043. The test for the status of a royalty—substance over form. To determine whether a royalty is lawful, it is clearly vital to establish whether that royalty is a charge for the distribution of a product or if it is being levied as remuneration for a public performance. But, the formal language used by the parties to describe the type of royalty does not decide the issue. This is well illustrated by the decision in *Basset v. Société des auteurs, compositeurs et éditeurs de musique ('SACEM')*,[113] the facts of which were as follows. SACEM, the French collecting society, collected

---

[111] Case 395/87 [1989] ECR 2521, [1991] 4 CMLR 248.
[112] See §4.166 below.
[113] Case 402/85 [1987] ECR 1747, [1987] 3 CMLR 173.

royalties from discotheques on behalf of composers, performers and producers of phonograms. SACEM charged the Appellant's discotheque a fee of 8.25 per cent of its turnover, which it said consisted of two components: 6.6 per cent in respect of performance rights and 1.65 per cent in respect of a supplementary 'mechanical rights'. The Appellant contended that the additional mechanical royalty amounted to a restriction on imports in breach of Article 30 because the recording used had been imported from another Member State where a royalty had already been paid at the point of sale, ie he argued that the right to a mechanical royalty had been exhausted. In ruling the supplementary mechanical royalty legitimate, the Court of Justice stated:

> It is undisputed that, as is normally the case with regard to copyright management, on the basis of the applicable international conventions, the aggregation of a performance fee and a supplementary mechanical reproduction fee charged on the public use in France of a recorded musical work takes place whether the records are of French origin or are manufactured or marketed in another Member State. It is true that public use in another Member State may give rise only to the collection of a performance royalty in favour of the author and the record manufacturer, but that circumstance does not imply that the amount of the royalty charged or its function are different from those of the royalties charged in France on such use.
>
> In other words, disregarding the concepts used by the French legislation and practice, the supplementary mechanical reproduction fee may thus be analysed as constituting part of the payment for an author's rights over the public performance of a recorded musical work. Moreover, the amount of that royalty, like that of the performance fee strictly so called, is calculated on the basis of the discotheque's turnover and not the number of records bought or played.
>
> It follows that, even if the charging of the fee in question were to be capable of having a restrictive effect on imports, it does not constitute a measure having equivalent effect prohibited under Article 30 of the Treaty inasmuch as it must be regarded as a normal exploitation of copyright and does not constitute a means of arbitrary discrimination or a disguised restriction on trade between Member States for the purposes of Article 36 of the Treaty.[114]

(10) Exclusive Rental Rights

1.044. Consumers have become aware that it is not economic to purchase a film on video-cassette and play it perhaps only three or four times before discarding it to a collection of forgotten cassettes. Consequently, a new market has rapidly evolved for the rental of video cassettes. Recognising the growth of this new market, the Court of Justice, in *Warner Brothers Inc. v. Christiansen*,[115] has extended its definition of the 'specific subject matter' of copyright to include exclusive rental rights. The facts of this case were as follows. Warner Brothers Inc, owners of rights in the James Bond film 'Never Say Never Again' in the United Kingdom, licensed its sale there on video-cassette. The Defendant, bought a copy of the film on video in the United Kingdom and imported it into Denmark where he proposed to hire it to the public from his shop in Copenhagen. In Denmark, unlike the United

---

[114] [1987] ECR 1747, [1987] 3 CMLR 173, para. 14 to 16. This principle was affirmed by the Court of Justice in Case C—270/86 *Cholay v. SACEM*, Judgment of 12 December 1990.
[115] Case 158/86 [1988] ECR 2605, [1990] 3 CMLR 684.

Kingdom, rental rights in video-cassettes were reserved exclusively for the owner of the copyright. Relying on this legislation, Metronome Video Aps, sued to prevent the Defendant from hiring out the video cassette to the public. The Danish Court referred the following question to the Court of Justice:

> Must the provisions of Chapter 2 in Title 1 of Part 2 of the EEC Treaty, on the elimination of quantitative restrictions between member-States, namely Articles 30 and 36, in conjunction with Article 222 of the Treaty, be interpreted as meaning that the owner of exclusive rights (copyright) in a video-recording which is lawfully put into circulation by the owner of the exclusive right or with his consent in a member-State under whose domestic copyright law it is not possible to prohibit the (resale and) hiring-out of the recordings, is prevented from restraining the hiring-out of the video-recording in another member-State into which it has been lawfully imported, where the copyright law of that State allows such prohibition without distinguishing between domestic and imported video-recordings and without impeding the actual importation of video-recordings.

The Court noted that a restriction on the hiring out of video cassette was likely to affect trade between Member States, given the size of the rental industry. Consequently, it amounted to a restriction in contravention of Article 30. However, such a restriction could be justified, in accordance with Article 36, for the protection of intellectual property. This is because a single royalty levied only on the initial sale of a video cassette was not a sufficient remuneration for the owner of the copyright in the recording given the number of times an industrial video cassette might be rehired. The terms of the second sentence of Article 36 were fulfilled because the Danish legislation was non-discriminatory applying both to video cassettes sold in Denmark as well as those marketed in other Member States. Accordingly the Court ruled:

> Articles 30 and 36 of the EEC Treaty do not prohibit the application of national legislation which gives an author the right to make the hiring-out of video-cassettes subject to his permission, when the video-cassettes in question have already been put into circulation with his consent in another Member State whose legislation enables the author to control the initial sale, without giving him the right to prohibit hiring-out.

1.045. Comment on Warner Bros Inc. v. Christiansen. By this judgment, the Court extends its definition of the 'specific subject matter' of copyright in a film to include exclusive rental rights. It confirms that those rights are not exhausted when a cassette sold in one Member State is imported into another Member State for hire there. Furthermore, it is not relevant that the owner of copyright can determine in which State he markets his video cassettes and therefore could choose a State which offers exclusive rental rights as opposed to one that does not.[116] If the history of the media industry reveals anything, it is that only human imagination limits the manner in which a person's artistic work can be delivered to an audience. *Warner Bros v. Christiansen* demonstrates that European Community legal concepts are malleable, readily responding to new marketing trends and technologies. If it can be proven that a novel form of disseminating a work is undermining an artist's

---

[116] See by way of contrast Joined Cases 55, 57/80 *Musik-vertrieb membran GmbH v.* GEMA [1981] ECR 147, [1981] 2 CMLR 44, where the author's freedom of choice as to the Member State in which to put his property on the market was a decisive factor in denying him protection against the operation of the exhaustion doctrine. See §1.011 above.

reward, the Court may add to or alter its definition of precisely what constitutes the 'specific subject matter' of copyright (or any other intellectual property right for that matter).

(11) Imposing 'Windows' in Licensing Agreements

1.046. Reason for 'windows' in licensing agreements. In granting an exhibition licence for a film, a licensor will often impose a 'window' (ie a period of set duration) between the exhibition of the film in the cinema and its subsequent broadcasting on television or distribution on video cassette. The licensor knows that a successful cinema release will yield more of a return for him than any other mode of exhibition. And by limiting the latter, he is forcing the public to see his film in the cinema. The Court of Justice has been called upon to judge the legality of 'windows' in two cases. The first concerned a window between a cinema exhibition and television broadcast and the second involved a window between a cinema exhibition and distribution on video cassette.

1.047. Window between a cinema exhibition and a broadcast on television. *Compagnie Générale pour la Diffusion de la Télévision, Coditel SA v. Ciné Vog Films SA,*[117] concerned a scenario where the Respondent had been licensed the exclusive right to exhibit a film in Belgium both in the cinema and on television. The licensor owner of the film had imposed a window of 40 months between the first cinema exhibition and any television broadcast. The Appellant, a cable retransmission company, pirated a copy of the film broadcast in an adjoining Member State and broadcast it in its cable nets in Belgium. Ciné Vog sued for breach of copyright. As well as ruling that Ciné Vog had the exclusive right to broadcast the film in Belgium, the Court of Justice sanctioned the 'window'. It stated that:

> . . . the owner of the copyright in a film and his assigns have a legitimate interest in. . . authorizing a television broadcast of the film only after it has been exhibited in cinemas for a certain period of time. . . the exploitation of copyright in films and the fees attaching thereto cannot be regulated without regard being had to the possibility of television broadcasts of those films. . . [118]

1.048. Window between cinema exhibition and distribution on video cassette. In Joined Cases *Cinéthèque SA v. Fédération Nationale de Cinémas Français,*[119] the Court of Justice sanctioned a window between a cinema exhibition and distribution of the film on video cassette. The producers of films had licensed their exhibition in the cinema simultaneously with their distribution on video cassette to unconnected undertakings. Section 89 of the French Act 82-652 of 29 July 1982 on audiovisual communication provided that no work being exhibited in cinemas could be simultaneously distributed to the public on video cassettes or video discs, before the expiry of a period to be determined by decree. The Defendant's exhibitors obtained injunctions prohibiting the marketing of the films on video cassette and the Tribunal de Grand Instance, Paris asked the Court, inter alia, to rule whether the interval required by the French legislation was in breach of

---

[117] Case 62/79 [1980] ECR 881, [1981] 2 CMLR 362. See also §1.037 above.
[118] *Ibid.*, paras. 13 and 14. Affirmed in Case 262/81 *Coditel SA v. Ciné Vog Films SA* [1982] ECR 3381, [1983] 1 CMLR 49.
[119] Joined Cases 60, 61/84 [1985] ECR 2605, [1986] 1 CMLR 365.

Articles 30 and 34 of the Treaty. The Court stated that although the French legislation did not have the purpose of regulating inter-State trade (merely safeguarding the cinema industry), it had the effect of impeding intra-Community trade because it prevented the products in question being made available for sale in France when the same products could be sold in other Member States. But, it said that the restriction could not be justified in the interests of protecting industrial or commercial property (under Article 36)[120] because its effect was to prevent the owners of the copyright in the films exercising their right to grant distribution licences. However, in permitting the restriction, the Court noted the universality of such restrictions:

> . . . the national legislation at issue in the main proceedings of these cases forms part of a body of provisions applied in the majority of Member States, whether in the form of contractual, administrative or legislative provisions and of variable scope, but the purpose of which, in all cases, is to delay the distribution of films by means of video cassettes during the first months following their release in the cinema in order to protect their exploitation in the cinema, which protection is considered necessary in the interests of the profitability of cinematographic production, as against exploitation through video cassettes. It must also be observed that, in principle, the Treaty leaves it to the Member States to determine the need for such a system the form of such a system, and any temporal restrictions which ought to be laid down.

It therefore ruled that the provisions could be justified in the 'general interest', providing they satisfied the 'proportionality' test required:

> Article 30 of the EEC Treaty does not apply to national legislation which regulates the distribution of cinematographic works by imposing an interval between one mode of distributing such works and another by prohibiting their simultaneous exploitation in cinemas and in video cassette form for a limited period, provided that the prohibition applies to domestically produced and imported cassettes alike and any barriers to intra-Community trade to which its implementation may give rise do not exceed what is necessary for ensuring that the exploitation in cinemas of cinematographic works of all origins retains priority over other means of distribution.[121]

1.049. Comment on Cinéthèque SA v. Fédération Nationale de Cinémas Français. Thus, the Court permits such a restriction in the 'general interest' because its purpose is to safeguard the film exhibition industry—a culture it values. That industry relies upon the exhibition of films in cinema to finance production. In fact, without the guarantee of the window between a cinema release and a distribution on video cassette, exhibition would not be profitable enough to make production economically viable. Although exceptions in the general interest may never be based on economic reasons, it is difficult to justify the result of this case on other rationales.

(12) Illustrations of the Effect of Community Law on Copyright

1.050. Illustration one (material and non-material works). A film production company owns the copyright in a film. It licenses a distributor to release the film in the form of a video cassette on to the German market. The film company secures

---

[120] See §1.009 above.

[121] As for other examples of restrictions permitted in the general interest, see §1.068 below.

a royalty of 10% of the selling price of each video cassette (the maximum permitted by national law). The cassettes which have been distributed in Germany are exported to France. French law does not set down maximum royalty rules. The film company are unable to assert their copyright to claim any further royalty because they chose to release their goods on the German market and their intellectual property rights have been exhausted. However, they may enter into a new distribution agreement in France marketing new video cassettes there and charge the higher royalty. Release of the film on video cassette on to the German and French market does not entitle a broadcast or screening of the film in the cinema, the rights of which have not been licensed.

The same film company licenses a single exhibition of the film to a German broadcasting company and supplies them with a copy on video tape. The broadcasting company transmits the film on its network in Germany. The film company's intellectual property rights in the non-material exploitation of the film are not exhausted. Thus, the German broadcasting company is limited to a single exhibition and no other party may retransmit the broadcast signal on television or exhibit the film in any other way such as, for example, in the cinema.

1.051. Illustration two (imports from third countries). A record company owns copyright worldwide in musical recordings made by a particular artist. It grants exclusive distribution rights in the recordings to an undertaking in Germany which manufactures compact discs containing the recordings and markets them in Germany. It also grants similar exclusive rights to undertakings in Switzerland and Norway. The European Community has entered into a trade agreement with Norway under the terms of a Treaty which has Articles similar to Articles 30 and 36 of the Treaty of Rome. An import enterprise in Germany buys the records placed on the markets in both Switzerland and Norway and imports them into Germany. The German undertaking is able to assert exclusive rights given to it under German law to oppose the imports of those recording from Switzerland and Norway. In neither case is 'trade between Member States' affected and the trade agreement with Switzerland makes no difference because that agreement does not strive to attain the conditions of a single market.

1.052. Illustration three (windows and rental rights). Spanish legislation provides that no copyright proprietor may market a video recording of a film there until the expiry of eight months after the date on which it is exhibited for the first time in Spain in the cinema. A film company with exclusive exhibition rights in a film licenses a cinema undertaking to exhibit the film in Spain. At the same time it licenses distribution of the film on video-cassette in France. It has already been shown in French cinemas. A chain of Spanish video rental shops buys the video-cassette put on the market in France and advertises them for hire in Spain. The exclusive cinema distributor is able to assert the national law to halt the video shop in its activities until the statutory eight month 'window' expires.

Spanish law recognises the right of a licensee to rent goods exclusively in Spain. The Spanish film company has licensed a chain of supermarkets to be its exclusive licensee for the rental of video cassettes in Spain. The chain may assert the right conferred on them by national legislation to stop any imports of those cassettes on to the Spanish market for the purpose of hire.

(13) Summary of Principles

1.053. A synthesis of the case law concerning Articles 30 and 36 yields the following principles:

(1) The owner of goods protected by copyright or a trademark has the exclusive right to put his product on the Community's market for the first time or determine who else may do so.

(2) The owner of a trademark has the absolute right to impede the importing into his territory of products bearing a confusingly similar mark which have been put on the Community's market in another Member State by a registered user there.

(3) The preceding principle applies even where the marks have a common historical origin provided that each has generated a reputation that distinguishes one from the other.

(4) It is undecided whether the exhaustion doctrine applies to direct sales of products by one licensee into another licensed territory.

(5) Consent is the key which opens the door to the Community's market. Thus, a copyright holder may assert his rights against products put on the market in another Member State after the expiry of copyright there. He may also assert his copyright against goods put on the market under a compulsory licence in another Member State. However, this does not apply if the compulsory licence comes into operation only after the copyright owner has put products protected by the same copyright on the market of his own free will.

(6) Remedies under Article 36 are limited by the terms of national laws. Laws which discriminate against imported goods will be struck down by the Court.

(7) The exhaustion doctrine does not apply to products imported into the Community from third countries. National copyright and trademark laws may be asserted under Article 36.

(8) The exhaustion doctrine does not apply even in cases where there is a trade agreement between the Community and a third country with terms similar to Articles 30 and 36 of the EEC Treaty. It might, however, be otherwise if the intention of such a trade agreement is to incorporate that country into the Community's single market.

(9) Payment of customs duties at a Community border with a third country does not exempt claims under Article 36 of the Treaty

(10) The exhaustion doctrine does not apply to a broadcast film or any other non-material medium protected by copyright. The copyright owner or assignee is entitled to authorise each performance in order to regulate his remuneration and can thus partition the Common Market in the process.

(11) Although the distribution royalty rights attached to a particular product may have been exhausted, a royalty may always be levied if that product is exploited for a performance.

(12) The Court looks at the substance and not the form of a royalty to determine its legality.

(13) The owner or assignee of copyright can assert his rights to enforce an exclusive right, granted by national legislation to hire out a video-cassette or similar product even though the product has been put on the Community's market with the owner's consent.

(14) The owner or assignee of copyright in a film is entitled, to 'exercise' his copyright to enforce a 'window' between the exhibition of the film in the cinema and its exhibition on television.

(15) The owner or assignee of copyright in a film is entitled, in the 'general interest' to enforce a 'window' between the exhibition of a film in the cinema and its subsequent release on video cassette.

II. HARMONISATION OF COPYRIGHT AND NEIGHBOURING RIGHTS

1. General Principles

1.054. Protection of national intellectual property laws under Community Law. National intellectual property laws of each Member State remain protected by Article 36 of the Treaty until measures have been taken by the Community's institutions to harmonize those particular laws. Thereafter, the Community's law prevails.[122]

1.055. Effect of Community harmonisation on international agreements. Most Member States are bound by international conventions governing copyright and neighbouring rights.[123] The Court has evolved case law which determines the effect of Community law on rights and obligations contained in those international conventions. These principles are dealt with elsewhere in this work.[124]

2. Implemented Harmonizing Legislation as at 1 January 1993

(1) Legal Protection of Computer Programs

1.056. Council Directive 91/250/EEC. Council Directive 91/250/EEC[125] provides for the protection of computer programs as 'literary works' as that term is used by the Berne Convention for the Protection of Literary and Artistic Works. Authors are given the exclusive right to reproduce, translate, adapt, arrange and distribute their works. The Directive provides for minimum terms of protection (broadly in conformity with the Berne Convention) and sets in place rules for the

---

[122] Case 35/76 *Simmenthal SpA v. Italian Minister for Finance* [1976] ECR 1871, [1977] 2 CMLR 1; Case 144/81 *Keurkoop BV v. Nancy Kean Gifts BV* [1982] ECR 2853, [1983] 2 CMLR 47; Case 241/87 *EMI Electrola GmbH v. Patricia Im- und Export* [1989] ECR 79, [1989] 2 CMLR 413; Case T—69/89 *Radio Telefis Eireann v. EC Commission* [1991] 4 CMLR 586; Case T—70/89 *The British Broadcasting Corporation and BBC Enterprises Ltd v. EC Commission* [1991] 4 CMLR 669; Case T—76/89 *Independent Television Publications Ltd v. EC Commission* [1991] 4 CMLR 745. As for the extent to which Article 100A(4) of the Treaty (introduced by the Single European Act) may allow Member States to justify under Article 36, a derogation from a Harmonizing Directive, see Kapteyn and VerLoren van Themaat, *op. cit.*, Chapter VII, 3.3.

[123] See §7.004 et seq. below.

[124] See §7.001 below.

[125] OJ No L 122, 17.05.91, p. 42. See §6.105 below.

seizure of infringing copies of a computer program. The Directive was adopted on 14 May 1991 and came into force on 1 January 1993.

(2) Rental, Lending, Fixation, Reproduction, Broadcasting and Communication to the Public and Distribution Rights

1.057. Council Directive 92/100/EEC. Council Directive 92/100/EEC[126] provides for the creation of two novel rights, namely, rental and lending rights, which it bestows on owners of copyright (ie authors) and owners of neighbouring rights (ie performers, broadcasters, phonogram producers and film producers). In addition, the Directive creates a fixation right (for performers and broadcasting organisations), a reproduction right (for performers, phonogram producers, film producers and broadcasting organisations), a broadcasting and communication to the public right (for performers and broadcasting organisations) and a distribution right (for performers, phonogram producers, film producers and broadcasting organisations). Phonogram producers and performers are given a right to remuneration for the secondary exploitation of their works.

The duration of authors' rights is not to be less than that provided for in the Berne Convention for the Protection of Literary and Artistic Works. The duration of neighbouring rights is not to expire before the end of the respective terms provided for in the Rome Convention, the rights of the producers of the first fixation of films not expiring before the end of the period of 20 years from the year in which the fixation was made. The Directive was adopted on 19 November 1992 and Member States had to introduce measures in compliance no later than the 1 July 1994.

3. Overview of Proposed Harmonizing Legislation as at 1 January 1993

(1) Cable and Satellite Transmissions

1.058. Simultaneous, unaltered and unabridged cable retransmissions. The proposed Council Directive[127] would provide rules for the exploitation of copyright material by simultaneous, unaltered and unabridged cable retransmissions. In general terms, the Directive would preserve the absolute right of the owner of copyright to authorise the exploitation of his work by cable transmission. (Statutory licensing systems as exist would continue until 31 December 1997.) The Directive would also stipulate that (save for works owned by broadcasting organisations) rights are to be negotiated solely through collecting societies. Where a rightholder refuses to assign the negotiation of his rights to a collecting society, an appropriate society would be mandated to represent him. The Directive would set in place a mediation mechanism to aid the process of negotiation of rights of broadcasting organisations.

---

[126] OJ No L 346, 27.11.92, p.61. See §6.123 below.

[127] Proposal on the co-ordination of certain rules concerning copyright and rights related to copyright applicable to satellite broadcasting and cable retransmission, COM (92) 526 final, OJ No C 25, 28.01.93.

1.059. Satellite transmissions. The proposed Council Directive[128] would safe-guard freedom of contract by providing that a 'communication to the public by satellite' of a copyright work requires the prior authorization of all the rightholders. The act of 'communication to the public' would occur only in the Member State where under the control and responsibility of the broadcasting organisations, the signals are introduced into an uninterrupted chain of communication leading to the satellite and down towards the earth. Collective agreements between a collecting society and broadcasting organisations concerning a particular category of work could be extended to other rightholders of the same category of works provided that there is a simulcast of a terrestrial broadcast and subject to the other rightholders' consent. Generally, the rights of performers, broadcasting organisations and phono-gram producers would be aligned with Council Directive 92/100/EEC.[129]

(2) Accession to the Berne Convention and Rome Convention

1.060. A proposed Council Decision would have bound the Community to both the Berne Convention for the Protection of Literary and Artistic Works and the Rome Convention.[130] However, that has been jettisoned and in accordance with a resolution by the Council of Ministers on 14 May 1992, Member States have themselves agreed to adhere to the Berne Convention (Paris Act) and the Rome Convention before 1 January 1995.

(3) Extension of Duration of Copyright and Neighbouring Rights

1.061. Under the proposed Directive,[131] the rights of an author of a literary or artistic work, which would include protected photographs, would run for the life of the author and for 70 years after his death. (The authors of a cinematographic or audiovisual work would be the natural persons who made the intellectual creation of the work and the principal director would be considered as one of its authors. A presumption of assignment of their rights could be provided for.) In the case of joint authorship that term would be calculated from the death of the last surviving author. In the case of anonymous works, works created by a legal person and collective works, the term would run for 70 years after the work has been lawfully made available to the public, provided in the case of collective works or works created by a legal person, which have not been made lawfully available to the public within 70 years from creation, the protection would expire.

The rights of performers would run for 50 years from the first lawful publication of the fixation of the performance, or if there has been no publication, after the first lawful communication to the public of the performance.

The rights of producers of phonograms would run for 50 years from first publication of the phonogram. However, they would expire 50 years after the fixation was made if the phonogram has not been published in that time.

The rights of producers of the first fixations of cinematographic works and of

---

[128] *Ibid.*

[129] OJ No L 346, 27.11.92, p.61. See §6.123 below.

[130] COM (90) 582 final.

[131] Amended Proposal for a Council Directive harmonising the term of protection of copyright and certain related rights, COM (92) 602 final, OJ No C 27, 30.01.93.

sequences of moving images, whether or not accompanied by sound, would expire 50 years after the first publication. However, they would expire 50 years after the fixation was made if those works has not been published during that time.

The rights of broadcasting organisations would run for 50 years from the first transmission of a broadcast.

A person who for the first time makes lawfully available to the public a work, the copyright protection of which has expired, is to the benefit from a protection equivalent to the economic rights of the author, to run for 25 years from the time the work was first lawfully made available.

The length of the proposed terms would be calculated from the first day of January of the year following the event which gives rise to them and when any of those terms begins to run in a Member State, it would be deemed to run in all Member States.

The Directive would provide a comparison of terms mechanism for determining the duration of protection of works protected by Member States but which are not by Community nationals and which do not have their origin in a Member State.

Moral rights would be maintained at least until the expiry of the economic rights.

(4) Protection of Databases

1.062. Under the proposed Council Directive,[132] Member States would protect databases as copyright works within the meaning of Article 2(5) of the Berne Convention for the Protection of Literary and Artistic Works ie they would have to be 'original' and protection would be without prejudice to protection of the materials comprising the database.

The author of the database is to be protected against the unauthorised utilisation of his database for commercial purposes. So, he would have the right to authorise reproduction, translation, adaptation, arrangement, alteration, distribution, including rental, communication, display or public performance of his work. The normal fair use exceptions would apply and when the materials cannot be found elsewhere their use would be licensed.

Authorship would be determined in accordance with the Berne Convention and the duration of protection is to be the same as that accorded to literary works by Member States.

III. ARTICLE 30—MEASURES HAVING EQUIVALENT EFFECT TO QUANTITATIVE RESTRICTIONS

1. Introduction

1.063. The threshold issue in any free movement of goods scenario, is whether the disputed action amounts to a restriction in breach of Article 30.[133] The term

---

[132] Proposal for a Council Directive on the legal protection of databases, COM (92) 24 final, OJ No C 156, 23.06.92, p.4.

[133] See generally: *Halsbury's Laws of England* (4th Edn), Vol 52, 12.01 et seq. and P Oliver, *Free Movement of Goods in the EEC* (2nd Edn, 1988).

'quantitative restrictions' with which Article 30 opens, speaks for itself. The phrase 'measures having equivalent effect' is less easy to define. Nevertheless, there is now a wealth of case law devoted to delineating the contours of this particular term.

2. General Principles

1.064. 'Cassis de Dijon' principle. The starting point in this topic is the principle established by the 'Cassis de Dijon' case, namely that a product lawfully produced and marketed in a Member State must be allowed to travel unimpeded throughout the Community.[134]

1.065. Hindering intra-Community trade. The Court of Justice has held that a measure is in breach of Article 30 if it hinders intra-Community trade. In *Association des Centres Distributeurs Edouard Leclerc v. Au Blé Vert Sàrl*,[135] it articulated the well-rehearsed general test thus:

> The Court has consistently held that under that Article, any national measure which is capable of hindering intra-Community trade, directly or indirectly, actually or potentially, is to be considered a measure having an effect equivalent to a quantitative restriction.[136] That would be the case, for instance, where national legislation treated domestic products differently from imported products or disadvantaged, in any manner whatsoever, the marketing of imported products vis-à-vis domestic products.

3. Offensive Measures

1.066. In general. Although the aforementioned passage refers to discrimination, and discrimination has been a particular focus of the cases[137] and legislation,[138] it is clear that Article 30 is breached even where national and imported products are treated indiscriminately but a barrier on imports is nevertheless created.[139] Thus a violation of Article 30 may in particular arise where a Member State imposes measures equally applicable to domestic and imported products governing the marketing of products, but where the restrictive effect of such measures on the free

---

[134] Case 120/78 *Rewe-Zentral AG v. Bundesmonopolverwaltung für Brantwein* [1979] ECR 649, [1979] 3 CMLR 494

[135] Case 229/83 [1985] ECR 1, [1985] 2 CMLR 286, para. 23.

[136] This phrase and the principle it embodies was forged by the Court of Justice in Case 8/74 *Procureur du Roi v. Dassonville* [1974] ECR 837, [1974] 2 CMLR 436, and it is consistently employed by the Court.

[137] See §1.071 below, Article 30 and discrimination.

[138] See, in particular, Commission Directive 70/50/EEC of 22 December 1969 on the abolition of measures having an effect equivalent to quantitative restrictions on imports and are not covered by other provisions adopted in pursuance of the EEC Treaty, Articles 1 and 2, OJ, Sp. Edn., 1970(I), p.17.

[139] Case 120/78 *Rewe-Zentral AG v. Bundesmonopolverwaltung für Branntwein* [1979] ECR 649, [1979] 3 CMLR 494 and Joined Cases 60, 61/84 *Cinéthèque SA v. Fédération Nationale de Cinémas Français* [1985] ECR 2605, [1986] 1 CMLR 365, per Advocate General Slynn. For an argument that Article 30 is concerned solely with prohibiting discrimination, see G Marenco, *Pour une interprétation traditionnelle de la notion de mesure deffet équivalent à une restriction quantitative* [1984] CDE, 291.

movement of goods exceeds the effects intrinsic to trade values.[140] And subtly, a barrier may exist where the importer is prevented, by pricing legislation, from passing on a price advantage arising from the importation of goods from another Member State.[141]

There is no 'de minimus' requirement in the operation of Article 30 ie it is not necessary to prove the existence of an 'appreciable effect' on trade between Member States before Article 30 comes into effect.[142] Furthermore, the fact that any barrier may be limited in time does not prevent it from falling within Article 30.[143] Ultimately, all that matters is that importation is prejudiced and that any prejudice cannot be justified by what are termed 'mandatory' requirements.[144]

1.067. Intellectual property laws. National intellectual property laws conferring exclusive rights on their owners will almost always result in action potentially offensive to Article 30.[145] It should be noted that claims for royalties on the importation of goods are within the scope of Article 30 (and not Articles 9 et seq. of the Treaty)[146] even though they are pecuniary in nature. This is because the national intellectual property laws under which claims are made, essentially give the rightholder the power to license others to exploit his property and consequently the power to oppose the importation of infringing copies of his work. The claim for a royalty is therefore subsidiary in nature being more in the way of a claim for damages.[147]

4. Excluded Restrictions

1.068. 'Mandatory' requirements. In the absence of harmonisation of rules by the Community, Member States are entitled to regulate all matters relating to the production and marketing of a product in its territory. Such measures are termed

---

[140] Case 155/73 *Sacchi* [1974] ECR 409, [1974] 2 CMLR 177 referring to Commission Directive 70/50/EEC of 22 December 1969 on the abolition of measures having an effect equivalent to quantitative restrictions on imports and are not covered by other provisions adopted in pursuance of the EEC Treaty, Article 3, OJ, Sp. Edn., 1970 (I), p. 17. The measure will be offensive if, in particular:

— the restrictive effects on the free movement of goods are out of proportion to their purpose;
— the same objective can be attained by other means which are less of a hindrance to trade.

See also Case 120/78 *Rewe-Zentral AG v. Bundesmonopolverwaltung für Branntwein* [1979] ECR 649, [1979] 3 CMLR 494; Case 53/80 *Officier van Justitie v. Koninklijke Kaasfabriek Eyssen BV* [1981] ECR 409, [1982] 2 CMLR 20; Joined Cases 60, 61/84 *Cinéthèque SA v. Fédération Nationale de Cinémas Français* [1985] ECR 2605, [1986] 1 CMLR 365, per Advocate General Slynn. See also §1.068 below 'Mandatory restrictions'.

[141] Case 82/77 *Openbaar Ministerie of the Netherlands v. van Tiggele* [1978] ECR 25, [1978] 2 CMLR 528 and Case 229/83 *Association des Centres Distributeurs Edouard Leclerc v. Au Blé Vert Sàrl* [1985] ECR 1, [1985] 2 CMLR 286. See §1.074 below.

[142] Case 16/83 *Prantl* [1984] ECJ 1299, [1985] 2 CMLR 238.

[143] Case 82/77 *Openbaar Ministerie of the Netherlands v. van Tiggele* [1978] ECR 25, [1978] 2 CMLR 528 and Joined Cases 60, 61/84 *Cinéthèque SA v. Fédération Nationale de Cinémas Français* [1985] ECR 2605, [1986] 1 CMLR 365, per Advocate General Slynn, where a prohibition on imports for a period of one year was caught. See §1.048 above.

[144] See §1.068 below.

[145] See §1.010 et seq. above generally, for the effect of Article 30 on national intellectual property laws.

[146] which govern the customs union.

[147] Joined Cases 55, 57/80 *Musik-Vertrieb membran GmbH v. GEMA* [1981] ECR 147, [1981] 2 CMLR 44, per Advocate General Warner.

'mandatory' requirements and are outside the scope of Article 30 provided that they are reasonable, proportional to their intended purpose and do not amount to an arbitrary restriction on trade between Member States.[148] They should, where relevant, be construed in the light of the European Convention for the Protection of Human Rights and Fundamental Freedoms.[149]

The Court has held mandatory requirements to include, amongst others, those concerning: the effective supervision by fiscal authorities;[150] the protection of health;[151] the protection of the consumer;[152] the fairness of commercial transactions[153] and the protection of culture and in particular cinematographic production.[154]

1.069. Internal transactions etc. Since Article 30 is focused on obstructions on imports, restrictions on purely internal transactions escape its grasp,[155] as do laws which discriminate against national products but favour imports.[156]

1.070. Abuse of Article 30 prohibited. The Treaty may not be abused. Thus Article 30 may not be relied upon by a party who exports goods to another Member State with the sole purpose of reimporting those goods in order to circumvent national legislation.[157] Intention is the crucial element and in its absence, reimported goods are protected by Article 30.

IV. MISCELLANEOUS FREE MOVEMENT ISSUES CONCERNING THE MEDIA

1. Discrimination Affecting Free Movement of Goods

1.071. Treaty terms. The Treaty expressly prohibits discrimination, for Article 7 provides that:

---

[148] Case 8/74 *Procureur du Roi v. Dassonville* [1974] ECR 837, [1974] 2 CMLR 436. Mandatory requirements are also referred to as an application of the 'rule of reason'. See generally: *Halsbury's Laws of England op. cit.*, Vol 52 12.83 et seq. and Oliver, *op. cit.*, 8.18 et seq.

[149] Joined Cases 60, 61/84 *Cinéthèque SA v. Fédération Nationale de Cinémas Français* [1985] ECR 2605, [1986] 1 CMLR 365, per Advocate General Slynn. See also Case 34/79 *R v. Henn and Darby* [1979] ECR 3795, [1980] 1 CMLR 246, per Advocate General Warner. See also §5.004 below.

[150] Case 120/78 *Rewe-Zentral AG v. Bundesmonopolverwaltung für Branntwein* [1979] ECR 649, [1979] 3 CMLR 494.

[151] *Ibid.*; Case 788/79 *Gilli and Andres* [1980] ECR 2071, [1981] 1 CMLR 146.

[152] *Ibid.*; Case 193/80 *Commission v. Italy* [1981] ECR 3019.

[153] *Ibid.* Case 58/80 *Dansk Supermarked A/S v. A/S Imerco* [1981] ECR, 181, [1981] 3 CMLR 590 and Joined Cases 60, 61/84 *Cinéthèque SA v. Fédération Nationale de Cinémas Français* [1985] ECR 2605, [1986] 1 CMLR 365, per Advocate General Slynn.

[154] Joined Cases 60, 61/84 *Cinéthèque SA v. Fédération Nationale de Cinémas Français* [1985] ECR 2605, [1986] 1 CMLR 365, per Advocate General Slynn. See §1.048 above.

[155] Joined Cases 314-316/81 and 83/82 *Procureur de la République v. Waterkeyn* [1982] ECR 4337, [1983] 2 CMLR 145 and Joined Cases 60, 61/84 *Cinéthèque SA v. Fédération Nationale de Cinémas Français* [1985] ECR 2605, [1986] 1 CMLR 365, per Advocate General Slynn.

[156] Case 355/85 *Driancourt and Thouars v. Cognet* [1986] ECR 3231. See §1.073 below.

[157] Case 229/83 *Association des Centres Distributeurs Edouard Leclerc v. Au Blé Vert Sàrl* [1985] ECR 1, [1985] 2 CMLR 286.

Within the scope of application of this Treaty, and without prejudice to any special provisions contained therein, any discrimination on grounds of nationality shall be prohibited.[158]

In addition, Article 37 of the Treaty requires the abolition of discrimination brought about by State monopolies. Article 37(1) states:

Member States shall progressively adjust any State monopolies of a commercial character so as to ensure that when the transitional period has ended no discrimination regarding the conditions under which goods are procured and marketed exists between nationals of Member States . . .

1.072. Discrimination against imported goods. The Court will condemn any undertaking which discriminates in favour of domestic goods. In Sacchi,[159] the Defendant argued that the existence in Italy of a RAI, the State company which held a monopoly in television broadcasting, including the transmission of advertisements, breached the Treaty rules on the free movement of goods. He said that the existence of the monopoly favoured domestic goods because it excluded him from operating a commercial cable channel which would retransmit foreign broadcasts containing advertising. The Court of Justice ruled that television monopolies were legal but held that they could not discriminate in favour of domestic products:

. . . although the existence of a monopoly with regard to television advertising is not in itself contrary to the principle of free movement of goods, such a monopoly would contravene this principle if it discriminated in favour of national material and products.[160]

Neither could such a monopoly discriminate in favour of domestic commercial operators:

. . . the fact that an undertaking of a Member State has an exclusive right to transmit advertisements by television is not as such incompatible with the free movement of products, the marketing of which such advertisements are intended to promote. It would however be different if the exclusive right were used to favour, within the Community, particular trade channels or particular commercial operators in relation to others.[161]

More significantly, the Court affirmed that the requirements that television be organised by Member States as a service in the public interest, could not justify imposing measures which would hinder trade even if those measures were applicable to domestic and imported goods alike.

In Sacchi,[162] the Court of Justice confirmed that Article 37 of the Treaty is concerned with monopolies trading in goods and cannot relate to a monopoly in

---

[158] The second paragraph of Article 7 gives the Council power to adopt rules to prohibit such discrimination.

[159] Case 155/73 [1974] ECR 409, [1974] 2 CMLR 177.

[160] Ibid., para. 7. See §4.181 below concerning Article 90(2) of the Treaty.

[161] Ibid., para. 8. This principle has been affirmed by the Court of Justice in Case C—260/89 Elliniki Radiophonia Tiléorassi—Anonimi Etairia v. Dimotiki Etairia Pliroforissis (DEP) [1991] I ECR 2925 in which it held lawful, a provision of Greek law which conferred on a single company, exclusive rights to make televised announcements and granted to that undertaking for that purpose the exclusive authority to import, hire or distribute material and products necessary for broadcasting. The Court, however, stated that it would be different if the grant of those rights directly or indirectly discriminated against imported products.

[162] Case 155/73 [1974] ECR 409, [1974] 2 CMLR 177.

the provision of services. This followed from the place of the provision in the Chapter on the elimination of quantitative restrictions and from the use of the words 'imports' and 'exports' in the second indent of Article 37(1) and of the words 'products' in Article 37(3) and (4). It was thus excluded from applying to broadcasting monopolies.

1.073. Discrimination against domestic goods. In *Driancourt and Thouars v. Cognet*,[163] the Defendant was charged with selling books at a 20% discount on the publisher's selling price in breach of French criminal law. The Court of Justice had already established that this law was in breach of Article 30 in as much as it applied either to books imported from other Member States or to books reimported from such States having been exported from France.[164] Mr Cognet argued that this law breached Community non-discrimination principles since it prejudiced national products (never having been reimported into France). For they were subject to retail price maintenance laws whilst imported books were freed from the constraints of the legislation. The Court of Justice held that Article 7 prohibits discrimination against individuals (ie traders), according to their nationality or to the place in which they are established. Since that was clearly not the case here, Article 7 did not apply.[165] With regard to any potential breach of Article 30, following from the different treatment accorded to national books, the Court ruled that:

> It should be added that Article 30 of the EEC Treaty does not forbid such a difference of treatment. The purpose of that provision is to eliminate obstacles to the importation of goods and not to ensure that goods of national origin always enjoy the same treatment as imported or reimported goods. The absence of restrictions as regards the selling price of reimported books does not prejudice the sale of such books. A difference in treatment between goods which is not capable of restricting imports or of prejudicing the marketing of imported or reimported goods does not fall within the prohibition contained in Article 30.

The Court also stated that:

> As regards the general principle of non-discrimination, it must be observed that Community law does not apply to treatment which works to the detriment of national products as compared with imported products or to the detriment of retailers who sell national products as compared with retailers who sell imported products and which is put into effect by a Member State in a sector which is not subject to Community rules or in relation to which there has been no harmonization of national rules.

2. Free Movement of Books subject to Fixed Retail Price Requirements

1.074. Many Member States impose fixed pricing requirements on the retailing of books. In *Association des Centres Distributeurs Edouard Leclerc v. Au Blé Vert Sàrl*,[166]

---

[163] Case 355/85 [1986] ECR 3231.

[164] See Case 229/83 *Association des Centres Distributeurs Edouard Leclerc v. Au Blé Vert Sàrl* [1985] ECR 1, [1985] 2 CMLR 286. See §1.074 below.

[165] Affirmed by the Court of Justice in Case 168/86 *Procureur Général v. Rousseau* [1987] ECR 995 and Case 160/86 *Ministère Public v. Verbrugge* [1987] ECR 1783, [1989] 2 CMLR 51, in respect of similar criminal proceedings.

[166] Case 229/83 [1985] ECR 1, [1985] 2 CMLR 286. See §4.074 et seq. below.

the Court of Justice had to consider Article 30 in its application to national retail price fixing laws. Under the French law of 10 August 1981, all publishers or importers of books were required to fix the retail prices for the books which they published or imported. Retailers then had to charge between 95% and 100% of that price for the sales of those books to the public. The Appellants sold books at prices undercutting the prices stipulated in the legislation and were sued by a number of bookshops and the French booksellers' association for breaching French law. The Court of Justice held that the national legislation resulted in a restriction in breach of Article 30 because it made it impossible for an importer to charge the retail price in the importing State that he considered adequate in the light of the cost price in the State in which it was published. In that sense it did not treat imported and domestic books equally. The Court also held that a provision requiring books which had been reimported, to be sold at the fixed price, contravened Article 30. Although it did not make a distinction between domestic and imported books, it discouraged the marketing of reimported books by preventing the importer from passing on in the retail price an advantage resulting from a lower price obtained in the exporting Member State.

The French Government argued that the legislation was necessary to conserve specialist booksellers from competition from those distribution channels which relied on reduced margins and limited number of book titles. It said also that its purpose was to avoid a small number of book distributors from imposing their will on publishers to the detriment of poetic, scientific and creative works. Refusing to shield the legislation behind Article 36, the Court held that:

> Since it derogates from a fundamental rule of the Treaty, Article 36 must be interpreted strictly and cannot be extended to cover objectives not expressly enumerated therein. Neither the safeguarding of consumers interests nor the protection of creativity and cultural diversity in the realm of publishing is mentioned in Article 36. It follows that the justification put forward by the French Government cannot be accepted.[167]

Following the decision, the French law was amended on terms that it did not apply to imported books. Neither would it apply to reimported books unless it was objectively proven that those books were reimported specifically to circumvent the legislation.

---

[167] *Ibid.*, para. 30. Followed by the Court of Justice in Case 95/84 *Boriello v. Darras and Tostain* [1986] ECR 2253 which concerned identical facts but a criminal rather than civil action.

CHAPTER TWO

Freedom of Establishment and Freedom to Provide Services

I. FREEDOM OF ESTABLISHMENT

1. Introduction

2.001. Treaty terms. Articles 52 to 58, which are contained in the part of the Treaty entitled 'Free Movement of Persons, Services and Capital', govern the right of establishment.[1] The Articles are as follows:

Article 52. Within the framework of the provisions set out below, restrictions on the freedom of establishment of nationals of a Member State in the territory of another Member State shall be abolished by progressive stages in the course of the transitional period. Such progressive abolition shall also apply to restrictions on the setting up of agencies, branches, or subsidiaries by nationals of any Member State established in the territory of any Member State.

Freedom of establishment shall include the right to take up and pursue activities as self-employed persons and to set up and manage undertakings, in particular companies or firms within the meaning of the second paragraph of Art. 58, under the conditions laid down for its own nationals by the law of the country where such establishment is effected, subject to the provisions of the Chapter relating to capital.

Article 53. Member States shall not introduce any new restrictions on the right of establishment in their territories of nationals of other Member States, save as otherwise provided in this Treaty.

Article 54.I. Before the end of the first stage, the Council shall, acting unanimously on a proposal from the Commission and after consulting the Economic and Social Committee and the Assembly, draw up a general programme for the abolition of existing restrictions on freedom of establishment within the Community. The Commission shall submit its proposal to the Council during the first two years of the first stage.

The programme shall set out the general conditions under which freedom of establishment is to be attained in the case of each type of activity and in particular the stages by which it is to be attained.

---

[1] Part Two, Title III, Chapter 2.

2. In order to implement this general programme or, in the absence of such programme, in order to achieve a stage in attaining freedom of establishment as regards a particular activity, the Council shall, acting on a proposal from the Commission, in co-operation with the European Parliament and after consulting the Economic and Social Committee, issue directives, acting unanimously until the end of the first stage and by a qualified majority thereafter.

3. The Council and the Commission shall carry out the duties developing upon them under the preceding provisions, in particular:

(a) by according, as a general rule, priority treatment to activities where freedom of establishment makes a particularly valuable contribution to the development of production and trade;

(b) by ensuring close co-operation between the competent authorities in the Member States in order to ascertain the particular situation within the Community of the various activities concerned;

(c) by abolishing those administrative procedures and practices, whether resulting from national legislation or from agreements previously concluded between Member States, the maintenance of which would form an obstacle to freedom of establishment;

(d) by ensuring that workers of one Member State employed in the territory of another Member State may remain in that territory for the purpose of taking up activities therein as self-employed persons, where they satisfy the conditions which they would be required to satisfy if they were entering that State at the time when they intended to take up such activities;

(e) by enabling a national of one Member State to acquire and use land and buildings situated in the territory of another Member State, in so far as this does not conflict with the principles laid down in Art. 39(2);

(f) by effecting the progressive abolition of restrictions on freedom of establishment in every branch of activity under consideration, both as regards the conditions for setting up agencies, branches or subsidiaries in the territory of a Member State and as regards the conditions governing the entry of personnel belonging to the main establishment into managerial or supervisory posts in such agencies, branches or subsidiaries;

(g) by co-ordinating to the necessary extent the safeguards which, for the protection of the interests of members and others, are required by Member States of companies or firms within the meaning of the second paragraph of Art. 58 with a view to making such safeguards equivalent throughout the Community;

(h) by satisfying themselves that the conditions of establishment are not distorted by aids granted by Member States.

Article 55. The provisions of this Chapter shall not apply, so far as any given Member State is concerned, to activities which in that State are connected, even occasionally, with the exercise of official authority.

The Council may, acting by a qualified majority on a proposal from the Commission, rule that the provisions of this Chapter shall not apply to certain activities.

Article 56.I. The provisions of this Chapter and measures taken in pursuance thereof shall not prejudice the applicability of provisions laid down by law, regulation or administrative action providing for special treatment for foreign nationals on grounds of public policy, public security or public health.

2. Before the end of the transitional period, the Council shall, acting unanimously on a proposal from the Commission and after consulting the Assembly, issue directives for the co-ordination of the aforementioned provisions laid down by law, regulation or administrative action. After the end of the second stage, however, the Council shall, acting by a qualified majority on a proposal from the Commission and in co-operation with the European Parliament, issue directives for the co-ordination of such provisions as, in each Member State, are a matter for regulation or administrative action.

Article 57.I. In order to make it easier for persons to take up and pursue activities as self-employed persons, the Council shall, on a proposal from the Commission and in co-operation with the European Parliament, acting unanimously during the first stage and by a qualified majority thereafter, issue directives for the mutual recognition of diplomas, certificates and other evidence of formal qualifications.

2. For the same purpose, the Council shall, before the end of the transitional period, acting on a proposal from the Commission and after consulting the Assembly, issue directives for the co-ordination of the provisions laid down by law, regulation or administrative action in Member States concerning the taking up and pursuit of activities as self-employed persons. Unanimity shall be required for directives the implementation of which involves in at least one Member State amendment of the existing principles laid down by law governing the professions with respect to training and conditions of access for natural persons. In other cases, the Council shall act by a qualified majority, in co-operation with the European Parliament.

3. In the case of the medical and allied, and pharmaceutical professions, the progressive abolition of restrictions shall be dependent upon co-ordination of the conditions for their exercise in the various Member States.

Article 58. Companies or firms formed in accordance with the law of a Member State and having their registered office, central administration or principal place of business within the Community shall, for the purposes of this Chapter, be treated in the same way as natural persons who are nationals of Member States.

'Companies or firms' means companies or firms constituted under civil or commercial law, including co-operative societies, and other legal persons governed by public or private law, save for those which are non-profit making.

2. Liberalisation and Harmonisation Programme

(1) Introduction

2.002. History of liberalisation programme. Article 52 of the Treaty required, during the course of the transitional period,[2] the abolition of those restrictions on the nationals of a Member State which prevented them from establishing themselves in the territory of another Member State.[3] In accordance with Article 54(1) of the Treaty, the Council was charged with the duty of drawing up a 'general programme' to fulfil the liberalisation demanded by the Treaty:

> The programme shall set out the general conditions under which freedom of establishment is to be attained in the case of each type of activity and in particular the stages by which it is to be attained.

A 'General Programme for the abolition of restrictions on freedom of establishment' (the 'General Programme') was duly enacted by the Council on 18 December 1961.[4] It set out, amongst other matters, the beneficiaries (Title I), the specific restrictions to be abolished (Title III), and a timetable within which the requirements were to be fulfilled (Title IV). It also contained five Annexes. These categorised the economic activities referred to in the timetable, in accordance with the 'International Standard Industrial Classification of all Economic Activities' ('ISIC').[5]

---

[2] That is, a period of twelve years which commenced on the entering into force of the Treaty and expired on 31 December 1969.

[3] See also Article 8 of the Treaty which sets out the general timetable for the transitional period.

[4] No 36/62, OJ 1962, p.7, Sp Edn (Second Series) IX, p.7.

[5] Issued by the Statistical Office of the United Nations. (See Statistical Papers, Series M No 4 Rev 1, New York, 1958). The Annexes classify activities into a 'Major Group' with 'Group' subdivisions.

Article 52 has had 'direct effect' since the expiry of the transitional period.[6] The status of the General Programme is that of a set of principles or guidelines for the implementation of the Treaty provisions and the interpretation of the directives issued pursuant to the General Programme. They do not therefore themselves create rights.[7]

2.003. Beneficiaries of the General Programme. Title I of the General Programme specifies its beneficiaries. They are divided into two categories. The first concerns those who wish to establish themselves in order to pursue activities as self-employed persons in a Member State. Qualifying persons are:

(1) nationals of Member States[8] and
(2) companies and firms formed under the laws of a Member State,[9] having either the seat prescribed by their Statutes, or their centre of administration, or their establishment situated within the Community.[10]

The second category concerns those who wish to set up agencies, branches or subsidiaries in a Member State. Qualifying persons are:

(1) nationals of Member States[11] who are established in a Member State[12] and
(2) companies and firms formed under the law of a Member State[13] having either the seat prescribed by their States, or their centre of administration, or their main establishment situated within the Community.[14] This is subject to the proviso that where only the seat prescribed by their statutes is situated within the Community, their activity must show a real and continuous link with the economy of a Member State.[15] The link must not be one of nationality, whether of the members of the company or firm, or of the persons holding managerial or supervisory posts therein, or of the holders of the capital.

2.004. Restrictions to be abolished. Title III of the General Programme generally requires Member States to eliminate both 'overt' and 'covert' discrimination, including (amongst others):

---

[6] Case 2/74 *Reyners v. Belgium* [1974] ECR 631, [1974] 2 CMLR 305. On the concept of direct effect, see generally: *Halsbury's Laws of England* (4th Edn, 1986), Vol 51, 3.41 et seq. and T C Hartley, *The Foundations of European Community Law* (2nd Edn, 1988), Chapter 7.

[7] See D Lasok, *Professions and Services in the European Economic Community* (1986), Chapter 2, Part II, citing amongst other cases: Case 71/76 *Thieffry v. Conseil de lordre des avocats à Paris* [1977] ECR 765, [1977] 2 CMLR 373 and Joined Cases 110, 111/78 *Ministère Public v. Van Wesemael* [1979] ECR 35, [1979] 3 CMLR 87.

[8] Or of overseas countries and territories with which association agreements have been concluded. For the Community concept of 'nationals', see *Halsbury's Laws of England op. cit.* Vol 52, 16.13 et seq. and D Lasok, *op. cit.*, Chapter 3, part I.

[9] Or of overseas countries and territories with which association agreements have been concluded. Concerning the rules on overseas territories, see *Halsbury's Laws of England op. cit.* Vol 52, 16.06 et seq.

[10] Or the overseas country or territory.

[11] Or of overseas countries and territories with which association agreements have been concluded.

[12] *Ibid.*

[13] *Ibid.*

[14] *Ibid.*

[15] *Ibid.*

A. Any measure which, pursuant to any provision laid down by law, Regulation or administrative action in a Member State, or as the result of the application of such a provision, or of administrative practices, prohibits or hinders nationals of other Member States in their pursuit of an activity as a self-employed person by treating nationals of other Member States differently from nationals of the country concerned.

B. Any requirements imposed, pursuant to any provision laid down by law, regulation or administrative action or in consequence of any administrative practice, in respect of the taking up or pursuit of an activity as a self-employed person where, although applicable irrespective of nationality, their effect is exclusively or principally, to hinder the taking up or pursuit of such activity by foreign nationals.

The General Programme also particularises restrictive provisions and practices which are to be abolished.[16]

(2) Liberalisation and Harmonisation of Film Services

(i) Introduction

2.005. The Title III restrictions to be abolished included, amongst others, the provisions and practices which, impeded the power of self-employed persons '(e) to acquire, use or dispose of intellectual property and all rights deriving therefrom.' The film industry is subsumed under Major Group ex 84 of Annex 1 of the General Programme, being 'Recreation Services'. Specifically, Group ex 841 includes 'Film production, distribution and projection, opening of theatres that specialise exclusively in the showing of films in the language of the country of origin.' The following Directives have been enacted.

(ii) Legislation

2.006. Council Directive 65/264/EEC—Specialist cinemas, import and screen quotas and dubbing of films. Council Directive 65/264/EEC[17] required Member States to abolish Title III restrictions on freedom of establishment (and freedom to provide services) in three areas: the opening of cinemas specialising in foreign films exhibited in their original language version; import and screen quotas and the dubbing of films.

2.007. Council Directive 68/369/EEC—Freedom of self-employed persons to provide services in film distribution. Council Directive 68/369/EEC[18] obliged Member States to abolish Title III restrictions on freedom of establishment of self-employed persons involved in film distribution.

2.008. Council Directive 70/451/EEC—Freedom of self-employed persons to provide services in film production. Under Council Directive 70/451/EEC,[19] Member States were required to abolish Title III restrictions on freedom of establishment (and freedom to provide services) that affected the right of self-employed persons to undertake activities in film production.

---

[16] See Title III.
[17] OJ Sp Edn 1965-1966, p. 62. See §6.015 below.
[18] OJ Sp Edn 1968 (II), p. 520. See §6.024 below.
[19] OJ Sp Edn 1970 (II), p. 620. See §6.032 below.

II. FREEDOM TO PROVIDE SERVICES

1. Introduction

2.009. Treaty terms. Articles 59 to 66 of the Treaty govern the freedom to provide services and like the establishment rules, are contained in that part of the Treaty entitled 'Free Movement of Persons, Services and Capital'.[20] They are as follows:

Article 59. Within the framework of the provisions set out below, restrictions on freedom to provide services within the Community shall be progressively abolished during the transitional period in respect of nationals of Member States who are established in a State of the Community other than that of the person for whom the services are intended.

The Council may, acting by a qualified majority on a proposal from the Commission, extend the provisions of this Chapter to nationals of a third country who provide services and who are established within the Community.

Article 60. Services shall be considered to be 'services' within the meaning of this Treaty where they are normally provided for remuneration, in so far as they are not governed by the provisions relating to freedom of movement for goods, capital and persons.

'Services' shall in particular include:

(a) activities of an industrial character;
(b) activities of a commercial character;
(c) activities of craftsmen;
(d) activities of the professions.

Without prejudice to the provisions of the Chapter relating to the right of establishment, the person providing a service may, in order to do so, temporarily pursue his activity in the State where the service is provided, under the same conditions as are imposed by that State on its own nationals.

Article 61. I. Freedom to provide services in the field of transport shall be governed by the provisions of the Title relating to transport.

2. The liberalisation of banking and insurance services connected with movements of capital shall be effected in step with the progressive liberalisation of movement of capital.

Article 62. Save as otherwise provided in this Treaty, Member States shall not introduce any new restrictions on the freedom to provide services which has in fact been attained at the date of the entry into force of this Treaty.

Article 63.I. Before the end of the first stage, the Council shall, acting unanimously on a proposal from the Commission and after consulting the Economic and Social Committee and the Assembly, draw up a general programme for the abolition of existing restrictions on freedom to provide services within the Community. The Commission shall submit its proposal to the Council during the first two years of the first stage.

The programme shall set out the general conditions under which and the stages by which each type of service is to be liberalised.

2. In order to implement this general programme or, in the absence of such programme, in order to achieve a stage in the liberalisation of a specific service, the Council shall, on a proposal from the Commission and after consulting the Economic and Social Committee and the Assembly, issue directives, acting unanimously until the end of the first stage and by a qualified majority thereafter.

---

[20] Part Two, Title III, Chapter 3.

3. As regards the proposals and decisions referred to in paragraphs 1 and 2, priority shall as a general rule be given to those services which directly affect production costs or the liberalisation of which helps to promote trade in goods.

Article 64. The Member States declare their readiness to undertake the liberalisation of services beyond the extent required by the directives issued pursuant to Art. 63(2), if their general economic situation and the situation of the economic sector concerned so permit.

To this end, the Commission shall make recommendations to the Member States concerned.

Article 65. As long as restrictions on freedom to provide services have not been abolished, each Member State shall apply such restrictions without distinction on grounds of nationality or residence to all persons providing services within the meaning of the first paragraph of Art. 59.

Article 66. The provisions of Arts. 55 to 58 shall apply to the matters covered by this Chapter.

2. Liberalisation and Harmonisation Programme

(i) Introduction

2.010. History of the liberalisation programme. Article 59 of the Treaty required, during the course of the transitional period,[21] the abolition of measures restricting nationals established in one Member State from providing their services to nationals established in the territory of another Member State.[22] Article 63 obligated the Council to draw up a general programme:

> The programme shall set out the general conditions under which and the stages by which each type of service is to be liberalised.

A 'General Programme for the abolition of restrictions on freedom to provide services' (the 'General Programme') was enacted by the Council on 18 December 1961.[23] It set out, amongst other matters, its beneficiaries (Title I), the specific restrictions to be abolished (Title III), and a Timetable within which the requirements were to be fulfilled (Title V) detailing the sectors in which restrictions were to be abolished. The Court of Justice has held that since the expiry of the transitional period, Article 59, first paragraph has had direct effect[24] as has Article 60, third paragraph.[25]

---

[21] that is, a period of twelve years which commenced on the entering into force of the Treaty and expired on 31 December 1969.

[22] See also Article 8 which sets out the general timetable for the transitional period.

[23] No 32/62, OJ 1962, p.3, Sp Edn (Second Series) IX, p.3. Although, as Advocate General Warner pointed out in Case 52/79 *Procureur du Roi v. Debauve* [1980] ECR 833, [1981] 2 CMLR 362, the existence of Article 63(2) illustrates that the General Programme was not essential for the implementation of Article 59 during the transitional period.

[24] See Joined Cases 110, 111/78 *Ministère Public v. Van Wesemael* [1979] ECR 35, [1979] 3 CMLR 87 and Case 52/79 *Procureur du Roi v. Debauve* [1980] ECR 833, [1981] 2 CMLR 362, per Advocate General Warner. For the concept of 'direct effect', see the references cited §2.002 fn 6 above. As for the status of the General Programme, see §2.002 fn 7 above.

[25] Case 33/74 *Van Binsbergen v. Bestuur van de Bedrijsvereniging voor de Mataalnijverheid* [1974] ECR 1299 [1975] 1 CMLR 298.

2.011. Beneficiaries of the General Programme. Title I of the General Programme specifies the beneficiaries. Persons qualifying are:

(1) nationals of Member States who are established within the Community;
(2) companies or firms formed under the law of a Member State and having the seat prescribed by their statues, or their centre of administration, or their main establishment situated within the Community. This is subject to the proviso that where only their main seat is situated within the Community their activity must show a real and continuous link with the economy of a Member State. Such a link cannot be one of nationality, whether of the members of the company or firm, or of the persons holding managerial or supervisory posts therein, or of the holders of the capital.

In both of the above cases, qualification is subject to the condition that the service is carried out either personally by the person contracting to provide it or by one of his agencies or branches established in the Community.

2.012. Restrictions to be abolished. Title III of the General Programme generally requires the abolition of both discriminatory and non-discriminatory restrictions, including (amongst others):

A. Any measures which, pursuant to any provision laid down by law, Regulation or administrative action in a Member State, or as a result of the application of such a provision, or of administrative practices, prohibits or hinders the person providing services in his pursuit of an activity as a self-employed person by treating him differently from nationals of the State concerned...

    Furthermore, any requirements imposed, pursuant to any provision laid down by law, Regulation or administrative action or in consequence of any administrative practice, in respect of the provision of services are also to be regarded as restrictions where, although applicable irrespective of nationality, their effect is exclusively or principally to hinder the provision of services by foreign nationals.

B. Any prohibition of, or hindrance to, the movement of the item to be supplied in the course of the service or of the materials comprising such item or of the tools, machinery equipment and other means to be employed in the provision of the service.[26]

C. Any prohibition of, or impediment to, the transfer of the funds needed to perform the service.[27]

D. Any prohibition of, or hindrance to, payments for services, where the provision of such services between the Member States is limited only by restrictions in respect of the payments therefor.

However, in respect of the provisions referred to in paragraphs C and D, Member States shall retain the right to verify the nature and genuineness of transfer of funds and of payments and to take all necessary measures in order to prevent contravention of their laws and regulations, in particular as regards the issue of foreign currency to tourists.

---

[26] Title III.B.
[27] Title III.C.

(2) Liberalisation of Film Services

(i) Introduction

2.013. The Title III restrictions to be abolished included, amongst others, those which impeded the power of foreign nationals '(e) to acquire use or dispose of intellectual property and all rights deriving therefrom.' The timetable set out in Title V specified that restrictions in the film industry were to be abolished before the end of the third stage of the transitional period. However, in States where existing rules restricted the importation of exposed and developed films, the bilateral quotas existing between Member States at the time of the entry into force of the Treaty were, before the end of the first stage, to be increased by one third.[28]

(ii) Legislation

2.014. Council Directive 63/607/EEC—Importation, distribution and commercial exploitation of films. Council Directive 63/607/EEC[29] provides rules to ensure that short films, newsreel films and full length films (of documentary value) which have the 'nationality' of a Member State may be imported into and distributed and commercially exploited within all other Member States.

2.015. Council Directive 65/264/EEC—Specialist cinemas, import and screen quotas and dubbing of films. Council Directive 65/264/EEC[30] required Member States to abolish Title III restrictions on freedom to provide services and (freedom of establishment) in three areas: the opening of cinemas specialising in foreign films exhibited in their original language version; import and screen quotas and the dubbing of films.

2.016. Council Directive 70/451/EEC—Freedom of self-employed persons to provide services in film production. Council Directive 70/451/EEC[31] required Member States to abolish Title III restrictions on freedom to provide services (and freedom of establishment) which affected the right of self-employed persons to undertake activities in film production.

(3) Liberalisation of Broadcasting Services

(i) Introduction

2.017. By 1985, there were still many sectors, including broadcasting, in which the Treaty's goal of establishing a 'common market' had not been fulfilled. In 1986, the Member States entered into the 'Single European Act' agreeing to adopt measures with the aim of establishing the 'internal market' over a period expiring on

---

[28] Article 106(3) of the Treaty also required the abolition of restrictions on transfers connected with invisible transactions listed in Annex III of the Treaty. Those transactions include authors' royalties.

[29] OJ Sp Edn 1963-1964, p. 52. See §6.001 below.

[30] OJ Sp Edn 1965-1966, p. 62. See §6.015 below.

[31] OJ Sp Edn 1970 (II), p. 620. See §6.032 below.

31 December 1992.[32] The Directive 'Television Without Frontiers'[33] has been adopted as part of the 1992 programme to set a harmonizing mechanism in motion.[34]

(ii) Legislation

2.018. Council Directive 89/552/EEC—'Television Without Frontiers'. After a considerable gestation period, Council Directive 89/552/EEC[35] was adopted on 3 October, 1989. It harmonizes legislation in the field of television broadcasting, production, advertising, sponsorship, as well as programme content and it confers on individuals, the right of access to broadcasting facilities.

The Directive's essential purpose is to create an internal market in broadcasting. It achieves this by stipulating, amongst other things, that Member States are to permit freedom of reception and retransmission on their territory of television signals which have been transmitted from other Member States in accordance with the rules prevailing there as harmonised by the terms of the Directive. This applies to all modes of transmission of television signals: terrestrial broadcasts and broadcasts by Direct Broadcast Satellite; transmissions by Fixed Service Satellite and cable retransmissions. The Directive does not, however, apply to broadcast material protected by copyright.

3. The Scope of Article 59—Case Law

(1) The Two Interpretations

2.019. The scope of Article 59 is the key issue for providers of any form of interstate service.[36] The central theme of general case law is this: is Article 59 intended only to abolish discrimination against persons established in one Member State who are intending to provide services to persons established in another Member State? Or does Article 59 have a wider purpose, namely, the abolition of all restrictions on those persons intending to provide such services. The sections below explain the development of the case law in this area.[37]

(2) Abolition of Discrimination

2.020. Overt and covert discrimination. The Court has consistently held that

---

[32] Article 8A of the EEC Treaty. That Article states: 'The internal market shall comprise an area without internal frontiers in which the free movement of goods, persons, services and capital is ensured in accordance with the provisions of this Treaty.'
[33] Council Directive 89/552/EEC of 3 October 1989 OJ No L 298, 17.10.89, p. 23.
[34] See §§2.018 above and 6.056 below.
[35] OJ No L 298, 17.10.89, p. 23. See §6.056 below.
[36] See generally, D Wyatt and A Dashwood, *The Substantive Law of the EEC*, (2nd Edn, 1987), Chapter 9 and D Lasok, *op. cit.*, Chapter 2, part IV.
[37] For a discussion of these issues, see Case C—76/90 *Säger v. Dennemeyer & Co Ltd*, [1991] I ECR 4221, per Advocate General Jacobs. See also G Marenco, The Notion of Restriction on the Freedom of Establishment and Provision of Services in the Case law of the Court, Yearbook of European Law, (1992), p.111 and the articles cited therein.

Article 59 is designed to prohibit both 'overt' and 'covert' discrimination.[38]

2.021. Discrimination only by human activity. The Court of Justice has ruled that the Treaty is concerned solely with eradicating discrimination caused by human activity. *Procureur du Roi v. Debauve*,[39] concerned a Belgian ban on the retransmission by cable of advertisements broadcast from neighbouring Member States. The national court demanded whether those rules introduced discrimination based on the geographical locality of the foreign broadcasting station: a foreign station would be able to transmit advertisements only within its natural reception zone and the reception zone of one foreign broadcaster might be less densely populated than the natural reception zones of others. The Court of Justice held that:

> . . . such differences, which are due to natural phenomena, cannot be described as 'discrimination' within the meaning of the Treaty; the latter regards only differences in treatment arising from human activity, and especially from measures taken by public authorities, as discrimination. Moreover, it should be pointed out that even if the Community has in some respects intervened to compensate for natural inequalities, it has no duty to take steps to eradicate differences in situations such as those contemplated . . .

2.022. Whether abolition of discrimination is the only object. The Court has occasionally expressed the view that Article 59 is focused solely on discrimination: that its terms are totally fulfilled provided only that any discrimination (whether overt or covert) is erased. Thus, for example, in *Société Générale Alsacienne de Banque SA v. Koestler*[40] the Court of Justice stated that:

> . . . whilst it prohibits discrimination, [the Treaty] does not impose any obligation to treat a foreigner providing services more favourably, with reference to his domestic law, than a person providing services established in the Member State where the services have been provided.

(3) Abolition of Restrictions

(i) Common Market for the Provision of Services

2.023. Treaty terms. Despite the aforementioned statement in *Société Générale Alsacienne de Banque SA v. Koestler*, the Court's judgments have more often been consistent with the notion that Article 59 has the wider purpose of removing all restrictions.[41] Indeed, the express terms of the Treaty encourage that interpretation.

---

[38] Case 279/80 *Webb* [1981] ECR 3305, [1982] 1 CMLR 719 (concerning covert discrimination). In Joined Cases 62, 63/81 *SECO SA v. Establissement D'Assurance contre la Vieillesse et l'Invalidité* [1982] ECR 223, the Court of Justice stated that Articles 59 and 60 '. . . prohibit not only overt discrimination based on the nationality of the person providing a service but also all forms of covert discrimination which, although based on criteria which appear to be neutral, in practice lead to the same result.' On the abolition of covert discrimination concerning free movement of workers, see Case 152/73 *Sotgiu v. Deutsche Bundespost* [1974] ECR 153. See also Case C–76/90 *Säger v. Dennemeyer & Co Ltd*, [1991] I ECR 4221, per Advocate General Jacobs.

[39] Case 52/79 [1980] ECR 833, [1981] 2 CMLR 362. See §2.032 below.

[40] Case 15/78 [1978] ECR 1971, [1979] 1 CMLR 89, para. 5.

[41] See e.g. Case 33/74 *Van Binsbergen v. Bestuur van de Bedrifsvereniging voor de Mataalnijverheid* [1974] ECR 1299 [1975] 1 CMLR 298, para. 10, and Case 39/75 *Coenen v. Sociaal-Economische Raad* [1975] ECR 1547, [1976] 1 CMLR 30, para. 6. where the Court of Justice held that: '*The restrictions to be abolished pursuant to this provision include all requirements imposed on the person providing the service by reason in particular of his nationality* or of the fact that he does not habitually reside in the State where the service is provided, which do not apply to persons established within the national territory or *which may prevent or otherwise obstruct the activities of the persons providing the service.*' (italics added)

According to Article 59, a 'Common Market' in services was to be progressively established during a period of twelve years to expire on December 31, 1969 (known as the transitional period).[42] But as Advocate General Warner pointed out in *Procureur du Roi v. Debauve*,[43] the existence of Article 65 illustrates that the framers of the Treaty perceived a distinction between the abolition of discrimination and the abolition of restrictions. Article 65 states:

> As long as restrictions on freedom to provide services have not been abolished, each Member State shall apply such restrictions without distinction on grounds of nationality or residence to all persons providing services within the meaning of the first paragraph of Art. 59.[44]

From this it appears that whilst a Common Market devoid of restrictions was the Treaty's ultimate goal, Article 65 required the instant abolition of discrimination. [45]

Furthermore, as the Advocate General noted, the final sentence of Article 60 also illustrates the wider purpose of Article 59. It states:

> Without prejudice to the provisions of the Chapter relating to the right of establishment, the person providing a service may, in order to do so, temporarily pursue his activity in the State where the service is provided, under the same conditions as are imposed by that State on its own nationals.[46]

In other words, a Member State may subject a foreign provider of services to the same conditions applied to nationals, when the foreign provider journeys to that Member State in order to provide his services there.[47] This envisages temporary presence in that Member State. However, no restrictions may be imposed when the foreign provider of the service remains within his own Member State whilst providing his services to persons in the other Member State.

2.024. Court's current view. In *Säger v. Dennemeyer*[48] & Co Ltd, the Court of Justice has held that the purpose of the Treaty is indeed to create a 'common market' in services and not merely abolish discrimination:

> ... Article 59 of the Treaty requires not only the elimination of all discrimination against a person providing services on the ground of his nationality but also the abolition of any restriction, even if it applies without distinction to national providers of services and to those of other Member States, when it is liable to prohibit or otherwise impede the activities of a provider of services established in another Member State where he lawfully provides similar services.[49]

---

[42] On the General Programme, See §2.010 above.

[43] Case 52/79 [1980] ECR 833, [1981] 2 CMLR 362.

[44] See also General Programme for the abolition of restrictions on freedom to provide services, Title IV which states that 'Until restrictions have been abolished, each Member State shall apply them in such a way as to accord to all beneficiaries falling within Title I, without distinction on grounds of nationality or residence, the most favourable treatment accorded under existing practices and bilateral or multilateral agreements ...' No 32/62, OJ 1962, p.3, Sp Edn (Second Series) IX, p.3.

[45] By way of contrast, the Treaty provisions on freedom of establishment (Articles 52 to 58) are solely concerned with abolishing discrimination: see for e.g. Case 6/64 Costa v. ENEL [1964] ECR 585, [1964] CMLR 425.

[46] See also now Case C—76/90 Säger v. Dennemeyer & Co Ltd, [1991] I ECR 4221 the judgment and per Advocate General Jacobs.

[47] in which case the distinction between the concepts of freedom of establishment and freedom to provide services is blurred, see Case 48/75 Royer [1976] ECR 497, [1976] 2 CMLR 619, para. 12.

[48] Case C—76/90 [1991] 1 ECR 4221, para. 12.

[49] This was also the conclusion reached by Advocate General Slynn in Case 279/80 Webb [1981] ECR 3305, [1982] 1 CMLR 719.

The fundamental point is that if a national of one Member State had to comply with special requirements[50] pertaining in another Member State in order to provide his services there, he would in practical terms have to establish himself in the latter State. That obligation would render worthless the whole chapter of the Treaty guaranteeing freedom to provide services.[51]

(ii) Restrictions in the 'General Interest'

2.025. General principles. Despite the Treaty's general requirement that all restrictions be eradicated, there may be occasions when a Member State may legitimately maintain a restriction in the 'general interest'. The 'general interest' is a concept used by the Court to make exceptions to fundamental obligations contained within the Treaty.[52] Sometimes those exceptions are absolute and at other times they anticipate the adoption of measures by the Community.[53] In Webb,[54] the Court of Justice permitted a restriction in the 'general interest'. It held that:

> . . . regard being had to the particular nature of certain services, specific requirements imposed on the provider of the services cannot be considered incompatible with the Treaty where they have as their purpose the application of rules governing such activities. However, the freedom to provide services is one of the fundamental principles of the Treaty and may be restricted only by provisions which are justified by the general good and which are imposed on all persons or undertakings operating in the said State in so far as that interest is not safeguarded by the provisions to which the provider of the service is subject in the Member State of his establishment.[55]

As well as being non-discriminatory, any restriction on services justified in the 'general interest' must be 'proportional' to the needs it seeks to protect.[56]

---

[50] albeit, non-discriminatory restrictions.

[51] Case 33/74 Van Binsbergen v. Bestuur van de Bedrifsvereniging voor de Mataalnijverheid [1974] ECR 1299 [1975] 1 CMLR 298; Case C—154/89 EC Commission v. France [1991] I ECR 659; Case C—180/89 EC Commission v. Italy (not yet reported); Case C—198/89 EC Commission v. Greece I ECR 727; Case C—76/90 Säger v. Dennemeyer & Co Ltd, [1991] 1 ECR 4221 both in the judgment and per Advocate General Jacobs.

[52] In fact, the principle that Article 59 has the wider purpose of eradicating restrictions — firmly established by the Court of Justice in Säger v. Dennemeyer — has been implicitly accepted for a long time with the Court's evolution of the 'general interest' principle. Commonly, the Court has reached the conclusion that a Member State is not conducting discrimination — whether overt or covert — but is nevertheless maintaining a restriction: a restriction which applies to nationals and non-nationals alike. Often the Court has permitted the Member State to maintain that restriction. However, the Court has implied that such a restriction is not permitted by the Treaty, for it has attempted to find some legal justification for it outside of the Treaty. It thus calls upon the concept of the 'general interest'.

[53] For an example of a temporary restriction, see §2.038 below.

[54] Case 279/80 [1981] ECR 3305, [1982] 1 CMLR 719, paras. 16 and 17.

[55] This principle was formulated in Case 33/74 Van Binsbergen v. Bestuur van de Bedrifsvereniging voor de Mataalnijverheid [1974] ECR 1299 [1975] 1 CMLR 298. For a discussion of these issues, see the Opinion of Advocate General Jacobs in Case C—76/90 Säger v. Dennemeyer & Co Ltd [1991] I ECR 4220.

[56] Case 39/75 Coenen v. Sociaal-Economische Raad [1975] ECR 1547, [1976] 1 CMLR 30; Case 52/79 Procureur du Roi v. Debauve [1980] ECR 833, [1981] 2 CMLR 362; Case 205/84 EC Commission v. Germany [1986] ECR 3755, [1987] 2 CMLR 69; Case 352/85 Bond Van Adverteerders v. The State (Netherlands) [1988] ECR 2085, [1989] 3 CMLR 113, per Advocate General Mancini; Case C—154/89 EC Commission v. France [1991] I ECR 659; Case C—180/89 EC Commission v. Italy (not yet reported); Case C—198/89 EC Commission v. Greece I ECR 727; Case C—353/89 EC Commission v. The Netherlands (not yet reported); Case C— 76/90 Säger v. Dennemeyer & Co Ltd [1991] I ECR 4221.

2.026. Current scope of the 'general interest' justification. Because the Court of Justice has held that the function of Article 59 is to create a 'common market' in services, it will not readily sanction restrictions in the 'general interest'. In *Säger v. Dennemeyer & Co Ltd*,[57] Advocate General Jacobs articulated the general test:

> . . . if an undertaking complies with the legislation of the Member State in which it is established it may provide services to clients in another Member State, even though the provision of such services would not normally be lawful under the laws of the second Member State. Restrictions imposed by those laws can only be applied against the foreign undertaking if they are justified by some requirement that is compatible to the aims of the Community. The case for taking that approach is particularly strong when the service is provided by means of post or telecommunications without the provider of the service moving physically between Member States.[58]

Permissable non-disriminatory restrictions include, in principle, those necessary: in order: to maintain professional conduct rules;[59] to maintain the social order;[60] to protect the rights of consumers;[61] to conserve the national and artistic heritage of a Member State;[62] to secure the proper appreciation of the artistic and archaeological heritage of a Member State[63] and on grounds of cultural policy to guarantee freedom of speech and plurality of broadcasting in a Member State.[64]

In exceptional circumstances, even a discriminatory restriction may be justified.[65] Furthermore, a national of one Member State may not circumvent a restriction operating there by establishing himself in another Member State and then relying on the Treaty to provide services to persons in his own Member State.[66] In other words, the freedom guaranteed by Article 59 may not be abused.

---

[57] Case C—76/90 *Säger v. Dennemeyer & Co Ltd* [1991] I ECR 4220, para. 27. See §2.024 above.

[58] The Court's approach in the domain of services now mirrors its jurisprudence on the free movement of goods where it has ruled that any restriction, not merely a non-discriminatory restriction is potentially in breach of Article 30. See §1.066 above.

[59] Joined Cases 110, 111/78 *Ministère Public v. Van Wesemael* [1979] ECR 35, [1979] 3 CMLR 87 and Case C—76/90 *Säger v. Dennemeyer & Co Ltd* [1991] I ECR 4220.

[60] Case 15/78 *Société Générale Alsacienne de Banque SA v. Koestler* [1978] ECR 1971, [1979] 1 CMLR 89

[61] Case 220/83 *EC Commission v. France* [1986] ECR 3663, [1987] 2 CMLR 113; Case C—180/89 *EC Commission v. Italy* (not yet reported) and Case C—198/89 *EC Commission v. Greece* [1991] I ECR 727.

[62] Case C—180/89 *EC Commission v. Italy* (not yet reported).

[63] Case C—154/89 *EC Commission v. France* [1991] I ECR 659 and Case C—198/89 *EC Commission v. Greece* [1991] I ECR 727.

[64] Case C—353/89 *EC Commission v. The Netherlands* (not yet reported). See §§2.041 and 2.045 below.

[65] Thus in Case—13/76 *Donà v. Mantero* [1976] ECR 1333, [1976] 2 CMLR 578, para. 14, a case concerning football players, the Court of Justice ruled that the Treaty would 'not prevent the adoption of rules or of a practice excluding foreign players from participation in certain matches for reasons which are not of an economic nature, which relate to the particular nature and context of such matches and are thus of sporting interest only, such as, for example, matches between national teams from different countries'. See also Case 36/74 *Walrave and Loch v. Association Union Cycliste Internationale* [1974] ECR 1405, [1975] 1 CMLR 320.

[66] Case 33/74 *Van Binsbergen v. Bestuur van de Bedrifsvereniging voor de Mataalnijverheid* [1974] ECR 1299 [1975] 1 CMLR 298. For a discussion of these issues, see the Opinion of Advocate General Jacobs in Case C—76/90 *Säger v. Dennemeyer & Co Ltd* [1991] I ECR 4220. In Case C—148/91 *Vereniging Veronica Omroep Organisatie v. Commissariat voor de Media* (not yet reported), the Court of Justice held that the Netherlands could prevent a national broadcasting organisation participating in the capital of a broadcasting organisation established in another Member State where the purpose had been to circumvent the rules regulating the structure of broadcasting organisations in the Netherlands by relying on freedom of transmission guaranteed by Article 59 of the Treaty.

4. Freedom to Provide Broadcasting Services—Case Law

(1) Introduction

2.027. Transmission of television signals across national frontiers is now commonplace in the Community and takes many forms: 'over the air' broadcasts, cable retransmissions, broadcasts by Direct Broadcast Satellites ('DBS') and transmissions by Fixed Service Satellite ('FSS').[67] Radio transmissions also often cross Community borders. The Court of Justice has evolved case law based on Article 59 et seq. of the Treaty which assists a broadcasting organisation wishing to make a transnational transmission but which is being hampered either by bodies constituted in the receiving Member State or by national legislation enacted there.

2.028. Key elements of a breach of Article 59. A party who wishes to avail itself of these provisions of the Treaty must prove:

(1) the existence of a remunerative service;
(2) an intention to provide that service to persons established in another Member State and
(3) a restriction on the provision of that service.

The following sections explain how each of those factors is to be identified.

(2) Television and Radio Transmissions as Services

2.029. Types of transmission. The European Community's case law in the realm of television transmissions had its beginnings in the *Sacchi*[68] case, where the Court of Justice held that:

In the absence of express provision to the contrary in the Treaty, a television signal must, by reason of its nature, be regarded as provision of services.[69]

The Court of Justice has held that the transmission of television signals constitutes a provision of services whether it is in the form of terrestrial transmissions (ie 'over the air' broadcasts),[70] transmissions by cable television[71] or transmissions by Fixed Service Satellites (ie 'distribution' and 'point-to-point' satellites).[72] No case has yet involved Direct Broadcast Satellites, simply because their signals are designed for direct reception over a large area, usually encompassing many

---

[67] For an explanation of the meaning of these technical terms, see §8.005 et seq. below.
[68] Case 155/73 [1974] ECR 409, [1974] 2 CMLR 177, para. 6.
[69] See also Council Directive 89/552/EEC of 3 October 1989 OJ No L 298, 17.10.89, p. 23, Recital 6 which states: '. . . television broadcasting constitutes, in normal circumstances, a service within the meaning of the Treaty.'
[70] Case 155/73 *Sacchi* [1974] ECR 409, [1974] 2 CMLR 177 and Case 52/79 *Procureur du Roi v. Debauve* [1980] ECR 833, [1981] 2 CMLR 362.
[71] Case 155/73, *Sacchi* [1974] ECR 409, [1974] 2 CMLR 177; Case 62/79 *Compagnie Générale pour la Diffusion de la Télévision, Coditel SA v. Ciné Vog Films SA* [1980] ECR 881, [1981] 2 CMLR 362; Case 52/79 *Procureur du Roi v. Debauve* [1980] ECR 833, [1981] 2 CMLR 362; Case 352/85 *Bond Van Adverteerders v. The State (Netherlands)* [1988] ECR 2085, [1989] 3 CMLR 113.
[72] Case 352/85 *Bond Van Adverteerders v. The State (Netherlands)* [1988] ECR 2085, [1989] 3 CMLR 113.

Member States, and there is thus no need for intervening services. However, like terrestrial broadcasts, a Direct Broadcast Satellite broadcast has so called 'shadow zones', that is, areas at the periphery of the satellite's beam where the signals are weakest. There may in such circumstances exist a demand for cable relay services which amplify the signals and distribute them to dwellings. It is submitted that the entire process (ie involving the satellite) would constitute the provision of services within the meaning of Article 59 of the Treaty.

The Court of Justice has confirmed that radio broadcasts are also services within the meaning of the Treaty.[73]

2.030. Advertising services. *Sacchi*[74] concerned a ban on the transmission of foreign programmes and advertising and the Court of Justice confirmed that, in particular:

> . . . the transmission of television signals, including those in the nature of advertisements, comes, as such, within the rules of the Treaty relating to services.

(3) Establishing Intention to Provide a Transnational Broadcasting Service

(i) General Principles

2.031. In *Procureur du Roi v. Debauve*, the Court of Justice laid the foundations of the test for establishing the requisite intention in broadcasting cases. It held that Article 59 of the Treaty may be invoked only by a party intending to provide a transnational service:

> . . . the provisions of the Treaty on freedom to provide services cannot apply to activities whose relevant elements are confined within a single Member State . . .[75]

The Court has fashioned principles which may be employed to determine whether or not the 'relative elements' cross national boundaries and these are analysed below.[76] It has confirmed that Article 59, first paragraph has direct effect.[77]

(ii) Types of Transmission

2.032. Cable relay of terrestrial broadcasts. *Procureur du Roi v. Debauve*,[78] involved cable relays of terrestrial broadcasts. It concerned Coditel, one of several Belgian companies whose business consisted of picking up by means of an aerial, terrestrial broadcasts made in neighbouring countries and piping those signals by cable to their subscribers throughout Belgium. In 1979, Coditel were prosecuted for failing to comply with the Belgian regulations which required the censorship of all

---

[73] Case C—288/89 *Stichting Collectieve Antennervoorziening Gouda v. Commissariaat voor de Media* (not yet reported) and C—353/89 *EC Commission v. Netherlands* (not yet reported).

[74] Case 155/73 [1974] ECR 409, [1974] 2 CMLR 177, para. 6.

[75] Case 52/79 [1980] ECR 833, [1981] 2 CMLR 362. This principle has been affirmed by the Court of Justice in Case C—154/89 *EC Commission v. France* [1991] I ECR 659; Case C—180/89 *EC Commission v. Italy* (not yet reported); Case C—198/89 *EC Commission v. Greece* [1991] I ECR 727.

[76] See §2.032 et seq. below.

[77] As from the expiry of the transitional period, see Case 52/79 *Procureur du Roi v. Debauve* [1980] ECR 833, [1981] 2 CMLR 362. per Advocate General Warner. For the meaning of the concept 'direct effect', see the references cited in §2.002 fn 6 above.

[78] Case 52/79 [1980] ECR 833, [1981] 2 CMLR 362.

advertising material.[79] In the same year Coditel were sued by S.A. Ciné Vog Films and Others for infringement of copyright and the cases were joined.[80] In its defence of the action for infringement of copyright Coditel asserted that it was contrary to the rules in the Treaty relating to the freedom to provide services to prevent them exhibiting a film in their cable nets. The Brussels Court d'Appel referred the following question to the Court:

> Are the restrictions forbidden by Article 59 of the Treaty establishing the European Economic Community only those that hinder the provision of services between nationals established in different Member States, or do they include restrictions on the provision of services between nationals established in the same Member State which however concern services the substance of which originates in another Member State.

Advocate General Warner affirmed that what must be hindered, is the provision of a service by a person in one Member State to persons in another Member State. The terms of the Treaty demand that 'intention' flows across a border. The Advocate General acknowledged that it would be impractical for the Court to hear evidence from individual programme producers as to the audience they had in mind and thus formulated an objective principle which can be applied to satisfy the requirement of intention. He said:

> The common sense answer seems to me to be that a television broadcast must be taken to be intended for all those who are able to receive it, whether directly or by cable diffusion, whether or not those responsible for the broadcast had them consciously in mind.

Furthermore, the Advocate General stated that evidence of transnational would also exist if a copyright owner has not availed itself of an international agreement, which would enable it to prohibit a cross-border broadcast.[81]

Technically, the term 'broadcast' is used for transmissions which are designed for direct reception by the general public.[82] It might therefor be argued that this case cannot be used as an authority for scenarios where the initial transmission is not 'broadcast' in this sense but transmitted by, for example, a Fixed Service Satellite. It is submitted however, that the Court was not using the term 'broadcast' as a term of art, but employed it in the more general sense as meaning any type of television transmission.

2.033. Transmissions by Fixed Service Satellite. There are two types of Fixed Service Satellites: distribution satellites and point-to-point satellites.[83] Typically with such services, a programme is prepared at a television station situated in one Member State. The signal is not, however, broadcast over the air there. Instead, it is transmitted via a Fixed Service Satellite to a cable operator situated in another Member State for onward transmission to the cable operator's subscribers.

---

[79] *Ibid.*

[80] Case 62/79 *Compagnie Générale pour la Diffusion de la Télévision, Coditel SA v. Ciné Vog Films SA* [1980] ECR 881, [1981] 2 CMLR 362.

[81] In the *Procureur du Roi v. Debauve*, it was decisive that the broadcaster of the initial signal had not invoked Article 1 of the European Agreement on the Protection of Television Broadcasts of 22 June 1960 which would have permitted it to prevent the Defendant relaying its signal by cable. See §7.164 below.

[82] See §8.002 et seq. below.

[83] For an explanation of the differences between the two technologies, see §8.005 et seq. below.

Although there is no reason why, in principle, these services should be unable to benefit from the principles annunciated in *Procureur du Roi v. Debauve*,[84] the Court of Justice was called upon to give a ruling of the rules concerning such transmissions in *Bond Van Adverteerders v. The State (Netherlands)*.[85] The case concerned the relay in the Netherlands, by cable, of a 'point-to-point' transmission sent by a satellite from a neighbouring Member State. The Dutch government had become concerned that with the development of point-to-point satellite broadcasting, foreign programming might became a threat to the national networks. Accordingly, it issued a decree which, subject to fulfilment of two conditions, permitted organisations to relay to their subscribers in the Netherlands programmes which they had picked up from abroad. The conditions were, that the programmes could not contain advertising which was specifically aimed at the Dutch public and they could not contain subtitles in Dutch. These rules seriously undermined the value of relaying foreign programmes by cable in the Netherlands. The Dutch advertiser's Association and a cable operator commenced proceedings against the Dutch government claiming that the legislation offended against Article 59 of the Treaty. The Court ruled that the requisite intention was present and that therefore the Dutch legislation breached the Treaty. It stated:

> It must be held that the transmission of programmes at issue involves at least two separate services. The first is provided by the cable network operators established in one Member State to the broadcasters established in other Member States and consists of relaying to network subscribers the television programmes sent to them by the broadcasters. The second is provided by the broadcasters established in certain Member States to advertisers established in particular in the Member State where the programmes are received, by broadcasting advertisements which the advertisers have prepared especially for the public in the Member State where the programmes are received.
>
> Each of those services are transfrontier services for the purposes of Article 59 of the Treaty. In each case the suppliers of the service are established in a Member State other than that of certain of the persons for whom it is intended.[86]

2.034. Summary of elements of 'intention'. In summary, transnational intention is deemed to exist if it is possible to identify:

(1) persons who are in fact able to receive in one Member State, a broadcast transmitted from another Member State and/or
(2) an international agreement which has not been invoked and which would enable the broadcaster of the signal in the transmitting Member State, to prohibit its reception in the receiving Member State.
(3) In a case involving Fixed Service Satellite transmissions, the principles in *Bond Van Adverteerders and Others v. The State (Netherlands)*, may be invoked.

2.035. Concept of being 'established'. The cases have not defined precisely what is meant by being 'established' in a Member State. Both *Procureur du Roi v.*

---

[84] Case 52/79 [1980] ECR 833, [1981] 2 CMLR 362.
[85] Case 352/85 [1988] ECR 2085, [1989] 3 CMLR 113.
[86] *Ibid.*, paras. 14 and 15. The Court overruled Advocate Mancini's Opinion that to benefit from Article 59, a television signal must simply have been broadcast in the Member State in accordance with its laws. The Court thus hammered home the principle that in cases involving Article 59, it is vital to establish an 'intention' to provide a transnational service.

Debauve[87] and *Bond Van Adverteerders and Others v. The State (Netherlands)*,[88] concerned national television networks. In the absence of any case law definition, it is submitted that the qualifications contained in Title I of the General Programme for the abolition of restrictions on freedom to provide services, should be applied.[89]

2.036. Establishing the existence of 'remuneration'. Whilst intention must be transnational, the cases illustrate that it is not necessary for payment to be made by a party in one Member State to a party in another Member State. Article 60 is satisfied simply because television is the type of service which is normally provided for remuneration, (usually either by licence fees or advertising revenue).[90] Thus in cases involving retransmission of signals by cable, the Court of Justice has deemed it unnecessary for the cable operators to pay fees either to the broadcasters whose terrestrial signals they retransmit[91] or to the broadcasters whose point-to-point signals they relay.[92]

(4) The Scope of Article 59 in respect of Broadcasting Services

(i) *Restrictions on the Broadcasting of Advertisements*

2.037. Introduction. In *Procureur du Roi v. Debauve*,[93] the Court of Justice had to examine the scope of Article 59 in the context of the broadcasting of advertisements. Belgian law prohibited any form of commercial advertising on Belgian television, save for a limited form of sponsorship. The Defendants operated a cable television service whereby they relayed foreign terrestrial broadcasts (which they could receive via antennae situated near the Belgian border) to their subscribers throughout Belgium. However, they neglected to blot out all advertising material (mainly because of the impracticalities of doing so) and were consequently prosecuted for breaching Belgian law.

2.038. Restrictions permitted in the 'general interest'. The Court held that the function of Article 59 was to create a 'common market' for the supply of services and not just to abolish discrimination.[94] However, it held that:

> In view of the particular nature of certain services such as the broadcasting and transmission of television signals, specific requirements imposed upon providers of services which are founded upon the application of rules regulating certain types of activity and which are justified by the general interest and apply to all persons and undertakings established within the territory of the said Member State cannot be said

---

[87] Case 52/79 [1980] ECR 833, [1981] 2 CMLR 436.
[88] Case 352/85 [1988] ECR 2085, [1989] 3 CMLR 113.
[89] See §2.011 above.
[90] Case 52/79 *Procureur Du Roi v. Debauve* [1980] ECR 833, [1981] 2 CMLR 362, per Advocate General Warner.
[91] *Ibid.*
[92] Case 352/85 *Bond Van Adverteerders v. The State (Netherlands)* [1988] ECR 2085, [1989] 3 CMLR 113.
[93] Case 52/79 [1980] ECR 833, [1981] 2 CMLR 362.
[94] See §2.023 above, affirmed by the Court of Justice in Case C—76170 *Säger v. Dennemeyer & Co Ltd* [1991] I ECR 4221.

to be incompatible with the Treaty to the extent to which a provider of services established in another Member State is not subject to similar regulations there.[95]

It was apparent that national laws governing broadcasting varied enormously from state to state and the Court thus felt it necessary to allow the continuance of non-discriminatory laws in the 'general interest' until harmonization had been achieved. The Court held:

> From information given to the Court during these proceedings it appears that the television broadcasting of advertisements is subject to widely divergent systems of law in the various Member States, passing from almost total prohibition, as in Belgium, by way of rules comprising more or less strict restrictions, to systems affording broad commercial freedom. In the absence of any approximation of national laws and taking into account the considerations of general interest underlying the restrictive rules in this area, the application of the laws in question cannot be regarded as a restriction upon freedom to provide services so long as those laws treat all such services identically whatever their origin or the nationality or place of establishment of the persons providing them.[96]

The necessary 'proportionality' test was fulfilled. Notwithstanding the existence of zones on the border where broadcasts from neighbouring Member States could be received naturally and larded with advertisements, the cable services enabled broadcasts to be received over a much wider area.

2.039. Council Directive: Television Without Frontiers. In *Procureur du Roi v. Debauve*,[97] the Court of Justice, in a single stroke, legitimized a barrier on foreign broadcasts and substantially cut down the value of Article 59 for broadcasters.[98] Harmonization was a pre-condition of any freeing up of broadcasting services. In fact, rules concerning the broadcasting of advertising have now been harmonised and Member States may no longer restrict the reception and retransmission of advertisements which comply with the terms of the Directive 'Television Without Frontiers'.[99]

(ii) Restrictions on the Broadcasting of Programmes

2.040. Legality of a broadcasting monopoly. The Court of Justice has ruled that, the conferring on a single undertaking, the right to both broadcast domestic programmes and retransmit programmes from other Member States could breach Article 59.[100] This was because it might lead the undertaking to favour its own programmes. In the case in issue, the Court emphasised that of fundamental

---

[95] [1980] ECR 833, [1981] 2 CMLR 362, para. 12. In Case C—288/89 *Stichting Collectieve Antennevoorziening Gouda v. Commissariaat voor de Media* (not yet reported) and Case C—353/89 *EC Commission v. The Netherlands* (not yet reported), the Court of Justice ruled that a restriction on the retransmission in the Netherlands of broadcasts (including advertising) coming from a neighbouring Member State could not be justified in the general interest merely on the ground that the foreign broadcasting organisation did not have a structure identical to that of the Dutch organisation. The Dutch government had argued that advertising coming from abroad had to be controlled by a body distinct from the broadcasters of programmes, as it was in the Netherlands so as to protect the non-commercial and pluralistic nature of broadcasting there. The Court ruled that such a restriction was designed for economic reasons to protect competition in advertising from abroad, and was thus unacceptable.

[96] *Ibid.*, para. 13. This was affirmed by the Court in Case 352/85 *Bond Van Adverteerders v. The State (Netherlands)* [1988] ECR 2085, [1989] 3 CMLR 113.

[97] Case 52/79 [1980] ECR 833, [1981] 2 CMLR 362.

[98] See §2.038 above.

[99] See §6.056 below.

[100] Case C—260/89 *Elliniki Radiophonia Tileorassi Anonimi Etairia v. Dimotiki Etairia Pliroforissi* [1991] I ECR 2925.

significance was the absence of a binding obligation on the monopoly to retransmit programmes from other Member States.[101] It was notable in that case that the monopoly was also entrusted with making programmes of national interest.

(iii) Miscellaneous Restrictions

2.041. Obligation to commission productions from national organisations. *EC Commission v. The Netherlands*[102] concerned an obligation on national broadcasting organisations in the Netherlands to commission their productions (100% in the case of radio and 25% in the case of television) from national undertakings. The Court of Justice noted that this amounted to a restriction in breach of Article 59 because it prevented organisations established in other Member States from providing their services to the Netherlands broadcasting organisation. The Defendant argued that this arrangement was justified in the general interest: for the protection of its culture. It said that it was necessary to commission a multitude of Dutch organisations in order to preserve the freedom of speech and representation of all the social, cultural, religious and philosophical components of the Netherlands. The Court rejected this. It acknowledged restrictions in the general interest might in principle be justified to guarantee freedom of speech, but that pluralism could not be affected by allowing the broadcasting organisations to call upon the services of undertakings established in other Member States.[103]

(5) Impeding Foreign Transmissions on Grounds of Public Policy

(i) General Principles

2.042. Discriminatory restrictions. In principle, the Treaty does permit discrimination, for Article 56(1)[104] states:

> The provisions of this Chapter and measures taken in pursuance thereof shall not prejudice the applicability of provisions laid down by law, regulation or administrative action providing for special treatment for foreign nationals on grounds of public policy, public security or public health.

Broadly speaking, the 'public policy' exception can be invoked only where there exists a genuine and sufficiently serious threat to one of the fundamental interests in society.[105] And it is subject to four qualifications. The first is that it may not be

---

[101] Advocate General Lenz noted that the retransmission of ten European programmes over a period of two years did nothing to dispel the Court's doubts as this was a mere practice which could change at any time.

[102] Case C—353/89 (not yet reported).

[103] See also Case C—211/91 *EC Commission v. Belgium* (not yet reported) where the Court of Justice struck down a provision of Belgium law which permitted the redistribution by cable of only those foreign broadcasts which were in a langauge of the Member State where the foreign station was established. On restrictions prohibited by competition law, see §4.181 below, Article 90(2).

[104] Part Two, Title III, Chapter 2.

[105] See Case 41/74 *Van Duyn v. Home Office* [1974] ECR 1337, [1975] 1 CMLR 1; Case 36/75 *Rutili v. Minister for the Interior* [1975] ECR 1219, [1976] 1 CMLR 140; Case 30/77 *R v. Bouchereau* [1977] ECR 1999, [1977] 2 CMLR 800. In Joined Cases 115, 116/81 *Adoui and Cornuaille v. Belgium* [1982] ECR 1665, [1982] 3 CMLR 631, it was stated that 'recourse by a national authority to the concept of public policy presupposes, in any event, the existence, in addition to the perturbation to the social order which any infringement of the law involves, of a genuine and sufficiently serious threat affecting one of the fundamental interest of society'. In that case, the Court held that a measure may be justified by a Member State on grounds of public policy, only where it is applied with equal rigour to the domestic situation but this is probably too strict a statement. On public policy generally, see *Halsbury's Laws of England op. cit.*, Vol 52, 16.23 et seq.

used to service economic ends.[106] The second is that since it is an exception to one of the fundamental principles of the Treaty, 'it must be interpreted in such a way that its effects are limited to that which is necessary in order to protect the interests it seeks to safeguard' ie it must satisfy a proportionality test.[107] Thirdly, because it allows a derogation from one of the fundamental rules in the Treaty, it must be interpreted strictly.[108] Finally, the Court of Justice has held that in appraising a measure justified on grounds of public policy, fundamental human rights must be taken into account. In *Elliniki Radiophonia Tileorassi Anonimi Etairia v. Dimotiki Etairia Pliroforissis*, the Court held that:

> . . . Where a Member State relies on the combined provisions of Articles 56 and 66 in order to justify rules which are likely to obstruct the exercise of the freedom to provide services, such justification, provided for by Community law, must be interpreted in the light of the general principles of law and in particular of fundamental rights—the observance of which is ensured by the Court
>   It follows that in such a case it is for the national court, and if necessary, the Court of Justice to appraise the application of those provisions having regard to all the rules of Community law, including freedom of expression, as embodied in Article 10 of the European Convention on Human Rights,[109] as a general principle of law the observance of which is ensured by the Court.[110]

2.043. Non-discriminatory restrictions. Although Article 56 of the Treaty sanctions discrimination, a Member State may invoke its terms in cases where it wishes to impose on foreign persons the same measure it imposes on its own nationals.[111]

---

[106] See Case 95/81 EC Commission v. Italy [1982] ECR 2187. See also Council Directive 64/221/EEC of 25 February 1964 on the co-ordination of special measures concerning the movement and residence of foreign nationals which are justified on grounds of public policy, public security or public health, OJ Sp Edn, 1963-1964, p.117. Article 2(2), which states that 'such grounds shall not be invoked to service economic ends'.

[107] Case 352/85 Bond Van Adverteerders v. The State (Netherlands) [1988] ECR 2085, [1989] 3 CMLR 113.

[108] Case 36/75 Rutili v. Minister for the Interior [1975] ECR 1219, [1976] 1 CMLR 140 and Case C—260/89 Elliniki Radiophonia Tileorassi Anonimi Etairia v. Dimotiki Etairia Pliroforissis [1991] I ECR 2925.

[109] For the text of Article 10 of the European Convention on Human Rights, see §5.016 below.

[110] [1991] I ECR 2925, paras. 33 and 34. In Case 36/75 Rutili v. Minister for the Interior [1975] ECR 1219, [1976] 1 CMLR 140, para. 32, the Court of Justice held that exceptions contained in Article 48(3), a provision which mirrors Article 56(1) 'are a specific manifestation of the more general principle, enshrined in Articles 8, 9, 10 and 11 of the Convention for the Protection of Human Rights and Fundamental Freedoms, signed in Rome on 4 November 1950 and ratified by all the Member States, and in Article 2 of Protocol No 4 of the same Convention, signed in Strasbourg on 16 September 1963, which provide, in identical terms, that no restrictions in the interests of national security or public safety shall be placed on the rights secured by the above quoted articles other than such as are necessary for the protection of those interests "in a democratic society"'. Schwartz has opined that Article 56 of the Treaty may not be interpreted differently from or more widely than the necessity clause in Article 10(2) of the ECHR. Thus Article 56 allows restrictions on the freedom to relay foreign programmes only where necessary in a free society as determined by the Community's institutions and not merely in the opinion of the Member States concerned. (see IE Schwartz, Broadcasting and the EEC Treaty, [1986] 11 E.L. Rev, 7.29). On fundamental human rights and the EEC Treaty, see generally Chapter 5, §5.001 et seq. below.

[111] See Case 52/79 Procureur du Roi v. Debauve [1980] ECR 833, [1981] 2 CMLR 362 where Advocate General Warner stated that '... Article 56, in allowing Member States to take, on grounds of public policy, public security or public health, measures providing for special treatment for foreign nationals, must a fortiori allow Member States to take on those grounds measures applying indiscriminately to foreign nationals and to their own nationals'.

(ii) Broadcasting Services

2.044. Application of public policy ground to broadcasting services. The precise contours of the public policy principle have been defined chiefly in cases concerning the freedom of movement of workers and the right of establishment.[112] However, Article 66 of the Treaty confirms that it is applicable to the rules governing the freedom to provide services. And the Court of Justice has confirmed that in principle, it is applicable to rules which govern broadcasting services.[113]

2.045. Maintaining plurality of broadcasting. *Bond Van Adverteerders v. The State (Netherlands),*[114] concerned a provision of Dutch law which prohibited the relaying of foreign transmissions containing either advertising aimed specifically at the Dutch public or subtitles in Dutch (the latter condition aiming to ensure compliance with the former). In the Netherlands, all television advertising was controlled by a central body, STER, which sold airtime and then distributed the revenue to a wide variety of television channels. The system was designed to maintain the pluralism of Dutch television, and thus to avoid commercial interests polluting Dutch culture. The Dutch Government argued that the ban on foreign advertising and subtitles was justified under Article 56 of the Treaty in the interests of 'public policy'. This was because it was designed both to complement its national advertising system which maintained the pluralism of Dutch television and to avoid foreign broadcasters engaging in unfair competition in the Netherlands.[115] The Court held that, the purpose of the prohibiting foreign advertising was to secure for STER, and hence Dutch television, all the revenue for advertising destined for the Netherlands. It was thus rooted in economic protectionism, a motive which disqualifies the public policy ground. Furthermore, the Court said that any measure justified on the grounds of public policy must be proportional to its intended object. This particular measure failed that test. The Court tentatively suggested that an acceptable obligation would be to give foreign broadcasters a choice between complying with objective restrictions (ie with prohibition on advertising certain products or services) or refraining from transmitting advertising at certain times, a condition which was imposed on national broadcasters.

2.046. Limitations on availability of channels. In *Elliniki Radiophonia Tileorassi— Anonimi Etairia v. Dimotiki Etairia Pliroforissis*[116] the Court of Justice ruled that maintaining a broadcasting monopoly which discriminated against foreign broadcasts could not be justified merely on the grounds that there were only a limited number of broadcasting frequencies available, especially where, as in the instant case, the monopoly used only a small proportion of those channels (in that case, 5 out of 49).

---

[112] See §2.042 fn 105 above.
[113] Case 352/85 *Bond Van Adverteerders v. The State (Netherlands)* [1988] ECR 2085, [1989] 3 CMLR 113, per Advocate General Mancini; Case C—260/89 *Elliniki Radiophonia Tileorassi Anonimi Etairia v. Dimotiki Etairia Pliroforissis* [1991] I ECR 2925; Case C—353/89 *EC Commission v. The Netherlands* (not yet reported).
[114] Case 352/85 [1988] ECR 2085, [1989] 3 CMLR 113.
[115] It could not apply the 'general interest' rule because the restriction on the transmission of foreign advertising was discriminatory.
[116] Case C—260/89 [1991] I ECR 2925.

CHAPTER THREE

Distinction Between Media Goods and Media Services

I. GENERAL PRINCIPLES

3.001. Definition of 'goods'. The Treaty has neglected to define what is meant by the term 'goods'. However, the Court of Justice has filled the gap by holding that goods are:

> ... products which can be valued in money and which are capable, as such, of forming the subject of commercial transactions.[1]

3.002. Definition of 'services'. Services are categorised as such, almost it seems, by default, for Article 60 states that:

> Services shall be considered to be 'services' within the meaning of this Treaty where they are normally provided for remuneration, in so far as they are not governed by the provisions relating to freedom of movement for goods, capital and persons.[2]

According to Article 60, services include, in particular, those of an industrial[3] and commercial character[4] and those of craftsmen[5] and of the professions.[6]

3.003. Distinction between goods and services. The sections below consider the distinction between media goods and media services. That distinction can be subtle and may depend upon the view taken generally in trade. Thus, for example, electricity falls within the category of goods because it is 'traded' as a commodity,

---

[1] Case 7/68 EC Commission v. Italy [1968] ECR 423, [1969] CMLR 1 concerning the interpretation of Article 9 of the Treaty.
[2] See Case 155/73 Sacchi [1974] ECR 409, [1974] 2 CMLR 177.
[3] Article 60(a).
[4] Article 60(b).
[5] Article 60(c).
[6] Article 60(d).

whilst television signals and the programmes they carry are deemed to be services even though transmitted by electrical energy.[7]

II. MEDIA GOODS

3.004. Trade in recording and recorded material, apparatus etc. The Court of Justice has held that the provisions concerning the freedom of movement of goods (Article 30 et seq.) govern trade in material, sound recordings, films, apparatus and other products used for the diffusion of television signals,[8] as well as the manner in which video cassettes and their master copies are marketed.[9]

3.005. Production of media. National laws which regulate the production of video cassettes, are also governed by Article 30 et seq. This is because a video disc or video cassette is a manufactured product which is the subject of a classification in the Common Customs Tariff and thus satisfies the terms of Article 60.[10] This makes it irrelevant whether or not those cassettes are to be put on the market.[11]

3.006. Rental of media. Peculiarly, the Court of Justice has held that the free movement of goods provisions govern the rental of video-cassettes. It has stated that 'although sale and hiring out are different in nature (the first entailing a transfer of title in the goods and the second conferring possession for a limited time), they none the less have the common characteristic that they necessarily involve making the product commercially available to the consumer'.[12]

III. MEDIA SERVICES

3.007. Exploitation of media (eg films, musical recordings etc) for performances. The importation, distribution and theatrical exhibition of films for the

---

[7] See Case 155/73 *Sacchi* [1974] ECR 409, [1974] 2 CMLR 177 per Advocate General Reischl commenting on Case 6/64 *Costa v. ENEL* [1964] ECR 585, [1964] CMLR 425.

[8] Case 155/73 *Saachi* [1974] ECR 409, [1974] 2 CMLR 177; Case 52/79 *Procureur du Roi v. Debauve* [1980] ECR 833, [1981] 2 CMLR 362; Case C—260/89 *Elliniki Radiophonia Tileorassis Anonimi Etairia v. Dimotiki Etairia Pliroforissis* [1991] I ECR 2925. See also Case 223/84 *Telefunken Fernseh und Rundfunk GmbH v. Oberfinanzdirektion Munchen* [1985] ECR 3335. For sound recordings, see in particular, Joined Cases 55, 57/80 *Musik-Vertrieb membran GmbH v. GEMA* [1981] ECR 147, [1981] 2 CMLR 44 (concerning vinyl discs); Case 402/85 *Basset v. Société des auteurs, compositeurs et éditeurs de musique* [1987] ECR 1747, [1987] 3 CMLR 173 (concerning vinyl discs), per Advocate General Lenz; Case 341/87 *EMI Electrola GmbH v. Patricia Im-und Export* [1989] ECR 79, [1989] 2 CMLR 413 (concerning vinyl discs), per Advocate General Darmon.

[9] Joined Cases 60, 61/84 *Cinéthèque SA v. Fédération Nationale des Cinémas Français* [1985] ECR 2605, [1986] 1 CMLR 365.

[10] *Ibid.*

[11] *Ibid.*

[12] Case 158/86 *Warner Brothers Inc v. Christiansen* [1988] ECR 2605, [1990] 3 CMLR 684, per Advocate General Mancini.

purposes of a public performance is governed by the freedom to provide service provisions (Article 59 et seq.),[13] as are performances of musical recordings.[14]

3.008. Television and radio transmissions. The Court of Justice has held that 'in the absence of express provision to the contrary in the Treaty, a television service must by reason of its nature, be regarded as provision of services' and is thus governed by Article 59 and seq.[15] Services include terrestrial broadcasts,[16] retransmissions by cable[17] and transmissions by Fixed Service Satellite.[18] They also include radio transmissions.[19] The cases confirm that the word 'remuneration', contained in Article 60, has a loose sense, for the purpose of the definition of 'services' in the Treaty is to identify the kinds of services to which it applies and to exclude those that are normally provided gratuitously.[20] Furthermore, Article 60 does not require the service to be paid for by those for whom it is performed.[21] Thus, for example, neither the method of financing broadcasting or the source from which it comes has been considered relevant.[22] The vital point is that television is normally paid for in one way or another.[23]

3.009. Sports professions. The Court of Justice has held that persons engaged in sports professions may be covered by the Treaty's provisions on freedom to provide services.[24] This is not, however, without qualification. Thus the Court has stated that 'Having regard to the objectives of the Community, the practice of sport is subject to Community law only in so far as it constitutes an economic activity within the meaning of Article 2 of the Treaty . . . This applies to the activities of

---

[13] See General Programme for the abolition of restrictions on freedom to provide services, Title V C(c), OJ, Sp. Edn, (Second Series), IX, p.3; Council Directive 63/607/EEC OJ Sp Edn 1963–1964, p. 52; Council Directive 65/264/EEC OJ Sp Edn 1965-1966, p. 62; Council Directive 68/369/EEC OJ Sp Edn 1968 (II) p. 520; Council Directive 70/451/EEC OJ Sp Edn 1970 (II) p. 620.

[14] Case 402/85 Basset v. *Société des auteurs, compositeurs et éditeurs de musique* [1987] ECR 1747, [1987] 3 CMLR 173 (concerning vinyl discs played in a discotheque), per Advocate General Lenz.

[15] Case 155/73 Sacchi [1974] ECR 409, [1974] 2 CMLR 177, para. 6, affirmed by the Court of Justice in Case C—260/89 *Elliniki Radiophonia Tileorassi Anonimi Etairia v. Dimotiki Etairia Pliroforissis* [1991] I ECR 2925. Furthermore, the General Programme on the abolition of restrictions on freedom to provide services specifically mentions the activity of broadcasting, OJ, Sp. Edn., (Second Series), IX, p. 3. See also Council Directive 89/552/EEC of 3 October 1989 OJ No L 298, 17.10.89, p.23, Recital 6 which states that '... television broadcasting constitutes, in normal circumstances, a service within the meaning of the Treaty'.

[16] Case 155/73, Sacchi [1974] ECR 409, [1974] 2 CMLR 177 and Case 52/79 *Procureur du Roi v. Debauve* [1980] ECR 833, [1981] 2 CMLR 362.

[17] Case 155/73, Sacchi [1974] ECR 409, [1974] 2 CMLR 177; Case 62/79 *Compagnie Générale pour la Diffusion de la Télévision, Coditel SA v. Ciné Vog Films SA* [1980] ECR 881, [1981] 2 CMLR 362; Case 52/79 *Procureur du Roi v. Debauve* [1980] ECR 833, [1981] 2 CMLR 362; Case 352/85 *Bond Van Adverteerders v. The State (Netherlands)* [1988] ECR 2085, [1989] 3 CMLR 113.

[18] Case 352/85 *Bond Van Adverteerders v. The State (Netherlands)* [1988] ECR 2085, [1989] 3 CMLR 113.

[19] Case C—288/89 *Stichting Collectieve Antennevoorziening Gouda v. Commissariaat voor de Media* (not yet reported) and Case C— 353/89 *EC Commission v. Netherlands* (not yet reported).

[20] Case 52/79 *Procureur du Roi v. Debauve* [1980] ECR 833, [1981] 2 CMLR 362, per Advocate General Warner.

[21] Case 352/85 *Bond Van Adverteerders v. The State (Netherlands)* [1988] ECR 2085, [1989] 3 CMLR 113.

[22] Whether by proceeds from licence fees or advertising revenue.

[23] Case 52/79 *Procureur du Roi v. Debauve* [1980] ECR 833, [1981] 2 CMLR 362, per Advocate General Warner.

[24] and freedom of establishment.

professional or semi-professional players, which are in the nature of gainful employment or remunerated service.'[25]

---

[25] Case 13/76 *Donà v. Mantero* [1976] ECR 1333, [1976] 2 CMLR 578, para. 12, which concerned football players. See also Case 36/74 *Walrave and Koch v. Association Union Cycliste Internationale* [1974] ECR 1405, [1975] 1 CMLR 320.

CHAPTER FOUR

Competition Law

I. INTRODUCTION

4.001. Outline of this chapter. This chapter contains those elements of the law of competition which impinge upon the media industry, an industry particularly rich in case law. The chapter does not intend to provide a comprehensive analysis of all competition law.[1] The purpose is rather to present to the practitioner a perspective of the wider picture, etching in detail in those areas which are of relevance to the media industries. Thus detailed analysis is made of exclusive exhibition licensing as well as the effects of Article 85(1) and Article 86 on collecting societies. This chapter also deals in particular with the special status that the Treaty, by virtue of Article 90(2), accords to undertakings entrusted with the operation of services of general economic interest. It considers to what extent broadcasting and other monopolies are able to shield themselves behind this Treaty provision.

4.002. The foundations of competition law. The foundations of the European Community's competition law are laid out in the opening Articles of the EEC Treaty. Article 2 contains one of the Treaty's grandest proclamations: a guiding precept. It states that:

> The Community shall have as its task, by establishing a common market and progressively approximating the economic policies of Member States, to promote throughout the Community a harmonious development of economic activities, a continuous and balanced expansion, an increase in stability, an accelerated raising of the standard of living and closer relations between the States belonging to it.

Article 3(f) then names as one of the Community's tasks 'the institution of a system ensuring that competition in the common market is not distorted'.

---

[1] For detail of general principles see, in particular, C W Bellamy and G D Child, *Common Market Law of Competition* (3rd Edn, 1987) and *Halsbury's Laws of England* (4th Edn, 1986), Vol 52, 19.01 et seq.

The Court of Justice makes it continually clear that Articles 2 and 3(f) are, in the realm of competition law, the Court's touchstones.[2] However, they are no more than the expression of general principles on which the Community is founded and cannot in themselves be invoked to determine whether a particular measure is contrary to the Community's law.[3] Therefore in seeking a remedy, recourse must be had to Article 85, Article 86 and Article 90 which lay down particular rules applicable to undertakings with a view to safeguarding the principles and attaining the objectives set out in Articles 2 and 3. Article 85 concerns agreements between undertakings, decisions of associations of undertakings and concerted practices. Article 86 concerns unilateral activity of one or more undertakings. Basically, Articles 85 and 86 seek to achieve the same aim on different levels, namely, 'the maintenance of effective competition within the Common Market'.[4]

II. ARTICLE 85—AGREEMENTS RESTRICTING COMPETITION

1. Introduction

4.003. Treaty terms. Article 85(1) essentially prohibits consensual activity which partitions the common market. The text of Article 85 is as follows:

Article 85.1. The following shall be prohibited as incompatible with the common market: all agreements between undertakings, decisions by associations of undertakings and concerted practices which may affect trade between Member States and which have as their object or effect the prevention, restriction or distortion of competition within the common market, and in particular those which:

(a) directly or indirectly fix purchase or selling prices or any other trading conditions;
(b) limit or control production, markets, technical development, or investment;
(c) share markets or sources of supply;
(d) apply dissimilar conditions to equivalent transactions with other trading parties, thereby placing them at a competitive disadvantage;
(e) make the conclusion of contracts subject to acceptance by the other parties of supplementary obligations which, by their nature or according to commercial usage, have no connection with the subject of such contracts.

Article 85.2. Any agreements or decisions prohibited pursuant to this Article shall be automatically void.

Article 85.3. The provisions of paragraph 1 may, however, be declared inapplicable in the case of:

● any agreement or category of agreements between undertakings;
● any decision or category of decisions by associations of undertakings;

---

[2] See e.g. Case 6/72 *Europemballage Corporation and Continental Can Co Inc v. EC Commission* [1973] ECR 215, [1973] CMLR 199 and Case 78/70 *Deutsche Grammophon Gesellschaft mbH v. Metro-SB-Grossmärkte GmbH & Co KG* [1971] ECR 487, [1971] CMLR 631.

[3] Case C—260/89 *Elliniki Radiophonia Tileorassi Anonimi Etairia v. Dimotiki Etairia Pliroforissis* [1991] I ECR 2925.

[4] Case 6/72 *Europemballage Corporation and Continental Can Co Inc v. EC Commission* [1973] ECR 215, [1973] CMLR 199.

- any concerted practice or category of concerted practices;

which contributes to improving the production or distribution of goods or to promoting technical or economic progress, while allowing consumers a fair share of the resulting benefit, and which does not:

(a) impose on the undertakings concerned restrictions which are not indispensable to the attainment of these objectives;
(b) affords such undertakings the possibility of eliminating competition in respect of a substantial part of the products in question.

4.004. Key elements of breach. An infraction of Article 85(1) consists of:

- an agreement
- between undertakings
- which may affect trade between Member States and
- which has as its object or effect the prevention, restriction or distortion of competition within the common market.

The sections that follow, consider in which cases, each of these elements is present. There is then an examination of the different types of restrictions on competition prevalent in the media industries.

2. Agreements

(1) Meaning of the Term 'Agreement'

4.005. The concept of an agreement. The concept of an agreement is nowhere defined by the Treaty. But the Commission has made it clear that in order for Article 85(1) to apply:

> . . . it is not essential that [the] agreement should take the form of a contract having all the elements required by civil law, it is sufficient that one of the parties voluntarily undertakes to limit its freedom of action with regard to the other.[5]

4.006. Circulars. The strictness of the Commission's approach was exhibited in an action it took against a manufacturer of vinyl discs. WEA— Filipacchi Music SA, a company in Paris, sent a circular to its French wholesale and retail customers, noting their obligation not to export light music on vinyl discs. The company had argued that its circular was only the expression of an opinion and that the consent given by the resale agents, which had signed it and stamped it with their house stamp, was no more than an acknowledgement of receipt. Noting that the Commission's action had restored the documents to their proper status, the Commission stated that 'a firm cannot use carefully worded clauses to avoid the ban on agreements contained in Article 85'.[6]

---

[5] Commission Decision 74/634/EEC Re Franco-Japanese Ballbearings Agreement OJ No L 343, 21.12.74, p. 19, [1975] 1 CMLR D8.
[6] Commission Second Report on Competition Policy (1972), point 40.

(2) Concerted Practices

(i) General Principles

4.007. Definition of concerted practice. Article 85(1) prohibits 'concerted practices' as well as 'agreements' (and 'decisions').[7] A concerted practice is behaviour which is co-ordinated but which falls short of having been formally agreed.[8] As the Court of Justice has noted:

> The system of competition rules established by Article 85 et seq. of the EEC Treaty is concerned with the economic effects of agreements or of any comparable form of concerted practice or coordination rather than with their legal form.[9]

4.008. Innocent parallel behaviour. Several undertakings involved in a single type of business may operate in tandem simply because commercial common sense pushes them in that direction and not because they have agreed to do so with each other. Thus the Court of Justice has held that parallel conduct resulting from the intelligent adaptation by each trader to the conduct of his competitors does not amount to an unlawful concerted practice.[10]

4.009. Concerted practices after termination of an agreement. A common form of concerted practice is that occurring after the termination of an agreement. In Joined Cases *EMI Records Ltd v. CBS United Kingdom Ltd*,[11] *EMI Records Ltd v. CBS Grammofon A/S*[12] and *EMI Records Ltd v. CBS Schallplatten GmbH*,[13] the Court of Justice held that even where an unlawful agreement has been terminated, undertakings may still be guilty of a breach of Article 85(1), by carrying on the behaviour in concert which the unlawful agreement had brought about. The Plaintiffs and Defendants owned rights in an identical trademark in the Community and in third countries respectively and it had at one time been agreed that they would not compete with each other. Although the restrictive covenants were no longer in force at the time of the action, the parties had continued to operate in compliance with their terms. The Court pronounced that for Article 85(1) to apply to agreements no longer in force it is sufficient that such agreements continue to produce their effects after they have formally ceased to be in force. The Court stated that:

> An agreement is only regarded as continuing to produce its effects if from the behaviour of the persons concerned there may be inferred the existence of elements of concerted practice and of coordination peculiar to the agreement and producing the same result as that envisaged by the agreement.[14]

It is noteworthy that the Court ignored Advocate General Warner's Opinion that this prohibition cannot extend to an agreement made and terminated before entry into force of the Treaty, or in the case of agreements affecting trade in new Member

---

[7] See, generally Bellamy and Child, *op. cit.*, 2-031 et seq.

[8] See generally *Halsbury's Laws of England* (4th Edn, 1986) Vol 52, 19.34.

[9] Case 243/83 *Binon and Cie SA v. Agence et Messageries de la Presse SA* [1985] ECR 2015, [1985] 3 CMLR 800, para. 17.

[10] *Ibid.*

[11] Case 51/75 [1976] ECR 811, [1976] 2 CMLR 235.

[12] Case 86/75 [1976] ECR 871, [1976] 2 CMLR 235.

[13] Case 96/75 [1976] ECR 913, [1976] 2 CMLR 235.

[14] [1976] ECR 811, [1976] 2 CMLR, para. 31; [1976] ECR 871, [1976] 2 CMLR 235, para. 28; [1976] ECR 913, [1976] 2 CMLR, para. 15. Affirmed in Case 243/83 *Binon and Cie SA v. Agence et Messageries de la Presse SA* [1985] ECR 2015, [1985] 3 CMLR 800.

States, the date of their accession to the Treaty. ie in the Advocate General's Opinion, the Treaty could not have retrospective effect.

(ii) Concerted Practices by Media Undertakings

4.010. Newspaper distribution agreement. *Binon and Cie SA v. Agence et Messageries de la Presse SA*[15] concerned a selective distribution agreement between the Defendant agency and Belgian and foreign publishers. It had been agreed that newspapers would be sold only to retailers approved by a consultative committee whose opinion was to be unanimously accepted by the publishers. That procedure was impugned by the Belgian Courts and replaced with a new mechanism whereby AMP delivered an opinion on every application and notified it to the publishers who were deemed to accept it unless they notified AMP to the contrary within a specified period. In practice, the publishers never rejected AMP's opinion and the Court of Justice held that they conducted a 'concerted practice' in breach of Article 85(1) by carrying on the behaviour that the original agreements had brought about.

4.011. Collecting societies refusing direct access to works. The dividing line between concerted practices and 'innocent parallel behaviour' can be almost imperceptively thin, as illustrated by a number of cases concerning 'reciprocal representation contracts' entered into by collecting societies. The Court of Justice had held that while so called 'reciprocal representation contracts' between collecting societies were generally lawful, Article 85(1) would be violated if the collecting societies agreed to refuse a foreign user direct access to their repertoire.[16]

Although the collecting societies had pruned clauses from those contracts which required them to operate in this way, they continued in parallel to refuse users direct access to their works. The Court of Justice held that so called 'parallel behaviour' may amount to strong evidence of a concerted practice if it leads to conditions of competition which do not correspond to the normal conditions of competition. However, concerted actions cannot be presumed where the parallel behaviour can be accounted for by reasons other than the existence of concerted action.[17] The Court noted that such a reason might be that the copyright societies of one Member State would be obliged, in the event of direct access to their repertories, to organise their own management and monitoring system in another country.

(3) Parent and Subsidiary Companies

4.012. The Court of Justice has held that an agreement between a parent and a subsidiary company is not caught be Article 85(1) if the undertakings form a single 'economic unit' within which the subsidiary has no real freedom to determine its

---

[15] Case 243/83 [1985] ECR 2015, [1985] 3 CMLR 800.

[16] Case 395/87 *Ministère Public v. Tournier* [1989] ECR 2521 [1991] ECR 2521, [1991] 4 CMLR 248; Case 110/88 *Lucazeau v. Société des auteurs, compositeurs et éditeurs de musique* [1989] ECR 2811, [1991] 4 CMLR 248; Case 241/88 *Société des auteurs, compositeurs et éditeurs de musique v. Debelle* [1989] ECR 2811, [1991] 4 CMLR 248; 242/88 *Société des auteurs, compositeurs et éditeurs de musique v. Soumagnac* [1989] ECR 2811, [1991] 4 CMLR 248. See §4.111 below.

[17] Affirming Case 48/69 *Imperial Chemical Industries v. EC Commission* [1972] ECR 619, [1972] CMLR 557.

course of action on the market, and if the agreements or practices are concerned merely with the internal allocation of tasks as between the undertakings.[18]

(4) Agency Agreement

(i) General Principles

4.013. The concept of the single economic unit. If, in an exclusive dealing arrangement, a distributor can prove that he is, in reality, an agent of the supplier, that is, an 'auxiliary organ of the principal undertaking', he will be outside of the ambit of Article 85(1). This is because Article 85(1) refers to 'agreements between undertakings' and where a commercial arrangement can be considered to be a single economic unit, there is only one undertaking.[19]

4.014. The Commission Announcement on Exclusive Agency Contracts with Commercial Agents. The Commission has issued a notice stating that in its view, contracts made with commercial agents are not covered by the prohibitions contained in Article 85(1) provided that, amongst other matters, the commercial agent does not undertake activities which would give him the status of an independent trader.[20] The notice states that:

> The Commission regards as the decisive criterion, which distinguishes the commercial agent from the independent trader, the agreement—express or implied, which deals with responsibility for the financial risks bound up with the sale or with the performance of the contract. Thus the Commission's assessment is not governed by the name used to describe the representative. Except for the usual del credere guarantee, a commercial agent must not by the nature of his functions assume any risk resulting from the transaction. If he does assume such risk, his function becomes economically akin to that of an independent trader and must therefore be treated as such for the purposes of the rules of competition.[21]

(ii) Media Agency Agreement

4.015. Distribution of newspapers and periodicals. In *Binon and Cie SA v. Agence et Messageries de la Presse SA*,[22] the Court of Justice held that Article 85(1) applied to a set of agreements between an agency which specialised in the

---

[18] Case 15/74 *Centrafarm BV v. Sterling Drug Inc* [1974] ECR 1147, [1974] 2 CMLR 480. In Case 78/70 *Deutsche Grammophon Gesellschaft mbh v. Metro-SB-Grossmärkte GmbH & Co KG* [1971] ECR 487, [1971] CMLR 631, Advocate General Roemer noted that an agreement between a parent and subsidiary could not invoke Article 85(1) where there was, in reality, a single economic unit, the subsidiary being subject to the instructions and control of the parent company. See also Case 22/71 *Béguelin Import Co v. GL Import Export SA* [1971] ECR 949, [1972] CMLR 81.

[19] Case 22/71 *Béguelin Import Co v. GL Import Export SA* [1971] ECR 949, [1972] CMLR 81.

[20] Announcement on Exclusive Agency Contracts with Commercial Agents, (1962) OJ 2921.

[21] In accordance with the notice, the Commission considers that 'an independent trader' is most likely to be involved where the contracting party described as a commercial agent:

— is required to keep or does in fact keep, as his own property, a considerable stock of the products covered by the contract, or

— is required to organise, maintain or ensure at this own expense a substantial service to customers free of charge, or does in fact organise maintain, or ensure such a service, or

— can determine or does in fact determine prices or terms of business.

[22] Case 243/83 [1985] ECR 2015, [1985] 3 CMLR 800. For the facts of the case, see §4.056 below.

distribution of newspapers and periodicals and publishers of newspapers and periodicals where the effect of the agreements was the approval of retail sales outlets was a matter for that agency or a body set up by it.

Advocate General Slynn in the Binon case outlined factors which the national court should take into account in determining whether an undertaking is an agent. Thus the Court should ascertain what expenses the undertaking meets, what its remuneration is and what risks it bears: an undertaking which takes on risks points to it being an independent trader. In the Binon case, for example, it was relevant to consider the risks to AMP arising from: the loss of newspapers; delayed payment or the bankruptcy of the retailer or the bankruptcy of the publisher. The fact that publishers agreed to take back unsold copies, and were only paid eventually for their net retail sales, was not conclusive that this was an agency situation. AMP had claimed it was part of 471 publishers. Advocate General Slynn stated that it is unlikely that an undertaking can claim to the part of the single economic unit of a large number of undertakings. Ultimately it is a question of reality and not of labels.[23]

(5) Granting Rights to Exploit Works Protected by Copyright or a Neighbouring Right

4.016. Absolute assignment of interest. An absolute assignment of copyright or a neighbouring right will not invoke Article 85(1) because in such a case, there is no agreement preventing the assignor from competing with the assignee. Thus Advocate General Reischl stated in *Coditel SA v. Ciné Vog Films SA:*[24]

> . . . an agreement in restraint of competition cannot ... be said to come into being when the copyright in a film is ... relinquished by way of a definitive transfer...this is a case of an isolated legal transaction and... as between the original proprietor of the right and his assign there is no subsisting legal relationship which may have repercussions on competition by limiting the freedom of action enjoyed by the original proprietor of the right.

As the Advocate General explained, it is not the contractual arrangement which prevents the original proprietor from exploiting the right himself or from granting licences in the territory in question, it is rather a consequence of the document of transfer itself ie the original proprietor no longer has any rights in the material assigned.[25]

4.017. Surrender of an interest. Although a surrender of an interest for a limited period is generally treated in the same way as an exclusive licence and therefore potentially caught by Article 85(1), it may, depending on all the circumstances, defeat the competition rules.[26]

---

[23] See also Case 26/76 *Metro SB-Grossmärkte GmbH & Co KG v. EC Commission* [1977] ECR 1875, [1978] 2 CMLR 1.

[24] Case 262/81 [1982] ECR 3381, [1983] 1 CMLR 49.

[25] *Ibid.*

[26] *Ibid.*, where Advocate General Reischl noted that 'It is a matter of analysing the clauses of the contract, dealing with the duration for example (which may be shorter than the copyright period), and of determining the party who ultimately assumes the commercial risk, in which task the terms and conditions governing payment may furnish important clues.'

3. Meaning of the Term 'Undertaking'

(1) General Principles

4.018. The Court of Justice has stated that 'an undertaking is constituted by a single organisation of personal, tangible and intangible elements, attached to an autonomous legal entity and pursuing a given long-term economic aim.'[27] But, as the Court has made abundantly clear, the application of competition law is not affected to any great extent by the legal mould in which the undertaking is cast.[28] It is essential only that the undertaking has its own legal personality, whether this is in the form of a commercial, co-operative or civil company or even an association.[29] In the final analysis, the competition rules[30] apply to any undertaking exercising an economic activity whether that activity involves the trading of goods or the provision of services[31] and whether or not it is intended to earn profits.[32]

(2) Examples of Media Undertakings

4.019. Collecting societies,[33] television broadcasting companies,[34] the manufacturers of musical recordings,[35] publishers, book clubs and booksellers[36] and artists,[37] have all been treated as undertakings by the Court of Justice. As far as public service television stations are concerned, the acquisition of broadcasting rights constitutes an economic activity which is sufficient to bring them within the definition of an 'undertaking.'[38] For what is involved, is the acquisition of goods for consideration, with the broadcasting organisations being in direct competition with

---

[27] Case 127/73 *Belgische Radio en Televisi (BRT) v. SV SABAM* [1974] ECR 51, [1974] 2 CMLR 238, per Advocate General Mayras citing the judgment in Case 19/61 *Mannesmann AG v High Authority* [1962] ECR 357, a case concerned with the application of the ECSC Treaty. See also Commission Decision 89/536/EEC Re Film Purchases by German Television Stations OJ No L 284, 03.10.89, p.36.

[28] *Ibid.*

[29] *Ibid.*

[30] Both Article 85 and Article 86.

[31] Case 127/73 *Belgische Radio en Televisi (BRT) v. SV SABAM* [1974] ECR 51, [1974] 2 CMLR 238, per Advocate General Mayras.

[32] Commission Decision 89/536/EEC, Re Film Purchases by German Television Stations OJ No L 284, 03.10.89, p.36.

[33] Case 127/73 *Belgische Radio en Televisi (BRT) v. SV SABAM* [1974] ECR 51, [1974] 2 CMLR 238, per Advocate General Mayras.

[34] Case 155/73 *Sacchi* [1974] ECR 409, [1974] 2 CMLR 177. In Commission Statement Re British Broadcasting Corporation [1976] 1 CMLR D89, the Commission confirmed that a public corporation qualified as an undertaking.

[35] Case 78/70 *Deutsche Grammophon Gesellschaft mbH v. Metro-SB-Grossmärkte GmbH & Co KG* [1971] ECR 487, [1971] CMLR 631.

[36] Joined Cases 43, 63/82 VBVB *and* VBBB v. *EC Commission* [1984] ECR 19, [1985] 1 CMLR 27 and Case T—66/89 Re The Net Book Agreements: *Publishers Association v. EC Commission* [1992] 5 CMLR 120.

[37] Case 7/82 *GVL v. EC Commission* [1983] ECR 483, [1983] 3 CMLR 645. The Commission has stated in respect of proceedings involving RAI/Unitel, that 'artists are undertakings within the meaning of Article 85(1) when they commercialize their artistic performances' (See Commission Eighth Report on Competition Policy (1978), point 129(i)).

[38] Commission Decision 89/536/EEC Re Film Purchases by German Television Stations OJ No L 284, 03.10.89, p.36.

other undertakings, the latter including, in particular, television stations.[39] Furthermore it is of no relevance that a broadcasting organisation may have a right to license material free of any charge.[40]

4. Object or Effect of Restricting, Preventing or Distorting Competition

(1) Introduction

4.020. Two stage test. The Court of Justice has evolved a two stage test to determine whether an agreement has 'the object or effect of restricting, preventing of distorting competition' since it has held that this phrase in Article 85(1) creates alternative and not cumulative conditions.[41]

4.021. Whether the object is to restrict competition. In the first instance, the Court looks at the object of the agreement in the light of its economic context, to see whether the intended effect of the agreement is appreciably to restrict competition, that is, the competition which would exist in the absence of the agreement.[42] Thus in *Miller International Schallplatten GmbH v. EC Commission*,[43] the Court of Justice stated that:

> In prohibiting agreements which may affect trade between Member States and which have as their object or effect the restriction of competition Article 85(1) of the Treaty does not require proof that such agreements have in fact appreciably affected such trade, which would moreover be difficult in the majority of cases to establish for legal purposes, but merely requires that it be established that such agreements are capable of having that effect.[44]

4.022. Whether the actual effect is to restrict competition. If the analysis of the intended effect of the agreement does not reveal the effect on competition to be sufficiently deleterious, the actual consequences of the agreement are considered.[45] Thus for the agreement to be caught by Article 85(1) it is necessary to find the presence of factors which show that competition has in fact been prevented or restricted or distorted to an appreciable extent.[46]

4.023. Distinction between horizontal and vertical restrictions. As an aid to analysis, the case law often categorises agreements as imposing either so called 'horizontal' or 'vertical' restrictions on competition, or both. A 'horizontal'

---

[39] *Ibid.*

[40] *Ibid.*

[41] Case 56/65 *Société Technique Minière v. Maschinenbau Ulm GmbH* [1966] ECR 235, [1966] 1 CMLR 357. See also Case 19/77 *Miller International Schallplatten GmbH v. EC Commission* [1978] ECR 131, [1978] 2 CMLR 334, per Advocate General Warner.

[42] *Ibid.*

[43] Case 19/77 [1978] ECR 131, [1978] 2 CMLR 334, para. 15.

[44] See also the opinion of Advocate General Warner.

[45] Case 56/65 *Société Technique Minière v. Maschinenbau Ulm GmbH* [1966] ECR 235, [1966] 1 CMLR 357.

[46] *Ibid.*

restriction is a restriction agreed between undertakings who occupy the same level of supply, for example, an agreement between one manufacturer and another or between one distributor and another. A 'vertical' restriction is a restriction agreed between undertakings at different levels on the supply chain, for example an agreement between a manufacturer and a distributor or between a distributor and a retailer.

(2) The Relevant Market

(i) General Principles

4.024. The effect of an agreement on competition can only be assessed by reference to the 'relevant market'. This has three components: the relevant product market; the relevant geographic market and the relevant temporal market.[47] The relevant product market is the market in those products which are considered to be interchangeable with the products in issue. The relevant geographic market is that part of the Community in which the effects of the agreement are felt. The relevant temporal market is the period of time over which the effects of the agreement are felt.

(ii) Media Relevant Market

4.025. Performances of pop music by well-known performers. In an action concerning an agreement to market performances of pop music by well-known performers,[48] the Commission stated that 'the records sold by this firm were interpretations by "hit" performers working solely for this firm: these performances are individual and can in no circumstances be regarded, because of their properties or their use, or their price, as similar, for the consumer, to the performance of other artists'.[49]

4.026. 'Light' and 'Classical' Music on Vinyl Disc. In an action concerning an agreement to market light music performances on vinyl discs,[50] the Commission found that there was 'no single market for classical music, light music and "pop" music'.[51] In another decision,[52] the Commission noted that 'The peculiar characteristics of light and serious music are such that they are only rarely interchangeable. Accordingly, recordings of light music may be said to constitute a separate market.' In that action, half of the manufacturer's repertoire consisted of music from the German 'hit parade' and German folk music. The Commission held that, as far as the relevant geographic market was concerned, 'Knowledge of the German language by purchasers in other Community countries may be said to be of minor importance as regards the sale of sound recordings of the German hit parade and folk music (songs in dialect and carnival songs, for example).'

---

[47] See generally, §4.117 et seq. below (abuse of a dominant position).
[48] Commission Decision of 22 December 1972, OJ No L 303, 31.12.72, p.52.
[49] Commission Second Report on Competition Policy (1972), point 40. See §4.107 below 'contracts with performers'.
[50] Commission Decision of 22 December 1972, OJ No L 303, 31.12.72, p.52.
[51] Commission Second Report on Competition Policy (1972), point 40. See §4.107 below 'contracts with performers'.
[52] Commission Decision 76/915/EEC Re Miller OJ No L 357, 29.12.76, p.40.

5.   De Minimus Agreements—Agreements Not 'Appreciably Restricting Competition'

(1)   General Principles

4.027. Introduction. The Court of Justice has determined that agreements which have an insignificant effect on the market are not in contravention of Article 85(1) of the Treaty. This may be due to the weakness of the parties concerned.[53] The Commission has also confirmed, that in its opinion, 'agreements, whose effects on trade between Member States and on competition are negligible, do not fall within the prohibition on restrictive agreements in Article 85(1) of the EEC Treaty'. 'Only those agreements are prohibited which have an appreciable impact on market conditions, in that they appreciably alter the market position, ie the sales outlets and supply possibilities, of non-participating undertakings and of consumers.'[54]

4.028. Agreements of minor importance. The Commission has stated that 'it considers it important to promote co-operation between undertakings where such co-operation is economically desirable without presenting difficulties from the point of view of competition policy; in particular, it wishes to facilitate co-operation between small and medium-sized undertakings'.[55] To this end it has issued a notice specifying those agreements which it considers fulfil these criteria in that they do not have an 'appreciable' impact on the market.[56] As a result of the notice there is no longer any need for undertakings to obtain negative clearance or to have the legal position established through an individual decision for agreements covered.[57]

In accordance with the notice, the Commission holds the view that agreements between undertakings engaged in the production or distribution of goods do not fall under the prohibition of Article 85(1) of the EEC Treaty if:[58]

● the products which are the subject of the agreement and other products of the participating undertakings considered by consumers to be similar by reason of their characteristics, price or use do not represent in a substantial part of the common market more than 5% of the total market for such products, and

---

[53] Case 5/69 *Völk v. Vervaecke* [1969] ECR 295, [1969] CMLR 273. According to Bellamy and Child, *op.cit.*, 2-141, an appreciable effect will usually be presumed by the Court where the parties concerned have more than 5% of the market for the products concerned. The authors state (2-140) that a market share of less may still be caught if, on the facts, a sufficiently appreciable effect can be demonstrated.

[54] Commission Notice of 19th December 1977 concerning Agreements of Minor Importance, para. 1, OJ No C 313, 29.12.77, p.3.

[55] *Ibid.*

[56] *Ibid.*

[57] *Ibid.*

[58] *Ibid.* The notice is expressly without prejudice to any interpretation which may be given by the Court of Justice of the European Communities.

● the aggregate annual turnover of the participating undertakings does not exceed 50 million units of account.[59]

The Commission also holds the view that the said agreements do not fall within the prohibition of Article 85(1) even if the above mentioned market share and turnover are exceeded by up to 10% within two successive financial years.[60]

Furthermore, the Commission itself points out that:

The quantitative definition of 'appreciable' given by the Commission is, however, no absolute yardstick; in fact, it is quite possible that, in individual cases, even agreements between undertakings which exceed the limits mentioned...may well have only a negligible effect on trade between Member States and on competition and are therefore not caught by Article 85(1).[61]

(2) Appreciable Effects by Media Undertakings

4.029. Record manufacturers. *Miller International Schallplatten GmbH v. EC Commission,*[62] concerned an agreement for the distribution of vinyl discs and music cassettes. The Applicant's share of the total market in sound recordings in the then Federal Republic of Germany hovered around the 5% mark in terms of volume and trade.[63] In fact, the Applicant specialised in the production of bargain-range long playing records and music cassettes and, within that category, in particular in the production of sound recordings for children and young persons, so that its share in those markets could be expressed as appreciably higher percentages. The Court of Justice held that accordingly, the agreement manifested an appreciable effect.

4.030. Exclusive contracts with performers. The Commission has held that, where little known performers are engaged on exclusive contracts, there will be no appreciable effect on competition. However, there are manifestly appreciable effects in the case of highly successful artists. Thus an agreement which prevented a

---

[59] For the purposes of this notice the participating undertakings are:

'1. The undertakings which are parties to the agreement.
2. Undertakings in which the undertakings which are parties to the agreement hold:
— at least 25% of the capital or of the working capital whether directly or indirectly, or
— at least half the voting rights, or
— the power to appoint at least half of the members of the supervisory board, the board of management or the bodies legally representing the undertaking, or
— the right to manage the affairs of the undertaking.
3. Undertakings which hold in an undertaking which is a party to the agreement:—at least 25% of the capital or working capital whether directly or indirectly, or
— at least half the voting rights, or
— the power to appoint at least half of the members of the supervisory board, the board of management or the bodies legally representing the undertaking party to the agreement, or
— the right to manage the affairs of the undertaking.

The aggregate turnover shall include the turnover in all goods and services achieved during the last financial year by the participating undertakings. The aggregate turnover shall not include dealings between undertakings which are parties to the agreement.'

[60] Commission Notice of 19th December 1977, concerning Agreements of Minor Importance, para. I, OJ No C313, 29.12.77, p.3.
[61] Ibid.
[62] Case 19/77 [1978] ECR 131, [1978] 2 CMLR 334.
[63] Being 5.19% in 1970, 5.05% in 1971, 4.91% in 1972, 5.87% in 1973, 5.05% in 1974 and 6.07% in 1975. Because these percentages relate to quantity, and Miller was essentially a low-price producer, its percentage of the market expressed in terms of value was necessarily lower.

worldwide broadcast from La Scala by the Italian state broadcasting company was held to manifest an appreciable effect on trade.[64]

6. Effect on Trade between Member States

(1) General Principles

4.031. Community law will only censure anti-competitive conduct which has an affect on inter-State trade. It follows that anti-competitive behaviour, the consequences of which are contained within the territorial boundaries of a single Member State, is outside the grasp of the competition rules.[65] But it should be emphasised that anti-competitive conduct confined to the territory of a single Member State is capable of having repercussions on patterns of trade and competition in the common market and in so far as it has such affects, it will invoke Article 85(1).[66]

The concept of what does or does not amount to an agreement affecting trade between Member States has evolved over the years. In *Etablissements Consten SARL and Grundig-Verkaufs-GmbH v. EC Commission*, an early case, the Court of Justice held that:

> . . . what is particularly important is whether the agreement is capable of constituting a threat, either direct or indirect, actual or potential, to freedom of trade between Member States in a manner which might harm the attainment of the objectives of a single market between States.[67]

The court made it clear in that case that Article 85 comes into play despite the fact that an agreement encourages an increase in trade (even a large one) between Member States. The crucial point is that trade flows will have been influenced by such an agreement and the possibility of uniting the markets of Member States may have been undermined.

In a refinement of the principle in *Société Technique Minière v. Maschinenbau Ulm GmbH*, the Court of Justice stated that:

> .. . it must be possible to foresee with a sufficient degree of probability on the basis of a set of objective factors of law or of fact that the agreement in question may have an

---

[64] Commission Decision 78/516/EEC Re RAI/UNITEL OJ No L 157, 15.6.78, p.39. (See also Commission Eighth Report on Competition Policy, (1979), point 129(i) Re RAI/Unitel.) The Commission noted that UNITEL's economic significance was determined to a certain extent by the influence which its shareholders had on its business activities. It was therefore necessary to know the identity of the shareholders and the extent of their potential influence. On restrictions on competition, see §4.107 below.

[65] Joined Cases 56, 58/64 *Etablissements Consten SARL and Grundig-Verkaufs-GmbH v. EC Commission* [1966] ECR 299, [1966] CMLR 418.

[66] Case T—66/89 Re The Net Book Agreements: *Publishers Association v. EC Commission* [1992] 5 CMLR 120. See also Case 8/72 *Vereeniging van Cementhandelaren v. EC Commission* [1972] ECR 977, [1973] CMLR 7; Case 322/81 *Nederlandsche Banden-Industrie Michelin NV v. EC Commission* [1983] ECR 3461, [1985] 1 CMLR 282; Case 246/86 *SC Balasco v. EC Commission* [1989] ECR 2117.

[67] Joined Cases 56, 58/64 *Etablissements Consten SARL and Grundig-Verkaufs-GmbH v. EC Commission* [1966] ECR 299, [1966] CMLR 418; affirmed Case 56/65 *Société Technique Minière v. Maschinenbau Ulm GmbH* [1966] ECR 235, [1966] CMLR 357; Case 5/69 *Völk v. Vervaecke* [1969] ECR 295 [1969] CMLR 273.

influence, direct or indirect, actual or potential, on the pattern of trade between Member States.[68]

In the words of one authority, 'The concept of "effect on trade between Member States" is thus best understood as a rule of jurisdiction, enabling Community law to regulate all restrictive agreements having appreciable repercussions at Community level.'[69]

(2) Effect on Trade by Media Undertakings

4.032. Political and not linguistic territories. In *VBVB and VBBB v. EC Commission*[70] the Court of Justice held that the phrase 'trade between Member States' contained in Article 85(1) is directed at political territories and not, for example, linguistic territories. The Applicants unsuccessfully argued that because their 'interstate' agreement concerned the Netherlands and the Flemish speaking region of Belgium, both of which shared the same language, this constituted a single geographic region which did not constitute two Member States within the meaning of Article 85(1).

4.033. Newspaper distribution. In *Binon and Cie SA v. Agence et Messageries de la Presse SA*,[71] it was necessary to consider that a restriction on competition in national newspapers might have an effect on the distribution of publications coming from other Member States.[72]

4.034. Net resale book regulation. In Re The Net Book Agreements: *Publishers Association v. EC Commission*,[73] the Court of First Instance upheld the Commission's Decision[74] that the 'Net Book Agreement' in issue, which set in place a price fixing mechanism for books in the United Kingdom and Ireland affected trade between Member States. Imports of books from the United Kingdom into Ireland accounted for 50% of total book sales in the latter country and 75% of those books were governed by the price fixing agreement. Furthermore, the Court held that were the Net Book Agreement to be restricted to operators in the United Kingdom, it would still affect trade between Member States bearing in mind the proportion of 'net books' which were eventually exported to Ireland.

The Net Book Agreement provided that books imported into the United Kingdom from other Member States by a publisher or exclusive distributor could be made 'net book' if those undertakings so wished. The Appellant argued that since the publisher or exclusive distributor was free to decide whether or not to make an imported book a 'net book', the Net Book Agreement did not affect trade between Member States. The Court rejected this conclusion as unfounded noting that if the

---

[68] Case 56/65 [1966] ECR 235, [1966] CMLR 357. This principle was approved by the Court of First Instance in Case T—66/89 Re The Net Book Agreements: *Publishers Association v. EC Commission* [1992] 5 CMLR 120.

[69] Bellamy and Child, *op. cit.*, 2-113.

[70] Joined Cases 43, 63/82 [1984] ECR 19, [1985] 1 CMLR 27.

[71] Case 243/83 [1985] ECR 2015, [1985] 3 CMLR 800.

[72] Per Advocate General Slynn citing Case 126/80 *Salonia v. Poidomani and Giglio* [1981] ECR 1563, [1982] 1 CMLR 64.

[73] Case T—66/89 [1992] 5 CMLR 120.

[74] Commission Decision 89/44/EEC Re Publishers Association—Net Book Agreements, OJ No L 22, 26.1.89, p. 13.

publisher or exclusive distributor decided to apply the standard conditions of sale to an imported title, those conditions would apply to inter alia, importation of new consignment of the same title and exportation from the United Kingdom to Ireland of a title originally imported in to the United Kingdom and sold as a 'net book'.

7. Negative Clearance of Article 85(1) and Exemption under Article 85(3)

4.035. Negative clearance. It may be that an agreement escapes the prohibition contained in Article 85(1). Upon an application by the undertakings concerned, the Commission may certify that there are no grounds under Article 85(1) for action on its part in respect of an agreement, decision or practice.[75] Such an agreement is said to have 'negative clearance'.

4.036. Application for exemption. Agreements in breach of Article 85(1) of the Treaty are automatically void in accordance with Article 85(2). And no prior decision is necessary to that effect by the Commission.[76] It may, however, be possible to seek an exemption under Article 85(3).[77]

The 'First Regulation implementing Articles 85 and 86 of the Treaty' provides for a notification procedure.[78] A decision by the Commission is issued for a specified period and may have conditions attached thereto.[79] It may be renewed[80] or revoked or amended.[81] In practice, few exemptions are granted and those that are awarded sometimes take years to reach their conclusion. Instead, the Commission often resorts to granting so called 'comfort letters' which confirm that the Commission finds no reason to intervene with the agreements notified.[82]

4.037. Component parts of Article 85(3). In practice, the Court and Commission generally break down Article 85(3) into component parts consisting of two positive and two negative conditions.[83] Undertakings must thus demonstrate that their agreement:

(a) contributes to improving the production or distribution of goods or to promoting technical or economic progress;

(b) allows consumers a fair share of the resulting benefit;

(c) does not impose on the undertakings concerned restrictions which are not indispensable for the attainment of these objectives; and

---

[75] Regulation 17, First Regulation implementing Articles 85 and 86 of the Treaty, Article 2, OJ Sp. Edn. 1959-62, p. 87.

[76] *Ibid.*

[77] See generally, Bellamy and Child, *op. cit.*, 3-001 et seq.

[78] Regulation 17, First Regulation implementing Articles 85 and 86 of the Treaty, OJ Sp. Edn. 1959-62, p. 87.

[79] *Ibid.*

[80] *Ibid.*

[81] *Ibid.*

[82] See generally, Bellamy and Child, *op. cit.*, 3-013.

[83] See e.g. Joined Cases 43, 63/82 VBVB *v.* VBBB [1984] ECR 19, [1985] 1 CMLR 27, per Advocate General VerLoren van Themaat who stated that '. . . it is generally incumbent upon the parties to show that the agreement is "pro-competitive" ie that it confers positive benefits beyond those to be expected from the free play and interplay of market forces.' See also Commission Decision 89/536/EEC Re Film Purchases by German Television Stations OJ No L 284, 03.10.89, p.36.

(d) does not afford those undertakings, the possibility of eliminating competition in respect of a substantial part of the products in question.

4.038. Notification not necessary. Notification is not necessary in the case of a narrowly defined category of agreements: essentially those to which the only parties are undertakings from a single Member State, the agreement does not relate either to imports or to exports between Member States and certain other conditions are fulfilled.[84]

4.039. Block Exemption. Because it would be impractical for the Commission to have to make an individual decision on each and every agreement potentially in breach of Article 85(1), it has been empowered to define categories of agreements which merit exemption and are accordingly exempted.[85] Using this power and employing the experience it has gained through individual decisions, the Commission has enacted a number of 'block exemptions'. It is not necessary to notify an agreement which satisfies the terms of a block exemption conferred by a Regulation: such an agreement is automatically exempted.[86] Agreements which do not come within the precise terms of a block exemption may be notified under the so called 'opposition procedure' provided for by the Regulations.

8. Exclusive Distribution Agreements

(1) General Principles

4.040. Exclusive dealership. The Court of Justice has held that a restriction on competition contained in an exclusive dealing agreement may fall outside of Article 85(1). It has stated that 'it may be doubted whether there is an interference with competition if the said agreement seems really necessary for the penetration of a new area by an undertaking'.[87]

4.041. Export bans. Nevertheless, export bans are consistently condemned by the Court as automatically in violation of Article 85(1) because they shelter price competition.[88] Thus the Court of Justice held in *Miller International Schallplatten GmbH v. EC Commission*:[89]

. . . by its very nature, a clause prohibiting exports constitutes a restriction on competition, whether it is adopted at the instigation of the supplier or of the customer since the agreed purpose of the contracting parties is the endeavour to isolate a part of the market.

---

[84] Regulation 17, First Regulation implementing Articles 85 and 86 of the Treaty, Article 4, OJ Sp. Edn. 1959-62, p. 87.
[85] Article 87(2)(b) of the Treaty.
[86] See e.g. §4.044 et seq. below.
[87] Case 56/65 *Société Technique Minière v. Maschinenbau Ulm GmbH* [1966] ECR 235, [1966] 1 CMLR 357.
[88] Joined Cases 56, 58/64 *Etablissements Consten SARL and Grundig-Verkaufs-GmbH v. EC Commission* [1966] ECR 299, [1966] CMLR 418.
[89] Case 19/77 [1978] ECR 131, [1978] 2 CMLR 334, para. 7.

Generally, the Commission's policy has been to exempt a ban on the distributor actively selling goods outside of the contract territory, but it will not approve of a prohibition on passive selling, that is, the distributor responding to unsolicited requests.[90]

4.042. Absolute exclusivity prohibited. An agreement in which a supplier grants a distributor absolute territorial protection against competition, by blocking parallel imports of goods marketed by other distributors (as well as imposing export bans on those distributors) will be in breach of Article 85(1) and is unlikely to gain an exemption under Article 85(3).[91]

(2) Media Exclusive Distribution Agreements

4.043. Distribution of sound recordings. *Miller International Schallplatten GmbH v. EC Commission*,[92] concerned an agreement for the distribution of sound recordings. The Applicant was a manufacturer of low price sound recordings (vinyl discs, tapes and cassettes), mostly of light and pop music as well as folk music for children. It entered into a number of exclusive dealing agreements in various Community territories, all of which provided that Miller's products could not be exported outside of the relevant distributor's contract territory. Miller charged its German distributors prices much higher than its customers elsewhere in the Community. The Commission condemned the agreement and Miller applied to the Court. Miller argued that, despite the ban on exports, none of its distributors was interested in intra-Community trade. The Court of Justice held that 'the fact that resellers, as customers of the applicant, prefer to limit their commercial operations to more restricted markets, whether regional or national, cannot justify the formal adoption of clauses prohibiting exports, either in particular contracts or in conditions of sale, any more than the desire of the producer to wall off sections of the Common Market'.

(3) Block Exemption for Exclusive Product Distribution Agreements— Regulation 1983/83

4.044. Introduction. The Commission believes that exclusive distribution agreements lead to a general improvement in distribution because an undertaking is able to concentrate its sales activities and does not need to maintain numerous business relations with a large number of dealers.[93] Given its experience with these types of agreements,[94] it has issued a 'block exemption' and agreements which are drafted in compliance with it gain automatic exemption from Article 85(1).

4.045. Commencement. Regulation 1983/83 entered into force on 1 July 1983 and will continue in force until 31 December 1997.[95]

---

[90] See, generally, Bellamy and Child, *op. cit.*, 3.018
[91] Joined Cases 56, 58/64 *Etablissements Consten SARL and Grundig-Verkaufs-GmbH v. EEC Commission* [1966] ECR 299, [1966] CMLR 418.
[92] Case 19/77 [1978] ECR 131, [1978] 2 CMLR 334.
[93] Recital (5).
[94] Recital (2).
[95] Article 10.

4.046. Geographic scope of block exemption. Exclusive distribution agreements to which only two undertakings are party from one Member State and which concern the resale of goods within that Member State are normally outside of Article 85(1).[96] However, they may be in violation where they affect trade between Member States and in so far as they do so they may also benefit from the block exemption (provided that they fulfil the terms of the Regulation).[97]

4.047. Exclusive distribution (restriction on competition). In accordance with the Regulation, Article 85(1) will not apply to agreements to which only two undertakings are party and whereby where one party (the supplier) agrees with the other (the distributor) to supply certain goods for resale within the whole or a defined area of the common market, only to that other (distributor).[98] Apart from the aforementioned obligation, the distributor may impose upon the supplier an obligation not to supply the contract goods to users in the territory.[99] However, no other restrictions on competition are permitted.[100]

4.048. Obligations of distributor (restrictions on competition). The Regulation allows the supplier to impose certain restrictions on competition on the distributor: they are the 'quid pro quo' for the exclusive distribution licence. Thus the supplier can demand that the distributor: does not manufacture or distribute goods which compete with the contract goods;[101] obtains the contract goods for resale only from the supplier;[102] refrains, outside the contract territory and in relation to the contract goods, from seeking customers, from establishing any branch and from maintaining any distribution depot.[103]

4.049. Obligations of distributor (general obligations). As well as restrictions on competition, the Regulation allows the supplier to impose a number of other obligations on the distributor. These is an obligation: to purchase complete ranges of goods or minimum quantities;[104] to sell the contract goods under trademarks or packed and presented as specified by the supplier;[105] to take measures for the promotion of sales, such measures including in particular,[106] advertising, the maintenance of a sales network or stock of goods, the provision of customer and guarantee services and the employment of staff having specialised or technical training.

4.050. Conditions which will invalidate the exemption. The Regulation stipulates a number of circumstances which will invalidate the exemption. These are as follows:

Reciprocal agreements. Where manufacturers of identical goods or of goods which are considered by users to be equivalent in view of their characteristics, price and

---

[96] Recital (3). See §4.040 above.
[97] *Ibid.*
[98] Article 1.
[99] Article 2(1).
[100] *Ibid.*
[101] Article 2(2)(a).
[102] Article 2(2)(b).
[103] Article 2(2)(c).
[104] Article 2(3)(a).
[105] Article 2(3)(b).
[106] Article 2(3)(c).

intended use, enter into reciprocal exclusive distribution agreements in respect of such goods.[107]

Non-reciprocal agreements. Where manufacturers of identical goods or of goods which are considered by users as equivalent in view of their characteristics, price, and intended use enter into non-reciprocal exclusive distribution agreements in respect of such goods, unless at least one of them has a total turnover of no more than 100 million ECU.[108] This remains applicable where during any period of two consecutive financial years the total turnover is exceeded by no more than 10%.[109]

Parallel Imports. The availability of parallel imports is a fundamental precondition for the permission for any territorially exclusive agreement distribution agreement. Therefore the exemption is withdrawn:

- Where users can obtain the contract goods in the contract territory only from the exclusive distributor and have no alternative source of supply outside the contract territory;[110] or

- Where either the supplier or the distributor or both of them makes is difficult for intermediaries or users to obtain the contract goods from other dealers inside the common market or, in so far as no alternative source of supply is available there, from outside the common market, in particular where one or both of them:[111]

(1) exercises their intellectual property so as to prevent dealers or users from obtaining outside, or from selling in, the contract territory properly marked or otherwise properly marketed contract goods;

(2) exercises other rights or takes other measures so as to prevent dealers or users from obtaining outside, or from selling in, the contract territory contract goods.

4.051. Withdrawal of exemption. The Commission may withdraw the benefit of the Regulation[112] when it finds in a particular case that an agreement which it exempts nevertheless has certain effects which are incompatible with the conditions set out in Article 85(3) of the Treaty. This will include, in particular, where: the contract goods are not subject, in the contract territory, to effective competition from identical goods or goods considered by users as equivalent in view of their characteristics, price and intended use;[113] access by other suppliers to the different

---

[107] Article 3(a). In accordance with Article 4(1), this also applies where the goods are manufactured by an undertaking connected with a party to the agreement. Connected undertakings are defined by Article 4(2), as (a) undertakings in which a party to the agreement, directly or indirectly: owns more than half the capital or business assets, or has the power to exercise more than half the voting rights, or has the power to appoint more than half the members of the supervisory board, board of directors or bodies legally representing the undertaking, or has the right to manage the affairs; (b) undertakings which directly or indirectly have in or over a party to the agreement the rights or powers list in (a); (c) undertakings in which an undertaking referred to in (b) directly or indirectly has the rights or powers listed in (a). In accordance with Article 4.3., undertakings in which the parties to the agreement or undertakings connected with them jointly have the rights or powers set out in paragraph 2(a) are considered to be connected with each of the parties to the agreement.

[108] Article 3(b).

[109] Article 5(2). Article 5(3), provides a formula for calculating turnover.

[110] Article 3(c).

[111] Article 3(d).

[112] Pursuant to Article 7 of Regulation No. 19/65/EEC.

[113] Article 6(a).

stages of distribution within the contract territory is made difficult to a significant extent;[114] for reasons other than those concerning parallel imports, it is not possible for intermediaries or users to obtain supplies of the contract goods from dealers outside the contract territory on the terms customary there;[115] or the exclusive distributor either without any objectively justified reason refuses to supply in the contract territory categories of purchasers who cannot obtain contract goods elsewhere on suitable terms or applies to them differing prices or conditions of sale[116] or he sells the contract goods at excessively high prices.[117]

4.052. Application to concerted practices. As well as agreements, the Regulation applies in all its terms to concerted practices.[118]

9. Selective Distribution Agreements

(1) General Principles

4.053. Definition of a 'selective distribution agreement'. A selective distribution system exists where a distributor agrees with its suppliers to restrict the persons to whom contract goods are sold in the course of distribution to those retailers approved by the supplier.[119]

4.054. Compatibility with Article 85(1). In *Binon and Cie SA v. Agence et Messageries de la Presse SA*,[120] the Court of Justice, held, following its judgment in *Metro SB-Grossmärkte GmbH & Co KG v. EC Commission*,[121] that:

> . . . selective distribution systems constitute an aspect of competition which accords with Article 85(1), provided that re-sellers are chosen on the basis of objective criteria of a qualitative nature relating to the technical qualifications of the re-seller and his staff and the suitability of his trading premises in connection with the requirements for the distribution of the product and that such criteria are laid down uniformly for all potential re-sellers and are not applied in a discriminatory fashion.

Generally speaking, it is necessary to ascertain whether the conditions adopted go beyond what is objectively needed for a proper distribution system or whether they impinge on competition to an unacceptable extent.[122] As the Court continually emphasises, the limitations inherent in a selective distribution system are acceptable only on condition that their long-term aim is an improvement in competition. Otherwise they would have no justification inasmuch as their sole effect would be to reduce price competition.[123]

---

[114] Article 6(b).
[115] Article 6(c).
[116] Article 6(d)1.
[117] Article 6(d)2.
[118] Article 9.
[119] See *Halsbury's Laws of England, op. cit.,* Vol 52, 19.316.
[120] Case 243/83 [1985] ECR 2015, [1985] 3 CMLR 800.
[121] Case 26/76 [1977] ECR 1875, [1978] 2 CMLR 1.
[122] Case 243/83 *Binon and Cie SA v. Agence et Messageries de la Presse SA* [1985] ECR 2015, [1985] 3 CMLR 800, per Advocate General Slynn.
[123] *Ibid.,* para. 31, affirming Case 107/82 *AEG-Telefunken AG v. EC Commission* [1983] ECR 3151, [1984] 3 CMLR 325.

4.055. Conditions for which exemption is necessary. The requirement that re-sellers are selected on the basis of 'qualitative' criteria means that 'quantitative' criteria will bring the agreement within Article 85(1).[124] As Advocate General Slynn noted in *Binon and Cie SA v. Agence et Messageries de la Presse SA*,[125] 'Quantitative criteria inevitably are capable of leading to a restriction of competition even by retailers who from a qualitative point of view are suitable for selection.' However, even if quantitative criteria are imposed, it may be possible to seek an exemption from the Commission under Article 85(3).[126]

(2) Media Selective Distribution Systems

(i) *Newspaper and Periodical Selective Distribution System*

4.056. Binon and Cie SA v. Agence et Messageries de la Presse SA. In *Binon and Cie SA v. Agence et Messageries de la Presse SA*,[127] the Court of Justice condemned a selective distribution agreement concerned with the distribution of newspapers and periodicals. Agence et Messageries de la Presse SA ('AMP') was responsible through itself and its subsidiaries, for the distribution to Belgian retailers of approximately 70% of Belgian newspapers and periodicals and virtually all newspapers and periodicals published abroad. AMP had a small 9.35% holding in Lecture gènèral SA, a Belgian retailer of newspapers and periodicals and Hachette, a major French publishing house had a 48.84% holding in AMP and one of 24.55% in Lecture gènèrale SA. In 1976, AMP and the newspaper and periodical publishers set up an exclusive distribution system whereby every retail outlet was subject to approval by a regional consultative committee and their opinion was usually followed by the publishers. Following legal action in Belgium, the arrangement was altered in 1983 and replaced with a system whereby each publisher individually decided whether to accept the request of a retailer. Under the new system, AMP delivered an opinion on every application for the opening of a new retail outlet, which was notified to the Belgian publishers. They were then regarded as following that opinion unless they informed AMP otherwise within eight days. SA Binon and Cie requested AMP to supply it with newspapers, magazines and publications for whose distribution it was responsible. Since AMP refused to supply it, Binon applied directly to various publishers but without success. At the same time AMP did not apply its stringent selection criteria to various outlets belonging to Lecture gènèral SA which it readily supplied with newspapers and periodicals.

4.057. Infraction of Article 85(1). The Court held that:

> Such a system may be established for the distribution of newspapers and periodicals, without infringing the prohibition contained in Article 85(1), given the special nature of those products as regards their distribution. As AMP rightly pointed out, newspapers and periodicals can, as a general rule, only be sold by retailers during an extremely limited period of time whereas the public, expects each distributor to be able to offer a representative selection of press publications, in particular those of the national press. For their part, publishers undertake to take back unsold copies and this gives rise to a continuous exchange of those products between publishers and distributors.

---

[124] Case 243/83 *Binon and Cie SA v. Agence et Messageries de la Presse SA* [1985] ECR 2015, [1985] 3 CMLR 800.

[125] Case 243/83 [1985] ECR 2015, [1985] 3 CMLR 800.

[126] *Ibid.*

[127] *Ibid.*

Consequently, the permissibility of a selective distribution system in this field from the point of view of Article 85(1) depends in particular on the criteria governing the choice of distributors. Those criteria must be objective and of a qualitative nature. The limitation of the number of retail outlets, for example by reference to a minimum number of inhabitants in the vicinity of an outlet, does not qualify as such a criterion.[128]

As well as being objective and uniform, the criteria governing choice of re-sellers must be non-discriminatory. The Court held that AMP's conduct was discriminatory and thus caught by Article 85(1) in so far as it consisted of applying criteria of a less strict manner to a retailer belonging to the group of undertakings to which it belonged than to an unconnected retailer.

The Court also noted that the cumulative effect of a number of exclusive agreements, even if only in respect of specific titles, was also a factor to consider in determining whether the agreements breached Article 85(1).[129]

4.058. Criteria which secured exemption. In *Binon and Cie SA v. Agence et Messageries de la Presse SA*, the Court stated that if quantitative criteria are imposed, then it may be possible to seek an exemption from the Commission under Article 85(3). Although it is for the national court to decide what amounts to quantitative and qualitative criteria, Advocate General Slynn in the Binon case gave some pointers. So for example, the requirement that the retailer keep a number of titles (350 in that case), that the outlets must be more than a fixed minimum distance apart and limits on outlets by reference to the number of inhabitants are all quantitative criteria and unlawful. The criteria of suitability of the premises and of the professional capacity of the retailer are qualitative and thus acceptable. The question is whether what is laid down is justified in relation to the sale of the particular commodity in issue and not generally in relation to other products.

10. Joint Ventures and Article 85(1)

(1) General Principles

4.059. Definition of a joint venture. A joint venture is in general defined as:

. . . an enterprise subject to joint control by two or more undertakings which are economically independent of each other.[130]

4.060. Assessing validity. The Commission has stated the principle it uses to assess the validity of a joint venture thus:[131]

The notified agreements have to be considered as a whole having particular regard to their economic consequences. The restrictions of competition are those resulting from the formation of the joint venture itself and from restrictive provisions contained in the other notified agreements.

---

[128] [1985] ECR 2015, [1985] 3 CMLR 800, paras. 32 and 33.
[129] Per Advocate General Slynn. See Case 23/67 *Brasserie de Haecht SA v. Wilkin* [1967] ECR 407, [1968] CMLR 26.
[130] Commission Thirteenth Report on Competition Policy (1983), point 53; see generally Bellamy and Child, *op. cit.*, 5-067.
[131] Commission Decision 89/467/EEC Re UIP OJ No L 226, 03.08.89, p.25, para. 37.

(2) Joint Ventures by Media Undertakings

(i) Distribution and exhibition of films

4.061. Commission decision: Re UIP. In Re UIP[132] the Commission exempted a joint venture agreement concerning the exploitation of films. Paramount Pictures Corporation (Paramount), MCA Inc (MCA) and Metro-Goldwyn-Mayer Film Co (MGM) were all engaged in the financing, production and distribution of feature films, and other entertainment programmes for exhibition in cinemas, television and through other media. At the time of the decision, they accounted for almost a quarter of the box office receipts from feature films in the Community. On 1 November 1981, they formed a company called 'UIP' the purpose of which was to distribute and license the feature films, short subjects and trailers produced by Paramount, MCA and MGM, in, amongst other territories, the European Community. UIP was granted an exclusive licence to distribute the films for cinema exhibition and on pay television (but not on broadcast television or on video cassette), for an initial period of ten years but which was to continue thereafter from year to year. In addition, MGM, MCA and Paramount granted UIP the exclusive right to produce, finance and distribute on their behalf, non-English language foreign local products, being films that were intended to be distributed solely in the territory where produced. UIP generally had subsidiaries acting as local distributors.

In this decision the product markets could be divided into two layers: the market in which the parent companies competed with other production companies in financing and producing feature films, and (primarily) the market in which distributors competed with each other to obtain the best terms and viewing slots from exhibitors for these films.

4.062. The relevant market—measure of market strength. The Commission noted that there are many possible measures of the size of the market for the exhibition of films in cinemas. Thus measurements may be made of the number of films or the number of tickets sold, or the amount of box office receipts or the part of box office receipts paid by the cinemas to the distributors for the exhibition licence. Of these, box office receipts (the amount paid by the public to see a film) seemed to be the most meaningful and was accordingly adopted by the Commission.[133]

The Commission stated that in looking at the competitive impact of a Community-wide joint venture in the film distribution and exhibition industry, it has to break the field down into smaller units:

> In evaluating these effects, the Commission bases its analysis on the concept of a Community market made up of sub-markets corresponding to the various Member States, the cinematographic environment of which varies from one to the other.[134]

The Commission explained that because the structure of the film industry is different in each Member State due to language barriers, governmental regulations and different patterns of distribution and exhibition, competition in the film industry tends to be localized.[135]

---

132 *Ibid.*
133 *Ibid.*
134 *Ibid.*, para. 38.
135 *Ibid.*

Furthermore it was no good measuring market power in this type of joint venture on the basis of a comparison of overall market share in the entire Community, because these were changeable from year to year depending solely on the success of particular films. Success depended on public response and that was a very subjective matter.[136]

4.063. Anti-competitive effects. The following anti-competitive effects were highlighted by the Commission:

(1) Article 85(1) applied to the horizontal relationship between Paramount, MCA and MGM/UA since they were potential competitors in the distribution of their films throughout the Community having in fact ceased to compete in this respect with the formation of the joint venture. They remained competitors in the production of feature films, as distributors of films for theatrical exhibition in the USA and Canada, and as distributors to broadcast television and as publishers of video cassettes in the Community.

(2) The creation of UIP had entailed a loss of decision-making autonomy which the parent companies would otherwise have enjoyed. The parent companies were bound to co-operate with each other in the decision-making process on important matters affecting the joint venture.

(3) The agreements had brought about a degree of consensus in the parent companies' films as regards the place and timing of the release. Prior to the release of any film, UIP had to consult and advise the respective parent company as to the general plans for distribution including the advertising campaign, estimated distribution costs and dates for release. In so doing, UIP was bound to adapt its advice to the interest of all the parents. Since UIP was required to maximize each of the three parent companies' profits, UIP and the parents had to agree the place and timing of release of all their films to their overall advantage and in such a way that no film would damage the prospects of other UIP films.

4.064. Terms which secured an exemption. In accordance with this decision, the general principle which secured an exemption under Article 85(3) was that the co-operation established in the agreements entailed economic benefits for the production and distribution of motion pictures and for consumers, which could not be achieved in the absence of the joint venture and which outweighed its disadvantages. The Commission identified in particular the following factors which warranted the exemption:

(1) The creation of UIP made possible a more effective and rationalised distribution of the product of the parent companies ensuring the maintenance of an economically viable distribution network in a deteriorating market where high financial risks were present.

(2) The UIP agreements had allowed the parent companies to achieve greater efficiency by avoiding the duplication of distribution organizations and by reducing to a considerable extent the distribution costs at central-office level and at the level of local operating branches. Such efficiency had increased film availability in the Community and stimulated production

---

[136] *Ibid.*

therein, especially in view of UIP's and each parent company's right to finance local products in the Community and the right of the parent to enter into co-production agreements and agreements concerning non-English-language foreign local products in this territory.

(3) The quality and the service offered had been improved. A less costly distribution organisation would result in a more efficient network of branch offices which would ensure exhibitors both ready access to films and regularity of supplies. Moreover, such improvements would permit UIP to develop closer ties with regional and small exhibitors so that it could better respond to their needs and demands. An increased supply of films would benefit cinema viewers by widening the range of choice.

(4) No independent non-integrated distribution organisation covering the entire Community existed and at national level the few distributors large enough to offer economies which could approach those realised by UIP were integrated upwards.

(5) The characteristics of films as a commodity decreased the likelihood of too-close collaboration between the parent companies derived from the creation of UIP. The Commission considers that feature films should not be considered necessarily as homogeneous products, each film having its own merits and commercial appeal which determine its success or failure. Moreover, it is very difficult to predict accurately the commercial success of a film prior to its screening.

(6) The restrictive character of the joint venture was limited by the fact that parameters vital for competition in the film industry were determined by the parent companies: they controlled the number of prints to be made, the selection of the film laboratory, and they bore their own costs for prints dubbing and advertising. The independence of the parties concerning the release and marketing of their respective films was reinforced since no UIP committee could discuss plans in that respect.

(7) The right of first refusal granted to UIP by the parent companies was necessary to ensure a sufficient flow of product reached UIP so that the joint venture could achieve the economies of scale sought by the partners.

Following intervention by the Commission, it was agreed that UIP and its partners would on the basis of their commercial judgment make themselves available to produce, finance, acquire distribution rights to, or distribute feature films of third parties in the Community; MGM, MCA and Paramount retained the individual right to produce finance or acquire distribution rights to non-English language foreign local products and to offer those to UIP for distribution. If UIP declined to distribute the product, the companies could distribute them themselves. With regard to co-production agreements, each party retained the right not to acquire any or all distribution rights to any picture produced under the terms of a co-production agreement with a third party. Where acquired by a third party, these rights could be exploited without regard to UIP.

4.065. Commission Decision: Re Screensport/EBU Members. In Re Screensport/EBU Members,[137] the Commission refused to grant an exemption for a trans-European joint venture sports channel. The members of the European Broadcasting Union and the Sky channel had entered into a joint venture sports channel. Under

---

[137] Commission Decision 91/130/EEC Re Screensport/EBU Members OJ No L 63, 09.03.91, p.32.

the terms of the joint venture, the new channel would receive material from programmes recorded by EBU members. The Commission held that the arrangement had the object and effect of restricting competition in two respects and was thus in breach of Article 85(1). This was manifest first, between the partners to the joint venture, to the extent that they were actual or potential competitors on the market for sports events. Prior to its conclusion, Sky was proposing to set up a transnational sports channel of its own. Any incentive for Sky to offer substantive competition to Eurosport was eliminated and any potential competition between the two 'parents' ceased as a result of Eurosport. Secondly, the agreements restricted competition between Eurosport and third parties seeking to broadcast sports events, in particular transnational dedicated sports channels. The Commission stated that any transnational sports channel relying on advertising revenue would have to broadcast sports events of international appeal. They were thus in a far more vulnerable position than a general entertainment transnational satellite service which might want a small selection of international events with which to pep up their ratings. The joint venture drained away a huge chunk of the market. Whilst the EBU consortium would grant sub-licences to third parties they were highly restricted. Thus for example they would not permit live transmissions. Another damaging factor was that Eurosport had become an organisation of considerable market strength which would make it virtually unassailable in its negotiations for rights to broadcast sports events. All of this would have a knock on effect with cable operators who would only want to retransmit the Eurosport channel. It was simply unlikely that another channel could survive economically.

The Commission refused to grant an exemption under Article 85(3). It rejected the claim that only through this scheme would Eurosport be able to recoup its investment. It held that there was not an improvement in the market but rather the joint venture had created a disproportionate distortion in the market. It stated that:

> The Commission takes the view that it is of vital importance in new, developing industries, requiring considerable investment in technology and development, that priority must be given to ensuring that competition at all levels should remain as open as possible so as to confer upon all potential market entrants an equal opportunity to compete.

As far as the benefit to consumers was concerned, the Commission accepted that in the short term they would benefit from the Eurosport channel with extensive coverage of sports events. However, since there was evidence that Sky would have gone ahead the consumer would be better served with a choice between at least two channels offering an equally wide variety of European sports programmes.

4.066. Commission statement on audiovisual competition policy. The Commission has made the following pronouncement which summarises its philosophy on joint ventures:

> The Commission's main concern here is to keep markets open and to prevent barriers to market entry. In particular, the Commission wishes to ensure that all broadcasting companies have appropriate access to attractive programmes and is therefore endeavouring above all to prevent programme material being withdrawn from the market as a result of collective long-term arrangements . . .
>
> Agreements or practices relating to the joint acquisition or distribution of television rights normally fall within the scope of Article 85(1). Exemption is possible if joint acquisition or distribution allows rationalisation advantages to be achieved and if no

barriers to market entry by competitors are set up. Where rights are jointly acquired by members of multinational associations, it must be ensured that non-members have appropriate access to the relevant programme material. This can be achieved through limitations on exclusivity or through the granting of sub-licenses.[138]

(ii) Promotion of New Technology

4.067. Establishment of satellite company. The Commission granted an exemption to a joint venture[139] between BBC Enterprises Ltd (a subsidiary of the BBC), Morgan Grenfell & Co. Ltd, a merchant bank, and Harold Holt Ltd, a concert promoter and musical agent. Under the joint venture, the parties set up a new satellite broadcasting company which intended to broadcast live music, opera and ballet by satellite from major European venues to be delivered through a subscriber cable network. In accordance with their agreement, each party agreed that for a period of three years they would keep information relating to a joint feasibility study and its results confidential and that they would not engage in competing activities. The parties were however, entitled to carry on their normal telecommunications or satellite business. And the venture was not such as to prevent third parties from entering the market for live TV broadcasts by satellite.

11. Agreements to Observe Prices

(1) General Principles

4.068. Article 85(1)(a) expressly bans agreements which 'directly or indirectly fix purchase or selling prices or any other trading conditions'. Accordingly, the Court of Justice has stated that:

> . . . provisions which fix the prices to be observed in contracts with third parties constitute, of themselves, a restriction on competition within the meaning of Article 85(1) which refers to agreements which fix selling prices as an example of an agreement prohibited by the Treaty.[140]

Price fixing is most common at the horizontal level ie between undertakings at the same level on the supply chain.

(2) Price Fixing by Media Undertakings

(i) Licensing of Television Material

4.069. Commission action against EBU. The Commission objected to a plan by members of the European Broadcasting Union (the 'EBU') to group together to fix joint rates and conditions for the use of television news items taken from the network by third parties. The Commission advised the Union that this would restrict competition within the common market because intended purchasers would no longer be able to negotiate separately with individual broadcasters. Accordingly,

---

[138] Communication from the Commission to the Council and Parliament on audiovisual policy, 2.2.2(b), COM (90) final.

[139] Commission Fourteenth Report on Competition Policy, (1984), point 86.

[140] Case 243/83 *Binon & Cie SA v. Agence et Messageries de la Presse SA* [1985] ECR 2015, [1985] 3 CMLR 800, para. 44. On price fixing generally, see Bellamy and Child, *op. cit.*, 4-002 et seq.

EBU members reverted to their previous practice of negotiating separately with purchasers.[141]

4.070. Commission statement on audiovisual policy. The Commission has said that it is opposed to any joint price fixing by media undertakings involved in granting rights to license television material:

> . . . the Commission is opposed to agreements within groups of TV broadcasters by which joint rates and conditions are fixed for the use of their programmes by third parties.[142]

12. Resale Price Maintenance

(1) General Principles

4.071. Definition of resale price maintenance systems. In *VBVB and VBBB v. EC Commission*,[143] Advocate General VerLoren van Themaat identified two forms of resale price maintenance, namely, 'individual' and 'collective resale price maintenance':

> In the case of individual resale price maintenance an individual producer or several individual producers make agreements with every distributor (and any intermediate trade links) as to the consumer price of an article. In the case of collective resale price maintenance a distinction may be made between two forms: a collective obligation for all producers in a given sector to impose resale price maintenance on their distributors (with individual maintenance) and a form in which (whether or not in conjunction with a similar collective obligation) maintenance is effected collectively, for example through all the producers and distributors concerned being obliged as against one another as well to uphold resale maintenance and/or for that purpose have set up collective maintenance machinery (for example the secretariat of their common organisation or some other organ of the cartel or a joint representative).

As the Advocate General made clear, the two forms do not always remain distinct, for even with individual resale price maintenance, it is possible that the collective maintenance of consumer prices has been voluntarily agreed.

4.072. Incompatibility with Article 85(1). In *VBVB and VBBB v. EC Commission*,[144] the Court of Justice made it clear that an agreement whose 'effect is to deprive distributors of all freedom of action as regards the fixing of the selling price up to the level of the final price to the consumer' infringes Article 85(1)(a). Furthermore such an agreement may violate Article 85(1)(b) in so far as it allows an undertaking to 'control outlets as far as the last stage in the other Member State from the point of view of price-fixing and thus to make impossible the introduction of sales methods capable of allowing consumers to be supplied in economically more favourable conditions'.[145]

---

[141] Commission Sixth Report on Competition Policy, (1976), point 62.
[142] Communication from the Commission to the Council and Parliament on audiovisual policy, 2.2.2(b), COM (90) final.
[143] Joined Cases 43, 63/82 [1984] ECR 19, [1985] 1 CMLR 27.
[144] *Ibid.*, para. 45.
[145] *Ibid.*

4.073. Whether justified as protection against unfair competition. In *VBVB and VBBB v. EC Commission*,[146] the applicants argued that their book resale price maintenance system was a guarantee against so called 'lossleading', that is, an act of unfair competition by which retailers sell products at abnormally low prices to attract competition. They said that Article 10 bis of the Paris Convention prohibited such an activity and that the Convention bound the Community and took precedence over the competition laws. The Court of Justice held that the fact that a system of resale price maintenance has the incidental effect of preventing unfair competition is not a reason for failing to apply Article 85(1) to a whole sector of the market such as the book trade. It is open to undertakings which have suffered injury to have recourse to legislation on trade practices such as exists on in all Member States.[147] But the fact that such abuses exist cannot in any circumstances justify an infringement of the Community rules on competition.

(2) Resale Price Maintenance by Media Undertakings

(i) Book Resale Price Maintenance Systems

4.074. VBVB and VBBB v. EC Commission. Most Member States tolerate, if not legislate for the institution of resale price fixing systems for books. In *VBVB and VBBB v. EC Commission*,[148] the Court of Justice had to consider a price fixing agreement between two large associations of book publishers, importers, wholesalers booksellers and book clubs. Vereniging ter Bevordering van het Vlaamse Boekwezen ('VBVB') and Vereeniging ter Bevordering van de Belangen des Boekhandels ('VBBB') were two associations which represented the majority of publishers and booksellers in Flanders and the Netherlands respectively. They had entered into a collective exclusive dealing system within which they operated a collective resale price maintenance system. The exclusive dealing system involved a prohibition of purchasing, stocking or encouraging the sale of books published in the other State by a publisher who was not recognised. Under the resale price maintenance system, the publishers in both associations were obliged to fix for each of his publications a retail price and had a duty to ensure that these prices were observed up to the stage of retail sale, subject to certain specified exceptions. The Commission impugned the system since it precluded any competition for one and the same title between booksellers in the two States and it forbade traders to engage in any personal effort which might permit them to increase their market share by reselling books below the price fixed by the publisher. The Commission's Decision formed the subject of the appeal.[149]

4.075. Terms in breach of Article 85(1). The Court drew attention to the prohibition on price fixing in Article 85(1)(a) which was in itself a sufficient breach of the Treaty. It also said that the agreement breached Article 85(1)(b) which prohibits agreements which 'limit or control production, markets, technical

---

[146] *Ibid.*

[147] Advocate General VerLoren van Themaat stated that since not all Member States have prohibited such an activity, it is not possible to speak of a general principle of law to which the Court must have regard.

[148] Joined Cases 43, 63/82 [1984] ECR 19, [1985] 1 CMLR 27.

[149] Commission Decision 8211231 EEC Re VBBB/VBVB OJ No L54, 25.02.82, p. 36.

development, or investment'. This was because it allowed the two associations to control outlets (ie the last stage in the distribution chain) in the other Member State through price fixing. It thus made impossible the introduction of sales methods capable of allowing consumers to be supplied in economically more favourable conditions. The Court accepted that the specific nature of books as an object of trade might justify certain special conditions in the matter of distribution and price, but the fact that the two large national associations of publishers and booksellers had extended to intra-Community trade the closely supervised rules which were in force within each of their States constituted a sufficiently marked restriction of competition in breach of Article 85(1).

4.076. Reasons for refusal of exemption under Article 85(3). The Applicants argued that their system merited an exemption under Article 85(3) on the basis that it improved the production and distribution of books. They said that only by maintaining price constraints could a publisher support the publication of abstruse titles that were less likely to sell quickly. Such a system of 'cross-subsidization' thus helped to disseminate a greater number of works. The counterpart of the reduction in price for successful books would be a corresponding increase in price of all other works. The Court held that the Applicants had not proved that their system would improve transnational production and distribution. It made no judgment on the merits of a purely national system. It was only concerned with the affect on trade between Member States because this is the threshold issue in an Article 85(1) analysis.

Advocate General VerLoren van Themaat focused in greater detail on the various arguments used to defend book resale price maintenance. In rejecting the notion that such a system was necessary to subsidise less popular books and thus ensure their survival, he made the following points:

(1) publishers can themselves finance losses on one product with profits from another;

(2) the possibility of this form of cross-subsidisation is enhanced because of the certainty of the success of reimpressions of a successful book;

(3) the existence of a large number of specialist book publishers refutes the argument that publishers must keep a broad range of titles only made possible by resale price maintenance;

(4) the risk for booksellers holding stocks of books is not as great as for publishing houses, because booksellers offering a general range can ensure that the number of reprints in their stock forms a greater proportion of the total number of titles than is the case with publishing houses;

(5) if publishers attach such importance to the maintenance of bookshops with a broad range of titles, they can offer lower purchase prices to those book shops.

4.077. Re The Net Book Agreements: Publishers Association v. EC Commission. In Re The Net Book Agreements: *Publishers Association v. EC Commission*,[150] the Court of First Instance upheld the Commission's Decision[151] that the so called 'Net Book Agreements' which set in place a collective resale price maintenance

---

[150] Case T—66/89 [1992] 5 CMLR 120.
[151] Commission Decision 89/44/EEC Re Publishers Association—Net Book Agreements OJ No L 22, 26.01.89, p.12.

system for books in the United Kingdom and Ireland, violated Article 85(1) and was ineligible for exemption under Article 85(3).

Two identical agreements had formed the subject of the action. The parties of one agreement were publishers who were members of the Publishers Association, whilst non-member publishers were parties of the other agreement. In accordance with the agreements, a so-called 'net book' could not be offered for sale or permitted to be sold to the public at less than the net published price. These conditions applied to all sales to the public in the United Kingdom and Ireland of books designated as a 'net book' by the publisher publishing or distributing the book. As an exception, 'net books' could be sold at a discount to libraries, book agents and quantity buyers authorised by the Publishers Association.

The agreements provided for an enforcement mechanism. The Council of the Publishers Association was appointed to monitor any breaches of the resale price maintenance system and publishers agreed to enforce any breaches if called upon to do so by the Council.

The Association published a 'Code of Allowances' reflecting the established general trade practice on reductions, new editions, cheap editions and remainders. Under 'Book Club Regulations', publishers were entitled to grant special rights to book clubs who were registered with the Association and who thus had agreed to certain conditions concerning the offering, selling and advertising of books. Since 1955, the Publishers Association had permitted an annual national book sale giving publishers and booksellers the opportunity to sell slow moving titles below the 'net price'. The Association published a 'Directory of Booksellers' listing booksellers who had undertaken to observe the standard conditions of sale of 'net books'.

The Publishers Association had put forward four arguments to demonstrate the indispensability of the collective price maintenance system:

(1) it was not possible in practice for publishers individually to give notice of their standard conditions to each bookseller;
(2) it was not possible for booksellers, especially those containing stocks of a large number of titles to comply with different conditions of sale for each book;
(3) booksellers had to be confident that their competitors would not buy or sell the same title at a price lower than the net price. Such confidence could not exist in an individual system of fixed prices because it would be impractical for an individual publisher to monitor or enforce adherence to his conditions; and
(4) only the Publishers Association was capable of monitoring and ensuring compliance with the standard pricing system.

4.078. Elements which breached Article 85(1). The Court rejected all of these justifications as groundless stating that:

(1) although a common system of notification alleviated the administrative burden on publishers, the imposition of standard conditions of sale which restricted competition in the Common Market went beyond what was necessary to set in place price maintenance. The practical convenience afforded by a common system of giving notice could not be allowed to justify the establishment of a common system of net prices. However, publishers were free to use the standard conditions as a starting point in negotiating individual agreements;

(2) booksellers would not be faced with an unmanageable administrative burden considering that the greater proportion of books were published by a limited number of publishers and that modern computer technology available alleviated considerable work. The booksellers that were eligible for discounts (ie book clubs, libraries, book agents and quantity buyers) were too limited in number for there to be an unmanageable burden placed upon booksellers generally. The Court suggested that as a practical matter to overcome administrative problems, it would be possible for the publishers to apply uniform conditions of discount, but it left open the question of whether a system (individual or collective) which did this, would violate the competition rules;

(3) under a collective as well as under an individual agreement on net prices, it was the same person ie the publisher who had the responsibility of granting the same conditions of sale to booksellers and enforcing those conditions. Even on the assumption that a collective system of price maintenance might subjectively reinforce booksellers' confidence, that was not capable in itself of justifying an agreement which by imposing uniform conditions, restricts the free play of competition in the Common Market;

(4) the Court stated that the Appellant had not put forward reasons why the monitoring and enforcement of standard conditions of sale was reliant on agreement (whether collective or individual) for price maintenance. The Court left open the question of the legality of a system which makes a single body, ie the Publishing Association, responsible for the monitoring and enforcement of standard conditions of sale.

4.079. Purely national book resale price maintenance systems. A purely national system of resale price maintenance will generally escape Article 85(1) because that provision comes into play only where there may be an effect on trade 'between Member States'.[152] However, an effect on inter-state trade may be perceptible if such agreements make the market in a single Member State impenetrable by undertakings from other Member States.[153]

In *VBVB and VBBB v. EC Commission*,[154] the Court of Justice canvassed the question of whether a purely national system of resale price maintenance for books might offend Article 85(1). Advocate General VerLoren van Themaat pointed out that even with a national system of resale price maintenance, provided that there is no exclusive distribution structure, producers from other Member States remain entirely free to export to the country in question and trade there. Although, he noted that resale price maintenance mechanisms produce barriers through high profit margins guaranteed to the home producers, this is usually only the case, where there is the potential for keen inter-brand competition. This is not possible with books since in consequence of their very pronounced difference in content— in contrast to many branded articles—books are not, in the eyes of the consumer, interchangeable.[155]

In fact, in *Association des Centres Distributeurs Edouard Leclerc v. 'Au Blé Vert' Sàrl*,[156] a case involving resale price maintenance legislation concerning books, the

---

[152] Case 8/72 *Vereeniging van Cementhandelaren v. EC Commission* [1972] ECR 977, [1973] CMLR 7. See §4.031 above.
[153] *Ibid.*
[154] Joined Cases 43, 63/82 [1984] ECR 19, [1985] 1 CMLR 27.
[155] per Advocate General VerLoren van Themaat.
[156] Case 229/83 [1985] ECR 1, [1985] 2 CMLR 286.

Court of Justice cleared national systems. The case concerned a French law under which all publishers or importers of books were required to fix the retail prices for the books which they published or imported. Retailers then had to charge a price for the sales to the public of between 95% and 100% of that price. The Applicants sold books at prices undercutting the aforementioned legislation. They were sued by a number of bookshops and the French booksellers' association for breaching French law. On appeal they argued that the national legislation breached in particular Articles 3(f)[157] and 5[158] of the Treaty. The Court stated that:

> . . . purely national systems and practices in the book trade have not yet been made subject to a Community competition policy with which the Member States would be required to comply by virtue of their duty to abstain from any measure which might jeopardize the attainment of the objectives of the Treaty.

It thus ruled that:

> As Community law stands, the second paragraph of Article 5 of the EEC Treaty, in conjunction with Articles 3(f) and 85, does not prohibit Member States from enacting legislation whereby the retail price of books must be fixed by the publisher or by the importer and is binding on all retailers, provided that such legislation is consonant with the other specific provisions of the Treaty, in particular those relating to the free movement of goods.

The Court was at pains to emphasise that whilst it is true that the rules on competition are concerned with the conduct of undertakings and not with national legislation, Member States were none the less obliged under the second paragraph of Article 5 of the Treaty not to detract, by means of national legislation, from the full and uniform application of Community law or from the effectiveness of its implementing measures. They were not entitled to introduce or maintain in force measures, even of a legislative nature, which might render ineffective the competition rules applicable to undertakings.[159]

(ii) Newspaper Resale Price Maintenance Systems

4.080. It is clear that certain industries could not survive without some form of resale price maintenance. In *Binon and Cie SA v. Agence et Messageries de la Presse SA*,[160] the Court of Justice recognised that a selective distribution agreement for the supply of newspapers and periodicals, which contained a price fixing mechanism, merited exemption under Article 85(3):

> If, in so far as the distribution of newspapers and periodicals is concerned, the fixing of the retail price by publishers constitutes the sole means of supporting the financial burden resulting from the taking back of unsold copies and if the latter practice

---

[157] See §4.002 above 'Foundations of competition law'.

[158] Article 5, para 2 states: '[Member States] . . . shall abstain from any measure which could jeopardize the attainment of the objectives of this Treaty.'

[159] This reaffirms a similar statement made by the Court of Justice in Joined Cases 43, 63/82 VBVB and VBBB v. EC Commission [1984] ECR 19, [1985] 1 CMLR 27.

[160] Case 243/83 [1985] ECR 2015, [1985] 3 CMLR 800, para. 46. For the facts of the case, see §4.056 above.

constitutes the sole method by which a wide selection of newspapers and periodicals can be made available to readers, the Commission must take account of those factors when examining an agreement for the purposes of Article 85(3).

13. Licensing the Exclusive Exploitation of Intellectual Property

(1) The Conceptual Conflict

4.081. Territorially exclusive licences pose a dilemma for the Court for they bring into conflict two provisions of the Treaty. On the one hand, there is Article 85(1) which clearly prohibits parties from granting exclusive licences which partition the Common Market. But, on the other hand, there is Article 36 which provides that restrictions on imports and exports are permitted on the grounds of, amongst other matters, the 'protection of industrial and commercial property'.[161] The words 'industrial and commercial property' have been held to include intellectual property[162] whose very purpose is to bestow exclusive rights on society's creators and innovators. And although Article 36 sits in that part of the Treaty which governs the free movement of goods, its principles are imported into the competition rules. This conflict is reinforced by Article 222 which states that the 'Treaty shall in no way prejudice the rules in Member States governing the system of property ownership.' And 'property ownership' must include intellectual property. The danger is thus that Article 36 will undermine Article 85(1) by shoring up the partitioning of markets within the Community.

(2) Reconciling the Conflict—The Existence/Exercise Doctrine

4.082. The first point to note, is that the Court of Justice decided long ago that Article 36 does not emasculate Article 85(1).[163] Over the years, the Court has been balancing the competing interests. It has fabricated a doctrine which enables both Article 36 and Article 85(1) to operate by deciding when the shield afforded by Article 36 slips away and the jaws of Article 85(1) bite off an offending term. The essential principle of the doctrine is that Article 36 safeguards the 'existence' of national intellectual property laws. However, it does not protect them in their entirety and there are circumstances when the owner of intellectual property will 'exercise' his rights in contravention of Article 85(1).[164] This is so when, according to the Court of Justice—which employs somewhat technical terms—the 'exercise' of the exclusive right constitutes:

---

[161] Such prohibitions or restrictions must not, however, constitute a means of arbitrary discrimination or a disguised restriction on trade between Member States (Article 36, second sentence).

[162] See §1.008 above.

[163] Joined Cases 56, 58/64 *Etablissements Consten SARL and Grundig-Verkaufs-GmbH v. EEC Commission* [1966] ECR 299, [1966] CMLR 418, concerning trademarks.

[164] For a general discussion of these concepts in the context of free movement of goods, see §1.003 above.

... the purpose, means or result of an agreement, decision or concerted practice, that is to say of a form of agreement which restricts competition.[165]

The distinction between the existence and exercise of intellectual property laws applies whether the licence concerns goods:

... On the assumption that those provisions [concerning industrial and commercial property in Article 36] may be relevant to a right related to copyright, it is nevertheless clear from that Article that, although the Treaty does not affect the existence of rights recognised by the legislation of a Member State with regard to industrial and commercial property, the exercise of such rights may nevertheless fall within the prohibitions laid down by the Treaty..;[166]

or the provision of services:

The distinction, implicit in Article 36, between the existence of a right conferred by the legislation of a Member State in regard to the protection of artistic and intellectual property, which cannot be affected by the provisions of the Treaty, and the exercise of such right, which might constitute a disguised restriction on trade between Member States, also applies where that right is exercised in the context of the movement of services.[167]

(3) The Alternative Models for the Distinction between the 'Existence' and 'Exercise' of Intellectual Property

4.083. Introduction. The distinction between the 'existence' and 'exercise' of intellectual property has been resolved by the adoption of two models. The first model, which is that favoured by the Commission, is conceptually complicated and rigid, whereas the second model yields to what is clearly a pragmatic inclination of the Court. The former is what may be called a 'per se' rule and the latter what may be termed a 'rule of reason' principle.

4.084. 'Per se' model. According to this model, there are certain rights which are so fundamental to the ownership of intellectual property, that terms in an agreement which enforce those rights are never in breach of Article 85(1). These are rights which form the 'specific subject matter' of intellectual property and they therefore relate to the 'existence' of intellectual property.[168] Their essential characteristic is that they empower the owner of the intellectual property. The ability to grant exclusive licences is not a 'power' because by agreeing to restrict the exploitation of his rights to a single licensee in a territory, a licensor is prevented from granting rights to other licensees. He is thus forced to curtail his rights. Accordingly, that sort of agreement cannot reflect the fundamental purpose of intellectual property and will constitute an unlawful 'exercise' of intellectual property. Under this doctrine, any agreement which confers exclusivity will automatically breach Article 85(1).[169] The concept has been nurtured mainly in

---

[165] Case 262/81 *Coditel SA v. Ciné Vog Films SA* [1982] ECR 3381, [1983] 1 CMLR 49, per Advocate General Reischl. In Case 78/70 *Deutsche Grammophon Gesellschaft mbH v. Metro-SB-Grossmärkte GmbH & Co KG* [1971] ECR 487, [1971] CMLR 631, para. 6, the Court of Justice stated that the exclusive right might fall under the prohibition set out by Article 85(1) 'each time it manifests itself as the subject, the means or the result of an agreement which ... has as its effect the partitioning of the market'.

[166] Case 78/70 *Deutsche Grammophon Gesellschaft mbH v. Metro-SB-Grossmärkte GmbH & Co KG* [1971] ECR 487, [1971] CMLR 631, para. 11.

[167] Case 262/81 *Coditel SA v. Ciné Vog Films SA* [1982] ECR 3381, [1983] 1 CMLR 49, para. 13.

[168] See §1.009 above.

[169] provided that the effects are 'appreciable'.

Commission Decisions involving patents, know-how and akin rights[170] but the same principles could be applied to copyright.

4.085. 'Rule of reason' model. Under an alternative approach the Court does not start from the assumption that exclusivity is contrary to Article 85(1) but rather looks at the exclusivity on its merits. It asks whether or not, in fact, the exclusive term is likely to prevent, restrict or distort competition. Only if this is so, is the exercise of the right unlawful. Thus, for example, in *Coditel SA v. Ciné Vog Films SA*,[171] the Court of Justice stated in respect of a film protected by copyright:

> ... the mere fact that the owner of the copyright in a film has granted to a sole licensee the exclusive right to exhibit that film in the territory of a Member State, and, consequently, to prohibit, during a specified period, its showing by others, is not sufficient to justify the finding that such a contract must be regarded as the purpose, the means or the result of an agreement, decision or concerted practice prohibited by the Treaty.

4.086. Exemption possible under Article 85(3). Where an agreement violates Article 85(1) under either model, it may be possible to obtain an exemption from the Commission under Article 85(3).[172]

(4) Licensing the Exclusive Distribution of an 'Old' Product Protected by Copyright

(i) Court Decisions

4.087. There are no recent decisions in which the Court has judged a territorially exclusive agreement licensing the exploitation of old products. The *Deutsche Grammophon Gesellschaft mbH v. Metro-SB-Grossmärkte GmbH & Co KG*[173] decision, which concerned an exclusive licence for the distribution of vinyl discs, did embrace the question of Article 85(1), but it is an old case which came before the Court at a time when it was just beginning to develop its jurisprudence in this area, so the Court did not spell out the relevant principles. However, Advocate General Roemer hinted that a 'rule of reason' approach was required.

(ii) Commission Decisions

4.088. There are no decisions on such an agreement. It is likely that the Commission would follow the 'per se' approach.

---

[170] Commission Decision 75/494 Re Kabel- und Metallwerke Neumeyer AG and Etablissements Luchaire SA Agreement, OJ No L222, 22.8.75, p.34, [1975] 2 CMLR D40; Commission Decision 85/410 Re Velcro/Aplix OJ No L 233, 30.08.85, p.22; Commission Decision 87/123 Re Boussois SA and Interpane-Entwicklungs- Und Beratungsgesellschaft mbH & Co KG OJ No L 50, 19.02.87, p.30, [1988] 4 CMLR 124; Commission Decision 88/563 Re DDD Limited and Delta Chemie OJ No L 309, 15.11.88, p. 34, [1989] 4 CMLR 535.

[171] Case 262/81 [1982] ECR 3381, [1983] 1 CMLR 49, para. 15.

[172] See §4.036 above.

[173] Case 78/70 [1971] ECR 487, [1971] CMLR 631.

(5) Licensing the Exclusive Distribution of a 'New' Product Protected by Copyright

(i) Court Decisions

4.089. It was an agreement licensing the exclusive distribution of a new product which gave birth to 'rule of reason' principles, although this did not concern copyright goods. The Court of Justice held that:

> Having regard to the specific nature of the products in question, the Court concludes that, in a case such as the present, the grant of an open exclusive licence, that is to say a licence which does not affect the position of third parties such as parallel importers and licensees for other territories, is not in itself incompatible with Article 85(1) of the Treaty.[174]

4.090. Meaning of an 'open' licence. The Court had approved of a so called 'open' licence. It took the following form:

(1) the licensor agreed to appoint only one licensee in a territory and not himself compete there;

(2) the exclusive licensee (the Appellant) could not be protected from exclusive licensees of other territories who might distribute the licensed products in the licensed territory. It followed that the Appellant could not be prevented from competing in the territory of another exclusive licensee;

(3) neither could the Appellant be protected from imports of products which had been put on the market in other territories in the Community with the licensors consent ie 'parallel imports'.

4.091. Limitations of an 'open' licence. The limitation of an 'open licence' is that it does not offer protection against a distributor licensed in another territory. If protection against this form of competition is required, an exemption under Article 85(3) is necessary.

4.092. Definition of a 'new' product. This ruling also begs the question: what constitutes a new product? Does a new recording of a known piece of music have the characteristics of 'newness'? And does a new edition of a book qualify as a new product? Probably they do. A new form of conveying those works to the public would qualify. Thus sound compact discs when first marketed ought to have been considered as 'new products' within the meaning of the Court's case law. And picture discs, it is submitted will qualify as 'new products.' They involve a substantial investment and marketing risks for those who manufacture and distribute them. In the final analysis 'newness' is a relative concept ranging from perhaps just one year for a copyright work and from five years in the case of fast moving technologies to twenty years for others.

(ii) Commission Decisions

4.093. Commission approach. Despite the Court's stance, the Commission takes a 'per se' approach to licensing of 'new' copyright products. In the context of an agreement licensing the distribution of a new edition of a book, it has stated that it is the 'Commission's opinion that any partitioning of the common market by means of copyright licences must be justified under Article 85(3) of the EEC Treaty.'[175]

---

[174] See Case 258/78 *Nungesser (L.C.) KG v. EC Commission* [1982] ECR 2015, [1983] 1 CMLR 278, para. 58, which concerned plant breeders' rights.

[175] Commission Ninth Report on Competition Policy, (1979), point 119.

4.094. Export bans. Bans on the export of licensed products to other Member States are consistently condemned by the Commission as in violation of Article 85(1) whether they concern books,[176] records[177] or other products[178] protected by copyright.

4.095. Obligation to grant Community-wide licence. In an interesting decision, the Commission obligated a copyright licensee to grant a Community-wide distribution agreement for a new edition of a paperback book.[179] Jonathan Cape Ltd held distribution rights throughout the Common Market in Hemingway's novel 'The Old Man and the Sea'. It gave Penguin Books Ltd the right to publish a paperback edition in a territory extending to all the Member States with the exception of Ireland and the United Kingdom. After a complaint that the edition was not available in Ireland and the United Kingdom, and following intervention by the Commission, Jonathan Cape Ltd entered into a separate agreement with another publisher for Community-wide publication of several of Hemingway's works, including 'The Old Man and the Sea'.

(6) Licensing the Exclusive Distribution of an 'Old' Service (ie Film) Protected by Copyright

(i) Court Decisions

4.096. There are no cases concerning the exclusive licence of an old 'service' (ie a film) protected by copyright.

(7) Licensing the Exclusive Exploitation of a New Service (ie Film) Protected by Copyright

(i) Court Decisions

4.097. Coditel SA v. Ciné Vog Films SA. In *Coditel SA v. Ciné Vog Films SA*,[180] the Court of Justice applied a 'rule of reason' approach to an exclusive exhibition licence. It concerned a film, 'Le Boucher' which was produced and owned by a French company 'Les Films La Boétie'. La Boétie concluded a contract with a Belgian company Ciné Vog Films on 8 July 1969 whereby Ciné Vog Films acquired the right to exhibit the film in Belgium and Luxembourg for seven years. This was subject to the proviso that it could not be broadcast on Belgian television until forty months after its first performance in the cinema there, which took place on 15 May 1970. The right to show the film on German television was assigned by La Boétie to a German television station which broadcasted it in January of 1971 at a

---

[176] See e.g. Commission Sixth Report on Competition Policy, (1976), point 153 et seq, Re Dutch Publishers Association. In Commission Ninth Report on Competition Policy, (1979), point 118 et seq, Re Ernest Benn Ltd, it stated that 'the Commission considers that export restrictions on books within the common market are contrary to the EEC competition rules in the same way as export restrictions on other goods'.

[177] Commission Second Report on Competition Policy, (1972), point 40, Re WEA-Filipacchi Music SA; Commission Sixth Report on Competition Policy, (1976), point 151, Re Miller; Commission Eleventh Report on Competition Policy, (1981), point 98, Re STEMRA (a collecting society).

[178] Commission Sixth Report on Competition Policy (1976), point 163, Re BBC, where the Commission noted that it had objected to the BBC's attempt (at the request of the Dutch head licensor) to prevent the exporting to another Member State of products manufactured by an undertaking granted a merchandising sublicence by the BBC.

[179] Commission Sixth Report on Competition Policy, (1976), point 164.

[180] Case 262/81 [1982] ECR 3381, [1983] 1 CMLR 49.

time when, under the terms of the agreement between La Boétie and Ciné Vog it was still forbidden to show the film on Belgian television. The broadcast was picked up by the Belgian Coditel group of companies and relayed by cable to their subscribers in Belgium without the authority of La Boétie or Ciné Vog.

Ciné Vog sued Coditel for infringement of their copyright and the Belgium Cour de Cassation asked the Court of Justice whether the exclusivity was in breach of Article 85(1). The Court ruled that:

> A contract whereby the owner of the copyright for a film grants an exclusive right to exhibit that film for a specific period in the territory of a Member State is not, as such, subject to the prohibitions contained in Article 85 of the Treaty. It is, however, where appropriate, for the national court to ascertain whether, in a given case, the manner in which the exclusive right conferred by that contract is exercised is subject to a situation in the economic or legal sphere the object or effect of which is to prevent or restrict the distribution of films or to distort competition on the cinematographic market, regard being had to the specific characteristics of that market.

Thus, the Court has determined that the grant of exclusivity is not, as such, in violation of Article 85(1). It is necessary for the national court to undertake an analysis of the market.

4.098. Factors which are relevant in the assessment. In *Coditel SA v. Ciné Vog Films SA*,[181] the Court indicated which factors it considered relevant in evaluating the market for the exhibition of films:

> The characteristics of the cinematographic industry and of its markets in the Community, especially those relating to dubbing and subtitling for the benefit of different language groups, to the possibilities of television broadcasts, and to the system of financing cinematographic production in Europe serve to show that an exclusive exhibition licence is not, in itself, such as to prevent, restrict or distort competition.

Thus, in reaching its decision, the Court took into account the particular characteristics of the film industry. As Advocate General Reischl explained in more depth:

> . . . films are often produced with the financial participation of the distributors.
> Of course, that does not happen unless there is a degree of security against the risks: a distributor will be prepared to advance a lump sum for financing a film only if he is accorded an exclusive right of exhibition on one particular market. If it were not for such a facility, many films would not be produced at all, which would impoverish the market and depress competition.
> An equally crucial factor is that a new film must, like a newly-developed article of merchandise, first be placed on the market and that [sic] this may often entail heavy expenditure on advertising and synchronization.
> However, when the producer himself cannot afford such costs, he will not find a licensee for the task unless he grants him an exclusive right of exhibition.[182]

4.099. Terms in an exclusive exhibition licence which will offend Article 85(1). In *Coditel SA v. Ciné Vog Films SA*,[183] the Court of Justice indicated the type of terms which will bring an exclusive exhibition licence outside of Article 85(1):

---

[181] *Ibid.*, para. 16.
[182] The Advocate General stated that 'This special situation is to be distinguished from the marketing of an old film with which the public is familiar and which has already covered its costs.'
[183] Case 262/81 [1982] ECR 3381, [1983] 1 CMLR 49, para. 19.

It must therefore be stated that it is for national courts, where appropriate, to make such inquiries and in particular to establish whether or not the exercise of the exclusive right to exhibit a cinematographic film creates barriers which are artificial and unjustifiable in terms of the needs of the cinematographic industry, or the possibility of charging fees which exceed a fair return on investment, or an exclusivity the duration of which is disproportionate to those requirements, and whether or not, from a general point of view, such exercise within a given geographic area is such as to prevent, restrict or distort competition within the common market.

(ii)   Commission Decisions on Exclusive Exhibition Agreements

4.100. Re Purchase of Films by German Television Stations. In Re Purchase of Films by German Television Stations,[184] the Commission analysed an exclusive film exhibition agreement. The decision concerned an association of several German public broadcasting organisations ('ARD') which operated a joint television channel. They concluded three agreements with a subsidiary of Metro-Goldwyn-Mayer/United Artists ('MGM/UA') under which ARD were entitled to broadcast on German television, films owned by MGM/UA for a total fee of $80 million. Under the first agreement, 'the library agreement', ARD acquired rights in 1350 feature films to be selected from MGM/UA's film library. They also had rights in at least 150 new films produced by MGM/UA for cinema or first television exhibition. They were granted the right to broadcast, during the same period, 416 hours of television films and series as well as any cartoons controlled by MGM/UA up to 1 January 1984.   Under the second agreement, the 'James Bond Agreement', ARD acquired rights in 14 named James Bond films from MGM/UA's existing library. This was supplemented by a further agreement which entitled them to exhibit all new James Bond films produced or acquired by MGM/UA between 1 January 1984 and 31 December 1998.

The contract territory consisted of both West and East Germany (as it then was), Austria, Liechtenstein, Luxembourg, the South Tyrol and the German speaking part of Switzerland. ARD was granted exclusivity for the whole library up to 31 December 1986. Although the films could generally only be broadcast in the German language, a limited number could be broadcast in two languages (German and English) with English subtitles or in their original English version. In addition, ARD was given exclusive rights to broadcast any of the films in German within the contract area for the period of the licences, save that, the agreement provided for two pay windows of up to a year in which 25% of the films could be licensed to third parties for exploitation on pay T.V.

ARD had, from 1 October 1983 until 1 January 1997, a right of first negotiation if MGM/UA wanted to concluded a an agreement similar to the library agreement with a third party. A similar right of negotiation applied if MGM/UA wished to concluded an output agreement on the films newly produced or acquired after 31 December 1998.

The licence term for any feature film or television film was usually 15 years, (some less, some more). Feature films (ie library films, news films and cartoons) could be shown any number of times, although MGM/UA could designate 75 Library films and 45 new films for not more than 15 showings. The James Bond films could be shown only 15 times.

---

[184] Commission Decision 89/536/EEC OJ No L 284, 03.10.89, p.36.

ARD were entitled to exploit their rights using terrestrial, cable, and satellite (including with certain restrictions, DBS satellites).

4.101. Terms in breach of Article 85(1). The Commission objected to the following terms of the agreement:

(1) The number of films went well beyond the normal quantity necessitated by the needs of programme acquisition. Because the stock of feature films could not be increased at will, large quantities of films could not be withdrawn from the market through long-term exclusive ties.

(2) Although the films acquired represented only 4.5% of the total stock worldwide, they represented a selected and therefore particulary interesting part of a library of one of the world's leading production and distribution companies. Since they included many films with mass appeal such as the James Bond Films or films given awards, the rights acquired had an importance that went beyond the purely numerical numbers involved. Furthermore they included new productions which were particulary attractive.

(3) The duration of the licence went well beyond the industry standard and beyond the previous practice of the ARD broadcasting organisations. Particulary offensive was the staggering of the licence period which meant that the exclusive tie extended beyond the actual licence period and prevented other television stations from having access to some of the films even before the actual licence period of ARD. This created an artificial barrier to other undertakings.

(4) The windows did not remove the offensive restriction because they lifted the granted exclusivity only within certain periods without third parties having full access to the films.

(5) The selection period arising from the large quantity of films was restrictive of competition. The fact that for the duration of the selection period, MGM/UA was not allowed to grant any licences to third parties made its entire library unavailable to other undertakings during this period. Since this also affected films which ARD did not subsequently select, an artificial barrier was created for other television stations.

(6) The right of first negotiation granted to ARD restricted MGM/UA in selecting parties with which it concluded agreements and adversely affected the negotiating position of other undertakings being another anti-competitive effect.

Under newly negotiated terms, it was agreed that ARD would allow the licensing of library films, new films, James Bond films, television products and cartoons, to third parties by means of windows during which ARD would not broadcast those products. It was agreed that ARD would supply the films in German or if not available, contribute 50% towards the costs of dubbing. Also ARD would release for licence to third parties without condition, any of the 416 hours of television programmes which it did not select, save for seven series in which it was given first rights of negotiation. It allowed, third parties to broadcast the films in a foreign language version in the licence territory, either from within the territory or from outside of it.

4.102. Factors which allowed exemption. Following the renegotiations, the Commission granted an exemption on the following basis:

(1) The large number of films involved meant that the MGM/UA library was systematically examined to see which of the available films were suitable for German television. The ARD broadcasting organisations which were familiar with the viewing habits of their viewers were in a better position to do this than MGM/UA who were unacquainted with their tastes. As a result of the selection procedure, it was realised that a number of old films were exploitable on German television and these were made accessible to German viewers for the first time.

(2) The staggered windows ensured that other broadcasting organisations were able to license the films when ARD did not exhibit them. Furthermore, this was possible before ARD exhibited them. The Commission stated that a two-year window period was useful to television companies. Also an improvement in the distribution of the films derived from the arrangement concerning the dubbing costs.

(3) New private stations benefited from the window arrangements in that ARD, in sublicensing films, would pay up to 50% of the costs of dubbing the films. This was seen as an improvement in film distribution because particularly in the start up phase, new private stations have considerable financial difficulties and could not afford high quality dubbing.

(4) The large number of film licences had also resulted in a lower price per film to be achieved than in the case of individual agreements relating to smaller quantity of films. Thus ARD had been able to afford more films than otherwise.

(5) Consumers received a fair share of the resulting benefit since more films were shown in Germany than would have existed in the absence of the agreement.

(6) All the restrictions were indispensable. The permitted exclusivity was necessary to allow a fair return for the investments ie licence fee, dubbing costs and selection administrative costs. The ban on pay-TV was acceptable since simultaneous exploitation of the films on pay-TV would considerably affect the value of the films for ARD. Terms that were not indispensable and which would not merit an exemption were the ban on foreign language broadcasts which would have prevented cross-frontier broadcasting of films by pan-European channels. There was no danger of eliminating all competition because of the existence of suitable German langauge films on the market.

4.103. Exclusive sports programmes licences. In 1978, following the Commission's intervention, the English Football League and London Weekend Television withdrew from an agreement which gave the independent television companies exclusive rights in England to record and transmit football matches. Since the agreement excluded the BBC, any broadcaster wanting to obtain recordings for transmission in other Member States could negotiate rights with only one party. It thus created a monopoly for the provision of certain broadcasts of significant public interest in the Community as a whole.[185]

4.104. Commission statement on audiovisual policy. The Commission has subsequently affirmed the stance it has taken in individual decisions, that:

---

[185] Commission Ninth Report on Competition Policy, (1979), points 116 and 117.

. . . the granting of exclusive television rights is not in itself anti-competitive; however, agreements which are excessive in their scope or duration or which impose additional restrictions on the parties may fall under Article 85(1).[186]

(8) Summary of Principles Governing Exploitation of Products and Films Protected by Copyright

4.105. A synthesis of Court Cases and Commission Decisions dealing with exclusive agreements licensing the distribution of goods or services protected by copyright, yields the following principles:

(1) The Court has not determined the rules applicable to an agreement licensing the exclusive distribution of an 'old' product. The Commission is likely to hold such an agreement in breach of Article 85(1) on the grounds that the power to grant exclusivity does not form part of the 'specific subject matter' of copyright. Any agreement must be justified under Article 85(3) and parallel imports may not be impeded.

(2) Because of the risk inherent in marketing new products, the Court considers that an exclusive licence for the distribution of a 'new product' is outside of the ambit of Article 85(1) if it takes the form of an 'open licence'. Thus the agreement must permit competition from licensees of other territories and from parallel imports. The Commission, however, treats any form of exclusive licence as being in breach of Article 85(1) and thus requiring exemption.

(3) The Court has not determined the rules applicable to an agreement licensing the exclusive distribution of an 'old' film. The Commission is likely to consider such an agreement in breach of Article 85(1), thus requiring exemption under Article 85(3).

(4) Both the Court and the Commission take the view that an exclusive licence of a 'new' film is not as such prohibited by Article 85(1) but may well be according to its actual affects on competition.[187] Restrictive agreements of excessive geographic scope and duration will be struck down.

(5) The Commission is likely to deny an exemption to an agreement licensing the exclusive exhibition on television of a large number of films for a period of excessive duration. It will, however, probably grant an exemption if sub-licensing to third parties is made possible during the term of the agreement and if there are specific benefits from large scale licensing.

(9) Terms Other Than Exclusivity

4.106. Terms other than exclusivity but which restrict competition may be found in a copyright licence concerning, for example, technical drawings. The Commission has stated that the following terms will normally be regarded as infringing Article 85(1) and as being incapable of exemption under Article 85(3):[188]

(1) no challenge clause;
(2) non-competition clause;

---

[186] Communication from the Commission to the Council and Parliament on audiovisual policy, 2.2.2(a), COM (90) 78 final.

[187] Although it goes without saying, Advocate General Reischl noted in Case 262/81 *Coditel SA v. Ciné Vog Films SA* [1982] ECR 3381, [1983] 1 CMLR 49, that parallel imports are not in point where film exhibition rights are concerned because there is no question of the circulation of goods.

[188] Commission Twelfth Report on Competition Policy, (1982), point 89.

(3) a clause requiring the payment of royalties on products not protected by any copyright of the licensor; and

(4) a clause requiring the licensee to transfer to the licensor the title to any copyright of the licensee in improvements made to the licensed product.

(10) Exclusive Contracts with Performers

4.107. The Commission has indicated its attitude to exclusive contracts with performing artists. Unitel, a producer of films for television, had entered into a contract with four principal La Scala opera singers for the production of a film of the opera 'Don Carlos'. In accordance with the contract, the singers agreed, amongst other matters, not to appear in cinema or television performances of the same opera if unapproved by Unitel. Unitel had refused to allow the Italian broadcasting company, RAI to broadcast live a performance of the opera. The Commission stated that:

> By entering into an exclusive contract with UNITEL, a singer is prevented from further commercializing his artistic performances in any of the Community Member States. Such a contract may therefore affect trade between Member States.[189]

After intervention by the Commission, Unitel agreed:

(1) to ensure that the making of films was not unduly delayed so that the non-competition clause was not extended inordinately;

(2) to waive its exclusive rights in the event of a live broadcast of particularly important cultural events (this was put into effect for the Bayreuth festival).

The Commission stated that 'In these circumstances, the exclusive obligation which the singers entered into, limited to one work only and one type of exploitation only, television films, is not normally caught by Article 85.'[190]

(11) Licensing the Exclusive Exploitation of a Product Protected by a Trademark

4.108. Exclusivity not 'per se' restrictive of competition. In Joined Cases *EMI Records Ltd v. CBS United Kingdom Ltd*,[191] *EMI Records Ltd v. CBS Grammofon A/S*[192] and *EMI Records Ltd v. CBS Schallplatten GmbH*,[193] the Court of Justice pronounced that:

> A trade-mark right, as a legal entity, does not possess those elements of contract or concerted practice referred to in Article 85(1). . . Nevertheless, the exercise of that right might fall within the ambit of the prohibitions contained in the Treaty if it were to manifest itself as the subject, the means, or the consequence of a restrictive practice.

In other words, exclusivity is not in itself a breach of Article 85(1). It is necessary to see whether there are particular factors which bring the agreement within the ambit of that Article.

---

[189] Commission Decision 78/516/EEC Re RAI/UNITEL OJ No L 157, 15.6.78, p.39.
[190] Commission Twelfth Report on Competition Policy, (1982), point 90. On 'appreciable effect', see §4.030 above.
[191] Case 51/75 [1976] ECR 811, [1976] 2 CMLR 235, paras. 26 and 27.
[192] Case 86/75 [1976] ECR 871, [1976] 2 CMLR 235, paras. 23 and 24.
[193] Case 96/75 [1976] ECR 913, [1976] 2 CMLR 235, para. 14.

4.109. EMI Records Ltd v. CBS Grammofon AS. Trademarks in the entertainment industry have featured in one set of Joined Cases, namely *EMI Records Ltd v. CBS United Kingdom Ltd*,[194] *EMI Records Ltd v. CBS Grammofon A/S*[195] and *EMI Records Ltd v. CBS Schallplatten GmbH*.[196] The cases examine the right of a manufacturer of records who has a registered trademark in all Community countries contractually to restrict an undertaking in a third country with ownership of the identical mark from importing goods bearing that mark into the Community. The facts of the cases were as follows. At the turn of the century, the trademark 'Columbia' belonged to an American company, Columbia Phonograph Company General, who traded worldwide. In 1917, under its new name of Columbia Graphophone Company, it transferred the interest and goodwill it had acquired in various countries including the Community territories of Belgium, Denmark, England, France, Italy and the Netherlands, to its English subsidiary. Along with this transfer, it assigned a number of trademarks including the name 'Columbia', but it retained its interest and goodwill and rights in that mark in the United States and various third countries. After 1922, the English and American companies passed their trademarks to various undertakings in America and England so that by 1975 they were owned respectively by the English company EMI Records Ltd and the American company CBS. Over the years each company established businesses in the 'other's' territories. In particular, CBS Inc operated a number of subsidiaries in the Community territories to which it imported its records. In general, it respected EMI's ownership in the trademark 'Columbia' by obliterating it with a sticker. However, on occasions, it failed to obliterate the mark and that is what led EMI Ltd to sue for infringement of its trademark.

4.110. Exclusivity deemed valid. The High Court in England asked the Court to pronounce on whether EMI Ltd's behaviour was in breach of the competition rules. The Court of Justice ruled that:

> The principles of Community law and the provision on the free movement of goods and on competition do not prohibit the proprietor of the same mark in all the Member States of the Community from exercising his trade-mark rights, recognised by the national laws of each Member State, in order to prevent the sale in the Community by a third party of products bearing the same mark, which is owned in a third country, provided that the exercise of the said rights does not manifest itself as the result of an agreement or of concerted practices which have as their object or effect the isolation or partitioning of the common market.

> In so far as that condition is fulfilled the requirement that such third party must, for the purposes of his exports to the Community, obliterate the mark on the products concerned and perhaps apply a different mark forms part of the permissible consequences of the protection which the national laws of each Member State afford to the proprietor of the mark against the importation of products from third countries bearing a similar or identical mark.

The agreement in issue had the effect of investing ownership of the trademark absolutely in the EMI companies in Member States of the Community. This was thus not an instance where Columbia Phonograph Company General, (CBS's predecessor in title) had licensed the exclusive exploitation of their mark. It followed that EMI were entitled to take any action which preserved their absolute right in the mark 'Columbia'. And that meant having the exclusive right to market products in their territory bearing their own mark.

---

[194] Case 51/75 [1976] ECR 811, [1976] 2 CMLR 235.
[195] Case 86/75 [1976] ECR 871, [1976] 2 CMLR 235.
[196] Case 96/75 [1976] ECR 913, [1976] 2 CMLR 235.

14. Collecting Societies and Article 85(1)

4.111. Reciprocal representation contracts. Collecting societies have veered dangerously close to Article 85(1) by establishing networks of 'reciprocal representation contract'. These are contracts in which a collecting society in one Member States agrees to be solely responsible for the collection of royalties for works which are exploited in that State but which are owned by the members of a collecting society established in another Member State. Traditionally, such contracts have stipulated that each society is to apply to the other's repertoire, the same scales, methods and means of collection and distribution of royalties as it applies to works in its own repertoire. Such contracts have a twofold purpose. First, they are intended to make all protected musical works, whatever their origin, subject to the same conditions for all users in a single Member State. In this way they ensure compliance with principles of 'national treatment' enshrined in international conventions.[197] Secondly, they enable collecting societies to rely, for the protection of their repertoire in another State, on the organisation established by the copyright management society operating there, without being obliged to add to that organization their own network of contracts with users and their own local monitoring arrangements.   The Court of Justice has held in a number of cases that, in view of their purposes, reciprocal representation contracts are not in themselves restrictive of competition so as to be caught by Article 85(1).[198] However, the competition rules are breached where a society agrees with a foreign society to refuse to allow users of recorded music established abroad, direct access to its repertoire should users so wish. Article 85(1) would also be violated if the collecting societies carried on a concerted practice having its object or effect the refusal by each society to grant direct access to its repertoire to users established in another Member State.[199]

4.112. Refusal to grant licences for certain works only (global licence). Anglo-American culture dominates the European audiovisual arena. Usually, therefore, discotheques throughout the Community favour British or American popular music, seldom wanting access to home grown repertoire. The collecting societies have, however, in general, refused to limit a licence to foreign works insisting that any licence must cover their entire repertoire. This naturally puts a high premium on royalties.

The Court of Justice has held that this practice does not necessarily have the 'object or effect of restricting competition in the common market' because a 'balance needs to be struck between the interests of the copyright-management society and a category of its customers'.[200]: It has stated that:

---

[197] Case 395/87 *Minstère Public v. Tournier* [1989] ECR 2521, [1991] 4 CMLR 248: ie Berne Convention for the Protection of Literary and Artistic Works, see §7.009 below.

[198] *Ibid.* Case 110/88 *Lucazeau v. Société des auteurs, compositeurs et éditeurs de musique* [1989] ECR 2811, [1991] 4 CMLR 248; Case 241/88 *Société des auteurs, compositeurs et éditeurs de musique v. Debelle* [1989] ECR 2811, [1991] 4 CMLR 248; Case 242/88 *Soumanagnac v. Société des auteurs, compositeurs et éditeurs de musique* [1989] ECR 2811, [1991] 4 CMLR 248.

[199] *Ibid.* As to the meaning of concerted practice, see §4.007 above. But note that innocent parallel behaviour may be excused (see §4.011 above).

[200] *Ibid.* per Advocate General Jacobs referring to the general principle formulated by the Court in Case 127/73 *Belgische Radio en Televisie (BRT) v. SABAM* [1974] ECR 51, [1974] 2 CMLR 238. See §4.153 below, abuse of a dominant position.

Copyright-management societies pursue a legitimate aim when they endeavour to safeguard the rights and interests of their members vis-à-vis the users of recorded music. The contracts concluded with users for that purpose cannot be regarded as restrictive of competition for the purposes of Article 85 unless the contested practice exceeds the limits of what is necessary for the attainment of that aim. Those limits may be exceeded if direct access to a sub-division of a repertoire, as advocated by the discotheque operators, could fully safeguard the interests of authors, composers and publishers of music without thereby increasing the costs of managing contracts and monitoring the use of protected musical works.

The result of that appraisal may differ from one Member State to another. It is for the national court to make the necessary findings of fact in each case.

Factors which may come into play include: the convenience of the global licence as a vehicle for the marketing of performing rights; the flexibility it offers to users such as discotheque owners who cannot predict their precise needs in advance; whether there is a viable alternative to the global licence; the additional cost of having to define and monitor a new category of music and the relative bargaining power of the parties.[201]

4.113. Export bans. The Commission has consistently required collecting societies to remove any export bans that may have been imposed on record manufacturers who produce and market copyright products protected by the societies.[202]

III. ARTICLE 86—THE ABUSE OF A DOMINANT POSITION

1. Introduction

4.114. Treaty terms. Article 86 prohibits undertakings abusing their dominant position within the common market. It states as follows:

Any abuse by one or more undertakings of a dominant position within the common market or in a substantial part of it shall be prohibited as incompatible with the common market in so far as it may affect trade between Member States. Such abuse may, in particular, consist in:

(a)   directly or indirectly imposing unfair purchase or selling prices or unfair trading conditions;

---

[201]   *Ibid.* The Advocate General found it also relevant to consider principles fashioned by the American Courts in determining the legality of 'blanket licences': In *Columbia Broadcasting System v. BMI and Ascap*, 441 US 1, 60 L Ed2nd 1, 99 S Ct 1551, the United States Supreme Court ruled that 'blanket licensing' could not be considered to be a 'per se' violation of the Sherman Act but had to be evaluated in terms of a 'rule of reason' market analysis. Other cases referred to by the Advocate General were: *Buffalo Broadcasting Inc. and Others v. Ascap and BMI*, United States Court of Appeal for the Second Circuit, 744 F. 2nd 917, 223 US PQ (BNA) 478, Copy. L. Rep. (CCH) P25, 710 and *BMI v. Moor-Law Inc.* 527 F. Supp. 758 (D. Del 1981), the latter case holding that there were no practicable alternatives to the blanket licence.

[202]   Commission Eleventh Report on Competition Policy, (1981), point 98, Re STEMRA and Commission Thirteenth Report on Competition Policy, (1983), point 147 et seq. Re BIEM-IFPI. See also §4.094 et seq. above generally on licensing copyright and §4.163 below on the abuse of a dominant position.

(b) limiting production, markets or technical development to the prejudice of
     consumers;
(c) applying dissimilar conditions to equivalent transactions with other trading
     parties, thereby placing them at a competitive disadvantage;
(d) making the conclusion of contracts subject to acceptance by the other parties of
     supplementary obligations which, by their nature or according to commercial
     usage, have no connection with the subject of such contracts.

4.115. Key elements of a breach. Article 86 is violated if:

● an undertaking
● in a dominant position in the Common Market
● abuses its position of dominance
● and that abuse has an effect on trade between Member States.

2. Definition of the Term 'Undertaking'

4.116. The definition of what type of enterprise constitutes an undertaking under
Article 86 is similar to that under Article 85.[203]

3. The Relevant Market

(1) General Principles

4.117. Article 86 prohibits 'Any abuse by one or more undertakings of a dominant
position within the common market or in a substantial part of it . . .'. The first point
to note is that, as Article 86 makes clear, behaviour is only abusive if the
undertaking has considerable market strength. In order to determine that strength
it is necessary to define the 'relevant market'. The relevant market has three
components. The first two components are the relevant product market and the
relevant geographic market. As the Court of Justice noted in *United Brands Co v.
EC Commission*:[204]

> The opportunities for competition under Article 86 of the Treaty must be considered
> having regard to the particular features of the product in question and with reference to
> a clearly defined geographic area in which it is marketed and where the conditions of
> competition are sufficiently homogeneous for the effect of the economic power of the
> undertaking concerned to be able to be evaluated.

The 'relevant product market' is thus that sphere of the market where the
products (or services) of the particular undertaking compete with other products
(or services). Essentially, the Court assesses the degree of 'interchangeability' of
products (or services) in a given area.[205] And it has imported some fairly technical

---

[203] See §4.018 et seq. above.
[204] Case 27/76 [1978] ECR 207, [1978] 1 CMLR 429, para. 11.
[205] Case 6/72 *Europemballage Corp and Continental Can Co Inc v. EC Commission* [1973] ECR 215,
[1973] CMLR 199.

tests from economic science to evaluate that environment.[206] The third factor which comes into play and completes the analysis, is the relative temporal market: that is, the period of time over which the products (or services) compete with other similar products (or services).[207] In fact, the Court shows a tendency to define the relevant market narrowly.

Having defined the breadth of the relevant market, the Court can discern whether the undertaking exercises the requisite dominance. But as Advocate General Mayras pointed out in *Belgische Radio en Televisie (BRT) v. SV SABAM*,[208] geographical coverage is not the factor which determines whether the undertaking has a dominant position '. . . within the Common Market or in a substantial part of it . . .'

> What is essential is the quantitative assessment of the market in relation to the whole of the common market, that is to say, its relative economic importance. For this purpose, one must consider above all the density of the population, the level of its resources, and the extent of its purchasing power.[209]

(2) The Media Relevant Product Market

4.118. Collecting societies. It has been stated (although it goes without saying) that in assessing the relevant market of a collecting society, it is not appropriate to consider whether substitute products exist because the asset in issue, is intangible.[210] A collecting society is dealing in copyright and neighbouring right material. The enquiry must thus focus on the availability of alternative services.[211] But the ambit of comparable services is, according to the Court of Justice, very limited. It is solely that of the management for reward of the royalties due to a performer from the secondary exploitation of recordings of his performance.[212] In other words, only the services of those who collect royalties for the exploitation of material on media such as radio and television. Thus excluded from the analysis are

---

[206] ie the cross elasticity of the product in issue: see Case 27/76 *United Brands Co v. EC Commission* [1978] ECR 207, [1978] 1 CMLR 429. For a detailed discussion of these concepts see Bellamy and Child, *op. cit.*, 8-005 et seq.

[207] See e.g. Case 27/76 *United Brands Co v. EC Commission* [1978] ECR 207, [1978] 1 CMLR 429.

[208] Case 127/73 [1974] ECR 51, [1974] 2 CMLR 238.

[209] On this basis, the Belgian territory was considered to be a 'substantial part of the Common Market' in a case involving a collecting society. In both Commission Decision 81/1030/EEC Re GVL OJ No L 370, 28.12.81, p.49 and Commission Decision 71/224/EEC Re GEMA OJ No L 134, 20.6.71, p.15, [1971] CMLR D35, the Commission held that the Federal Republic of Germany constituted a substantial part of the Common Market. In Case T—69/89 *Radio Telefís Eireann v. EC Commission* [1991] 1 ECR 2925 [1991] 4 CMLR 586, the Court of First Instance held that the geographical market represented by Ireland and Northern Ireland was a substantial part of the Common Market. In Case C—260/89 *Elliniki Radiophonia Tileorassi Anonimi Etairia v. Dimotiki Etairia Pliroforissis* [1991] 1 ECR 2925, the Court of Justice noted that the territory of a Member State over which a statutory monopoly extended might constitute a substantial part of the common market and on that basis, Greece was indeed a substantial part of the Common Market.

[210] Case 127/73 *Belgische Radio en Televisie (BRT) v. SV SABAM* [1974] ECR 51, [1974] 2 CMLR 238, per Advocate General Mayras.

[211] *Ibid.*

[212] Case 7/82 *GVL v. EC Commission* [1983] ECR 483, [1983] 3 CMLR 645, upholding Commission Decision 81/1030/EEC Re GVL OJ No L 370, 28.12.81. p.49.

undertakings which manage the primary exploitation of performances.[213] These are agents or similar persons who negotiate the terms of recording contracts. Also excluded are transactions between artists and the users of their works.[214] This narrows the field down considerably.

4.119. Broadcasting organisations. The relevant market of certain broadcasting company operations can be narrow in the court's perspective. Sometimes there are simply no comparable products or services. Thus in the Magill cases,[215] an action examining practices in the publishing of television programme listings, the Court of First Instance held that programme listings produced by individual television broadcasting companies were obviously not interchangeable with each other. More significantly, weekly listings with their advance information were not even inter-changeable with daily listings. This was illustrated by the demand for weekly television guides. Consequently, the relevant market in which dominance and its abuse could be assessed for a daily listing encompassed solely the daily listing of an individual television broadcasting company. And the relevant market for a weekly listing encompassed solely the weekly listing of programmes broadcast by an individual television broadcasting company. The Court of First Instance affirmed that the weekly lists, ie the 'products', represented specific markets which could not be 'identified either with the market for the broadcasting services or with the market for information on television programmes in general'.[216]

The Commission has held that the relevant product market for TV broadcasting is influenced and determined by the programme mix.[217] Certain TV channels offer a wide variety of different types of programmes eg news, general entertainment, films, sports, music and documentaries whilst other channels focus, even exclusively on one of the aforementioned types of programmes, to reach a specific audience. Accordingly, free access TV, which usually provides a wide programming mix,[218] is a distinct market from pay TV, which usually broadcasts specialist programmes (ie films or sport or music)[219] and thus caters for the needs of a targeted audience. The relevant geographic market is influenced and determined mainly by the existence of language and cultural barriers but can surpass national boundaries. The evolution of satellite broadcasting as well as the expansion of cable networks are leading to the development of pan-European channels. The Commission noted that whilst cultural differences may still hinder the development of such channels, linguistic problems can be overcome by dubbing, subtitling or greater language familiarity.[220] Sports programmes are particularly amenable for transnational broadcasting.

---

[213] *Ibid.*

[214] *Ibid.* per Advocate General Reischl.

[215] Case T—69/89 *Radio Telefis Eireann v. EC Commission* [1991] 4 CMLR 586; Case T—70/89 *The British Broadcasting and BBC Enterprises Ltd v. EC Commission* [1991] 4 CMLR 669; Case T—76/89 *Independent Television Publications Ltd v. EC Commission* [1991] 4 CMLR 745, all upholding Commission Decision 89/205/EEC Re Magill TV Guide/ITP, BBC and RTE, OJ No L 78, 21.03.89 p.43.

[216] *Ibid.*

[217] Case IV/M.110, *Re the Concentration between ESPN inc, Compagnie Generale D'Images and Canal+ and WH Smith TV Ltd*, 10.9.91, [1993] 4 CMLR M1.

[218] Normally financed by public authorities and/or advertising.

[219] Normally funded by subscription charges.

[220] In fact, the Commission left open the exact definition of the relevant product and geographic market for free access TV.

4. Effect on Trade Between Member States

(1) General Principles

4.120. According to the express terms of Article 86, an abuse of a dominant position is only unlawful if it affects trade between Member States.[221] So, Article 86 cannot be invoked if the effects of an abuse are contained within the territorial boundaries of a single Member State.[222] Affecting trade between Member States amounts to any practice which might harm the attainment of the objectives of a single market between the Member States, in particular by partitioning the natural markets or affecting the structure of competition within the common market.[223] But, it is enough that abusive conduct should be capable of affecting trade between Member States. It is therefore not necessary for the Court to find that there is a real and present effect on inter-State trade.[224] The Court of Justice has held that the expression 'trade in goods' contained in Article 86, can apply to the provision of services.[225] Furthermore, it has held that trade between Member States may be affected even where the product or service is to be exported or provided in non-Member States.[226]

(2) Effect on Trade by Media Undertakings

4.121. Collecting Societies. Article 86 may apply to the manner in which a collecting society offers copyright management services.[227] In GVL v EC Commission,[228] the Court of Justice, upholding the Commission's Decision against GVL, held that a refusal by a collecting society to administer in its Member State, the rights of non-national artists resident in other Member States, would have an affect on inter-state trade. By preventing the crossfrontier movement of services in this

---

[221] See also Article 85(1), page §4.031 et seq. above.
[222] Case 85/76 *Hoffmann-La Roche & Co AG v. EC Commission* [1979] ECR 461, [1979] 3 CMLR 211; Case 22/79 *Greenwich Film Production v. SACEM* [1979] ECR 3275, [1980] 1 CMLR 629; Case 7/82 *GVL v. EC Commission* [1983] ECR 483, [1983] 3 CMLR 645; Case T—69/89 *Radio Telefis Eireann v. EC Commission* [1991] 4 CMLR 586; Case T—70/89 *The British Broadcasting and BBC Enterprises Ltd v. EC Commission* [1991] 4 CMLR 669; Case T—76/89 *Independent Television Publications Ltd v. EC Commission* [1991] 4 CMLR 745; Case C—260/89 *Elliniki Radiophonia Tileorassi Anonimi Etairia v. Dimotiki Etairia Pliroforissis* [1991] I ECR 2925.
[223] Joined Cases 6, 7/73 *Istituto Chemioterapico Italiano SpA and Commercial Solvents Corpn v. EC Commission* [1974] ECR 223, [1974] 1 CMLR 309; Case 22/76 *United Brands Co v. EC Commission* [1978] ECR 207, [1978] 1 CMLR 429; Case 85/76 *Hoffman-La Roche & Co AG v. EC Commission* [1979] ECR 461, [1979] 3 CMLR 211; Case 22/78 *Hugin Kassaregister AB v. EC Commission* [1979] ECR 1869, [1979] 3 CMLR 345; Case 7/82 *GVL v. EC Commission* [1983] ECR 482, [1983] 3 CMLR 645; Case T—69/89 *Radio Telefis Eireann v. EC Commission* [1991] 4 CMLR 586; Case T—70/89 *The British Broadcasting and BBC Enterprises Ltd v. EC Commission* [1991] 4 CMLR 669; Case T—76/89 *Independent Television Publications Ltd v. EC Commission* [1991] 4 CMLR 745.
[224] Case 322/81 *Michelin v. EC Commission*; Case C—41/90 *Höfner and Elser v. Macroton* [1991] ECR 1979; Case T—69/89 *Radio Telefis Eireann v. EC Commission* [1991] 4 CMLR 586; Case T—70/89 *The British Broadcasting and BBC Enterprises Ltd v. EC Commission* [1991] 4 CMLR 669; Case T—76/89 *Independent Television Publications Ltd v. EC Commission* [1991] 4 CMLR 745.
[225] Case 22/79 *Greenwich Film Production v. SACEM* [1979] ECR 3275, [1980] 1 CMLR 629 and Case 311/84 *Centre Belge d'Etudes de Marché-Télé-Marketing SA v. Compagnie Luxembourgeoise de Télédiffusion SA* [1985] ECR 1105, [1986] 2 CMLR 558. See §4.156 below.
[226] Case 22/79 *Greenwich Film Production v. SACEM* [1979] ECR 3275, [1980] 1 CMLR 629.
[227] *Ibid.*
[228] Case 7/82 [1983] ECR 482, [1983] 3 CMLR 645.

fashion, the society was impeding the creation of a uniform market within the Community.[229] It should be noted that artists qualify as 'trading partners' under the Treaty.[230]

The insistence by a collecting society that a member assign to it his rights for the whole world may affect trade between Member States. This is because such action would hinder the freedom of authors and composers to shop around for the services of collecting societies in other Member States who might administer the collection of their royalties in third countries.[231]

4.122. Broadcasting organisations. The Court of Justice has held that Article 86 may apply to the manner in which a broadcasting organisation offers transmission time for the broadcasting of either advertisements[232] or programmes.[233] But it has stated that where a local undertaking was prevented from providing an internal transmission service being a service which would be exhibiting solely local programmes, prima facie, Article 86 would not apply.[234] In the Magill cases,[235] the Court of First Instance held that by refusing to grant to Magill a licence to reproduce the Applicant's programme listings, the Applicant's not only eliminated a competing undertaking from the market but also excluded any competition, thus maintaining the partitioning of the markets.

5. Meaning of the Term 'Dominant'

(1) General Principles

4.123. The EEC Treaty failed to define the meaning of 'dominance' and so the Court has filled the gap. In *Centre Belge d'Etudes de Marché-Télé-Marketing SA v. Compagnie Luxembourgeoise de Télédiffusion SA*[236] the Court of Justice reaffirmed the definition first found in *United Brands Co v. EC Commission*, stating:

> . . . an undertaking occupies a dominant position for the purposes of Article 86 where it enjoys a position of economic strength which enables it to hinder the maintenance of effective competition on the relevant market by allowing it to behave to an appreciable extent independently of its competitors and customers and ultimately of consumers.[237]

---

[229] In Commission Decision 81/1030/EEC Re GVL OJ No L 370, 28.12.81. p.49, para. 64, the Commission stated that: 'The economic discrimination suffered by foreign artists also affected their cross-frontier competitive position. This discrimination was likely to place foreign artists in a less favourable position than favoured German and domestic artists, with whose performances they were in competition within the Community, and hence to affect trade between Member States.'

[230] *Ibid.*

[231] Case 22/79 *Greenwich Film Production v. SACEM* [1979] ECR 3275, [1980] 1 CMLR 629.

[232] Case 155/73 *Sacchi* [1974] ECR 409, [1974] 2 CMLR 177; Case 311/84 *Centre Belge d'Etudes de Marché-Télé-Marketing SA v. Compagnie Luxembourgeoise de Télédiffusion SA* [1985] ECR 3261; [1986] 2 CMLR 558 [1986] 2 CMLR 558, per Advocate General Lenz.

[233] Case C—260/89 *Elliniki Radiophonia Tileorassi Anonimi Etairia v. Dimotiki Etairia Pliforissis* [1991] I ECR 2925.

[234] *Ibid.* per Advocate General Lenz.

[235] Case T— 69/89 *Radio Telefis Eireann v. EC Commission* [1991] 4 CMLR 586; Case T—70/89 *The British Broadcasting and BBC Enterprises Ltd v. EC Commission* [1991] 4 CMLR 669; Case T—76/89 *Independent Television Publications Ltd v. EC Commission* [1991] 4 CMLR 745.

[236] Case 311/84 [1985] ECR 3261, [1986] 2 CMLR 558, para. 16.

[237] See also Case 322/81 *Michelin v. EC Commission* [1983] ECR 3461, [1985] 1 CMLR 282.

The fact that the absence of competition or its restriction on the relevant market is brought about or encouraged by provisions laid down by law in no way precludes the application of Article 86.[238]

But a group of traders engaged in the same business activity do not necessarily acquire a dominant status simply because they are all obliged, by national legislation to fix prices for the goods manufacture or supplied by them,[239] provided that each can determine the level of the price independently.[240]

(2) Dominant Media Undertakings

4.124. Newspaper retailers and book manufacturers In a case concerning the supply of newspapers and periodicals, the Court of Justice held that an undertaking which owned 190 out of a total of approximately 3500 retail outlets could not be regarded as occupying a dominant position on the retail market.[241]

In *Syndicat des libraires de Normandie v. L'Aigle distribution SA*,[242] the Court of Justice held that the fact that all publishers and importers of books were obliged, by national legislation, to fix the retail price of any books published or imported by them, did not of itself confer on them a dominant position, provided that those rules did not in any was interfere with the freedom of each of those traders to determine those price levels independently.

6. Meaning of the Term 'Abuse'

4.125. General principles. The concept of 'an abuse' is not defined by Article 86 which merely sets out particular examples.[243] Briefly, the examples cited are: imposing unfair prices or unfair trading conditions; limiting production, markets or technical development to the prejudice of consumers; applying dissimilar conditions to equivalent transactions with trading parties, thereby placing them at a competitive disadvantage and making the conclusion of contracts subject to acceptance by the parties of supplementary obligations which, by their nature or according to commercial usage, have no connection with the subject of such contracts. Since these are mere instances of an abuse, albeit common instances, an abuse has to be determined according to the individual case.[244]

---

[238] Case 26/75 *General Motors Continental NV v. EC Commission* [1975] ECR 1367, [1976] 1 CMLR 95; Case 13/77 *GB-INNO-BM NV V. Vereniging van de Kleinhandelaars in Tabak* [1977] ECR 2115, [1978] 1 CMLR 283; Case 41/83 *Italy v. EC Commission* [1985] ECR 880, [1985] 2 CMLR 368; Case 311/84 *Centre Belge d'Etudes de Marché-TéléMarketing SA v. Compagnie Luxembourgeoise de Télédiffusion SA* [1985] ECR 3261, [1986] 2 CMLR 558.

[239] The combined effect of which could be to hinder effective competition.

[240] Case 254/87 *Syndicat des libraires de Normandie v. L'Aigle distribution SA* [1988] ECR 4457. See §4.124 below.

[241] Case 243/83 *Binon and Cie SA v. Agence et Messageries de la Presse SA* [1985] ECR 2015, [1985] 3 CMLR 800.

[242] Case 254/87 [1988] ECR 4457. The facts of the case were substantially the same as those found in Case 229/83 *Association des Centres Distributeurs Edouard Leclerc v. Au Blé Vert' Sàrl* [1985] ECR 1, [1985] 2 CMLR 286. See §1.074 above.

[243] Case 127/73 *Belgische Radio en Televisie (BRT) v. SV SABAM* [1974] ECR 313, [1974] 2 CMLR 238, per Advocate General Mayras.

[244] *Ibid.*

4.126. The Court of Justice's appraisal of an abuse. In *Hoffman-La Roche & Co AG v. EC Commission*,[245] the Court of Justice defined the essence of an abuse thus:

> The concept of abuse is an objective concept relating to the behaviour of an undertaking in a dominant position which is such as to influence the structure of a market where, as a result of the very presence of the undertaking in question, the degree of competition is weakened and which, through recourse to methods different from those which condition normal competition in products or services on the basis of the transactions of commercial operators, has the effect of hindering the maintenance of the degree of competition still existing in the market or the growth of that competition.

However, according to Bellamy and Child, a synthesis of the case law reveals that generally abuses are either:

(a) anticompetitive, that is action which further reduces or impedes effective competition, or;

(b) exploitative, that is, unfair or unreasonable action aimed at the dominant undertaking's suppliers and customers.[246]

7. Effect of Violation on Validity of Agreements

4.127. Article 86 prohibits the type of conduct which it enumerates in a number of subsections. But it does not say that agreements which are in violation of its provisions are automatically void, (in contrast to Article 85(2)). And the Court of Justice has declared that 'it would be unthinkable that Article 86 should be held indiscriminately to avoid contracts in a manner detrimental to the victims of the abuse or to third parties'.[247] It has therefore held,[248] that the relevant national authorities must undertake a pruning exercise:

> If abusive practices are exposed, it is. . . for the court to decide whether and to what extent they affect the interests of authors or third parties concerned, with a view to deciding the consequences with regard to the validity and effect of the contracts in dispute or certain of their provisions.[249]

8. Examples of Specific Abuses

(1) Denying 'Raw Materials' to an Undertaking Competing on an Ancillary Market

(i) *General Principles*

4.128. A company in a dominant position with control of a rare resource is well placed to, as it were, 'starve' his competitors to death. Such a company might, for

---

[245] Case 85/76 [1979] ECR 461, [1979] 3 CMLR 211, para. 91.

[246] Bellamy and Child, *op. cit.*, 8-039.

[247] Case 22/79 *Greenwich Film Production v.* SACEM [1979] ECR 3275, [1980] 1 CMLR 629, per Advocate General Warner.

[248] in a case involving abuses by collecting societies.

[249] Case 127/73 *Belgische Radio en Televisie* [1974] ECR 51, [1974] 2 CMLR 238, para. 14, affirmed in Case 22/79 *Greenwich Film Production v.* SACEM [1979] ECR 3275, [1980] 1 CMLR 629.

example, supply the 'raw material' only to a connected undertaking. In *Istituto Chemioterapico Italiano SpA and Commercial Solvents Corpn v. EC Commission*,[250] the Court of Justice thus held that an undertaking which holds a dominant position in a market in raw materials and which, with the object of reserving those materials for its own production of derivatives, refuses to supply a customer who also produces those derivatives, with the possibility of eliminating all competition from that customer, is abusing its dominant position within the meaning of Article 86.

(ii) Examples of Exclusionary Conduct by Media Undertakings

4.129. Centre Belge d'Etudes de Marché Télé Marketing SA v. Compagnie Luxembourgeoise de Télé diffusion SA. In *Centre Belge d'Etudes de Marché Télé Marketing SA v. Compagnie Luxembourgeoise de Télédiffusion SA*,[251] the Court of Justice confirmed that the principle forged in *Istituto Chemioterapico Italiano SpA and Commercial Solvents Corp v. EC Commission* applies equally in the case of a company in a dominant position in the provision of broadcasting services. The facts were as follows. The Plaintiff company had been engaged in tele-marketing. This is a practice whereby an advertiser places an advertisement in one of the media with a telephone number which the target audience can call to obtain information on the product. The Plaintiff had run the first tele-marketing operation aimed at Belgium on the RTL channel. Informations Publicités Benelux SA was responsible for advertising operations on RTL and granted the Plaintiff the exclusive right for a year to conduct tele-marketing operations on the Belgium television station RTL which were aimed at the Benelux countries. At the termination of the contract, Informations Publicités Benelux SA informed advertisers that in future only the number of Informations Publicités Benelux SA was to be broadcasted. The Plaintiff considered that it had been excluded from the market which it had essentially built up in Belgium and issued an injunction.

4.130. Breach of Article 86. On a 177 reference, the Court held that the Commercial Solvent's principle:

> . . . also applies to the case of an undertaking holding a dominant position on the market in a service which is indispensable for the activities of another undertaking on another market. If, as the national court has already held in its order for reference, tele-marketing activities constitute a separate market from that of the chosen advertising medium, although closely associated with it, and if those activities mainly consist in making available to advertisers the telephone lines and team of telephonists of the tele-marketing undertaking, to subject the sale of broadcasting time to the condition that the telephone lines of an advertising agent belonging to the same group as the television station should be used amounts in practice to a refusal to supply the services of that station to any other tele-marketing undertaking. If, further, that refusal is not justified by technical or commercial requirements relating to the nature of the television, but is intended to reserve to the agent any tele-marketing operation broadcast by the said station, with the possibility of eliminating all competition from another undertaking, such conduct amounts to an abuse prohibited by Article 86, provided that the other conditions of that Article are satisfied.[252]

The Court thus held that:

---

[250] Joined Cases 6, 7/73 [1974] ECR 223, [1974] 1 CMLR 309.
[251] Case 311/84, [1985] ECR 3261, [1986] 2 CMLR 558.
[252] *Ibid.*, para. 26.

An abuse within the meaning of Article 86 is committed where, without any objective necessity, an undertaking holding a dominant position on a particular market reserves to itself or to an undertaking belonging to the same group an ancillary activity which might be carried out by another undertaking as part of its activities on a neighbouring but separate market, with the possibility of eliminating all competition from such undertaking.

4.131. The Magill cases—abuse of copyright in programme listings. The Magill cases[253] provide a good example of this type of exclusionary abuse and are dealt with below in the section concerning the abuse of intellectual property rights.[254]

(2) Imposing Unfair Prices

(i) General Principles

4.132. Article 86(a) states that an abuse, may in particular, consist in:

... directly or indirectly imposing unfair purchase or selling prices or unfair trading conditions.

The Court of Justice has held that the relationship between the economic value of a product supplied and the price charged is the factor which determines whether or not that price is fair.[255] A fair price is a price that would come about given sufficiently effective competition.[256] Similar concepts apply to prices in respect of services.[257]

(ii) Abuses by Media Undertakings

4.133. Film Licence Fees. Comité des Industries Cinématographiques des Communautés Européennes v. EC Commission. Comité des Industries Cinématographiques des Communautés Européennes v. EC Commission,[258] concerned a claim by a representative of film makers, distributors and technical industries that a group of television monopolies in France had breached Article 86 by taking unfair advantage of their statutory monopoly to fix abnormally low film licence fees. Although the case is substantially concerned with the Applicant's complaint that the Commission had failed to take proper action, it deals with the substantive issue of the pricing of licence fees.

In support of their complaint, the Applicant had made two key points. First, they pointed out that the French television companies allocated just 3.3 per cent of their budget for the purchase of film broadcasting rights whereas the films themselves constituted the 'main programme' when broadcast on television in terms of audience ratings and the cost of advertising time. Secondly, they noted that the average film licence fee paid by the French companies was less than the cost to them of making a television film.

---

[253] Case T—69/89 Radio Telefis Eireann v. EC Commission [1991] 4 CMLR 586; Case T—70/89 The British Broadcasting and BBC Enterprises Ltd v. EC Commission [1991] 4 CMLR 669; Case T—76/89 Independent Television Publications Ltd v. EC Commission [1991] 4 CMLR 745.

[254] See §4.151 below.

[255] Case 26/75 General Motors Continental NV v. EC Commission [1975] ECR 1367, [1976] 1 CMLR 429 and Case 27/76 United Brands Co v. EC Commission [1978] ECR 207, [1978] 1 CMLR 429.

[256] Case 27/76 United Brands Co v. EC Commission [1978] ECR 207, [1978] 1 CMLR 429.

[257] See e.g. Case 395/87 Ministère Public v. Tournier [1989] ECR 2521, [1991] 4 CMLR 248; §4.166 below and Case 298/83 Comités Industries Cinématographiques des Communautés Européennes v. EC Commission [1985] ECR 1105, [1986] 1 CMLR 486; see §4.133 below.

[258] Case 298/83 [1985] ECR 1105, [1986] 1 CMLR 486.

The Commission had decided that films were heterogeneous products and that the economic value of a film was very variable depending on: the artistic quality of the film; the film's success in cinemas; the size of the potential television audience; whether the film was being shown for the first time and the time for which broadcasting rights were granted. Accordingly any putative abuse had to be established in relation to each film for which broadcasting rights had been purchased.

The Commission pointed out that no comparison could be made between the production costs of a film and the licence fee paid by a television company to broadcast that film. This was because the 'amortisation' of a film was based not only on the sale of broadcasting rights to a television company but also on showings in the cinema and exploitations of new technologies. Furthermore, there was no value in comparing the licence fees with the cost of production of a film by a television company because a television film remains the property of the television company which made it. They could exploit it through all manner of media.

The Court of Justice confirmed the validity of the Commission's analysis declaring that any allegation of an abuse in the pricing of film licences must be examined on an individual basis.

(3) Mergers

(i) General Principles

4.134. Continental Can. In *Europemballage Corp and Continental Can Co Inc v. EC Commission*[259] the Court of Justice established the principle that whilst the union of two undertakings into a single entity may avoid any Article 85 infractions, it can fall foul of Article 86. The Court held that:

> ... The restraint of competition which is prohibited if it is the result of behaviour falling under Article 85, cannot become permissible by the fact that such behaviour succeeds under the influence of a dominant undertaking and results in the merger of the undertakings concerned. In the absence of explicit provisions one cannot assume that the Treaty, which prohibits in Article 85 certain decisions of ordinary associations of undertakings restricting competition without eliminating it, permits in Article 86 that undertakings, after merging into an organic unity, should reach such a dominant position that any serious chance of competition is practically rendered impossible. Such a diverse legal treatment would make a breach in the entire competition law which could jeopardize the proper functioning of the Common Market. If, in order to avoid the prohibitions in Article 85, it sufficed to establish such close connections between the undertakings that they escaped the prohibition of Article 85 without coming within the scope of that of Article 86, then, in contradiction to the basic principles of the Common Market, the partitioning of a substantial part of this market would be allowed.

The Court based its reasoning on the wording of Article 2 and particularly 3(f) of the Treaty:

> ... if Article 3(f) provides for the institution of a system ensuring that competition in the Common Market is not distorted, then it requires a fortiori that competition must not be eliminated. . . [260]

---

[259] Case 6/72 [1973] ECR 215, [1973] CMLR 199, para. 25.
[260] *Ibid.*, para. 24. See §4.002 above ('Foundations of competition law').

As the Court noted, Article 86 is not only aimed at practices which may cause damage to consumers directly, but also at those which are detrimental to them through their impact on an effective competition structure, such as is mentioned in Article 3(f) of the Treaty. It thus held that:

> Abuse may therefore occur if an undertaking in a dominant position strengthens such position in such a way that the degree of dominance reached substantially fetters competition, ie. that only undertakings remain in the market whose behaviour depends on the dominant one.

4.135. Merger Regulation. Council Regulation 4064/89 of 21 December 1989 on the control of concentrations between undertakings,[261] has been adopted to govern large scale mergers.

(ii) Mergers of Media Undertakings

4.136. The unique problem. The merging of media undertakings takes on a significance not generally present in the merging of other types of business. For media undertakings are the vocal organs of a society. They play a vital role in both maintaining political balance and offering a medium through which individuals can address a vast audience. The merging of media undertakings can undermine these important tasks. The most obvious example is the merging of national newspapers where one is absorbed by the other. Often newspapers espouse the political views of their proprietors. A balance of views can be maintained so long as there are a number of newspapers with proprietors of differing political persuasions. If, however, a country has few newspapers and two of those that exist merge, that country may become dominated by a press representing only one political stance. Furthermore the union of two newspapers into a single entity, may reduce the opportunity in general for expression of opinion.

4.137. Commission Statement on Audiovisual Policy. The Commission has expressed its policy on mergers and their effect on pluralism, as follows:[262]

> ... the Commission considers that the establishment of the European audiovisual space does not derive merely from its wish to promote the audiovisual industry but also from the importance attached by the Community to the requirements of a democratic society, such as, notably, the respect for pluralism in the media and for freedom of expression. The Community's audiovisual policy seeks therefore, also, to ensure that the audiovisual sector is not developed at the expense of pluralism but, on the contrary, that it helps to strengthen it by encouraging, in particular, the diversity of the programmes offered to the public.
>
> Whereas the activities of media operators have increasingly assumed a European dimension, the response to the effects these may have, in certain cases, on pluralism has, for the time being, not gone beyond national limits. [However] National legislation, existing or planned, could be circumvented and would not therefore by sufficient to guarantee pluralism in all cases. Moreover, this situation, characterised by a multiplicity and disparity of national laws, may produce the opposite effect of limiting the activity of operators who could contribute to a growth of pluralism in the Member States.
>
> Nor is the application of Community competition law, in particular Articles 85 and 86 of the Treaty, able to cover all situations in which a threat to pluralism is posed,

---

[261] OJ No L 395, 30.12.89, p.1.
[262] Communication from the Commission to the Council and Parliament on audiovisual policy, 2.2.3, COM (90) final.

notably in the case of multimedia ownership. Likewise, the Regulation on mergers, adopted on 21 December 1989, covers only large mergers which affect competition on the market in question. This is why that Regulation provides that Member States may continue to apply their national legislation on the protection of pluralism and freedom of expression when the Commission does not take steps to counter a merger in the media.

4.138. Media mergers and the Merger Regulation. The Merger Regulation[263] authorises, subject to approval of the Commission, Member States to take appropriate measures to protect the plurality of the media.

9. Article 86 and the Abuse of Intellectual Property Rights

(1) The Conceptual Problem

4.139. Article 86 prohibits an abuse of a dominant position. But parties who are accused of breaching this Treaty provision in the exploitation of their intellectual property rights have tried to shield themselves behind Article 36 of the Treaty. Article 36 is a provision which rests in the chapter of the Treaty containing the laws which seek to abolish restrictions on the free movement of goods. Article 36 states that restrictions (on the free movement of goods) are permitted on the grounds of, amongst other reasons, the protection of 'industrial and commercial property'. The Court of Justice has interpreted this phrase to refer to 'intellectual property' and thus include copyright[264] and trademarks.[265] Although Article 36 is in a different part of the Treaty, the Court has brought it into play in the competition rules. It would be difficult to construct two provisions more likely to collide in their respective purposes: Article 86 curtailing abuses of monopolies and Article 36 defending the existence of monopolies brought about by the ownership of intellectual property.

In general, the tussle has been resolved by the Court making a distinction between the 'existence' of intellectual property rights and the 'exercise' of those rights. The doctrine holds that Article 36 protects the existence of intellectual property. This means that it protects only rights which constitute the 'specific subject matter' of intellectual property and only in so far as they do not constitute 'a means of arbitrary discrimination or a disguised restriction of trade between Member States'.[266] Thus the shield of Article 36 slips away with the 'exercise' of rights which do not constitute the 'specific subject matter' of intellectual property. However, as is explained below, the Court departs from these general principles where the issue is Article 86.

(2) Holding a Dominant Position

4.140. Exploitation of copyright. Before an abuse can be assessed, it must be possible to point to the existence of a dominant position.[267] The Court of Justice

---

[263] Council Regulation (EEC) No 4064/89, OJ No L 257, 21.09.90, p.14, Article 21(3).

[264] Case 78/70 *Deutsche Grammophon Gesellschaft mbH v. Metro-SB-Grossmärkte GmbH & Co KG* [1971] ECR 487, [1971] CMLR 631.

[265] Joined Cases 56, 58/64, *Établissements Consten SARL and Grundig-Verkaufs-GmbH v. EEC Commission* [1966] ECR 299, [1966] CMLR 418.

[266] Case 78/70 *Deutsche Grammophon Gesellschaft mbH v. Metro-SB-Grossmärkte GmbH & Co KG* [1971] ECR 487, [1971] CMLR 631.

[267] See §4.123 above.

has held that the mere ownership and exploitation of exclusive rights of reproduction does not confer 'dominance'. Thus in *Deutsche Grammophon Gesellschaft mbH v. Metro-SB-Grossmärkte GmbH & Co KG*,[268] it stated that:

> It is clear from this provision that the action prohibited by it presupposes the existence of a dominant position within the common market or in a substantial part of it. A manufacturer of sound recordings who holds a right related to copyright[269] does not occupy a dominant position within the meaning of Article 86 of the Treaty merely by exercising his exclusive right to distribute the protected articles.[270]

4.141. Exploitation of a trademark. The principle that ownership of intellectual property does not, of itself, confer dominance, applies to products protected by a trademark. Thus, in Joined Cases *EMI Records Ltd v. CBS United Kingdom Ltd*,[271] *EMI Records Ltd v. CBS Grammofon A/S*[272] and *EMI Records Ltd v. CBS Schallplatten GmbH*,[273] the Court of Justice held that:

> Although the trade-mark right confers upon its proprietor a special position within the protected territory this, however, does not imply the existence of a dominant position within the meaning of the above mentioned article [Article 86]. . .

(3) Factors Employed to Assess Dominance of Particular Rights Holders

(i) Exploitation of Copyright and Neighbouring Rights

4.142. General principles. In *Deutsche Grammophon Gesellschaft mbH v. Metro-SB-Grossmärkte GmbH & Co KG*,[274] the Court of Justice held that dominance means that:

> . . . the manufacturer, alone or jointly with other undertakings in the same group, should have the power to impede the maintenance of effective competition over a considerable part of the relevant market, having regard in particular to the existence of any producers marketing similar products and to their position on the market.[275]

Advocate General Roemer explained that 'it must be considered whether it is possible for an undertaking, by virtue of its share of the market (including the shares of other undertakings belonging to the same group), its know-how, its raw materials, its capital and its exclusive rights, to determine prices for a substantial part of the common market (such as the territory of a Member State) or to control production and distribution, and whether an undertaking has scope for independent action and can act to a large extent without regard to competitors, customers or suppliers'.[276]

4.143. Contracts with performers. In *Deutsche Grammophon Gesellschaft mbH v. Metro-SB-Grossmärkte GmbH & Co KG*,[277] the Court of Justice elaborated on factors which can be employed to assess the dominance of record manufacturers who have exclusive recording contracts with performers. It stated that:

---

[268] Case 78/70 [1971] ECR 487, [1971] CMLR 631, para. 16.
[269] For the significance of the phrase 'a right related to copyright', see §1.007 above.
[270] Advocate General Roemer stated that '. . . the mere fact that an undertaking holds industrial property rights and a corresponding entitlement to their conservation does not constitute a dominant position.'
[271] Case 51/75 [1976] ECR 811, [1976] 2 CMLR 235, para. 36.
[272] Case 86/75 [1976] ECR 871, [1976] 2 CMLR 235, para. 33.
[273] Case 96/75 [1976] ECR 913, [1976] 2 CMLR 235, para. 19.
[274] Case 78/70 [1971] ECR 487, [1971] CMLR 631, para. 17.
[275] These criteria were forged in Case 40/70 *Sirena Srl v. Eda Srl* [1971] ECR 69, [1971] CMLR 260.
[276] Case 78/70 *Deutsche Grammophon Gesellschaft mbH v. Metro-SB-Grossmärkte GmbH & Co KG* [1971] ECR 487, [1971] CMLR 631.
[277] Case 78/70 [1971] ECR 487, [1971] CMLR 631.

If recording artists are tied to the manufacturer by exclusive contracts consideration should be given, inter alia, to their popularity on the market, to the duration and extent of the obligations undertaken and to the opportunities available to other manufacturers of sound recordings to obtain the services of comparable performers.

If there are competing manufacturers, it is necessary to establish whether they, or their shares of the market are at all comparable with one another or whether it is possible to divide the market up according to the type of music and performers. With regard to performers, although it may be assumed that a dominant position arises in certain sectors of the market because of exclusive contracts with certain performers, this will only be in rare cases ie where the performers in question are unusually successful and numerous exclusive contracts exists.[278]

4.144. Copyright in programme listings. In the Magill cases[279] the Court of First Instance held that as a result of their exclusive right (arising from their copyright) to reproduce and market television listings, the respective Applicant publishing companies held dominant positions on the market. Third parties who wished to publish a general television magazine were in a situation of economic dependence on the publishing companies. And the latter were thus able to hinder the emergence of any effective competition on the market for information on their weekly programmes.

4.145. Film exhibition. Should the Commission be called upon to judge dominance of a Community wide film exhibition agreement, it is likely to consider the market in each Member State separately.[280] This is because 'the Commission bases its analysis on the concept of a Community market made up of sub-markets corresponding to the various Member States, the cinematographic environment of which varies from one to the other'.[281]

(ii) Exploitation of a Trademark

4.146. In Joined Cases *EMI Records Ltd v. CBS United Kingdom Ltd*,[282] *EMI Records Ltd v. CBS Grammofon A/S*[283] and *EMI Records Ltd v. CBS Schallplatten GmbH*[284] which concerned trademark rights, the Court of Justice stated that dominance would not exist:

> . . . in particular where, as in the present case, several undertakings whose economic strength is comparable to that of the proprietor of the mark operate in the market for the products in question and are in a position to compete with the said proprietor.

(4) The Abuse of Intellectual Property Rights

(i) The Substantive Test

4.147. Introduction. If a dominant position is established, the ultimate question is whether or not the owner of the rights is 'exercising' his rights in breach of Article 86 so that Article 36 will offer no protection. It was explained above that the Court of Justice has generally held that an undertaking which 'exercises' rights

---

[278] *Ibid.*, per Advocate General Roemer
[279] Case T—69/89 *Radio Telefís Eireann v. EC Commission* [1991] 4 CMLR 586; Case T—70/89 *The British Broadcasting and BBC Enterprises Ltd v. EC Commission* [1991] 4 CMLR 669; Case T—76/89 *Independent Television Publications Ltd v. EC Commission* [1991] 4 CMLR 775.
[280] Commission Decision 89/467/EEC Re UIP OJ No L 226, 03.08.89, p.25. see §4.062 above.
[281] *Ibid.*
[282] Case 51/75 [1976] ECR 811, [1976] 2 CMLR 235, para. 36.
[283] Case 86/75 [1976] ECR 871, [1976] 2 CMLR 235, para. 33.
[284] Case 96/75 [1976] ECR 913, [1976] 2 CMLR 235, para. 19.

which form the 'specific subject matter' of intellectual property will be protected by
Article 36. Whilst this is true of Article 85, the Court adopts what might be
termed a 'commercially pragmatic' stance in considering potential abuses of
intellectual property under Article 86. Even exercising rights which form the
'specific subject matter' of intellectual property may be censured by the Court.

4.148. Copyright. In the Magill cases,[285] the Court of First Instance thus held
that:

> It is common ground that in principle the protection of the specific subject-matter of a
> copyright entitles the copyright-holder to reserve the exclusive right to reproduce the
> protected work. The Court of Justice expressly recognised that in its judgment of 17
> May 1988 in Case 158/86, *Warner Brothers v. Christiansen*... in which it held that '[t]he
> two essential rights of the author, namely the exclusive right of performance and the
> exclusive right of reproduction, are not called in question by the rules of the
> Treaty'.[286]

> However, while it is plain that the exercise of the exclusive right to reproduce a
> protected work is not in itself an abuse, that does not apply when, in the light of the
> details of each individual case, it is apparent that that right is exercised in such ways and
> circumstances as in fact to pursue an aim manifestly contrary to the objectives of Article
> 86. In that event, the copyright is no longer exercised in a manner which corresponds
> to its essential function, within the meaning of Article 36 of the Treaty, which is to
> protect the moral rights in the work and ensure a reward for the creative effort, while
> respecting the aims of, in particular, Article 86.[287] ... In that case, the primacy of
> Community Law, particulary as regards principles as fundamental as those of the free
> movement of goods and freedom of competition, prevails over any use of a rule of
> national intellectual property law in a manner contrary to those principles.[288]

In the Magill[289] cases, in justifying its decision, the Court of First Instance stated
that:

> Within the system of the Treaty, Article 36 must be interpreted 'in the light of the
> Community's objectives and activities as defined by Articles 2 and 3 of the EEC Treaty',
> as the Court of Justice held in its judgment of 9 February 1982 in Case 270/8 (*Polydor
> v. Harlequin* [1982] ECR 329, para. 16.). That assessment must take into account, in
> particular, the requirements arising out of the establishment of a system of free
> competition within the Community, referred to in Article 3(f), which take the form,
> inter alia, of the prohibitions laid down in Articles 85 and 86 of the Treaty.

---

[285] Case T—69/89 *Radio Telefis Eireann v. EC Commission* [1991] 4 CMLR 586, paras. 70 and 71;
Case T—70/89 *The British Broadcasting and BBC Enterprises Ltd v. EC Commission* [1991] 4
CMLR 669, paras. 57 and 58; Case T—76/89 *Independent Television Publications Ltd v. EC
Commission* [1991] 4 CMLR 745, paras 55 and 56.

[286] The Court also referred to the judgment in Case 341/87 *EMI Electrola v. Patricia Im- und Export*
[1989] ECR 79 [1989] 2 CMLR 413.

[287] The Court referred to both Case 187/80 *Merck & Co v. Stephar* [1981] ECR 2063, [1983] 3
CMLR 463 and Case 19/85 *Pharmon v. Hoechst* [1985] ECR 2281, [1985] 3 CMLR 775, with
regard to patents, and to Case 158/86 *Warner Brothers v. Christiansen* [1988] ECR 2605, [1990] 4
CMLR 684 with regard to copyright.

[288] In Case 78/70 *Deutsche Grammophon Gesellschaft mbH v. Metro-SB-Grossmärkte GmbH & Co KG*
[1971] ECR 487, [1971] CMLR 631, Advocate General Roemer stated that 'if an economic study
of the market leads to discovery of the existence of a dominant position in that market and if
that dominant position is used for the purpose of an abuse within the second paragraph of
Article 86 by the exercise of industrial property rights, in certain circumstances there may be an
abuse of those rights'.

[289] Case T—69/89 *Radio Telefis Eireann v. EC Commission* [1991] 4 CMLR 586, para. 68; Case
T—70/89 *The British Broadcasting and BBC Enterprises Ltd v. EC Commission* [1991] 4 CMLR
669, para. 55; Case T—76/89 *Independent Television Publications Ltd v. EC Commission* [1991] 4
CMLR 745, para. 53.

4.149. Proportionality principle. To justify its liberal interpretation of Article 36, the Court employs a proportionality principle. As it noted in the Magill cases:

> Article 36 thus emphasises that the reconciliation between the requirements of the free movement of goods and the respect to which intellectual property rights are entitled must be achieved in such a way as to protect the legitimate exercise of such rights, which alone is justified within the meaning of that Article, and to preclude any improper exercise thereof likely to create artificial partitions within the market or pervert the rules governing competition within the Community.

(5) Abuses of Intellectual Property Rights by Media Undertakings

(i)   Pricing Abuses

4.150. Deutsche Grammophon Gesellschaft mbH v. Metro-SB-Grossmärkte GmbH & Co KG. *Deutsche Grammophon Gesellschaft mbH v. Metro-SB-Grossmärkte GmbH & Co KG,*[290] is one of the earliest cases to concern a potential abuse of intellectual property rights. The facts were as follows. The Appellant owned exclusive recording contracts with a number of high profile artists and distributed recordings of those artists in various Member States through both subsidiary companies and unconnected undertakings. Each distribution agreement obliged the distributor to ensure that the records were marketed at a price fixed by the Appellant. The Respondent had been supplied in France with records by Polydor, one of the Appellant subsidiaries, and imported them into Germany. Since it was not bound by any undertaking to observe a fixed retail price, it sold the records to its customers at around a third less than the Appellant's usual selling price. The Appellant realised that the Respondent was not bound to maintain the regulated prices, and accordingly refused to supply it with recordings through Polydor. But the Respondent managed to obtain those recordings from a third party supplied by Polydor and once again sold them at a discount in Germany. The Appellant obtained an injunction in Germany prohibiting the Respondent from selling any Polydor records there and on an Article 177 reference to the Court, the German Appeal Court, asked whether the Appellant was abusing its dominant position by attempting to regulate the retail price of its records in this manner in Germany. The Court of Justice held that:

> The difference between the controlled price and the price of the product reimported from another Member State does not necessarily suffice to disclose such an abuse; it may however [ie the disparity in prices may], if unjustified by any objective criteria and if it is particularly marked, be a determining factor in such abuse.[291]

Advocate General Roemer hammered home the principle that if 'the differences in price are considerable and disproportionate, and constitute decisive evidence of an abuse of a dominant position within the market, according to previous case-law the use of industrial property rights for the purposes of partitioning the market and the maintenance of the price difference must be held to constitute an abuse and fall within the prohibitions of Article 86 of the EEC Treaty'.[292] To determine whether the differences were based upon objective criteria 'it is necessary to consider not only the manufacturer's selling prices but also the retail prices, and to be aware that

---

[290]   Case 78/70 [1971] ECR 487, [1971] CMLR 631.

[291]   *Ibid.,* para. 19. See also Case 24/67 *Parke, Davis & Co v. Probel* [1968] ECR 55, [1968] CMLR 47 and Case 40/70 *Sirena Srl v. Eda Srl* [1971] ECR 69 [1971] CMLR 260.

[292]   Case 78/70 *Deutsche Grammophon Gesellschaft mbH v. Metro-SB-Grossmärkte GmbH & Co KG* [1971] ECR 487, [1971] CMLR 631, per Advocate General Roemer.

the different burdens of value added tax. . . .[in this particular case, 11% in Germany and 33⅓% in France] must be taken into account and that different costs may be due to the marketing structure and the amount of the copyright royalties to be paid [to the relevant collecting society].'[293]

(ii) Preventing the Emergence of a New Product in a Derivative Market

4.151. Magill cases. In the Magill[294] cases the Court of First Instance held that the Applicants had abused their copyright in programme listings. By reserving the exclusive right to publish their weekly television programme listings, they were preventing the emergence on the market of a new product, namely a general television magazine likely to compete with their own magazines. The Applicants were thus using their copyright in the programme listings which they produced as part of their broadcasting activities in order to secure a monopoly in the derivative market of weekly television guides. It was significant that one of the Applicants had authorised reproduction of highlights of those listings free in the United Kingdom and Northern Ireland and even allowed the publication of weekly listings free of charge in other Member States. The Court held that:

Conduct of that type—characterised by preventing the production and marketing of a new product, for which there is potential consumer demand, on the ancillary market of television magazines and thereby excluding all competition from that market solely in order to secure the Applicant's monopoly—clearly goes beyond what is necessary to fulfil the essential function of the copyright as permitted in Community law. The Applicant's refusal to authorise third parties to publish its weekly listings was, in this case, arbitrary in so far as it was not justified either by the specific needs of the broadcasting sector, with which the present case is not concerned, or by those peculiar to the activity of publishing television magazines. It was thus possible for the Applicant to adapt to the conditions of a television magazine market which was open to competition in order to ensure the commercial viability of its weekly publication, the Radio Times [TV Times] [RTE Guide]. The Applicant's conduct cannot, therefore, be covered in Community law by the protection conferred by its copyright in the programme listings.

The Court distinguished this decision from its judgment in *Volvo v. Veng*[295] and *CICRA v. Renault*,[296] where the Court of First Instance held lawful the refusal by car manufacturers to license third parties to manufacture and market spare parts for which the car manufacturers owned design rights. In those cases the manufacture and marketing of spare parts fell within the manufacturer's main activities. In the Magill cases, on the other hand, the Applicant's main activity concerned broadcasting, the publication of programme listings being an ancillary activity. An analogy could therefore be made between the Applicant's actions and the arbitrary refusal by a car manufacturer to supply spare parts—produced in the course of his main activity of car making—to an independent repairer carrying on his business on the derivative market of automobile maintenance and repair. It was also similar to a case where a car manufacturer refused to produce spare parts for certain models

---

[293] Ibid.
[294] Case T—69/89 *Radio Telefís Eireann v. EC Commission* [1991] 4 CMLR 586; Case T—70/89 *The British Broadcasting and BBC Enterprises Ltd v. EC Commission* [1991] 4 CMLR 669; Case T—76/89 *Independent Television Publications Ltd v. EC Commission* [1991] 4 CMLR 745, upholding the Commission's Decision against the Applicants.
[295] Case 238/87 [1988] ECR 6211.
[296] Case 53/87 [1988] ECR 6039.

even though there was still a market for those products. In short, the Applicant's action 'was in particular characterised, in that regard, by a failure to take consumer needs into consideration. . . '

10. Abuses of Intellectual Property by Collecting Societies

(1) General Principles—The Balancing Exercise

4.152.   Introduction. Despite their key role in preserving the Community's creative talent, both the Court and the Commission have found certain practices of collecting societies to be incompatible with Article 86.   These practices, as well as the Court and Commission's approach, are analysed below.[297]

4.153. The Courts of Justice's view. *In Belgische Radio en Televisie (BRT) v. SV SABAM*,[298] the Court of Justice outlined its task and forged certain general principles which it uses to assess the legality of practices conducted by collecting societies. It held that:

> According to the terms of Article 86(a) an abuse must be regarded as consisting, in particular, in directly or indirectly imposing unfair trading conditions.
>
> It is therefore necessary to investigate whether the copyright association, through its statutes or contracts concluded with its members, is imposing, directly or indirectly, unfair conditions on members or third parties in the exploitation of works, the protection of which has been entrusted to it.
>
> For this appraisal account must be taken of all the relevant interests, for the purpose of ensuring a balance between the requirement of maximum freedom for authors, composers, and publishers to dispose of their works and that of the effective management of their rights by an undertaking which in practice they avoid joining.

The Court went on to rule that:

> The fact that an undertaking entrusted with the exploitation of copyrights and occupying a dominant position within the meaning of Article 86 imposes on its members obligations which are not absolutely necessary for the attainment of its object and which thus encroach unfairly upon a member's freedom to exercise his copyright can constitute an abuse.
>
> If abusive practices are exposed, it is for the national court to decide whether and to what extent they affect the interests of authors or third parties concerned, with a view to deciding the consequences with regard to the validity and effect of the contracts in dispute or certain of their provisions.

4.154. The Commission's view. The Commission has similarly acknowledged the need for collecting societies. This perceived need is reflected in its approach to potential Article 86 violations, an approach which echoes that of the Court of Justice. Thus in Re GEMA Statutes,[299] it stated:

> In its Decision of 22 June 1971 relating to GEMA, (OJ No L 134, 20.6.1971), the

---

[297] On the problems encountered by collecting societies in administering entrusted rights, see W Nordemann, Current difficulties encountered by copyright societies within the European Economic Community, RIDA [1988], 135, 31.

[298] Case 127/73 [1974] ECR 313, [1974] 2 CMLR 238, paras. 6 to 8.

[299] Commission Decision 82/204/EEC OJ No L 94, 08.04.82, p.12, [1982] 2 CMLR 482, para. 37.

Commission also recognised the need for joint copyright protection by collecting societies to counterbalance the user's market strength. Collecting society membership is above all necessary in relation to communication to the public and broadcasting rights, where copyright holders are up against powerful users of music and the demand side i.e. the listener, can exert only a very limited influence on these users. Only through the collecting societies therefore can the copyright holders obtain the fair compensation due for their intellectual labour.

(2) Specific Abuses of Members

(i) Excessive Obligations Concerning Assignment of Works, Duration of Assignment and Geographical Coverage

4.155. Belgische Radio en Televisie (BRT) v. SV SABAM. Collecting societies have often insisted that their members forfeit any right to exploit their copyright works themselves not only in their own State but throughout all Member States of the Community (and sometimes throughout the world). The legitimacy of this form of 'mandatory assignment' of copyright was considered first by the Court of Justice in *Belgische Radio en Televisie (BRT) v. SV SABAM*.[300] Since 1940, SABAM had been the only undertaking in Belgium having the task of exploiting copyright, in particular in the field of musical compositions. No composer, author or music publisher could, in reality, avoid the obligation to have recourse to SABAM's services in order to exercise his rights. As a condition of membership, SABAM demanded the global assignment of all present and future copyrights without drawing any distinction between specific categories of such rights and it continued to exercise the rights assigned for five years following the withdrawal of an artist's membership. The Court of Justice stated that:

> To determine whether, in these circumstances, the practices mentioned in the referring judgment constitute an abuse within the meaning of Article 86 of the Treaty account must however be taken of the fact that an undertaking of the type envisaged is an association whose object is to protect the rights and interests of its individual members against, in particular, major exploiters and distributors of musical material, such as radio broadcasting bodies and record manufacturers.
>
> For an association effectively to protect its rights and interests it must enjoy a position based on the assignment in its favour, by the associated authors, of their rights to the extent required for the association to carry out its activity on the necessary scale.
>
> Consequently, it is desirable to examine whether the practices in dispute exceed the limit absolutely necessary for the attainment of this object, with due regard also to the interest which the individual author may have that his freedom to dispose of his work is not limited more than need be.
>
> For this purpose, a compulsory assignment of all copyrights, both present and future, no distinction being drawn between the different generally accepted types of exploitation, may appear an unfair condition, especially if such assignment is required for an extended period after the member's withdrawal.

Advocate General Mayras pointed out that:

> . . . an author or composer, and even a publisher of musical material—unless, in respect of this last case, it is a very powerful undertaking—has not, in practice, the power to exercise his rights himself. He does not have at his disposal the means to supervise the

---

[300] Case 127/73 [1974] ECR 313, [1974] 2 CMLR 238.

different uses which can be made of his work. In addition, some exploiters of musical material (record manufacturers, public authorities and private companies concerned with radio and television broadcasting) occupy such a strong position on the market that it enables them completely to control authors and composers by requiring the assignment of some of their works, especially those which are very successful and whose exploitation is particularly profitable.

In spite of these observations, it was confirmed that the duration and generalised nature of the assignment applying as it did, to both present and future rights could not be justified in view of the principles voiced by the Court.

4.156. Greenwich Film Production v. SACEM. *Greenwich Film Production v. SACEM*[301] concerned a dispute over the requirement of SACEM, the French collecting society, that two of its members assign the management of their works to SACEM for the entire world. Two author members had assigned to the Appellant company, via an intermediary publisher, the right to exploit certain of their works in third countries. Relying on its absolute rights, SACEM however sued the Appellant for royalties due to SACEM for the public performance of the works in issue. On appeal, the Appellant argued that SACEM was abusing its dominant position by demanding a global assignment of works. The Court of Justice first had to consider whether there was an effect on trade 'between' Member States,[302] even though, the territory in issue was outside of the Community. The Court stated that there was no reason to distinguish between production intended for sale within the Common Market and that intended for export, because restrictions on the latter could affect the competitive structure of the Common Market.[303] As Advocate General Warner explained '. . . it would hinder the freedom of authors to 'shop around' for the services of performing right societies in other Member States in respect of some categories of their rights or in respect of the exploitation of their rights in some countries. . . a French author or composer might think the British Performing Right Society better placed than the SACEM to look after the exploitation of his copyright in English-speaking countries.' The Court thus held that:

> . . . It is possible in those circumstances that the activities of such associations may be conducted in such a way that their effect is to partition the Common Market and thereby restrict the freedom to provide services which constitutes one of the objectives of the Treaty. Such activities are thus capable of affecting trade between Member States within the meaning of Article 86 of the Treaty, even if the management of copyrights, in certain cases, relates only to the performance of musical works in non-member countries. In considering whether Article 86 is applicable the performance of certain contracts cannot be assessed in isolation but must be viewed in the light of the activities of the undertaking in question as a whole.[304]

4.157. Terms acceptable in accordance with Commission Decisions. The precise contours of acceptable terms, have been defined by the Commission chiefly in a series of Decisions against GEMA, the German collecting society, which managed rights on behalf of composers, authors and music publishers. In Re

---

[301] Case 22/79 [1979] ECR 3275, [1980] 1 CMLR 629.

[302] See §4.121 above.

[303] The Court affirmed Joined Cases 6, 7/73 *Istituto Chemioterapico Italiano SpA and Commercial Solvents Corpn v. EC Commission* [1974] ECR 223, [1974] 1 CMLR 309.

[304] [1979] ECR 3275, [1980] 1 CMLR 629, para. 12.

GEMA, the Commission held that the collecting society was culpable of an abuse by requiring an author to assign his present and future copyright for all categories of his work and all forms of exploitation throughout the whole world.[305] The Commission held that while there was usually no objection to a collecting society requiring the exclusive assignment of all the works of an artist for the territory in which the society carried on direct activity, members had to be free to assign their rights to another collecting society for those countries in which the collecting society did not carry on any direct activity.[306] This was subsequently qualified, in Re GEMA (No.2), by the proviso that the longer the duration of commitment to the society, the narrower must be its scope, in terms of the categories of work and the mode of exploitation, if the conduct is not to amount to an abuse.[307] The Commission has approved of an agreement where on resignation of membership a society was entitled to continue to exercise copyright for three years when the author had been offered the opportunity of assigning his rights for particular forms of exploitation (ie performance rights) and one year when he assigned his rights for specific categories of forms of exploitation (ie performance by broadcasting).[308]

(ii) Discrimination against an Artist who is a National of another Member State by Refusing to Accord any Rights

4.158. GVL v. EC Commission. The Commission has decided[309] and the Court of Justice confirmed[310] that a collecting society is culpable of an abuse within the meaning of Article 86 if it refuses to administer the rights of an artist who is a national of another Member State. The Gesellschaft zur Verwertung von Leistungsschutzrechten mbH known as 'GVL' was solely responsible for the management of the exploitation of performers' rights in Germany. Prior to the Commission's action, GVL refused to conclude management agreements with foreign artists, (including those from other Member States), who were not resident in Germany.

4.159. Breach of Article 7 of the Treaty. The Commission held that the prohibitions contained in Article 86 had to be interpreted in the light of the general principles enshrined in the EEC Treaty. One of those principles is embodied in Article 7 which provides that any discrimination on the grounds of nationality shall be prohibited. As a rule, therefor, any discriminatory treatment by a dominant undertaking on grounds of nationality must be regarded automatically as an infringement of Article 86.[311]

In upholding the Decision the Court of Justice stated that:

Such a refusal by an undertaking having a de facto monopoly to provide its services for all those who may be in need of them but who do not come within a certain category of persons defined by the undertaking on the basis of nationality or residence must be

---

[305] Commission Decision 71/224/EEC Re GEMA OJ No L 134, 20.06.71, p.15, [1971] CMLR D35.
[306] *Ibid.*
[307] Commission Decision 72/268/EEC Re GEMA (No 2) OJ No L 166, 24.07.72, p.12, [1972] CMLR D115.
[308] Commission action against SABAM referred to in Case 127/73 *Belgische Radio en Televisie (BRT) v. SV SABAM* [1974] ECR 51, [1974] 2 CMLR 238, per Advocate General Mayras. See also Commission Decision 72/268/EEC Re GEMA (No 2) OJ No L 166, 24.07.72, p.12, [1972] CMLR D115, where the Commission approved of a three year period.
[309] Commission Decision 81/1030/EEC Re GVL OJ No L370, 28.12.81, p.49, [1982] 1 CMLR 221.
[310] Case 7/82 GVL *v. EC Commission* [1983] ECR 483, [1983] 3 CMLR 645.
[311] Affirming the Court of Justice's decision in Case 155/73 *Sacchi* [1974] ECR 409, [1974] 2 CMLR 177.

regarded as an abuse of a dominant position within the meaning of the first paragraph of Article 86 of the Treaty.[312]

Advocate General Reischl stated as regards the burden of proof that:

> Thus as regards the management of secondary exploitation rights the only question is whether an artist really does hold the rights which he claims and the burden of proof in relation to this lies on the artist, regardless of his residence.

4.160. Breach of Article 86(c) of the Treaty. As well as transgressing Article 7, the Commission held that GVL's behaviour specifically contravened Article 86(c) of the Treaty. That Article states that an abuse may, in particular, consist of:

> applying dissimilar conditions to equivalent transactions with other trading parties, thereby placing them at a competitive disadvantage.

The Commission said that:

> The transaction ('trade') within the meaning of Article 86 (c) between artists and GVL consists in the fact that GVL's service, namely affording management of rights is provided only in return for valuable consideration, i.e. GVL's administrative share of the royalties collected.[313]

The specific prohibition of discrimination laid down in Article 86(c) of the Treaty comes into operation only where there is a disturbance of competition at the level of the trading partners of the dominant undertaking. The Court confirmed that 'the competition being referred to must be understood as competition in a very general sense where the trading partners of the dominant undertaking have a direct relationship with their consumers when rendering their service'.[314] Thus artists are deemed to compete with each other by selling their performances to 'consumers' in the most remunerative way possible. Although the Court accepted that the quality of the performance—a matter over which the collecting society has no influence—can be decisive to the success of an artist, it emphasised that he may also be dependent on representation by a collecting society. For an artist who is not well known, his ability to compete with other artists can depend on how competitively he can offer his services. Since this can be determined by his resources, an artist who is not able to claim remuneration for the exploitation of his work in a particular Member State, is placed at a competitive disadvantage in the market in general.[315]

The Commission confirmed that a dominant undertaking cannot counter the accusation of discrimination by maintaining that the 'trading partner' criterion is lacking, when it prevents some of its natural trading partners from becoming actual trading partners by imposing an additional requirement such as residence in a particular Member State.

Finally, it should be noted that an undertaking may not justify its discriminatory behaviour by asserting that other Member States do not offer the same rights. The point is, that a Member State must offer the identical rights to all members of the Community, regardless of their nationality or residence and regardless of a disparity in Community laws.[316]

---

[312] [1983] ECR 483, [1983] 3 CMLR 645, para. 36.

[313] OJ No L370, 28.12.81, p.49, para. 49. Affirmed by the Court, per Advocate General Reischl, stating that it is irrelevant that the respective artists are not competing with each other for the collecting society's services.

[314] Per Advocate General Reischl.

[315] Ibid.

[316] Ibid.

(iii) Discrimination against a Member who is a National of another Member State by Refusing to Accord Equivalent Rights

4.161. The Commission has held that the collecting society GEMA, was abusing its dominant position by refusing voting rights to foreign artists who were not resident in the Federal Republic of Germany.[317] Prejudice consisted of two elements. First, unlike nationals, these persons could not influence the management policy of GEMA ie by voting or holding office. The Commission said that it was no defence that GEMA treated both nationals and non-nationals equally in the general distribution of fees. Secondly, they were deprived of certain direct financial benefits.[318] The Commission held that where a society such as GEMA, required a minimum revenue over a given period before according office, income received by the applicant from previous membership of a foreign society must be taken into account in calculating that figure.

(iv) Miscellaneous Abuses

4.162. The Commission has held that a collecting society may not refuse rights of office to national publishers simply because they have economic or legal connections with foreign publishers because that type of restriction must be regarded as inimical to economic and personal contacts abroad.[319] Neither may such a society limit loyalty bonuses to certain members only, if all the members contribute towards the funds from which those payments are made.[320] It is also unlawful for a society to prevent its members from appealing to the courts for review of the distribution of payments.[321] It is no answer to say that the society is subject to administrative supervision, for such control does not guarantee to each member that individual account will be taken of his rights in calculating payments.[322]

(3) Specific Abuses of Users

(i) Restricting the Importation of Recordings

4.163. According to well-settled case law of the Court of Justice, it is unlawful under the doctrine of exhaustion of rights, to impede the importation of sound recordings that have been lawfully placed on the market in another Member State following payment of royalties.[323] The Commission has held that it is was an abuse for a collecting society to oppose cross-frontier deliveries of recordings between

---

[317] Commission Decision 71/224/EEC Re GEMA OJ No L 134, 20.06.71, p.15, [1971] CMLR D35.

[318] See also Case 127/73 *Belgische Radio en Televisie (BRT) v. SV SABAM* [1974] ECR 51, [1974] 2 CMLR 238, where Advocate General Mayras commented that provisions, previously in force in SABAM's statutes which (a) prevented nationals of other Member States from participating in the administration of the association and (b) denied them benefits from the mutual aid fund even though they were obliged to contribute to the latter, would have been in breach of Article 86.

[319] Commission Decision 71/224/EEC Re GEMA OJ No L 134, 20.06.71, p.15, [1971] CMLR D35. Nevertheless, the Commission stated that the voting rights of such users may be curtailed.

[320] *Ibid.*

[321] *Ibid.*

[322] *Ibid.*

[323] Joined Cases 55, 57/80 *Musik-Vertrieb membran GmbH v. GEMA* [1981] ECR 147, [1981] 2 CMLR 44 and Case 395/87 *Ministère Public v. Tournier* [1989] ECR 2521, [1991] 4 CMLR 248. See §§1.006 and 1.010 above.

companies belonging to the same group. The Commission rejected the society's claim that the records were not in free circulation (ie that rights had not been exhausted) because they had not yet been supplied to retailers.[324]

(ii) Claiming Additional 'Mechanical Royalties'

4.164. The Commission has held it to be an abuse for a collecting society to charge a manufacturer royalties on recordings imported into its state where royalties have already been paid by the manufacturer in another Member State.[325]

Sometimes manufacturers obtain a manufacturing licence from a collecting society in one Member State to whom they pay royalties but have the pressings made by a subcontractor in another Member State. This is known as 'custom pressing'. GEMA had announced its intention to charge royalties on all custom pressing work carried out in the Federal Republic of Germany, regardless of the fact that a royalty had already been paid by the manufacturer in another Member State. The Commission objected stating that in its opinion, 'a licence granted by a Community copyright protection society is valid throughout the Community, and authorises manufacture, even by way of custom pressing, in any member-State.'[326]

(iii) Continuing Obligation to Pay Performance Royalties

4.165. The difference between lawful and unlawful royalty charges can be quite subtle. In *Basset v. Société des auteurs, compositeurs et éditeurs de Musique (SACEM)*,[327] the owner of a discotheque sued SACEM, the French collecting society for abusing its dominant position by charging a 'mechanical royalty' in addition to a performance royalty for the use of the phonograms protected by the society. The Court of Justice looked to the substance of the charge rather than its form and stated that 'leaving aside the concepts used by French legislation and practice, the supplementary royalty in respect of mechanical rights can be described as forming part of the royalty payment for public performance of a recorded musical work.' It therefore fulfilled a function which was equivalent to that of the performing right charged on the same occasion in another Member State.[328] Decisively, the Court found that the amount of the additional mechanical royalty was calculated, like that of a proper performance royalty on the basis of the discotheque's turnover and not on the basis of the number of discs purchased or performed. Accordingly, the Court ruled:

> The prohibitions laid down in Article 86 of the EEC Treaty, properly construed, do not apply to the conduct of a national copyright-management society simply because it charges a royalty called a 'supplementary mechanical reproduction fee', in addition to a performance royalty, on the public performance of sound recordings, even where such

---

[324] Commission Statement of 9 January 1984, Re Performing Rights Societies IP (84) 7, [1984] 1 CMLR 308. But as for whether this reasoning is consistent with the Court's case law, see §1.017 fn 53 above.

[325] Commission Decision 71/224/EEC Re GEMA OJ No L 134, 20.06.71, p.15, [1971] CMLR D35.

[326] Commission Statement of 6 February 1985, Re Performing Rights Societies [1985] 2 CMLR 1.

[327] Case 402/85 [1987] ECR 1747, [1987] 3 CMLR 173.

[328] See Case 395/87 *Ministére Public v. Tournier* [1989] ECR 2521, [1991] 4 CMLR 248. See §1.043 above.

a supplementary fee is not provided for in the Member State where those sound recordings were lawfully placed on the market.[329]

(iv) Level of Royalty

4.166. In *Ministère Public v. Tournier*,[330] and a series of joined subsequent cases,[331] the Court of Justice was asked to judge the legality of the level of royalties charged by a collecting society to discotheque owners where those rates were markedly different from the rates charged in other Member States. The Court formulated the following general principle to be applied in assessing such cases:

> When an undertaking holding a dominant position imposes scales of fees for its services which are appreciably higher than those charged in other Member States and where a comparison of the fee levels has been made on a consistent basis, that difference must be regarded as indicative of an abuse of a dominant position. In such a case it is for the undertaking in question to justify the difference by reference to objective dissimilarities between the situation in the Member State concerned and the situation prevailing in all the other Member States.

The Court examined the merit of a number of arguments which might be asserted to justify differences:

(1) It rejected arguments based on differences in operating costs: 'Where—as appears to be the case here, according to the record of the proceedings before the national court—the staff of a management society is much larger than that of its counterparts in other Member States and, moreover, the proportion of receipts taken up by collection, administration and distribution expenses rather than by payment to copyright holders is considerably higher, the possibility cannot be ruled out that it is precisely the lack of competition on the market in question that accounts for the heavy burden of administration and hence the high level of royalties'.

(2) A high level of prices charged by the discotheques could not in itself be used to justify differences since these might be due to a number of factors, one of which might be the high level of the collecting societies' charges.

(3) A higher level of protection in a Member State might justify differential royalty charges, but the existence of an 'additional mechanical royalty' (as in France) did not indicate a higher level of protection.

(4) A flat-rate royalty could only be impugned under Article 86 if other methods of collection might be capable of attaining the same legitimate aim, namely, the protection of the interests of authors, composers and publishers of music, without thereby increasing the costs of managing contracts and monitoring the use of protected works.[332]

---

[329] The Court did not discount the possibility that the level of the mechanical royalty was excessive but stated that this was a matter upon which only the national court could give a ruling.

[330] Case 395/87 [1989] ECR 2521, [1991] 4 CMLR 248.

[331] Case 110/88 *Lucazeau v. Société des auteurs, compositeurs et éditeurs de musique* [1989] ECR 2811, [1991] 4 CMLR 248; Case 241/88 *Société des auteurs, compositeurs et éditeurs de musique v. Debelle* [1989] ECR 2811, [1991] 4 CMLR 248; Case 242/88 *Société des auteurs, compositeurs et éditeurs de musique v. Soumanagnac* [1989] ECR 2811, [1991] 4 CMLR 248.

[332] See also Case 402/85 *Basset v. Societe des auteurs, compositeurs et editeurs de Musique (SACEM)* [1987] ECR 1747, [1987] 3 CMLR 173, where Advocate General Lenz stated that 'when charging royalties to discothèques and other users of phonograms, it is essential to proceed on the basis of a global rate,..' in fact, specifically provided for by the French copyright Act of 11 March 1957.

Advocate General Jacobs underscored the difficulties in determining whether a price charged for the use of copyright material is a fair price. He said that the orthodox principles usually employed by the Court cannot be directly transposed into this situation,[333] ie it is not appropriate to make a comparison between the costs of production and the selling price 'because it is impossible to determine the costs of the creation of a work of the imagination such as a musical work'. Nevertheless, some objective method was called for such as making 'a comparison between the level of the royalty (taking account for this purpose of the total revenue generated by the royalty) on the one hand, and the necessary costs of the effective management of performing rights and the need to ensure reasonable remuneration of copyright owners on the other hand.' The Advocate General pointed out that it was misleading to focus on the amount of the royalty paid to one particular class of copyright owner, because copyright in a musical work was owned and exploited by a number of different persons for a number of different purposes. On the other hand, the relationship between the level of the royalty and amount actually paid to copyright owners as a whole would be a useful method. In this case, it appeared that the amount of the royalty set aside for management costs was disproportionately high in relation to the amount paid to copyright owners.

An accusation of discrimination had been levelled at SACEM. In response, the Advocate General said that it would appropriate to consider the level of royalties paid by other important music users of material protected by the collecting society. If these were less and there lacked objective justification for the difference, then an abuse, especially in contravention of Article 86(c) might be established.

The Commission has objected to societies charging manufacturers royalties according to the rates prevailing in the country where the records were eventually sold by retailers, rather than basing royalties on the manufacturer's published selling prices. This form of levy meant that a single manufacturer had to pay widely differing royalties depending on the country of sale. It also prevented any cost or price advantages that arose in the country of manufacture from being passed on to the consumers in the country of sale. Since royalties were based not on the sales revenue of the manufacturer but on the level of retail prices, over which the manufacturers had no direct influence, this system lacked any objective basis of assessment.[334]

(v) Charging for Unprotected Works

4.167. The Commission has held it an abuse for a collecting society to require royalties for works which are not protected by copyright.[335] GEMA had attempted to charge manufacturers who tried to obtain an increased sale of a record by adding works in the public domain to an attractive portion of music in which they owned rights.

---

[333] See e.g. Case 27/76 *United Brands Co v. EC Commission* [1978] ECR 207, [1978] 1 CMLR 429, where the Court of Justice indicated that it is necessary to consider whether the difference between the costs actually incurred in producing the product and the price actually incurred is excessive and, if the answer to that is affirmative, whether a price has been imposed which is unfair in itself compared with competing products. See §4.132 et seq. above.

[334] Commission Statement of 9 January 1984 Re Performing Rights Societies, IP (84) 7, [1984] 1 CMLR 308.

[335] Commission Decision 71/224/EEC Re GEMA OJ No L134, 20.06.71, p.15, [1971] CMLR D35.

(4) Miscellaneous Issues

(i) Prohibiting Tying Agreements Between Users and Artists

4.168. GEMA concluded exploitation contracts with users who included, amongst others, radio and television stations, sound recording manufacturers, theatre orchestras and discotheque owners. In the case of performing or broadcasting rights, royalties were determined according to the type, duration and frequency of use and in the case of mechanical reproduction according to the number of copies of the sound recording sold. Certain of GEMA's members had sought to influence the playing time and regularity of the performance of their works by the users by promising to reimburse the users with some of the fees they received from GEMA. By doing so, the members increased the royalties which were paid by GEMA. The preferential selection of certain works was limiting the access of other members' work to broadcasting time thus reducing their potential royalties. Another scam was solely operated by the users who charged the copyright owner for the exploitation of works in respect of which the user would be have to pay a royalty to GEMA. GEMA had sought approval from the Commission for incorporating a clause in its governing statute which would put a stop to users operating in this way.

The Commission confirmed that it was vital that an association such as GEMA should not be influenced by parties representing the user's interest or those persons economically dependent on them, and that it should adopt a uniform treatment to all its users. It said, therefor that the proposed clause could amount to an abuse in breach of Article 86 if it was 'not indispensable or excessive':

> GEMA would exceed the bounds of necessity if it wanted to induce the users to withhold all preferential treatment of its individual member's works or to treat them all the same. This would be completely inconsistent with the user's need to select only certain music works out of the numerous works offered them. Similarly GEMA is not entitled to prevent the beneficiaries from paying the users for publicity, distinguished as such, to promote the sale of copies of certain works (paid advertising).[336]

It is important to note that the Commission did not rule out the legality, under competition law, of an arrangement whereby a beneficiary gives a share of its revenue to a user. It censured such action only where the object is to favour works unjustifiably. It stated:

> By the new provision, GEMA restricts itself to prohibiting the beneficiaries from granting shares of royalty revenue to users, only where the purpose is to favour certain works of said beneficiaries. In such cases the granting of the share and the preferential treatment must be directly linked by a specific objective.
>
> The mere fact of participation pursuant to company law or the existence of joint publishing agreements between beneficiaries and parties to collective agreements are not in themselves caught by the new provision. GEMA only wishes to prevent those contracts whereby the users seek, by exploiting certain works frequently and taking no account of public taste and qualitative criteria, to share in the royalties collected by GEMA, helping themselves, as it were, without any restrictions. In this way GEMA protects its membership as a whole.[337]

---

[336] Commission Decision 82/204/EEC Re GEMA Statutes OJ No L 94, 08.04.82, p.12, [1982] 2 CMLR 482, para. 45.

[337] Ibid., para. 52. The Commission left open the question of whether an individual author who has not assigned his copyright to a collecting society may be entitled to enter into an arrangement with a user under which the user is paid by the copyright owner for preferential treatment of his work. It would probably strike down such an arrangement as constituting a perversion of the principles governing copyright.

(5) Summary of Principles Applying to Collecting Societies

4.169. A synthesis of Court cases and Commission decisions yields the following general principles:

(1) In deciding whether a collecting society is acting in breach of Article 86, both the Court and the Commission conduct a balancing exercise. A balance must be struck between on the one hand, ensuring the maximum freedom of copyright owners to dispose of their works as they wish and on the other, the necessity of having powerful collecting societies for effective copyright management.

(2) An obligation to assign all categories of works for the Member State in which the collecting society carries on direct activity is lawful. But Members must be free to appoint collecting societies carrying on activities in foreign Member States, to represent them there. When membership ceases, any continuing obligation for representation in respect of existing works must be reasonable.

(3) Discrimination against non-national artists, either by refusing to enter into a management contract or entering into a contract but not on terms equivalent with those entered into with nationals, qualifies as an abuse generally in contravention of Article 86 and specifically in breach of Article 86(c) and Article 7 of the Treaty.

(4) Collecting societies are culpable of an abuse if they charge royalties on recordings already placed on the market, or impede the movement of those goods in any way. However, it is not an abuse to charge an 'additional mechanical royalty' for a performance of a work where this is, in essence, a performance royalty calculated in accordance with usual practices applying to performance royalties.

(5) An abuse may exist where a collecting society charges royalties at a level considerably higher than societies in other Member States, unless it can justify that disparity by objective criteria.

(6) A collecting society does not act in breach of Article 86 where it prohibits its members and users from entering into contracts between themselves to favour certain of the member's works.

IV. SPECIAL RULES APPLYING TO UNDERTAKINGS

1. Introduction

4.170. Many of the undertakings in the media industry are 'state' monopolies. The Treaty contains a set of rules, in Article 90, which dictate the relationship of the competition rules to such monopolies and in certain narrowly defined cases, allow exceptions to the competition rules. The sections below analyse the functions of Articles 90(1) and 90(2) and explain the remedies available. Article 90(3) confers upon the Commission, the role of enforcing Articles 90(1) and 90(2). The enforcement procedure is outside the scope of this work.[338]

---

[338] For analysis of the enforcement procedure, see Bellamy and Child, *op. cit.*, 13-001 et seq.

2. Article 90(1)—Public Undertakings and Undertakings with Exclusive Rights

(1) Introduction

4.171. Treaty terms. Article 90(1) is concerned with public undertakings and undertakings granted exclusive rights[339] by Member States. It states:

> In the case of public undertakings and undertakings to which Member States grant special or exclusive rights, Member States shall neither enact nor maintain in force any measure contrary to the rules contained in this Treaty, in particular to those rules provided for in Art. 7[340] and Arts. 85 to 94.

4.172. Definition of a 'public undertaking'. The Treaty does not define a 'public undertaking'. However, the Commission has defined such a body as 'any undertaking over which the public authorities may exercise directly or indirectly a dominant influence by virtue of their ownership of it, their financial participation therein, or the rules which govern it'.[341]

(2) Prohibition of Abuses by Undertakings Granted Exclusive Rights

(i) General Principles

4.173. Public undertakings. Despite the fact that the Treaty enables the State to confer monopolies on particular undertakings, the Court of Justice has emphasised that the prohibitions in Article 86 continue to apply:

> The interpretation of Articles 86 and 90 taken together leads to the conclusion that the fact that an undertaking to which a Member State grants exclusive rights has a monopoly is not as such incompatible with Article 86.[342]

And, of course, Article 86 will continue to operate where the State has widened the sphere of activities of an undertaking on which it has conferred exclusive rights:

> It is therefore the same as regards an extension of exclusive rights following a new intervention by this State.[343]

These two points have been summarised by the Court of Justice thus:

> ... Article 86 of the EEC Treaty must be interpreted as applying to an undertaking holding a dominant position on a particular market even where that position is due not to the activity of the undertaking itself but to the fact that by reason of provisions laid down by law there can be no competition or only very limited competition on that market.[344]

---

[339] But note that this Article is not referring to undertakings empowered with special functions. The latter are governed by Article 90(2). See §4.176 *et seq.* below.

[340] Article 7 states: 'Within the scope of application of this Treaty, and without prejudice to any special provisions contained therein, any discrimination on grounds of nationality shall be prohibited.'

[341] Commission Directive 80/723/EEC, OJ No L 195, 29.07.80 p.35.

[342] Case 155/73 *Sacchi* [1974] ECR 409, [1974] 2 CMLR 177, para. 14. The Court in Sacchi confirmed that Articles 85 and 86 continue to have direct effect.

[343] *Ibid.* In that case, the extension of RAI's television monopoly to include cable transmissions would have been sanctioned by the Treaty.

[344] Case 311/84 *Centre Belge d'Etudes de Marche-Tele-Marketing SA v. Compagnie Luxembourgeoise de Telediffusion SA* [1985] ECR 3261, [1986] 2 CMLR 558, para. 18.

Thus the Court of Justice has held that since the second sentence of Article 5 of the Treaty states that Member States 'shall abstain from any measure which could jeopardise the attainment of the objectives of this Treaty':

> Article 86 of the EEC Treaty prohibits any abuse by one or more undertakings of a dominant position, even if such abuse is encouraged by a national legislative provision.[345]

4.174. Private undertakings. Just as Article 86 prohibits an abuse of a dominant position by a public undertaking, so too it prohibits Member States from encouraging or permitting an abuse by a private undertaking:

> . . . Likewise, Member States may not enact measures enabling private undertakings to escape from the constraints imposed by Articles 85 to 94 of the Treaty.[346]

(ii) Prohibition of Abuses by Media Undertakings

4.175. Discrimination against foreign broadcasts. In Sacchi,[347] a case concerning the Italian broadcasting company RAI, the Court of Justice confirmed that broadcasting monopolies were lawful:

> Nothing in the Treaty prevents Member States, for considerations of public interest, of a non-economic nature, from removing radio and television transmissions, including cable transmissions, from the field of competition by conferring on one or more establishments an exclusive right to conduct them.

But the Court of Justice confirmed the general principle that any discrimination was prohibited:

> . . . for the performance of their tasks these establishments remain subject to the prohibitions against discrimination and, to the extent that this performance comprises activities of an economic nature, fall under the provisions referred to in Article 90 relating to public undertakings and undertakings to which Member States grant special or exclusive rights.

These principles have been affirmed by the Court of Justice in Elliniki Radiophonia Tiléorassi—Anonimi Etairia v. Dimotiki Etairia Pliroforissis:[348] where it held that:

> . . . Article 90(1) of the Treaty prohibits the granting of an exclusive right to transmit and an exclusive right to retransmit television broadcasts to a single undertaking, where those rights are liable to create a situation in which that undertaking is led to infringe Article 86 by virtue of a discriminatory broadcasting policy which favours its own programmes. . .

In that case, it was emphasised that it was of no matter that the monopoly had in fact retransmitted ten European programmes broadcast by satellite within a two year period since this was a mere practice not laid down by statute.[349]

---

[345] Case 13/77 GB-INNO-BM NV v. Vereniging van de Kleinhandelaars in Tabak [1977] ECR 2155, [1978] 1 CMLR 283, para. 34. See also Case C—260/89 Elliniki Radiophonia Tileorassi Anonimi Etairia v. Dimotiki Etairia Pliroforissis [1991] I ECR 2925.

[346] Case 13/77 GB-INNO-BM NV v. Vereniging van de Kleinhandelaars in Tabak [1977] ECR 2155, [1978] 1 CMLR 283, para. 33. See also Case C—260/89 Elliniki Radiophonia Tileorassi Anonimi Etairia v. Dimotiki Etairia Pliroforissis [1991] I ECR 2925.

[347] Case 155/73 [1974] ECR 409, [1974] 2 CMLR 177, para. 34.

[348] Case C—260/89 [1991] 1 CMLR 2925, para. 38.

[349] Per Advocate General Lenz. The Advocate General went as far as to say that the best means of ensuring no danger of discrimination, was to abolish the retransmission monopoly.

3. Application of the Treaty to Undertakings Entrusted with Special Functions—Article 90(2)

(1) Introduction

4.176. Treaty terms. Article 90(2) contains rules for undertakings entrusted with special functions by Member States. It states:

Undertakings entrusted with the operation of services of general economic interest or having the character of a revenue-producing monopoly shall be subject to the rules contained in this Treaty, in particular to the rules on competition, in so far as the application of such rules does not obstruct the performance, in law or in fact, of the particular tasks assigned to them. The development of trade must not be affected to such an extent as would be contrary to the interests of the Community.

(2) Definition of these Undertakings

(i) General Principles

4.177. Precisely what types of undertaking constitute 'Undertakings entrusted with the operation of services of general economic interest or having the character of a revenue-producing monopoly' is far from clear. As the Court of Justice has emphasised, the concept of 'general economic interest' in particular is in fact extremely wide and overlaps with that of public economic services of an industrial or commercial nature.[350] Private undertakings may come under that provision, but they must be entrusted with the operation of services of general economic interest by an act or measure of the public authority.[351] And the requirement that they be assigned with a task by the State excludes those undertakings which have taken up an opportunity to conduct such a task as opposed to having had a task specifically conferred upon them.[352] It also has the effect of excluding undertakings to which the State has not assigned any task and which manages private interests.[353] Finally, since Article 90(2) is a provision which permits, in certain circumstances, a derogation from the rules of the Treaty, the Court imposes a strict definition of those undertakings which can take advantage of it.[354]

(ii) Whether Particular Types of Media Undertakings Qualify

4.178. Collecting societies. In *Belgische Radio en Televisie (BRT) v. SV SABAM*,[355] the Court of Justice refused to grant the Belgian collecting society, SABAM, the status of an undertaking entrusted with a service of a general economic interest. It ruled that:

---

[350] Case 127/73 *Belgische Radio en Televisie (BRT) v. SV SABAM* [1974] ECR 313, [1974] 2 CMLR 238, per Advocate General Mayras,

[351] *Ibid.* By way of example, see Commission Decision 82/861/EEC Re British Telecommunications OJ No L 360, 21.12.82, p. 36, [1983] 1 CMLR 457, where the Commission held that British Telecommunications, a public limited company, fell within the definition since the Telecommunication Act of 1981 had entrusted it with the task of operating the telecommunication system in the United Kingdom. (It should be noted that the Court, in *Belgische Radio en Televise(BRT) v. SV SABAM*, did not endorse the Opinion of Advocate General Mayras that the special role must be conferred upon the undertaking by a legislative act).

[352] Commission Decision 71/224/EEC Re GEMA OJ No L 134, 20.06.71, p.15, [1971] CMLR D35.

[353] Case 127/73 *Belgische Radio en Televisie (BRT) v. SV SABAM* [1974] ECR 313, [1974] 2 CMLR 238. See §4.178 below.

[354] *Ibid.*

[355] Case 127/73 [1974] ECR 313, [1974] 2 CMLR 238.

An undertaking to which the state has not assigned any task and which manages private interests, including intellectual property rights protected by law, is not covered by the provisions of Article 90(2) of the EEC Treaty.

There was no connection between SABAM and the State. The undertaking had not been entrusted with its task by a public authority; it was a co-operative association the creation of which was solely due to private initiative and it was governed by the ordinary Belgium law relating to that category of association.[356] In *GVL v. EC Commission*,[357] the Court of Justice similarly refused to grant Article 90(2) status to a German collecting society, Gesellschaft zur Verwertung von Leistungsschutzrechten mbH. German law did not confer the management of copyright and accompanying rights on a specific undertaking. It simply defined, in general terms, the rules applying to the activities of companies which intended to undertake the collective exploitation of such rights: their rights and duties. And the fact that the monitoring of those activities went further than the public supervision of many other undertakings could not make a difference.[358] Likewise, in Re GEMA,[359] the Commission stated that the obligations imposed on GEMA, by national legislation, to institute an insurance and aid fund and to take account in the establishment of its prices, of religious, cultural and social interests and interests of youth constituted services of a 'general cultural and social interest' but not of a general economic interest within the meaning of Article 90(2).[360]

4.179. Broadcasting organisations. In *Sacchi*,[361] the Court of Justice held that the Italian television company RAI, which had been conferred a monopoly of broadcasting services by a sovereign act of state, did qualify as a service of a 'general economic interest'. And in *Radio Telefís Eireann v. EC Commission*,[362] the Court of First Instance accepted that the Irish language television channel RTE was such a service on the grounds of its 'cultural, social and educational tasks'. The Commission has also consistently accepted that broadcasting organisations do qualify.[363]

These decisions beg the question, what makes television, a service of 'general economic interest' amenable to Article 90(2) status when a collecting society is denied this privilege? Advocate General Reischl answered that question in Sacchi thus:

Television is without doubt a means of mass-communication of great cultural and educational significance, an instrument which, on account of the intensity of its effect, is particulary capable of influencing public opinion.

---

[356] Per Advocate General Mayras.

[357] Case 7/82 [1983] ECR 483, [1983] 3 CMLR 645, upholding Commission Decision 81/1030/EEC Re GVL OJ No L 370, 28.12.81, p.49.

[358] Per Advocate General Reischl.

[359] Commission Decision 71/224/EEC Re GEMA, OJ No L 134, 20.06.71, p.15, [1971] CMLR D35.

[360] With regard to the phrase 'cultural and social interest', note the apparent contradiction in the ruling in Case 155/73 Sacchi [1974] ECR 409, [1974] 2 CMLR 177 and in particular Case T—69/89 *Radio Telefís Eireann v. EC Commission* [1991] 4 CMLR 586 where the Court has stated that it is the 'cultural' importance of broadcasting organisations which qualifies it as a service within the meaning of Article 90(2).

[361] Case 155/73 [1974] ECR 409, [1974] 2 CMLR 177.

[362] Case T—69/89 [1991] 4 CMLR 586.

[363] See e.g. Commission Decision 89/536/EEC Re Film Purchases by German Television Stations OJ No L 284, 3.10.89, p.36 Commission Decision 91/130/IEC Re Screensport/EBU Members OJ No L 63, 09.03.91, p.32.

The observations are likewise not without significance for commercial television. . . Even in this connection there exists the possibility of influencing public opinion and therefore the necessity for a control from various points of view (health policy, ethical and similar).

As the Advocate General earlier explained,[364] it is for this reason, that most Member States control their broadcasting organisations under public law and ensure that all facets of public opinion are represented:

> . . . the general structure of television programmes, ie the selection of what will be transmitted over this effective means of mass-communication, can, according to the proper view, not be left to private groups. Rather, it is a public task, which in the interests of the maintenance of the freedom of radio reporting can be dealt with only in a way which ensures the appropriate participation of all social groups. Looked at in this light, the exclusion of purely private groups, even in the context of commercial television, does not indeed go beyond what is indispensable for the purpose of properly providing for the matter. . .

Significantly, the Advocate General did not consider it necessary to find 'a general economic interest' in their activity[365] but regarded it as 'decisive that the basic concept of Article 90(2), a concept which is found on other forms (reservations in favour of the public administration) in other Articles in the Treaty (Articles 48, 55 and 56), is the only one appropriate for dealing with the matter of television.'

In its Decision, Re Screensport/EBU Members,[366] the Commission rejected the Applicant's claim that their transnational sports channel fed as it was by material from national broadcasting organisations fulfilled the function of a service of general economic interest and thus qualified for Article 90(2) privileges. It stated that:

> While it may be possible that the public mission obligations imposed by Member States on their national broadcasting organisations renders them undertakings entrusted with services of general economic interest to this extent, it is highly doubtful that, given the national character of these obligations, they could be interpreted as extending to transnational activities of a collective nature. . .

(3) Relationship Between Article 90(2) and the Competition Rules

(i)   General Principles

4.180. The general rule, according to the express terms of Article 90(2), is that where the activities of these undertakings have an economic nature, the competition rules will apply unless the prohibitions are incompatible with the performance of their tasks.[367]

---

[364] In the context of a discussion on the free movement of goods.

[365] It is irrelevant whether the broadcasting organisation is 'commercial' or 'non-commercial'.

[366] Commission Decision 91/130/EEC Re Screensport/EBU Members OJ No L 63, 09.03.91, p.32, para. 69.

[367] Case 155/73 Sacchi [1974] ECR 409, [1974] 2 CMLR 177; Case 311/84 Centre Belge d'Etudes de Marché Télé-Marketing SA v. Compagnie Luxembourgeoise de Télédiffusion SA [1985] ECR 3261, [1986] 2 CMLR 558; Case T—69/89 Radio Telefis Eireann v. EC Commision [1991] 4 CMLR 586 and Commission Decision 89/536/EEC Re Film Purchases by German television stations OJ L No 284, 03.10.89, p.36.

(ii) Activities of Media Undertakings

4.181. Prohibition of discrimination, unfair practices etc. Any form of discrimination against foreign nationals or undertakings is prohibited. In Sacchi,[368] the Court of Justice held that:

> . . . if certain Member States treat undertakings entrusted with the operation of television, even as regards their commercial activities, in particular advertising, as undertakings entrusted with the operation of services of general economic interest, the same prohibitions apply [as defined by Article 86] as regards their behaviour within the market, by reason of Article 90(2) so long as it is not shown that the said prohibitions are incompatible with the performance of their tasks. . .
>
> Such would certainly be the case with an undertaking possessing a monopoly of television advertising, if it imposed unfair charges or conditions on users of its services[369] or if it discriminated between commercial operators or national products on the one hand, and those of other Member States on the other, as regards access to television advertising.[370]

Thus, the Court ruled that whilst the grant of the exclusive right to transmit television signals does not as such constitute a breach of Article 7 of the Treaty:

> Discrimination by undertakings enjoying such exclusive rights against nationals of Member States by reason of their nationality is however incompatible with this provision.

In Re Film Purchases by German Television Stations, the Commission held that Article 90(2) would not stand in the way of applying the competition rules to the manner in which a public broadcasting organisation acquired exclusive rights to exhibit films.[371] There was no indication that the application of those rules would thwart the public service duty of broadcasting organisations to provide programmes. The competition rules would simply regulate the terms (ie duration and scope) of the licensing agreements.

Similarly, in its decision concerning the Magill TV Guide,[372] the Commission held that ITP, BBC and RTE were abusing their dominant position by refusing to allow other undertakings to publish weekly programme listings. The Commission held that even if the broadcasting companies were under a statutory duty to publish their individual programme listings in the form of TV guides, the requirement that they license others to do so, in no way obstructed the performance of that particular

---

[368] Case 155/73 [1974] ECR 409, [1974] 2 CMLR 177, paras. 15 to 17.

[369] Advocate General Reischl gave as an example of abusive behaviour, the arbitrary and discriminatory allocation of broadcasting times.

[370] This has been affirmed by the Court of Justice in Case 311/84 *Centre Belge d'Etudes de Marché Télé-Marketing SA v. Compagnie Luxembourgeoise de Télédiffusion SA* [1985] ECR 3261, [1986] 2 CMLR 558, above at §4.129. In Case C—353/89 *EC Commission v. The Netherlands* (not yet reported), the Court of Justice held that Article 90(2) could not justify an obligation on national broadcasting organisations to commission some or all of their productions from national undertakings (see §2.040 above). See also Case C—260/89 *Elliniki Radiophonia Tileorassi–Anonimi Etairia v. Dimotiki Etairia Pliroforissis* [1991] I ECR 2925, in which Advocate General Lenz noted that removing a broadcaster's monopoly on both the transmission of national broadcasts and the retransmission of broadcasts from other territories, would not obstruct the task of producing programmes of national identity, a task which had been entrusted on the Defendant by national law.

[371] Commission Decision 89/536/EEC Re Film Purchases by German television stations OJ No L 284, 03.10.89, p.36.

[372] Commission Decision 89/205/EEC OJ No L78, 21.03.89, p. 43. See §4.151 above.

task within the meaning of Article 90(2). This finding was challenged in
of First Instance solely in relation to the Irish company ('RTE'). It was r
RTE had been authorised to publish the RTE Guide with a view no
presenting and promoting its programmes, in particular its cultural and Irish-
language programmes, but also to contribute to its funding and it argued that being
a channel devoted to promoting Irish language and culture, it needed its monopoly
in the programme guide to promote its programmes. Whilst recognising the
Applicant's public duties, the Court held that it was difficult to discern how the
publication of general television magazines by third parties and the Applicant's
consequent adaptation to the requirements of the market, would undermine the
performance of the cultural, social and educational tasks assigned to RTE.[373]

Although, in *GVL v. EC Commission*,[374] the Court held that the Applicant could
not qualify as a service of a general economic interest, Advocate General Reischl
pointed out that even if Article 90(2) could in principle be said to apply to GVL,
an increased administrative burden on GVL could not amount to an obstruction as
defined by that Article.

4.182. Commission statement on audiovisual policy. The Commission has
affirmed that:

> Articles 85, 86 and 90 of the EEC Treaty apply to undertakings in the audiovisual
> industry in the same way as to undertakings in other economic areas.[375]

---

[373] Case T—69/89 *Radio Telefis Eireann v. EC Commission* [1991] 4 CMLR 586.
[374] Case 7/82 *GVL v. EC Commission* [1983] ECR 483, [1983] 3 CMLR 645.
[375] Communication from the Commission to the Council and Parliament on audiovisual policy,
2.2.2(a), COM (90) 78 final. In Commission Sixth Report on Competition Policy, (1976), point
163 (Re BBC), the Commission noted that 'a public broadcasting company, entrusted with the
operation of services of general economic interest within the meaning of Article 90 of the EEC
Treaty, is subject to the rules in the Treaty, and notably the rules on competition, in its
commercial exploitation of copyright'. (See §4.094 fn 178 above, for details.)

CHAPTER FIVE

Fundamental Human Rights and Community Law

I. RELATIONSHIP OF FUNDAMENTAL HUMAN RIGHTS TO EUROPEAN COMMUNITY LAW

1. General Principles

(1) Introduction

5.001. Integral part of Community Law. In 1969 in *Staunder v. City of Ulm*,[1] the Court of Justice declared that a particular Community measure would not prejudice '. . . the fundamental human rights enshrined in the general principles of Community law and protected by the Court.' And with that judgment, the role of fundamental human rights in the interpretation of Community law was secured.[2] Since then, the Court of Justice has regularly affirmed that human rights are a touchstone against which the law may be tested.[3] In Nold (J), *Kohlen- und*

---

[1] Case 29/69 [1969] ECR 419, [1970] CMLR 112, para. 17.

[2] On fundamental human rights and EEC law, see T C Hartley, *The Foundations of European Community Law* (2nd Edn, 1988), Chapter 5, p. 132 and H G Schermers and D F Waelbroeck, *Judicial Protection in the European Communities* (5th Edn, 1992), §§63 et seq and the literature referred to therein. Hartley explains (p. 132) that '. . . the conversion of the European Court to a specific doctrine of human rights has been as much a matter of expediency as conviction.' The Court of Justice was anxious to prevent the German constitutional courts from declaring invalid Community law which infringed fundamental human rights protected by the German constitution.

[3] See e.g. Case 11/70 *Internationale Handelsgesellschaft mbH v. Einfuhr- und Vorratsstelle für Getreide und Futtermittel* [1970] ECR 1125, [1972] CMLR 255, where the Court of Justice stated that '. . . respect for fundamental rights forms an integral part of the general principles of law protected by the Court of Justice.'; Case 4/73 Nold (J), *Kohlen- und Baustoffgroßhandlung v. EC Commission* [1974] ECR 491, [1974] 2 CMLR 338; Case 44/79 *Hauer v. Land Rheinland-Pfalz* [1979] ECR 3727, [1980] 3 CMLR 42; Case 136/79 *National Panasonic (UK) Ltd v. EC Commission* [1980] ECR 2033, [1980] 3 CMLR 169; Joined Cases 60, 61/84 *Cinéthèque SA v. Fédération Nationale de Cinémas Français* [1985] ECR 2605, [1986] 1 CMLR 365; Case 5/88 *Hubert Wachauf v. Federal Republic of Germany* [1989] ECR 2609, [1991] 1 CMLR 328; Case C—260/89 *Elliniki Radiophonia Tileorassi Anonimi Etairia v. Dimotiki Etairia Pliroforissis* [1991] I ECR 2925.

Baustoffgroßhandlung v. EC Commission,[4] Advocate General Trabucchi spelled out the obligation:

> . . . if the task of the Court of Justice as an institution is that of ensuring that in the application of the Treaties the law is observed, this means that the Court should be particularly sensitive when dealing with problems which concern those fundamental rights forming the basis of every civil society. The respect for liberty, for property ownership, the declaration of principles of equality, of non-discrimination, of proportionality—to cite only a number of those which are really fully recognised—form a part of that concept of law which governs and forms the framework for the whole Community system and from which that system, even in its application to individual cases, may never deviate.

5.002. Governing legality of both Community and subsidiary legislation. Generally, the cases in which human rights are invoked, challenge the validity of legislation enacted by the Community's institutions. But the Court of Justice has affirmed that Member State legislation implementing Community legislation, is also subject to review in the light of fundamental human rights which form an integral part of the Community's law.[5]

(2) Sources and Inspiration

5.003. Constitutional traditions and international treaties. The very existence of the EEC, illustrates that upon its inception, the Member States shared common values.[6] Many of those shared values are articulated in their respective written constitutions. Indeed, in the Internationale Handelsgesellschaft case,[7] the Court of Justice declared that fundamental principles of human rights were '. . . inspired by the constitutional traditions common to the Member States. . . ' As Advocate General Trabucchi explained in Nold (J), *Kohlen- und Baustoffgroßhandlung v. EC Commission*,[8] those principles have their origins in ancient history:

> . . . we find them in the ancient laws, as the written basis of human society, we find them in the codes of the nineteenth century, which were conceived precisely for the purpose of setting out the validity of those declarations in the form of Articles; we now find them more formally proclaimed in modern Constitutions . . .

In Nold,[9] the Court of Justice affirmed the sanctity of fundamental rights and held that in defining those rights, inspiration was drawn not only from the constitutional traditions of Member States, but also from international obligations which they have undertaken:

> . . . fundamental rights form an integral part of the general principles of law, the observance of which it ensures.

---

[4] Case 4/73 [1974] ECR 491, [1974] 2 CMLR 338.
[5] See Case 5/88 *Wachauf v. Germany* [1989] ECR 2609, [1991] 1 CMLR 328, in which Advocate General Jacobs stated (para. 22) that '. . . when acting in pursuance of powers granted under Community law, Member States must be subject to the same constraints, [respect for the right to property] in any event in relation to the principle of respect for fundamental rights, as the Community legislator.'
[6] The same can be said of the European Coal and Steel Community and the European Atomic Energy Community.
[7] Case 11/70 *Internationale Handelsgesellschaft mbH v. Einfuhr- und Vorratsstelle für Getreide und Futtermittel* [1970] ECR 1125, [1972] CMLR 255.
[8] Case 4/73 [1974] ECR 491, [1974] 2 CMLR 338.
[9] *Ibid.*, para. 13.

In safeguarding these rights, the Court is bound to draw inspiration from constitutional traditions common to the Member States, and it cannot therefore uphold measures which are incompatible with fundamental rights recognized and protected by the Constitutions of those States.

Similarly, international treaties for the protection of human rights on which the Member States have collaborated or of which they are signatories, can supply guidelines which should be followed within the framework of Community law.

5.004. Particular importance of the European Convention on Human Rights. The European Convention for the Protection of Human Rights and Fundamental Freedoms has been ratified by all Member States of the Community.[10] Its special role in inspiring Community principles was acknowledged by the Court of Justice in *Hauer v. Land Rheinland-Pfalz*[11] where it endorsed the aforementioned principles, annunciated in Nold, and held that:

> That conception [ie that international treaties may inspire Community law] was later recognised by the joint declaration of the European Parliament, the Council and the Commission of 5 April 1977,[12] which, after recalling the case law of the Court, refers on the one hand to the rights guaranteed by the constitutions of the Member States and on the other hand to the European Convention on for the Protection of Human Rights and Fundamental Freedoms of 4 November 1950 ...

Furthermore, in the Preamble to the Single European Act, the Member States pledge:

> ... to work together to promote democracy on the basis of the fundamental rights recognised in the constitutions and laws of the Member States, in the Convention for the Protection of Human Rights and Fundamental Freedoms and the European Social Charter, notably freedom, equality and social justice, ...

Whilst emphasising that the Convention does not bind, and is not part of the law of the Community as such,[13] the Court of Justice has consistently affirmed the particular significance of the Convention.[14] Thus in defining Community law,

---

[10] On the case law of the Convention, see §5.018 et seq. below.

[11] Case 44/79 [1979] ECR 3727, [1980] 3 CMLR 42, para. 15.

[12] That declaration states: 'The European Parliament, the Council and the Commission, Whereas the Treaties establishing the European Communities are based on the principle of respect for the law; Whereas, as the Court of Justice has recognised, that law comprises, over and above the rules embodied in the treaties and secondary Community legislation, the general principles of law and in particular the fundamental rights, principles and rights on which the constitutional law of the Member States is based; Whereas, in particular, all the Member States are Contracting Parties to the European Convention for the Protection of Human Rights and Fundamental Freedoms signed in Rome on 4 November 1950, Have adopted the following declaration; I. The European Parliament, the Council and the Commission stress the prime importance they attach to the protection of fundamental rights, as derived in particular from the constitutions of the Member States and the European Convention for the Protection of Human Rights and Fundamental Freedoms. 2. In the exercise of their powers and in pursuance of the aims of the European Communities they respect and will continue to respect these rights. (OJ C No 103, 1977, p.1.)

[13] Case 48/75 Royer [1976] ECR 497, [1976] 2 CMLR 619; Case 118/75 Watson and Belman [1976] ECR 1185, [1976] 2 CMLR 552; Joined Cases 60, 61/84 Cinéthèque SA v. Fédération Nationale de Cinémas Français [1985] ECR 2605, [1986] 1 CMLR 365, per Advocate General Slynn.

[14] See e.g. Case 222/84 Johnson v. Chief Constable of RUC [1986] ECR 1651, [1986] 3 CMLR 240, para. 18, in which the Court stated that 'As the European Parliament, Council and Commission recognised in their Joint Declaration of 5 April 1977 (Official Journal C 103, p.1) and as the Court has recognised in its decisions, the principles on which that Convention is based must be taken into consideration in Community law.'; Case C—260/89 Elliniki Radiophonia Tileorassi Anonimi Etairia v. Dimotiki Etairia Pliroforissis [1991] I ECR 2925, para. 41, in which the Court stated that 'The European Convention on Human Rights has special significance ...'

the Court of Justice has taken inspiration from: Article 6 (right to a fair and public trial within a reasonable time);[15] Article 7 (right to freedom from retrospective effect of penal legislation);[16] Article 8 (right to respect for private and family life, home and correspondence);[17] Article 9 (right to freedom of thought, conscience and religion);[18] Article 10 (right to freedom of expression);[19] Article 13 (right to an effective remedy before national authorities);[20] First Protocol, Article 1 (right to peaceful enjoyment of possessions);[21] Fourth Protocol, Article 2 (right of freedom to move within and freedom to choose residence in a country)[22] and the 'national security' and 'public safety' exceptions to the principles enshrined in Articles 8, 9, 10 and 11 of the Convention.[23]

5.005. Compatibility of national law with international obligations. It is not the role of the Court of Justice to determine the compatibility of national law with an international Convention. In *Elliniki Radiophonia Tileorassi Anonimi Etairia v. Dimotiki Etairia Pliroforissis*,[24] the Court of Justice held:

> As the Court has held (see the judgment in Joined Cases C-60 and C-61/84 *Cinéthèque v. Fédération Nationale des Cinémas Français* [1985] ECR 2605, paragraph 25, and the judgment in Case C-12/86 *Demirel v. Stadt Schwäbisch Gmund* [1987] ECR 3719, paragraph 28), it has no power to examine the compatibility with the European Convention on Human Rights of national rules which do not fall within the scope of Community law. On the other hand, where such rules do fall within the scope of Community law, and reference is made to the Court for a preliminary ruling, it must

---

[15] Joined Cases 209—215, 218/78 *Van Landewyck (Heintz) Sàrl v. EC Commission* [1980] ECR 3125, [1981 3 CMLR 134; Case 98/79 *Pecastaing v. Belgium* [1980] ECR 691, [1980] 3 CMLR 685; Joined Cases 100—103/80 *Musique Diffusion Française SA v. EC Commission* [1983] ECR 1825, [1983] 3 CMLR 221; Case 222/84 *Johnson v. Chief Constable of RUC* [1986] ECR 1651, [1986] 3 CMLR 240, para. 18, in which the Court stated that 'The requirement of judicial control stipulated by that article reflects a general principle of law which underlies the constitutional traditions common to the Member States. That principle is also laid down in Articles 6 and 13 of the European Convention for the Protection of Human Rights and Fundamental Freedoms of 4 November 1950.'; Case 222/86 *Union nationale des entraîneurs et Cadres techniques professionnels du football v. Heylens* [1987] ECR 4097.

[16] Case 63/83 *R v. Kirk* [1984] ECR 2689, [1984] 3 CMLR 522.

[17] Case 136/79 *National Panasonic (UK) Ltd v. EC Commission* [1980] ECR 2033, [1980] 3 CMLR 169; Case 5/85 *AKZO Chemie BV v. EC Commission* [1986] ECR 2585, [1987] 3 CMLR 716; Case 46/87 *Hoechst AG v. EC Commission* [1987] ECR [1988] 4 CMLR 430.

[18] Case 130/75 *Prais v. EC Council* [1976] ECR 1589, [1976] 2 CMLR 708.

[19] Case 34/79 *R v. Henn and Darby* [1979] ECR 3795, [1980] 1 CMLR 246, per Advocate General Warner (obscene publications); Joined Cases 43, 63/82 *VBVB and VBBB v. EC Commission* [1984] ECR 19, [1985] 1 CMLR 27 (resale price maintenance on books) see §5.014 below; Joined Cases 60, 61/84 *Cinéthèque SA v. Fédération Nationale de Cinémas Français* [1985] ECR 2605, [1986] 1 CMLR 365 (windows between theatrical exhibition and distribution on video cassette) in which Advocate General Slynn stated: 'That freedom of speech, or expression is part of Community law in those areas where it is relevant to the activities of the Community, may . . . be accepted.' See §5.011 below; Case C—260/89 *Elliniki Radiophonia Tileorassi Anonimi Etairia v. Dimotiki Etairia Pliroforissis* [1991] 1 ECR 2925 (retransmission of foreign broadcasts) see §§2.041 et seq. above and 5.013 below.

[20] Case 222/84 *Johnson v. Chief Constable of RUC* [1986] ECR 1651, [1986] 3 CMLR 240 and Case 222/86 *Union nationale des entraîneurs et Cadres techniques professionnels du football v. Heylens* [1987] ECR 4097.

[21] Case 4/73 *Nold (J) Kohlen- und Baustoffgroßhandlung v. EC Commission* [1974] ECR 491, [1974] 2 CMLR 338 (concerning the ECSC Treaty) and Case 44/79 *Hauer v. Land Rheinland-Pfalz* [1979] ECR 3727, [1980] 3 CMLR 42.

[22] Case 36/75 *Rutili v. Minister for the Interior* [1975] ECR 1219, [1976] 1 CMLR 140.

[23] *Ibid.*

[24] Case C—260/89 [1991] I ECR 2925, para. 42.

provide all the criteria of interpretation needed by the national court to determine whether those rules are compatible with the fundamental rights the observance of which the Court ensures and which derive in particular from the European Convention on Human Rights.

(3) Subject Matter of Protection

5.006. Protection of substance of fundamental rights. The Court recognises the 'existence' of fundamental rights but it will temper the manner in which they are exercised in a particular circumstance.[25] Were it otherwise, their greater purpose—being the preservation of a civilised society—might not be fulfilled. As Advocate General Trabucchi stated in Nold (J), *Kohlen- und Baustoffgroßhandlung v. EC Commission*:[26]

> . . . it is for the very purpose of ensuring fundamental respect for these rights that their exercise must be regulated. Recognition by the Constitution [of a Member State] does not mean that the subject matter is no longer subject to any rules, but that the rules must be inspired and limited by an effective and essential recognition of the principles. Therefore, one cannot in general invoke one of these basic norms to avoid in an actual concrete situation those obligations and burdens which the legal order [ie Member State constitution and international treaties] has established or authorised . . . for the precise purpose of obtaining a functional application of those rules which are in accordance with the spirit of the system. Any violation must actually strike at the existence of the right recognised constitutionally as an indisputable characteristic of human personality. The Court ensures respect for these fundamental rights, which the Community must adopt by recognising that there are limits to the activity of organs and individuals and by, if necessary recognising liability. But both forms of recognition conform to the realities and to the requirements of the various forms of protection. . . . the very importance of these essential forms of recognition of fundamental rights requires that they should not be invoked as a general ground by which to deny a more specific obligation or to impede the demands of social conduct which require that everyone should accept limitations and sacrifices in exercising his rights.
>
> Indeed, the right of the individual is always also the result of limiting an aspect of liberty. Like every freedom, an individual right is not without its limits: every right must therefore be exercised in accordance with the rules which govern it.

On the manner in which fundamental human rights may be regulated in order to secure the proper functioning of the common market, the Advocate General continued thus:

> The Community order certainly cannot disregard the right of every citizen to engage in trade. The protection of the public interest, both by national legal orders and by the Community legal order, does however limit in several respects the exercise of trading activity. An example in the Community sphere is the case of the rules on competition, which prohibit many types of behaviour, transactions and practices. Also, out of respect for the principle of free movement of goods within the Community, the limitation can go as far as to prohibit specific uses of property, as has occurred in the field of trademark rights or rights similar to copyright. Such important limitations are justified by the general interest in the proper functioning of the common market; this is not the only consideration; one must regard these limitations as established for the purpose of supporting the other fundamental criterion relating to the safeguarding of the essential right to trade . . .

---

[25] This reasoning mirrors the Court's approach in the domain of intellectual property. See §1.004 above.

[26] Case 4/73 [1974] ECR 491, [1974] 2 CMLR 338.

In *Wachauf v. Germany*,[27] the Court of Justice underscored these principles affirming that the substance of human rights may never be violated. It ruled that the precise fashion in which they are exercised may be controlled on the grounds of 'general interest' provided that a proportionality test is fulfilled:

> The fundamental rights recognised by the Court are not absolute, however, but must be considered in relation to their social function. Consequently, restrictions may be imposed on the exercise of those rights, in particular in the context of a common organisation of a market, provided that those restrictions in fact correspond to objectives of general interest pursued by the Community and do not constitute, with regard to the aim pursued, a disproportionate and intolerable interference, impairing the very substance of those rights.[28]

5.007. Particular fundamental rights. On property rights, in particular the Court of Justice in Nold,[29] held that:

> If rights of ownership are protected by the constitutional laws of all the Member States and if similar guarantees are given in respect of their right freely to choose and practice their trade or profession, the rights thereby guaranteed, far from constituting unfettered prerogatives, must be viewed in the light of the social function of the property and activities protected thereunder.
>
> For this reason, rights of this nature are protected by law subject always to limitations laid down in accordance with the public interest.
>
> Within the Community legal order it likewise seems legitimate that these rights should, if necessary, be subject to certain limits justified by the overall objectives pursued by the Community, on condition that the substance of these rights is left untouched.

The Court has recognised many other specific fundamental rights including, freedom of expression[30] and the maintenance of democracy.[31]

(4) Unity of Community law

5.008. Supremacy of 'Community' law. Whilst the Court is inspired by principles enshrined in the constitutions of Member States and international treaties to which they are parties, it is the *Community's law* against which any measure must be assessed. As the Court of Justice established in the Internationale Handelsgasellschaft case,[32] were it to defer to specific national laws or principles contained in international agreements, the supremacy of 'Community' law—ie the notion of an overarching supreme system—would be undermined. In *Hauer v. Land Rheinland-Pfalz*,[33] the Court thus held that:

> As the Court declared in its judgment of 17 December 1970 Internationale Handelsgesellschaft [1970] ECR 1125, the question of a possible infringement of fundamental rights by a measure of the Community institutions can only be judged in the light of

---

[27] Case 5/88 [1989] ECR 2609, [1991] 1 CMLR 328, para. 18.
[28] See also Case 44/79 *Hauer v. Land Rheinland-Pfalz* [1979] ECR 3727, [1980] 3 CMLR 42, per Advocate General Caportorti.
[29] Case 4/73 Nold (J), *Kohlen- und Baustoffgroßhandlung v. EC Commission* [1974] ECR 491, [1974] 2 CMLR 338, para. 14. See also Case 44/79 *Hauer v. Land Rheinland-Pfalz,* [1979] ECR 3727, [1980] 3 CMLR 41.
[30] Case 100/88 *Oyowe and Traore v. EC Commission* [1989] ECR 4285.
[31] Case 139/79 *Maizena GmbH c. EC Council* [1980] ECR 3393.
[32] Case 11/70 *Internationale Handelsgesellschaft mbH v. Einfuhr- und Vorratsstelle für Getreide und Futtermittel* [1970] ECR 1125, [1972] CMLR 255.
[33] Case 44/79 [1979] ECR 3727, [1980] 3 CMLR 42, para. 14.

Community law itself. The introduction of special criteria for assessment stemming from the legislation or constitutional law of a particular Member State would, by damaging the substantive unity and efficacy of Community law, lead inevitably to the destruction of the unity of the Common Market and the jeopardising of the cohesion of the Community.[34]

5.009. Exclusive jurisdiction of the Community's courts. The supremacy of Community law means that ultimately, only the Community's courts can enshrine fundamental rights in Community law. In *Hauer v. Land Rheinland-Pfalz*,[35] Advocate General Capotorti stated that:

In accordance with these premises it is necessary to reject the idea that it is permissible to appeal to the highest national courts, rather than to this Court, in order to secure the protection of fundamental rights as against the Communities, in particular when infringements as a result of the legislative activity of the Communities are alleged. It is the exclusive task of the Community Court to guarantee such protection, within the scope of its jurisdiction: the uniform application of Community law and its primacy over the legal orders of the Member States must not be endangered by the intervention of national courts, when it is a question of ascertaining whether or not Community provisions are in conformity with the principles concerning human rights.

2. Fundamental Human Rights and the Media

(1) Article 30 and Freedom of Expression

5.010. Interpreted in the light of the Convention. In *Cinéthèque SA v. Fédération Nationale de Cinémas Français*,[36] Advocate General Slynn stated that:

. . . it is right . . . that the exceptions in Article 36 and the scope of 'mandatory requirements' taking a measure outside Article 30 should be construed in the light of the Convention . . .[37]

5.011. Enforcing 'windows' between film exhibition and release on video cassette. In *Cinéthèque SA v. Fédération Nationale de Cinémas Français*,[38] it was argued that French legislation which prohibited the distribution of films on video cassette until the expiry of one year after they had been first exhibited in the cinema, breached the rights contained in Article 10 of the European Convention on Human Rights. The Court of Justice held that it was not within its power to judge the compatibility of national laws with international conventions.[39] Nevertheless, Advocate General Slynn stated that Article 10 would not be breached simply by national legislation regulating the sequence of particular methods of exhibiting filmed material.

---

[34] Affirmed by the Court in Joined Cases 41, 121, 796/79 *Testa, Maggio and Vitale v. Bundesanstalt für Arbeit* [1980] ECR 1979, [1981] 2 CMLR 552 and Case 234/85 *Staatsanwalt v. Keller* [1986] ECR 2 897, [1987] 1 CMLR 875, para. 7, where the Court of Justice stated that '. . . a claim that a Community measure infringes fundamental rights laid down in the Constitution of a Member State cannot in itself affect the validity of that measure or its effect within that State. . . '
[35] Case 44/79 [1979] ECR 3727, [1980] 3 CMLR 42.
[36] Joined Cases 60, 61/84 [1985] ECR 2605, [1986] 1 CMLR 365.
[37] Affirming Case 36/75 *Rutili v. Minister for the Interior* [1975] ECR 1219, [1976] 1 CMLR 140 and Case 34/79 *R v. Henn and Darby* [1979] ECR 3795, [1980] 1 CMLR 246, per Advocate General Warner.
[38] Joined Cases 60, 61/84 [1985] ECR 2605, [1986] 1 CMLR 365.
[39] See §5.005 above.

(2) Article 59 and Freedom of Expression

5.012. Broadcasting generally. The application of the Convention to broadcasting has been affirmed in Council Directive 89/552/EEC:[40] 'Television Without Frontiers', which states that the right of free movement of broadcasts and the free distribution of television services is:

> ... a specific manifestation in Community law of a more general principle, namely, freedom of expression as enshrined in Article 10(1) of the Convention for the Protection of Human Rights and Fundamental Freedoms ratified by all Member States.

5.013. Prohibiting television transmissions on grounds of 'public policy'. The Court of Justice has held that in invoking Article 56 of the Treaty to impede the transmission of foreign broadcasts, fundamental human rights must be taken into consideration.[41]

(3) Article 85(1) and Freedom of Expression

5.014. Resale price maintenance for books. The Court is reluctant to yield to arguments that Article 85 impinges upon basic human rights such as the right to freedom of expression enshrined in Article 10 of the European Convention on Human Rights. In *VBVB and VBBB v. EC Commission*,[42] the Court of Justice rejected the Applicants' claim that it was necessary to impose a system of resale price maintenance for books to encourage publishers to issue a multiplicity of titles and thus ensure the publication of less readily saleable works such as works of science and poetry. By attacking the French law, the Applicants maintained that the Commission was trying to impose an indirect form of censorship. The Court acknowledged that economic conditions can sometimes have effects on freedom of expression, and that it might be possible to interpret the European Convention on Human Rights in such a way as to include guarantees of the possibility of publishing books in economically profitable conditions. However, the Court said that the Applicants had failed to establish a link in this case:

> To submit the production of and trade in books to rules whose sole purpose is to ensure freedom of trade between Member States in normal conditions of competition cannot be regarded as restricting freedom of publication which, it is not contested, remains entire at the level of both publishers and distributors.

Advocate General VerLoren van Themaat, applying the Court's judgment in Nold, stated that:

> ... basic rights must always operate subject to given social and economic circumstances. Indeed, considerations of profit will never make it possible for publishers with or without resale price maintenance (at least without an external subsidy) to publish all the manuscripts offered to them. It is therefore naturally going too far to speak of indirect censorship ...

---

[40] of 3 October 1989, OJ 1989 L N0 298, p.23, Recital 8. See §§2.028 and 3.008 above.
[41] See §2.041 et seq. above.
[42] Joined Cases 43, 63/82 [1984] ECR 19, [1985] 1 CMLR 27.

II. ARTICLE 10 OF THE EUROPEAN CONVENTION FOR THE PROTECTION OF HUMAN RIGHTS AND FUNDAMENTAL FREEDOMS

1. Introduction

5.015. Convention institutions. All Member States of the European Community and most European States are signatories to the European Convention for the Protection of Human Rights and Fundamental Freedoms (the 'Convention') which entered into force on 3 September 1953. The Convention is administered by the European Commission of Human Rights ('the European Commission of Human Rights') and the European Court of Human Rights (the 'European Court').[43]

5.016. Convention terms. The Convention provides a panoply of rights. Freedom of expression is guaranteed by Article 10. It states the following:

1. Everyone has the right to freedom of expression. This right shall include freedom to hold opinions and to receive and impart information and ideas without interference by public authority and regardless of frontiers. This Article shall not prevent States from requiring the licensing of broadcasting, television or cinema enterprises.
2. The exercise of these freedoms, since it carries with it duties and responsibilities, may be subject to such formalities, conditions, restrictions or penalties as are prescribed by law and are necessary in a democratic society, in the interests of national security, territorial integrity or public safety, for the prevention of disorder or crime, for the protection of health or morals, for the protection of the reputation or rights of others, for preventing the disclosure of information received in confidence, or for maintaining the authority and impartiality of the judiciary.

5.017. Constituent elements. Article 10 is violated by the existence of:

(1) an interference by public authority;
(2) which restricts a person's freedom of expression;

unless that restriction is:

(3) prescribed by law and
(4) necessary in a democratic society.

2. Qualifying Applicants

5.018. General principles. The Convention states that 'Everyone has the right to freedom of expression.'[44] The term 'Everyone' is widely construed. As the European Court stated in *Autronic AG v. Switzerland*: 'The Article applies to "everyone",

---

[43] On the practice of the Convention, see generally P van Dijk and G J H van Hoof, *Theory and Practice of the European Convention on Human Rights*, (2nd Edn, 1990).
[44] Article 10(1).

whether natural or legal persons. . . . [Moreover] it is applicable to profit-making corporate bodies.'[45]

5.019. Specific categories of applicants. As well as individual citizens,[46] Article 10 has been held to apply to: writers;[47] artists;[48] politicians;[49] political associations;[50] activists;[51] religious organisations;[52] publishers,[53] and their proprietors;[54] newspapers;[55] broadcasting organisations;[56] television production companies;[57] persons engaged in the liberal professions;[58] the manufacturers of consumer electronic products[59] and supermarket corporations.[60]

---

[45] Application NO 12726/87 *Autronic AG v. Switzerland* Series A NO 178, (1990) 12 EHRR 485, para. 47.

[46] Application NO 3071/67 *X v. Sweden* 26 Collection of Decisions 71; Application NO 4750/71 *X v. United Kingdom* 29 Collection of Decisions 40; Application NO 6452/74 *G Sacchi v. Italy* 5 DR 43; Application NO 8266/78 *X v. United Kingdom* (Radio Caroline) 16 DR 190; Application NO 8962/80 *X and Y v. Belgium* 28 DR 112, (1983) 5 EHRR 268; Application NO 9777/82 *X v. Belgium* (1984) 6 EHRR 467; Application NO 10248/83 *Aebi v. Switzerland* 41 DR 141, (1986) 8 EHRR 252.

[47] Application NO 10799/84 *Radio 24, S, W and A v. Switzerland* 37 DR 236 (radio journalist); Application NO 11034/84 *Weber v. Switzerland* Series A NO 177, (1990) 12 EHRR 508 (a journalist); Application NO 11508/85 *Barfod v. Denmark* Series A NO 149, (1991) 13 EHRR 493 (a journalist); Application NO 11662/85 *Oberschlick v. Austria* Series A 204 (a journalist); Application NO 13778/88 *Thorgeir Thorgeirson v. Iceland* Series A NO 239, (1992) 14 EHRR 843 (a journalist).

[48] Application NO 10737/84 *Müller v. Switzerland* Series A NO 133, (1991) 13 EHRR 212.

[49] Application NO 11798/85 *Castells v. Spain* Series A NO 236 (1992) 14 EHRR 445, (an opposition politician).

[50] Application NO 4515/70 *X and the Association of Z v. United Kingdom* 14 Yearbook 538 and Application NO 9297/81 *X Association v. Sweden* 28 DR 204.

[51] Application NO 11034/84 *Weber v. Switzerland* Series A NO 177, (1990) 12 EHRR 508.

[52] Application NO 7805/77 *X and Church of Scientology v. Sweden* 16 DR 68.

[53] Application NO 5178/71 *De Geillustreede Pers NV v. The Netherlands* 8 DR 5, [1978] ECC 164; Application NO 8710/79 *Gay News Ltd and Lemon v. United Kingdom* (1983) 5 EHRR 123; Application NO 9615/81 *X v. United Kingdom* (1983) 5 EHRR 581. In Application NO 9615/81 *X v. United Kingdom*, the European Commission of Human Rights stated that the rights conferred by Article 10 may be '. . . invoked not only by the author or the editor of a certain publication, but also by the publisher who purports to disseminate the information or ideas contained therein by making the necessary arrangements for its production and marketing.'

[54] Application NO 5493/72 *Handyside v. United Kingdom* Series A NO 24, (1979–80) 1 EHRR 737 (book publisher); Application NO 8710/79 *Gay News Ltd and Lemon v. United Kingdom* (1983) 5 EHRR 123, (magazine publisher); Application NO 9815/82 *Lingens v. Austria* Series A NO 103, (1986) 8 EHRR 407, (magazine publisher); Application NO 10572/83 *Markt Intern and Beerman v. Germany* Series A NO 165, (1990) 12 EHRR 161 (magazine publisher).

[55] Application NO 6538/74 *The Sunday Times v. The United Kingdom* Series A NO 30, (1979–80) 2 EHRR 245; Application NO 13166/87 *The Sunday Times v. United Kingdom* Series A NO 217, (NO 2) (1992) 14 EHRR 229; Application NO 13585/88 *The Observer and The Guardian v. United Kingdom* Series A NO 216, (1992) 14 EHRR 153.

[56] Application NO 10799/84 *Radio 24, S, W and A v. Switzerland* 37 DR 236 (private radio stations); Application NO 10746/84 *Verein Alternatives Lokalradio Bern and Verin Radio Dreyeckland Basel v. Switzerland* 49 DR 126 (private radio stations); Application NO 10890/84 *Groppera Radio AG v. Switzerland* Series A NO 173, (1990) 12 EHRR 321 (transmitter of terrestrial signals); Applications NOs 11553/85 and 11658/85 *Hodgson, Woolf Productions and National Union of Journalists and Channel Four Television v. United Kingdom* (1988) 10 EHRR 503; Application NO 12726/87 *Autronic AG v. Switzerland* Series A NO 178, (1990) 12 EHRR 485 (receiver of Fixed Service Satellite signals).

[57] Applications NOs 11553/85 and 11658/85 *Hodgson, Woolf Productions and National Union of Journalists and Channel Four Television v. United Kingdom* (1988) 10 EHRR 503.

[58] Application NO 8734/79 *Barthold v. Germany* Series A NO 90, (1985) 7 EHRR 383 (a veterinary surgeon).

[59] Application NO 12726/87 *Autronic AG v. Switzerland* Series A NO 178, (1990) 12 EHRR 321.

[60] Application NO 11532/85 *Hammerdahls Stormarknad AB v. Sweden* (1986) 8 EHRR 45.

3. Subject Matter of Protection

(1) General Categories Protected

5.020. Political opinions. Article 10 may apply to political opinions such as are espoused by politicians[61] or contained in advertisements for political parties.[62]

5.021. Publications. Books,[63] newspapers,[64] magazines[65] and 'papers'[66] are encompassed by the terms of Article 10.

5.022. Television transmissions (terrestrial, cable and satellite). The European Court has held that '"Broadcasting" is mentioned in the Convention precisely in relation to freedom of expression. . . . [Thus] both broadcasting of programmes over the air and cable retransmission of such programmes are covered by the right enshrined in the first two sentences of Article 10(1), without there being any need to draw distinctions according to the content of the programmes.'[67] The European Court has extended that principle to broadcasts by satellite stating that '. . . the reception of television programmes by means of a dish or other aerial comes within the right laid down in the first two sentences of Article 10(1), without its being

---

[61] Application NO 11798/85 *Castells v. Spain* Series A NO 236, (1992) 14 EHRR 445 (an opposition politician). See §§5.051 and 5.104 below.

[62] Application NO 4515/70 *X and the Association of Z v. United Kingdom* 14 Yearbook 531 concerning the refusal of the BBC and ITV to grant broadcasting time for an organisation which wished to express its views. See §§5.039 and 5.092 below.

[63] Application NO 5493/72 *Handyside v. United Kingdom* Series A NO 24, (1979–80) 1 EHRR 737. See §5.121 below.

[64] Application NO 6538/74 *The Sunday Times v. The United Kingdom* Series A NO 30, (1979–80) 2 EHRR 245; Application NO 13166/87 *The Sunday Times v. United Kingdom* (NO 2) Series A NO 217, (1992) 14 EHRR 229; Application NO 13585/88 *The Observer and The Guardian v. United Kingdom* Series A NO 216, (1992) 14 EHRR 153; Application NO 13704/88 *Schwabe v. Austria* Series A NO 242; Application NO 13778/88 *Thorgeir Thorgeirson v. Iceland* Series A NO 239, (1992) 14 EHRR 843. See §5.095 et seq. below.

[65] Application NO 5178/71 *De Geillustreerde Pers NV v. The Netherlands* 8 DR 5, [1978] ECC 164 (television listing magazine); Application NO 8710/79 *Gay News Ltd and Lemon v. United Kingdom* (1983) 5 EHRR 123 (magazine); Application NO 9615/81 *X v. United Kingdom* (1983) 5 EHRR 581, (pornography); Application NO 9815/82 *Lingens v. Austria* Series A NO 103, (1986) 8 EHRR 407, (political magazine); Application NO 10572/83 *Markt Intern and Beerman v. Germany* Series A NO 165, (1990) 12 EHRR 161 (trade magazine); Application NO 11508/85 *Barfod v. Denmark* Series A NO 149, (1991) 13 EHRR 493 (regional magazine); Application NO 11662/85 *Oberschlick v. Austria* Series A NO 204 (a political periodical); Application NO 11798/85 *Castells v. Spain* Series A NO 236 (1992) 14 EHRR 445 (weekly magazine).

[66] Application NO 9777/82 *X v. Belgium* (1984) 6 EHRR 467.

[67] Application NO 10890/84 *Groppera Radio AG v. Switzerland* Series A NO 173, (1990) 12 EHRR 508, para. 55, Judge Valticos dissenting, stating that the content of the broadcasts disqualified it for protection under Article 10 which is focused on political views and the discussion of ideas and artistic expression. The broadcasts in issue were, in fact, mainly light music, popular programmes and commercials. See also Application NO 4515/70 *X and the Association of Z v. United Kingdom* Yearbook 14, 538; Application NO 9297/81 *X Association v. Sweden* 28 DR 204; Application NO 9297/81 *X Association v. Sweden* 28 DR 204; Applications NOs 11553/85 and 11658/85 *Hodgson, Woolf Productions and National Union of Journalists and Channel Four Television v. United Kingdom* (1988) 10 EHRR 503, which concerned terrestrial broadcasts. See §5.076 et seq. below.

necessary to ascertain the reason and purpose for which the right is to be exercised.'[68]

5.023. Radio transmissions. The European Commission of Human Rights has treated radio transmissions as protected by Article 10.[69]

5.024. Other forms of technical transmission. The European Commission of Human Rights has considered that, in principle, citizen's band radio transmissions are a form of expression encompassed by Article 10.[70]

5.025. Films etc distributed in material form. Article 10 applies, in principle, to 'the making and distribution of films' eg video cassettes which are distributed for home consumption.[71]

5.026. Works of art. In *Müller v. Switzerland*,[72] a case which concerned paintings, the European Court held that despite the absence of any reference to artistic works in the Convention, they are included within Article 10. The Court stated that Article 10 '. . . includes freedom of artistic expression— notably within freedom to receive and impart information and ideas—which affords the opportunity to take part in the public exchange of cultural, political and social information and ideas of all kinds.' As the Court noted, confirmation that this is so is provided by the final sentence of paragraph (1) which refers to 'broadcasting, television or cinema enterprises', media whose activities extend to the field of art.[73]

5.027. Advertisements. The European Commission of Human Rights has held that so-called commercial 'speech' is covered by the protection conferred by Article 10(1).[74]

5.028. Professional publicity. In *Barthold v. Germany*,[75] the European Court held that the Applicant's views on the need for a particular service together with factual data and assertions regarding himself and the running of his practice, constituted the expression of 'opinions' and the imparting of 'information' and were therefore

---

[68] Application NO 12726/87 *Autronic AG v. Switzerland* Series A NO 178, (1990) 12 EHRR 485, para. 47, Judges Bindschedler–Robert and Matscher dissenting who stated that 'In our opinion, Article 10 presupposes a minimum of identification between the person who wishes to exercise the right protected by that Article and the "information" which is transmitted or received.' According to those judges, that connection did not exist in the instant case, for the sole purpose of reception of the broadcasts was to demonstrate the efficacy of the Applicant's technology.

[69] Application NO 8266/78 *X v. United Kingdom* (Radio Caroline) 16 DR 190 (pirate radio station operating on the high seas); Application NO 10746/84 *Verein Alternatives Lokalradio Bern and Verein Radio Dreyeckland Basel v. Switzerland* 49 DR 126 (private radio station); Application NO 10799/84 *Radio 24, S, W and A v. Switzerland* 37 DR 236 (private radio station). In Application NO 10746/84 *Verein Alternatives Lokalradio Bern and Verein Radio Dreyeckland Basel v. Switzerland*, the Commission stated that '. . . the right to freedom of expression recognised in Article 10 includes among other things the freedom to impart information and ideas through broadcasting. . . .' See §5.080 et seq. below.

[70] Application NO 8962/80 *X and Y v. Belgium* 28 DR 112 (1983), 5 EHRR 268. See §5.090 below.

[71] Application NO 12381/86 *X v. United Kingdom* (1988) 10 EHRR 123.

[72] Application NO 10737/84 Series A NO 133, (1991) 13 EHRR 212, para. 27. See §5.123 below.

[73] The Court also noted (para. 27) that 'Confirmation that the concept of freedom of expression is such as to include artistic expression is also to be found in Article 19(2) of the International Covenant on Civil and Political Rights, which specifically includes within the right of freedom of expression information and ideas "in the form of art."'

[74] Application NO 7805/77 *X and Church of Scientology v. Sweden* 16 DR 68. As to the level of protection afforded to advertisements, see §5.033 below.

[75] Application NO 8734/79 Series A NO 90, (1985) 7 EHRR 383.

covered by Article 10(1). The Court noted that it was not possible to divide the material into, on the one hand, those elements that went more to the presentation of the Applicant's services (and hence amounted to an advertisement), from on the other hand, the expression of the need for a particular service. It was therefore unnecessary to consider whether the material constituted an advertisement.

5.029. Commercial information with a limited readership. In *Markt Intern and Beerman v. Germany*,[76] the European Court held that the dissemination of information to a particular commercial sector, amounted to the imparting of informations and was therefore protected by Article 10:

> It is clear that the article in question was addressed to a limited circle of tradespeople and did not directly concern the public as a whole; however, it conveyed information of a commercial nature. Such information cannot be excluded from the scope of Article 10(1) which does not apply solely to certain types of information or ideas or forms of expression.

5.030. Data eg programme listings. Mere lists of data such as programme listings may qualify as 'information' under Article 10. The European Commission of Human Rights has stated that:

> 'in the ordinary sense of the word, information includes the expression of facts and of news and that television and radio programme data can be regarded as being either of them. The European Commission of Human Rights considers therefore that the lists of programme data in question constitute 'information' as opposed to 'opinions' or 'ideas' within the meaning of Article 10 of the Convention.'[77]

5.031. Protection of the form in which ideas are conveyed. In *Oberschlick v. Austria*,[78] the European Court held that:

> Article 10 protects not only the substance of the ideas and information expressed, but also the form in which they are conveyed.

(2) Limitations on Particular Categories

5.032. Information ie news of facts. A distinction has been made between on the one hand, the protection afforded to information of facts and on the other hand, protection given to the expression of opinion. The European Commission of Human Rights has held that in the case of the former, it is merely the free flow of the information to the public which is safeguarded, and not the right of everybody to disseminate that information. Thus in *De Geillustreerde Pers NV v. The Netherlands*,[79] it stated that:

> . . . in the area of 'information', ie in the area of facts and news as opposed to 'ideas' and 'opinions' the protection which Article 10 of the Convention seeks to secure concerns the free flow of such information to the public in general.

5.033. Advertising. The European Commission of Human Rights has held that although commercial 'speech' is not outside of the protection conferred by Article 10(1):

---

[76] Application NO 10572/83 Series A NO 165, (1990) 12 EHRR 161, para. 26.
[77] Application NO 5178/71 *De Geillustreerde Pers NV v. The Netherlands* 8 DR 5, [1978] ECC 164, para. 81.
[78] Application NO 11662/85 Series A 204, para. 57.
[79] Application NO 5178/71 8 DR 5, [1978] ECC 164, para. 85.

. . . it considers that the level of protection must be less than that accorded to the expression of 'political' ideas, in the broadest sense, with which the values underpinning the concept of freedom of expression in the Convention are chiefly concerned.[80]

(3) Protection of both the Inoffensive and the Shocking

5.034. Article 10 is designed to safeguard all forms of expression. Subject to certain carefully delineated exceptions, it is not discriminating in its application. As the European Court has stated in *Lingens v. Austria*[81] and numerous other cases:

. . . freedom of expression, as secured in paragraph 1 of Article 10, constitutes one of the essential foundations of a democratic society and one of the basic conditions for its progress and for each individual's self-fulfilment. Subject to paragraph 2, it is applicable not only to 'information' or 'ideas' that are favourably received or regarded as inoffensive or as a matter of indifference, but also to those that offend, shock or disturb. Such are the demands of that pluralism, tolerance and broadmindedness without which there is no 'democratic society'.[82]

4. Meaning of 'interference by public authority'

5.035. Introduction. It is the 'interference by public authority' which invokes the Convention. Whilst this is a broad concept, the interference normally consists of: a criminal conviction; or an injunction; or the interference by civil authorities or the refusal of access to the media. The first two forms of interference are often accompanied by a confiscation order whilst the third form usually consists of a refusal to award, or the withdrawal of, a licence.

5.036. Criminal convictions. Penalties imposed have included: a conviction under obscene publications legislation and the seizure, subsequent forfeiture and destruction of copies of a book and a matrix from which they were reproduced;[83] the seizure and subsequent forfeiture under obscenity legislation of pornographic magazines;[84] a conviction under obscenity legislation and subsequent confiscation of works of art;[85] a conviction for defamation;[86] a conviction for insulting the

---

[80] Application NO 7805/77 *X and Church of Scientology v. Sweden* 16 DR 68, para. 5.
[81] Application NO 9815/82 Series A NO 103, (1986) 8 EHRR 407, para. 41.
[82] This principle was first formulated in Application NO 5493/72 *Handyside v. United Kingdom* Series A NO 24, (1979–80) 1 EHRR 737 and has been affirmed by the European Court in: Application NO 10737/84 *Müller v. Switzerland* Series A NO 133, (1991) 13 EHRR 212; Application NO 11662/85 *Oberschlick v. Austria* Series A 204; Application NO 11798/85 *Castells v. Spain* Series A NO 236, (1992) 14 EHRR 445; Application NO 13166/87 *The Sunday Times v. United Kingdom* (NO 2) Series A NO 217, (1992) 14 EHRR 229; Application NO 13585/88 *The Observer and The Guardian v. United Kingdom* Series A NO 216, (1992) 14 EHRR 153; Application NO 13778/88 *Thorgeir Thorgeirson v. Iceland* Series A NO 239, (1992) 14 EHRR 843. On the operation of Article 10 (2) to justify censorship, see Application NO 9777/82 *X v. Belgium* (1984) 6 EHRR 467 (see §5.110 below).
[83] Application NO 5493/72 *Handyside v. United Kingdom* Series A NO 24, (1979–80) 1 EHRR 737.
[84] Application NO 9615/81 *X v. United Kingdom* (1983) 5 EHRR 581.
[85] Application NO 10737/84 *Müller v. Switzerland* Series A NO 133, (1991) 13 EHRR 212.
[86] Application NO 9815/82 *Lingens v. Austria* Series A NO 103, (1986) 8 EHRR 407; Application NO 11508/85 *Barfod v. Denmark* Series A NO 149 (1991) 13 EHRR 493; Application NO 11662/85 *Oberschlick v. Austria* Series A 204; Application NO 13704/88 *Schwabe v. Austria* Series A NO 242; Application NO 13778/88 *Thorgeir Thorgeirson v. Iceland* Series A NO 239, (1992) 14 EHRR 843.

government together with suspension from public office;[87] a conviction and fine under a common law offence of blasphemous libel;[88] a conviction and fine for revealing to the press the existence of prosecution investigations, contrary to confidentiality laws;[89] a conviction and one year's imprisonment under legislation prohibiting wartime collaborators from writing, publishing or printing any newspapers or other publications which had a political character;[90] a conviction and suspended sentence under legislation prohibiting the operation of pirate radio stations[91] and a conviction for using a citizen's band radio without official permission.[92]

5.037. Injunctions. Measures imposed have included: an injunction prohibiting the publication of an article concerning a live action contrary to contempt of court laws;[93] an injunction preventing the reporting of trial proceedings by way of dramatic reconstruction contrary to contempt of court laws;[94] an injunction issued pursuant to consumer protection legislation to prohibit an advertisement;[95] an injunction issued pursuant to unfair competition legislation prohibiting a professional from publicising his practice;[96] an injunction issued pursuant to unfair competition legislation restraining a publisher of a trade journal from publishing critical information about particular companies contrary to unfair competition legislation.[97]

5.038. Civil interference including the conferring of monopoly rights. Measures imposed have included: legislation conferring broadcasting rights upon a state monopoly;[98] the refusal to award a broadcasting licence to a third party;[99] the jamming of a broadcast;[100] a statute conferring upon a broadcasting organisation, the sole right to publish details of radio and television programmes;[101] an administrative decision permitting the redistribution of only terrestrial transmissions which complied with the provisions of the International Telecommunication Convention and the Radio Regulations;[102] and administrative and judicial

---

[87] Application NO 11798/85 *Castells v. Spain* Series A NO 236, (1992) 14 EHRR 445.

[88] Application NO 8710/79 *Gay News Ltd and Lemon v. United Kingdom* (1983) 5 EHRR 123.

[89] Application NO 11034/84 *Weber v. Switzerland* Series A NO 177, (1990) 12 EHRR 508.

[90] Application NO 9777/82 *X v. Belgium* (1984) 6 EHRR 467.

[91] Application NO 8266/78 *X v. United Kingdom* (Radio Caroline), 16 DR 190.

[92] Application NO 8962/80 *X and Y v. Belgium* 28 DR 112, (1983) 5 EHRR 268.

[93] Application NO 6538/74 *The Sunday Times v. The United Kingdom* Series A NO 30, (1979–80) 2 EHRR 245; Application NO 13166/87 *The Sunday Times v. United Kingdom* (NO 2) Series A NO 217, (1992) 14 EHRR 229; Application NO 13585/88 *The Observer and The Guardian v. United Kingdom* Series A NO 216, (1992) 14 EHRR 153.

[94] Applications NOs 11553/85 and 11658/85 *Hodgson, Woolf Productions and National Union of Journalists and Channel Four Television v. United Kingdom* (1988) 10 EHRR 503.

[95] Application NO 7805/77 *X and Church of Scientology v. Sweden* 16 DR 68.

[96] Application NO 8734/79 *Barthold v. Germany* Series A NO 90, (1985) 7 EHRR 383.

[97] Application NO 10572/83 *Markt Intern and Beerman v. Germany* Series A NO 165, (1990) 12 EHRR 161.

[98] Application NO 3071/67 *X v. Sweden* 26 Collection of Decisions 71 (both radio and television).

[99] Application NO 4750/71 *X v. The United Kingdom* 40 Collection of Decisions 29 (refusal to license private commercial radio station); Application NO 10746/84 *Verein Alternatives Lokalradio Bern and Verein Radio Dreyeckland Basel v. Switzerland* 49 DR 126 (refusal to license private commercial radio station); Application NO 10799/84 *Radio 24 AG S, W and A v. Switzerland* 37 DR 236 (refusal to license private commercial radio station).

[100] Application NO 4750/71 *X v. The United Kingdom* 40 Collection of Decisions 49 (jamming of commercial radio stations).

[101] Application NO 5178/71 *De Geillustreerde Pers NV v. The Netherlands* 8 DR 5, [1978] ECC 164.

[102] Application NO 10890/84 *Groppera Radio AG v. Switzerland* Series A NO 173, (1990) 12 EHRR 508.

decisions which prevented an undertaking from lawfully receiving transmissions made by a Fixed Service Satellite.[103]

5.039. Refusing access to the media. Measures have included: the refusal of a State broadcasting organisation to allow a political organisation to broadcast its views[104] and the refusal of a commercial broadcasting organisation to broadcast advertisements for a particular political organisation.[105]

5.040. Interference with the media ie production of television programmes. The European Commission of Human Rights has stated that an order transforming the format of a television programme, comes within the notion of 'interference' under the Convention:

> . . . an interference with the manner of conveying information to the public, as opposed to the content of information constitutes an interference with freedom of expression under paragraph 1 of this provision [Article 10(1)]. In reaching this view the Commission has attached particular importance to the role played by production and presentation techniques in the making of television programmes.[106]

5. Prescribed by Law

(1) General Principles

5.041. Introduction. The measure impugned under Article 10 must have been 'prescribed by law . . . ' This is a rule inspired by the concept of natural justice. No party should be bound by the arbitrary acts of those in authority. Any prescriptive rule must thus satisfy certain rules evolved by the European Commission of Human Rights and the European Court.

5.042. Clear, accessible and precise. In *The Sunday Times v. The United Kingdom*,[107] the European Court defined the yardstick against which any prescriptive law must be measured:

> In the Court's opinion, the following are two of the requirements that flow from the expression 'prescribed by law'. First, the law must be adequately accessible: the citizen must be able to have an indication that is adequate in the circumstances of the legal rules applicable to a given case. Secondly, a norm cannot be regarded as a 'law' unless it is formulated with sufficient precision to enable the citizen to regulate his conduct: he must be able—if need be with appropriate advice—to foresee, to a degree that is reasonable in the circumstances, the consequences which a given action may entail. Those consequences need not be foreseeable with absolute certainty: experience shows this to be unattainable. Again, whilst certainty is highly desirable, it may bring in its train excessive rigidity and the law must be able to keep pace with changing circumstances. Accordingly, many laws are inevitably couched in terms which, to a

---

[103] Application NO 12726/87 *Autronic AG v. Switzerland* Series A NO 178, (1990) 12 EHRR 485.
[104] Application NO 4515/70 *X and the Association of Z v. The United Kingdom* 14 Yearbook 538 and Application NO 9297/81 *X Association v. Sweden* 28 DR 204.
[105] Application NO 4515/70 *X and the Association of Z v. The United Kingdom* 14 Yearbook 538.
[106] Applications NOs 11553/85 and 11658/85 *Hodgson, Woolf Productions and National Union of Journalists and Channel Four Television v. United Kingdom* (1988) 10 EHRR 503, para. 2. In that case, the Applicants were able to impart substantially the same information in an amended version of their programme and the European Commission of Human Rights stated that the interference was less serious than a total prohibition.
[107] Application NO 6538/74 Series A NO 30, (1979–80) 2 EHRR 245, para. 49.

greater or lesser extent, are vague and whose interpretation and application are questions of practice.[108]

5.043. Non-existence of case law. A measure is accessible and foreseeable even where there is no case law precedent for its application to a particular situation. In *Castells v. Spain*,[109] the Applicant argued that because his case was the first of its type to come before the national courts and academic opinion was divided on the effect of the legislation in issue, it failed the prescription test. The European Court held that the text of the legislation covered in a general fashion several scenarios and was inevitably capable of being brought into play in new situations.

5.044. Dependent on the nature of the legislation. In *Groppera Radio AG v. Switzerland*,[110] the European Court stated that:

. . . the scope of the concepts of foreseeability and accessibility depends to a considerable degree on the content of the instrument in issue, the field it is designed to cover and the number and status of those to whom it is addressed.

5.045. Presumption of validity of court order. A court order which has been issued pursuant to legislation is presumed to be valid until proved otherwise. Thus the European Commission of Human Rights has stated that:

When a court order is grounded on a statutory provision it must be regarded as 'lawful' until set aside by a decision of a superior court. It is not rendered unlawful when . . . there exists no appeal against it.[111]

5.046. Common law and statute. The prescriptive law to which Article 10 refers, may be both statute and common law. As the European Commission of Human Rights held in *Gay News Ltd and Lemon v. United Kingdom*:[112]

. . . not only written statutes, but also rules of common or other customary law may provide a sufficient legal basis both for the restrictions of fundamental rights subject to exception clauses such as the one contained in Article 10(2) of the Convention, and for the criminal convictions envisaged in Article 7 of the Convention.

In *The Sunday Times v. United Kingdom*,[113] the European Court held that:

The Court observes that the word 'law' in the expression 'prescribed by law' covers not

---

[108] See Application NO 10465/83 *Olsson v. Sweden* Series A NO 130, (1989) 11 EHRR 259 and Application NO 10737/84 *Müller v. Switzerland* Series A NO 133, (1991) 13 EHRR 212. In Application NO 8734/79 *Barthold v. Germany* Series A NO 90, (1985) 7 EHRR 383, para. 45, the European Court held that '. . . the interference must have some basis in domestic law, which itself must be adequately accessible and be formulated with sufficient precision to enable the individual to regulate his conduct, if need be with appropriate advice.' In Applications NOs 11553/85 and 11658/85 *Hodgson, Woolf Productions and National Union of Journalists and Channel Four Television v. United Kingdom* (1988) 10 EHRR 503, para. 2, the European Commission of Human Rights stated that 'The mere fact that a legislative provision may give rise to problems of interpretation does not mean that it is so vague and imprecise as to lack the quality of "law" in this sense (see in this respect, App. No 9174/80 *Zamir v. United Kingdom* (1986) 8 EHRR 108, para 93–94).'

[109] Application NO 11798/85 Series A NO 236, (1992) 14 EHRR 445.

[110] Application NO 10890/84 Series A NO 173, (1990) 12 EHRR 508, para. 68.

[111] Applications NOs 11553/85 and 11658/85 *Hodgson, Woolf Productions and National Union of Journalists and Channel Four Television v. United Kingdom* (1988) 10 EHRR 503, para. 2.

[112] Application NO 8710/79 (1983) 5 EHRR 123, para. 6.

[113] Application NO 6538/74 Series A NO 30, (1979–80) 2 EHRR 245, para. 47.

only statute but also unwritten law . . . It would clearly be contrary to the intention of the drafters of the Convention to hold that a restriction imposed by virtue of the common law is not 'prescribed by law' on the sole ground that it is not enunciated in legislation: this would deprive a common law State which is Party to the Convention of the protection of Article 10(2) and strike at the very roots of that State's legal system.[114]

5.047. Prohibition of retrospective law—Article 7. Article 7 of the Convention prohibits the retrospective application of criminal law. It states that:

> No one shall be held guilty of any criminal offence on account of any act or omission which did not constitute a criminal offence under national or international law at the time when it was committed. Nor shall a heavier penalty be imposed than the one that was applicable at the time the criminal offence was committed.

5.048. Prohibition of retrospective legislation. As the European Commission of Human Rights made clear in *Gay News Ltd and Lemon v. United Kingdom*,[115] Article 7 imposes a specific obligation which must be implied in the interpretation of any prescription under Article 10:

> . . . Article 7(1) of the Convention forbids the retrospective application of the criminal law to the detriment of the accused and stipulates in a general way the principle of the legality of criminal offences and penalties (*nullum crimes, nulla poena sine lege*). What is, amongst other things, prohibited is the application of the penal law *in malum partem* in relation to facts which the text of the law cannot reasonably extend to.[116]

5.049. Prohibition of retrospective common law. In relation to common law, the European Commission of Human Rights in *Gay News Ltd and Lemon v. United Kingdom*,[117] stated that:

> The Commission considers that the same principles [annunciated above][118] also apply to the interpretation and application of the common law. While this branch of the law presents certain particularities for the very reason that it is by definition law developed by the courts, it is nevertheless subject to the rule that the law-making function of the courts must remain within reasonable limits. In particular in the area of the criminal law it is excluded, by virtue of Article 7(1) of the Convention, that any acts not previously punishable should be held by the courts to entail criminal liability, or that existing offences should be extended to cover facts which previously clearly did not constitute a criminal offence. This implies that constituent elements of an offence such as, eg. the particular form of culpability required for its completion may not be essentially changed, at least not to the detriment of the accused, by the case law of the courts. On the other hand it is not objectionable that the existing elements of the offence are clarified and adapted to new circumstances which can reasonably be brought under the original concept of the offence.

---

[114] In that case the Court stated (para. 47) in relation to the contempt of court laws of the United Kingdom that '. . . the Court does not attach importance here to the fact that contempt of court is a creature of the common law and not of legislation.'

[115] Application NO 8710/79 (1983) 5 EHRR 123, para. 8.

[116] On the application of Article 7 to statute (see cases cited in *Gay News Ltd and Lemon v. United Kingdom*).

[117] Application NO 8710/79 (1983) 5 EHRR 123, para. 9.

[118] See §5.048 above.

In that case, the English courts before whom the charge was heard all held that intent to blaspheme was not a necessary element for a finding of guilt. It was simply necessary to prove that the Applicants had intended to publish the offending piece ie liability was strict. The Applicants argued that this interpretation was contrary to the Convention having been evolved solely by the Courts before whom the matter was tried. The Commission however, rejected the application stating that new law had not been created because there had not been any previous judgment in which it was held that an intention to blaspheme was a required element.

5.050. Articles intended for export. A Contracting State does not trespass its jurisdiction by applying domestic legislation to articles intended for export. The European Commission of Human Rights has held that legislation under which articles for export have been seized is 'prescribed by law' under the Convention, notwithstanding that those articles might not be seized under the laws existing in the importing country.[119]

(2) Particular Laws

5.051. Defamation and political insults. In *Lingens v. Austria*,[120] *Barfod v. Denmark*,[121] *Oberschlick v. Austria*,[122] *Schwabe v. Austria*[123] and *Thorgeir Thorgeirson v. Iceland*,[124] the European Court held that a conviction for criminal defamation pursuant to a statute was a measure prescribed by law and in *Castells v. Spain*,[125] the European Court held that a conviction for insulting the government was prescribed by law.

5.052. Contempt of court. *The Sunday Times v. The United Kingdom*[126] concerned an injunction preventing the publication of an article concerning active litigation.[127] The Attorney General had obtained an injunction preventing publication on the grounds that by bringing pressure to bear on the parties to settle the claims, the newspaper would be committing a contempt of court. The injunction was reversed by the Court of Appeal but confirmed by the House of Lords. In justifying the concept of contempt of court, certain Law Lords confirmed the 'pressure principle' whilst others held that the Applicants' articles sought to prejudge, or were likely to cause public prejudgment of the issues raised in pending litigation. The Applicants argued that the notion of 'prejudgment' had not been sufficiently defined so as to constitute a measure 'prescribed by law'. The European Court held, not without mild reservation, that the 'prejudgment principle' was sufficiently defined having been referred to in case law and reference works on the subject.

5.053. Obscenity. In *Müller v. Switzerland*,[128] the European Court held that:

---

[119] Application NO 9615/81 X v. *United Kingdom* (1983) 5 EHRR 581, in which the European Commission of Human Rights held that the English courts had not trespassed their jurisdiction by holding that magazines which were likely to be read solely by forcing subjects resident abroad, were obscene within the meaning of English law, (under the Obscene Publications Act 1959).
[120] Application NO 9815/82 Series A NO 103, (1986) 8 EHRR 407. See §5.101 et seq. below.
[121] Application NO 11508/85 (1991) 13 EHRR 493. See §5.108 et seq. below.
[122] Application NO 11662/85 Series A 204. See §5.101 et seq. below.
[123] Application NO 13704/88 Series A NO 242. See §5.101 et seq. below.
[124] Application NO 13778/88 Series A NO 239, (1992) 14 EHRR 843. See §5.109 below.
[125] Application NO 11798/85 Series A NO 236, (1992) 14 EHRR 445. See §5.104 et seq. below.
[126] Application NO 6538/74 Series A NO 30, (1979–80) 2 EHRR 245. See §5.111 et seq. below.
[127] For the facts, see §5.115 below.
[128] Application NO 10737/84 Series A NO 133, (1991) 13 EHRR 212, para. 29. See §5.123 below.

The Court has . . . already emphasised the impossibility of attaining absolute precision in the framing of laws, particulary in fields in which the situation changes according to the prevailing views of society. The need to avoid excessive rigidity and to keep pace with changing circumstances means that many laws are inevitably couched in terms which, to a greater or lesser extent, are vague. Criminal law provisions on obscenity fall within this category.

The Court held that the national legislation fulfilled the necessary requirements: there had been a number of consistent decisions in the national appeal court which had been published and which were followed by the lower courts.

5.054. Blasphemy. In *Gay News Ltd and Lemon v. United Kingdom*,[129] the European Commission of Human Rights found that law under which the Applicants were charged with having 'unlawfully and wickedly published or caused to be published a blasphemous libel concerning the Christian religion, namely an obscene poem and illustration vilifying Christ in His life and in His crucifixion', was prescribed by law.

5.055. Political censorship. The European Commission of Human Rights has found that a law which prohibited persons who collaborated with the Germans during World War Two from writing, publishing or printing any newspaper or other publication of a political character, was prescribed by law.[130]

5.056. Unfair competition. In *Barthold v. Germany*,[131] the European Court held that unfair competition legislation which conferred a broad discretion on the courts, did satisfy the 'prescription' rules:

The Court has . . . already had the occasion to recognise the impossibility of attaining absolute precision in the framing of laws. Such considerations are especially cogent in the sphere of conduct governed by . . . competition, this being a subject where the relevant factors are in constant evolution in line with developments in the market and in means of communication.

In *Markt Intern and Beerman v. Germany*,[132] the European Court affirmed the aforementioned principle and went on to state that:

. . . The interpretation and application of such legislation are inevitably questions of practice.

In this instance, there was consistent case law on the matter from the Federal Court of Justice. This case law, which was clear and abundant and had been the subject of extensive commentary, was such as to enable commercial operators and their advisers to regulate their conduct in the relevant sphere.

5.057. International telecommunications legislation. In *Groppera Radio AG v. Switzerland*,[133] the International Telecommunication Convention and the Radio Regulations were found to be sufficiently accessible to qualify as 'prescribed by law'. The former were published in an official federal collection. The latter, although not published in national reference works, could be accessed either at the national telecommunication organisation office or at the offices of the International Telecommunication Union. The European Court noted that the regulations were highly technical and complex, but, said that it was reasonable to assume that any

---

129 Application NO 8710/79 (1983) 5 EHRR 123. For the facts of the case, see §5.125 et seq. below.
130 Application NO 9777/82 X v. Belgium (1984) 6 EHRR 467. See §5.110 below.
131 Application NO 8734/79 Series A NO 90, (1985) 7 EHRR 383, para. 47. See §5.132 below.
132 Application NO 10572/83 Series A NO 165, (1990) 12 EHRR 161, para. 30. See §5.133 below.
133 Application NO 10890/84 Series A NO 173, (1990) 12 EHRR 321. See §5.082 et seq. below.

broadcaster engaged in satellite transmissions would seek professional advice to enable them to comply with the terms of those rules. Nevertheless this is not without qualification. Thus in *Autronic AG v. Switzerland*,[134] despite the European Court stating that 'Having regard to the particular public for which they are intended, these enactments are sufficiently accessible', it held that 'Their status as "law" within the meaning of Article 10(2), however, remains doubtful, because it may be asked whether they do not lack the required clarity and precision . . . the international provisions seem to leave a substantial margin of appreciation to the national authorities.'

5.058. Legal principles underlying an injunction. In *The Observer and The Guardian v. United Kingdom*,[135] the European Court rejected the Applicant's argument that the common law principles upon which a court in the United Kingdom granted an injunction, namely those formulated in the 'American Cyanimid'[136] case, were neither adequately accessible nor sufficiently foreseeable.

6. Legitimate Aim—Necessary in a Democratic Society

(1) Convention Categories

5.059. The freedom generally safeguarded by Article 10 'carries with it duties and responsibilities' and therefore must yield to such 'formalities, conditions, restrictions or penalties' which are '. . . necessary in a democratic society'. The Convention itself lists the permissible grounds. They are generally referred to both by the European Commission of Human Rights and the European Court as 'legitimate aims', being those that are:

(1) in the interests of national security, territorial integrity or public safety;
(2) for the prevention of disorder or crime;
(3) for the protection of health or morals;
(4) for the protection of the reputation or rights of others;
(5) for preventing the disclosure of information received in confidence;
(6) or for maintaining the authority and impartiality of the judiciary.

(2) The Necessity of the Aim

5.060. Concept of necessity—a pressing social need. The concept of a 'necessary' aim eludes easy definition. In *Handyside v. United Kingdom*,[137] the European Court held that:

. . . whilst the adjective 'necessary', within the meaning of Article 10(2), is not synonymous with 'indispensable' (cf., in Articles 2(2) and 6(1), the words 'absolutely necessary' and 'strictly necessary' and, in Article 15(1) the phrase 'to the extent strictly required by the exigencies of the situation'), neither has it the flexibility of such expressions as 'admissible', 'ordinary' (cf. Article 4(3)), 'useful', (cf the French text of the first paragraph of Article I of Protocol No 1), 'reasonable' (cf. Articles 5(3) and 6(1)) or 'desirable'.[138]

---

[134] Application NO 12726/87 Series A NO 178, (1990) 12 EHRR 485, para. 57. See §5.086 et seq. below.

[135] Application NO 13585/88 Series A NO 216, (1992) 14 EHRR 153.

[136] See *American Cyanimid Co v. Ethicon Ltd* [1975] AC 396.

[137] Application NO 5493/72 Series A NO 24, (1979–80) 1 EHRR 737, para. 48.

[138] Affirmed by the European Court in Application NO 8734/79 *Barthold v. Germany* Series A NO 90, (1985) 7 EHRR 383 and Application NO 6538/74 *The Sunday Times v. The United Kingdom* Series A NO 30, (1979–80) 2 EHRR 245.

The Court stated that, in essence, the concept of necessity implies a 'pressing social need'.[139]

5.061. Convention categories merely a starting point. The fact that the impugned legislation fits into a category listed in Article 10(2), is not sufficient to make it 'necessary' within the meaning of the Convention. A careful appraisal of the issues has to be made in the case in point and thus national authorities cannot rely upon absolute principles they have themselves developed in a particular area of law. As the European Court noted in *The Sunday Times v. The United Kingdom*:[140]

> It is not sufficient that the interference involved belongs to that class of the exceptions listed in Article 10(2) which has been invoked; neither is it sufficient that the interference was imposed because its subject-matter fell within a particular category or was caught by a legal rule formulated in general or absolute terms: the Court has to be satisfied that the interference was necessary having regard to the facts and circumstances prevailing in the specific case before it.

(3) Relationship between National and European Court

5.062. Initial assessment by national court. Despite the fact that 'necessity' is difficult to define, the European Court stated in *Handyside v. United Kingdom*[141] that:

> . . . The Court points out that the machinery of protection established by the Convention is subsidiary to the national systems safeguarding human rights . . . The Convention leaves to each Contracting State, in the first place the task of securing the rights and freedoms it enshrines. The institutions created by it make their own contribution to this task but they become involved only through contentious proceedings and once all domestic remedies have been exhausted (Article 26) . . .[142]
>
> . . . it is for the national authorities to make the initial assessment of the reality of the pressing social need implied by the notion of 'necessity' in this context.[143]

5.063. Domestic margin of appreciation. Acknowledging the difficulty of delineating the contours of a 'necessary' measure, the European Court allows Contracting States a so called 'margin of appreciation'.[144] This margin is given both to the

---

[139] Application NO 5493/72 *Handyside v. United Kingdom* Series A NO 24, (1979–80) 1 EHRR 737, affirmed in Application NO 6538/74 *The Sunday Times v. The United Kingdom* Series A NO 30, (1979–80) 2 EHRR 245; Application NO 8734/79 *Barthold v. Germany* Series A NO 90, (1985) 7 EHRR 383; Application NO 10737/84 *Müller v. Switzerland* Series A NO 133, (1991) 13 EHRR 212; Applications NOs 11553/85 and 11658/85 *Hodgson, Woolf Productions and National Union of Journalists and Channel Four Television v. United Kingdom* (1988) 10 EHRR 503; Application NO 13166/87 *The Sunday Times v. United Kingdom* (NO 2) Series A NO 217, (1992) 14 EHRR 229.

[140] Application NO 6538/74 Series A NO 30, (1979–80) 2 EHRR 245, para. 65.

[141] Application NO 5493/72 Series A NO 24, (1979–80) 1 EHRR 737, para. 48.

[142] Affirmed by the European Court in Application NO 6538/74 *The Sunday Times v. The United Kingdom* Series A NO 30, (1979–80) 2 EHRR 245.

[143] On exhaustion of domestic remedies, see van Dijk and van Hoof, *op. cit.*, 2.6 et seq.

[144] Application NO 5493/72 *Handyside v. United Kingdom* Series A NO 24, (1979–80) 1 EHRR 737; Application NO 6538/74 *The Sunday Times v. The United Kingdom* Series A NO 30, (1979–80) 2 EHRR 245; Application NO 8734/79 *Barthold v. Germany* Series A NO 90, (1985) 7 EHRR 383, Application NO 9815/82 *Lingens v. Austria* Series A NO 103, (1986) 8 EHRR 407; Application NO 13166/87 *The Sunday Times v. United Kingdom* (NO 2) Series A NO 217, (1992) 14 EHRR 229.

domestic legislator who enacts prescriptive measures as well as the judicial and other bodies that are called upon to interpret and apply the laws in force.[145]

5.064. Court's supervisory role. The European Court's role is thus one of supervisor. It regulates the measures taken by the national authorities. In *Handyside v. United Kingdom*,[146] the European Court stated:

> . . . Article 10(2) does not give the Contracting States an unlimited power of appreciation. The Court, which, with the Commission, is responsible for ensuring the observance of those States' engagements (Article 19), is empowered to give the final ruling on whether a 'restriction' or 'penalty' is reconcilable with freedom of expression as protected by Article 10.[147] The domestic margin of appreciation thus goes hand in hand with a European supervision. Such supervision concerns both the aim of the measure challenged and its 'necessity'; it covers not only the basic legislation but also the decision applying it, even one given by an independent court. . .[148]
>
> It follows from this that it is in no way the Court's task to take the place of the competent national courts but rather to review under Article 10 the decisions they delivered in the exercise of their power of appreciation.[149]

5.065. Supervision is strict. Whilst European supervision will vary according to the case, it is strict because of the importance of the rights guaranteed by Article 10. As the European Court is wont to reiterate, the exceptions enumerated in Article 10(2) are narrowly construed and the necessity for restricting the rights conferred by Article 10(1) must be convincingly established.[150]

---

[145] Application NO 5493/72 *Handyside v. United Kingdom* Series A NO 24, (1979–80) 1 EHRR 737; (see judgments cited in Handyside) and Application NO 6538/74 *The Sunday Times v. The United Kingdom* Series A NO 30, (1979–80) 2 EHRR 245.

[146] Application NO 5493/72 Series A NO 24, (1979–80) 1 EHRR 737, para. 49.

[147] Affirmed in Application NO 9815/82 *Lingens v. Austria* Series A NO 103, (1986) 8 EHRR 407; Application NO 10737/84 *Müller v. Switzerland* Series A NO 133, (1991) 13 EHRR 212; Application NO 13166/87 *The Sunday Times v. United Kingdom* (NO 2) Series A NO 217, (1992) 14 EHRR 229.

[148] Affirmed by the European Court in Application NO 6538/74 *The Sunday Times v. The United Kingdom* Series A NO 30, (1979–80) 2 EHRR 245; Application NO 9815/82 *Lingens v. Austria* Series A NO 103, (1986) 8 EHRR 407; Application NO 10572/83 *Markt Intern and Beerman v. Germany* Series A NO 165, (1990) 12 EHRR 161; Application NO 10737/84 *Müller v. Switzerland* Series A NO 133, (1991) 13 EHRR 212; Application NO 10890/84 *Goppera Radio AG v. Switzerland* Series A NO 173, (1990) 12 EHRR 321 (in that case, the court made reference only to the national authorities); Application NO 11034/84 *Weber v. Switzerland* Series A NO 177, (1990) 12 EHRR 508; Application NO 11508/85 *Barfod v. Denmark* (1991) 13 EHRR 493; Application NO 12726/87 *Autronic AG v. Switzerland* Series A NO 178, (1990) 12 EHRR 485 (in that case the court made reference only to the national authorities); Application NO 13166/87 *The Sunday Times v. United Kingdom* (NO 2) Series A NO 217, (1992) 14 EHRR 229.

[149] Affirmed in Application NO 6538/74 *The Sunday Times v. The United Kingdom* Series A NO 30, (1979–80) 2 EHRR 245; Application NO 13166/87 *The Sunday Times v. United Kingdom* (NO 2) Series A NO 217, (1992) 14 EHRR 229. In Application NO 13778/88 *Thorgeir Thorgeirson v. Iceland* Series A NO 239, (1992) 14 EHRR 843, para. 58, the European Court stated that '. . . it is primarily for the national authorities, notably the courts, to interpret and apply domestic law.' (See *Kruslin v. France* (1990) 12 EHRR 547.)

[150] Application NO 7805/77 *X and Church of Scientology v. Sweden* 16 DR 68 (on the strictness of supervision on cases concerning 'commercial ideas', see 5.033 above); Application NO 8734/79 *Barthold v. Germany* Series A NO 90, (1985) 7 EHRR 383; Application NO 11034/84 *Weber v. Switzerland* (Series A NO 177, (1990) 12 EHRR 508; Application NO 12726/87 *Autronic AG v. Switzerland* Series A NO 178, (1990) 12 EHRR 485; Application NO 13585/88 *The Observer and The Guardian v. United Kingdom* Series A NO 216, (1992) 14 EHRR 153; Application NO 13778/88 *Thorgeir Thorgeirson v. Iceland* Series A NO 239, (1992) 14 EHRR 843.

(4) Factors Relevant to Assessment by European Court

5.066. Appraisal made in the light of the case as a whole. In exercising its supervisory jurisdiction, the European Court (and the European Commission of Human Rights) cannot confine itself to considering the impugned measures in isolation: it must look at them in the light of the case as a whole.[151] The Court must therefore consider the variety of reasoning and solutions in judicial decisions in the various stages of the case in issue.[152]

5.067. Relevancy, sufficiency and proportionality. The reasons adduced by the authorities to justify their action, must be 'relevant and sufficient'.[153] And most importantly, they must be proportionate to the perceived danger.[154]

5.068. Good faith of national court irrelevant. In *The Sunday Times v. The United Kingdom*,[155] the European Court emphasised that it is not enough for a Contracting State to act reasonably within the parameters of its own law: the Convention establishes a yardstick against which any State interference must be measured:

> This does not mean that the Court's supervision is limited to ascertaining whether a respondent State exercised its discretion reasonably, carefully and in good faith. Even a

---

[151] Application NO 5493/72 *Handyside v. United Kingdom* Series A NO 24, (1979–80) 1 EHRR 737; Application NO 6538/74 *The Sunday Times v. The United Kingdom* Series A NO 30, (1979–80) 2 EHRR 245; Application NO 9815/82 *Lingens v. Austria* Series A NO 103, (1986) 8 EHRR 407; Application NO 10243/83 *Times Newspapers Ltd and Others v. United Kingdom*; Application NO 10572/83 *Markt Intern and Beerman v. Germany* Series A NO 165, (1990) 12 EHRR 161; Application NO 10737/84 *Müller v. Switzerland* Series A NO 133, (1991) 13 EHRR 212; Application NO 11508/85 *Barfod v. Denmark* (1991) 13 EHRR 493; Application NO 13166/87 *The Sunday Times v. United Kingdom* (NO 2) Series A NO 217, (1992) 14 EHRR 229; Application NO 13704/88 *Schwabe v. Austria* Series A NO 242.

[152] Application NO 6538/74 *The Sunday Times v. The United Kingdom* Series A NO 30, (1979–80) 2 EHRR 245.

[153] Applications NO 5493/72 *Handyside v. United Kingdom* Series A NO 24, (1979–80) 1 EHRR 737; Application NO 6538/74 *The Sunday Times v. The United Kingdom* Series A NO 30, (1979–80) 2 EHRR 245; Application NO 8734/79 *Barthold v. Germany* Series A NO 90, (1985) 7 EHRR 383; Application NO 9815/82 *Lingens v. Austria* Series A NO 103, (1986) 8 EHRR 407; Application NO 10737/84 *Müller v. Switzerland* Series A NO 133, (1991) 13 EHRR 212 and Applications NOs 11553/85 and 11658/85 *Hodgson, Woolf Productions and National Union of Journalists and Channel Four Television v. United Kingdom* (1988) 10 EHRR 503; Application NO 13166/87 *The Sunday Times v. United Kingdom* (NO 2) Series A NO 217, (1992) 14 EHRR 229; Application NO 13585/88 *The Observer and The Guardian v. United Kingdom* Series A NO 216, (1992) 14 EHRR 153.

[154] Application NO 5493/72 *Handyside v. United Kingdom* Series A NO 24, (1979–80) 1 EHRR 737; Application 7805/77 *X and Church of Scientology v. Sweden* 16 DR 68; Application NO 6538/74 *The Sunday Times v. The United Kingdom* Series A NO 30, (1979–80) 2 EHRR 245; Application NO 8734/79 *Barthold v. Germany* Series A NO 90, (1985) 7 EHRR 383; Application NO 9815/82 *Lingens v. Austria* Series A NO 103, (1986) 8 EHRR 407; Application NO 10737/84 *Müller v. Switzerland* Series A NO 133, (1991) 13 EHRR 212; Application NO 10572/83 *Markt Intern and Beerman v. Germany* Series A NO 165, (1990) 12 EHRR 161; Application NO 11508/85 *Barfod v. Denmark* (1991) 13 EHRR 493; Applications NOs 11553/85 and 11658/85 *Hodgson, Woolf Productions and National Union of Journalists and Channel Four Television v. United Kingdom* (1988) 10 EHRR 503; Application NO 13166/87 *The Sunday Times v. United Kingdom* (NO 2) Series A NO 217, (1992) 14 EHRR 229; Application NO 13585/88 *The Observer and The Guardian v. United Kingdom* Series A No 216, (1992), 14 EHRR 153.

[155] Application NO 6538/74 Series A NO 30, (1979–80) 2 EHRR 245, para. 59.

Contracting State so acting remains subject to the Court's control as regards the compatibility of its conduct with the engagements it has undertaken under the Convention.[156]

5.069. Comparison of similar cases. The decisions (or even inactivity) of domestic courts in purportedly analogous cases is of no relevance to the European Court in determining the case in issue. In *Handyside v. United Kingdom*,[157] it stated that:

> In principle, it is not the Court's function to compare different decisions taken, even in apparently similar circumstances, by prosecuting authorities and courts . . .

5.070. Mélange of legal solutions. Not all Contracting States have developed identical legal solutions to a given problem. The fact that a measure under consideration might not have been granted under a different legal system does not invalidate that particular measure, for the main purpose of the Convention is 'to lay down certain international standards to be observed by the Contracting States in their relations with persons under their jurisdiction'.[158] But, as the European Court has noted, this:

> . . . does not mean that absolute uniformity is required and, indeed, since the Contracting States remain free to choose the measures which they consider appropriate, the Court cannot be oblivious of the substantive or procedural features of their respective domestic laws.[159]

5.071. Importance of national law where inspiration for specific Convention principle. In *The Sunday Times v. United Kingdom*,[160] the European Court held that even where a part of Article 10(2) was inspired by a legal concept existing in a particular Contracting State (in that case, the common law concept of contempt of court):

> . . . it cannot have adopted them as they stood: it transposed them into an autonomous context. It is 'necessity' in terms of the Convention which the Court has to assess, its role being to review the conformity of national acts with the standards of that instrument.

(5) Paramountcy of Freedom of Expression

5.072. In assessing the rights conferred by Article 10, it is generally not a question of balancing competing interests. Rather, the general principle is the preservation of freedom of expression to which certain exceptions are allowed:

---

[156] Affirmed in Application NO 13166/87 *The Sunday Times v. United Kingdom* (NO 2) Series A NO 217, (1992) 14 EHRR 229. This may not always be the case. Thus, for example, in Application NO 10572/83 *Markt Intern and Beerman v. Germany* Series A NO 165, (1990) 12 EHRR 161, para. 37, which concerned unfair competition laws, the European Court stated that '. . . the European Court of Human Rights should not substitute its own evaluation for that of the national courts in the instant case where those courts, on reasonable grounds, had considered the restrictions to be necessary.' The explanation for this is probably that in cases which concern laws which are fast changing, the margin of discretion is wider.

[157] Application NO 5493/72 Series A NO 24, (1979–80) 1 EHRR 737, para. 56.

[158] Application NO 6538/74 *The Sunday Times v. The United Kingdom* Series A NO 30, (1979–80) 2 EHRR 245, para. 61.

[159] *Ibid.*; See Application No 1474/62 and others, The Belgium Lingustic Case (Merits) (1968) Series A NO 6, (1968) 1 EHRR 252.

[160] Application NO 6538/74 Series A NO 30, (1979–80) 2 EHRR 245, para. 60.

The Court is faced not with a choice between two conflicting principles, but with a principle of freedom of expression that is subject to a number of exceptions which must be narrowly interpreted.[161]

(6) Margin of Appreciation allowed National Courts

5.073. Contempt of court. The European Court imposes what it considers to be a universal concept of unacceptable judicial control. Contrasting its attitude in this domain from its approach on obscenity laws, it stated in *The Sunday Times v. United Kingdom* that:[162]

... Precisely the same cannot be said of the far more objective notion of the 'authority' of the judiciary. The domestic law and practice of the Contracting States reveal a fairly substantial measure of common ground in this area. This is reflected in a number of provisions of the Convention including Article 6, which have no equivalent as far as 'morals' are concerned. Accordingly, here a more extensive European supervision corresponds to a less discretionary power of appreciation.[163]

In the different, but to a certain extent comparable, contexts of Articles 5(3) and 6(1), the Court has on occasion reached conclusions different from those of the national courts on matters in respect of which the latter were also competent and qualified to make the initial assessment.

5.074. Obscenity. Obscenity is one of those areas of law in which a great deal of latitude is allowed to the national courts. In *Handyside v. United Kingdom*,[164] the European Court stated that:

... it is not possible to find in the domestic law of the various Contracting States a uniform European conception of morals. The view taken by their respective laws of the requirements of morals varies from time to time and from place to place, especially in our era which is characterised by a rapid and far-reaching evolution of opinions on the subject. By reason of their direct and continuous contact with the vital forces of their countries, State authorities are in principle in a better position than the international judge to give an opinion on the exact content of these requirements as well as on the 'necessity' of a 'restriction' or 'penalty' intended to meet them.[165]

5.075. Unfair competition. A wide margin of appreciation is left to the national authorities in the field of unfair competition:

... Such a margin of appreciation is essential in commercial matters and, in particular, in an area as complex and fluctuating as that of unfair competition. Otherwise,

---

[161] Application NO 6538/74 *The Sunday Times v. The United Kingdom* Series A NO 30, (1979–80) 2 EHRR 245, para. 65. In a Dissenting Opinion, Judges Wiarda, Cremona, Thor Vilhjalmsson, Ryssdal, Ganshof van der Meersch, Sir Gerald Fitzmaurice, Bindschedler-Robert, Leisch and Matscher, considered that a balancing exercise between two equally competing rights must be carried out.

[162] Application NO 6538/74 Series A NO 30, (1979–80) 2 EHRR 245, para. 59. See §5.111 et seq. below.

[163] In a Dissenting Opinion, Judges Wiarda, Cremona, Thor Vilhjalmsson, Ryssdal, Ganshof van der Meersch, Sir Gerald Fitzmaurice, Bindschedler-Robert, Leisch and Matscher, stated that precisely because the ground of 'maintaining the authority and impartiality of the judiciary' was inserted at the request of the United Kingdom to protect its contempt laws, the national courts were better placed to assess its scope (subject of course to supervision by the European Court).

[164] Application NO 5493/72 Series A NO 24, (1979–80) 1 EHRR 737, para. 48. See §5.121 et seq. below.

[165] The Court also noted (para. 57) that 'The Contracting States have each fashioned their approach in the light of the situation obtaining in their respective territories; they have had regard, inter alia, to the different views prevailing there about the demands of the protection of morals in a democratic society.'

the European Court of Human Rights would have to undertake a re-examination of the facts and all the circumstances of each case. The Court must confine its review to the question whether the measures taken on the national level are justifiable in principle and proportionate.[166]

7. Licensing of Media as a Legitimate Aim

(1) Introduction

5.076. Necessity of licensing. The final sentence of Article 10 of the Convention provides that 'This Article shall not prevent States from requiring the licensing of broadcasting, television or cinema enterprises'. The key issue is whether that sentence gives absolute power to Contracting States to license those media as they wish or whether Contracting States are constrained in any way by the second paragraph of Article 10 ie licensing must be justified by a general interest ground (ie a legitimate aim), necessary in a democratic society. In *Groppera Radio AG v. Switzerland*,[167] the European Court determined that the final sentence of Article 10 cannot be interpreted in isolation, but must be interpreted in the context of Article 10 as a whole:

> . . . the purpose of the third sentence of Article 10(1) of the Convention is to make it clear that States are permitted to control by a licensing system the way in which broadcasting is organised in their territories, particularly in its technical aspects. It does not, however, provide that licensing measures shall not otherwise be subject to the requirements of paragraph 2, for that would lead to a result contrary to the object and purpose of Article 10 taken as a whole.[168]

As the Court explained in *Groppera Radio AG v. Switzerland*, the phrase was in fact inserted (at an advanced stage of the preparatory work on the Convention) for both practical and political reasons. Licensing was considered necessary in practice because of the limited number of frequencies available (ie because of the scarcity of the resource) and the large capital investment required for constructing transmitters. The sanctioning of licensing also reflected a political concern, on the part of several States, that broadcasting should be the preserve of the State.[169]

5.077. Non-arbitrary or discriminatory. The European Commission of Human Rights has stated that national authorities do not have absolute freedom in determing whether to grant or withhold a licence:

---

[166] Application NO 10572/83 *Markt Intern and Beerman v. Germany* Series A NO 165, (1990) 12 EHRR 161, para. 33. In a dissenting opinion, Judges Golcuklu, Pettiti, Russo, Spielmann, De Meyer, Carrillo Salcedo and Valticos, stated that the margin of appreciation defined by the court in these matters was too wide. See §5.133 et seq. below.

[167] Application NO 10890/84 Series A NO 173, (1990) 12 EHRR 321.

[168] This principle was affirmed by the European Court in Application NO 12726/87 *Autronic AG v. Switzerland* Series A NO 178, (1990) 12 EHRR 485. In Application NO 9297/81 *X Association v. Sweden* 28 DR 204, para. 1, the Commission of Human Rights stated that '. . . a State that establishes a system requiring licensing has special duties to ensure that the rights under Article 10 of the Convention remain protected.'

[169] The Court noted that a similar provision was to be inserted in Article 19 of the 1966 International Covenant on Civil and Political Rights in order to license the technology so as to avoid chaos in the use of frequencies: it was not intended to license the information imparted by that technology. Ultimately no such phrase was incorporated because of the fear that it might undermine freedom of expression and because licensing was deemed to be encompassed by the reference to 'public order' in paragraph (3) of the Article (see UN Doc A/5000, 16th session of United Nations General Assembly, 5 December 1961, para. 23).

States do not ... have an unlimited margin of appreciation concerning licensing systems. Although broadcasting enterprises have no guarantee of any right to a licence under the Convention, it is nevertheless the case that the rejection by a State of a licence application must not be manifestly arbitrary or discriminatory, and thereby contrary to the principles set out in the preamble to the convention and the rights secured therein.

For this reason, a licensing system not respecting the requirements of pluralism, tolerance and broadmindedness without which there is no democratic society ... would thereby infringe Article 10 para. 1 of the Convention.[170]

5.078. Preventing the circumvention of licensing systems. The European Commission of Human Rights has declared that:

... since a State may enact legislation requiring the licensing of broadcast enterprises, it must also be legitimate for that State to enact legislation which ensures compliance with the licence in question, in particular by preventing means of circumventing the conditions stated in the licence.[171]

Impugned measures have included advertising for a pirate radio station[172] and the use of cable to transmit radio signals received outside of a geographic zone permitted under a licence.[173]

(2) Maintaining Broadcasting Monopolies

(i) Television Monopolies

5.079. In X v. Sweden,[174] the Applicant argued that the use of the plural 'enterprises' contained in the final sentence of Article 10(1) indicated that the reservation of broadcasting to a single State 'enterprise' was prohibited by the Convention. The European Commission of Human Rights, however, ruled that the plural was grammatically consistent with the previous reference in the text to 'States' in general as opposed to a 'State'. Accordingly, in deciding the issue it was relevant to consider the practice at that time in the various States party to the Convention. That consideration revealed that many such States had established both television and radio broadcasting monopolies. The European Commission of Human Rights therefore held that '. . . the term "licensing" mentioned in the Convention cannot be understood as excluding in any way a public television

---

[170] Application NO 10746/84 *Verein Alternatives Lokalradio Bern and Verein Radio Dreyeckland Basel v. Switzerland* 49 DR 126, para. 1.

[171] Application NO 10799/84 *Radio 24 AG S, W and A v. Switzerland* 37 DR 236, para. 4, affirming Application NO 8266/78 *X v. United Kingdom* (Radio Caroline) 16 DR 190.

[172] In Application NO 8266/78 *X v. United Kingdom* 16 DR 190, the Applicant challenged the right of the United Kingdom to prohibit advertising for a pirate radio station. The Commission held the Application inadmissible (para. 3) on the grounds that '. . . whilst such measures might constitute an interference with the Applicant's freedom of expression and, in particular, his right to impart information, the restriction imposed is justified as being in accordance with the law and necessary in a democratic society for the prevention of crime, namely the promotion and encouragement of unlicensed "pirate" stations in their illegal activities.'

[173] In Application NO 10799/84 *Radio 24 AG S, W and A v. Switzerland* 37 DR 236, the European Commission of Human Rights held valid, legislation which prevented cable companies transmitting to subscribers, signals broadcast by a private radio station, which were received by the cable company's antennae located outside of a ten kilometre broadcasting radius granted to the radio stations under licence. The Commission stated (para. 4) that 'Such a reglementation is intended to lead to and guarantee an effective order during the period in which experimental local radio broadcasts are being permitted' (see Application NO 8962/80 *X and Y v. Belgium* 28 DR 125).

[174] Application NO 3071/67 26 Collection of Decisions 71 (application declared inadmissible).

monopoly as such . . . ' Nevertheless, this has now been qualified. In *Saachi v. Italy*,[175] it was once again challenged. Italian law reserved television (and radio) broadcasting to the State enterprise save that independent undertakings were allowed to establish a single channel cable television. The Applicant had set up a multichannel cable network and was prosecuted by the authorities. He argued that a single channel cable system could never be economically viable and therefore broadcasting was effectively reserved to the State. The Commission cited the ruling in *X v. Sweden*[176] but stated that 'Notwithstanding this precedent, the Commission would not now be prepared purely and simply to maintain this point of view without further consideration.' In fact the point was left open for the Commission ruled the application inadmissible on technical grounds.

(ii)   Radio Monopolies

5.080. Right to maintain monopoly. In *X v. United Kingdom*[177] the Applicant argued that the Wireless Telegraphy Act 1949 which allowed the maintenance of radio broadcasting monopolies in the United Kingdom and gave the government the right to jam radio broadcasts, was in breach of Article 10 of the Convention. The Applicant wished to set up a private commercial radio station in the United Kingdom. The European Commission of Human Rights applied the reasoning employed in *X v. Sweden*[178] and ruled that the United Kingdom Government had the right to ban private broadcasting within the United Kingdom. In fact, many Contracting States grant licences to private radio stations. The European Commission of Human Rights has stated[179] that the limitations on the natural resource of frequencies, justifies their limitation:

> . . . considerably more enterprises are capable of producing radio broadcasts as a result of technical advances in broadcasting [than has been possible at an earlier period]. However, given the continued limitation on the number of frequencies available, it is clear that, by definition, there is always an unmet demand for licences.

5.081. Criteria for selecting local radio (minority programming). In *Verein Alternatives Lokalradio Berne and Verein Radio Dreyeckland Basel v. Switzerland*, the Applicants challenged the right of the Swiss authorities to withhold a licence to broadcast local radio. The Swiss authorities had set up local broadcasting trials and of the 214 organisations which applied for a concession, only 36 were granted. The Applicants, whose application for a licence in the Berne and Basel area had been rejected, argued that the selection was political. For whilst they had made provision for local audiences whose mother tongue was a foreign language, only one of the 20 concessions granted had made similar arrangements. The European Commission of Human Rights acknowledged that there was a political dimension to the awarding of licences but held that this was insufficient in the circumstances to amount to a violation of Article 10:

> The Commission considers that the political element in the decision, acknowledged by the Government, does not necessarily signify that the decision was arbitrary. The

---

[175] Application NO 6452/74 5 DR 43, 46 (application declared inadmissible).
[176] Application NO 3071/67 26 Collection of Decisions 71.
[177] Application NO 4750/71 40 Collection of Decisions 26 (application declared inadmissible).
[178] See §5.079 above.
[179] Application NO 10746/84 *Verein Alternatives Lokalradio Bern and Verein Radio Dreyeckland Basel v. Switzerland* 37 DR 236, para. 1.

Commission takes into consideration the particular political circumstances in Switzerland which necessitate the application of sensitive political criteria such as cultural and linguistic pluralism, balance between lowland and mountain regions and a balanced federalist policy.[180]

(3) Freedom of Reception and Retransmission of Signals

(i) Cable Retransmission of Terrestrial Broadcasts

5.082. Groppera Radio. In *Groppera Radio AG v. Switzerland*,[181] the European Court held lawful, national legislation preventing cable companies from retransmitting signals infringing international telecommunication treaties. The Applicant operated, without a licence from the Italian authorities, the most powerful VHF transmitter in Europe broadcasting from a mountain peak close to the Italian border with Switzerland. A Swiss undertaking picked up those signals and distributed them to their cable subscribers in Switzerland. In 1983, the Swiss government issued an ordinance which prohibited a licensed community cable distribution system retransmitting terrestrial broadcasts which did not comply with, amongst other instruments, the provisions of the International Telecommunication Convention and the Radio Regulations. The broadcasts by Groppera Radio contravened the Radio Regulations because they were not licensed. The Swiss authorities requested that the Italian authorities put an end to Groppera Radio's activities but to no avail. The Swiss undertaking continued to operate its system in violation of the ordinance and proceedings were taken against it which the Applicant later joined.

In the action, the Swiss government argued that its interference was necessary for two reasons:

(1) the prevention of disorder in telecommunications; and
(2) the protection of the rights of others ie maintaining pluralism of the press.

5.083. Prevention of disorder. The European Court acknowledged that the prevention of disorder in telecommunications was a legitimate aim under the Convention. The 'order' in question was that laid down in the International Telecommunications Convention and the Radio Regulations. The Italian broadcaster had violated the following three principles of international frequency order:

(1) the *licensing principle*, whereby the establishment or operation of a broadcasting station by a private person or by an enterprise was subject to the issue of a licence;
(2) the *co-ordination* principle, which required special agreements to be concluded between States where the frequency used was between certain levels as in the case in issue, there being no agreements between Italy and Switzerland; and
(3) the principle of *economic use of the frequency spectrum*. Broadcasting frequencies were a scarce resource and the Italian broadcaster had the most powerful transmitter in Europe.

---

[180] 37 DR 236, para. 1. The Commission was influenced by the fact these were merely broadcasting trials and that the contentious licence was to run for a maximum of five years.

[181] Application NO 10890/84 Series A NO 173, (1990) 12 EHRR 321.

5.084. Protection of the rights of others. The Court also acknowledged that restricting the use of the frequency spectrum in order to ensure pluralism, in particular pluralism of information, by allowing a fair allocation of frequencies internationally and nationally, was a legitimate aim under the Convention.

5.085. Necessary in a democratic society. The Court affirmed that Switzerland had operated within the margin of appreciation permitted. The Court weighed up, on the one hand, the interests of protecting international telecommunications order, and on the other hand, the rights of the cable company and Applicant. The Swiss authorities had never jammed the Applicant's broadcasts. Instead they had approached the Italian authorities. There was no censorship directed at the content of the broadcasts but rather the action was designed to prevent an evasion of law: the Applicant was in reality a Swiss-owned broadcaster who was transmitting from Italy in order to breach Swiss law.

(ii)   Reception of Signals Transmitted by Fixed Service Satellite

5.086. Autronic. In *Autronic AG v. Switzerland*,[182] the European Court held that the Swiss authorities refusal to license reception of Fixed Service Satellite signals by the Applicant, amounted to a violation of Article 10 of the Convention. The Applicant was an undertaking specialising in consumer electronics and sold satellite dish aerials. It wished to demonstrate the efficacy of its equipment at a trade fair by receiving signals which were transmitted by a Soviet Fixed Service Satellite. Consequently it applied to the Swiss authorities for a licence. The Swiss authorities refused the request having been denied consent by the Soviet authorities. In defending an action, the authority pleaded two grounds:

(1) the prevention of disorder in telecommunications; and
(2) the need to prevent the disclosure of confidential information.

5.087. Prevention of disorder. The European Court agreed that the prevention of disorder was a legitimate aim under the Convention. It accepted the government's contention that pluralism would be threatened and anarchy would reign if there was no control over the use of the finite number of available telecommunication frequencies.

5.088. Prevention of disclosure of confidential information. Article 22 of the International Telecommunication Convention required Contracting States to ensure the secrecy of signals transmitted by Fixed Service Satellite. It stated: '1. Members agree to take all possible measures, compatible with the system of telecommunication used, with a view to ensuring the secrecy of international correspondence.' Numbers 1992–1994 of the Radio Regulations laid down more specific rules, prohibiting: '(a) the unauthorised interception of radiocommunications not intended for the general use of the public; (b) the divulgence of the contents, simple disclosure of the existence, publication or any use whatsoever, without authorisation, of information of any nature whatever obtained by the interception of the radio communications mentioned [in sub-paragraph (a)].' The European Court accepted that, in accordance with these provisions, the prevention of disclosure of confidential information was a legitimate aim.

---

[182] Application 12726/87 Series A NO 178, (1990) 12 EHRR 485.

5.089. Necessary in a democratic society. The European Court held that the prevention of reception of signals broadcast by telecommunication satellite was not 'necessary in a democratic society'. Merely receiving signals could not upset the international telecommunication order. As to confidentiality, the Court focused upon the specific types of satellite. It noted that many States permitted the direct reception of signals transmitted by their Fixed Service Satellites and that the European Convention on Transfrontier Television which required this, had been signed by many countries.[183] Accordingly the distinction between Direct Broadcast Satellites and Fixed Service Satellites had become blurred. The very fact that the broadcasts in issue were not encoded and were intended for reception by the general public in the then Soviet Union, precluded describing them as not intended for the general use of the public within the meaning of the Radio Regulations.[184]

(iii) CB Radio Transmissions

5.090. The European Commission of Human Rights has ruled that a Contracting State may authorise or prohibit the use of CB radios on grounds of 'the prevention of disorder or crime' and 'the protection of . . . the rights of others.' It held that:

> . . . It seems that use of radiophonic broadcasting and receiving equipment requires or justifies, given their nature, sufficient regulation and control by the national authorities to allow and to guarantee an efficient and rational use of the possibilities of telecommunication.
>
> The Commission notes that such a system of regulation and control clearly develops from the potential, practical applications of the technology which, in this field, has seen and is seeing a rapid evolution. The reasons invoked to justify the control of radio communication . . . were the necessity to maintain order and to prevent crime, especially because illegally used machines risked interfering with the working of telegraphic and telephonic equipment and because their use could have seriously prejudiced the 'the protection of private life'.[185]

(iv) Erection of Private Aerial

5.091. The Convention patently secures freedom of reception, but it does not secure freedom of reception by any means. An Applicant[186] had complained that his freedom of reception was impaired by the refusal of the Swiss authorities to allow him to erect an individual aerial. The Swiss authorities had installed community aerials to avoid the proliferation of individual constructions and to improve the reception of programmes. It was established that the community aerial enabled the Applicant to receive all the television and radio signals he could have received with an individual aerial. Moreover he could pick up more distant private emissions as well as pirate stations. Furthermore, the Applicant, being a radio ham had a short wave aerial sanctioned by the authorities which permitted the reception

---

[183] See §7.280 below.

[184] In a dissenting opinion, Judges Binschedler–Robert and Matscher found there to be no violation of Article 10. In their view the distinction between a Direct Broadcast Satellite and a Fixed Service Satellite was still valid and accordingly a Contracting State was obliged to adhere to the provisions of the Radio Regulations.

[185] Application NO 8962/80 X and Y v. Belgium, 28 DR 112, (1993) 5 EHRR 268, para. 10 (application declared inadmissible).

[186] Application NO 10248/83 Aebi v. Switzerland 41 DR 141, (1986) 8 EHRR 252 (application declared inadmissible).

of many distant signals. It seemed that the Applicant wanted the external aerial in order to carry out technical experiments. The Commission held that the authorities' action had not impeded his freedom of reception and rejected the claim as manifestly ill-founded.

8. Restricting Access to Broadcasting Facilities

(1) Political Advertisements

5.092. Nationalistic propaganda. In X and the *Association of Z v. United Kingdom*,[187] the Applicant challenged the refusal of the BBC and the ITA to allow it access to broadcasting time for the purpose of publicising its views. The Applicant asserted that such action breached Article 10 as well as Article 14 (which prohibits discrimination) of the Convention. The objects of the association were to 'gather together in a single organisation all British people who wish to determine the destiny of Britain' and 'to demand that in all matters affecting the British way of life and the British constitution, the issue shall be determined directly by the people of Britain'. The BBC allowed general access to broadcasting time if an organisation had representation in parliament and during elections if the organisation had a sufficient number of candidates in the field. The Applicant could not fulfil these qualifications. The European Commission of Human Rights held that:

> It is evident that the freedom to 'impart information and ideas' included in the right to freedom of expression under Art. 10 of the Convention, cannot be taken to include a general and unfettered right for any private citizen or organisation to have access to broadcasting time on radio and television in order to put forward its opinion. On the other hand, the Commission considers that the denial of broadcasting time to one or more specific groups or person may, in particular circumstances, raise an issue under Art. 10 alone or in conjunction with Art. 14 of the Convention. Such an issue would, in principle, arise, for instance, if one political party was excluded from broadcasting facilities at election time while other parties were given broadcasting time.[188]

The Independent Television Code of Advertising Standards and Practice (1969) and the Television Act 1964 upon which it was based, governed advertisements in commercial independent television in the United Kingdom. That legislation provided that first, no advertisements could be inserted by any body, in a broadcast, where the objects of those advertisements were wholly or mainly of a religious or political nature and secondly, that advertisements could not be directed towards any religious or political end. The purpose of these rules was to prevent those persons with the longest purse from having access to the broadcasting medium. The Commission stated that the notion of licensing in Art 10, third sentence implied that in granting a licence, the State could subject radio and television broadcasting to certain regulations. It thus ruled that '. . . the provisions of Art. 10(1) should be interpreted as permitting the State, in granting a licence, to exclude, as in the present case, certain specified categories of advertisement.'

---

[187] Application NO 4515/70 14 Yearbook 538 (application declared inadmissible).
[188] *Ibid.*, para. 1, affirmed in Application NO 9297/81 X *Association v. Sweden* 28 DR 204. On discrimination, see §5.135 et seq. below.

5.093. Representation of business Interests. In X *Association v. Sweden*,[189] the Commission of Human Rights rejected the Applicant's claim that a refusal to broadcast a programme representing their views, constituted a breach of Article 10. The national broadcasting monopoly had transmitted a programme which was critical of a local building project. The Applicant, a student association of a liberal and conservative trend, which alleged that the broadcasting monopoly disseminated unilateral information, wished to broadcast their own programme to redress the balance. In fact, the broadcasting authority had represented the views of those in favour of the project and the Applicant had not complained that it was prevented from exercising his rights under Article 10 through other media and channels. Referring to the statement in X *and the Association of Z v. United Kingdom*,[190] cited above, the Commission held that the Applicant had failed to establish its case.

9. Prior Censorship

(1) Classification of Video Works

5.094. Vetting of pornography. An Applicant had complained that legislation which set up a classification system for video recordings violated Article 10.[191] The Act in question provided for the establishment of an authority from which appeal could be made only to a government department. It replaced a system under which decisions were made by a board with appeal to a jury. The Act exempted from control certain types of film including those designed to inform, educate or instruct and those concerned with sport, religion or music, or video games. The purpose of the Act was essentially to 'restrict the widespread availability of video works which, to any significant extent, depict human sexual activity, human genital organs or human urinary or excretory functions and mutilation or torture of, or other acts of gross violence towards, humans or animals'. The Applicant refused to pay fees due to the authority in respect of two films he had submitted to its predecessor and he argued that the system amounted to state censorship in violation of Article 10.

The European Commission of Human Rights held that it did not appear that '. . . the mere existence of the censorship authority . . . imposes a restriction or condition on the exercise of freedom of expression in the context of video film-making and distribution which is, by virtue of the mere existence of the legislation, contrary to Art. 10 or any other provision of the Convention.' Furthermore, it stated that '. . . in view of the express provision for an appeal from the determination of the censorship authority created by the Video Recordings Act 1984, there is nothing to show from the application as submitted that a national remedy against an alleged interference with the rights protected by the Convention would not be available under the machinery set up by the Video Recordings Act 1984'.

---

[189] Application NO 9297/81 28 DR 204 (application declared inadmissible).
[190] Application NO 4515/70 14 Yearbook 538 (application declared inadmissible).
[191] Application NO 12381/86 X *v. United Kingdom* (1988) 10 EHRR 123 (application declared inadmissible).

10. Freedom of the Press

(1) General Principles

5.095. Press duty as 'public watchdog'. The European Court respects, indeed guards, the role of the press as purveyor of information on matters of public interest. In *Thorgeir Thorgeirson v. Iceland*,[192] it stated:

> ... Whilst the press must not overstep the bounds set, inter alia, for 'the protection of the reputation of . . . others,' it is nevertheless incumbent on it to impart information and ideas on matters of public interest. Not only does it have the task of imparting such information and ideas: the public also has a right to receive them. Were it otherwise, the press would be unable to play its vital role of 'public watchdog'.[193]

5.096. Press' task as forum for public opinion. Because the European Court considers that the press has a vital role to play in ventilating public opinion, it has rejected the opinion of national courts that the task of the press is merely to impart information, the interpretation of which has to be left primarily to the reader.[194]

5.097. Protection of value statements. The importance of the press's function as forum for public opinion has been emphasised by the European Court's condemnation of a law which effectively undermined that role. In *Lingens v. Austria*,[195] it ruled that as a general principle, legislation which provides justification in fact as the only defence against a charge of libel concerning value statements, constitutes a violation of the Convention:

> In the Court's view, a careful distinction needs to be made between facts and value judgments. The existence of facts can be demonstrated, whereas the truth of value judgments is not susceptible of proof . . .
> As regards value judgments [the requirement of proving the truth of statements] is impossible of fulfilment and it infringes freedom of opinion itself, which is a fundamental part of the right secured by Article 10 of the Convention.

5.098. Protection of free flow of information—not of medium itself. The European Commission of Human Rights has affirmed that in the domain of information, the Convention guarantees the public's right of access to information, and not the right of a particular enterprise to impart that information.[196]

5.099. Confiscation of documents. The European Court has condemned a sentence which required the confiscation of documents. It held that such a measure infringed proportionality principles:

> In the context of political debate such a sentence would be likely to deter journalists from contributing to public discussion of issues affecting the life of the community. By

---

[192] Application NO 13778/88 Series A NO 239, (1992) 14 EHRR 843, para. 63.
[193] This principle has been enunciated in Application NO 9815/82 *Lingens v. Austria* Series A NO 103, (1986) 8 EHRR 407 and Application NO 11798/85 *Castells v. Spain* Series A NO 236, (1992) 14 EHRR 445.
[194] Application NO 9815/82 *Lingens v. Austria* Series A NO 103, (1986) 8 EHRR 407.
[195] Application NO 9815/82 Series A NO 103, (1986) 8 EHRR 407, para. 46; affirmed in Application NO 11662/85 *Obershclick v. Austria* Series A 204; Application NO 13704/88 *Schwabe v. Austria* Series A NO 242.
[196] Application NO 5178/71 *De Geillustreerde Pers NV v. The Netherlands* 8 DR 5, [1978] EEC 164.

the same token, a sanction such as this is liable to hamper the press in performing its task as purveyor of information and public watchdog.[197]

5.100. Meaning of proportionality in freedom of press. In *Barfod v. Denmark*,[198] the European Court indicated precisely what is meant by 'proportional' measures in cases involving freedom of the press:

> ... proportionality implies that the pursuit of the aims mentioned in Article 10(2) has to be weighed against the value of open discussion of topics of public concern. When striking a fair balance between these interests, the Court cannot overlook ... the great importance of not discouraging members of the public, for fear of criminal or other sanctions, from voicing their opinions on issues of public concern.

(2) Libel of Politicians

(i) Libel by Members of the Public

5.101. Paramountcy of political debate. The European Court has consistently underscored the importance of political debate:

> Freedom of the press ... affords the public one of the best means of discovering and forming an opinion of the ideas and attitudes of political leaders. More generally, freedom of political debate is at the very core of the concept of a democratic society which prevails throughout the Convention.[199]

5.102. Status of politician. Whilst politicians should not be unprotected by libel laws, they must be more accepting of sharp criticism than persons who do not occupy such public appointments. Thus the European Court has held that:

> The limits of acceptable criticism are accordingly wider as regards a politician as such than as regards a private individual. Unlike the latter, the former inevitably and knowingly lays himself open to close scrutiny of his every word and deed by both journalists and the public at large, and he must consequently display a greater degree of tolerance. No doubt Article 10(2) enables the reputation of others—that is to say, of all individuals—to be protected, and this protection extends to politicians too, even when they are not acting in their private capacity; but in such cases the requirements of such protection have to be weighed in relation to the interests of open discussion of political issues.[200]

5.103. Specific cases. In *Lingens v. Austria*,[201] the European Court condemned a libel judgment. Mr Wiesenthal, President of the Jewish Documentation Centre had accused the then President of the Austrian Liberal Party, Mr Friedrich Peter, of having served in the first SS infantry brigade during the Second World War. Mr Bruno Kreisky, the then Austrian Chancellor defended Mr Friedrich against the

---

[197] Application NO 9815/82 *Lingens v. Austria* Series A NO 103, (1982) 8 EHRR 407, para. 44.

[198] Application NO 11508/85 (1991) 13 EHRR 493, para. 29.

[199] Application NO 9815/82 *Lingens v. Austria* Series A NO 103, (1982) 8 EHRR 407, para. 42, affirmed by the European Court in Application NO 11662/85 *Oberschlick v. Austria* Series A NO 204.

[200] Application NO 9815/82 *Lingens v. Austria* Series A NO 103, (1982) 8 EHRR 407, para. 42, affirmed in Application NO 11662/85 *Oberschlick v. Austria* Series A NO 204 and Application NO 13704/88 *Schwabe v. Austria* Series A NO 242 in which the Court stated, (para. 29) that '... Where what is at stake is the limits of acceptable criticism in the context of public debate on a political question of general interest, the Court, in the exercise of its supervisory function, has to satisfy itself that the national authorities did apply standards which were in conformity with those principles, and moreover, that in doing so they based themselves on an acceptable assessment of the relevant facts.'

[201] Application NO 9815/82 Series A NO 103, (1986) 8 EHRR 407.

attacks made by Mr Wiesenthal. Mr Lingens, the Applicant was a journalist and editor of a magazine. He published two articles in which he criticised Mr Kreisky's defence of his compatriot. The Applicant highlighted Mr Peter's past history and was critical of Mr Kreisky's role as protector of him and other politicians who had been involved with the Nazis. He stated that had Mr Kreisky's criticism of Mr Wiesenthal been made by anyone else '. . . this would probably have been described as the basest opportunism'. He also said that such criticism was 'immoral' and 'undignified', that Mr Peter's history made him unfit for office, that 'This is a minimum requirement of political ethics' and that it was a 'monstrosity' that Mr Kreisky wished to hush up the issue. Mr Lingens was prosecuted for political libel under the Austrian Criminal Code.[202] The domestic court found that the expressions 'basest opportunism', 'immoral' and 'undignified' were defamatory because they were directly or indirectly aimed at Mr Kreisky personally, whereas the words 'minimum requirement of political ethics' and 'monstrosity' could be justified as political criticism. The convictions were upheld on appeal and both Mr Lingens and Mr Kreisky applied to the European Court.

The European Court underlined the importance of free political debate and held that politicians had to be more accepting of criticism than the private citizen. The Court underscored the principle that in assessing the impugned statements it must place them in their context. In this case, the Applicant had made comments about a leading figure's support for another politician at the time of a general election when both individuals might find themselves jointly leading a coalition government. As the Court noted '. . . in this struggle each used the weapons at his disposal; and these were in no way unusual in the hard-fought tussles of politics.'

In *Oberschlick v. Austria*,[203] the European Court similarly condemned a libel judgment. During a parliamentary campaign, the Secretary General of the Austrian Liberal Party (Mr Walter Grabher-Meyer) suggested that family allowances for Austrian women should be increased by 50% in order to obviate their seeking abortions for financial reasons, whilst those paid to immigrant mothers should be reduced to 50% of their current levels. He justified his statement by saying that immigrant families were placed in a discriminatory position in other European countries. The Applicant laid a criminal information against Mr Grabher-Meyer, but the public prosecutor decided not to prosecute him. On the same day that the public prosecutor made its decision, the Applicant published the criminal information in *Forum*, a political periodical. It charged incitement to hatred and encouragement of policies promulgated by the outlawed national socialist party, an activity which was prohibited by the Prohibition Act. The Applicant was sued for defamation under Article 111 of the Criminal Code. He was found guilty, affirmed on appeal, on the basis that he had not proved the truth of his statements, namely, that Mr Grabher-Meyer was motivated by Nazi principles.

The European Court held that the insertion of the text of the criminal information in *Forum* contributed to a public debate on a political question of general importance and noted that differential treatment of nationals and foreigners in the social field had given rise to considerable discussion in many Contracting

---

[202] Article 111(1) of the Code stated that 'Anyone who in such a way that it may be perceived by a third person accuses another of possessing a contemptible character or attitude or of behaviour contrary to honour or morality and of such a nature as to make him contemptible or otherwise lower him in public esteem shall be liable to imprisonment not exceeding six months or a fine.' Article 111(3) provided for a defence of justification.

[203] Application NO 11662/85 Series A 204.

States. The Court said that a politician who expresses himself in shocking terms exposes himself to a strong reaction on the part of journalists and the public.

The Court condemned the libel judgment as violating Article 10, for the Applicant had been found guilty on the basis of a value statement. He had stated the fact of the criminal information and then proceeded to make a comparative analysis between the statements of Mr Grabher-Meyer and the doctrine of the Nazis. Given the importance of the issue at stake, the Applicant's conviction was not 'necessary in a democratic society . . . for the protection of the reputation . . . of others'.[204]

In *Schwabe v. Austria*,[205] a further libel judgment was condemned by the European Court. A provincial Mayor was convicted of negligently causing bodily harm whilst under the influence of alcohol and abandoning the victim. Mr Wagner, a high-ranking official of the Austrain Socialist Party demanded the resignation of the Mayor. The Applicant then issued a press release noting that Mr Wagner had not demanded the resignation of one of his deputies who had been convicted for negligent homicide (the deputy had not been convicted for intoxication even though tests showed him to have imbibed an illegal amount). The Applicant suggested that Mr Wagner had applied double standards. The domestic court convicted the Applicant of criminal libel on the grounds that he had cited a criminal conviction which had been spent under rehabilitation of offenders laws and he had implied that the offences were identical.

The European Court found that the Applicant had not made a direct comparison between the convictions and in violation of Article 10 of the Convention, had in fact been found guilty for making a value statement concerning his belief of the double moral standards of Mr Wagner on a matter of public concern.

(ii) Freedom of Expression of Opposition Politicians

5.104. Castells v. Spain. In *Castells v. Spain*,[206] the European Court held that freedom of expression had been violated by the conviction of an opposition politician. The Applicant was an elected senator in the party supporting independence for the Basque Country. He wrote an article in which he accused the Spanish Government of involvement in a number of murders of Basque dissidents. He was prosecuted and convicted under Article 161 of the Institutional Act 8/1983 of 25 June 1983 which stated that: 'The following shall be liable to long-term prison sentences: 1. Those who seriously insult, falsely accuse or threaten . . . the Government . . . '. Article 20(1) of the Constitution of 1978 guaranteed (a) the right freely to express and disseminate thoughts, ideas and opinions by word of mouth, in writing or by any other means of reproduction. However, according to Spanish law, the defence of truth was not admissible in cases of insults to State institutions, which included the government (save in the case of statements against civil servants in the performance of their duties). As well as receiving a prison sentence, the Applicant was disbarred from public office for a year and a day.

5.105. Necessity of freedom of expression of elected representatives. The European Court held that the law was for the protection of the reputation of others (this article complained of the inactivity and collusion of the authorities including

---

[204] Judges Matscher and Bindschedler–Robert dissenting on the grounds that the publication of the criminal information gave the impression that a prosecution was proceeding.
[205] Application NO 13704/88 Series A NO 242.
[206] Application NO 11798/85 Series A NO 236, (1992) 14 EHRR 445.

the police) as well as for the 'prevention of disorder'. The Court underscored the particular importance of ensuring the freedom of expression of elected members of parliament:

> While freedom of expression is important for everybody, it is especially so for an elected representative of the people. He represents his electorate, draws attention to their preoccupations and defends their interests. Accordingly, interferences with the freedom of expression of an opposition Member of Parliament . . . call for the closest scrutiny on the part of the Court.

5.106. Exercisable both in parliament and the press. The Court noted that whilst the Applicant could have chosen to express his views from the floor of the Senate, the fact that he made his statement in a periodical, did not alter his rights:

> Freedom of the press affords the public one of the best means of discovering and forming an opinion of the ideas and attitudes of their political leaders. In particular, it gives politicians the opportunity to reflect and comment on the preoccupations of public opinion; it thus enables everyone to participate in the free political debate which is at the very core of the concept of a democratic society.

5.107. Broad freedom in political matters. The Court then acknowledged that freedom of speech was not absolute but that particular latitude should be given to those who criticise the government:

> The freedom of political debate is undoubtably not absolute in nature. A Contracting State may make it subject to certain 'restrictions' or 'penalties', but it is for the Court to give a final ruling on the compatibility of such measures with the freedom of expression enshrined in Article 10.
>
> The limits of permissible criticism are wider with regard to the Government than in relation to a private citizen, or even a politician. In the democratic system the actions or omissions of the Government must be subject to the close scrutiny not only of the legislative and judicial authorities but also of the press and public opinion. Furthermore, the dominant position which the Government occupies makes it necessary for it to display restraint in resorting to criminal proceedings, particularly where other means are available for replying to the unjustified attacks and criticisms of its adversaries or the media. Nevertheless it remains open to the competent State authorities to adopt, in their capacity as guarantors of public order, measures, even of a criminal law nature, intended to react appropriately and without excess to defamatory accusations devoid of foundation or formulated in bad faith.

The Court held that the facts stated by the Applicant in his article were capable of confirmation. The refusal of the national courts to allow him to adduce evidence confirming his statement was not an interference necessary in a democratic society. Accordingly, the Government had violated his rights under Article 10 of the Convention.[207]

---

[207] In concurring Opinions, Judges de Meyer and Pekkanen stated that the mere fact that the Applicant was punished for criticising the Government was sufficient to find a violation of Article 10 without it being necessary to establish the truth of the allegations.

(3) Libel on Matters of Public Concern

(i) Composition of Judicial Authorities

5.108. In *Barfod v. Denmark*,[208] the European Court upheld a conviction of criminal libel against the Applicant who made a criticism of two judges. Local authorities had introduced taxes on Danes who worked on American bases in Greenland. Certain workers challenged that decision. It was, however, upheld by the High Court whose bench consisted of one professional judge and two lay judges both employed by the local government. The Applicant wrote an article in which he implied that the two lay judges were politically motivated stating that they '... did their duty ... The vote was two to one in favour of the Local Government and with such a bench of judges it does not require much imagination to guess who voted how.' The Applicant was convicted of criminal libel. His appeal to the Danish High Court was dismissed despite the High Court's acknowledgement that, in accordance with the Danish constitution, the judges ought to have disqualified themselves because of their interest in the proceedings. The European Court held that while the Applicants would have been permitted to criticise the composition of the bench, they had overstepped the mark by making remarks directed personally at the judges.[209] It stated that:

It was quite possible to question the composition of the High Court without at the same time attacking the two lay judges personally ...

Concerning the issue of the judges' employment, the European Court noted:

... Although this fact may give rise to a difference of opinion as to whether the court was properly composed, it was certainly not proof of actual bias ...

The State's legitimate interest in protecting the reputation of the two lay judges was accordingly not in conflict with the Applicant's interest in being able to participate in free public debate on the question of the structural impartiality of the High Court.

(ii) Libel of Police Authorities

5.109. In *Thorgeir Thorgeirson v. Iceland*,[210] the European Court held that a criminal conviction for defamation of the police violated the Convention. The Applicant was a journalist and writer resident in Reykjavik. The conviction of a policeman on charges of brutality, was followed by a public debate about police activities. In the course of this debate, the Applicant wrote two articles in a daily newspaper levelling an accusation of brutality against the Icelandic police in general. The first article outlined a particular incident. The second was a response to the police defence of their activities in a television programme in which they called into question the integrity of the Applicant. At the instigation of the police federation, he was prosecuted under the Penal Code by the public authorities for libel. The national court found him guilty of criminal libel on the grounds that, he could not justify the allegations he had made. In the first article, he had referred to the police as, amongst other things, 'beasts in uniform'. He spoke of 'Individuals

---

[208] Application NO 11508/85 (1991) 13 EHRR 493.
[209] In a dissenting Opinion, Judge Golcuklu stated that by making the remarks he did, the Applicant was doing no more than attacking the composition of the bench. On the issue of insulting allegations, see also Application NO 12230. X v. Germany (1989) 11 EHRR 46.
[210] Application NO 13778/88 Series A NO 239, (1992) 14 EHRR 843.

reduced to a mental age of a new-born child as a result of strangleholds that policemen and bouncers learn and use with brutal spontaneity instead of handling people with prudence and care . . .', 'victims of the police brutes' and 'allowing brutes and sadists to act out their perversions'. In the second article he had said that: 'Their behaviour was so typical of what is gradually becoming the public image of our police force defending itself: bullying, forgery, unlawful actions, superstitions, rashness and ineptitude.'

The European Court held that the legislation pursued a legitimate aim being for the protection of the rights of others. It held following Castells that:

> . . . the Applicant expressed his views by having them published in a newspaper. Regard must therefore be had to the pre-eminent role of the press in a State governed by the rule of law.

Significantly, the Court held that the requirement placed on the Applicant to establish the truth of what he was stating was an unreasonable, if not impossible, task. The Applicant's intention was not a general attack on the whole police force but rather had been to urge the Minister of Justice to set up and investigate incidents of police brutality: he had stated that the violence was restricted to a small number of officers. The incident reported in his first article had not been proved untrue and there had been many reports of police brutality. The articles bore on a matter of serious public concern. Thus the language employed, though strong could not be considered as excessive.

(4) Censorship

(i) Political Material

5.110. Revisionist publications. The European Commission of Human Rights has sanctioned censorship of offensive political material.[211] The Applicant had been the 'author-editor' for the publication of a text entitled 'Letter to the Pope about Auschwitz'. The paper questioned whether 6,000,000 Jews had been exterminated, especially at Auschwitz, and compared the Nazi atrocities with other wartime atrocities. The real author had collaborated with the Germans during the Second World War following which she had been prohibited under the criminal law from writing, publishing or printing any newspaper or other publication throughout the whole of her life. Following an earlier Application, namely, *De Becker v. Belgium*,[212] the Belgian law was amended so that it applied only to publications of a political character.

The Commission found that legitimate aims were pursued by the legislation, namely, the protection of morals as well as the protection of the rights of others and the prevention of disorder.

The Commission rejected the objection that the Auschwitz atrocities only belonged to the sphere of history and that the survivors were few in number. It said that the families of the survivors continued to have a right to the protection of their parents' memory. Concluding that the interference was necessary in a democratic society, the Commission held:

---

[211] Application NO 9777/82 *X v. Belgium* (1984) 6 EHRR 467, (application declared inadmissible).
[212] Application NO 214/56 (1979–80) 1 EHRR 43.

More generally, the Commission notes that current events show that anti-democratic ideologies similar to those which inspired the atrocities have not disappeared in Europe. Although in *Handyside v. United Kingdom*, the European Court of Human Rights took care to indicate that freedom of expression applies to information or ideas which offend, shock or disturb the State or any sector of the population, this was subject to the qualification of Art. 10(2). The Commission thus considers that confronted by a publication which, by its particular objectionable contents, would offend an important sector of the population, the national authorities were entitled to regard as insufficient a mere prohibition even accompanied by a confiscation of the publications . . . unless accompanied by criminal proceedings and penalties.

11. Contempt of Court

(1) General Principles

5.111. Maintaining the authority and impartiality of the judiciary. Quite evidently, contempt of court laws come within the ambit of '. . . maintaining the authority and impartiality of the judiciary.' The key issue is to determine what is meant by the term 'judiciary'. In *The Sunday Times v. The United Kingdom*,[213] the European Court examined the scope of this term:

> The term 'judiciary' (*pouvoir judiciaire*) comprises the machinery of justice or the judicial branch of government as well as the judges in their official capacity. The phrase 'authority of the judiciary' includes, in particular, the notion that the courts are, and are accepted by the public at large as being, the proper forum for the ascertainment of legal rights and obligations and the settlement of disputes relative thereto; further, that the public at large have respect for and confidence in the court's capacity to fulfil that function.

In the Sunday Times case, the European Court concluded that in fact the law of contempt is designed to protect the 'rights of others' and that accordingly, it is not appropriate to invoke that category as a separate ground:

> . . . in so far as the law of contempt may serve to protect the rights of litigants, this purpose is already included in the phrase 'maintaining the authority and impartiality of the judiciary': the rights so protected are the rights of individuals in their capacity as litigants, that is, as persons involved in the machinery of justice, and the authority of that machinery will not be maintained unless protection is afforded to all those involved in or having recourse to it. It is therefore not necessary to consider as a separate issue whether the law of contempt has the further purpose of safeguarding 'the rights of others'.[214]

5.112. Right to a fair trial. The Convention and its jurisprudence guarantees the right to a fair trial. As the European Commission of Human Rights has stated:[215]

---

[213] Application NO 6538/74 Series A NO 30, (1979–80) 2 EHRR 245, para. 55.

[214] *Ibid.*, para. 56, affirmed by the European Court in Applications NOs 11553/85 and 11658/85 *Hodgson, Woolf Productions and National Union of Journalists and Channel Four Television v. United Kingdom* (1988) 10 EHRR 503; Application NO 13166/87 *The Sunday Times v. United Kingdom* (NO 2) Series A NO 217, (1992) 14 EHRR 229; Application NO 13585/88 *The Observer and the Guardian v. United Kingdom* Series A NO 216, (1992) 14 EHRR 153.

[215] Applications NOs 11553/85 and 11658/85 *Hodgson, Woolf Productions and National Union of Journalists and Channel Four Television v. United Kingdom* (1988) 10 EHRR 503, para. 2. On the importance of Article 6 of the Convention, see also Application NO 13585/88 *The Observer and The Guardian v. United Kingdom* Series A NO 216, (1992) 14 EHRR 153.

. . . the prominent place held in a democratic society by the right to a fair trial as guaranteed by Art. 6(1) of the Convention as well as the importance attached to the public reporting of trials as one of the means whereby confidence in the courts, superior and inferior, can be maintained. As the European Court of Human Rights has stated: 'By rendering the administration of justice visible, publicity contributes to the achievement of the aims of Art. 6(1), namely a fair trial . . . ' (see Axen v. Germany (1984) 6 EHRR 195, para. 25).

5.113. Public's right to information. The European Court operates from the assumption that the public will never be entirely insulated from a trial. Furthermore, in principle, the press may not be muzzled without good reason. In *The Sunday Times v. The United Kingdom*, the Court held:

> . . . There is general recognition of the fact that the courts cannot operate in a vacuum. Whilst they are the forum for the settlement of disputes, this does not mean that there can be no prior discussion of disputes elsewhere, be it in specialised journals, in the general press or amongst the public at large. Furthermore, whilst the mass media must not overstep the bounds imposed in the interests of the proper administration of justice, it is incumbent on them to impart information and ideas concerning matters that come before the courts just as in other areas of public interest. Not only do the media have the task of imparting such information and ideas: the public also has a right to receive them.[216]

5.114. Prior censorship. The European Court sanctions prior censorship of material but must be satisfied of its absolute necessity. Thus it has held that:[217]

> . . . Article 10 of the Convention does not in terms prohibit the imposition of prior restraints on publication, as such. This is evidenced not only by the words 'conditions', 'restrictions', 'preventing' and 'prevention' which appear in that provision, but also by the Court's Sunday Times judgment of 26 April 1979[218] and its Markt Intern Verlag GmbH and Klaus Beerman judgment of 20 November 1989.[219] On the other hand, the dangers inherent in prior restraints are such that they call for the most careful scrutiny on the part of the Court. This is especially so as far as the press is concerned, for news is a perishable commodity and to delay its publication, even for a short period, may well deprive it of all its value and interest.

(2) Specific Instances

(i) Newspaper Investigation

5.115. *The Sunday Times v. The United Kingdom*[220] concerned contempt of court proceedings arising from a newspaper investigation. Distillers, a drug manufacturer had marketed in the United Kingdom, a drug for pregnant women called 'thalido-

---

[216] Application NO 6538/74 Series A NO 30, (1979–80) 2 EHRR 245, para. 65. This principle was affirmed by the Court in Application NO 13166/87 *The Sunday Times v. United Kingdom* (NO 2) Series A NO 217, (1992) 14 EHRR 229; Application NO 13585/88 *The Observer and The Guardian v. United Kingdom* Series A NO 216, (1992) 14 EHRR 153. See also Applications NO 11553/85 and NO 11658/85 *Hodgson, Woolf Productions and National Union of Journalists and Channel Four Television v. United Kingdom* (1988) 10 EHRR 503.

[217] Application NO 13166/87 *The Sunday Times v. United Kingdom* (NO 2) Series A NO 217, (1992) 14 EHRR 229, para. 51 and Application NO 13585/88 *The Observer and The Guardian v. United Kingdom* Series A NO 216, (1992) 14 EHRR 153.

[218] See §5.115 et seq. below.

[219] See §5.133 below.

[220] Application NO 6538/74 Series A NO 30, (1979–80) 2 EHRR 245.

mide'. The drug had not been adequately tested and women who took it gave birth to children with deformed limbs. Distillers were sued for negligence. However, they appeared dilatory in their attempts to settle the actions and the Sunday Times newspaper took up the cause of the victims, publishing several articles. In one proposed but unpublished article, the Applicant was to outline a number of negligent factors laying the blame at the door of the drugs company. Prior to publication, the Attorney General obtained an injunction preventing publication, which though reversed by the Court of Appeal, was upheld by the House of Lords. The injunction was eventually lifted when only a few cases remained unsettled.

The European Court considered that the legitimate aim being pursued by the Government was 'maintaining the authority and impartiality of the judiciary' and not the protection of the rights of others ie litigants. The Court considered that the various reasons employed to justify the injunction came within the scope of this ground. They included, amongst others:

(1) prejudging the issue would have led to disrespect for the processes of the law and interference with the administration of justice: exposing the Defendant to public and prejudicial discussion of the merits of their case would inhibit suitors generally from having recourse to the courts;

(2) prejudgment by the press inevitably led to replies by the parties to an action thereby creating the danger of a 'trial by newspaper' incompatible with the proper administration of justice.

5.116. Legitimate aims generally. The European Court affirmed that, generally, legitimate aims in contempt proceedings include:

(1) preventing interference with negotiations towards the settlement of a pending suit;

(2) preventing interference with a procedural situation in the strictly forensic sense;

(3) preventing interference with the procedure for judicial approval of a settlement.

5.117. In a democratic society—prevention of trial by jury. The European Court acknowledged the dangers of the public being led to form an opinion before adjudication of that matter. Parties should not have to undergo so called 'trial by newspaper':

> . . . Such concern is in itself 'relevant' to the maintenance of the 'authority of the judiciary' as that expression is understood by the [domestic] Court . . . If the issues arising in litigation are ventilated in such a way as to lead the public to form its own conclusion thereon in advance, it may lose its respect for and confidence in the courts. Again, it cannot be excluded that the public's becoming accustomed to the regular spectacle of pseudo-trials in the news media might in the long run have nefarious consequences for the acceptance of the courts as the proper forum for the settlement of legal disputes.

Nevertheless, the Court found that the injunction was not justified in the instant case. Of chief importance was the public interest aspect of the litigation: the question of whether a large corporation would be found legally and morally responsible towards individuals to whom it had given appalling deformities or whether they would receive compensation from the State and also the rights and remedies flowing from harmful medicines. The families of the victims had a right to whatever information might benefit their cause. Furthermore, at the time when the Sunday Times intended to publish the article, litigation had become stationary. The fact that had the Sunday Times article been published, Distillers would have been bound to canvass the arguments in advance of the trial was outweighed by the public interest in knowing the information: in fact bringing to light certain facts could have put a brake on speculation. Also the national court betrayed its own arguments, for it had lifted the injunction when cases were still pending.[221]

(ii) Presenting a Dramatic Reconstruction

5.118. Trials are theatrical events which lend themselves readily to theatrical reconstructions. It is tempting for the media, in presenting news of an ongoing trial, to resort to reconstructions. *Hodgson, Woolf Productions and National Union of Journalists and Channel Four Television v. United Kingdom*[222] concerned the attempts of a broadcasting organisation to run a television series in this way. Woolf Productions were preparing to produce a series of programmes which would present trials of public interest in the form of an extended news report. Hodgson and various other journalists were engaged to edit the reports. One programme in the series concerned the trial of a senior civil servant who had allegedly given information to the press on the sinking of a ship during the time of Britain's war in the Falkland Islands. The Applicants proposed that actors would read a transcript which had been checked for accuracy and fairness: the actors were to be hired not for dramatic effect (and there was no intention to present the case in a theatrical way), but in order to ensure that no undue emphasis was given to any particular words. At the opening of the trial, the trial judge made an order under the Contempt of Court Act 1981, (with the defence counsel's support) postponing the proposed presentation until the jury had given their verdict. The judge's grounds were that, however unintentionally, the employment of actors would give dramatic effect to the presentation and that jury members who might watch the programme could be influenced by what the production had chosen to reconstruct: ie they might recall the evidence of the day not from what the witnesses had said but from how the actors had presented their evidence. As the trial judge noted, 'The important point is that actors are being used in a dramatic setting, and it is difficult to think why actors are being used unless it be to give dramatic effect to the words used.' Channel Four changed the format, replacing the actors with newsreaders and presented the programme as extended news. The Applicants argued that the judge did not need to prohibit the programmes, for there were other actions open to him. The European Commission of Human Rights held that the trial judge was allowed a wide margin of discretion in such cases:

> . . . the need to ensure a fair trial and to protect members of a jury from exposure to prejudicial influences corresponds to a 'pressing social need'. Such an interpretation is reflected in the importance attached in a democratic society to the right to a fair trial.

---

[221] In a Dissenting Opinion, the minority judges stated that the purpose of the injunction was to avoid publication at a premature moment. In the English Courts, the Law Lords acknowledged that a juncture might arrive when the interest of press freedom might outweigh the considerations of the justice system: when the general lines of a settlement to be applied in these cases had emerged.

[222] Application NOs 11553/85 and 11658/85 *Hodgson, Woolf Productions and National Union of Journalists and Channel Four Television v. United Kingdom* (1988) 10 EHRR 503 (application declared inadmissible).

Furthermore, where a trial judge is confronted, in the opening of a highly publicised and controversial trial, with a potentially prejudicial media report, great weight must be attached to his on-the-spot assessment of the dangers of prejudicing the jury and thereby harming the fairness of the trial. Such a calculation, involving as it does the proper balance to be struck between the applicant's freedom of expression and the fair administration of justice, is a matter which falls within the Contracting State's margin of appreciation subject, of course, to supervision by the organs of the Convention.

The Commission acknowledged that the judge could have, for example, prohibited the jury from watching the programme but stated that:

> . . . where there is a real risk of prejudice the appropriate response, in the circumstances, is one which must lie, in principle, with the person responsible for ensuring the fairness of the trial, namely, the trial judge.

In view of the fact that, following the order, the Applicants were able to impart substantially the same information, the order had been necessary in a democratic society.

(iii) Non-disclosure in the Interests of National Security

5.119. In *The Observer and the Guardian v. United Kingdom*,[223] the European Court considered whether an injunction prohibiting the publication of material, could be justified on grounds of national security. The British Government was seeking an injunction in the Australian courts to prevent a former MI5 officer, publishing in Australia, a book concerning activities in the service during his period of engagement. Prior to the trial, the Applicant newspapers, which had been campaigning for an independent enquiry on the role of the security services, published certain information which was contained in the forthcoming book. The Attorney General obtained an injunction from the English courts (upheld on appeal) preventing the Applicants from publishing any material which might have originated from Mr Wright. They were not prohibited from publishing a fair and accurate report of proceedings in the trial in Australia and also information already made public. The British Government lost the case in Australia but the injunctions were maintained pending an appeal. In the interim, summaries of allegations appeared in The Independent—a British daily national newspaper. Another British newspaper, The Sunday Times, began serialising instalments of the book. That action was swiftly met with injunctions. Then, Mr Wright's book was published in the United States. No action was taken by the British Government to prevent its publication there, neither did they seek to prevent individual copies being taken back to the UK by tourists.

The European Court held that the injunction pursued legitimate aims being both for 'maintaining the authority of the judiciary' and for the 'protection of national security'. Furthermore throughout the period up until publication of the book in the United States, it was 'necessary in a democratic society' and proportionate. The Applicants had revealed their intention to publish the whole book. The Court noted that '. . . it was not unreasonable to suppose that where a former employee

---

[223] Application NO 13585/88 *The Observer and The Guardian v. United Kingdom* Series A NO 216, (1992) 14 EHRR 153. See also on similar facts, Application NO 13166/87 *The Sunday Times v. United Kingdom* (NO 2) Series A NO 217, (1992) 14 EHRR 229.

of a security service—an 'insider'. . .—proposed to publish without authorisation, his memoirs, there was at least a risk that they would comprise material the disclosure of which might be detrimental to that service; it has to be borne in mind that in such a context damaging information may be gleaned from an accumulation of what may appear at first sight to be unimportant details.' The measures were proportionate for they did not contain a blanket ban, neither did they prevent the Applicants from maintaining their campaign.[224] However, after publication of the book in the United States, the injunction ceased to be legitimate since the information became public knowledge. In fact, most of the information contained in Mr Wright's book was public knowledge having been disclosed in other works of a similar nature. This was reflected in a 'metamorphoses' of the Government's case in the Australian courts. Initially it argued that the injunction was necessary to prevent the disclosure of confidential information. However, once it was realised that the information was already public, the Government argued that it was necessary to punish Mr Wright so as to deter others from divulging information obtained in confidence during their employment. The European Court held that this was not legitimate and that the injunction:

> . . . prevented newspapers from exercising their right and duty to purvey information, already available, on a matter of legitimate public concern.

(iv) Disclosure of Judicial Investigation

5.120. In *Weber v. Switzerland,*[225] the European Court was called upon to examine legislation which prohibited the disclosure of a judicial investigation. Mr Weber was a journalist who ran an organisation concerned with nature conservation. An individual who had received a request for a donation from the organisation, wrote to a national newspaper accusing the Applicant of pursuing his cause purely for financial gain living '. . . by devious means, sponging off decent people who still believe that these drop-outs have their uses and in so doing demonstrate their distrust of the whole country's democratically—and how democratically!—elected authorities.' Mr Weber lodged a complaint for defamation which was pursued by an investigating judge. The judge demanded certain accounts which the Applicant refused to hand over and the Applicant lodged a criminal complaint alleging misuse of official authority and coercion—which was dismissed. The Applicant divulged at a press conference that investigations were being made against the writer, that he had handed over certain accounts and he denounced 'the plot hatched against him by the Vaud authorities in order to intimidate him'. The writer of the letter was eventually charged with defamation immediately following which, the Applicant organised a press conference informing the public that a defamation charge had been brought and charging the authorities with intimidation over the demands of certain accounts. This was reported in two daily newspapers. The Applicant was charged with breach of confidentiality of a judicial investigation and convicted and ordered to pay a fine. He argued, inter alia, a breach of Article 10.

---

[224] In one of several dissenting opinions, a minority of five judges stated that the injunction had never been justified:

Under no circumstances, however, can prior restraint, even in the form of judicial injunctions, either temporary or permanent, be accepted, except in what the Convention describes as a 'time of war or other public emergency threatening the life of the nation' and, even then, only 'to the extent strictly required by the exigencies of the situation' (Article 15).

[225] Application NO 11034/84 Series A NO 177, (1990) 12 EHRR 508.

The Code of Criminal Procedure dictated that all judicial investigations had to remain confidential until they were finally completed. The European Court held the legislation under which the Applicant was prosecuted had a legitimate aim under the Convention for it '. . . was intended to ensure the proper conduct of the investigation and was therefore designed to protect the authority and impartiality of the judiciary.' However, the Court found that it was not necessary in a democratic society due to the fact that the information had already become public knowledge as a result of the first press conference: it followed that the action might have been legitimate had it occurred at the first conference. Furthermore, the investigating judge had charged the Defendant the day before the second conference.

12. Obscenity

(1) Literary Works

5.121. Books intended for education. The European Court has defined the contours of the immorality ground in *Handyside v. United Kingdom*.[226] The Applicant, a publisher, had been prosecuted in the United Kingdom under the Obscene Publications Act 1959 (as amended by the Obscene Publications Act 1964) following distribution of 'The Little Red Schoolbook', a translation of a work by two Danish authors. The book, which was intended as a reference work for school children of the age of twelve upwards, contained material which in the domestic court's view, subordinated cultivating a sense of responsibility for the community, to the development of the expression of the child itself. For example, in one part of the book, the authors reassured their readers that they should not feel guilty about doing those things of which parents might not approve, and cited as examples smoking pot and engaging in under-age sex. Whilst there was acknowledgement that such activities were illegal, that acknowledgement was in another part of the book.

The European Court stated that the British legislation had a legitimate aim under Article 10(2), namely the protection of morals. It noted that 'Basically the book contained purely factual information that was generally correct and often useful . . . However, it also included, above all in the section on sex and in the passage headed "Be yourself" in the chapter on pupils . . . sentences or paragraphs that young people at a critical stage of their development could have interpreted as encouragement to indulge in precocious activities harmful for them or even to commit certain criminal offences.' It thus held that:

> . . . In these circumstances, despite the variety and the constant evolution in the United Kingdom of views on ethics and education, the competent English judges were entitled, in the exercise of their discretion, to think at the relevant time that the Schoolbook would have pernicious effects on the morals of many of the children and adolescents who would read it.

It was argued that the British authority's actions had been disproportionate to the need in that, rather than seizing copies, they could have demanded that the Applicant expurgate his work or limit its advertising and distribution. The European Court dismissed this as impractical noting that 'Article 10

---
[226] Application NO 5493/72 Series A NO 24, (1979–80) 1 EHRR 737.

of the Convention certainly does not oblige the Contracting States to introduce such prior censorship.'[227]

5.122. Pornography intended for export. The European Commission of Human Rights has held that the United Kingdom acted within its rights by seizing and forfeiting pornographic magazines which were intended for export.[228] The Commission acknowledged that ' . . . the moral standards and legal policies regarding obscene publications vary greatly from one country to another, and that the restriction of such material must in principle be decided having regard to the standards of the possible readership.' Nevertheless, it found that this was not the only consideration. The purpose of the legislation was to prevent persons in the United Kingdom 'publishing obscene matter for gain'. Thus whatever the ultimate destination of the material, it was the publishing act itself which was morally and legally disapproved in the United Kingdom. It was therefore a legitimate aim for the United Kingdom to prevent its country from becoming the source of a flourishing export trade. Moreover, the Commission acknowledged that it was '. . . undesirable and impracticable to apply a moral double standard according to whether the publication is intended for a domestic or foreign audience.'

(2) Works of Art

5.123. In *Müller v. Switzerland*,[229] the European Court held that the national authorities had acted within their rights by prosecuting the Applicant, an artist, under obscenity laws and confiscating his works. He had, at the invitation of another artist created works on the spot for a public exhibition in Freiburg. His pictures contained many sexually explicit images and the national court which convicted him under Switzerland's obscenity laws stated that 'The overall impression is of persons giving free rein to licentiousness and even perversion.'

The European Court held that the prosecution pursued legitimate aims being the 'protection of . . . morals' as well as the 'protection of . . . the rights of others'. It noted that '. . . there is a natural link between protection of morals and protection of the rights of others.'

The Court confirmed that its approach in these cases mirrors that in *Handyside v. United Kingdom*,[230] namely, that morals are always in a state of evolution and that consequently Contracting States are in a better situation to appraise these issues than the European Court. But the Court stated that this is not without qualification:

> . . . Those who create, perform, distribute or exhibit works of art contribute to the exchange of ideas and opinions which is essential for a democratic society. Hence the obligation on the State not to encroach unduly on their freedom of expression.
>
> Artists and those who promote their work are certainly not immune from the possibility of limitations as provided for in paragraph (2) of Article 10. Whoever exercises his freedom of expression undertakes, in accordance with the express terms of that paragraph, 'duties and responsibilities'; their scope will depend on his situation and

---

[227] Judge Mosler dissenting on the basis that the measures were not proportionate since there were a large number of books still in circulation which could not, in practice, be seized.

[228] Application NO 9615/81 X v. *United Kingdom* (1983) 5 EHRR 581 (application declared inadmissible).

[229] Application NO 10737/84 Series A NO 133, (1991) 13 EHRR 212.

[230] See §5.121 above.

the means he uses. In considering whether the penalty was 'necessary in a democratic society', the Court cannot overlook this aspect of the matter.

The domestic court had determined that the paintings, '. . . with their emphasis on sexuality in some of its crudest forms' were '. . . liable grossly to offend the sense of sexual propriety of persons of ordinary sensitivity' and the European Court held this assessment to be valid being within the margin of appreciation allowed it.[231] Moreover, no age limit was placed upon those persons entering the exhibition. Significantly the fact that the paintings had not given rise to a public outcry, that the press was supportive of the artist and that he had exhibited similar work elsewhere in Switzerland without event, did not make any difference. This was because it did not '. . . in all the circumstances of the case, respond to a genuine social need . . . '

5.124. Confiscation of works. As to the confiscation, the European Court held that the legislation was designed to protect public morals by preventing a repetition of the offence and accordingly it had a legitimate aim. The Court noted that:

> A principle of law which is common to the Contracting States allows confiscation of 'items whose use has been lawfully adjudged illicit and dangerous to the general interest' (see *Handyside v. United Kingdom*, para. 63). In the instant case, the purpose was to protect the public from any repetition of the offence.

The Court acknowledged that the confiscation of an original work prevented the artist from making use of that work by exhibiting it in places where public morals were less highminded. Nevertheless, it held that the legislation was proportionate since the Applicant could at any time have applied to the national court to have the order varied or discharged if there was no danger of recurrence. The Applicant did not make such an application until 1988 when the court submitted to his request.

13. Blasphemy

5.125. In *Gay News Ltd and Lemon v. United Kingdom*,[232] the European Commission of Human Rights held valid, a conviction of blasphemous libel. The First Applicant was the publisher and the Second Applicant the editor of a magazine called 'Gay News'. An issue in 1976 carried a poem by a Professor James Kirkup entitled 'The Love that Dares to Speak its Name' which 'purported to describe in explicit detail acts of sodomy and fellatio with the body of Christ immediately after His death and ascribed to Him during His lifetime promiscuous homosexual practices with the Apostles and other men'. The poem was accompanied by a drawing illustrating the subject matter.

The Applicants were prosecuted privately (though with the authorities' consent) under section 8 of the Law of Libel Amendment Act 1888 for having 'unlawfully and wickedly published or caused to be published a blasphemous libel concerning

---

[231] In a dissenting Opinion, Judge Spielmann stated that the margin of appreciation given to the national authorities was too generous: that the Contracting States should not be given carte blanche to determine what was or was not morally acceptable since that which was considered obscene at one moment in history had been exonerated at another citing as his example the quashing in 1949 of a conviction against Baudelaire, Poulet-Malassis and de Broisse in 1857.

[232] Application NO 8710/79 (1983) 5 EHRR 123, (application declared inadmissible).

the Christian religion, namely an obscene poem and illustration vilifying Christ in His life and in His crucifixion'. The English Court convicted the Defendant. It found that the prosecution needed to establish only that the Defendant intended to publish material which was in fact blasphemous: ie the test was one of strict liability.

5.126. Necessary in a democratic society. The Commission stated that the offence of blasphemous libel was designed to prevent a publication offending a person's religious belief: the legislation therefore had a legitimate aim which was 'the protection of the . . . rights of others.' The Commission held that the protection of religious beliefs was necessary in a democratic society:

> . . . If it is accepted that the religious feelings of the citizen may deserve protection against indecent attacks on the matters held sacred by him, then it can also be considered as necessary in a democratic society to stipulate that such attacks, if they attain a certain level of severity, shall constitute a criminal offence triable at the request of the offended person. It is in principle left to the legislation of the State concerned how it wishes to define the offence, provided that the principle of proportionality, which is inherent in the exception clause of Article 10(2), is being respected.

The English legislation fulfilled those requirements, even though liability was strict. Moreover, the intended audience was of no relevance:

> . . . In particular it does not seem disproportionate to the aim pursued that the offence is one of strict liability incurred irrespective of the intention to blaspheme and irrespective of the intended audience and of the possible avoidability of the publication by a certain member of the public.

The fact remained, that the magazine was on sale to the general public and happened to find its way into the private prosecutor's hands.

14. Publishing Monopolies

(1) General Principles

5.127. Freedom of information. The mere existence of a press monopoly inevitably leads to the charge that freedom of expression is in fact or in danger of being threatened. But, for the purposes of Article 10, a distinction must be made between on the one hand, the right to disseminate information, and on the other, the right to express opinions. In *De Geillustreerde Pers NV v. Netherlands*,[233] the European Commission of Human Rights stated that:

> . . . in the area of 'information', ie in the area of facts and news as opposed to 'ideas' and 'opinions' the protection which Article 10 of the Convention seeks to secure concerns the free flow of such information to the public in general.

5.128. Freedom to publish copyright material. Whilst the Convention guarantees the right of publication of information or literary works, that right is restricted to the originator of that information or the copyright holder, as the case may be:

---

[233] Application NO 5178/71 8 DR 5, [1978] ECC 164, para. 85.

The Commission considers that the freedom under Article 10 to impart information of the kind described above, is only granted to the person or body who produces, provides or organises it. In other words the freedom to impart such information is limited to information produced, provided or organised by the person claiming that freedom, being the author, the originator or otherwise the intellectual owner of the information concerned.[234]

5.129. No protection of commercial interests. In *De Geillustreerde Pers NV v. The Netherlands*,[235] the European Commission of Human Rights held that the Convention is not intended, and cannot be invoked, to protect commercial interests:

. . . the Commission considers that the protection of the commercial interests of particular newspapers or groups of newspapers is not as such contemplated by the terms of Article 10 of the Convention. These matters might perhaps raise an issue under this provision where a State fails in its duty to protect against excessive press concentrations, but this obviously is not the position in the present case.

(2) Matter Protected by Copyright

5.130. Monopoly right to publish programme listings. In *De Geillustreerde Pers NV v. The Netherlands*,[236] the European Commission of Human Rights considered whether a broadcasting organisation's monopoly right to publish programme listings and the refusal to allow others to publish the same material, constituted a violation of Article 10. The Netherlands Broadcasting Foundation, compiled for each week, television and radio programme data supplied to it by the various broadcasting organisations. Its monopoly right over the publishing of that information was secured by the Netherlands Broadcasting Act 1967. This right served two purposes. In the first place, the number of subscriptions to the magazines determined the financial subsidy which the Netherlands Broadcasting Foundation allocated to the broadcasting organisation to enable its operation. Secondly, it provided a direct source of revenue for those organisations. The Applicant, a publisher of weekly magazines' wished to publish programme data compiled by that organisation but was refused permission. The Commission noted the special characteristics of programme listing material:

. . . such lists of programme data are not simple facts, or news in the proper sense of the word. They are rather a compilation of facts and they are news in the sense that they provide an orientation guide for television viewers or radio listeners prior to or during a particular week with a view to assisting them in the selection of forthcoming programmes. The characteristic feature of such information is that it can only be produced and provided by the broadcasting organisations being charged with the production of the programmes themselves and that it is organised by the Foundation being the co-ordinating body of these organisations.

The Commission therefore held that there was no question of state censorship:

---

[234] Application NO 5178/71 *De Geillustreerde Pers NV v. The Netherlands* 8 DR 5, [1978] ECC 164, para. 84.
[235] Application NO 5178/71 8 DR 5, [1978] ECC 164, para. 88.
[236] *Ibid.*

... there can be no question in the present case that the freedom of the press in general is threatened in the sense that the public is deprived of any specific information, ie, in the present case, the programme data, by censorship or otherwise by reason of any undue State monopoly on news. On the contrary, every person in the Netherlands may inform himself about the forthcoming radio and television programmes through a variety of mass media representing various sections and tendencies of society. To that extent, there is, in the Commission's opinion, no merit in the applicant company's claim that the public is prevented from receiving unbiased information about these programmes owing to the fact that it can only obtain such information by reading the broadcasting organisation's own magazines.

15. Consumer Protection

(1) Advertising and Marketing of Goods

5.131. In *X and Church of Scientology v. Sweden*,[237] the European Commission of Human Rights upheld an injunction preventing a religious community advertising the sale of a religious artefact. The Applicant church had placed an advertisement in its periodical for an 'E-Meter' which purportedly measured the mental state of an individual. The E-Meter was defined as 'A religious artefact used to measure the state of electrical characteristics of the "static field" surrounding the body and believed to reflect or indicate whether or not the confessing person has been relieved of the spiritual impediment of his sins.' The Commission noted that most European countries had legislation which restricted the free flow of commercial 'ideas' in the interests of protecting consumers from misleading or deceptive practices. It stated that the level of protection afforded to 'commercial ideas' ought to be less than that given to 'political ideas'. Accordingly '. . . the test of "necessity" in the second paragraph of Article 10 should therefore be a less strict one when applied to restraints imposed on commercial "ideas".' Of relevance, were the national court's findings that the magazine was not restricted to members of the religious community and that the advertisement did not limit the sale to priests or those studying for the priesthood. It was important to protect consumers in matters of marketing activities by religious communities. The injunction had not prevented the sale of the meter, merely the use of a certain wording and the Commission thus felt that the injunction was proportional and 'necessary in a democratic society'.

16. Unfair Competition

(1) Advertising Services

5.132. In *Barthold v. Germany*,[238] the European Court examined the merits of unfair competition legislation. The Applicant was a vet in Hamburg offering a

---

[237] Application NO 7805/77 16 DR 68 (application declared inadmissible).
[238] Application NO 8734/79 Series A NO 90, (1985) 7 EHRR 383.

round-the-clock service. A committee on which he sat refused to put into effect his proposals for establishing 24-hour treatment for animals. In a report of this issue, a journalist recounted how a cat owner had tried in vain to find a vet during the night, before calling Dr Barthold who had saved the cat from death. The Article stated that 'The fact that there is a demand for an emergency service at night is illustrated by Dr Barthold by reference to the number of calls received by his practice between 8 pm and 8 am.' Other vets considered Dr Barthold to have violated rules of unfair competition secured by a statute, namely the Unfair Competition Act of 7 June 1909 and through a regulatory body obtained an injunction forbidding him from giving any publicity to the press about his practice and his personal experiences (the injunction did not extend to professional journals). He was not prevented from giving his opinion on the need of a night service and providing his name and photograph and stating his post as the head of a particular service.

The European Court found that the legislation upon which the injunction was founded had a legitimate aim, namely, the protection of the rights of others: it was issued in order to prevent the Applicant from acquiring a commercial advantage over professional colleagues prepared to conduct themselves in compliance with the rule of professional conduct that required vetinary surgeons to refrain from advertising. However, the legislation was too severe. It provided that there was an intent to act for the purposes of commercial competition as long as that intent had not been entirely overridden by other motives. The Court ruled that this rigorous test violated Article 10:

> A criterion as strict as this in approaching the matter of advertising and publicity in the liberal professions is not consonant with freedom of expression. Its application risks discouraging members of the liberal professions from contributing to public debate on topics affecting the life of the community if ever there is the slightest likelihood of their utterances being treated as entailing, to some degree, an advertising effect. By the same token, application of a criterion such as this is liable to hamper the press in the performance of its task of purveyor of information and public watchdog.

(2) Criticism of Competing Products

5.133. In *Markt Intern and Beermann v. Germany*,[239] the Applicant was a publishing firm which sought to defend the interests of small and medium-sized retail businesses against competition from large distribution companies such as supermarkets and mail-order firms. It published an article outlining a complaint against a cosmetics company that the company had not honoured its pledge to refund customers unsatisfied by its products and demanded whether other subscribers had similar experiences. The application concerned the ruling by the Federal Court of Justice that the Applicant refrain from publishing the information: it was based on a 1909 Act.[240] The national court had found that the Applicant's conduct was designed to benefit a particular commercial sector and therefore served commercial interests. The publication of the article had been premature considering that the

---

[239] Application NO 10572/83 Series A NO 165, (1990) 12 EHRR 161.
[240] Section 1 of the 1909 Act stated that 'any person who in the course of business commits, for the purposes of competition, acts contrary to honest practices may be enjoined from further engaging in those acts and held liable in damages.'

club had promised an enquiry and bearing in mind the weapon which publication gave to subscribers of the publication.

The European Court found that the legislation pursued a legitimate aim, namely, the protection of the reputation and the rights of others. It held that the national court had operated within the margin of appreciation allowed, considering the type of publication in dispute:

> In a market economy an undertaking which seeks to set up a business inevitably exposes itself to close scrutiny of its practices by its competitors. Its commercial strategy and the manner in which it honours its commitments may give rise to criticism on the part of consumers and the specialised press. In order to carry out this task, the specialised press must be able to disclose facts which could be of interest to its readers and thereby contribute to the openness of business activities.
>
> However, even the publication of items which are true and describe real events may under certain circumstances be prohibited: the obligation to respect the privacy of others or the duty to respect the confidentiality of certain commercial information are examples. In addition, a correct statement can be and often is qualified by additional remarks, by value judgments, by suppositions or even insinuations. It must also be recognised that an isolated incident may deserve closer scrutiny before being made public; otherwise an accurate description of one such incident can give the false impression that the incident is evidence of a general practice. All these factors can legitimately contribute to the assessment of statements made in a commercial context, and it is primarily for the national courts to decide which statements are permissible and which are not.[241]

17. Restricting Commercial Conditions for the Sale of Material

(1) Price Restraints

5.134. Resale price maintenance for newspapers. In *Hammerdahls Stormarknad v. Sweden*,[242] the European Commission of Human Rights held that freedom of expression within the meaning of Article 10 does not include the freedom to trade goods under whatever conditions of sale the Applicant so wishes. The Applicant company operated a supermarket where newspapers were sold. A distributor of newspapers and magazines refused to supply the Applicant with newspapers because he sold them at prices lower than the prices fixed by the distributor. The Commission rejected the claim noting that the Applicant was not prevented from selling newspapers.

---

[241] Series A NO 165, (1990) 12 EHRR 161, para. 35. In a dissenting opinion, Judges Golcuklu, Pettiti, Russo, Spielmann, De Meyer, Carrillo Salcedo and Valticos, stated that the measures did not satisfy the necessity test because consumers needed to be protected from highly effective distribution techniques and advertising frequently lacking objectivity. The socio-economic press was as vital for the development of society as the political and cultural press. The event reported had in fact occurred. The fact that a person defends a given interest, even economic, should not deprive him of freedom of expression. In a dissenting opinion, Judges Martens and MacDonald held that the commercial press is to be treated in the same way as any other type of press notwithstanding that they may represent a particular interest because all press are partisan.
[242] Application NO 11532/85 (1986) 8 EHRR 45 (application declared inadmissible).

18. Prohibition of Discrimination

(1) Introduction

5.135. Convention terms. Article 14 of the Convention prohibits discrimination. It states:

> The enjoyment of the rights and freedoms set forth in the Convention shall be secured without discrimination on any ground such as sex, race, colour, language, religion or other opinion, national or social origin, association with a national minority property, birth or other status.

(2) General Principles

5.136. Dependence on other Convention articles. Article 14 does not have an independent existence and must therefore be read in conjunction with another Article in Section I of the Convention.[243] Nevertheless, a measure which might otherwise be justified in accordance with Article 10 may infringe that Article when read in conjunction with Article 14.[244]

5.137. Key elements of violation. A violation will be found where:[245]

(1) the facts disclose a differential treatment;
(2) the distinction does not have a legitimate aim ie it has no objective and reasonable justification having regard to the aim and effects of the measure under consideration; and
(3) there is no reasonable proportionality between the means employed and the aim sought to be realised.

5.138. Meaning of differential treatment. In order to find the existence of differential treatment it is necessary that the party alleging that a distinction is made between himself and another is in a position comparable to that of the other who is allegedly favoured.[246]

(3) Specific Instances

5.139. Preserving publication monopolies. In *De Geillustreerde Pers NV v. The Netherlands*,[247] the Applicant argued that Dutch legislation which gave to a broadcasting organisation, a monopoly for the publication of its programme listing, contravened Article 14. The legislation allowed the broadcasting organisation the exclusive right to publish weekly programme listings in its own magazine. It also obligated the broadcasting organisation to supply summaries for publication in daily newspapers and thrice weekly newspapers as well as in foreign weekly newspapers.

---

[243] Application NO 5178/71 *De Geillustreerde Pers NV v. The Netherlands* 8 DR 5, [1978] ECC 164.
[244] *Ibid.*
[245] *Ibid*; Application NO 13585/88 *The Observer and The Guardian v. United Kingdom* Series A NO 216, (1992) 14 EHRR 153; Application NO 13166/87 *The Sunday Times v. United Kingdom* (NO 2) Series A NO 217, (1992) 14 EHRR 229.
[246] Application NO 5178/71 *De Geillustreerde Pers NV v. The Netherlands* 8 DR 5, [1978] ECC 164 and Application NO 6538/74 *The Sunday Times v. The United Kingdom* Series A NO 30, (1979–80) 2 EHRR 245.
[247] Application NO 5178/71 8 DR 5, [1978] ECC 164.

The Applicant, being a weekly magazine was excluded. The European Commission of Human Rights stated that comparing the Applicant's magazine with that of the broadcasting organisations, revealed, prima facie discrimination, but it held that such discrimination had a legitimate aim. This was twofold. First, the volume of subscriptions to the broadcasting organisation's magazine was employed to indicate the number of subscribers to the channel and hence determine the amount of funding it deserved from the Netherlands Broadcasting Foundation. Secondly, it provided a source of income for the channel. There was no ostensible discrimination in favour of the other national press permitted to publish the details and summaries for there was substantial differences between them and the Applicant as regards content, presentation and purpose. Finally, the Commission accepted that there might be similarities between the foreign weekly magazines and the magazines of foreign broadcasters and the Applicant's magazine in terms of format. Nevertheless any inequality had an objective and justifiable basis. It was designed to serve those persons abroad who were interested in Dutch broadcasts and similar arrangements existed for Dutch people interested in foreign broadcasts.

5.140. On religious grounds. In *Gay News Ltd and Lemon v. United Kingdom*,[248] the European Commission of Human Rights found that blasphemy laws which defended only Christianity, were not discriminatory for they did not discriminate between different offenders. The Commission stated that:

> . . . the applicants cannot complain of discrimination because the law of blasphemy protects only the Christian but no other religion. This distinction in fact relates to the object of legal protection, but not to the personal status of the offender.

5.141. Selecting certain newspapers (contempt of court). In *The Sunday Times v. The United Kingdom*,[249] the European Court held that the fact that injunctions were sought against the Applicant newspapers and not others, was not sufficient evidence to find discrimination contrary to Article 14.

5.142. Inadequate provision for foreign language programmes. In *Verein Alternatives Lokalradio Bern and Verein Radio Dreyeckland Basel v. Switzerland*,[250] the Applicants argued that a refusal to grant them a licence to broadcast local radio was discriminatory for they intended to make greater provision for foreign language programming than those organisations actually granted a licence. The Commission of Human Rights held that the Applicants had failed to establish such discrimination, for the distinctiveness of the programming was a relevant factor in awarding the licences. But it stated that:

> The Commission nevertheless considers that refusal to grant a broadcasting licence may raise a problem under Article 10, in conjunction with Article 14 of the Convention in specific circumstances. Such a problem would arise, for example, if the refusal to grant a licence resulted directly in a considerable proportion of the inhabitants of the area concerned being deprived of broadcasts in their mother tongue.[251]

The Commission noted that, in fact, the foreign language populations of Berne and Basle could receive programmes in their mother tongue, broadcast by private radio states or foreign stations.

---

[248] Application NO 8710/79 (1983) 5 EHRR 123, para. 14.
[249] Application NO 6538/74 Series A NO 30, (1979–80) 2 EHRR 245.
[250] Application NO 10746/84 49 DR 126.
[251] *Ibid.*, para. 2.

5.143. Parties within different jurisdictions. In *The Observer and The Guardian v. United Kingdom*,[252] the European Court held that foreign newspapers were not in a similar situation to national newspapers, for the former were not subject to the jurisdiction of the English courts. No discrimination could thus be said to arise from the fact that the Applicants were prevented from publishing material whilst no measures were taken to prevent publication of the same material by the foreign press. With regard to the publication of that same material, the European Court held, in *The Sunday Times v. United Kingdom (NO 2)*,[253] that foreign publishers were not comparable with the Applicant.

5.144. Distinctions between the press and parliament. In *The Sunday Times v. The United Kingdom*,[254] the Court of Appeal in lifting an injunction which had silenced a national newspaper's report on live proceedings, noted the undesirability of there being differences in treatment between on the one hand parliament, whose proceedings were published, and on the other hand, proceedings in courts. The newspapers wished to report on issues about which there had been considerable debate within parliament. Despite this fact, the European Court stated that '. . . the Court is of the opinion that the press and parliamentarians cannot be considered to be "placed in comparable situations" since their respective "duties and responsibilities" are essentially different'.[255]

---

[252] Application NO 13585/88 Series A NO 216, (1992) 14 EHRR 153.
[253] Application NO 13166/87 Series A NO 217, (1992) 14 EHRR 229.
[254] Application NO 6538/74 Series A NO 30, (1979–80) 2 EHRR 245.
[255] *Ibid.*, para. 72. In fact, as the Court noted, the parliamentary debate did not cover exactly the same ground as the proceedings in court.

CHAPTER SIX

European Community Directives

I. FREEDOM OF IMPORTATION, DISTRIBUTION AND EXPLOITATION OF FILMS

1. Introduction

6.001. Commencement. Council Directive 63/607/EEC[1] was executed on 15 October 1963 and Member States had to adopt measures in compliance with it within six months of notification.[2]

6.002. Scope of Directive. The Directive implements the provisions of the General Programme for the abolition of restrictions on freedom to provide services as it applies to the film industry. However, nothing in the Directive affects the operation of rules applicable in a Member State to the exhibition of its own films or films treated as such.[3]

6.003. Beneficiaries. The Directive confers rights on 'beneficiaries',[4] that is, natural persons and companies or firms covered by Title I of the General Programme for the abolition of restrictions on freedom to provide services.[5]

6.004. Definition of a 'film'. A film is defined as a 'copy which conforms to the master copy of a completed cinematographic work intended for public or for private exhibition and in which subsist all rights of commercial exploitation arising under

---

[1] OJ Sp Edn 1963–1964, p. 52.
[2] Article 12. In the case of Member States who subsequently acceded to the Treaty, the Directive was to be implemented by their date of accession.
[3] Article 9.
[4] Article 1.
[5] OJ 2, 15.1.62, p.32, OJ Sp Ed (Second Series) IX, p.3. For the definition of Title I beneficiaries, see §2.011 above.

international conventions or under other international arrangements.[6] Films are divided into three categories: full-length films;[7] short films[8] and newsreel films.[9] These categories are based on the film industry standard film width of 35 mm. Films of other widths are deemed to fall into one of the three aforementioned categories depending on their length and subject matter.[10]

6.005. The definition of a film having the nationality of a Member State. The status of Member State nationality confers certain rights of importation, distribution and exploitation of films. To possess the nationality of a particular Member State, a film must satisfy the following conditions:

(1) the film must be produced by a beneficiary;[11]
(2) studio-filming must take place in studios situated in a Community territory.[12]
(3) the original version must be recorded in the language or one of the languages of that Member State, except for any parts of the dialogue which the screen play requires to be in another language;[13]
(4) the screenplay, adaptation, dialogue and, if specially composed for the film, musical score, must be written or composed by persons who are nationals of that Member State or who come within its cultural domain;[14]
(5) the director must be a national of that Member State or a person who comes within its cultural domain;[15] and
(6) the majority of the executants ie principal players, executive producer, director of photography, sound engineer, editor, art director and wardrobe chief, must be nationals of that Member State or come within its cultural domain.[16]

Provided that the Member State in question accords its nationality to the film, its status is not affected by:

(i) participation in the activities referred to in (4), (5), and (6) above, by nationals of other Member States, or by persons who come within the cultural domain of any such State;[17]
(ii) participation in the activities referred to in (4) and (6) above by nationals of third countries who are not persons coming within the cultural domain of

---

[6] Article 2.
[7] Article 2(a). Full length films are 35 mm films equal to or exceeding 1600 m in length.
[8] Article 2(b). Short films are 35 mm films less than 1600 m in length.
[9] Article 2(c). Newsreel films are 35 mm films equal to or exceeding 200 m in average length, the purpose of which is to provide regular reports and filmed accounts of current affairs and events. Newsreel films in colour may be less than 200 m in length.
[10] Article 2. para.3.
[11] Article 3(a). ie an undertaking which satisfies the provisions of Title I of the General Programme for the abolition of restrictions on freedom to provide services.
[12] Article 3(b). However, in accordance with Article 3(b), if the subject of the film requires the filming of outdoor scenes in a third country, up to 30% of the studio-filmed scenes may be shot in the territory of that third country.
[13] Article 3(c). In accordance with Article 3(c), where the film is recorded in more than one version, one of those versions must be in the language, or in one of the languages, of that Member State.
[14] Article 3(d).
[14] Article 3(e).
[16] Article 3(f).
[17] Article 3. para.2.

a Member State provided that such nationals do not constitute more than two-fifths of the total number of persons participating in such activities;[18]

(iii) the fact that the person referred to in (5) above is a national of a third country and does not come within the cultural domain of a Member State provided that all the activities referred to in (4) above and not less than four-fifths of the functions referred to in (6) above are performed by nationals of Member States.[19]

2. Freedom of Importation, Distribution and Commercial Exploitation

6.006. Documentary films. Member States may not restrict in any way the importation, distribution and commercial exploitation of short films,[20] newsreel films[21] and full-length films of documentary value.[22] Films of documentary value include those having cultural, scientific, technical or industrial subjects, or instructional or educational films for young people, or films promoting the Community ideal.[23]

6.007. Original version films. Member States may not restrict in any way the importation into, distribution and commercial exploitation within Member States, of full-length films having the nationality of another Member State and being for exhibition in their original version.[24] This prohibition applies regardless of whether such films contain subtitles in the language or one of the languages of the State in which they are exhibited.[25]

6.008. Dubbed films. Member States must allow the importation into, distribution and commercial exploitation within their territories of one another's films dubbed in the language of the State in which they are to be shown.[26] The Directive permits the existence of import quotas for such films but provides that they must not amount to less than seventy films per year.[27]

6.009. Reissued films. The commercial exploitation of reissued films is subject to agreement between the competent authorities of the Member States concerned.[28]

6.010. Import quotas. The Directive prohibited Member State introducing import quotas for any category films, where none existed.[29]

---

[18] *Ibid.*

[19] Article 3. para.2.

[20] Article 5(a).

[21] Article 5(b). Member States were permitted to maintain, until the end of the transitional period, any existing restrictions on the distribution and commercial exploitation of newsreels containing items not intended for exhibition in more than one country.

[22] Article 5(c).

[23] *Ibid.*

[24] Article 6.

[25] *Ibid.*

[26] Article 7(1).

[27] *Ibid.*

[28] Article 7(2).

[29] Article 7(3).

6.011. Special rules applying to co-productions and co-operation agreements with producers from third countries. Films made by producers from Member States as co-productions or in co-operation with producers from third countries may qualify as having the nationality of a Member State. Such films must be allowed to circulate freely for the purposes of distribution and commercial exploitation among all Member States.[30] A film is considered to be a co-production where it is made under the terms of reciprocal international agreements.[31] It is considered to be a co-operation agreement where it is made in conformity with national laws.[32] In either case, the artistic and technical contribution of the Member State or Member States must not be less than 30%.[33]

3. Miscellaneous Provisions

6.012. Prints dupes and advertising material. Any import authorization granted for a film carries with it, the right to import prints, dupes and advertising material relating to that film.[34]

6.013. Tax or other measures of equivalent effect. No tax or other measure having equivalent effect, the application of or exemption from which might result in discrimination can be imposed in respect of the granting of any authorization for the importation, distribution or commercial exploitation of any film which has the nationality of a Member State.[35]

6.014. Nationality certificates. Member States may refuse to issue an authorization for the importation into and commercial exploitation in their territories of any film which is not accompanied by a certificate issued by the exporting Member State confirming that the film has satisfied the nationality test.[36]

Member States have been enjoined to adopt a standard certificate for establishing the nationality of a film.[37]

II. OPENING OF SPECIALIST CINEMAS, SCREEN AND IMPORT QUOTAS AND DUBBING OF FILMS

1. Introduction

6.015. Commencement. Council Directive 65/264/EEC[38] was executed on 13 May 1965 and Member States were bound to adopt measures in compliance within six months of notification.[39]

---

[30] Article 4. para.5.
[31] *Ibid.* para.2.
[32] *Ibid.* para.3.
[33] *Ibid.* para.4.
[34] Article 8.
[35] Article 10.
[36] Article 11 (in accordance with the provisions of Articles 3 and 4 of the Directive).
[37] Commission Recommendation 64/242/EEC, JO 1964, p. 1025.
[38] OJ Sp Edn 1965–1966, p.6.
[39] Article 9.

6.016. Scope of Directive. The Directive implements the provisions of the General Programmes for the abolition of restrictions on freedom of establishment[40] and freedom to provide services[41] as they apply to the film industry.

6.017. Beneficiaries. The Directive confers rights on 'beneficiaries',[42] that is, natural persons and companies or firms covered by Title I of the General Programmes for both the abolition of restrictions on freedom of establishment[43] and freedom to provide services.[44]

6.018. Definition of a 'film having the nationality of a Member State'. This definition is imported from Council Directive 63/607/EEC above.[45] Films which satisfy the terms of the definition are guaranteed certain freedoms as detailed below.

2. Opening of Specialist Cinemas

6.019. Abolition of restrictions. Member States were required[46] to abolish the Title III restrictions on freedom of establishment and freedom to provide services relating to the opening of cinemas specialising exclusively in the exhibition of foreign films in the language of their country of origin.[47] This rule did not, however, apply in Member States in which films were usually shown in their country of origin.[48]

6.020. State aid. The Directive stipulates that any and every kind of aid available in one Member State for the opening of a specialist cinema must be available without discrimination to operators who are nationals of other Member States of the Community.[49] Furthermore, beneficiaries from Member States must not in any circumstance be treated less favourably than natural persons, companies or firms from third countries.[50] However, the act of opening of a specialist cinema in one Member State does not entitle any other Member State to grant any direct or indirect aid, whether financial or other for the opening of a specialist cinema in the latter Member State.[51] This is because such action would have the effect of distorting the natural conditions of establishment.[52] Thus, in particular, no aid may

---

[40] OJ 2, 15.1.62, p.36, OJ Sp. Edn (Second Series), IX, p.7.
[41] OJ 2, 15.1.62, p.32, OJ Sp. Edn (Second Series), IX, p.3.
[42] Article 1.
[43] OJ 2, 15.1.62, p.36, OJ Sp. Edn (Second Series), IX, p.7. For the definition of Title I beneficiaries see §2.003 above.
[44] OJ 2, 15.1.62, p.32, OJ Sp. Edn (Second Series), IX, p.3. For the definition of Title 1 beneficiaries, see §2.011 above.
[45] In accordance with Article 2 of Council Directive 65/264/EEC, a film is to be regarded as having the nationality of one or more Member States under that Directive where it satisfies the provisions of Articles 3 and 4 of Council Directive 63/607/EEC. See §6.005 above.
[46] By the end of the transitional period ie 31 December 1969.
[47] Article 1(a). In accordance with Article 1(a), this applied regardless of whether or not such films contained subtitles.
[48] Article 3.
[49] Article 4. para.3.
[50] *Ibid.* para.4.
[51] *Ibid.* para.1.
[52] *Ibid.*

be granted in such circumstances for: the construction, reconstruction or modern-isation of any cinema; the execution of work in connection with safety, hygiene or technical improvements; the purchasing of equipment; the renting of full length films or the covering of risks or trading losses.[53]

3. Abolition of Screen Quotas, Import Quotas and Dubbing Regulation

6.021. Screen quotas. Member States which required cinemas to set aside a minimum number of days per calendar year for the exhibition of domestic films, were required to allow films having the nationality of one or more Member States to be included in the quota under the same conditions applicable to domestic films, by 31 December 1966.[54] Those Member States which did not[55] impose screen quotas could introduce them provided that films having the nationality of another Member State were included.[56] However, quotas may not be applied to cinemas specialising in the exhibition of foreign films in their language of origin.[57]

6.022. Import quotas. Member States were required, to abolish quotas restricting the importing of films having the nationality of one or more Member States, by 31 December 1966.[58] The abolition of these quotas carries with it the right to import, without restriction, prints, dupes and advertising material relating to those films.[59]

6.023. Dubbing of films in importing country. Provisions which required that foreign films were to be dubbed in the importing country were to be repealed by 31 December 1966,[60] for films having the nationality of one or more Member States.[61]

III. FREEDOM OF ESTABLISHMENT AND FREEDOM TO PROVIDE SERVICES IN FILM DISTRIBUTION

1. Introduction

6.024. Commencement. Council Directive 68/369/EEC[62] was executed on 15

---

[53] *Ibid.* para.2.
[54] *Ibid.* para.1. and Article 1(b).
[55] On the day of notification of Council Directive 63/264/EEC.
[56] Article 5. para.2, provided that they were to include films having the nationality of other Member States.
[57] *Ibid.* para.3.
[58] Article 7. para. 1, and Article 1(b). However, the Federal Republic of Germany was entitled, during the transitional period, to retain the power to limit the importation of films having the nationality of one or more Member States in respect of which the national authority had granted a certificate more than four years before the date on which the application to import was submitted to the competent authorities.
[59] *Ibid.* para.3.
[60] ie by the end of the transitional period.
[61] Article 1(c) and Article 8.
[62] OJ Sp Edn 1968 (II) p.520.

October 1968 and Member States were required to adopt measures in compliance within six months of its notification.[63]

6.025. Scope of Directive. The Directive is concerned with the freedom of establishment and freedom to provide services of self-employed persons involved in film distribution.[64]

6.026. Beneficiaries. The Directive confers rights on 'beneficiaries',[65] that is, natural persons, companies or firms covered by Title I of the General Programmes for both the abolition of restrictions on freedom of establishment[66] and freedom to provide services.[67]

6.027. Definition of 'distribution' and 'renting' of films. The distribution and renting of films is regarded as 'comprising any activity involving the making over of the rights of commercial exploitation of a film with a view to its being distributed on a commercial basis in a specific market and the temporary transfer of the right of public exhibition to any person who directly organises the exhibition of films in the host country.'[68] Distribution is taken to include the renting of films.[69]

2. Restrictions to be Abolished

6.028. Member States were required to abolish the Title III restrictions on freedom of establishment and freedom to provide services affecting the activities of self-employed persons involved in film distribution.[70] In particular, these included restrictions which:

- prevented beneficiaries from establishing themselves or providing services in the host country under the same rights as nationals of that country;[71]
- by reason of administrative practices resulted in treatment being applied to beneficiaries that is discriminatory by comparison with treatment applied to nationals;[72]
- arose out of specific measures in particular Member States which prevented or limited establishment or provision of services by beneficiaries.[73]

3. Prohibition of Distortion of Conditions of Establishment

6.029. No Member State may grant to any of its nationals who go to another

---

[63] Article 7. In accordance with Article 4(3), this included, designating the authorities and bodies competent to issue documents specified in Article 4.
[64] As defined in Annex IV to the General Programme for the abolition of restrictions on freedom of establishment, ex Group 841, ex Major Group 84. Article 2(1) para.1.
[65] Article 1.
[66] OJ 2, 15.1.62, p.36, OJ Sp. Edn (Second Series), IX, p.7. For definition of Title I beneficiaries, see §2.003 above.
[67] OJ 2, 15.1.62, p.32, OJ Sp. Edn (Second Series), IX, p.3. For the definition of Title I beneficiaries, see §2.011 above.
[68] Article 2(2).
[69] Article 2(1), para.2.
[70] Article 1.
[71] Article 3(1)(a).
[72] Article 3(1)(b).
[73] Article 3(2). The Directive required the abolition of: in Belgium, the obligation to hold a carte professionelle; in France, the obligation to hold a carte d'identité d'étranger commerçant; in Luxembourg, the limited period of validity of authorisations granted to foreign nationals.

Member State for the purposes of pursuing any film distribution activity, any aid which is liable to distort the conditions of establishment.[74]

4. Special Requirements

6.030. Proof of good repute, solvency and financial standing. Where the host Member State requires of its own nationals wishing to take up any film distribution activity, proof of good repute and/or proof that they have not previously been declared bankrupt, that State must accept as sufficient evidence for nationals of other Member States, the production of an extract from the 'judicial record' or, failing this, of an equivalent document issued by a competent judicial or administrative authority in the country of origin or the country from which the foreign national comes showing that these requirements have been met.[75] Where the country of origin or the country from which the foreign national comes does not issue such documentary proof it may be replaced by a declaration on oath made by the person concerned (before a judicial or administrative authority, a notary, or a competent professional or trade body,) in the country of origin or in the country from which that person comes.[76] However, documents issued in accordance with these provisions may not be produced more than three months after their date of issue.[77] Where the host Member State requires proof of financial standing, that State must regard certificates issued by banks in the country of origin or in the country from which the foreign national comes, as equivalent to certificates issued in its own territory.[78]

6.031. Membership of professional or trade association. Member States must ensure that beneficiaries have the right to join professional or trade organisations under the same conditions and with the same rights and obligations as their own nationals.[79] The right to join such professional or trade organisations must entail eligibility for election or appointment to high office in those organisations.[80] However, such posts may be reserved for nationals where, in pursuance of any provision laid down by law or regulation, the organisations concerned is connected with the exercise of official authority.[81]

IV. FREEDOM OF ESTABLISHMENT AND FREEDOM TO PROVIDE SERVICES IN FILM PRODUCTION

1. Introduction

6.032. Commencement. Council Directive 70/451/EEC[82] was executed on 29

---

[74] Article 6.
[75] Article 4(1) para.1.
[76] *Ibid.* para.2.
[77] Article 4(2).
[78] Article 4(4). In accordance with Article 4(3), Member States were required to designate authorities and bodies competent to issue documents covered by Article 4 within six months of notification of the Directive.
[79] Article 5(1).
[80] Article 5(2).
[81] *Ibid.* In accordance with Article 5(3), in the Grand Duchy of Luxembourg, membership of the Chambre de commerce or of the Chambre des métiers, shall not give beneficiaries the right to take part in the election of the administrative organs of those Chambers.
[82] OJ Sp Edn 1970 (II) p.620.

September 1970 and Member States were required to adopt measures in compliance within six months of its notification.[83]

6.033. Scope of Directive. The Directive is concerned with the freedom of establishment and freedom to provide services of self-employed persons involved in film production.[84] However, it does not apply to the activities of the persons who are directly involved with the producer in the making of a film.[85]

6.034. Beneficiaries. The Directive confers rights on 'beneficiaries',[86] that is, natural persons, companies and firms covered by Title I of the General Programmes for both the abolition of restrictions on freedom of establishment[87] and freedom to provide services.[88]

2. Restrictions to be Abolished

6.035. Member States were required to abolish the Title III restrictions affecting freedom of establishment of self-employed persons involved in film production.[89] In particular this included restrictions which:

- prevented beneficiaries from establishing themselves or providing services in the host country under the same conditions and the same rights as nationals of that country;[90]
- by reason of administrative practices resulted in treatment being applied to beneficiaries that was discriminatory in comparison with that applied to nationals;[91]
- arose out of specific measures in particular Member States which prevented or limited establishment or provision of services by beneficiaries.[92]

---

[83] Article 7. In accordance with Article 6(3), this included the designation of authorities and bodies competent to issue the document specified in Article 6.

[84] As referred to in Annex IV to the General Programme for the abolition of restrictions on freedom of establishment: ex Group 841, ex Major Group 84. Article 2. para.1, OJ 2, 15.1.62, p.36, OJ Sp. Edn (Second Series), IX, p.7.

[85] Article 2. para.2.

[86] Article 1.

[87] OJ 2, 15.1.62, p.36, OJ Sp. Edn (Second Series), IX, p.7. For the definition of Title I beneficiaries, see §2.003. above.

[88] OJ 2, 15.1.62, p.32, OJ Sp. Edn (Second Series), IX, p.3. For the definition of Title I beneficiaries, see §2.011 above.

[89] Article 1.

[90] Article 3(1)(a).

[91] Article 3(1)(b).

[92] Article 3(2). The Directive required the abolition of: in Belgium, the obligation to hold a carte professionelle, the requirement that film producers be of Belgian nationality or that there be reciprocal arrangements and the requirement also that producers of newsreel films be of Belgian nationality; in France, the obligation to hold a carte d'identité d'étranger commerçant, the requirement that a person wishing to receive financial aid towards production should be of French nationality and the exclusion from the right to renew commercial leases; in Italy, the requirement that producers be of Italian nationality; in Luxembourg, the limited period of validity of authorisations granted to foreign nationals.

3. Distortion of Conditions of Establishment

6.036. No Member State may grant to any of its nationals who go to another Member State for the purposes of pursuing any film distribution activity, any aid which is liable to distort the conditions of establishment.[93]

4. Special Requirements

6.037. Membership of professional or trade organisations. Member States must ensure that beneficiaries have the right to join professional or trade organisations under the same conditions and with the same rights and obligations as their own nationals.[94] The right to join such professional or trade organisations must entail eligibility for election or appointment to high office in those organisations.[95] However, such posts may be reserved for nationals where, in pursuance of any provision laid down by law or regulation, the organisation concerned is connected with the exercise of official authority.[96]

6.038. Proof of good repute, solvency and public standing. Where the host Member State requires of its own nationals wishing to take up any film distribution activity, proof of good repute and/or proof that they have not previously been declared bankrupt, that State must accept as sufficient evidence for nationals of other Member States, the production of an extract from the 'judicial record' or, failing this, of an equivalent document issued by a competent judicial or administrative authority in the country of origin or the country from which the foreign national comes showing that these requirements have been met.[97] Where the country of origin or the country from which the foreign national comes does not issue such documentary proof of no previous bankruptcy, it may be replaced by a declaration on oath made by the person concerned (before a judicial or administrative authority, a notary, or a competent professional or trade body), in the country of origin or in the country from which that person comes.[98] However, documents issued in accordance with these provisions may not be produced more than three months after their date of issue.[99] Where the host Member State requires proof of financial standing, that State must regard certificates issued by banks in the country of origin or in the country from which the foreign national comes, as equivalent to certificates issued in its own territory.[100]

---

[93] Article 4.
[94] Article 5(1).
[95] Article 5(2).
[96] *Ibid.* In accordance with Article 5(3), in the Grand Duchy of Luxembourg, membership of the Chambre de commerce or of the Chambre des métiers shall not give beneficiaries the right to take part in the election of the administrative organs of those Chambers.
[97] Article 6(1) para.1.
[98] *Ibid.* para.2.
[99] Article 6(2).
[100] Article 6(4). In accordance with Article 6(3), Member States were required to designate authorities and bodies competent to issue documents covered by Article 6 within six months of notification of the Directive.

V. REGULATION OF MISLEADING ADVERTISING

1. Introduction

6.039. Commencement. Council Directive 84/450/EEC[101] was adopted on 10 September 1984[102] and Member States had to bring into force measures in compliance by 1 October 1986.[103]

6.040. Scope of Directive. The purpose of the Directive is to protect consumers, persons carrying on a trade or business or practising a craft or profession and the interests of the public in general, against misleading advertising and the unfair consequences which it produces.[104] Misleading advertising may cause consumers to take decisions prejudicial to them, when acquiring goods or other property, or using services.[105] The differences between the laws of the Member States has not only led, in many cases, to inadequate levels of consumer protection, but has also hindered the execution of advertising campaigns beyond national boundaries and thus affected the free circulation of goods and services.[106] The Directive was aimed at ameliorating these disparities.

6.041. Beneficiaries. The Directive gives rights to persons or organisations regarded under national law, as having a legitimate aim in prohibiting misleading advertising.[107]

6.042. Definition of 'advertising'. Advertising means 'the making of a representation in any form in connection with a trade, business, craft or profession in order to promote the supply of goods or services, including immoveable property, rights and obligations.'[108]

6.043. Definition of 'misleading advertising'. Misleading advertising means 'any advertising which in any way, including its presentation, deceives or is likely to deceive the persons to whom it is addressed or whom it reaches and which, by reason of its deceptive nature, is likely to affect their economic behaviour or which, for those reasons, injures or is likely to injure a competitor.'[109]

6.044. Definition of a 'person'. A person means any natural or legal person.[110]

2. Remedies

6.045. Legal Provisions. Member States must ensure that, in the interests of consumers as well as competitors and the general public, adequate and effective means exist for the control of misleading advertising.[111] Such means must include

---

[101] OJ No L 250, 19.09.84, p.17.
[102] Article 9.
[103] Article 8. para.1.
[104] Article 1.
[105] Recital 4.
[106] *Ibid.*
[107] Article 4(1) para.2.
[108] Article 2(1).
[109] Article 2(2).
[110] Article 2(3).
[111] Article 4(1) para.1.

legal provisions under which persons or organizations regarded under national law as having a legitimate interest in prohibiting misleading advertising, may take legal action against such advertising,[112] and/or bring such advertising before an administrative authority competent either to decide on complaints or to initiate appropriate legal proceedings.[113] However, it is for each Member State to decide which of these facilities are to be available and whether to enable the courts or administrative authorities to require prior recourse to other established means of dealing with complaints, including self-regulatory bodies.[114] The Directive acknowledges that in certain cases it may be desirable to prohibit misleading advertising even before it has been published.[115] However, Member States are not under an obligation to introduce rules requiring the systematic prior vetting of advertising.[116]

6.046. Powers of the courts or administrative authorities. In setting in place the legal provisions mentioned above, Member States must confer upon the courts or administrative authorities certain powers which can be exercised where they deem such measures to be necessary taking into account all the interests involved and in particular, the public interest.[117] Thus Member States must enable the courts or administrative authorities to: order the cessation of, or to institute appropriate legal proceedings for an order for the cessation of misleading advertising;[118] or, if misleading advertising has not yet been published but publication is imminent, powers to order the prohibition of, or to institute appropriate legal proceedings for an order for the prohibition of such publication.[119] These rights must be available even without proof of actual loss or damage or of intention or negligence on the part of the advertiser.[120]

6.047. Accelerated procedure. Member States must make provision for legal measures to be taken under an accelerated procedure. They have a choice between adopting measures which provide for relief with interim effect or those which provide for relief with definitive effect.[121]

6.048. Eliminating continuing effects of misleading advertising. Member States may confer upon courts or administrative authorities, powers enabling them to eliminate the continuing effects of misleading advertising the cessation of which has been ordered by a final decision.[122] Such powers can require publication of that decision in full or in part and in such form as they deem adequate and require also the publication of a corrective statement.[123]

6.049. Rules concerning administrative authorities. The administrative authorities empowered under the Directive must be composed so as not to cast

---

[112] Article 4(1)(a).
[113] Article 4(1)(b).
[114] Article 4(1) para.2 and Article 5.
[115] Recital 12.
[116] *Ibid.*
[117] Article 4(2) para.1.
[118] *Ibid.*
[119] *Ibid.*
[120] *Ibid.*
[121] *Ibid.* para.2.
[122] *Ibid.* para.3.
[123] *Ibid.*

doubt on their impartiality.[124] They must have adequate powers, where they decide on complaints, to monitor and enforce the observance of their decisions effectively[125] and they must normally give reasons for their decisions.[126] Where powers are exercised exclusively by an administrative authority, reasons for its decisions must always be given.[127] Furthermore, Member States must enact procedures whereby improper or unreasonable exercise of its powers by the administrative authority or improper or unreasonable failure to exercise those powers can be the subject of judicial review.[128]

6.050. Self-regulatory bodies. The Directive does not exclude the voluntary control of misleading advertising by self-regulatory bodies and the recourse to such bodies by persons or organisations regarded under national law as having a legitimate interest in prohibiting misleading advertising.[129] However, proceedings before such bodies must only be in addition to the court or administrative proceedings referred to in the Directive.[130]

6.051. Evidence. Member States must confer upon the courts or administrative authorities, powers, enabling them in civil or administrative proceedings, to require the advertiser to furnish evidence of the accuracy of factual claims in advertising if, taking into account the legitimate interests of the advertiser and any other party to the proceedings, such a requirement appears appropriate on the basis of the particular case.[131] Courts and administrative authorities may consider factual claims as inaccurate if the evidence demanded is not furnished or is deemed insufficient by them.[132]

3. Factors used to Assess whether Advertising is Misleading

In determining whether advertising is misleading, account must be taken of all its features, and in particular information on the following:[133]

6.052. Characteristics of the goods or services. Account must be taken of information concerning the characteristics of the goods or services, such as their availability, nature, execution, composition, method and date of manufacture or provision, fitness for purpose, uses, quantity, specification, geographical or commercial origin or the results to be expected from their use, or the results and material features of tests or checks carried out on them.[134]

6.053. Price. Account must be taken of information concerning the price of the goods or services or the manner in which the price is calculated, and the conditions on which the goods are supplied or the services provided.[135]

---

[124] Article 4(3)(a).
[125] Article 4(3)(b).
[126] Article 4(3)(c).
[127] Article 4(3) para.2.
[128] *Ibid.* para.2.
[129] Article 5.
[130] *Ibid.*
[131] Article 6(a).
[132] Article 6(b).
[133] Article 3.
[134] Article 3(a).
[135] Article 3(b).

6.054. Advertiser. Account must be taken of information concerning the nature, attributes and rights of the advertiser, such as his identity and assets, his qualifications and ownership of industrial, commercial or intellectual property rights or his awards and distinctions.[136]

4. More Extensive Domestic Law

6.055. The Directive does not preclude Member States from retaining or adopting provisions with a view to ensuring more extensive protection for consumers, persons carrying on a trade, business, craft or profession, and the general public.[137]

VI. TELEVISION WITHOUT FRONTIERS

1. Introduction

6.056. Commencement. Council Directive 89/552/EEC[138] was adopted on 3 October 1989,[139] and Member States were obliged to bring into force laws in compliance with its terms not later than 3 October 1991.[140]

6.057. Scope of the Directive. The Directive concerns solely broadcasting services. Excluded from the Directive are, therefor, telecommunication services providing items of information or other messages on individual demand ie telephone, telecopying, electronic data banks and other similar services.[141] These services fall within the umbrella of the telecommunication Directives.[142] The Directive also does not affect the responsibility of Member States in their organisation of broadcasters under their jurisdiction.[143] So it leaves untouched systems which govern the licensing, administrative control or taxation of television.[144] Neither does it interfere with the financing and content of programmes since the preservation of the cultural independence of Member States is of fundamental importance.[145] Nevertheless, it is without prejudice to existing or

---

[136] Article 3(c).
[137] Article 7.
[138] OJ No L 298, 17.10.89, p.23.
[139] Article 27.
[140] Article 25(1). In accordance with Article 3(2), Member States must ensure by appropriate means, that television broadcasters under their jurisdiction comply with the provisions of the Directive.
[141] Article 1(a).
[142] See e.g. Council Directive 90/387/EEC of 28 June, 1990 on the establishment of the internal market for telecommunications services through the implementation of open network provisions OJ No L 192, 24.07.90, p.1.
[143] Recital 13. Recital 16 states that Member States must ensure the prevention of any acts 'which may promote the creation of dominant positions which would lead to restrictions on pluralism and freedom of televised information and of the information sector as a whole.'
[144] Recital 13.
[145] *Ibid.*

future Community law in particular those satisfying mandatory requirements which may protect consumers, and the fairness of commercial transactions, or regulate competition in the industry.[146]

2. Freedom of Reception and Retransmission

(1) General Principles

6.058. The Directive is designed to bring about a Community wide audio-visual arena. It achieves this by stipulating that a television broadcast made in a Member State which complies with the minimum standards determined by the Directive, must be freely received and retransmitted in every other Community State.[147] This right embodies the principle of freedom of expression contained in Article 10(1) of the European Convention for the Protection of Human Rights and Fundamental Freedoms.[148] Thus 'the issuing of directives on the broadcasting and distribution of television programmes must ensure their free movement in the light of the said Article and subject only to the limits set by paragraph 2 of that Article and by Article 56(1) of the Treaty.'[149]

(2) Specific Rules

6.059. Member States must ensure the freedom of reception and retransmission in their territories of television broadcasts transmitted from other Member States which conform with the rules stipulated by the Directive.[150] This means that, one Member State which acts purely as a host to signals which are relaying programmes between two other Member States, is responsible for securing the free flow of those transmissions through its territory.[151] But the Directive excludes protection for broadcasts intended exclusively for reception in third countries and which are not received directly or indirectly in one or more Member States.[152] So for example, a broadcaster in France who transmits a signal to the United States of America may not invoke the Directive to prevent the French authorities from impeding his broadcast. But the situation is less clear if the same broadcaster, in the process of 'exporting' his signal, uses in addition to a French frequency, a telecommunication frequency in another Member State. Although in such a case the signal is received indirectly in another Member State[153] it might not be protected on the grounds that the Directive's function is to create an internal market within the Community and not outside of it.

---

[146] Recital 17.
[147] Article 2(2). See §6.059 below.
[148] Recital 8.
[149] *Ibid.* On the European Convention for the Protection of Human Rights and Fundamental Freedoms, see §5.015 et seq. On Article 56(1) of the Treaty, see §2.041 et seq. above.
[150] Article 2(2).
[151] Article 1(a).
[152] Article 2(3).
[153] *Ibid.*

(3) Grounds for Censorship

6.060. The requirement that the originating Member State has verified that broadcasts comply with its law,[154] is generally sufficient to ensure the free movement of broadcasts, without there being the necessity of any secondary control in the receiving Member State.[155] Therefore secondary control is probably generally unlawful. However, the receiving Member State may exceptionally and under specific conditions (namely, where there is a danger to minors) provisionally suspend the retransmission of broadcasts.[156]

3. Obligations of Transmitting Member States

6.061. A Member State must ensure that any television broadcast transmitted by broadcasters under its jurisdiction or by broadcasters who, whilst not being under its jurisdiction, make use of a frequency or satellite capacity granted by, or a satellite up-link situated in that Member State, comply with the law applicable to broadcasts intended for the public there. In other words they must conform with the Directive.[157] Television broadcasting is defined as 'the initial transmission by cable, over the air or by satellite in unencoded or encoded form of television programmes intended for reception by the public.'[158] But, it also includes the communication of programmes between undertakings for onward transmission to the public.[159] So one Member State which acts as a host to signals transmitted between two Fixed Service Satellites carrying programmes between two other Member States, must also ensure that those programmes comply with the Directive.[160] This may seem an onerous duty.

4. Advertising and Sponsorship

(1) Advertising General Principles

6.062. Introduction. The Directive regulates six aspects of advertising, namely its: definition, form, timing, duration and daily volume and content. Member States are given a discretion to impose stricter or more detailed rules in certain circumstances.

---

[154] As harmonized by the Directive.
[155] Recitals 12 and 15.
[156] Articles 2(2) and 22 and Recital 15. See §6.088 below.
[157] Article 2(1). Article 3(2) states that 'Member States shall, by appropriate means, ensure, within the framework of their legislation, that television broadcasters under their jurisdiction comply with the provisions of this Directive'.
[158] Article 1(a). 'Encoded form' refers to broadcast signals which can be viewed only after they are unscrambled by equipment supplied by the broadcaster to the subscriber (ie as in most forms of satellite T.V.).
[159] *Ibid.*
[160] This is despite the fact that Recital 15 states that in order to ensure their free movement of broadcasts throughout the Community, it is sufficient that the Member States in which the broadcast originated ensures compliance with Community Law.

6.063. Definition of 'advertising'. Television advertising is defined as 'any form of announcement broadcast [made] in return for payment or for similar consideration by a public or private undertaking in connection with a trade, business, craft or profession in order to promote the supply of goods or services, including immoveable property, or rights and obligations, in return for payment.'[161]

6.064. Form. Generally, television advertising must be clearly recognisable as such and kept separate from other parts of the programme service[162] and this may be achieved by either optical and/or acoustic means.[163]

6.065. Advertising spots. The Directive permits isolated advertising spots but states that they shall remain the exception.[164] Spot advertising is defined as 'direct offers to the public for the sale, purchase or rental of products or for the provision of services in return for payment.'[165]

6.066. Subliminal techniques. Advertising may not use subliminal techniques.[166]

6.067. Surreptitious advertising. Surreptitious advertising is prohibited.[167] Surreptitious advertising means 'the representation in words or pictures of goods, services, the name, the trademark or the activities of a producer of goods or provider of services in programmes, when such representation is intended by the broadcaster to serve advertising and might mislead the public as to its nature. Such representation is considered to be intentional in particular if it is done in return for payment or for similar consideration.'[168]

(2) Timing of Advertising

(i) General Principles

6.068. Generally advertisements must be inserted between programmes.[169] However, advertisements may be inserted during programmes if they do not prejudice either the integrity and value of the programme (taking into account natural breaks in and the duration and nature of the programme) or the rights of the rightholders.[170] The Directive establishes the following regime to satisfy this requirement.

(ii) Specific Rules

6.069. Programmes with autonomous parts (eg sports programmes, musical concerts). In programmes consisting of autonomous parts, or in sports programmes and similarly structured events and performances comprising intervals, advertise-

---

[161] Article 1(b).
[162] Article 10(1).
[163] Ibid.
[164] Article 10(2).
[165] Article 1(b).
[166] Article 10(3).
[167] Article 10(4).
[168] Article 1(c).
[169] Article 11(1).
[170] Ibid.

ments may only be inserted between the parts or in the intervals.[171] These would include, for example, broadcasts of lectures, plays and musical concerts.

6.070. Audio-visual programmes (feature films and films made for television). Transmissions of audiovisual works such as feature films and films made for television (but excluding series, serials, light entertainment programmes and documentaries) may be interrupted once for each complete period of 45 minutes provided that their programmed duration is more than 45 minutes.[172] A further interruption is allowed if their programmed duration is at least 20 minutes longer than two or more complete periods of 45 minutes.[173]

6.071. Light entertainment. Light entertainment programmes such as series or serials have, out of all types of programme, the most scope for insertion of advertisements. The Directive simply requires a period of at least 20 minutes to elapse between each successive advertising break within such a programme.[174]

6.072. Religious services. Advertisements may not be inserted in any broadcast of a religious service.[175]

6.073. News, documentaries, religious and children's programmes. Advertisements may be inserted in news and current affairs programmes, documentaries, religious programmes and children's programmes where their programmed duration is less than 30 minutes.[176] If their programmed duration is 30 minutes or longer, advertisements are permitted provided that a period of at least 20 minutes elapses between each successive advertising break.[177]

6.074. Discretion to lay down other conditions. Member States may with due regard to Community law lay down other rules regarding the timing of advertisements, in respect of broadcasting intended solely for the national territory which may or may not be received, directly or indirectly, in one or more other Member States.[178]

(3) Content of Advertising

(i) General Principles

6.075. Generally, television advertising must not prejudice respect for human dignity;[179] include any discrimination on grounds of race, sex or nationality;[180] be offensive to religious or political beliefs;[181] encourage behaviour prejudicial to health or to safety;[182] or encourage behaviour prejudicial to the protection of the environment.[183]

---

[171] Article 11(2).
[172] Article 11(3).
[173] Ibid.
[174] Article 11(4).
[175] Article 11(5).
[176] Ibid.
[177] Ibid.
[178] Article 20.
[179] Article 12(a).
[180] Article 12(b).
[181] Article 12(c).
[182] Article 12(d).
[183] Article 12(e).

(ii) Specific Rules

6.076. Tobacco. All forms of advertising for cigarettes and other tobacco products are absolutely prohibited.[184] This coverall provision catches indirect forms of advertising, that is, advertising which whilst not directly mentioning the tobacco product, seeks to circumvent the ban by using brand names, symbols or other distinctive features either of tobacco products or of undertakings whose known or main activities include the production or sale of such products.[185]

6.077. Medicine. Advertising for medicinal products and medical treatment available only on prescription in the Member State within whose jurisdiction the broadcaster falls is prohibited.[186]

6.078. Alcohol. The rules here follow the principle that unlike tobacco with its clear link with cancer, it is the abuse of alcohol that causes problems, not its controlled and sensible use. Television advertising for alcoholic beverages must fulfil the following six conditions. It must not: be aimed specifically at minors or, in particular, depict minors consuming alcoholic beverages;[187] link the consumption of alcohol to enhanced physical performance or to driving;[188] create the impression that the consumption of alcohol contributes towards social or sexual success;[189] claim that alcohol has therapeutic qualities or that it is a stimulant, a sedative or a means of resolving personal conflicts;[190] encourage immoderate consumption of alcohol or present abstinence or moderation in a negative light;[191] place emphasis on high alcoholic content as being a positive quality of the beverages.[192]

6.079. Minors. The Directive dictates the general principle that advertising must not cause moral or physical detriment to minors.[193] Accordingly advertising must not: directly exhort minors to buy a product or a service by exploiting their inexperience or credulity;[194] directly encourage minors to persuade their parents or others to purchase the goods or services being advertised;[195] exploit the special trust minors place in parents, teachers or other persons;[196] unreasonably show minors in dangerous situations.[197] A public safety advertisement showing a child in a dangerous situation should escape the ban.

(4) Sponsorship

6.080. Definition. Sponsorship is defined as 'any contribution made by a public or private undertaking not engaged in television broadcasting activities or in the

---

[184] Article 13.
[185] Recital 29.
[186] Article 14.
[187] Article 15(a).
[188] Article 15(b).
[189] Article 15(c).
[190] Article 15(d).
[191] Article 15(e).
[192] Article 15(f).
[193] Article 16.
[194] Article 16(a).
[195] Article 16(b).
[196] Article 16(c).
[197] Article 16(d).

production of audiovisual works, to the financing of television programmes with a view to promoting its name, its trademark, its image, its activities or its products.'[198]

6.081. Stipulations and restrictions. The Directive permits sponsorship of all programmes other than news and current affairs programmes.[199] Sponsored television programmes must meet the following requirements: the sponsor may not in any circumstances influence the content and scheduling of a programme in such a way as to affect the responsibilities and editorial independence of the broadcaster in respect of the programmes;[200] the sponsor must be clearly identified as such by his name and/or logo appearing at the beginning and/or the end of the programmes;[201] the sponsored programme must not encourage the purchase or rental of the sponsor's products or services or those of a third party, by, in particular, making special promotional references to those products or services.[202] Television programmes may not be sponsored by natural or legal persons whose principal activity is the manufacture or sale of products, or the provision of services, the advertising of which is prohibited by the Directive ie the manufacturers of tobacco products,[203] and those medicinal products available only on prescription.[204]

(5) Daily Volume of Advertising

(i) General Principles

6.082. Generally, the amount of advertising cannot exceed 15% of the daily transmission time.[205] However, this proportion can be increased to 20% if it includes spot advertising ie direct offers to the public for the sale, purchase or rental of products or for the provision of services, provided that the amount of spot advertising does not exceed 15% of daily transmission time.[206] The amount of spot advertising must not exceed 10 minutes in any one-hour period[207] and one hour of each day.[208]

(ii) Discretion of Member States to Impose Stricter Rules

6.083. In the public interest. Member States are given a discretion to lay down stricter or more detailed rules concerning the permitted daily volume of advertising and the procedures for television broadcasting for television broadcasters under their jurisdiction so as to reconcile demand for televised advertising with the public interest, taking account in particular: the role of television in providing information, education, culture and entertainment[209] and the protection of pluralism of information and of the media.[210]

---

[198] Article 1(d).
[199] Article 17(3).
[200] Article 17(1)(a).
[201] Article 17(1)(b).
[202] Article 17(1)(c).
[203] Article 17(2). See Article 13.
[204] *Ibid.* See Article 14.
[205] Article 18(1).
[206] *Ibid.*
[207] Article 18(2).
[208] Article 18(3). This is without prejudice to Article 18(1).
[209] Article 19(a). The Directive recognises the value of public service broadcasting. It is perfectly in order for a Member State to prohibit advertising on certain channels such as occurs with the BBC in the United Kingdom.
[210] Article 19(b).

6.084. Internal advertising. Member States may, with due regard for Community law, lay down other rules in respect of broadcasts intended solely for the national territory which may not be received, directly of indirectly, in one or more other Member States.[211]

(6) Availability of Remedies under National Law

6.085. Member States must, within the framework of their laws, ensure that in the case of television broadcasts that do not comply with the provisions concerning advertising and sponsorship, appropriate measures are applied to secure compliance with these provisions.[212]

5. Protection of Minors

The protection of minors is a particular focus of the Directive and it prescribes a number of rules designed to protect their interests.

6.086. Programmes which might seriously impair the physical, mental or moral development of minors. Member States are bound to take appropriate measures to ensure that television broadcasts made by broadcasters under their jurisdiction do not include programmes which might seriously impair the physical, mental or moral development of minors, being in particular those that involve pornography or gratuitous violence.[213] This provision extends to other programmes which are likely to impair the physical, mental or moral development of minors, if the broadcaster ensures that minors in the area of transmission will not normally hear or see them.[214] The broadcaster can achieve this either by selecting the time of the broadcast or by employing a technical measure[215] ie by encoding the service and providing the consumer with a decoder.

6.087. Incitement to hatred on grounds of race, sex, religion or nationality. There is an absolute ban on the transmission of a broadcast which might incite children to hatred on grounds of race, sex, religion or nationality.[216]

6.088. Suspension of freedom of retransmission. Member States may provisionally suspend freedom of retransmission if:[217]

---

[211] Article 20.

[212] Article 21.

[213] Article 22.

[214] *Ibid.* There are, it is suggested, two interpretations of this clause. According to the first interpretation, there is an absolute ban on pornography or gratuitous violence. But other types of programme which might seriously impair the physical, mental or moral development of minors, are allowed, if minors would not normally hear or see such broadcasts. According to the second interpretation, programmes containing pornography or gratuitous violence are allowed (ie must be freely received and retransmitted in Member States other than the transmitting Member State) provided that minors would not normally hear or see such broadcasts. It is submitted that the first interpretation is correct. In any case, the reception and retransmission of such programmes might be suspended on grounds of public policy. See §2.041 et seq. above.

[215] Article 22.

[216] *Ibid.* Precisely why this is limited to children is unclear. In principle, a broadcaster will escape the jaws of this provision by broadcasting such material at a time when children are unlikely to form an audience or by technical means which will exclude them.

[217] *Ibid.* and Recital 8.

- a broadcast coming from another Member State manifestly, seriously and gravely infringes the above rules relating to minors;[218] and
- the broadcaster has in the previous 12 months infringed the above provision on at least two occasions;[219] and
- the Member State has notified the broadcaster and the Commission in writing of the alleged infringements and of its intention to restrict retransmission in the event of a further violation;[220] and
- consultations with the transmitting broadcaster and the Commission have not produced a settlement within 15 days of the notification and the alleged infringement persists.[221]

The Commission is to ensure that the suspension is compatible with Community law and it may ask the Member State to put an end to a suspension which is contrary to Community law as a matter of urgency.[222] The Commission's powers are without prejudice to the application of any procedure, remedy or sanction obtainable in the Member State which has jurisdiction over the offending broadcaster.[223]

6. Right of Reply

6.089. Duties of Member States. Redress is provided for parties whose interests have been prejudiced by a broadcast. Thus, without prejudice to other provisions adopted by the Member States under civil, administrative or criminal law, any person (either natural or legal ie the latter including companies) whose legitimate interests, being in particular their reputation and good name, have been damaged by an assertion of incorrect facts in a television programme, must have a right of reply or equivalent remedy.[224] This right must exist in relation to all broadcasters under the jurisdiction of a Member State.[225]

Member States must adopt measures needed to establish the right of reply or the equivalent remedies and must determine the procedure to be followed therewith.[226] In particular, they must, ensure that a sufficient time span is allowed between the offending broadcast and the implementation of the remedy,[227] and that the right or equivalent remedies can be exercised appropriately by persons (either natural or legal) resident or established in other Member States.[228]

6.090. Rejection of right. Member States may provide rules for the rejection of these rights. Thus an application for the exercise of the right of reply or the equivalent remedy may be rejected if: it is not justified to protect the complainant's

---

[218] Article 2(2)(a).
[219] Article 2(2)(b).
[220] Article 2(2)(c).
[221] *Ibid.*
[222] Article 2(2) para.2.
[223] *Ibid.*
[224] Article 23(1). See also Recital 33 which states that 'television broadcasters are normally bound to ensure that programmes present facts and events fairly . . .'
[225] Article 23(2).
[226] Article 23(3).
[227] *Ibid.*
[228] *Ibid.*

legitimate interests, ie their reputation and good name;[229] or would involve the broadcaster committing a punishable act;[230] or would render the broadcaster liable to civil law proceedings or would regress standards of public decency.[231] Member States are to adopt provisions whereby disputes as to the exercise of the right of reply or the equivalent remedies can be subject to judicial review.[232]

7. The Production, Promotion and Distribution of Television Programmes

6.091. Introduction. There has been much concern that Europe's vast television market will be invaded by non-European material in the absence of sufficient European industry.[233] As a result, a substantial proportion of the Directive is geared towards generating a 'European' television production industry and stimulating new sources of television production.[234] The Directive prescribes two rules which are designed to set this in motion. The first rule is that Member States must reserve a majority of their transmission time for 'European works'.[235] The second rule is that broadcasters must reserve at least 10% of their transmission time for European works which are independent productions.[236] These rules are not, however, absolute since in both cases Member States are themselves to gauge the precise proportions having regard to their broadcaster's informational, educational, cultural and entertainment responsibilities to their viewing public.[237] The Directive permits the application of national support schemes for the development of European production in so far as they comply with Community law.[238]

6.092. Reservation for European Works. The general rule is that Member States are to ensure where practicable and by appropriate means, that broadcasters reserve a majority proportion of their transmission time, excluding the time appointed to news, sports events, games, advertising and teletext services, for European works.[239] This proportion is to be achieved progressively on the basis of suitable criteria, having regard to the broadcaster's informational, educational, cultural and entertainment responsibilities to its viewing public.[240]

The Directive by its express terms acknowledges that it may not be possible to achieve its stated objective. It therefor provides a standstill rule. Accordingly, where the 'majority' proportion cannot be attained it must not be lower than the average which existed in Member States in 1988,[241] save for the Hellenic and Portuguese Republics in which case the year is to be 1990.[242]

---

[229] Article 23(4).
[230] *Ibid.*
[231] *Ibid.*
[232] Article 23(5).
[233] See e.g. Commission Interim Report: 'Realities and Tendencies in European Television; Perspectives and Options', COM (83) 229 final.
[234] Recital 24.
[235] Article 4(1).
[236] Article 5.
[237] Article 4(1) and Article 5.
[238] Recital 23.
[239] Article 4(1).
[240] *Ibid.*
[241] Article 4(2) para.1.
[242] *Ibid.* para.2.

6.093. Reservation for European Works of independent producers. Member States are to ensure, where practicable and by appropriate means, that broadcasters reserve at least 10% of their transmission time, excluding the time appointed to news, sports events, games, advertising and teletext services, or alternatively at the discretion of the Member State, at least 10% of their programming budget, for European works created by producers who are independent of broadcasters.[243] This proportion is to be achieved progressively on the basis of suitable criteria, having regard to broadcaster's informational, educational, cultural and entertainment responsibilities to its viewing public.[244] It is to be accomplished by earmarking an adequate proportion for recent works, that is to say works transmitted within five years of their production.[245]

The aim of the Directive is to stimulate new sources of television production, especially the creation of small and medium-sized enterprises with the objective of offering new opportunities and outlets to creative talents and new possibilities of employment for the 'cultural profession'.[246] Therefore, whilst the definition of an 'independent' producer is a matter for Member States, that concept should take account of the aforementioned objectives by giving due consideration to small and medium-sized producers and making it possible to authorize financial participation by the co-production subsidiaries of television organisations.[247]

6.094. Definition of European works. The Directive provides a complex formula for determining qualification as a European work. Essentially, European works are those works which originate from either:

(1) Member States of the Community[248] or European third States which are parties to the European Convention on Transfrontier Television,[249] or from

(2) other European third countries and which fulfil certain conditions.[250]

Further, to prove 'origination' in any of the relevant European States, three criteria must be satisfied, namely:

(1) European authorship; and
(2) European worker participation; and
(3) European finance or other involvement in production.

6.095. European works of Member States of the European Community and States which are parties to the European Convention on Transfrontier Television. A work is a European work of those States if it is:

(1) mainly made with authors and workers residing in one or more of those States[251] and
(2) it is either:

---

[243] Article 5.
[244] Ibid.
[245] Ibid.
[246] Recital 24.
[247] Ibid.
[248] Article 6(1)(a).
[249] Article 6(1)(b). For parties to the Convention, see Table H of Appendix III.
[250] Article 6(1)(c).
[251] Article 6(1)(a), Article 6(1)(b) and Article 6(2).

(a) made by one or more producers established in one or more of those States;[252] or

(b) production of the work is supervised and actually controlled by one or more producers established in one or more of those States;[253] or

(c) the contribution of co-producers of those States to the total co-production costs is preponderant and the co-production is not controlled by one or more producers established outside of those States.[254]

6.096. European Works of European third countries. A work is a European work of third countries if it is:

(1) mainly made with authors and workers residing in one or more European States[255] and

(2) it is either:
   (a) made exclusively or in co-production with producers established in one or more Member States of the European Community;[256] or
   (b) made exclusively or in co-production with producers established in one or more European third countries with which the European Community will conclude agreements in accordance with procedures set out in the Treaty.[257]

6.097. Hybrid European works. Works which do not satisfy these criteria may still be eligible for partial European status. Accordingly works which are made mainly with authors and workers residing in one or more Member States shall be considered to be European works to an extent corresponding to the proportion of the contribution of Community co-producers to the total production costs.[258]

6.098. Timetable. Fulfilment of the above requirements will of course be a slow process and the Commission considers that progress should be monitored. So the Directive provides that from 3 October 1991, Member States are to provide the Commission with a progress report every two years.[259] The Council is to review the implementation of the Directive and proposals for its amendment by the Commission no later than the end of the fifth year from the adoption of the Directive.[260]

6.099. Obligation to observe 'windows'. Member States must ensure that the television broadcasters under their jurisdiction do not broadcast any cinematographic work, unless otherwise agreed between its rights holders and the broadcaster, until two years have elapsed since the work was first shown in cinemas in one of the Member States of the Community.[261] In the case of cinematographic works co-produced by the broadcaster, this period is to be one year.[262]

---

[252] Article 6(2)(a).
[253] Article 6(2)(b).
[254] Article 6(2)(c).
[255] Article 6(3).
[256] *Ibid.*
[257] *Ibid.*
[258] Article 6(4).
[259] Article 4(3). Article 4(3) provides detailed rules concerning the making of this report.
[260] Article 4(4).
[261] Article 7. On 'windows' and Community law, see §1.046 et seq. above.
[262] *Ibid.*

6.100. Discretion of Member States to lay down more detailed or stricter rules on grounds of language policy. Member States may, where they consider it necessary for purposes of language policy as regards some or all programmes of television broadcasters under their jurisdiction, lay down stricter or more detailed rules in particular on the basis of language criteria.[263] Community law must be observed[264] and these rules must not be applicable to the retransmission of broadcasts originating in other Member States.[265]

6.101. Exclusions of local television broadcasts. The requirements concerning the promotion, distribution and production of television programmes do not apply to those local television broadcasts which do not form part of a national network.[266]

8. Relationship to International Agreements Protecting Copyright and Neighbouring Rights

6.102. The Directive leaves unaffected international agreements concerning broadcasting activities which the Directive does not co-ordinate.[267] This includes all international agreements which govern the exploitation by broadcasting of material protected by copyright and neighbouring rights.

9. Freedom to Lay Down More Detailed or Stricter Rules

6.103. Member States remain free to require television broadcasters under their jurisdiction to lay down more detailed of stricter rules in the areas covered by the Directive.[268]

10. Continuing Supervision by Commission

6.104. Not later than the end of the fifth year after the date of adoption of the Directive and every two years thereafter, the Commission is to submit to the European Parliament, the Council and Economic and Social Committee, a report on the application of the Directive, and if necessary, make further proposals to adapt it to developments in the field of television broadcasting.[269]

VII. PROTECTION OF COMPUTER PROGRAMS

1. Introduction

6.105. Commencement. Council Directive 91/250/EEC[270] was adopted on 14 May 1991 and Member States were required to bring into force the laws, regulations

---

[263] Article 8. See Article 3(1) and Recital 21.
[264] Article 8.
[265] Recital 26.
[266] Article 9.
[267] Article 24.
[268] Article 3(1).
[269] Article 26.
[270] OJ No L 122, 17.05.91, p.42.

and administrative provisions necessary to comply with its terms no later than 1 January 1993.[271]

6.106. Scope of Directive. The Directive establishes the status of computer programs as 'literary works' under copyright law and determines who and what should be protected, the exclusive rights on which protected persons should be able to rely in order to authorise or prohibit certain acts and the duration of protection.[272] The provisions of the Directive are without prejudice to any other legal provisions such as those concerning patent rights, trademarks, unfair competition, trade secrets, protection of semi-conductor products or the law of contract.[273] And it does not affect derogations provided for under national legislation in accordance with the Berne Convention for the Protection of Literary and Artistic Works.[274]

6.107. Date of works affected. The provisions of the Directive apply to programs created before January 1 1993 without prejudice to any acts concluded and rights acquired before that date.[275]

6.108. Interaction with competition rules (Articles 85 and 86). The provisions of the Directive are without prejudice to the application of the competition rules under Articles 85 and 86 of the Treaty if a dominant supplier refuses to make information available which is necessary for 'interoperability' as defined by the Directive.[276]

6.109. Publication of 'interfaces'. The provisions of the Directive are without prejudice to specific requirements of Community law already enacted in respect of the publication of interfaces in the telecommunications sector or Council Decisions relating to standardization in the field of information technology and telecommunication.[277]

2. Object of Protection

6.110. Protection as 'literary works'. Member States must protect computer programs, by copyright, as 'literary works' within the meaning of the Berne Convention for the Protection of Literary and Artistic Works.[278] The term 'computer programs' is deemed to include their preparatory design material,[279] provided that the nature of the preparatory work is such that a computer program can result from it at a later stage.[280] Protection applies to the expression in any form of a computer program,[281] including those that are incorporated into hardware.[282] A computer program is to be protected if it is original in the sense that it is the

---

[271] Article 10.
[272] Recital 6.
[273] Article 9(1).
[274] Recital 29. See §7.085 et seq. below.
[275] Article 9(2).
[276] Recital 27.
[277] Recital 28.
[278] Article 1(1). For the concept of 'literary works', see §7.011 below.
[279] *Ibid.*
[280] Recital 7.
[281] Article 1(2). This is in accordance with the legislation and jurisprudence of the Member States as well as the international copyright conventions (Recital 15).
[282] Recital 7.

author's own intellectual creation and no other criteria may be applied to determine its eligibility for protection.[283] Thus no tests as to the qualitative or aesthetic merits of a program should be applied.[284] However, ideas and principles, which underlie any element of a computer program, including those which underlie its interfaces, are not to be accorded copyright protection.[285] Thus, to the extent that logic, algorithms and programming languages comprise ideas and principles, those ideas and principles are not protected under the Directive.[286] The 'interfaces' are those parts of the program which provide for the interconnection and interaction between elements of software and hardware.[287]

6.111. Authorship of computer programs. The author of a computer program is deemed to be the natural person or group of natural persons who has created the program or, where the legislation of a Member State permits, the legal person designated as the rightholder by that legislation.[288] Where collective works are recognised by the legislation of a Member State, the person considered by the legislation of the Member State to have created the work is deemed to be its author.[289] In respect of a computer program created by a group of 'natural' persons jointly, the exclusive rights are deemed to be jointly owned.[290] Where a computer program is created by an employee in the execution of his duties or following instructions given by his employer, the employer is to be exclusively entitled to exercise all economic rights in the program so created, unless otherwise provided by contract.[291]

6.112. Beneficiaries of protection. In accordance with the Directive, protection is to be granted to all natural or legal persons eligible under national copyright legislation as applied to literary works.[292]

3. Restricted Acts

6.113. Reproduction. Rightholders are to be given the exclusive right to do or to authorise the permanent or temporary reproduction of a computer programme by any means and in any form, in part or in whole.[293] In so far as loading, displaying, running, transmission or storage of the computer program necessitates such reproduction, such acts are to be subject to authorization by the rightholder.[294] However, in the absence of specific contractual provisions, these acts do not require the authorization by the rightholder where they are necessary for the use of the computer program by the lawful acquirer in accordance with its intended purpose, including error correction.[295] And the rightholder cannot prohibit these acts by contract.[296]

---

[283] Article 1(3).
[284] Recital 8.
[285] Article 1(2).
[286] Recital 14.
[287] Recital 11.
[288] Article 2(1).
[289] Ibid.
[290] Article 2(2).
[291] Article 2(3).
[292] Article 3.
[293] Article 4(a).
[294] Ibid.
[295] Article 5(1).
[296] Recitals 17 and 18.

6.114. Translation, adaption and arrangement. Rightholders are to be given the exclusive right to do or authorise the translation, adaptation, arrangement and other alteration of a computer program and the reproduction of the results thereof, without prejudice to the rights of the person who alters the program.[297] However, in the absence of specific contractual provisions, these acts do not require the authorization by the rightholder where they are necessary for the use of the computer program by the lawful acquirer in accordance with its intended purpose, including error correction.[298]

6.115. Distribution and rental. Rightholders are to be given the exclusive right to do or authorise any form of distribution to the public, including rental, of the original computer program or of copies thereof.[299] This is subject to the proviso that the first sale in the Community of a copy of a program by the rightholder or with his consent exhausts the distribution right within the Community of that copy, with the exception of the right to control further rental of the program or a copy thereof.[300] The term 'rental' means the making available for use, for a limited period of time and for profit-making purposes, of a computer program or a copy thereof.[301] This term does not include 'public lending', an activity which is outside of the control of the Directive.[302]

4. Exceptions to Restricted Acts

6.116. Making of back-up copies. The making of a back-up copy by a person having a right to use the computer program may not be prevented by contract in so far as it is necessary for that use.[303] Any contractual provision contrary to this is null and void.[304]

6.117. Right to study program. The person having a right to use a copy of a computer program is entitled, without the authorization of the rightholder, to observe, study or test the functioning of the program in order to determine the ideas and principles which underlie any element of the program if he does so while performing any of the acts of loading, displaying, running, transmitting or storing the program which he is entitled to do,[305] and provided that these acts do not infringe the copyright in the program.[306] Any contractual provision contrary to this is null and void.[307]

5. Decompilation

6.118. Reproduction, translation etc of a code. As a general principle, the unauthorised reproduction, translation, adaptation or transformation of the form of

---

[297] Article 4(b).
[298] Article 5(1).
[299] Article 4(c).
[300] *Ibid.*
[301] Recital 16.
[302] *Ibid.*
[303] Article 5(2).
[304] Article 9(1).
[305] Article 5(3).
[306] Recital 19.
[307] Article 9(1).

the code in which a copy of a computer program has been made available constitutes an infringement of the exclusive rights of the author.[308]

6.119. Authorization permitted without consent. The authorization of the rightholder is not to be required where reproduction of the code and translation of its form are indispensable to obtain the information necessary to achieve the interoperability of an independently created computer program with other programs, provided that this is compatible with fair practice.[309] This will be satisfied where: these acts are performed by the licensee or by another person having the right to use a copy of a program, or on their behalf by a person authorised to do so;[310] the information necessary to achieve interoperability has not previously been readily available to the aforementioned persons[311] and these acts are confined to the parts of the original program which are necessary to achieve interoperability.[312]

The above provisions do not permit the information obtained through its application either: to be used for goals other than to achieve the interoperability of the independently created program;[313] or to be given to others, except when necessary for the interoperability of the independently created computer program;[314] or to be used for the development, production or marketing of a computer program substantially similar in its expression, or for any other act which infringes copyright.[315]

In accordance with the provisions of the Berne Convention for the protection of Literary and Artistic Works, the aforementioned provisions may not be interpreted in such a way as to allow their application to be used in a manner which unreasonably prejudices the rightholder's legitimate interests or conflicts with a normal exploitation of the computer program.[316]

Any contractual provisions contrary to these provisions are null and void.[317]

6. Special Measures of Protection

6.120. Member States are to provide,[318] in accordance with their national legislation, appropriate remedies against a person committing any of the following acts:

- any act of putting into circulation a copy of a computer program knowing, or having reason to believe, that it is an infringing copy;[319]
- the possession, for commercial purposes, of a copy of a computer program knowing, or having reason to believe, that it is an infringing copy;[320]

---

[308] Recital 20.
[309] Article 6(1) and Recital 22. In accordance with Recital 12, 'Interoperability' is defined by the Directive as 'the ability to exchange information and mutually to use the information which has been exchanged.'
[310] Article 6(1)(a).
[311] Article 6(1)(b).
[312] Article 6(1)(c).
[313] Article 6(2)(a).
[314] Article 6(2)(b).
[315] Article 6(2)(c).
[316] Article 6(3). See §7.085 et seq. below (Fair Use under the Berne Convention).
[327] Article 9(1).
[318] Without prejudice to Articles 4 (restricted acts), 5 (exceptions to the restricted acts) and 6 (decompilation).
[319] Article 7(1)(a).
[320] Article 7(1)(b).

● any act of putting into circulation, or the possession for commercial purposes of, any means the sole intended purpose of which is to facilitate the unauthorised removal or circumvention of any technical device which may have been applied to protect a computer program.[321]

Any infringing copy of a computer program must be liable to seizure in accordance with the legislation of the Member State concerned.[322] And Member States may provide for the seizure of any means used to facilitate the unauthorised removal or circumvention of any technical device referred to above.[323]

7. Term of Protection

6.121. General principles. In accordance with the Directive Member States are to grant protection for the life of the author and for fifty years after his death or after the death of the last surviving author.[324] Where the computer program is an anonymous or pseudoanonymous work, or where a legal person is designated as the author by national legislation,[325] the term of protection must be fifty years from the time that the computer program is first lawfully made available to the public.[326] The term of protection is deemed to begin on the first of January of the year following the aforementioned events.[327]

6.122. Discretion to maintain pre-existing terms. Member States which already have a term of protection longer than that stipulated above are allowed to maintain their present term until such time as the term of protection for copyright works is harmonized by Community law in a more general way.[328]

VIII. RENTAL, LENDING, FIXATION, REPRODUCTION AND DISTRIBUTION RIGHTS

1. Introduction

6.123. Commencement. Council Directive 92/100/EEC[329] was adopted on 19 November 1992 and Member States were required to bring into force the laws, regulations and administrative provisions necessary to comply with its terms not later than 1 July 1994.[330]

6.124. Scope of Directive. The Directive institutes a rental and lending right for authors of copyright works and owners of neighbouring rights in works. The

---

[321] Article 7(1)(c).
[322] Article 7(2).
[323] Article 7(3).
[324] Article 8(1).
[325] In accordance with Article 2(1).
[326] Article 8(1).
[327] *Ibid.*
[328] Article 8(2).
[329] OJ No L 346, 27.11.92, p.61.
[330] Article 15(1).

Directive also confers a fixation right, a reproduction right, a broadcasting and communication to the public right and a distribution right for owners of neighbouring rights in works. The conferring of these neighbouring rights is to leave intact and in no way affect the protection of copyright in those works.[331] The Directive is expressly without prejudice to Article 4(c) of Council Directive 91/250/EEC of 14 May 1991 on the legal protection of computer programs.[332]

6.125. Date of works protected. The Directive applies to all copyright works, performances, phonograms, broadcasts and first fixations of films which are on 1 July 1994, still protected by the legislation of the Member States in the field of copyright and neighbouring rights or meet the criteria for protection under the provisions of the Directive on that date.[333] The Directive is without prejudice to any acts of exploitation performed before 1 July 1994.[334]

Subject to specific exceptions noted below, the Directive does not affect any contracts concluded before the date of its adoption.[335] However, Member States may provide, subject to the rules governing the unwaivable right to equitable remuneration, that when rightholders who acquire new rights under national provisions adopted in implementation of the Directive have, before 1 July 1994, given their consent for exploitation, they shall be presumed to have transferred the new exclusive rights.[336]

6.126. Exclusion of public performances, broadcasting and exhibition. The Directive does not apply to the making available of phonograms or films (cinematographic or audiovisual works or moving images, whether or not accompanied by sound) for the purpose of public performance or broadcasting, making available for the purpose of exhibition or making available for 'on-the-spot' use.[337]

6.127. Preservation of 'windows'. The rental and lending rights and the neighbouring rights harmonized by the Directive may not be exercised in a way which is contrary to the rule of media exploitation chronology as recognised by the Court of Justice ie they may not disrupt the system of 'windows' usually negotiated by rightholders, for example between the exploitation of a film in a cinema and its distribution on cassette.[338]

6.128. Obligation to comply with Article 36 of the Treaty. Rights may not be exercised in a way which constitutes a disguised restriction on trade between Member States.[339]

2. Rental and Lending Right

(1) General Principles

6.129. Rental and lending right. Member States are to provide a right to authorize or prohibit the rental and lending of originals and copies of copyright and

---

[331] Article 14.
[332] Article 3. See §6.115 above.
[333] Article 13(1).
[334] Article 13(2).
[335] Article 13(6). Exceptions are contained in Article 13(3), 13(8) and 13(9).
[336] Article 13(7).
[337] Recital 14.
[338] Recital 21. See Joined Cases 60, 61/84 *Cinéthèque SA v. Fédération Nationale des Cinémas Français* [1985] ECR 2605, [1986] 1 CMLR 365. See §1.048 above.
[339] Recital 21. ie Rights must be exercised in conformity with Article 36 of the EEC Treaty.

certain other works.[340] 'Rental' is defined as 'making available for use, for a limited period of time and for direct or indirect economic or commercial advantage.'[341] 'Lending' means 'making available for use, for a limited period of time and not for direct or indirect economic or commercial advantage, when it is made through establishments which are accessible to the public.'[342] Insomuch as lending by an establishment accessible to the public gives rise to a payment the amount of which does not go beyond what is necessary to cover the operating costs of the establishment, there is no direct or indirect economic or commercial advantage within the meaning of the Directive.[343] (Such institutions might include, for example, public libraries, specialised libraries and school libraries).

Lending does not include making available 'between' establishments which are accessible to the public,[344] neither does it include the making available for the purpose of exhibition (ie in a gallery), or making available for on-the-spot reference use.[345] Both rental and lending rights may be transferred, assigned or subject to the granting of contractual licences.[346]

Member States may provide that the rights holders are deemed to have given their authorization to the rental and lending of an object covered by the Directive which is proven to have been made available to third parties for this purpose or to have been acquired before 1 July 1994.[347] However, in particular where such an object is a digital recording, Member States may provide that rightholders shall have a right to obtain an adequate remuneration for the rental or lending of that object.[348]

6.130. Works protected and identity of rightholders. These exclusive rental and lending right are given to: the author in respect of the original and copies of his work;[349] the performer in respect of fixations of his performance;[350] the phonogram producer in respect of his phonograms;[351] and to the producer of the first fixations of a film in respect of the original and copies of his film.[352] The term 'film' means a 'cinematographic or audiovisual work or moving images, whether or not accompanied by sounds.'[353] The principal director of a cinematographic or audiovisual work is to be considered its author or one of its authors and Member States may provide for others to be considered as its co-authors.[354] However, Member States need not accord the status of author to the principal director in the case of cinematographic or audiovisual works created before 1 July 1994.[355] Furthermore, they may determine the date as from which that status will apply, provided that this

---

[340] Article 1(1).
[341] Article 1(2).
[342] Article 1(3).
[343] Recital 14.
[344] Recital 13.
[345] Ibid.
[346] Article 2(4).
[347] Article 13(3).
[348] Ibid.
[349] Ibid.
[350] Ibid.
[351] Ibid.
[352] Ibid.
[353] Ibid.
[354] Article 2(2).
[355] Article 13(4).

date is no later than 1 July 1997.[356] The Directive does not cover rental and lending rights in relation to buildings and to works of applied art.[357]

(2) Derogation from the Exclusive Public Lending Right

6.131. Member States may derogate from the exclusive lending right in respect of public lending, provided that at least authors obtain a remuneration for such lending.[358] Member States are free to determine this remuneration taking account of their cultural promotion objectives.[359] This is subject to the proviso that any such measures must comply with Community law in general and Article 7 of the Treaty in particular.[360]

When Member States do not apply the exclusive lending right as regards phonograms, films and computer programs, they must introduce remuneration at least for authors.[361] This is subject to the proviso that they may exempt certain categories of establishments from the payment of this remuneration.[362] The Commission must, in co-operation with Member States draw up before 1 July 1997, a report on public lending in the Community.[363]

(3) Presumptive Assignment of Rental Rights in Respect of Films

6.132. Performers. When a contract concerning film production is concluded, individually or collectively, by performers with a film producer, the performer covered by this contract is to be presumed, subject to contractual clauses to the contrary to have transferred his rental right.[364] This is subject to the unwaivable right to equitable remuneration guaranteed by the Directive.[365] Member States may provide that the signing of a contract between a performer and a film producer concerning the production of a film has the effect of authorizing rental, provided that such a contract provides for an equitable remuneration.[366]

6.133. Authors. Member States may provide that when a contract concerning film production is concluded, individually or collectively by authors with a film producer, the author covered by this contract shall be presumed, subject to contractual clauses to the contrary, to have transferred his rental rights.[367] This must be subject to an unwaivable right to an equitable remuneration as set out in the Directive.[368]

---

[356] Article 13(5).
[357] Article 2(3).
[358] Article 5(1).
[359] Article 5(2).
[360] Recital 18. Article 7 of the Treaty prohibits any discrimination on grounds of nationality.
[361] Article 5(2).
[362] Article 5(3).
[363] Article 5(4).
[364] Article 2(5).
[365] Ibid.
[366] Article 2(7). The remuneration is to be calculated in accordance with Article 4.
[367] Article 2(6).
[368] Article 2(7). ie as guaranteed by Article 4.

6.134. Unwaivable right to equitable remuneration. Where an author or performer has transferred or assigned his rental right concerning a phonogram or an original or copy of a film to a phonogram or film producer, that author or performer retains the right to obtain an equitable remuneration for the rental of the work.[369] Member States may determine the date as from which the unwaivable right to an equitable remuneration shall exist, provided that this date is no later than 1 July 1997.[370] For contracts concluded before 1 July 1994, the unwaivable right to an equitable remuneration is to apply only where authors or performers or those representing them have submitted a request to that effect before 1 January 1997.[371] In the absence of agreement between rightholders concerning the level of remuneration, Member States may fix the level of equitable remuneration.[372]

The right to obtain an equitable remuneration for rental cannot be waived by authors or performers.[373] But the administration of this right may be entrusted to collecting societies representing authors or performers.[374] Member States may regulate whether and to what extent administration by collecting societies of the right to obtain an equitable remuneration may be imposed as well as the question from whom this remuneration may be claimed or collected.[375] Thus the equitable remuneration may be paid on the basis of one or several payments and any time on or after the conclusion of the contract.[376] But is must take account of the importance of the contribution of the authors and performers concerned to the phonogram or film.[377]

(4) Effect of Sale of Works on Rental and Lending Right

6.135. Rights of rental or lending are not exhausted by any sale, or other act of distribution, of originals and copies of the works specified above.[378]

2. Fixation Right

6.136. Performers. Member States must provide for performers, the exclusive right to authorize or prohibit the fixation of their performances.[379]

6.137. Broadcasting organisations. Member States must also provide for broadcasting organisations the exclusive right to authorize or prohibit the fixation of their broadcasts, whether these broadcasts are transmitted by wire or over the air, including by cable or satellite.[380] However, a cable distributor does not have these rights where it merely retransmits by cable the broadcasts of broadcasting organisations.[381]

---

[369] Article 4(1).
[370] Article 13(8).
[371] Article 13(9).
[372] Ibid.
[373] Article 4(2).
[374] Article 4(3).
[375] Article 4(4).
[376] Recital 16.
[377] Recital 17.
[378] Article 1(4).
[379] Article 6(1).
[380] Article 6(2).
[381] Article 6(3).

3. Reproduction Right

6.138. Introduction. Member States must provide to certain defined parties the right to authorize or prohibit the direct or indirect reproduction of their works.

6.139. Works protected and identity of rightholders. This right applies: to performers in respect of fixations of their performances;[382] to phonogram producers in respect of their phonograms;[383] to producers of the first fixations of films in respect of the original and copies of their films;[384] and to broadcasting organizations in respect of fixations of their broadcasts, whether those broadcasting have been transmitted by wire or over the air, including by cable or satellite.[385] These rights of reproduction may be transferred, assigned or made subject to the granting of contractual licences.[386]

4. Rights in Respect of Broadcasting and Communication to the Public

6.140. Rights of performers. Member States must provide for performers the exclusive right to authorize or prohibit the broadcasting by wireless means and the communication to the public of their performances, except where the performance is itself already a broadcast performance or is made from a fixation.[387]

6.141. Use of a commercial phonogram. Member States must provide a right to ensure that a single equitable remuneration is paid by the user, if a phonogram published for commercial purposes, or a reproduction of such a phonogram is used for broadcasting by wireless means or for any communication to the public, and ensure that this remuneration is shared between the relevant performers and phonogram producers.[388] Member States may, in the absence of an agreement between the performers and phonogram producers, lay down the conditions as to the sharing of this remuneration between them.[389]

6.142. Rights of broadcasting organisations. Member States must provide for broadcasting organisations the exclusive right to authorize or prohibit the rebroadcasting of their broadcasts by wireless means, as well as the communication to the public of their broadcasts if such communication is made in places accessible to the public against payment of an entrance fee.[390]

6.143. Extension of protection. Member States may provide for more far-reaching protection for owners of any of the above rights.[391]

---

[382] Article 7(1).
[383] *Ibid.*
[384] *Ibid.*
[385] *Ibid.*
[386] Article 7(2).
[387] Article 8(1).
[388] Article 8(2).
[389] *Ibid.*
[390] Article 8(3).
[391] Recital 20.

5. Distribution Right

6.144. The Directive institutes a 'distribution right' by which certain defined parties are given the right to make their respective works including both originals and copies available to the public by sale or otherwise. The distribution right is given: to performers in respect of fixations of their performances;[392] to phonogram producers in respect of their phonograms;[393] to producers of the first fixations of films in respect of the original and copies of their films[394] and to broadcasting organizations in respect of fixations of their broadcasts, whether these broadcasts are transmitted by wire or over the air, including by cable or satellite.[395] The distribution right will not be exhausted within the Community in respect of any of the aforementioned objects, except where the first sale in the Community of that object is made by the rightholder or with his consent.[396] This distribution right is without prejudice to the rules concerning the rental and lending or works.[397] However, the distribution right may be transferred, assigned or made subject to the granting of contractual licences.[398]

6. Presumptive Assignment of Performers' Neighbouring Rights

6.145. Member States may provide that when a contract concerning film produc-tion is concluded, individually or collectively, by performers with a film producer, the performer covered by this contract shall be presumed, subject to contractual clauses to the contrary, to have transferred his reproduction right, broadcasting and communication to the public right and distribution right.[399] Furthermore Member States may provide that the signing of a contract concluded between a performer and a film producer concerning the production of a film has the effect of authorising, the reproduction, broadcasting and communication to the public and distribution of his work.[400] This is so provided that such a presumption is compatible with the International Convention for the Protection of Performers, Producers of Phonograms and Broadcasting Organisations (the 'Rome Conven-tion').[401] And the presumption must be without prejudice to the right of the performer to receive an equitable remuneration for the exploitation of his work.[402]

---

[392] Article 9(1).
[393] *Ibid.*
[394] *Ibid.*
[395] *Ibid.*
[396] Article 9(2).
[397] Article 9(3).
[398] Article 9(4).
[399] Recital 19 and Article 2(5).
[400] Article 2(7) and Recital 19.
[401] Recital 19.
[402] Article 2(5). The terms of the right to equitable remuneration are governed by Article 4.

7. Limitation of Rights—Fair Use

6.146. Member States are given the right to provide limitations to the exclusive rights of fixation, reproduction, broadcasting and communication to the public and distribution in respect of: private use;[403] the use of short excerpts in connection with the reporting of current events;[404] the ephemeral fixation by a broadcasting organisation by means of its own facilities for the purposes of its own broadcasts;[405] use solely for the purposes of teaching or scientific research.[406] Moreover, irrespective of the above, any Member State may provide the same kind of limitations with regard to the protection of performers, producers of phonograms, broadcasting organisations and of producers of the first fixation of films, as it provides for in connection with the protection of copyright in literary and artistic works.[407] However, compulsory licences may only be permitted to the extent to which they are compatible with the Rome Convention (International Convention for the Protection of Performers, Producers of Phonograms and Broadcasting Organizations).[408]

8. Duration of Authors' Rights

6.147. Without prejudice to further harmonization of laws, authors' rights dealt with by the Directive must not expire before the end of the term provided for by the Berne Convention for the Protection of Literary and Artistic Works.[409]

9. Duration of Neighbouring Rights

6.148. Without prejudice to further harmonization, the rights of performers, phonogram producers and broadcasting organisations dealt with in the Directive must not expire before the end of the respective terms provided by the Rome Convention.[410] Furthermore, the rights referred to in the Directive for producers of the first fixations of films must not expire before the end of a period of 20 years computed from the end of the year in which the fixation was made.[411]

---

[403] Article 10(1)(a). However, in accordance with Article 10(3), this is without prejudice to any existing or future legislation on remuneration for reproduction for private use.
[404] Article 8(1)(b).
[405] Article 10(1)(c).
[406] Article 10(1)(d).
[407] Article 10(2).
[408] *Ibid.*
[409] Article 11. See §7.077 below.
[410] Article 12. See respectively §§7.202, 7.211 and 7.220.
[411] *Ibid.*

CHAPTER SEVEN

International Conventions

I. RELATIONSHIP BETWEEN COMMUNITY LAW AND INTERNATIONAL CONVENTIONS

7.001. Conventions in force before the entry into force of the EEC Treaty.
The Treaty of Rome gives some protection to international conventions ratified by Member States before the Treaty came into force, for Article 234[1] states:

> The rights and obligations arising from agreements concluded before the entry into force of this Treaty between one or more Member States on the one hand, and one or more third countries on the other, shall not be affected by the provisions of this Treaty.[2]

However, the Treaty would be undermined if parties could assert obligations that Member States had accepted prior to their accession to the Community and the Court of Justice has therefore interpreted Article 234 narrowly. It has ruled that it protects only those obligations accepted by Member States towards non-member countries.[3] In *Conegate Ltd v. HM Customs and Excise,*[4] the Court of Justice thus held that:

---

[1] First paragraph.

[2] Article 234 continues: 'To the extent that such agreements are not compatible with this Treaty, the Member State or States concerned shall take all appropriate steps to eliminate the incompatibilities established. Member States shall, where necessary, assist each other to this end and shall, where appropriate, adopt a common attitude. In applying the agreements referred to in the first paragraph, Member States shall take into account the fact that the advantages accorded under this Treaty by each Member State form an integral part of the establishment of the Community and are thereby inseparably linked with the creation of common institutions, the conferring of powers upon them and the granting of the same advantages by all the other Member States. See also Article 5 of the First Accession Treaty which states that 'Art. 234 of the EEC Treaty and Arts. 105 and 106 of the Euratom Treaty shall apply, for the new Member States, to agreements or conventions concluded before accession.'

[3] Case 10/61 *EC Commission v. Italy* [1962] ECR 1 and Case 812/79 *Attorney-General v. Burgoa* [1980] ECR 2787, [1981] 2 CMLR 193.

[4] Case 121/85 [1986] ECR 1007 [1986] 1 CMLR 739.

Article 234 is intended to ensure that the application of the Treaty does not affect either the duty to observe the rights of non-member countries under an agreement previously concluded with a Member State, or the observance by that Member State of its obligations under that Agreement. Agreements concluded prior to the entry into force of the Treaty may not therefore be relied upon in relations between Member States in order to justify restrictions on trade within the Community.

In *Musik-Vertrieb membran GmbH v. GEMA*,[5] the Court of Justice held that Article 13 of the Berne Convention for the Protection of the Literary and Artistic Works (Brussels Act) to which the Member States had acceded prior to their accession to the Community, was in breach of Articles 30 and 36 of the Treaty and could therefore not be enforced. Article 13 allowed Contracting States to authorise under compulsory licence, the reproduction of musical works, the recording of which had already been authorised by the rights owners, provided that those reproductions were not imported into other Contracting States. The prohibition on the importing of those reproductions offended Article 30 and was struck down by the Court. Similarly, in the Magill cases,[6] the Court of First Instance held that the Applicants could not defeat Community competition law, in particular Article 86 of the Treaty, by asserting Article 9(1) of the Berne Convention for the Protection of Literary and Artistic Works (Brussels Act), a provision which the United Kingdom had ratified before its accession to the Treaty.[7] That Article gave to authors of literary and artistic works, the exclusive right to authorise the reproduction of their works.[8]

7.002. Conventions entered into by a Member State after accession to the EEC Treaty. Member States may not set aside the rules arising out of the Treaty by concluding an international treaty or convention after their accession to the Community. In the Magill cases,[9] the Court of First Instance held that the Applicants could not defeat Community competition law, in particular Article 86 of the Treaty,[10] by asserting Article 9(2) of the Berne Convention for the Protection of Literary and Artistic Works (Paris Act), a provision which the United Kingdom had ratified after its accession to the Treaty. That Article permits Contracting States to permit the fair use of copyright works provided that such reproduction does not conflict with a normal exploitation of the work and does not unreasonably prejudice the legitimate interests of the author.[11] The Applicants had argued that their legitimate interests would be prejudiced contrary to that Article.

7.003. Conventions entered into by the Community. Article 228 provides a procedure to enable the Community to enter into international treaties or conventions

---

[5] Joined Cases 55, 57/80 [1981] ECR 147, [1981] 2 CMLR 44. For the facts of the case, see §1.011 above.

[6] Case T—69/89 *Radio Telefis Eireann v. EC Commission* [1991] 4 CMLR 586; Case T—70/89 *British Broadcasting Corporation and BBC Enterprises Ltd v. EC Commission* [1991] 4 CMLR 669; Case T—76/89 *Independent Television Publications Ltd v. EC Commission* [1991] 4 CMLR 745. For the facts of the cases, see §4.151 above.

[7] The Court noted that the Applicants were bound by Article 234 of the Treaty in accordance with Article 5 of the Act of Accession.

[8] See §7.047 below.

[9] Case T—69/89 *Radio Telefis Eireann v. EC Commission* [1991] 4 CMLR 586; Case T—70/89 *British Broadcasting Corporation and BBC Enterprises Ltd v. EC Commission* [1991] 4 CMLR 669; T—76/89 *Independent Television Publications Ltd v. EC Commission* [1991] 4 CMLR 745. For the facts of the cases, see §4.151 above.

[10] As well as Regulation No. 17, Article 3.

[11] See §7.048 below.

on behalf of Member States.[12] The obligations created by those conventions are then absorbed into the Community's jurisprudence. As the Court of Justice held in Re the Draft Treaty on a European Economic Area:[13]

> ... international agreements concluded by means of the procedure set out in Article 228 of the Treaty are binding on the institutions of the Community and its Member States ... as the Court of Justice has consistently held, the provisions of such agreements and the measures adopted by institutions set up by such agreements become an integral part of the Community legal order when they enter into force.

II. THE BERNE CONVENTION FOR THE PROTECTION OF LITERARY AND ARTISTIC WORKS

1. Introduction

7.004. History. The ideal of creating a global and egalitarian regime for the protection of literary and artistic works—a regime in which an author would be guaranteed fundamental rights in his own country and equivalent protection in other states—had been nurtured since the middle of the last century. But despite a number of countries displaying their enthusiasm for this worthy cause by adopting accords in which were framed proposed general principles, concrete progress was not made until 1878. 1878 was a momentous year for authors (indeed, for the creative community as a whole), for it saw the formation, at a literary congress, of the International Literary Association (later to become the International Literary and Artistic Association and now known as the 'ALAI'). The ALAI was an august body of literary luminaries—it boasted Victor Hugo as its first president—which, due no doubt to the vested interest of its members, took up the cause of authors' rights with fervour. Over the next few years it lobbied assiduously for an international regime of protection, organised numerous congresses in pursuit of its ideal and constantly nudged governments into action. The ALAI's labour soon bore fruit and in 1883 a meeting was organised to consider its proposal for a draft convention. This led to an international conference held in Berne in 1884, which was to be a turning point in the quest for the worldwide protection of authors' rights.

At the close of the 1884 conference, the delegates adopted draft instruments which, in ensemble, were designed to confer internationally enforceable rights on authors. They sought to establish a Union for the protection of authors of literary and artistic works, they provided for 'national treatment' and articulated exclusive rights of translation, adaptation and performance.[14] In all, they paved the way for a binding convention.

There followed a lengthy process of negotiation. Existing rights were refined, others were added.[15] Finally on 9 September 1886, ten States breathed life into the draft which had been settled at a conference in 1885 and the Berne Convention for the

---

[12] Article 4(1) of the First Accession Act states: 'The agreements or conventions entered into by any of the Communities with one or more third States, with an international organisation or with a national of a third State, shall, under the conditions laid down in the original Treaties and in this Act, be binding on the new Member States.'

[13] Opinion 1/91 [1992] 1 CMLR 245.

[14] For an analysis of these in detail see S. Ricketson, *The Berne Convention for the Protection of Literary and Artistic Works: 1886-1986* (1987), 2.28 et seq.

[15] *Ibid.*

Protection of Literary and Artistic Works (the 'Convention') was born. It entered into force on 5 December 1887.

The original Act of 1886 contained many provisions which have endured over the years, albeit in refined form. In the first place, the 1986 Act created a Union for the protection of authors of literary and artistic works.[16] There was a definition of recognised categories of works.[17] Although this was generally an open class, 'covering every production whatsoever in the literary, scientific, or artistic domain',[18] the Convention specifically provided for the inclusion of photographic[19] and choreographic works[20] to which it attached certain conditions.

The concept of 'national treatment' was enshrined: authors who belonged to a Union country were to enjoy in another Union country (whether or not their works were published there), the rights which the latter conferred on its nationals for the protection of their works.[21] Convention rights were also granted to a person who did not belong to a Union country for those of their works which were published in a Union country.[22]

Protection was conditional solely on the author complying with all conditions and formalities demanded in the country of origin of the work.[23] National treatment applied to the term of protection save for the proviso that the duration of protection could not exceed the period legislated in the country of origin of the work.[24]

It was assumed that the Convention protected the author's exclusive right of reproduction[25] and it therefore enshrined only two specific rights: it gave the author the right to authorise translations[26] and public performances of his works.[27] The translation right continued for a period of ten years from the date of first publication.[28]

There were exceptions to protection: Articles from newspapers or periodicals could be reproduced in original form or in translation unless the author or publisher expressly forbade those acts.[29] Articles containing 'political discussion' were unprotected as were 'news of the day' or miscellaneous information[30] and 'portions' of protected works could be used in publications of an educational or scientific nature if the legislation of the member country so permitted.[31]

7.005. The Berne 'Union'. The opening Article of the Convention establishes the Berne Union with the following words:

> The countries to which this Convention applies constitute a Union for the protection of the rights of authors in their literary and artistic works.[32]

---

[16] Article I.
[17] Article IV.
[18] *Ibid.*
[19] Final Protocol, Article 1.
[20] Final Protocol, Article 2.
[21] Article II.
[22] Article III.
[23] Article II.
[24] *Ibid.*
[25] Article X detailed types of illicit reproduction.
[26] Article V. In accordance with Article VI, lawful translations were protected as original works and enjoyed all the rights flowing from that status under the Convention.
[27] Article IX.
[28] Article V.
[29] Article VII.
[30] *Ibid.*
[31] Article VIII.
[32] Article 1.

The Union has an Assembly,[33] which deals with all matters concerning the Union's maintenance and development as well as the implementation of the Convention[34] and it gives directions concerning the preparation of revision conferences.[35] The work of the Assembly is undertaken by an Executive Committee[36] and funded by the Union budget.[37]

Although the Union has certain tasks, it does not play an essential role in the administration of the international copyright regime established by the Convention. That regime would continue to function should the Union cease to exist. So what is its raison d'être? As Ricketson explains, the Convention and thus its creature, the Union, came into being in an era when there existed a thirst for the creation of symbols of international co-operation.[38] The framers of Berne thus appeared to have been swept up by fashion. Nevertheless, it is fair to say that the Berne Union does perform two important functions. In the first place, it serves a symbolic role, 'embodying the ultimate ideal of universal codification' of copyright law.[39] But more importantly it provides continuity. For whilst there have been several revisions of Berne and not all countries have acceded to the same acts, they are united in their membership of the Union. And should any of them cease to be members, the Union would continue to exist after their departure.[40]

7.006. Revisions of the Convention. To meet the challenges posed by new types of media and new technologies, the Convention has undergone many metamorphoses during its century long evolution. It is a process that continues. The chronology is as follows.[41] The Convention was enacted in 1886 in Berne and an addition followed in 1896 (Additional Act of Paris). In 1908, it was revised (the Berlin Act) and there soon followed, in 1914, an additional Protocol (Additional Protocol of Berne). The Convention was revised in 1928 (Rome Act) and again in 1948 (Brussels Act). The next revision came in 1967 (Stockholm Revision) but the substantive amendments did not take effect until the last revision in 1971 (Paris Act).

7.007. Act analysed below. Generally accession to each Act of the Convention entails acceptance of all its provisions: reservations are exceptional.[42] The Act analysed below is the Paris Act of 24 July, 1971 as amended on 2 October, 1979. However, some Union Members have not acceded to revisions later than the Rome Act of 1928, and therefore, to aid practical application of the Convention, the footnotes indicate the date when provisions were introduced as well as their substance.[43] Where there is no such footnote annotation, the relevant provision has been in existence at least since the adoption of the Rome Act.

7.008. Scope of the Convention. The Convention with its numerous revisions, provides a regime of protection for solely authors of literary and artistic works. It thus offers no protection to performers and other proprietors of neighbouring rights. They

---

[33] Article 22(1)(a).
[34] Article 22(2)(a)(i).
[35] Article 22(2)(a)(ii).
[36] Article 23
[37] Article 25.
[38] Ricketson, *op. cit.*, 4.23 et seq.
[39] *Ibid.*
[40] See generally, *ibid.* 4.32.
[41] For details of the dates of each revision and the dates of their entry into force, see §7.094 below.
[42] Article 30(1). As to permitted reservations, see §7.095 below.
[43] For detailed analysis of the process of evolution of each Article of the Convention see Ricketson, *op. cit.*

are guaranteed protection under other conventions such as the International Convention for the Protection of Performers, Producers of Phonograms and Broadcasting Organisations (the 'Rome Convention').[44]

7.009. Regime of protection. The Convention was conceived as a tool to help shape a framework of rights for authors throughout the world. The regime of protection reflects that role. Thus, in the first place, the Convention places an obligation on one Member country of the Union to confer on authors of another Member of the Union, the equivalent treatment which the former grants to its own nationals. This is known as conferring 'national treatment' and it acts as a catalyst. The concept is based on the belief that the foreign author will force his own government to bring the measure of protection available in his own country up to the level which that author is guaranteed abroad. However, 'national treatment' would be of little use on its own to that same author for countries with a poor level of protection. Therefore secondly, the Convention enshrines certain absolute minimum rights which override national laws.

7.010. Interpretation of the Convention. The Intergovernmental Report[45] of the Stockholm revision conference compiled by Professor Svante Bergström, the Rapporteur-General (the 'Bergström Report') and unanimously adopted by the Committee may be used as an interpretative guide to the Convention. It is referred to below.

The World Intellectual Property Organisation has written a Guide to the Berne Convention[46] and it is an invaluable tool in the analysis of the Convention. However, as the Guide itself points out, it is not to be regarded as an authentic interpretation of the treaty but rather has the aim of presenting 'an account of the origins, aims, nature and scope of the provisions concerned'.[47] Its purpose is thus to aid in the implementation of the Convention and ultimately, therefore, it is for the authorities to form their own opinions about the interpretation of the Convention.[48]

2. Protected Works

(1) The Concept of 'Literary and Artistic Works'

7.011. The Convention confers rights on authors of 'literary and artistic works', an expression which embraces every production in the literary, scientific and artistic domain, whatever may be the mode or form of its expression.[49] The Convention focuses its attention on the form and not the substance of a work: protection is never conditional on the content.[50] As the WIPO Guide puts it:

> The scientific work is protected by copyright not because of the scientific character of its contents: a medical textbook, a treatise on physics, a documentary on interplanetary space are protected not because they deal with medicine, physics or the surface of the moon, but because they are books and films.[51]

---

[44] See §7.188 et seq. below.
[45] Copyright [1967] Issue 9, 183.
[46] The Guide has been written by Mr Claude Masouyé and Mr William Wallace.
[47] WIPO Guide to the Berne Convention (1978), Preface.
[48] Ibid.
[49] Article 2(1).
[50] WIPO Guide to the Berne Convention (1978), 2.2.
[51] Ibid.

Therefore, novelty, character, quality and merit are irrelevant. All that matters is that a work is 'original', meaning simply that it is the product of intellectual activity. The WIPO Guide elegantly illustrates the difference between 'originality' and 'novelty' thus:

> ... two artists, placing their easels on the same spot and each making a picture of the same landscape, each separately creates a work; the second painting is not novel, because the same subject has already been dealt with by the first painter, but it is original because it reflects the personality of its maker. Equally, two craftsmen carving the figure of an elephant in wood each creates an original even though the two elephants are indistinguishable and there is no question of novelty.[52]

By eschewing the notion that 'novelty' is a precondition of protection, the Convention recognises that all works, whatever may be their type—artistic, cinematographic, dramatic, literary, musical, plastic and others—are derivative in the sense that they carry the influence of much that preceded them. With very few exceptions, cultural history confirms that no creator is an island entire of itself. Furthermore to impose a concept of 'novelty' requires the existence of a person or a court to make aesthetic judgments, a task which is arguably impossible to fulfil.

(2) Categories of Works

(i) General Principles

7.012. The Convention[53] sets out examples of the categories of works it protects. However, since the term 'literary and artistic works' is all-embracing, these categories are merely illustrative and therefore non-exhaustive. Thus the Convention gives to Union members the power to introduce other specific categories themselves.[54] Nevertheless, it is clear that a work does involve some kind of 'intellectual creation' and this is the test to be applied in determining whether a category of work not mentioned in the list qualifies for protection.[55] The classifications made by the Convention are:

(ii) Specific Categories

7.013. 'books, pamphlets and other writings'. These are protected irrespective of their content, their length, their purpose (entertainment, education, information, discussion, advertisement, propaganda) and their form (manuscript, typescript, printing).[56]

7.014. 'lectures, addresses, sermons and other works of the same nature'. Although the Convention protects such works, it is left to the discretion of countries of the Union to determine the conditions under which lectures, addresses and other works of the same nature which are delivered in public, may be broadcast, communicated to the public by wire and made the subject of public communication[57] when such use is justified by their informatory purpose.[58] In other words, these works may

---

[52] WIPO Guide to the Berne Convention (1978), 2.8.
[53] in Article 2(1).
[54] WIPO Guide to the Berne Convention (1978), 2.7.
[55] S M Stewart, *International Copyright and Neighbouring Rights* (2nd Edn, 1989), 5.30.
[56] WIPO Guide to the Berne Convention (1978), 2.6.(a).
[57] As envisaged by Article 11 bis(1). See §7.051 below.
[58] Article 2 bis(2). Note that compulsory licences cannot apply to sermons (Bergström Report, para. 156.). See §7.026 below.

be subject to compulsory licences. The term 'informatory purpose' means 'newsworthi-ness'. But, it is not the subject matter of the work that need be newsworthy, merely the fact that the work has taken place: 'the character of the news must apply not to the subject dealt with in the lecture, address etc., but to the actual utilisation with the object of informing the public'.[59] So, for example, a controversial lecture about a seventeenth century writer would qualify.[60] However the Convention preserves the right of the author to make collections of such works even if they have already been disseminated by the media[61] because to deny him this privilege cannot be justified on the grounds of freedom of information.[62]

7.015. 'dramatic or dramatico-musical works'. This category includes, for example, pieces for theatre, musicals and operas.[63]

7.016. 'choreographic works and entertainments in dumb show'. There is no need for these to be fixed in a material form in order to be protected (although member countries may dictate this condition)[64] for imposing such a requirement would, for example leave, broadcast works of this nature unprotected.[65]

7.017. 'musical compositions with or without words'. The phrase 'with or without words' means that any words accompanying the music are protected as well as the music.[66]

7.018. 'cinematographic works to which are assimilated works expressed by a process analogous to cinematography'. This category refers to 'films in the classic sense whether silent or "talkies", whatever their type (documentaries, newsreels, reports or feature films made to a script), whatever their length, whatever their method of making (films on location, films made in studios, cartoons, etc.) or the technical process used (films on celluloid, video tape, etc.) whatever they are intended for (showing in cinemas or television transmission) and finally whoever is their maker (commercial production companies, television organisations or mere amateurs)'.[67] The word 'expressed' is employed by the Convention to convey that uniquely, for this particular work, it is the method of making the work public that gives it its identity as a work.[68] By contrast, a broadcast does not qualify as a work because it is regarded as a method of making a work public (ie of expressing a work).[69] Nevertheless, since the list of works in the Convention is non-exhaustive it is open to member countries to include a broadcast as a work.

7.019. 'works of drawing, painting, architecture, sculpture, engraving and lithography'. This category is designed to encompass all artistic works whether in two or

---

[59] Bergström Report, para. 156.
[60] WIPO Guide to the Berne Convention (1978), 2 bis.3.
[61] Article 2 bis(3).
[62] WIPO Guide to the Berne Convention (1978), 2 bis.5.
[63] Ibid. 2.6.(c).
[64] See §7.029 below.
[65] WIPO Guide to the Berne Convention (1978) 2.6.(d). Prior to the Stockholm Revision, choreographic works and entertainments in dumb show were protected only where 'the acting form of which is fixed in writing or otherwise'. This has now been deleted (see Bergström Report, para. 118).
[66] WIPO Guide to the Berne Convention (1978), 2.6.(e).
[67] Ibid. 2.6.(f). The Rome Act assimilated cinematographic works to photographic works if the work lacked an original character (Article 14(2), Rome Act). The Brussels Act did away with this exception.
[68] Ibid.
[69] Ibid. 2.6.(f).

three dimensions, independent of their type (ie figurative or abstract) and their purpose (pure or commercial art).[70]

7.020. 'photographic works to which are assimilated works expressed by a process analogous to photography'. The concept of assimilation is used here to ensure that any form of technical or chemical process not yet invented will be covered.[71] However, it is possible for member countries to exclude certain categories of photographs ie national legislators might want to deprive photographs produced by automatic means (ie passport photographs) of protection.[72]

7.021. 'works of applied art'. This would include, for example, jewellery, furniture, wallpaper, clothing etc.[73]

7.022. 'illustrations, maps, plans, sketches and three-dimensional works relative to geography, typography, architecture or science'. Although the Convention is highly specific with this category of work, it is important to emphasise that this list is merely illustrative.

7.023. Translations, adaptations, arrangements and alterations. Translations, adaptations, arrangements of music and other alterations of a literary or artistic work are protected as original works, without prejudice to the rights of the author of the original work.[74] They merit protection because they are products of intellectual creativity. It goes without saying that in order to translate, adapt, arrange or alter a protected work, the consent of the author is needed, unless the work is in the public domain.[75] And to make use of a translation, it is necessary to obtain the consent of both the author and the translator.[76]

7.024. Collections of literary and artistic works. Collections of literary or artistic works such as encyclopedias and anthologies, which, by reason of the selection and arrangement of their contents, constitute intellectual creations are protected as such, without prejudice to the copyright in each of the works forming part of such collections.[77] Thus merely listing the works or extracts without a personal contribution is not enough to confer protection.[78]

(3) Power to Limit the Protection of Certain Works

7.025. Official texts. It is a matter for legislation in the countries of the Union to determine the protection to be granted to official texts of a legislative, administrative and legal nature, and to official translations of such texts.[79] However, the reference to texts of an 'administrative' nature does not permit countries to refuse protection to all Government publications, for instance, textbooks.[80]

---

[70] *Ibid.* 2.6.(g).
[71] *Ibid.* 2.6.(h).
[72] *Ibid.*
[73] *Ibid.* 2.6.(i). Works of applied art were introduced by the Brussels Act (Article 2(1), Brussels Act). See §7.027 below.
[74] Article 2(3).
[75] WIPO Guide to the Berne Convention (1978), 2.16.
[76] *Ibid.* 2.17.
[77] Article 2(5).
[78] WIPO Guide to the Berne Convention (1978), 2.19.
[79] Article 2(4).
[80] Bergström Report, para. 136.

7.026. Political speeches and speeches in legal proceedings. It is a matter for the legislation in the countries of the Union to exclude, wholly or in part, from protection, political speeches and speeches delivered in the course of legal proceedings.[81] The justification of this provision is freedom of information.[82] Nevertheless, the Convention gives to the author the exclusive right of making a collection of such works[83] because freedom of information is already served by the right to publish the works individually.

7.027. Works of applied art. It is a matter for legislation in the countries of the Union to determine the extent of the application of their laws to works of applied art and industrial designs and models as well as the conditions under which such works, designs and models shall be protected.[84] Works which are protected in their country of origin solely as designs and models are entitled in another country of the Union only to such protection as is granted in that country to designs and models.[85] However, if no such special protection is granted in that country, such works must be protected as artistic works.[86] These rules are without prejudice to the rules that the Convention sets out for the duration of protection of these works.[87]

(4) Works Excluded from Protection

7.028. 'News of the day'. 'News of the day' or 'miscellaneous facts having the character of mere items of press information' are categorically denied protection under the Convention.[88] This is because they do not possess the requisite element of creativity. It follows therefore that creativity applied to the presentation of such news or information may well make it a protected work.[89]

(5) Requirement of Fixation

7.029. There are substantial differences among the domestic laws of the countries of the Union as to whether or not fixation is a requirement for copyright protection. Those countries which impose such requirements (normally the common law systems) deem them necessary so as to identify the work and avoid confusion with other works.[90] The Convention respects this diversity and provides that it is a matter for legislation in the Countries of the Union to prescribe, should they so wish, that works in general or any specified categories of works will not be protected unless they have been fixed in some material form.[91]

---

[81] Article 2 bis(1).
[82] WIPO Guide to the Berne Convention (1978), 2 bis.1.
[83] Article 2 bis(3).
[84] Article 2(7).
[85] *Ibid.*
[86] *Ibid.* This provision was introduced by the Stockholm Revision.
[87] Article 2(7). ie a minimum period of twenty five years from the making of the work must be conferred as set out in Article 7(4). This was introduced by the Stockholm Revision.
[88] Article 2(8).
[89] WIPO Guide to the Berne Convention (1978), 2.27.
[90] *Ibid.* 2.9. Although as the Guide notes, even in some of those copyright regimes, works are deemed to have an existence before their moment of fixation, the fixation merely 'perfecting' the copyright.
[91] Article 2(2). This provision was introduced by the Stockholm revision.

(6) Formalities and the Protection of Works

7.030. The enjoyment and exercise of rights under the Convention cannot be subject to any formality.[92] The word 'formality' is not defined but should be understood to mean a condition which is necessary for the right to exist ie administrative obligations laid down by national laws, which if not fulfilled lead to the loss of copyright. They include for example, the requirement that a copy of the work is deposited with specific institutions or that it is registered with a public body or that a registration fee is paid.[93] The Convention's prohibition of such formalities applies whether rights are conferred under the principle of 'national treatment' or by the specific provisions of the Convention.[94]

(7) Protection of Works Existing on Convention's Entry into Force

7.031. The Convention applies to all works which, at the moment of the Convention's coming into force, have not fallen into the public domain in the country of origin through the expiry of the term of protection.[95] If, however, through the expiry of the term of protection which was previously granted, a work has fallen into the public domain of the country where protection is claimed, that work is not to be protected anew.[96] In other words, a work which was once protected in the country where protection is claimed but which is now in the public domain, will not be protected there when that country accedes to the Convention, despite the fact that the term of protection in the country of origin has not expired.

The application of these principles is subject to any provisions contained in special conventions to that effect existing or to be concluded between countries of the Union.[97] In the absence of such provisions, the respective countries are to determine, each in so far as it is concerned, the conditions of application of this principle.[98] The aforementioned provisions apply also in the case of new accessions to the Union and to cases in which the protection is extended by the application of Article 7 or by the abandonment of reservations.[99]

3. Who is Protected

There are several criteria which may qualify an author for protection under the Convention. These 'points of attachment' are as follows:

7.032. Authors who are nationals of Union countries. Protection applies to authors who are nationals of one of the countries of the Union, for their works, whether or not they have been published.[100] Where an author's nationality changes from time to time, he should be protected if during a period of nationality, his work is made available to the public.[101]

---

[92] Article 5(2).
[93] WIPO Guide on the Berne Convention (1978), 5.5. It should be noted, as the Guide points out, that countries are entirely free to impose whatever formalities they so wish as a condition of protection for works which originate in their own country.
[94] See §7.043 et seq. below.
[95] Article 18(1).
[96] Article 18(2).
[97] Article 18(3).
[98] *Ibid.*
[99] Article 18(4).
[100] Article 3(1)(a).
[101] Bergström Report, para. 30.

7.033. Authors who have habitual residence in Union countries. Authors who are not nationals of one of the countries of the Union but who have their habitual residence in one of them are, for the purposes of the Convention, assimilated to nationals of that country and protected under the Convention.[102] This category includes stateless persons and refugees.[103] In the case where an author has his habitual residence in a country of the Union only from time to time, then he will probably be protected if during a period of residence, his work[104] is made available to the public.[105] If the work was first made available to the public by an unauthorised person, the author can claim protection if he has his habitual residence in a country of the Union at that date.[106]

7.034. Non-national authors. Authors who are not nationals of one of the countries of the Union, are protected if their works are first published in one of the countries of the Union, or simultaneously in a country outside the Union and in a country of the Union.[107] A work is considered as having been published simultaneously in several countries if it has been published in two or more countries within thirty days of its first publication.[108]

7.035. Meaning of the term 'published works'. The expression 'published works' means 'works published with the consent of their authors, whatever may be the means of manufacture of the copies, provided that the availability of such copies has been such as to satisfy the reasonable requirements of the public, having regard to the nature of the work'.[109] However, a performance of a dramatic, dramatico-musical, cinematographic or musical work, the public recitation of a literary work, the communication by wire or the broadcasting of literary or artistic works, the exhibition of a work of art and the construction of a work of architecture, does not constitute publication.[110] Performances, recitations, and the broadcasting and communication to the public of a work produce only a fleeting impression of a work whereas the concept of 'publication' involves distributing a work in tangible form.[111] The requirement of 'consent' means that infringing copies do not acquire copyright under the Convention. It also has the effect of excluding duplicates of a work which have been made under compulsory licence.[112]

---

[102] Article 3(2). This provision was introduced by the Stockholm Revision. The criterion of habitual residence was preferred to that of domicile because the concept of the latter varies from State to State whilst that of the former is purely a question of fact (see WIPO Guide to the Berne Convention (1978), 3.4).

[103] Bergström Report, para. 28.

[104] not having been published.

[105] Bergström Report, para. 29. As the Report notes, this is a point which the courts must decide in the country in which protection is claimed.

[106] Bergström Report, para. 29.

[107] Article 3(1)(b).

[108] Article 3(4). The 30 day period was an addition made by the Brussels Act (Article 3, Brussels Act). Prior to that Act, the word 'simultaneously' was interpreted strictly and meant publication on the same day.

[109] Article 3(3). The Rome Act defined published works simply as 'works copies of which have been issued to the public'. (Article 4(4), Rome Act). The Brussels Act required the work to be 'made available in sufficient quantities' and declared that any means of manufacture of copies amounted to publication (Article 4(4), Brussels Act). The requirement that the works be published 'with the consent of their authors' and that they satisfy the reasonable requirements of the public was introduced by the Stockholm Revision.

[110] Article 3(3). The recitation of a literary work as well as the broadcasting and communication of a work by wire were mentioned for the first time in the Brussels Act (Article 4(4), Brussels Act).

[111] WIPO Guide to the Berne Convention (1978), 3.9.

[112] Ibid. 3.8.

The dual criteria of the 'nature of the work' and the 'reasonable requirements of the public' are designed to cover the diversity of works protected by the Convention and the fact that works may be sold, exhibited, hired out, lent etc. The WIPO Guide to the Berne Convention states that this wording avoids abuse: 'it is not enough to show, in the window of a single bookshop, a dozen copies of a book which has enjoyed massive success in some other country outside the Union. Again, a single copy of a cinematographic work sent to a festival to be shown before a restricted audience does not meet the conditions'.[113]

7.036. Authors of cinematographic works. Authors of cinematographic works who fail to meet the aforementioned conditions on publication are nevertheless protected where the maker of the cinematographic work has his headquarters or habitual residence in one of the countries of the Union.[114] It is generally accepted that, in the case of co-productions, the work will enjoy protection under the Convention where one of its makers has his habitual residence or headquarters in the Union country.[115]

7.037. Authors of works of architecture. Regardless of nationality, protection is given to: authors of works of architecture erected in a country of the Union or; to authors of other artistic works incorporated in a building or other structure located in a country of the Union.[116] However this rule applies only to the original work. No protection can thus be given to a copy of the work in a country of the Union if the original were in a country outside of the Union.[117]

7.038. Meaning of the term 'author'. The Convention does not define the term 'author' due to the multiplicity of different laws applying in members of the Union. Thus the question of who or what can be an author, is probably governed by the law in which protection is claimed.

7.039. Successors and assignees. Generally, protection operates for the benefit of the author and his successors in title.[118] The author's rights can be disposed of by contract. Thus an assignee enjoys the rights assigned as if he were the author.[119]

4. Protection in the Country of Origin

7.040. General principles. Generally protection of a work in the country of origin is governed by its domestic law and completely outside of the ambit of the Convention.[120] However, when the author is not a national of the country of origin of the work for which he is protected under the Convention, he must enjoy in that country, the same rights as national authors ie the Convention confers on him

---

[113] *Ibid.* 3.6.
[114] Article 4(a). This provision was introduced by the Stockholm Revision.
[115] WIPO Guide to the Berne Convention (1978), 4.5.
[116] Article 4(b). This provision was introduced by the Stockholm Revision.
[117] Bergström Report, para. 63.
[118] Article 2(6). This provision was introduced by the Brussels Act (Article 2(4), Brussels Act).
[119] WIPO Guide to the Berne Convention (1978), 2.22.
[120] Article 5(3). ie a country can impose whatever formalities it wishes on such works as a pre-condition of protection. See by way of contrast, §7.030 above (Article 5(2)).

'national treatment'.[121] In other words, where the author is a national of one country of the Union and the work originates in another country of the Union, that author is guaranteed 'national treatment' in the latter country.[122] But the Convention will not intervene any further.

7.041. Meaning of country of origin. The country of origin is considered to be: in the case of works first published in a country of the Union, that country;[123] in the case of works published simultaneously in several countries of the Union which grant different terms of protection, the country whose legislation grants the shortest term of protection;[124] in the case of works published simultaneously in a country outside the Union and in a country of the Union, the latter country;[125] in the case of unpublished works or of works first published in a country outside the Union, the country of the Union of which the author is a national,[126] provided that when these are cinematographic works the maker of which has his headquarters or his habitual residence in a country of the Union, the country of origin is that country,[127] and when these are works of architecture erected in a country of the Union or other artistic works incorporated in a building or other structure located in a country of the Union, the country of origin is that country.[128]

5. Possible Restrictions of Protection in respect of Certain Works of Nationals of Countries Outside of the Union

7.042. Where any country outside the Union fails to protect in an adequate manner the works of authors who are nationals of one of the countries of the Union, the latter country may restrict the protection given to the works of authors who are, at the date of the first publication (there), nationals of the other country and are not habitually resident in one of the countries of the Union.[129] If the country of first publication avails itself of this right, the other countries of the Union are not required to grant to works thus subjected to special treatment a wider protection than that granted to them in the country of first publication.[130] However, no restrictions introduced by virtue of the preceding provisions affect the rights which an author may have acquired in respect of a work published in a country of the Union before such restrictions were put into force there.[131]

---

[121] Article 5(3). This provision was introduced by the Stockholm Revision, although it was implicit in previous Acts.
[122] Bergström Report, para. 54.
[123] Article 5(4)(a).
[124] Ibid.
[125] Article 5(4)(b).
[126] Article 5(4)(c).
[127] Article 5(4)(c)(i). This provision was introduced by the Stockholm Revision.
[128] Article 5(4)(c)(ii). This provision was introduced by the Stockholm Revision.
[129] Article 6(1).
[130] Ibid.
[131] Article 6(2). In accordance with Article 6(3), notice of such restriction is given by declaration to the Director-General of WIPO, specifying the countries in regard to which protection is restricted and the restrictions to which rights of authors who are nationals of those countries are subjected. The Director-General then communicates this declaration to all the other countries of the Union. See Table A of Appendix III.

6. Rights Protected

(1) The Right to National Treatment

7.043. General principles. As a fundamental right, authors of works protected under the Convention, enjoy in countries of the Union[132] the rights which their respective laws presently or at any time after the entry into force of the Convention, grant to their nationals in respect of those works ie they are to be accorded 'national treatment'.[133] As is the case with the minimum rights guaranteed by the Convention, such countries cannot make the conferring of 'national rights' subject to the existence of formalities.[134]

7.044. The relationship between national treatment and specific rights granted by the Convention. As a general rule, the extent of protection, as well as the means of redress afforded to the author to protect his rights, is governed exclusively by the laws of the country where protection is claimed.[135] However, this is subject to the minimum rights specifically fashioned by the Convention and which are detailed below.[136]

(2) Rights of Translation

7.045. General principles. Authors of literary and artistic works are given the exclusive right to make and authorize others to make a translation of their works throughout the term of protection of their rights in the original work.[137]

---

[132] See §7.040 above in respect of protection in the country of origin of a work.
[133] Article 5(1).
[134] Article 5(2). A country can impose formalities, as a condition of protection of domestic works.
[135] *Ibid.*
[136] *Ibid.*
[137] Article 8. In accordance with Article 30(2)(b) of the Paris Act, any country outside the Union may declare, in acceding to the Convention, '. . . subject to Article V(2) of the Appendix that it intends to substitute, temporarily at least, for Article 8 of this Act concerning the right of translation, the provisions of Article 5 of the Union Convention of 1886, as completed at Paris in 1896, on the clear understanding that the said provisions are applicable only to translations into a language in general use in the said country.' Article 30(2)(b) provides for material reciprocity in respect of works whose country of origin is a country availing itself of this reservation. See Table A of Appendix III.

Article V of the Union Convention of 1886 as completed at Paris in 1896 provides that:

Authors who are subjects or citizens of any of the countries of the Union, or their lawful representatives, shall enjoy in the other countries the exclusive right of making or authorizing the translation of their works until the expiration of ten years from the publication of the original work in one of the countries of the Union.

For works published in incomplete parts ('livraisons') the period of ten years shall commence from the date of publication of the last part of the original work.

For works composed of several volumes published at intervals as well as for bulletins or collections ('cahiers') published by literary or scientific societies, or by private persons, each volume, bulletin, or collection shall be with regard to the period of ten years, considered as a separate work.

In the cases provided for by the present Article, and for the calculation of the terms of protection, 31st December of the year in which the work was published shall be regarded as the date of publication.

7.046. Minor reservations. Although not explicit, it is accepted that the normal minor reservations will apply to translated works.[138] But the moral rights of the author must be protected.[139]

(3) Rights of Reproduction

7.047. General principles. Authors of literary and artistic works are given the exclusive right of authorizing the reproduction of those works, in any manner or form.[140] This phrase is wide enough to cover all processes known or yet to be discovered.[141] The Convention confirms that any sound or visual recording is considered to be a reproduction.[142] It has been pointed out that the Convention extends the ordinary meaning of a right of reproduction: the Convention concept not only includes the duplication of the original (a true reproduction right) but also the first fixation of the work on to the matrix.[143] It should be noted however, that despite this broad interpretation, the term reproduction does not include a public performance[144] so that for example the dramatist who assigns to a publisher the right to print (ie to reproduce) his play does not give him a right to perform it.[145] Of more significance is the fact that the Convention does not mention the author's right of 'distribution' although this must, in practical terms, flow from the right of reproduction.[146]

7.048. Fair use. It is left to the countries of the Union to permit reproduction of such works in special cases, provided that these do not conflict with a normal exploitation of the work and do not unreasonably prejudice the legitimate interests of the author.[147] It follows that 'If it is considered that reproduction conflicts with the normal exploitation of the work, reproduction is not permitted at all. If it is considered that reproduction does not conflict with the normal exploitation of the work, the next step would be to consider whether it would unreasonably prejudice the legitimate interests of the author and only if such is not the case would it be possible in special cases to introduce a compulsory licence, or to authorise further use without payment'.[148] 'A practical example might be photocopying for various purposes. If it consists of producing very large numbers of copies, it may not be permitted as it conflicts with a normal exploitation of the work. If it implies a rather large number of copies for use in industrial undertakings, it may not unreasonably prejudice the legitimate interests of the author, provided that, according to national legislation, an equitable remuneration is paid. If a great number of copies is made, photocopying may be permitted without further payment, particularly for individual or scientific use'.[149]

---

[138] Bergström Report, para. 203. ie those permitted by Articles 2 bis(2), 9(2), 10(1) and (2), 10 bis(1) and(2).

[139] ie Article 6 bis. See Bergström Report, para. 210. and para. 205.

[140] Article 9(1). This provision was introduced by the Stockholm Revision (although it was implicitly acknowledged since the Convention's conception, that unauthorised reproductions were prohibited).

[141] WIPO Guide to the Berne Convention (1978), 9.2

[142] Article 9(3).

[143] See Stewart, *op. cit.*, 5.38.

[144] Bergström Report, para. 75.

[145] WIPO Guide to the Berne Convention (1978), 9.3.

[146] *Ibid.* 9.4.

[147] Article 9(2).

[148] Bergström Report, para. 85.

[149] *Ibid.* para. 85.

(4) Public Performance Rights in respect of Dramatic, Dramatico-musical and Musical Works

7.049. General principles. Authors of dramatic, dramatico-musical and musical works have the exclusive right to authorise the public performance of their work including such public performance by any means or process.[150] They also have the right to authorize any communication to the public of the performance of their work.[151] Identical rights are attached to translations of their works.[152] The general public must have access to a performance to make it a public performance but a performance before a small invited audience whether in a home or in a hired hall would probably not invoke the Convention.[153]

7.050. Minor reservations. Where national legislation so provides, dramatic, dramatico-musical and musical work may be performed without the author's consent where the Convention generally allows this.[154] But the moral rights of the author must be protected.[155]

(5) Broadcasting and Cable Transmission Rights

7.051. Right to authorise an initial broadcast. Authors of literary and artistic works have the exclusive right to authorise an initial broadcast of their works to the public as well as the communication of those works to the public by any other means of wireless diffusion of signs, sounds or images.[156] The phrase 'signs, sounds or images' indicates that both radio and television broadcasts are envisaged by these terms. As to the applicability of satellites, there is no doubt that direct broadcast satellite transmissions are covered by the term 'broadcast' since such signals are intended for direct reception by the public and Fixed Service Satellite transmissions which also permit this may well qualify.[157]

7.052. Right to authorise a subsequent rebroadcast or communication to the public by cable. Authors are given the exclusive right to authorise the communication to the public by wire or by rebroadcasting of a broadcast work when made

---

[150] Article 11(1)(i). This provision was introduced by the Rome Act (Article 11(1), Rome Act), the words 'by any means or process' being added by the Stockholm Revision.

[151] Article 11(1)(ii). This provision was introduced by the Stockholm Revision. It covers a cable transmission whether just of the sounds (relay of a work by wire to a sound system) or images and sounds (cable television).

[152] Article 11(2). This provision was introduced by the Rome Act (Article 11(2), Brussels Act).

[153] Stewart, *op. cit.*, 5.41.

[154] The Bergström Report states (para. 210) that although it was not made explicit in the Convention, it was the intention that States could enact the usual 'minor reservation' (ie those permitted by Articles 2 bis(2), 9(2), 10(1) and (2), 10 bis(1) and(2)) to the Article 11 rights. The General Report of the Brussels Conference had taken this view.

[155] ie Article 6 bis. See Bergström Report, para. 210. and para. 205.

[156] Article 11 bis(1)(i). The Rome Act introduced a provision governing broadcasting simply giving authors 'the exclusive right of authorising the communication of their works to the public by radiocommunication' (Article 11 bis(1), Rome Act). The Brussels Act extended the general right of authorisation to include a television broadcast by giving authors the exclusive right of authorising 'the radio-diffusion of their works or the communication thereof to the public by any other means of wireless diffusion of signs, sounds or images' (Article 11 bis(1), Brussels Act).

[157] For a discussion of which technology the term broadcast may encompass, see §8.005 et seq. below.

by an organisation other than the original one.[158] This provision was designed to trap the myriad cable operators whose business consists of retransmitting to their subscribers, broadcast signals which they simply tapped into without authority.[159] Thus it probably does not encompass cable retransmissions which are not made for profit eg community antennae in blocks of flats.[160]

7.053. Right to authorise a communication to the public by loudspeaker etc. Authors have the exclusive right of authorising the public communication of a broadcast work when this communication is effected by loudspeaker or any other analogous instrument transmitting signs, sounds or images.[161] This provision envisages, for example, the relaying of a broadcast signal to a television in a hotel, or to a screen in a public auditorium or even a transmission to a screen in an aircraft.

7.054. Exercise of the right to make an initial transmission, retransmission or communicate a broadcast work to the public. It is a matter for legislation in the countries of the Union to determine the conditions under which the above rights may be exercised but these conditions apply only in the countries where they have been prescribed.[162] In other words, the Convention permits Union members to institute systems of compulsory licences but makes it clear that they are restricted to those territories which enact them. And, in no circumstances can any of those rights be prejudicial to the moral rights of an author or his right to obtain equitable remuneration which in the absence of agreement, is to be fixed by a competent authority.[163]

7.055. Fixation of broadcasts. Authorization to make a broadcast in any of the above circumstances does not, unless the contrary is agreed, imply permission to record, by means of instruments recording sounds or images, the work broadcast.[164] However the Convention recognises that nowadays most broadcasts are pre-recorded. Thus contracting States have a discretion to allow the broadcasting organisation to make, by means of its own facilities, an 'ephemeral' recording for the purpose of facilitating its own broadcast.[165] The word 'ephemeral' probably means that such recordings may be kept for a period of up to six months.[166] Domestic legislation may authorise the preservation of these recordings in official archives, on the ground of their exceptional documentary character.[167]

---

[158] Article 11 bis(1)(ii). This provision was introduced by the Brussels Act (Article 11 bis(1)(ii), Brussels Act).

[159] See §8.022 et seq. below.

[160] See §8.042 below.

[161] Article 11 bis(1)(iii). This provision was introduced by the Brussels Act (Article 11 bis(1)(iii), Brussels Act).

[162] Article 11 bis(2). From the enactment of the Rome Act until the Brussels Act, compulsory licences covered only radio-diffusion since this was the only act prohibited by the Rome Act (Article 11 bis(2), Rome Act). The Brussels Act widened the scope of the compulsory licence so that it applied also to television broadcasting, a communication to the public by loudspeaker or analogous instrument and a subsequent communication to the public by cable (Article 11 bis(2), Brussels Act).

[163] Article 11 bis(2).

[164] Article 11 bis(3). This provision was introduced by the Brussels Act (Article 11 bis(3), Brussels Act).

[165] *Ibid.*

[166] Stewart, *op. cit.*, 5.44.

[167] Article 11 bis(3). This provision was introduced by the Brussels Act (Article 11 bis(3), Brussels Act).

(6) Public Recitation Rights

7.056. Authors of literary works have the exclusive right of authorising the recitation to the public of their works by any means or process,[168] and any communication to the public of a recitation of their works.[169] Authors of literary works enjoy these same rights in translations of such works during the full term of their rights in the original works.[170] The fair use principles that apply to the public performance rights[171] probably apply equally to these rights.

(7) Rights of Adaptation, Arrangement and Alteration

7.057. Authors of literary or artistic works are given the exclusive right to authorise adaptations, arrangements and other alterations of their works.[172] The adaptation becomes a new work protected under the Convention even if it is made without the authority of the owner of the original work or if the original work is in the public domain.[173] Those who wish to exploit such a derivative work, need the authority of both the author of the original work as well as the author of the adaptation.

(8) Compulsory Licences in Respect of Musical Works

7.058. General principles. Generally, the Convention preserves the right of authors of musical works to authorise the reproduction,[174] public performance,[175] broadcasting and communication to the public of their works.[176] Although the reproduction right normally encompasses the right to authorise sound recordings, the Convention provides an exception. For each country of the Union may limit the exclusive right granted to both the author of a musical work and to the author of any words, the recording of which together with the musical work has already been authorised by those authors, to authorise the sound recording of that musical work, together with such words, if any.[177] Thus once the authors have given their consent for a recording of their works, the Convention permits the institution of a regime of compulsory licences for the production of further recordings by others (ie phonogram producers).[178] But there are certain conditions. Thus compulsory licences may not be imposed on musical works recorded from an authorised public performance.[179] And compulsory licences introduced in accordance with these

---

[168] Article 11 ter(1)(i). This provision was introduced by the Brussels Act (Article 11 ter, Brussels Act).
[169] Article 11 ter(1)(ii). This provision was introduced by the Stockholm Revision.
[170] Article 11 ter(2). This provision was introduced by the Stockholm Revision.
[171] See §7.050 above.
[172] Article 12. This provision was introduced by the Brussels Act (Article 12, Brussels Act).
[173] Stewart, *op. cit.*, 5.45.
[174] Article 9(1). See Bergström Report, para. 229.
[175] Article 11(1). See Bergström Report, para. 229.
[176] Article 11 bis.
[177] Article 13(1).
[178] The Rome and Brussels Acts had allowed compulsory licences for the adaptation of their works to instruments which could reproduce them mechanically and the performance of those works (Article 13(2), Rome and Brussels Acts). The Stockholm revision referred to 'sound recordings'.
[179] Bergström Report, para. 235.

rules, can apply only in the country in which they have been imposed.[180] Most importantly, they must not, in any circumstances, prejudice the right of these authors to obtain equitable remuneration which, in the absence of an agreement, is to be fixed by a competent authority.[181]

7.059. Non-applicability to cinematographic works. Musical works may not be produced under compulsory licences[182] for incorporation in a cinematographic work.[183]

7.060. Recordings made under the Rome and Brussels Acts. The Convention permitted the reproduction of recordings made in a country of the Union, in accordance with Article 13(3), signed at Rome on 2 June 1928, and at Brussels on 26 June 1948, to be reproduced in that country without the permission of the author of the musical work for a period of two years after that country had become bound by the Paris Act.[184]

7.061. Seizure of recordings. Recordings which are made in accordance with the above rules and imported without permission from the parties concerned into a country where they are treated as infringing recordings may be seized.[185]

(9) Rights in Cinematographic Works

(i) Right of Authors of Original Works

7.062. Cinematographic adaptation, reproduction, distribution, public performance and communication to the public by wire. Authors of literary or artistic works have the exclusive right to authorise the cinematographic adaption and reproduction of their works and the distribution of the works thus adapted or reproduced.[186] They also have the exclusive right of authorising a public performance and the communication to the public, by wire, of their works thus adapted or reproduced.[187] In addition they have the right to authorise a broadcast of their works.[188]

7.063. Adaptation of cinematographic works. Authors of literary and artistic works which have been adapted (ie turned, incorporated etc) into a cinematographic work, retain the exclusive right to authorise the adaptation of that cinematographic work into any other artistic form.[189] This is without prejudice to the right of the author of the cinematographic production to give permission for the adaptation of his work (ie film).[190]

---

[180] Article 13(1). As to whether this provision is compatible with European Community Law, see §1.019 above.
[181] *Ibid.*
[182] In accordance with Article 13, the Convention generally permits, under certain circumstances, the reproduction of musical works under compulsory licence. See §7.058 above.
[183] Article 14(3). This provision was introduced by the Brussels Act (Article 14(4), Brussels Act).
[184] Article 13(2).
[185] Article 13(3). However, see §7.058 fn 180 and §1.019 above.
[186] Article 14(1)(i). This provision was introduced by the Rome Act (Article 14(1), Rome Act). Note that, by contrast, authors covered by the general right of reproduction in Article 9(1) are not explicitly given exclusive rights of distribution.
[187] Article 14(1)(ii). The right of performance was introduced by the Brussels Act (Article 14(1), Brussels Act) and the right of communication to the public by wire by the Stockholm Revision.
[188] This is in accordance with the general terms of Article 11 bis. See 7.051 above.
[189] Article 14(2). This provision was introduced by the Brussels Act (Article 14(3), Brussels Act).
[190] *Ibid.*

(ii) Rights of Owner of Cinematographic Works

7.064. Protection of cinematographic work as a literary or artistic work. Without prejudice to the copyright in any work which may have been adapted or reproduced in the making of a cinematographic work, the cinematographic work is protected as an original work.[191] Thus the owner of copyright in a cinematographic work enjoys all the rights of an author of an original work.[192] He has therefore exclusive rights of adaptation, reproduction, distribution, public performance, communication to the public by wire and broadcasting.

7.065. Adaptation of a cinematographic work. A cinematographic work may not be adapted into any other form without the consent of the author of the cinematographic production[193] (as well as the consent of authors of the literary or artistic works from which it has been derived).[194] The subtitling or dubbing of a film is an example of an 'adaptation'.

(iii) Identity of Owner of Cinematographic Works

7.066. Differences in international legal systems. International law fails to reach a consensus on who is or should be the owner of rights in a cinematographic work. There are two principal regimes: the copyright regime and the droit d'auteur regime. The former grants copyright to the maker of the film from the beginnings of the creation. The 'maker' is usually a corporation which takes the initiative in and responsibility for the making of the film. The droit d'auteur regime cannot accept that authors' rights can originate in a corporation. Thus rights belong in the first instance to those who have brought contributions to the making of the film. Ownership is then transferred to the 'maker' which may be a corporate entity. This process differs according to individual systems. Under one, the so called system of 'presumption of legitimation', the contributors are deemed to have transferred to the maker their rights to exploit the film unless the opposite is proven.

7.067. Basic Convention principle. Taking into account the diversity of legal regimes, the Convention takes a neutral position: the identity of the owners of copyright in a cinematographic work is a matter for legislation to determine in the country where protection is claimed.[195] This principle applies not only where copyright as a whole belongs to one particular person but also where only some of the elements of copyright are assigned.[196]

(iv) 'Droit d'Auteur' Systems

7.068. Presumption of legitimation. Where national legislation includes amongst the owners of copyright in a cinematographic film, authors who have

---

[191] Article 14 bis(1). This provision was introduced by the Rome Act (Article 14(3), Rome Act). The Rome Act stipulated (Article 14(2)) that cinematographic productions could be protected as 'literary and artistic works' only if the author had given the work an original character. If that character was absent, they could enjoy the status solely of photographic works and be granted the limited protection afforded to such works by the Convention. The Brussels Act did away with the distinction, thus treating all cinematographic works as 'literary and artistic' works.
[192] Article 14 bis(1). This provision was introduced by the Stockholm Revision.
[193] This follows from the fact that the film is protected as an original work.
[194] Article 14(2).
[195] Article 14 bis(2)(a). This provision was introduced by the Stockholm Revision. As for the proof of identity of the film maker, see below §7.090.
[196] Bergström Report, para. 317(iii).

brought contributions to the making of the work (ie where the country employs the droit d'auteur system), such authors, if they have undertaken to bring such contributions, may not in the absence of any contrary or special stipulation object to the: reproduction, distribution, public performance, communication to the public by wire, broadcasting or any other communication to the public, or to the subtitling or dubbing of texts, of the work.[197] ie they are deemed to agree to the film being exploited by the 'maker' under a 'presumption of legitimation' imposed by the Convention. The words 'undertaken to bring such contributions' simply means that such persons must have consented to the making of the film.[198] By 'contrary or special stipulation' is meant any restrictive condition which is relevant to the film maker.[199]

7.069. Presumption a mandatory requirement. The 'presumption of legitimation' is a mandatory requirement in droit d'auteur systems where rights are deemed to originate in 'contributors'.[200] Thus 'It is not possible for those countries of the Union which regard authors of contributions as owners of copyright in the cinematographic work to maintain or introduce legislation that does not include a presumption of legitimation . . .'.[201] And it follows, that the presumption only applies in countries which regard contributors as owners of copyright.[202] Hence countries which use the system of 'film copyright' fall outside of its application.

However, it may be noted that cinematographic works from 'film copyright' countries can be affected by the presumption.[203] If, for example, the cinematographic work of a British maker is exported to France, the maker will benefit in France from the presumption of legitimation, provided the necessary conditions are fulfilled.[204]

7.070. Where written undertaking of 'contributors' necessary. The Convention allows Union countries to impose a requirement that the undertaking of the contributors must be in writing. It then sets in place a complex set of rules to determine which countries may demand that written undertaking. Thus, it is a matter for the legislation of the country where the maker of the cinematographic work has his headquarters or habitual residence to determine whether or not the above undertaking must be in a written agreement or written act of the same effect.[205] However, it is a matter for the legislation of the country of the Union where protection is claimed to provide that this undertaking must be in the form of a written agreement or written act of the same effect.[206] The words 'written act of the same effect' means a 'legal instrument in writing defining sufficiently adequately the conditions of the engagement of persons bringing contributions to the making of the cinematographic work. This notion applies, for example, to a collective employment contract or to a general settlement to which those persons have agreed'.[207]

---

[197] Article 14 bis(2)(b). This provision was introduced by the Stockholm Revision.
[198] Stewart, *op. cit.*, 5.51.
[199] Article 14 bis(d).
[200] Bergström Report, para. 321.
[201] *Ibid.*
[202] Bergström Report, para. 317(iv).
[203] *Ibid.*
[204] *Ibid.*
[205] Article 14 bis(2)(c).
[206] In accordance with Article 14 bis(2)(d), countries of the Union so providing are obliged to notify this requirement to the Director-General of WIPO. See Table A of Appendix III.
[207] Bergström Report, para. 322.

In other words, if the country where protection is claimed requires an act in writing, it is irrelevant that the country of the maker does not. For this reason, countries who have this requirement must notify this to the Director General of WIPO who can then communicate it to the other Union countries. There would otherwise be chaos in the enforcement of rights in cinematographic works.

7.071. Contributor's right to remuneration. It should be noted that the 'presumption of legitimation' does not affect the right of the authors (ie contributors) to obtain remuneration for the exploitation of the cinematographic work. Countries of the Union are therefore free to introduce any system of remuneration they wish: for example, to provide for the benefit of the authors a participation in the distribution receipts.[208]

7.072. Right of maker to make changes in the cinematographic work. The right of the maker to make, even without the authorisation of the authors (ie contributors), changes in the cinematographic work (eg editorial changes or the addition of dubbing or subtitling), is solely a matter for national legislation and subject to the interpretation of the agreement between the authors and the maker.[209] However, the moral rights guaranteed by the Convention[210] must be respected.[211] So for example, normally the contributors may not object to the film being subtitled for a foreign audience (where the agreement is silent on this point or there is no provision under national law to regulate this) but a grossly unfaithful translation may well invoke the contributor's moral rights.

7.073. Authors not covered by the 'presumption of legitimation'. Unless national legislation provides to the contrary, the 'presumption of legitimation' does not apply to authors of scenarios, dialogues and musical works created for the making of the cinematographic work.[212] This is because the authors referred to are allowed their own copyright protection under the Convention. Equally, unless otherwise provided, the 'presumption of legitimation' will not apply to the principal director of the film.[213] And where it is the case that the director is not covered, Union countries must notify the Director General of WIPO by means of a written declaration which will then be immediately communicated by him to all the other countries of the Union.[214]

(10) Rights to Proceeds of Sales of Works (the 'droit de suite')

7.074. The author, or after his death the persons or institutions authorised by national legislation, are given the inalienable right to an interest in any sale of original works of art and original manuscripts of writers and composers subsequent to the first transfer by the author of such work.[215] This protection can be claimed in a country of the Union only if the country to which the author belongs so

---

[208] *Ibid.* para. 323.
[209] *Ibid.* para. 324.
[210] In Article 6 bis.
[211] Bergström Report, para. 324.
[212] Article 14 bis(3). This provision was introduced by the Stockholm Revision.
[213] *Ibid.* In some countries the director is treated as an employee of the film company (WIPO Guide to the Berne Convention (1978), 14 bis.14).
[214] Article 14 bis(3). This provision was introduced by the Stockholm Revision.
[215] Article 14 ter(1). This provision was introduced by the Brussels Act (14 bis(1), Brussels Act).

permits and only to the extent permitted by the country where such protection is claimed.[216] ie the Convention institutes a system of 'material reciprocity'. This is deemed necessary because many Union countries do not recognise the 'droit de suite'. The country to which the author belongs is the country of origin of the work and not the country where the author resides.[217] It is a matter for national legislation to determine both the procedure for collection and the amounts of the remuneration.[218]

(11) Moral Rights

7.075. General principles. Independently of the author's economic rights, and even after the transfer of those rights, the author is given the right to claim authorship of his work and to object to any distortion, mutilation or other modification of, or other derogatory action in relation to that work which would be prejudicial to his honour or reputation.[219] Furthermore, after the author's death, these rights must be maintained at least until the expiry of the economic rights, and are to be exercised by the persons or institutions authorised by the legislation of the country where protection is claimed.[220] However, countries which at the moment of accession to the Convention,[221] do not provide for the protection of all these moral rights after the author's death, may provide that some of these rights cease to be maintained after his death.[222]

7.076. Means of redress. The means of redress for safeguarding these moral rights is to be governed by the legislation of the country where protection is claimed.[223]

7. Duration of Rights

7.077. General principles—'national treatment'. The general rule is that the term of protection is governed by the legislation of the country where protection is claimed ie the concept of 'national treatment' applies.[224] This is, however, subject to the following qualification. If the term of protection in that country exceeds the term in the country of origin of the work, then the latter will prevail unless the legislation in the country where protection is claimed provides for the supremacy of its own law.[225] This institutes a form of material reciprocity which is an exception to the general rule of national treatment.

---

[216] *Ibid.*

[217] Stewart, *op. cit.*, 5.53.

[218] Article 14 ter(3). This provision was introduced by the Brussels Act (Article 14 bis(3), Brussels Act).

[219] Article 6 bis(1). The Brussels Act broadened the protection to cover action in relation to the said work (Article 6 bis(1), Brussels Act).

[220] Article 6 bis(2). This provision was introduced by the Brussels Act (Article 6 bis(2), Brussels Act). Prior to the Brussels Act, the Convention had not specified whether or not these rights were to cease on death (see Article 6 bis, Rome Act).

[221] Paris Act.

[222] Article 6 bis(2).

[223] Article 6 bis(3).

[224] Article 7(8).

[225] *Ibid.* The Stockholm Revision introduced the 'supremacy' principle.

7.078. Minimum terms. In default of any period stipulated in the country where protection is claimed, the Convention guarantees a minimum period of protection which is the life of the author and fifty years after his death.[226] Although the term runs from the date of death, the term is deemed to begin on the first of January of the year following the death.[227] The WIPO Guide notes that this minimum period 'seems to provide a fair balance between the interests of authors and the need for society to have free access to the cultural heritage which lasts far longer than those who contributed to it'.[228] The minimum is subject to specific rules which are dealt with below.

7.079. Cinematographic works. In the case of cinematographic works, countries may provide that the term of protection shall expire fifty years after the work has been made available to the public with the consent of the author, or, failing such an event, within fifty years from the making of the work.[229] Although the term runs from the date of the aforementioned events, it is deemed to commence on the first day of January of the year following the date of availability of the work or the making of the work as the case may be.[230] The concept of making a film available to the public includes not only the provision of copies of films for showing to the public but also the showing itself whether in cinemas or on television.[231] It is important to note that the film must be made available with the consent of the author: it is thought wrong that a showing to which the author had never agreed should set the running of the term in motion.[232]

7.080. Anonymous or pseudonymous works. In the case of anonymous or pseudonymous works, the term of protection granted by the Convention expires fifty years after the work has been lawfully made available to the public.[233] Although the term runs from the date on which the work is lawfully made available to the public, it is deemed to commence on the first of January of the year following this act.[234] The Convention uses the term 'lawfully made available' so as to include works of folklore which might be made publicly available by a public authority and whose action is lawful even if the authority does not have the author's consent.[235]

When the pseudonym adopted by the author leaves no doubt as to his identity, the term of protection is the life of the author and fifty years after his death.[236] Furthermore, if the author of an anonymous or pseudonymous work discloses his identity during the fifty year period mentioned above, the term of protection becomes also the life of the author and fifty years after his death.[237] Although the

---

[226] Article 7(1).
[227] Article 7(5). This provision was introduced by the Brussels Act (Article 7(6), Brussels Act).
[228] WIPO Guide to the Berne Convention (1978), 7.4.
[229] Article 7(2). This provision was introduced by the Stockholm Revision. According to the Brussels Act (Article 7(3), Brussels Act), the term of protection was governed by the country where protection was claimed, but could not exceed that in the country of origin of the work.
[230] Article 7(5).
[231] WIPO Guide to the Berne Convention (1978), 7.6.
[232] Ibid.
[233] Article 7(3). A provision governing anonymous works was introduced by the Brussels Act (Article 7(4), Brussels Act) with the term running from the date of publication of the work. The Stockholm Revision introduced the concept of availability of the work.
[234] Article 7(5). This provision was introduced by the Brussels Act (Article 7(6), Brussels Act).
[235] Bergström Report, para. 183.
[236] Article 7(3). This provision was introduced by the Brussels Act (Article 7(4), Brussels Act).
[237] Ibid.

term of protection runs from the date of death, it is, in both cases, deemed to begin on the first of January of the year following death.[238]

The countries of the Union are not required to protect anonymous or pseud-onymous works in respect of which it is reasonable to presume that their author has been dead for fifty years.[239] This allows, for example, the publication of old manuscripts.

7.081. Photographs and works of applied art. It is a matter for legislation in the countries of the Union to determine the term of protection of photographic works and works of applied art in so far as they are protected as artistic works.[240] However, this is subject to the proviso that for those works, the term must last at least until the end of a period of twenty-five years from the making of the work.[241] Although the term runs from that date of making of the work, it is deemed to begin on the first of January of the year following this event.[242]

7.082. Joint authorship. All the preceding provisions apply in the case of a work of joint authorship, provided that the terms measured from the death of the author are to be calculated from the death of the last surviving author.[243] In the case of a work of joint authorship published in a country of the Union, the term is calculated from the death of the last surviving author, regardless of whether or not he is a national of a country of the Union.[244]

7.083. Possibility of longer terms. Countries of the Union are permitted to grant longer terms than those minimum stipulated by the Convention.[245]

7.084. Privilege accorded to Countries bound by the Rome Act of the Berne Convention. Countries which are bound by the Rome Act,[246] and which at the time of signature of the Paris Act,[247] granted shorter terms of protection than the minimum terms introduced by the Paris Act,[248] could maintain those terms when they acceded to the Paris Act.[249]

8. Specific Exceptions to Exclusive Rights—Fair Use

7.085. Reproduction of quotations. The Convention permits the making of quotations from a work which has already been lawfully made available to the public, including quotations from newspaper articles and periodicals in the form of

---

[238] Article 7(5). This provision was introduced by the Brussels Act (Article 7(6), Brussels Act).
[239] Article 7(3). This provision was introduced by the Stockholm Revision.
[240] Article 7(4). In both the Rome Act (Article 7(3), Rome Act) and Brussels Act (Article 7(3), Brussels Act), the term was that prevailing in the country where protection was claimed, subject to the proviso that it could not be longer than that in the country of origin.
[241] Article 7(4). The limitation of the term was introduced by the Stockholm Revision.
[242] Article 7(5). This provision was introduced by the Brussels Act (Article 7(6), Brussels Act).
[243] Article 7 bis.
[244] Bergström Report, para. 199.
[245] Article 7(6). This provision was introduced by the Brussels Act (Article 7(2), Brussels Act).
[246] Act of 1928.
[247] It should be emphasised that the relevant date is signature and not ratification or acceptance of their ratification of or accession to the Paris Act.
[248] ie the terms stipulated in: Article 7(1), Article 7(2), Article 7(3) and Article 7(4).
[249] Article 7(7).

press summaries, provided that this is compatible with fair practice, and the extent does not exceed that justified by the purpose.[250] Where use is made of works in accordance with the above, mention must be made of the source, and of the name of the author if it appears thereon.[251]

7.086. Reproduction of literary or artistic works for the purposes of teaching. It is a matter for legislation in the countries of the Union, and for special agreements existing or to be concluded between them, to permit the utilization, to the extent justified by the purpose, of literary or artistic works by way of illustration in publications, broadcasts or sound or visual recordings for teaching, provided that this utilisation is compatible with fair practice.[252] Teaching encompasses instruction at all levels—in educational institutions and universities, municipal and State schools and private schools. But education outside these institutions, for instance general teaching available to the public, but not included in the aforementioned categories, is excluded.[253] Where use is made of works in accordance with the above, mention must be made of the source, and of the name of the author if it appears thereon.[254]

7.087. Reproduction of articles in newspapers or periodicals. It is a matter for the legislation in the countries of the Union to permit the reproduction by the press, the broadcasting or the communication to the public by wire, of articles published in newspapers or periodicals on current economic, political or religious topics, and of broadcast works of the same character, but only in cases where the reproduction, broadcasting or such public communication is not expressly reserved by the owner of the rights.[255] Nevertheless, the source must always be clearly indicated: the legal consequences of a breach of this obligation is to be determined by the legislation in the country where protection is claimed.[256]

7.088. Reproduction of literary or artistic works seen or heard in the course of an event. It is a matter for the legislation in the countries of the Union to determine conditions under which literary or artistic works seen or heard in the course of an event may for the purpose of reporting current events be reproduced and made available to the public by means of photography, cinematography, broadcasting or communication to the public by wire.[257]

9. Enforcing Protected Rights

(1) Proof of Ownership

7.089. General principles. The Convention provides that in order that the author of literary or artistic work protected by the Convention shall, in the absence

---

[250] Article 10(1). The Brussels Act introduced a provision entitling the use of quotations from newspaper articles and periodicals (Article 10(1), Brussels Act). The Stockholm Revision extended the right to quote from all works.

[251] Article 10(3). This provision was introduced by the Brussels Act (Article 10(3), Brussels Act).

[252] Article 10(2). Prior to the Stockholm Revision, excerpts could be included solely in publications.

[253] Bergström Report, para. 97.

[254] Article 10(3).

[255] Article 10 bis(1). Prior to the Stockholm Revision, the provision did not encompass exploitation by broadcasting or communication to the public. Neither did it include the exploitation of a broadcast work.

[256] *Ibid.*

[257] Article 10 bis(2). The Brussels Act introduced this provision in respect of reporting 'by means of photography or cinematography or by radio-diffusion' (Article 10 bis, Brussels Act). The Stockholm Revision redefined it to include 'broadcasting or communication to the public by wire'.

of any proof to the contrary, be regarded as such, and consequently entitled to institute infringement proceedings in the countries of the Union, it is sufficient for his name to appear on the work in the usual manner.[258] This is applicable even if this name is a pseudonym, provided that the pseudonym adopted by the author leaves no doubt as to his identity.[259]

7.090. Cinematographic works. The person or body corporate whose name appears on a cinematographic work in the usual manner is, in the absence of proof to the contrary, to be presumed to be the maker of that work.[260]

7.091. Anonymous and pseudonymous works. In the case of anonymous works, and pseudonymous works where there is doubt as to the author's identity, the publisher whose name appears on the work is, in the absence of proof to the contrary, to be deemed to represent the author, and in this capacity he is entitled to protect and enforce the author's rights.[261] This provision ceases to apply when the author reveals his identity and establishes his claim to authorship of the work.[262]

7.092. Unpublished works by unknown authors. In the case of unpublished works where the identity of the author is unknown, but where there is every ground to presume that he is a national of the Union, it is a matter for legislation in that country to designate the competent authority which shall represent the author and shall be entitled to protect and enforce his rights in the countries of the Union.[263] Countries of the Union which make such a designation must notify the Director-General by means of a written declaration giving full information concerning the authority thus designated. The Director-General is immediately to communicate this declaration to the other countries.[264] Although not explicit, it is clear that this provision will be mainly applicable to works generally described as 'folklore'.[265]

(2) Seizure of Infringing Copies

7.093. Infringing copies of a work are liable to be seized in any country of the Union where the work enjoys legal protection.[266] This also applies to reproductions coming from a country where the work is not protected or has ceased to be protected.[267] Seizure is to take place in accordance with the legislation of each country of the Union.[268]

---

[258] Article 15(1).
[259] *Ibid.* The provision was introduced by the Brussels Act (Article 15(1), Brussels Act).
[260] Article 15(2). This provision was introduced by the Stockholm Revision.
[261] Article 15(3). Prior to the Stockholm Revision the publisher was deemed to represent the pseudoanonymous author even where there might have been no doubt as to his identity.
[262] *Ibid.* This provision was introduced by the Brussels Act (Article 15(2), Brussels Act).
[263] Article 15(4)(a). This provision was introduced by the Stockholm Revision.
[264] Article 15(4)(b). This provision was introduced by the Stockholm Revision. See Table A of Appendix III.
[265] Bergström Report, para. 252.
[266] Article 16(1).
[267] Article 16(2).
[268] Article 16(3).

10. General Provisions

7.094. Commencement and parties. The Convention was signed at Berne on 9 September 1886 and came into force on 5 December 1887. On 4 May 1896, an addition was made (Additional Act of Paris) which came into force on 9 December 1897. On 13 November 1908, the Convention was revised (the Berlin Act) and the revision came into force on 9 September 1910. That was followed, on 20 March 1914, by an additional Protocol (Additional Protocol of Berne) which took effect on 20 April 1915. On 2 June 1928 the Convention was once again revised (Rome Act) and that revision entered into force on 1 August 1931. The following revision was made on 26 June 1948 (Brussels Act) and came into force on 1 August 1951. The Convention was revised on 14 July 1967 (Stockholm Revision) but the substantive amendments did not take effect until the last revision on 24 July 1971 (Paris Act). The current version is that of the Paris Act of July 24, 1971 as amended on October 2, 1979. It entered into force on 10 October 1974 and it is to remain in force indefinitely.[269]

The Paris Act was open for ratification by any Union country which had signed it and is currently open for accession by any Union country.[270] Any country outside of the Union may accede to the Convention (Paris Act) hence becoming a member of the Union.[271] Parties to the Union undertakes to adopt, in accordance with its constitution, measures necessary to comply with the convention,[272] and they must be in a position to give effect to its provisions under domestic law when bound by the Convention.[273] Any country may denounce the Convention,[274] however, it may not be exercised before the expiration of five years from the date upon which it becomes a member of the Union.[275]

7.095. Reservations. Generally, ratification or accession automatically entails acceptance of all the provisions and admission to all the advantages of the Convention.[276] This is subject to certain provisos. The first is that there are reservations which may be specifically declared.[277] Also, any Union country, may, upon ratification or accession retain the benefit of any reservations it previously formulated.[278] Any country may withdraw a reservation at any time.[279]

7.096. Internal regulation (censorship and abuses of monopoly). The provisions of the Convention do not in any way affect the right of the Government of each country of the Union to permit, to control, or to prohibit, by legislation or regulation, the circulation, presentation, or exhibition of any work or production in regard to which the competent authority may find it necessary to exercise that right.[280] This provision refers mainly to censorship and to the prevention of abuses

---

[269] Article 35(1). See Table A of Appendix III.
[270] Article 28(1)(a).
[271] Article 29(1).
[272] Article 36(1).
[273] Article 36(2).
[274] Article 35(2).
[275] Article 35(4).
[276] Article 30(1).
[277] ie Article 28(1)(b), Article 33(2) and the Appendix.
[278] Article 30(2)(a). A declaration has to be made to that effect at the time of ratification or accession. See Table A of Appendix III.
[279] Article 30(2)(c). Notification is to be addressed to the Director General.
[280] Article 17.

of monopoly. As far as censorship is concerned, it is generally agreed that the censor has the power to control a work which it is intended to make available to the public with the consent of the author, and on the basis of that control, either to 'permit' or 'prohibit' dissemination of the work.[281] However, 'According to the fundamental principles of the Berne Union, countries of the Union should not be permitted to introduce any kind of compulsory licence on the basis of Article 17. In no case where the consent of the author was necessary for the dissemination of the work, according to the rules of the Convention, should it be possible for countries to permit dissemination without the consent of the author'.[282]

Since abuses of monopoly are considered to be issues of public policy, they are always a matter for domestic legislation and countries of the Union are therefore able to take all necessary measures to prevent such abuses.[283]

7.097. Obligation to protect. The Convention states that 'The works mentioned in this Article shall enjoy protection in all countries of the Union'.[284] The effect of this wording is to confer rights directly on individuals in Union countries which consider Conventions to be part of their law upon ratification. Individuals within those countries may then themselves bring actions based on the Convention.[285] However, countries that follow the British legal tradition where legislation must be enacted to 'enable' a Convention, are unaffected by this provision.

7.098. Relationship of convention to internal law and international agreements. The Convention is without prejudice to national legislation which provides wider protection than the Convention confers.[286] Moreover, the countries of the Union have reserved the right to enter into special agreements amongst themselves in so far as such agreements grant to authors more extensive rights or embody other provisions not contrary to the Convention.[287] The provisions of existing agreements which satisfy these conditions continue in effect.[288]

7.099. Settlement of disputes. Any dispute between two or more countries of the Union concerning the interpretation or application of the Convention, not settled by negotiation, may, by any one of the countries concerned, be brought before the International Court of Justice unless the countries concerned agree on some other method of settlement.[289] A country may at the date of accession declare that it does not consider itself bound by this rule, in which case, it cannot be invoked by another country.[290]

7.100. Extension to territories. Any country may at any time declare that the Convention applies to all or part of those territories, designated in the declaration, for whose international relations it is responsible.[291]

---

[281] Bergström Report, para. 262.
[282] *Ibid.*
[283] *Ibid.* para. 263.
[284] Article 2(6). This provision was introduced by the Brussels Act (Article 2(4), Brussels Act).
[285] WIPO Guide to the Berne Convention (1978), 2.20.
[286] Article 19.
[287] Article 20.
[288] *Ibid.*
[289] Article 33(1).
[290] Article 33(2). See Table A in Appendix III.
[291] Article 31(1). In accordance with Article 31(2), any country which has made such a declaration may declare at any time that the Convention ceases to be applicable to those territories.

7.101. Compulsory licences in developing countries. The Convention contains special provisions which apply to developing countries.[292] This gives permission for the institution of compulsory licences provided that certain conditions are fulfilled.[293]

III. THE UNIVERSAL COPYRIGHT CONVENTION

1. Introduction

7.102. History. Throughout the first half of the twentieth century, the Berne Convention for the Protection of Literary and Artistic Works had spearheaded the quest for an international regime of protection for authors'. Yet despite having been in existence since 1886, it had not become 'universal', even by 1950. This was due in part to its origin. For Berne was a child of the 'droit d'auteur' tradition. That tradition was inspired by the French Revolution and according to its philosophy, the 'individual' was the source of all creativity and the sole focus of protection.[294] The mere act of creating a work was sufficient to justify a property right in it. And to burden the author with any formal or procedural requirements would be in conflict with the doctrine.[295] It followed that the term of protection was determined by reference to the author's life.

These principles were— or at least were perceived to be—in stark contrast to the philosophy of the 'common law' copyright system which the English speaking nations[296] had evolved to protect authors' rights and which had been embraced by many latin American countries. 'Copyright' was designed to stimulate artistic creation by rewarding an author for his creative endeavour.[297] It made protection dependent upon the fulfilment of certain formalities and it measured the term of protection from the date of first publication of the work.[298]

The United Nations Educational, Scientific and Cultural Organisation— UNESCO for short—took on the challenge of uniting the two distinct 'worlds' of authors' rights with a new 'universal' convention. It was persuaded that a universal 'copyright' system would bring about 'a wider dissemination of works of the human mind and increase international understanding'.[299] However, in order to achieve its ambition, UNESCO had to reconcile the seeming incompatibilities between the two systems.[300] Its proposed solution was twofold. First, it would incorporate a

---

[292] Article 21(1). See Appendix to the Berne Convention. In accordance with Article 21(2), subject to the possibility that a State may exclude the Appendix, it forms an integral part of the Paris Act.

[293] See Appendix, Articles II to VI.

[294] A notable disadvantage of the droit d'auteur system was that it could not recognise a corporation, such as a broadcasting organisation, as an original owner of rights. See §§7.155 and 7.164 below.

[295] See Article 5(2) of the Berne Convention for the Protection of Literary and Artistic Works, see §7.030 above.

[296] ie the United States and England.

[297] A Bogsch, *The Law of Copyright under the Universal Convention* (3rd Rev Edn, 1972), on Preamble.

[298] It found no difficulty in conferring rights upon corporations.

[299] Universal Copyright Convention, Preamble.

[300] Bogsch has doubted that there is any contradiction between the copyright and droit d'auteur systems. 'How could one encourage creation without protecting the individual who creates? And since all authors create for the public, their protection necessarily is beneficial to the development of the arts.' Bogsch, *op. cit.*, on Preamble.

limited formality requirement in the new convention: protection depending solely upon their being an imprint of the symbol '©' accompanied by the name of the copyright proprietor and the year of first publication.[301] Secondly, contracting states would be permitted to maintain their own term for the works of their nationals where based upon the date of publication. But they would be required to grant to a foreign author a minimum term to endure throughout that author's life and for twenty five years after his death.

But before UNESCO could realise its wish it had to overcome one other hurdle. Berne's limited geographical sweep was due, in part, to the comprehensiveness of its regime which had proved too demanding for many third world countries.[302] UNESCO thus set out to entice States who would not accede to Berne because of its guarantee of certain minimum rights. But support from the Berne Union, would be forthcoming only if it could be reassured that its members would not defect to the new, less demanding convention. A solution to that particular problem was eventually found and it is called the 'Berne safeguard clause': a mechanism which ensures the survival and supremacy of the Berne Convention. Essentially, it provides that in a case where two countries are Contracting States of both the Berne and Universal Conventions, works whose origin is in a country of the Berne Union, will be governed exclusively by the Berne Convention. The Berne safeguard clause also prevents a country other than a developing country[303] denouncing the Berne Convention and then acceding to the Universal Convention.

Because of the Berne safeguard clause, relationships among Member States of the European Community are governed by the Berne Convention. Nevertheless, their relations with third countries may by determined by the Universal Convention.

7.103. Scope of the Convention. The Convention enacts protection for authors and other copyright proprietors in their literary, scientific and artistic works.[304] It does not, therefore, give protection to owners of neighbouring rights.

7.104. Regime of Protection. The regime of protection consists of two elements. The first element is the guarantee that one Contracting State will provide to authors of another Contracting State, the same protection which the former grants to its own nationals ie it must confer 'national treatment'.[305] This right is then qualified by a set of very limited specific rights and obligations.[306] The Convention places the onus on Contracting States to enact legislation protecting the rights it sets out and thus it does not, merely by accession, confer these rights upon individuals.[307]

7.105. Interpretation of the Convention. The report of the Rapporteur General of the 1952 conference, Sir John Blake (the 'Blake Report')[308] and the report of the

---

301 Article III.I.
302 This was to be a source of crises when the Berne Convention was revised in 1967.
303 which, in order to benefit from the generous compulsory licensing system incorporated in the Universal Convention defects to that Convention.
304 Article I.
305 Article II.I. and Article II.2.
306 *Ibid.*
307 Stewart, *op. cit.*, 6.20.
308 which brought the Convention into being.

Rapporteur General of the 1971 conference, namely AL Kaminstein (the 'Kaminstein Report'),[309] may both be used as interpretive guides to the Convention. Reference is made to them below.

2. Works Protected

7.106. General principles. In acceding to the Convention, 'Each Contracting State undertakes to provide for the adequate and effective protection of the rights of authors and other copyright proprietors in literary, scientific and artistic works, including writings, musical, dramatic and cinematographic works, and paintings, engravings and sculpture'.[310] It has been suggested that the phrase 'literary, scientific and artistic works', should be considered together, as an expression meaning 'works susceptible to copyright protection'.[311]

The seven listed categories are not limitive but merely examples and thus 'literary, scientific and artistic works' can include other categories recognised by the customs of civilised countries. However, the seven categories should be protected regardless of the custom in the Contracting States.[312]

The word 'scientific' is employed so as to cover such things as logarithm tables and works on nuclear physics.[313] The term 'writing' has a non-technical sense meaning 'a work of the human intellect expressed in language and fixed by means of conventional signs susceptible of being read', and thus its form, length, genre and packaging are irrelevant.[314] However, 'writing' does not include purely oral works even if their literary genre frequently takes the form of writing. Thus addresses, sermons, lectures and speeches are not writings if not written down before or after their oral delivery.[315] Cinematographic works include[316] silent or sound pictures irrespective of their destination,[317] the person of their producers,[318] their genre,[319] length and mode of realization[320] or technical process employed.[321] Paintings probably include drawings and 'engravings' includes lithographs.[322] Sculpture are three dimensional works of art produced by, for examples, carving, cutting, hewing wood and stone and modelling plaster.[323] The Convention does not necessarily require the protection of photographic works and works of applied art.[324]

---

[309] which added the economic rights.
[310] Article I.
[311] Bogsch, *op. cit.*, on Article 1 (point 4).
[312] *Ibid.*
[313] Blake Report on Article I.
[314] Bogsch, *op. cit.* on Article 1 (point 4). However, some writing on account of their contents may be excluded such as official documents emanating from the legislative, administrative and judicial public authorities.
[315] *Ibid.*
[316] *Ibid*, on Article 1 (point 7).
[317] theatrical exhibition, television broadcasting or exhibition for a restricted group of spectators.
[318] ie commercial producers, amateurs or broadcasting organisations.
[319] ie film dramas, documentaries, newsreels.
[320] ie cartoons are included.
[321] ie pictures on transparent films or electronic tapes.
[322] Bogsch, *op. cit.*, Article 1 (point 8).
[323] *Ibid*, on Article 1 (point 9).
[324] *Ibid*, on Article 1 (point 10).

7.107. Works published by international agencies. The protection afforded by the Convention may apply[325] to works published for the first time by the United Nations, the Specialised Agencies in relationship therewith, or by the Organisation of American States,[326] as well as to the unpublished works of those bodies.[327]

3. Protection Afforded to Published Works

(1) Guarantee of 'National Treatment'

7.108. Published works of nationals of another Contracting State. The Convention stipulates that a Contracting State must accord to the published works of nationals of another Contracting State, the equivalent protection it confers on its own nationals for the works that they have first published in its territory ie it must confer 'national treatment'.[328]

7.109. Works first published in another Contracting State. Furthermore, Contracting States must grant 'national treatment' to works which have been first published in another Contracting State, whether or not by a national of that State.[329] In order to determine whether a country qualifies as a country of 'first publication', all publications made in any country of the world must be considered.[330] Simultaneous publication on the same day in both a non-Contracting State and Contracting State would probably qualify the work for protection. However, a 'simultaneous' publication in a Contracting State between the second and thirtieth day from publication in a non-Contracting State would not qualify the work.[331]

(2) Meaning of the Term 'Publication'

7.110. General principles. Publication is defined as 'the reproduction in tangible form and the general distribution to the public of copies of a work from which it can be read or otherwise visually perceived'.[332] The public performance or the broadcasting of a work do not qualify because a performance is not a reproduction.[333] The word 'copies' means duplicates and not imitations or adaptations of a work.[334]

Technically, a work is not 'published' until copies (note that this is in the plural) are distributed to the general public. The meaning of 'distribution' is unclear but

---

[325] to Contracting States who are parties to Protocol 2. In accordance with 2.2(a) of the Protocol, the Protocol was subject to ratification and acceptance by signatory States and is generally open to accession.

[326] Protocol 2.I(a).

[327] Protocol 2.I(b).

[328] Article II.I. It is unsure whether the Convention obligates a Contracting States to protect a work first published on its own territory if the author of the work is a national of another Contracting State (see Bogsch, *op. cit.*, on Article II (point 6)).

[329] *Ibid.* It is uncertain whether the Convention obliges a country to protect a work of its own national if the work was first published in any other Contracting State (see *ibid.* on Article II (point 5)).

[330] *Ibid*, on Article II (point 14) ie the consideration is not limited to Contracting States.

[331] *Ibid*, on Article II (point 14). cf the concept of 'simultaneous publication' in the Berne Convention for the Protection of Literary and Artistic Works, see §7.034 above.

[332] Article VI.

[333] A Bogsch, *op. cit.*, on Article VI (point 9).

[334] *Ibid*, on Article VI (point 3).

probably means making the work available to the public gratuitously or non-gratuitously (although lending or leasing may not qualify).[335] The phrase 'the general public' is similarly incapable of precise definition and much will turn on the facts. But, a distribution to a circle of friends would probably not be covered by those words.[336] It has been suggested that cinematographic works are protected regardless of whether they are shown in a cinema or on television or on a screen to a narrower group of spectators.[337]

7.111. Whether particular media qualify. Phonogram recordings are excluded from the definition of published works on two counts. First, phonogram recordings are not 'copies' of a work because they merely embody the interpretation of a work.[338] Secondly they or any other exclusively aural medium of a literary, dramatic or musical work cannot 'be read or otherwise visually perceived'.[339] Cinematographic media, however, come within the definition of a copy because, a film enjoys the status of an individual work. But the soundtrack on a film if separately reproduced is outside the ambit of the definition of a copy of a work: it is treated in the same way as a phonogram recording.[340]

(3) Formalities (for Published Works)

7.112. Introduction. The Convention sets out a set of rules which are deemed to satisfy any formality requirements or which dictate that no formality rules may be imposed by a Contracting State as a prerequisite for the existence of copyright protection.

7.113. General principles. Any Contracting State which, under its domestic law, requires as a condition of the existence of copyright protection, compliance with formalities such as deposit, registration, notice, notarial certificates, payment of fees or manufacture or publication in that Contracting State, are to regard these requirements as satisfied with respect to all works protected in accordance with the Convention and first published outside its territory, and the author of which is not one of its nationals, if from the time of the first publication all the copies of the work published with the authority of the author or other copyright proprietor bear the symbol © accompanied by the name of the copyright proprietor and the year of first publication placed in such manner and location as to give reasonable notice of claim of copyright.[341] The constituent conditions are strictly construed and any slight deviation would probably nullify the copyright protection. However, if a contracting State grants protection for more than one term of copyright and the first term is for a period longer than one of the minimum periods prescribed by the Convention, such a State is not required to comply with the aforementioned provisions in respect of the second or any subsequent term of copyright.[342]

---

[335] *Ibid*, on Article VI (point 11).
[336] Stewart, *op. cit.* 6.33.
[337] *Ibid*. 6.04.
[338] Bogsch, *op. cit.*, on Article VI (point 6).
[339] *Ibid*, on Article VI (point 10).
[340] *Ibid*, on Article VI (point 7).
[341] Article III.I.
[342] Article III.5.

7.114. Identity of the 'copyright proprietor' and form of notice. The identity of the copyright proprietor varies according to whether the work is published in a country which operates a divisible or an indivisible copyright regime. Thus in cases where copyright in a single work can be owned by different persons for different forms of exploitation, the name of the part owner is to be specified.[343] On the other hand, in those systems in which copyright can be owned only by one person, other persons (ie known as licensees) having the right to exploit the work in different forms but having no ownership of copyright, then the licensor's name should always be specified.[344] The name can be that of a natural person or a legal entity (including a trade name), but pseudonyms are probably excluded.[345] The form of the name (which may be a corporate name) should be that prevailing in the country where the work is published or the language in which the work appears but the symbol must always be a 'c' of the Latin alphabet.[346] The year can be indicated in any form (words, figures, Roman numerals) having a connection with the work or the nationality of the copyright proprietor at the place of first publication.[347] Where new editions contain new copyrightable matter, then the date of that new edition as well as the date of earlier publications should be included.[348]

7.115. Location of the copyright notice. To satisfy the formality requirements, the copyright notice should be 'located so as to give reasonable notice of claim of copyright'. The Intergovernmental Copyright Committee has stated how the requirement would be satisfied in respect of certain works as follows:[349]

> **Books or pamphlets:** on the title page or the page immediately following, or at the end of the book or pamphlet, or in the case of a single sheet, on either of the sides;
>
> **Printed Music:** on the title page or first page of music, or at the end of the printed music;
>
> **Newspapers, magazines or other periodicals:** under the main title or the 'masthead';
>
> **Maps, prints or photographs:** on their face side, either on the actual map or picture (but somewhere near the title or the margin) or on the margin;
>
> **Independent parts of a whole:** (if a separate copyright is claimed in the independent parts), under the title of the independent part;
>
> **Motion pictures:** on the frames which carry its title (whether appearing at the beginning or the end) or in the credits.

7.116. Maintenance of procedural formalities. The aforementioned provisions do not preclude any Contracting State from providing that a person seeking judicial relief, must, in bringing the action, comply with procedural requirements, such as that the complainant must appear through domestic counsel or that the complainant must deposit with the court or an administrative office, or both, a copy of the work involved in the litigation.[350] However, a failure to comply with such

---

[343] ie the name of the owner of the rights in the published copies in issue.

[344] Bogsch, *op. cit.*, on Article III (point 6).

[345] *Ibid.*

[346] *Ibid.*

[347] *Ibid,* on Article III (point 7). See Bogsch generally for a discussion of the problems of ante- and post-dated notices.

[348] *Ibid.* (See Bogsch generally for a discussion of the problems of ante- and post-dated notices).

[349] Advisory opinion of the Intergovernmental Committee of the Convention given in 1957, cited by *Ibid,* on Article III (point 9).

[350] Article III.3.

requirements does not affect the validity of the copyright.[351] Furthermore such a requirement cannot be imposed upon a national of another Contracting Sate if such a requirement is not imposed on nationals of the State in which protection is claimed ie the principle of 'national treatment' must always prevail.[352]

7.117. Preservation of domestic law. Any Contracting State may require different formalities or make other conditions for the acquisition and enjoyment of copyright in respect of works first published in its territory or the works of its nationals wherever these may be published.[353]

4. Protection Afforded to Unpublished Works

7.118. Obligation to protect unpublished works. In each Contracting State there must be legal means of protecting without formalities the unpublished works of a national of another Contracting State.[354] This is required because of the limited definition of 'publication'. Thus, for example, sales of a work in recorded form (phonograms) do not amount to publication so that the music and the text of a song although recorded and the records sold in large quantities, can be 'unpublished'.[355]

7.119. Guarantee of 'national treatment'. A Contracting State must grant to the unpublished works of a national of another Contracting State, the equivalent protection it confers on unpublished works of its own nationals ie it must confer 'national treatment'.[356]

5. Meaning of the Term 'national'

7.120. General principles. The concept of a 'national' is central to the rights granted by the Convention.[357] The term is not defined but can probably apply to corporate bodies, legal entities, government bodies and other artificial persons as well as individual citizens.[358] Ultimately, it is a matter for each Contracting State to interpret the word 'nationals' according to its own rule of law; the Convention is not to be regarded as imposing on any Contracting State the obligation of recognising for copyright purposes legal and moral persons as well as physical persons, but only requiring that a State should apply the same interpretation to foreign nationals as to its own nationals; for example, a State protecting the works of its own incorporated bodies should protect also the works of such bodies of other Contracting States.[359] In fact, the use of the term 'other copyright proprietors'[360] implies that copyright may belong to corporate proprietors. But to benefit from

---

[351] *Ibid.*
[352] *Ibid.*
[353] Article III.2.
[354] Article III.4.
[355] Stewart, *op. cit.*, 6.14.
[356] Article II.2.
[357] See Article II.I. and Article II.2.
[358] Blake Report on Article II.
[359] Kaminstein Report, para. 52, affirming the Blake Report.
[360] ie Article I states that 'Each Contracting State undertakes to provide for the adequate and effective protection of the rights of authors and other copyright proprietors.'

protection, the national must be the author not only because of his close connection with the work but because the recognition of the nationality of other persons would lead to arbitrary results and abuses. It would, for example, allow licensee authors of a non-Contracting State to obtain protection by assigning their rights to a national of a Contracting State.[361] The use of the term 'other copyright proprietors' also suggests that those persons who acquire the rights of the author are to be in the same position of the author. Thus protection probably endures for an author's successors in title such as assignees, heirs or legatees.[362] If the nationality of an author changes, the relevant nationality is probably as follows: in the case of unpublished works, the nationality he had at the date of creation of the work and in the case of published works, the nationality at the date of first publication.[363]

7.121. Domiciled persons and refugees. For the purposes of the Convention, a Contracting State may give national status to a person domiciled there.[364] Furthermore, where agreed to by Contracting States, stateless persons and refugees who have their habitual residence in a Contracting may also be assimilated to the nationals of that State.[365] A 'stateless person' is a person who is not a citizen, subject or national of any country for whatever reason.[366] The meaning of the word 'refugees' is not capable of precise definition, but the interpretations given to the term in various national instruments, including the Geneva Convention of 28 July 1951, should be taken into account.[367]

6. Minimum Rights Guaranteed (1971 Revision)

7.122. Economic rights (reproduction, public performance, broadcasting, translation rights etc). The equivalent protection ('national treatment') principle annunciated above[368] is subject to the specific rights enshrined in the Convention. Thus, regardless of national rules, Contracting States must guarantee the basic right of securing the author's economic interests.[369] These include the exclusive right of an author to authorise the reproduction by any means, public performance and broadcasting of a work.[370] These rights apply to works in their original form or in any form recognisably derived from the original.[371] Thus the author has the exclusive right to authorise the reproduction, performance or broadcasting of any work recognisably derived from the original.[372] The author's economic rights also includes the exclusive right of the author to make, publish and authorise the

---

[361] Bogsch, *op. cit.*, on Article II (point 19).
[362] *Ibid*, on Article I (point 3).
[363] *Ibid*, on Article II (point 19). See Bogsch generally for a discussion of the various arguments.
[364] Article II.3.
[365] Protocol I.I. In accordance with Protocol I.2(a), Protocol I was subject to ratification or acceptance by signatory States and is open to accession. In accordance with Protocol I.2(a), on the entry into force of the Protocol in respect of a State not a party to Protocol I annexed to the 1952 Convention, the latter Protocol is deemed to enter into force in respect of such a State.
[366] Bogsch, *op. cit.*, on Protocol I (point 2).
[367] Kaminstein Report, para. 141.
[368] See §§7.108 and 7.109 above.
[369] Article IV bis.I.
[370] *Ibid.* As to the meaning of the term 'broadcast', see §8.002 et seq. below.
[371] *Ibid.*
[372] Kaminstein Report, para. 41.

making and publication of translations of works protected under the Convention.[373] This list is non-exhaustive.[374]

7.123. Exceptions to economic rights (fair use). Any Contracting State may, by its domestic legislation, make exceptions to the exclusive economic rights of authors conferred by the Convention, provided that these exceptions do not conflict with the spirit and provisions of the Convention.[375] Contracting States must thus undertake a form of balancing exercise in making any exceptions. This is because the 'spirit' of the Convention comprehends the convictions contained in the Universal Declaration of Human Rights[376] namely that everyone has a right 'freely to participate in the cultural life of the Community' and that everyone equally has a right 'to the protection of the moral and material interests resulting from any scientific, literary or artistic production of which he is the author'.[377] Therefore, any State whose legislation provides exceptions to the economic rights, must nevertheless accord a reasonable degree of effective protection to each of the rights to which exception has been made.[378] Thus Contracting States are not entitled to withhold entirely all exclusive rights of reproduction, performance and broadcasting of a work.[379] And any exception to those rights must be applied on a logical basis and not arbitrarily, the protection offered being effectively enforced by the laws of the Contracting State.[380] In particular, developed countries, eg those in the West, are not permitted to institute the more generous statutory licensing system[381] that the Convention confers on developing Contracting States.[382] For this would conflict with the 'provisions of the Convention'.[383]

7.124. Moral rights. No Contracting State is obliged to grant moral rights to an author under the Convention, although it is hoped that they will do so.[384]

7. Grant of Compulsory Licences for Translations of Works

(1) Rights of Author

7.125. To make and publish translations. Generally, the author has the exclusive right to make, publish and authorise the making and publication of translations of works protected under the Convention.[385] 'Publication' is defined by the Convention as 'the reproduction in tangible form and the general distribution to the public

---

[373] Article 5.1.
[374] Kaminstein Report, para. 43.
[375] Article IV bis.2.
[376] paras. 1 and 2.
[377] Kaminstein Report, para. 46.1.
[378] Article IV bis.2.
[379] Kaminstein Report, para. 46.4.
[380] *Ibid.*
[381] Under Article V bis, V ter and V quater.
[382] Kaminstein Report, para. 46.2. This is cited as a 'general system' in the Report, referring 'either to a system applying to a specific type of work with respect to all forms of uses, or to a system applying to all types of works with respect to a particular form of use'.
[383] Kaminstein Report, para. 46.3.
[384] *Ibid*, para. 43.
[385] Article V.1.

of copies of a work from which it can be read or otherwise visually perceived'.[386]
Thus the recording of a translation, or the public performance of a translation are
not prohibited in accordance with the author's aforementioned right. Nevertheless,
these acts are prohibited in Contracting States which are parties to the 1971
Revision of the Convention.[387]

(2) Right of Third Party to Receive Compulsory Licence

7.126. Introduction. Notwithstanding the author's general right to authorise
translations of his work, the Convention institutes two systems of compulsory
licensing for the making of translations of a published work. One can be exploited
by both developed and developing countries[388] but the other, which is more
generous, may be exploited only by developing countries.[389] Only the former is
dealt with below.

7.127. Qualifying seven year rule. If, after the expiration of a period of seven
years from the date of the first publication of a writing, a translation of such writing
has not been published in a language in general use[390] in a Contracting State, by the
owner of the right of translation or with his authorization, any national[391] of such
a Contracting State may obtain a non-exclusive licence[392] from the competent
authority thereof to translate the work into that language and publish the work so
translated.[393] It has been suggested that writing means 'any work the form of
expression of which is language, susceptible of translation into another language, if
it exists in a written form'. Thus dramatic works, cinematographic scripts and also
the words of songs and libretti of dramatico-musical works, are probably 'writings'
provided that they exist in written form and may be subject to a compulsory
licence.[394] Contracting States are to determine themselves which are the national
languages for this purpose and can declare that a regional language qualifies.[395] The
concept of a 'national' language is not the same as that of an 'official' language and
encompasses any language which is the mother tongue of a minority in a
region.[396]

7.128. Permitted form of translation. The licence will cover only the 'publication' of writings. 'Publication' is generally defined by the Convention as 'the
reproduction in tangible form and the general distribution to the public of copies
of a work from which it can be read or otherwise visually perceived'. This means,
as Bogsch notes that, neither the recording, public performance nor broadcasting of

---

[386] Article VI.
[387] In accordance with Article IV bis.I. See §7.122 et seq. above.
[388] Article V.
[389] Articles V bis, V ter, V quater. See §7.154 below.
[390] A Contracting State may designate which of its languages are 'in general use' and this can
include a regional language (see Blake Report on Article V).
[391] Which includes legal entities, government bodies, corporate bodies and other artificial persons
(see Kaminstein Report, para. 52.).
[392] and personal licence (see Blake Report on Article V).
[393] Article V.2(a).
[394] Bogsch, *op. cit.*, on Article V (point 3).
[395] Blake Report on Article V.
[396] Indeed, official languages are not necessarily covered by the term at all (see Bogsch, *op. cit.* on
Article V (point 4)).

a work qualify as a 'publication' and therefore recordings, public performances and broadcasts and any other use which does not amount to a 'publication' are outside the scope of these provisions and a compulsory licence may not be issued in respect of them.[397]

7.129. Conditions to be satisfied. A 'national'[398] seeking a compulsory licence must, in accordance with the procedure of the State concerned, establish either:

(1) that he has requested, and been denied, authorization by the proprietor of the right to make and publish the translation, or

(2) that, after due diligence on his part, he was unable to find the owner of the right.[399]

A licence may also be granted on the same conditions if all previous editions of a translation in a language in general use in the Contracting State are out of print.[400] The licence must not be transferrable by the licensee.[401]

7.130. Copies of application to the publisher. If the owner of the right of translation cannot be found, then the applicant for a licence must send copies of his application to the publisher whose name appears on the work and, if the nationality of the owner of the right of translation is known, to the diplomatic or consular representative of the State of which the owner is a national, or to the organisation which may have been designated by the government of that State.[402] The licence must not be granted before the expiration of a period of two months from the date of despatch of the copies of the application.[403]

7.131. Protection of author's economic and moral rights. Due provision must be made by domestic legislation: to ensure that the owner of the right of translation receives a compensation which is just and conforms to international standards: to ensure payments and transmittal of such compensation and to ensure a correct translation of the work.[404] Bogsch suggests that a 'correct' translation is 'a translation which conveys with the greatest possible fidelity the thoughts expressed in the original' and that 'correct' does not therefore mean 'literal'.[405] The original title and the name of the author of the work must be printed on all copies of the published translation.[406] And a licence must not be granted when the author has withdrawn from circulation all copies of the work.[407]

7.132. Conditions for export. The licence must be valid only for the publication of the translation in the territory of the Contracting State where it has been applied for.[408] Copies so published may be imported and sold in another Contracting State if a language in general use in that other Contracting State is the same language as that into which the work has been translated, and if the domestic law in that other

---

[397] *Ibid*, on Article V (point 2).
[398] As for the concept of a 'national', see §7.120 et seq. above.
[399] Article V.2(b).
[400] *Ibid.*
[401] Article V.2(e).
[402] Article V.2(c).
[403] *Ibid.*
[404] Article V.2(d).
[405] Bogsch, *op. cit.* on Article V (point 7).
[406] Article V.2(e). If the name was a pseudonym, that pseudonym must be printed.
[407] Article V.2(f).
[408] Article V.2(e).

Contracting State makes provision for such licences and does not prohibit such importation and sale.[409] Where the foregoing conditions do not exist, the importation and sale of such copies in a Contracting State are to be governed by its domestic law and its agreements.[410]

8. Duration of Protection

(1) General Principle—National Treatment

7.133. The Convention determines that, as a general principle, the duration of protection of a work is governed by the law of the Contracting State in which protection is claimed.[411] This is, however, subject to a number of minimum guarantees[412] (which are specified below).

(2) Guarantee of Specific Periods of Protection

7.134. Life of the author. The term of protection must not be less than the life of the author and twenty five years after his death.[413]

7.135. From date of first publication—where 'author's life' employed as criteria for certain works. Some Contracting States, in respect of certain works, do not compute the term of protection with reference to the life of an author. The Convention therefore provides that where any Contracting State, upon the date of the coming into force of the Convention there, has limited the term of twenty five years for certain classes of works to a period computed from the date of first publication of the work, that State is entitled to maintain these exceptions and extend them to other classes of works.[414] This is subject to the proviso that the term of protection must not be less than twenty-five years from the date of first publication.[415]

7.136. From date of first publication—where 'author's life' never employed as criteria. Certain Contracting States do not use the life of the author at all as a reference in computing the term of protection. The Convention therefore provides that where any Contracting State, upon the date of the Convention coming into force there, does not compute the term of protection upon the basis of the life of the author, that State is entitled to compute the term of protection from the date of first publication of the work or from the registration prior to publication, as the case may be.[416] This is subject to the proviso that the term of protection must not be less than twenty-five years from the date of first publication or from its registration prior to publication, as the case may be.[417]

---

[409] *Ibid.*
[410] *Ibid.*
[411] Article IV.I.
[412] *Ibid.*
[413] Article IV.2(a).
[414] *Ibid.*
[415] *Ibid.*
[416] Article IV.2(b).
[417] *Ibid.*

7.137. Successive terms. If the legislation of a Contracting State grants two or more successive terms of protection, the duration of the first term must not be less than one of the minimum periods specified above.[418]

7.138. Special rules for photographic works and works of applied art. The aforementioned provisions do not apply to photographic works or to works of applied art. The term of protection in Contracting States which protect such works as artistic works, must not be less than ten years for each of those classes of works.[419]

(3) Material Reciprocity

7.139. Introduction. The rule of 'national treatment' is subject to the proviso that a Contracting State need not protect a work for a period which exceeds that pertaining in the country of origin of the work. It should be emphasised that this is a right and not a duty. The specific rules are as follows.

7.140. Unpublished works. In the case of unpublished works, no Contracting State is obliged to grant protection to a work for a longer period than that fixed for the class of works to which the work in question belongs, by the law of the Contracting State of which the author is a national.[420]

7.141. Published works. In the case of published works, no Contracting State is obliged to grant protection to a work for a longer period than that fixed for the class of works to which the work in question belongs, by the law of the Contracting State in which the work has been first published.[421] In the case of simultaneous publication in two or more Contracting States, the work is treated as though first published in the State which affords the shortest term; any work published in two or more Contracting States within thirty days of its first publication is considered as having been published simultaneously in those said Contracting States.[422] The work of a national of a Contracting State is treated as though first published in the Contracting State of which the author is a national.[423]

7.142. Successive terms. For the purpose of application of the preceding provisions, if the law of any Contracting State grants two or more successive terms of protection, the period of protection in that State is considered to be the aggregate of those terms.[424] However, if a specified work is not protected by such State during the second or any subsequent term for any reason, the other Contracting State is not obliged to protect it during the second of any subsequent term.[425]

9. General Provisions

7.143. Commencement and parties. The Convention was adopted on 6 September, 1952[426] and entered into force on 16 September 1955.[427] A revised version

---

[418] Article IV.2(c).
[419] Article IV.3.
[420] Article IV.4(a).
[421] *Ibid.*
[422] Article IV.6.
[423] Article IV.5.
[424] Article IV.4(b).
[425] *Ibid.*
[426] Article VIII of the 1952 version.
[427] Article IX of the 1952 version.

was adopted on the 24 July 1971[428] and entered into force on 10 July 1974. The latter was open for signature and subsequent ratification or acceptance by all signatories of the 1952 version,[429] and is generally open for accession by any State.[430] Each State undertakes to adopt, in accordance with its Constitution, such measures as are necessary to ensure the application of the Convention[431] and a State must be in a position under its domestic law to give effect to the terms of the Convention at the date that it comes into force there.[432] Any Contracting State may denounce the Convention in its own name or on behalf of any of the countries or territories for whose international relations it is responsible and to whom it has extended the Convention.[433] However, such notice cannot take effect until twelve months after the date of receipt of the notification.[434]

7.144. Non-retroactivity. The Convention does not apply to works or rights in works which, at the effective date of the Convention in a Contracting State where protection is claimed, are permanently in the public domain in that Contracting State.[435] As well as covering works in which copyright has expired, this covers works which have never been protected because they were ineligible for protection or because 'constituent formalities' have not been complied with.[436]

7.145. Reservations. Reservations to the Convention are not permitted.[437]

7.146. Relationship between members of the 1952 version and members of the 1971 version. By acceding to the 1971 Convention, a Contracting State which has not already done so, automatically accedes to the 1952 Convention.[438] Moreover, no State may accede solely to the 1952 Convention.[439] This assures the existence of a common text between any two Convention members, thus providing a legal basis for their mutual copyright obligations, but at the same time allows the 1971 text eventually to supersede the 1952 text as it attracts more and more ratification and accessions.[440]

7.147. Relations between States parties to different versions. Relations between a State which is a party to the 1971 Convention and a State which is a party only to the 1952 Convention is governed exclusively by the 1952 Convention.[441] This is subject to the proviso that any State which is a Party only to the 1952 Convention may declare[442] that it will apply the 1971 text to the works of its nationals or works first published in its territory by all States party to the 1971

---

[428] Article VIII.I.
[429] *Ibid.*
[430] Article VIII.2.
[431] Article X.I.
[432] Article X.2.
[433] Article XIV.I. In accordance with XIV.I. such a denunciation also constitutes denunciation of the 1952 Convention.
[434] Article XIV.2.
[435] Article VII.
[436] Bogsch, *op. cit.* on Article VII (point 4). (see Bogsch generally for a discussion of the status of works 'provisionally' in the public domain).
[437] Article XX.
[438] Article IX.3.
[439] *Ibid.*
[440] Kaminstein Report, para. 120.
[441] Article IX.4.
[442] Notification is deposited with the Director-General. See Table B of Appendix III.

Convention.[443] If a Contracting State makes such a declaration it cannot select from among the States party to the 1971 Convention those it will allow to apply the new text to its works but must extend protection to all such States.[444]

7.148. Example. The Kaminstein Report gives an example[445] of the working together of these rules where State X is a party to the 1952 Convention only, and States Y and Z are party to both the 1971 and 1952 text:

(1) The general rule is that, although the relations between States Y and Z are governed by the 1971 text, their separate relations with State X are each governed by the 1952 text.

(2) If State X chooses to file a notification allowing States parties to the 1971 text to apply that text to its works, the privileges must extend to both States Y and Z equally without requiring any acceptance on their part.

(3) If State X does make the notification and does not ratify the 1971 Convention, it cannot claim any rights under the 1971 Convention with respect to its own works.

7.149. Relationship of the (Universal) Convention to the Berne Convention for the Protection of Literary and Artistic Works. The Convention emphasises that, generally, it does not in any way affect the provisions of the Berne Convention or the membership in the Union created by the Berne Convention.[446] Specifically, the Universal Copyright Convention is not applicable to the relationships among countries of the Berne Union in so far as it relates to the protection of works having as their country of origin, within the meaning of the Berne Convention, a country of the Berne Union.[447] The practical effect of this is to make the Berne Convention predominant over the Universal Copyright Convention as between two countries, both of which belong to the two conventions.[448]

Furthermore, a work whose origin is a country which has withdrawn from the Berne Union after 1 January 1951, cannot be protected by the Universal Copyright Convention in any country which is in the Berne Union.[449] This has the practical effect of precluding a Berne country from leaving the Berne Union and then relying on the Universal Copyright Convention for protection of its works in countries which were both members of the Berne Union and the Universal Copyright Convention.[450] It is however, subject to the a major proviso in the case of developing countries. Where a Contracting State is regarded as a developing country in conformity with the established practice of the General Assembly of the

---

[443] Article IX.4.

[444] Kaminstein Report, para. 124.

[445] *Ibid*, para. 125.

[446] Article XVII.I. Article XVII.2 provides that an express declaration is appended to the Universal Copyright Convention and that 'This declaration is an integral part of this Convention for the States bound by the Berne Convention on January 1, 1951, or which have or may become bound to it at a later date. The signature of this Convention by such States shall also constitute signature of the said Declaration, and ratification, acceptance or accession by such States shall include the Declaration as well as the Convention'. The terms of Article XVII and its Appendix Declaration constitute what is referred to as the 'Berne Safeguard Clause' (see Kaminstein Report, para. 138.). See generally Bogsch, *op. cit.*, on Article XVII and Appendix Declaration Relating Thereto.

[447] Appendix declaration relating to Article XVII (c).

[448] Kaminstein Report, para. 138.

[449] Appendix declaration relating to Article XVII (a).

[450] Kaminstein Report, para. 138.

United Nations and has deposited[451] at the time of its withdrawal from the Berne Union a notification to that effect, the preceding provision will not be applicable as long as such a State avails itself of the exceptions provided for in the Universal Copyright Convention for developing countries.[452]

7.150. The relationship of the Convention to other conventions entered into between two American States. The Convention does not abrogate multilateral or bilateral copyright conventions or arrangements that are or may be in effect exclusively between two or more American Republics.[453] Nevertheless, in the event of any difference either between the provisions of such existing conventions or arrangements and the provision of the Universal Copyright Convention, or between the provisions of the Universal Copyright Convention and those of any new convention or arrangement which may be formulated between two or more American Republics the convention or arrangement most recently formulated shall prevail between the parties thereto.[454] However, rights in works acquired in any Contracting State under existing conventions or arrangements before the date that the Universal Copyright Convention came into force in such a State are not affected.[455]

7.151. The relationship of the Convention to other conventions. The Convention does not abrogate multilateral or bilateral conventions or arrangements in effect between two or more Contracting States.[456] However, in the event of any difference between the provisions of such existing conventions or arrangements and the provisions of the Universal Copyright Convention, the provisions of the latter are to prevail.[457] This is subject to the proviso that rights in works acquired in any Contracting State under existing conventions or arrangements before the date on which the Universal Copyright Convention came into force in such a State, are not affected.[458]

7.152. Settlement of disputes. A dispute between two or more Contracting States concerning the interpretation or application of the Convention, which is not settled by negotiation, should, unless the States concerned agree on some other method of settlement, be brought before the International Court of Justice for determination.[459]

7.153. Extension to territories. Any Contracting State may declare either at the time of ratification, acceptance or accession, or at any time thereafter, that the Convention applies to all or any of the countries or territories for whose international relations it is responsible.[460] In the absence of such a notification, the Convention will not apply to any such country or territory.[461]

---

[451] With the Director-General of the United Nations Educational, Scientific and Cultural Organisation. See Table B of Appendix III.

[452] Appendix declaration relating to Article XVII (b).

[453] Ibid.

[454] Ibid.

[455] Ibid.

[456] Article XIX.

[457] Ibid.

[458] Ibid. Article XIX is expressly without prejudice to Articles XVII (the Berne Safeguard clause) and XVIII (conventions between two American States).

[459] Article XV.

[460] Article XIII.I. Notification is addressed to the Director-General of the United Nations Educational, Scientific and Cultural Organisation. See Table B of Appendix III.

[461] Article XIII.2.

7.154. Compulsory licences for developing countries. The Convention allows a Contracting State regarded as a developing country in conformity with the established practice of the General Assembly of the United Nations,[462] to benefit from generous compulsory licences.[463] Broadly speaking, these allow translations of works to be made earlier than the period stipulated for other countries.[464] They also permit the developing country to distribute copies of a work at a price reasonably related to that normally charged in the State for comparable works or a lower price, if such works have not been distributed there by the owner of the rights.[465]

IV. EUROPEAN AGREEMENT CONCERNING PROGRAMME EXCHANGES BY MEANS OF TELEVISION FILMS

1. Introduction

7.155. History. In protecting intellectual property, certain legal systems employ the concept of droit d'auteur as opposed to copyright. With its inextricable link between creativity and the human mind, the system of droit d'auteur confers rights in the first instance solely upon individuals and cannot recognise a corporation as an original owner of copyright. This has in the past deprived broadcasting organisations who 'make' programmes or films of any protection against the piracy of their works. The European Agreement Concerning Programme Exchanges by Means of Television Films (the 'Agreement') was entered into by Member States of the Council of Europe as a 'special arrangement'[466] sanctioned by the Berne Convention,[467] to cope with this deficiency. As Stewart points out, 'there is no doubt that according to the philosophy of "copyright" as opposed to the philosophy of the "droit d'auteur" there is sufficient originality and intellectual effort in the making of a broadcast to justify a copyright in it'.[468]

7.156. Scope of the Agreement. The Agreement confers on broadcasting organisations, rights of control over the exploitation of their television films.

2. Rights Protected

7.157. Right to authorise a broadcast of a television film. A broadcasting organisation under the jurisdiction of a Party to the Agreement, is given the right, in other Parties to the Agreement, to authorise the exploitation for television of television films of which it is the maker.[469] The right of authorization conferred by

---

[462] Article V bis.
[463] See generally Bogsch, *op. cit.* and Stewart, *op. cit.*, 6.38 et seq.
[464] Article V ter.
[465] Article V quater.
[466] Recital 5
[467] Article 20 of Berne Convention for the Protection of Literary and Artistic Works (Paris Act).
[468] Stewart, *op. cit.*, 11.01.
[469] Article I.

this Agreement is, however, subject to any restrictive condition to the contrary agreed between the maker and the persons who contribute to the making of the television film.[470]

7.158. Definition of 'television films'. 'Television films' are loosely defined as all 'visual or sound and visual recordings intended for television'.[471]

7.159. Definition of a 'maker' of films. A broadcasting organisation is deemed to be the maker if it has taken the initiative in, and responsibility for, making the film.[472]

7.160. Assignment of rights to a broadcasting organisation. Although the Agreement confers rights solely on broadcasting organisations, it provides that if the television film has been made by a person other than a broadcasting organisation, the former (ie the maker) may transfer to the broadcasting organisation rights accorded by the Agreement.[473] This is, however, subject to the condition that both the maker and the broadcasting organisation are under the jurisdiction of countries which are Parties to the Agreement.[474] It is also subject to any restrictive condition to the contrary agreed between the maker and the persons who contribute to the making of the television film.[475]

3. General Provisions

7.161. Commencement and parties. The Agreement was adopted on 15 December, 1958 and came into force on the 1 July, 1961.[476] It was open to signature and subsequent ratification with[477] or without[478] reservation, by Members of the Council of Europe.[479] Any other country which is not a Member of the Council of Europe may accede to the Convention, subject to the prior approval by the Committee of Ministers of the Council of Europe.[480] The Agreement is to remain in force for an unlimited period.[481] Any Contracting Party may denounce the Agreement at one year's notice.[482]

7.162. Relationship between the Agreement and copyright and neighbouring rights. The Agreement is entirely without prejudice to any moral right recognised in relation to television films;[483] the copyright in literary, dramatic or artistic works from which the television film is derived;[484] the copyright in a musical work, with or without words, accompanying a television film;[485] the copyright in films other

---

[470] *Ibid* and Article 4.
[471] Article 2.1.
[472] Article 2.2.
[473] Article 3.1.
[474] Article 3.2.
[475] Article 3.1. and Article 4.
[476] In accordance with Article 7.1.
[477] Article 6.1(b).
[478] Article 6.1(a).
[479] Article 6.1. See Table C of Appendix III.
[480] Article 8.1. See Table C of Appendix III.
[481] Article 12.1.
[482] Article 12.2. Notification is given to the Secretary-General of the Council of Europe.
[483] Article 5(a).
[484] Article 5(b).
[485] Article 5(c).

than television films;[486] and the copyright in the exploitation of television films otherwise than on television.[487]

7.163.   Extension to territories. Generally, the Agreement applies to the metropolitan territories of Contracting States.[488] However, any Contracting Party may, at the time of signature, ratification or accession, or at any later date, declare by notice that the Agreement applies to any territory or territories mentioned in the declaration and for whose international relations it is responsible.[489] Any declaration made in accordance with the preceding provision may be withdrawn with one year's notification.[490]

V. THE EUROPEAN AGREEMENT FOR THE PROTECTION OF TELEVISION BROADCASTS

1. Introduction

7.164. History. By 1960, the Eurovision movement was in full swing, its grand ideal being the creation of a European audio-visual arena. But it soon ran into difficulties caused essentially by the limitations in certain intellectual property regimes. For the organisers of musical and dramatic performances and the promoters of sports meetings would consent to their events being broadcast in other countries only on the condition that they would be viewed privately.[491] But European legal regimes which centred on the concept of 'droit d'auteur' could not offer them the protection they demanded: such systems could not recognise corporate bodies (ie broadcasting organisations) as owners of authors or neighbouring rights. Therefore, television organisations were powerless to restrain the broadcasting, fixation or public performance of their broadcasts in another State.[492] To plug the gap, the Contracting States of the Council of Europe entered into the European Agreement on the Protection of Television Broadcasts (the 'Agreement').

The Agreement was to be regional in scope and of limited duration since the International Convention for the Protection of Performers, Producers of Phonograms and Broadcasting Organisations (the 'Rome Convention'), which would later provide a full panoply of neighbouring rights, was already in contemplation.[493] The Council of Europe did not wish to frustrate a worldwide initiative to harmonise protection for broadcasters. Thus the European Agreement was to terminate (except in regard to fixations that had already been made and were therefore protected by the Agreement), 'at such time as a Convention on "neighbouring

---

[486] Article 5(d).
[487] Article 5(e).
[488] Article 11.I.
[489] Article 11.2. In accordance with Article 11.2, notice is to be addressed to the Secretary-General of the Council of Europe. See Table C of Appendix III.
[490] Article 11.3 and Article 12.2.
[491] Recital 3.
[492] Recital 4.
[493] Recital 7.

rights", including the protection of television broadcasts and open to European countries, amongst others, shall have entered into force for at least a majority of the Members of the Council of Europe . . .'[494] However, as Stewart explains, the protection afforded by the Rome Agreement turned out to be less than that conferred by this (the European) Agreement and the Council of Europe's Contracting States fought to save the broader protection given them by their own specially tailored instrument.[495] In 1965, a Protocol was enacted to ensure conformity with the Rome Convention. Three Additional Protocols were subsequently added extending the term of the Agreement.

7.165. Scope of the Agreement. The Agreement confers protection on broadcasting organisations for their original and relayed broadcasts.

7.166. Regime of protection. The Agreement provides a basic level of protection with a set of minimum rights. However, a contracting State which grants to organisations constituted in its territory and under its laws or transmitting from its territory, greater protection than is generally conferred by the Agreement, must extend such protection to broadcasts made from another contracting State ie it must confer 'national treatment'.[496]

7.167. Status of rights created by the Agreement. The precise status of the right created by the Agreement is unclear. In respect of an original broadcast made by a broadcasting organisation, the right is akin to a copyright. In respect of a relayed broadcast, the right resembles a neighbouring right.

2. Who is Protected

7.168. Protection is granted to broadcasting organisations constituted in a Contracting State under its laws or transmitting from that State.[497] A Contracting State may, however, by reservation, limit the operation of the Agreement to benefit only those broadcasting organisations which are both constituted in the territory and under the laws of another Contracting State and transmitting from that same territory.[498] This will exclude pirate stations operating from the High Seas.

Contracting States may, by reservation, withhold the protection granted by the Agreement from broadcasts made by a broadcasting organisation constituted in its territory and under its laws or transmitting from its territory where those broadcasts enjoy equivalent protection under its domestic laws.[499]

3. Broadcasts Protected

7.169. Definition of a 'broadcast'. The Agreement confers protection on 'television broadcasts'. This term is not defined but probably includes both terrestrial

---

[494] Article 13.1.
[495] Stewart, *op. cit.*, 11.04.
[496] Article 1.2. ie by broadcasting organisations constituted in its territory and under its laws or transmitting from its territory.
[497] Article 1.
[498] Article 3.1(f). See Table D of Appendix III.
[499] Article 3.1(e). See Table D of Appendix III.

broadcasts and broadcasts by satellite.[500] Although the Agreement affords protection to both the visual and sound element of a broadcast,[501] protection is not conferred on the sound element when broadcast separately.[502]

The Agreement confers a right on all broadcasts made by a broadcasting organisation in a Contracting State regardless of whether they are original (ie made by that broadcasting organisation) or relayed from another Contracting State.[503] The effect of this is that each time a broadcast is relayed, it becomes a new broadcast separately protected.[504]

7.170. National and international broadcasts. Since the Agreement grants rights of one form or another to all television broadcasts in the territories of all the Contracting States, it covers national as well as international situations.[505]

4. Rights Protected

7.171. 'National treatment' in another Contracting State. Broadcasting organisations constituted in the territory and under the laws of a Party to the Agreement or transmitting from such a territory must enjoy, in the territory of any other Party to the Agreement, the same protection as that other Party extends to organisations constituted in its territory and under its laws or transmitting from its territory ie the latter must confer 'national treatment'.[506] However, the following minimum rights are guaranteed.

7.172. Retransmission over the air or by cable. Broadcasting organisations have the right to authorise or prohibit the rebroadcasting of their broadcasts[507] or the diffusion of such broadcasts to the public by wire (ie cable retransmission).[508]

In its original form, the Agreement stipulated that a Contracting State could, by reservation, withhold protection against all cable retransmissions.[509] However, following amendment by the Protocol on 22 January 1965, the Agreement now imposes a limit. It states that Contracting States may withhold protection 'as regards broadcasting organisations constituted in their territory or transmitting from such territory, and restrict the exercise of such protection as regards broadcasts by broadcasting organisations constituted in the territory of another Party to this Agreement or transmitting from such territory, to a percentage of the transmissions by such organisations, which shall not be less than 50 per cent of the average weekly duration of the broadcasts of each of these organisations'.[510] Although far from clear, this probably means that a Contracting State may withhold protection

---

[500] For an analysis of which particular transmissions may qualify under those terms, see §8.002 et seq. below.
[501] Article 5.
[502] Ibid.
[503] Stewart, op. cit. 11.05.
[504] Ibid. 11.06 citing Straschnov, The European Agreement for the Protection of TV Broadcast, Copyright [1960], 263. However, for the purposes of computing the duration of protection, time runs from the first broadcast in a Contracting State.
[505] Stewart, op. cit. 11.06.
[506] Article 1.2.
[507] Article 1.1(a).
[508] Article 1.1(b).
[509] Article 3.1(a).
[510] Ibid as amended by Article 2.1. of the Protocol.

for up to 50 per cent of the output of its broadcasting organisations and withhold protection against retransmission in its territory of incoming signals up to 50 per cent of the output of the foreign transmitting broadcasting organisation. However any contracting State which before the enactment of the Protocol availed itself of the option to withhold all protection for cable retransmissions, may continue to do so.[511]

7.173. Communication to the public by means of any instrument for the transmission of signs, sounds or images. Broadcasting organisations have the right to authorise or prohibit the communication of their broadcasts to the public by means of any instrument for the transmission of signs, sounds or images.[512] A Contracting State may, by exercising a reservation, withhold protection against this form of exploitation of broadcasts where the public are not a 'paying audience' as defined by that State's domestic law.[513]

7.174. Fixation. Broadcasting organisations have the right to authorise or prohibit any fixation of their broadcasts, a fixation including the making of a still photograph.[514] They also have the right to authorise or prohibit any reproduction of those fixations.[515]

A Contracting State may, by exercising a reservation, withhold protection where the fixation or reproduction of the fixation is made for private use or solely for educational purposes.[516] ie this covers the making of a video recording for private use. Furthermore, a Contracting State may, by exercising a reservation, withhold protection against the making, for any purpose, of a still photograph of a broadcast and the making of a reproduction of such photographs.[517] However, if a Contracting State has availed itself of this reservation then any other Contracting State whose broadcasts are affected by this reservation may reciprocate with an equivalent reservation.[518]

7.175. Use of fixation for retransmission or public communication. Broadcasting organisations have the right to authorise or prohibit the rebroadcasting of their broadcasts, or the diffusion or their broadcasts by wire (ie cable retransmission) or the communication of their broadcasts to the public all with the aid of fixations or reproductions of fixations except where the organisation in which the rights vest, has authorised the sale of those fixations to the public.[519] However, Contracting States may, by exercising a reservation, withhold protection from broadcasting organisations against a rebroadcasting of their broadcasts or diffusion of their broadcasts by wire (cable retransmission) or the communication of their broadcast to the public all of which have been made with the aid of a still photograph or a reproduction of such a still photograph.[520] If a Contracting State has availed itself of this reservation then any other Contracting State whose

---

[511] Article 2.4 of the 1965 Protocol. See Table D of Appendix III.
[512] Article 1.1(c).
[513] Article 3.1(b). See Table D of Appendix III.
[514] Article 1.1(d).
[515] *Ibid.*
[516] Article 3.1(c). See Table D of Appendix III.
[517] Article 3.1(d). See Table D of Appendix III.
[518] Article 4.4.
[519] Article 1.1(e).
[520] Article 3.1(d). See Table D of Appendix III.

broadcasts are affected by this reservation, may reciprocate with an equivalent reservation.[521]

5. Duration of Protection

7.176. Old rules. Under the terms of the original Agreement, protection was to continue until the end of the tenth calendar year following the year in which the first broadcast was made from the territory of a Party to the Agreement.[522] This was subject to two provisos. The first was that protection would end when the Agreement was terminated following the enactment of a Convention on 'neighbouring rights'[523] ie when the Rome Convention, then in preparation, was enacted. The second proviso was that any particular Contracting State which applied a longer period under its domestic law, had to confer that longer period of protection on broadcasts coming from another Contracting State[524] (ie it had to confer national treatment).[525] However, this was qualified by the rule that no Contracting State was required to confer on broadcasts coming from another Contracting State,[526] longer protection than that granted by the other Contracting State.[527]

7.177. New rules. Following amendment of the Agreement by the Protocol of 22 January 1965, the period of protection was extended. Protection must now last for a period of not less than twenty years from the end of the year in which the first broadcast was made from a Contracting State.[528] This is still subject to the proviso that any particular Contracting State which applies a longer period under its domestic law, must confer that longer period of protection on broadcasts coming from[529] another Contracting State.[530] But the rule that no Contracting State was required to confer a longer period of protection than that conferred by another Contracting State, has been abolished.[531]

6. Exceptions to Protection—Fair Use

7.178. Reporting current events. For the purpose of reporting current events, the Agreement leaves it to the discretion of the Contracting States to provide exceptions to the protection of broadcasts in the case of rebroadcasting, diffusion by wire (ie cable retransmission), fixation or reproduction of fixations or public

---

[521] Article 4.4.
[522] Article 2.1.
[523] *Ibid* and Article 13.1
[524] ie broadcasts of any broadcasting organisations constituted in the territory and under the laws of another Party or transmitting from the territory of another Party.
[525] Article 2.1 and Article 1.2.
[526] ie broadcasts of any broadcasting organisations constituted in the territory and under the laws of another Party or transmitting from the territory of another Party.
[527] Article 2.2.
[528] Article 2.1 as amended by Article 1.1 of the Protocol of January 22, 1965.
[529] ie broadcasts of any broadcasting organisations constituted in the territory and under the laws of another Party or transmitting from the territory of another Party.
[530] Article 1.1 of the Protocol of 22 January 1965.
[531] Article 1.2. of the Protocol of 22 January 1965.

performance of short extracts from a broadcast where the broadcast itself constitutes the whole or part of the event in question.[532] In other words, no material can be taken from a broadcast which is itself documenting the particular event for informatory purposes (as opposed to relaying the complete or part of the event). Thus, an excerpt could be pruned from a broadcast of a football match or concert, but no excerpts can be taken from news, Tele-Journal or similar programmes which report those events.[533] This fair use exception applies only where it is prescribed by national law.

7.179. Ephemeral fixations for the use of a broadcast. The Agreement leaves it to the discretion of the Contracting States to provide exceptions to the protection of broadcasts in the case of ephemeral fixations made by a broadcasting organisation by means of its own facilities for the purpose of making its own broadcast.[534] This exception applies only where it is prescribed by national law.

7. Seizure

7.180. Fixations imported from non-contracting states. The Agreement requires the seizure of a fixation of a broadcast, including a still photograph or reproductions of such photographs, which are made in a territory not a party to the Agreement and which are imported into a contracting State where they would be unlawfully there without the consent of the broadcasting organisation in which the rights vest.[535] Seizure is to be effected in accordance with the domestic law of the relevant Contracting States.[536]

7.181. Fixations imported from Contracting States. The Agreement allows Parties to deny protection against the making of a fixation of a broadcast or a still photograph of a broadcast as well as the making of reproductions of those fixations.[537] However, not all Contracting States will have exercised this reservation. The Agreement therefore requires the seizure of those materials if they are imported into a territory where they would be unlawful without the consent of the broadcasting organisations in which the rights vest.[538] Seizure is to be effected in accordance with the domestic law of the relevant Contracting States.[539]

7.182. Material reciprocity. Both of the aforementioned rules are subject to the following proviso. This is that no protection need be offered to a broadcasting organisation constituted in the territory and under the laws of another Contracting State or transmitting from such a territory if that Contracting State has withheld protection under the Agreement against the exploitation in its own territory of broadcasts by such fixations.[540] In other words, the Agreement institutes a form of 'material reciprocity'.

---

[532] Article 3.2(a).
[533] Stewart, *op. cit.*, 11.10.
[534] Article 3.2(b).
[535] Article 4.
[536] Article 4.3.
[537] Article 3.1(d), see §7.174 above.
[538] Article 4.2.
[539] Article 4.3.
[540] Article 4.4.

8. General Provisions

7.183. Commencement and parties. The Agreement was enacted on June 22, 1960, and entered into force on 1 July 1961.[541] It was open to signature and subsequent ratification, with or without reservation, by the Members of the Council of Europe.[542] Any European Government which is not a Member of the Council of Europe or any non-European Government having political ties with a Member of the Council of Europe may accede to the Agreement, subject to the prior approval of the Committee of Ministers of the Council of Europe.[543] A Contracting State may denounce the Agreement by giving one years notice to that effect.[544]

Following the enactment of the Rome Convention,[545] the Agreement was amended by a Protocol on 22 january 1965, which came into force on 24 March 1965.[546] The Protocol stipulated that the Agreement was to remain in force indefinitely.[547] But it also provided, amongst other things, that as from 1 January 1985, no State could remain or become a Party to the Agreement unless it was also a Party to the Rome Convention.[548] Furthermore, it was declared to bind States who were Parties to the Agreement.[549] The Agreement was further amended by three Additional Protocols. They confirmed the maintenance in force of the Agreement, and were declared to bind Contracting States of the original Agreement and its former Protocol(s).[550] The First Protocol entered into force on 31 December 1974. The Second Additional Protocol entered into force on 1 January 1985. The Third Additional Protocol has not entered into force.

7.184. Reservations. The Agreement permits a number of reservations and these are dealt with in context above.[551]

7.185. Relationship of Agreement to other rights. The Agreement does not affect any rights in respect of a television broadcast which may accrue to third parties such as authors, performers, film makers, manufacturers of records or organisers of entertainments.[552] The Agreement is also without prejudice to the protection of television broadcasts that may be accorded outside of the Agreement.[553]

7.186. Arbitration for public communication and diffusion by wire. The Agreement provides that a Contracting State must offer protection against the communication of a broadcast to the public by means of any instrument for the transmission of signs, sounds or images,[554] as well as the diffusion of those broadcasts

---

[541] In accordance with Article 8.
[542] Article 7.1(a) and (b). See Table D of Appendix III.
[543] Article 9.1. See Table D of Appendix III.
[544] Article 14. Notice is given to the Secretary General of the Council of Europe.
[545] International Convention for the Protection of Performers, Producers of Phonograms and Broadcasting Organisations. See §7.188 below.
[546] In accordance with Article 4.3 of the Protocol, no State may become a party to the Agreement without also becoming a party to the Protocol.
[547] Article 3.1 of the Protocol amending Article 13 of the Agreement.
[548] Protocol, Article 3.
[549] Article 4.3.
[550] See Table D of Appendix III.
[551] See §§7.168, 7.173, 7.174 and 7.175 above.
[552] Article 6.1.
[553] Article 6.2.
[554] Article 1.1(c). See §7.173 above.

to the public by wire.[555] Nevertheless, it sanctions the establishment of a body with jurisdiction to determine whether a broadcasting organisation in which the right vests, has unreasonably refused permission to exploit the broadcast in either of these ways or granted permission but on unreasonable terms.[556] Stewart submits that 'unreasonable refusal' or 'unreasonable terms' suggest cases of discrimination or abuse of power. The tribunal could not for instance overrule the motivated refusal of a broadcasting organisation to grant a licence to a cable operator if that organisation, as a matter of policy, refuses to license any cable operators or if the broadcasting organisation refuses because contracts with authors or performers or organisers of sporting events forbid it.[557]

7.187. Extension to territories. The Agreement applies to the metropolitan territories of the Contracting States.[558] In addition, a Party may at any time declare that the Agreement shall extend to any or all of the territories for whose international relations it is responsible.[559] A Contracting State may separately denounce the Agreement in respect of a territory to which it has been extended.[560]

VI. THE INTERNATIONAL CONVENTION FOR THE PRO-TECTION OF PERFORMERS, PRODUCERS OF PHONO-GRAMS AND BROADCASTING ORGANISATIONS

1. Introduction

7.188. History. The International Convention for the Protection of Performers, Producers of Phonograms and Broadcasting Organisations (the 'Convention' or the 'Rome Convention') was the first Treaty to give wide-ranging protection to performers and others who exploit literary and artistic works. Although it did not come into existence until the 1960s, its conception can be traced back to the early part of the twentieth century—the moment, in fact, when sounds were first fixed by the gramophone recording. For the invention of the gramophone changed the fortune of performers by allowing their hitherto ephemeral art, to be preserved for all time (or at least a long time) and disseminated on a commercial scale. The gramophone recording thus not only deprived performers of regular work but meant that their performances (their means to a living) could be exploited in private with little chance of the profit finding its way back to them.

The cinema, as well as radio and television broadcasting soon joined the gramophone recording as a way of bringing the performer to his audience. Though, no doubt, these new technologies were an enhancement for society enabling inexpensive enjoyment of the arts, they increased the vulnerability of performing artists. But—as often happens—the beneficiaries of one technology became the victims of another and it was not long before the owners of the new media, ie record

---

[555] Article 1.1(b). See §7.172 above.
[556] Article 3.3 of the Agreement as amended by Article 2.3 of the Protocol.
[557] Stewart, *op. cit.* 11.11.
[558] Article 12.1.
[559] See Table D of Appendix III.
[560] Article 12.3. and Article 14.

producers and broadcasting organisations, found that their own works were being exploited without their consent. It thus rapidly became apparent that it was not only performers who were in need of protection. The Berne and later Universal Conventions had enshrined rights in favour of authors. The time was ripe for the creation of a global 'neighbouring rights' regime.

During the many revisions of Berne in the first half of the century, the matter of incorporating performers' rights was often touched upon but was always rejected. One reason lay in the fact that such rights posed a conceptual difficulty. The copyright Conventions are concerned with the rights of authors. Because 'performers' derive their creativity from the work of authors, their art is thus a step removed from the focus of those Conventions. But perhaps more credibly, authors were simply loath to yield to the demands of artists who might undermine an author's freedom to enjoy his work. It has been suggested[561] that another reason for the difficulty in combining performers' rights in the same instruments which protected authors, lay in the fact that those claiming performing rights were often not individuals but organisations. A Convention such as Berne, being based on the concept of the 'droit d'auteur', ie on the idea of the 'individual' being the source of creative work, could thus not accommodate 'corporate' bodies as an original owner of rights.

Fortunately, performers had a particularly strong voice in the form of the International Labour Organisation. Indeed it had begun studying the question of protection for performers in 1926 and had carried on championing the cause of these neglected 'workers' (producing a draft convention in 1956). Ultimately, the International Union for the Protection of Literary and Artistic Works, UNESCO and the International Labour Office gathered together to draw up a treaty (separate from the copyright conventions) enshrining rights for performers, record producers and broadcasting organisations and the Rome Convention came into being. Stewart notes these three rights are interconnected: 'There are few records without a performance (birdsong or sound effects are rare exceptions) and few broadcasts without either a performance or records or both'.[562] The framers of the Rome Convention thus wanted to create a balance between these three right holders and a separate instrument seemed the most practical way of achieving their ideal.

7.189. Scope of the Convention. The Convention sets up an almost exhaustive regime of protection of neighbouring rights ie those of performers, the producers of phonograms and broadcasting organisations. But it is entirely without prejudice to the rights of authors.[563]

7.190. Regime of Protection. Protection under the Convention is composed of two elements. The first element is the guarantee that foreign performances, phonograms and broadcasts protected under the Convention will be given so called 'national treatment'.[564] 'Simply stated, national treatment is the treatment that a State grants under its domestic law to domestic performances, phonograms and broadcasts'.[565] The second element, which is grafted on to and which may modify 'national treatment', is a series of specifically protected rights and also limitations—

---

[561] Stewart, *op. cit.*, 8.02.
[562] *Ibid.*
[563] Article 1.
[564] Article 2.1.
[565] Kaminstein Report on Article 2.

the 'Conventional Minima'.[566] But even with the Conventional Minima, the Convention is flexible in its approach, for, as the WIPO Guide prosaically puts it 'As well as the basic table d'hôte menu . . . there exist à la carte provisions which allow each country a choice of the obligations which it must undertake'.[567]

7.191. Interaction of 'National Treatment' and the 'Conventional Minima'. The domestic laws of a particular Contracting State may be less generous than the Conventional Minima. Nevertheless, a Contracting State which does not grant the Conventional Minima to its own nationals must grant those Minima to nationals of other Contracting States.[568] It may be that on the contrary, domestic laws are more generous than the Conventional Minima because Contracting States are able to limit specific rights. Where the Convention allows a limitation on a particular right, and is thus less charitable than domestic law, the Contracting State may assert the Convention to deny 'national treatment' to the foreign performance, phonogram or broadcast.[569]

7.192. Interpretation of the Convention. The Intergovernmental Report compiled by AL Kaminstein, the Rapporteur-General (the 'Kaminstein Report') and adopted by the Committee which approved the final draft of the Convention may be used as an interpretative guide to the Convention and copious reference is made to it below.

At the request of Member States which were parties of the Intergovernmental Committee of the Rome Convention, the World Intellectual Property Organisation has written a Guide to the Rome Convention.[570] It is an invaluable tool in the analysis of the Convention. However, as the Guide itself points out, it is not to be regarded as an authentic interpretation of the treaty but rather has the aim of presenting 'an account of the origins, aims, nature and scope of the provisions concerned'.[571] Its purpose is thus to aid in the implementation of the Convention. Ultimately, therefore it is for the authorities to form their own opinions about the interpretation of the Convention.[572]

Reference is also made to the Model Law Concerning the Protection of Performers, Producers of Phonograms and Broadcasting Organisations (the 'Model Law'), an instrument which has been drafted by the Intergovernmental Committee of the Convention to provide a legislative framework for the implementation of the Convention.

2. Protection Granted to Performers

(1) Who is Protected

7.193. The Convention grants protection to performers if either: the performance takes place in another Contracting State;[573] or the performance is incorporated in

---

[566] Article 2.2.
[567] WIPO Guide to the Rome Convention (1981), Introduction para. XXI.
[568] Ibid. 2.2.
[569] Ibid. This may be contrary to EEC competition law, See §4.158 et seq. above.
[570] The Guide has been written by Mr Claude Masouyé and Mr William Wallace.
[571] WIPO Guide to the Rome Convention (1981), Preface.
[572] Ibid.
[573] Article 4(a).

a phonogram which is protected under the Convention;[574] or, the performance, not being fixed on a phonogram, is carried by a broadcast which is protected under the Convention.[575] Performers are defined as 'actors, singers, musicians, dancers, and other persons who act, sing, deliver, declaim, play in, or otherwise perform[576] literary or artistic works'.[577] The term 'literary or artistic works' has the same meaning as in the Berne and Universal Conventions,[578] and in particular includes musical, dramatic and dramatico-musical works.[579] This treatment of the term 'literary or artistic works' means that the Convention does not protect persons who, although undoubtably performers, do not perform 'works' as this is meant in the copyright sense, for example, variety and circus artists.[580] Thus sports personalities, in particular, are excluded from protection.[581] However, Contracting States are given the right to extend the protection provided for in the Convention to 'artists' who do not perform literary or artistic works.[582]

The term 'performer' is broad enough to include persons who perform for the purposes of fixation rather than in the presence of an audience, as well as persons whose performances are later joined by technical editing or mixing processes with independent performances made at different times and places by other performers.[583] If several performers participate in the same performance, Contracting States can determine the manner in which they will be represented in exercising their rights under the Convention.[584]

(2) Rights Protected

7.194. National treatment. A Contracting State must grant to performers protected by the Convention, the identical treatment that it gives to performers who are its own nationals.[585] This is, however, subject to the following minimum protection and limitations.[586]

7.195. Concept of 'the possibility of preventing' certain acts. The Convention does not bestow on performers 'exclusive' rights (as it does on phonogram producers and broadcasting organisations). Rather, it provides that performers have 'the possibility of preventing' certain specified acts which thus become unlawful without their consent.[587] There are two principal reasons for the Convention using this terminology. The first is that it allows countries to protect performers' rights in any

---

[574] Article 4(b). For the protection of phonograms, see §7.204 et seq. below.
[575] Article 4(c). For the protection of broadcasts, see §7.215 et seq. below.
[576] A performance includes a recitation and presentation (Kaminstein Report on Article 3).
[577] Article 3(a). Performers thus include conductors of musicians or singers (Kaminstein Report on Article 3).
[578] Kaminstein Report on Article 3. See §§7.011 and 7.106 above.
[579] Although it is immaterial whether the work performed is or is not protected by copyright (WIPO Guide to the Rome Convention (1981), 3.1).
[580] Kaminstein Report on Article 8. But the term 'literary and artistic works' is generally regarded as broad enough to include oral works, pantomimes and improvisations (see Model Law, commentary on Section 1(iii)).
[581] WIPO Guide to the Rome Convention (1981), 3.2.
[582] Article 9.
[583] Model Law, commentary on Section 1(iii).
[584] Article 8.
[585] Article 4.
[586] Article 2.2.
[587] Article 7.1.

way they deem appropriate[588] (which can include exclusive rights if they so wish). Thus a country can use the criminal law, making the exploitation of a performance without consent punishable.[589] But, the institution of a compulsory licence system is incompatible with the Convention since, under such a system, a performer 'could not prevent, but would have to tolerate, the acts in question'.[590] The other reason the Convention employs this terminology is rooted in politics. During negotiations for the Convention, authors and other right holders expressed their fears that by giving a performer an exclusive right to authorize the exploitation of his perform-ance, the Convention would fetter them in the exploitation of their works. It was felt that a performer might demand further remuneration from the author for a repeat performance or he might hinder phonogram producers and broadcasting organisations in the exploitation of their recordings and broadcasts.[591] The Con-vention was thus forced to pay lip service to these parties with wording that makes no difference in practice in Contracting States which want to enshrine exclusive rights.

7.196. Broadcasting rights. The Convention grants to performers, the possibility of preventing the broadcasting of their live performance without their consent.[592] Broadcasting is defined as 'the transmission by wireless means for public reception of sounds or of images and sounds'.[593] Only transmission by hertzian waves or other wireless means constitutes 'broadcasting'.[594] This includes both radio or television transmissions,[595] but excludes wire diffusion (ie sound relay or cable television) although Contracting States can themselves enact legislation to prevent this act if they so wish.[596] The words 'for public reception' make it clear that transmission to a single person or a defined group (eg ships at sea, aircraft or a fleet of taxis) are not broadcasts for the purpose of the Convention.[597] The status of a satellite transmis-sion has in the past been unclear. As the WIPO Guide noted (in March 1981) 'The question whether the transmission of a programme by means of a space satellite with a view to it being seen by the public constitutes "broadcasting" within that definition is a matter of controversy'.[598] It is submitted that it is now beyond doubt that a Direct Broadcast Satellite transmission is covered by the term 'broadcast' and is protected.[599]

The broadcasting right lapses once the performance has been broadcast.[600] This is because any further exploitation is governed by the agreement between the performers and the broadcasting organisation.[601] There is also no right to authorise

---

[588] ie employment law, law of unfair competition, unjust enrichment, criminal law etc (Kaminstein Report on Article 7). Section 2 of the Model Law confers on performers the absolute right to authorise the acts covered by the Convention.

[589] Kaminstein Report on Article 7.

[590] Ibid.

[591] WIPO Guide to the Rome Convention (1981), 7.8.

[592] Article 7.1(a).

[593] Article 3(f).

[594] Kaminstein Report on Article 3.

[595] WIPO Guide to the Rome Convention (1981), 3.16.

[596] Ibid. 3.17.

[597] Kaminstein Report on Article 3.

[598] WIPO Guide to the Rome Convention (1981), 13.8.

[599] It probably also includes a transmission made by distribution satellite where the signal can be received by members of the public without the intervention of a cable distributor. For a general discussion of these issues, see §8.005 below.

[600] Article 7.1(a).

[601] Article 7.2(1). See §7.198 below 'Relations between Performers and Broadcasting Organisations'.

the broadcast of a performance taken from an authorised fixation;[602] examples include an authorised ephemeral recording, commercial disc or a recording made for broadcasting purposes.[603]

7.197. Communication to the public. The Convention grants to performers, the possibility of preventing the communication to the public, of their live performance without their consent.[604] The 'communication to the public' envisaged by the framers of the Convention was that where a live performance, for example, a recital in a concert hall, was transmitted to another public not present in the hall, by loudspeaker or by wire. It was thus designed to protect a performer against unauthorised live sound relay.[605] But today it is more likely to be invoked to prevent transfrontier relays of live performances by cable television which the wording will cover.

The public communication right does not apply where the performance used has already been broadcast.[606] Thus for example, it would not cover the scenario in which a broadcast of a live performance is received on domestic televisions in hotels or restaurants and then relayed by cable to larger screens. The public communication right also does not apply if the performance is relayed from an authorised fixation.[607] The classic example is a juke-box 'performance'. The playing of the record in the juke-box is a 'communication to the public by wire' but the Convention will not apply because the relay is made from an authorised fixation.

7.198. Relations between performers and broadcasting organisations regulating 'broadcasting rights'. Where a performer has consented to a broadcast of his performance, then subject to one proviso, the Convention leaves it up to the Contracting States where protection is claimed to regulate protection against exploitation of that performance (ie exploitation of the fixation) by the broadcasting organisation.[608] Such protection may, although it need not, guard against rebroadcasting (by the same broadcasting organisation), fixation for broadcasting purposes, and the reproduction of such fixation for broadcasting purposes.[609] The proviso is that where performers and broadcasting organisations have in their contract agreed terms concerning the exploitation of a broadcast performance, the domestic law must yield to those terms,[610] ie only if the contract is silent can domestic law intervene and define the parties respective rights. The term 'contract' includes collective agreements between performers and broadcasting organisations, decisions of arbitration boards if 'arbitration was the mode of settlement ordinarily applying between performers and broadcasters.'[611]

7.199. Fixation and reproduction of a fixation. Performers have the possibility of preventing an unauthorised fixation of their unfixed (ie live) performance,[612] ie

---

[602] Article 7.1(a).
[603] *Ibid.* See WIPO Guide to the Rome Convention (1981), 7.13. But see §7.212 below.
[604] Article 7.1(a).
[605] WIPO Guide to the Rome Convention (1981), 7.12.
[606] Article 7.1(a).
[607] *Ibid.*
[608] Article 7.2(2).
[609] Article 7.2(1). The Model Law, Section 2(1) (a) (i) gives to performers the right to authorise a broadcast made from an ephemeral fixation despite the fact that the performer consented to the ephemeral fixation in the first place.
[610] Article 7.2(3).
[611] Kaminstein Report on Article 7.
[612] Article 7.1(b).

they can prevent 'bootlegging'. They also have the possibility of preventing a reproduction of a fixation of their performance. This latter right is permitted in three circumstances.[613] The first is where the original fixation was made without the performer's consent.[614] The second is where the reproduction is made for purposes different from those for which the performers gave their consent for the fixation,[615] an example being where a disc is incorporated in the soundtrack of a motion picture without the performer's consent.[616] The third circumstance is where the original fixation was made: for the purposes of private use; or for the reporting of current events; or or as an ephemeral fixation by a broadcasting organisation for its own broadcasts; or for teaching or scientific research, and the reproduction is made for different purposes.[617]

7.200. Limitation of protection resulting from the incorporation of a performance in a film. Once a performer has consented to the incorporation of his performance in a 'visual or audio-visual fixation' ie a film, he is denied any of the specific rights afforded to him under the Convention.[618] He cannot prevent any use which is made of his fixed performance, whether the fixation was intended for cinema showing or on television. So his performance may, for example, be inserted in other films or broadcasts or made into video cassettes.[619] But it should be emphasised that performers have complete freedom of contract in the first instance as far as the making of a visual or audio-visual fixation is concerned.[620] And these rules do not prevent a performer from benefiting from the Convention's obligation on Contracting States to grant 'national treatment' to a performer.[621]

7.201. Conclusion on performers' rights. It can be seen that performers are, to a certain extent, treated as second class citizens under the Convention. Any control that they may have had over their work is wrested from them at the moment that they 'deliver' their performance to a commercial undertaking which is to exploit it. As the WIPO Guide to the Rome Convention notes: 'By the simple decision to appear or not on the stage or in the studio, the performer carries in himself the exclusive right to authorise his performance. But from the moment that modern technology intervenes (phonograms, broadcasting), their performance, once fixed, may be used in ways never envisaged.'

(3) Duration of Protection

7.202. General principles. Under the principle of 'national treatment', the duration of pretection is governed by the law in which protection is claimed.[622] However, the Convention determines that protection must last at least until the end of a period of twenty years computed from the end of the year in which the performance took place.[623] Stewart points out that 'under the Convention the right

---

[613] Article 7.1(c).
[614] Article 7.1(c)(i).
[615] Article 7.1(c)(ii).
[616] WIPO Guide to the Rome Convention (1981), 7.18.
[617] Article 7.1(c)(iii).
[618] Article 19. ie Article 7 rights cease to apply.
[619] WIPO Guide to the Rome Convention, (1981), 19.2.
[620] Kaminstein Report on Article 19.
[621] Ibid.
[622] Article 2. See WIPO Guide to the Rome Convention, (1981), 14.3.
[623] Article 14(b).

of the performer is only "the possibility of preventing" (Article 7) and if that is implemented by a protection under criminal law only, time for prescription would run from the date of the offence, that is the infringement, regardless of how long after the performance that infringement took place. Equally, if the protection is based on the law of unfair competition there is no time-limit'.[624] No Contracting State is bound to apply the provisions of the Convention to performances which took place before the date of coming into force of the Convention in that Contracting State.[625]

7.203. Performances incorporated in phonograms. Where the performance is incorporated in a phonogram protected under the Convention, the performer may benefit from the period of protection granted to such phonograms.[626]

3. Protection Granted to Producers of Phonograms

(1) Who is Protected

7.204. General principles. Contracting States must grant protection to producers of phonograms if: the producer of the phonogram is a national of another Contracting State;[627] or the first fixation of the sound was made in another Contracting State;[628] or the phonogram was first published in another Contracting State.[629] A phonogram is defined as 'any exclusively aural fixation of sounds of a performance or of other sounds'.[630] It thus excludes a fixation of film or television images and sounds[631] but can include, for example, bird-song and natural noises.[632] Since a phonogram is defined as a 'fixation', the work is protected from the moment it is recorded.[633] Thus, where the 'first fixation' criterion is relied upon, it is of no importance whether or not the phonogram is multiplied into a number of copies and these are put at the disposition of the public.[634]

7.205. Meaning of 'producer'. A producer of phonograms is 'the person who, or the legal entity which, first fixes the sounds of a performance or other sounds,'[635] and can include broadcasting organisations as regards their own recordings.[636] Where the producer is a company, it is likely that it will be given the nationality of the country under whose law it is organised.[637] When an employee of a legal entity fixes the sounds in the course of his employment, the employer, rather than the employee is to be considered the producer.[638]

---

[624] Stewart, *op. cit.*, 8.38.
[625] Article 20.2.
[626] Article 14(a).
[627] Article 5.1(a).
[628] Article 5.1(b).
[629] Article 5.1(c).
[630] Article 3(b).
[631] WIPO Guide to the Rome Convention (1981), 3.7.
[632] *Ibid*, 3.8.
[633] *Ibid*, 3.6.
[634] *Ibid*.
[635] Article 3(c).
[636] WIPO Guide to the Rome Convention, (1981), 3.10.
[637] Stewart, *op. cit.*, 8.11.
[638] Kaminstein Report on Article 3.

7.206. Meaning of 'publication'. 'Publication' is defined as the 'offering of copies of a phonogram to the public in [a] reasonable quantity',[639] and what constitutes 'reasonable' depends on the phonogram in issue. The term offer should be widely construed and any sort of advertisement would probably qualify. It is suggested that the offering of a reasonable quantity for hire in a record library would also qualify.[640] Under the principle of 'simultaneous publication', if the phonogram was first published in a non-Contracting State but within thirty days it was published in a Contracting State, it is treated as if it was first published in a Contracting State.[641]

7.207. Alternative criteria for protection. Contracting States may declare at any time that they will not apply the criteria of publication or alternatively fixation.[642] In this case, protection is limited to one or other of those criteria and to producers who are nationals of another Contracting State. The general rule is that no country may exclude the criterion of nationality, however, any Contracting State which on 26 October 1961, granted protection to producers of phonograms solely on the basis of the criteria of fixation, may, at the time of ratification, acceptance or accession, declare that it will apply that criterion alone.[643] This reservation was included to accommodate Nordic counties which had recently passed new laws on neighbouring rights.[644]

7.208. Affixation of a notice. If, as a condition of protecting the rights of producers of phonograms (or of performers in relation to phonograms), a Contracting State requires compliance under its domestic law with certain formalities, the Convention dictates the conditions under which these shall be deemed to have been fulfilled.[645] Thus, protection must be granted if, in commerce, all the copies of the published phonogram or their containers (ie sleeves) bear a notice consisting of the symbol Ⓟ, accompanied by the year date of first publication, placed in such a manner as to give reasonable notice of the claim of protection.[646] If the copies of the phonograms or their containers do not identify the producer or the licensee of the producer (by carrying his name, trademark or other appropriate designation), the notice must include the name of the owner of the rights of the producer.[647] Moreover, if the copies of the phonograms or their containers, do not identify the principal performers, the notice must also include the name of the person who, in the country in which the fixation was effected, owns the rights of such performers.[648]

(2) Rights Protected

7.209. National treatment. A Contracting State must grant to producers of phonograms in another Contracting State, the identical rights it gives to producers

---

[639] Article 3(d).
[640] Stewart, *op. cit.*, 8.14.
[641] Article 5.2.
[642] Article 5.3. This is effected by means of a notification deposited with the Secretary General of the United Nations. See Table E of Appendix III.
[643] Article 17. See Table E of Appendix III.
[644] See also Kaminstein Report on Article 5.
[645] Article 11.
[646] *Ibid.*
[647] *Ibid.*
[648] *Ibid.*

of phonograms who are its own nationals,[649] ie it must confer 'national treatment' on them. This is, however, subject to the following minimum rights and limitations.[650]

7.210. Right of reproduction. Contracting States must grant to producers of phonograms the right to authorise or prohibit the direct or indirect reproduction of their phonograms,[651] or parts of their phonograms.[652] Reproduction is defined as the 'making of a copy or copies of a fixation.'[653] 'Direct or indirect reproduction' means, amongst other things, reproduction by means of moulding and casting, recording the sounds made by a pre-existing phonogram or it may mean reproduction by recording 'off the air' a broadcast of a phonogram.[654] The performance of a work, its public recitation or broadcasting or its exhibition to the public[655] (or any other activity which does not result in new permanent tangible copies)[656] does not amount to the making of new copies under the Convention and are thus excluded.

(3) Duration of Protection

7211. Under the principle of 'national treatment,' the duration of protection is governed by the law in which protection is claimed.[657] However, the Convention determines that, for phonograms and for performances incorporated thereon, the term of protection must last at least until the end of a period of twenty years which is computed from the end of the year in which the fixation was made.[658] No Contracting State is bound to apply the Convention to phonograms fixed there before the Convention came into force there.[659]

4. Protection Granted to Performers and Producers of Phonograms for the 'Secondary Exploitation' of their Works

7.212. General principles. In the event that a phonogram published for commercial purposes, or a reproduction of such a phonogram, is used directly for broadcasting[660] or for any communication to the public, a single equitable remuneration must be paid to the producer, or to the performer or both.[661] The requirement that

---

[649] Article 5.
[650] Article 2.2.
[651] Article 10.
[652] Kaminstein Report on Article 10.
[653] Article 3(e).
[654] Kaminstein Report on Article 10.
[655] *Ibid.* on Article 3.
[656] *Ibid.*
[657] Articles 2 and 5. See WIPO Guide to the Rome Convention (1981), 14.3.
[658] Article 14(a).
[659] Article 20.2.
[660] Broadcasting means the 'transmission by wireless means for public reception of sounds or of images and sounds' ie it includes both radio and television but excludes cable relays.
[661] Article 12.

the phonogram must have been published for commercial purposes means that copies of the phonogram must have been offered to the public in a reasonable quantity.[662] It thus excludes unpublished phonograms or recordings made by a broadcasting organisation. The term 'used directly', means that only the person who takes the decision to make use of the phonogram is the one who must pay.[663] This leads to the inequitable result that use by way of rebroadcasting (ie where one broadcasting organisation simultaneously broadcasts the signal of another broadcasting organisation)[664] does not constitute a direct use and the rebroadcaster would not be called upon to make a second payment.[665] However, the mere transfer by a broadcasting organisation of a commercial disc to tape and the broadcast from the tape, would not make the use indirect.[666]

7.213. Collection of remuneration. Contracting States have a choice of laying down who should be paid ie whether it is to be the producer, the performer or both. The purpose of this is to save broadcasting organisations and other users from having to deal with a number of different beneficiaries,[667] In the absence of any agreement between the parties, it is left to domestic law to lay down rules for the sharing of this remuneration.[668] The WIPO Guide advances arguments as to who is deserving of the royalties received from broadcasting organisations stating that 'each State must review the arguments, weigh the importance of each and eventually choose, from the bundle of solutions the Convention offers, that which seems fairest and best suited to its own economic situation'.[669] The Model Law [670] adopts a regime under which payent is made to the producer with a provision requiring him to pay a share to the performers, although noting that the Convention does not require that the remuneration be shared equally or in any other particular proportion. The Convention is silent as to the intervals at which payment should be made but the Model Law states that 'the appropriate delay following the use would depend on the circumstances, and would need to be long enough to avoid harassment of the broadcaster or other user'.[671]

7.214. Limitation of rights. Contracting States are given the right to deny, at any time, protection of the above rights, in the various degrees sanctioned by the Convention.[672] Thus they may deny this protection completely.[673] Or they may deny the protection only in respect of certain uses[674] ie a country may decide not to grant payments in the case of uses in broadcasting or in the case of public communication.[675] Alternatively, Contracting States may deny this protection

---

[662] Article 3(d).
[663] WIPO Guide to the Rome Convention (1981), 12.7.
[664] Article 3(g).
[665] Kaminstein Report on Article 12.
[666] Ibid.
[667] WIPO Guide to the Rome Convention, (1981), 12.12.
[668] Article 12. See generally Stewart, op. cit., 8.28. for a discussion of this topic.
[669] WIPO Guide to the Rome Convention, (1981), 12.28.
[670] Section 5.
[671] Model Law, commentary on Section 5.
[672] See Table E of Appendix III. In accordance with Article 16.2, if the notification is made after the date of the deposit of the instrument of ratification, acceptance or accession, the declaration becomes effective six months after deposit of the notification.
[673] Article 16.1(a)(i).
[674] Article 16.1(a)(ii).
[675] Kaminstein Report on Article 16.

where the producer is not a national of another Contracting State.[676] (This allows for the purposes of Article 12, the application of the nationality criterion alone.) Furthermore, where the producer is a national of another Contracting State, Contracting States may limit the protection to the extent and term which that other Contracting State grants to phonograms first fixed by a national of the State making the declaration[677] ie the State making the reservation can cut back the protection it grants to the extent of the protection it receives.[678] However, the fact that the other Contracting State does not grant protection to the same beneficiary or beneficiaries does not constitute a difference which justifies a limitation under this Article.[679] Thus a state that grants protection to both performers and producers may not refuse protection to a State that protects only the performer or producer.[680] Finally, any State which, on 26 October, 1961 granted protection to producers of phonograms solely on the basis of fixation may apply this criteria alone.[681]

5. Protection Granted to Broadcasting Organisations

(1) Who is Protected

7.215. Protection is granted to broadcasting organisations if either the headquarters of the broadcasting organisation is situated in another Contracting State[682] (meaning that State under which the laws of the broadcasting organisation entity is organised)[683] or the broadcast was transmitted from a transmitter situated in another Contracting State.[684] However, Contracting States may declare that they will only protect broadcasts where both the headquarters of the broadcasting organisation is situated in another Contracting State and the broadcast was transmitted from a transmitter situated in the same Contracting State.[685] This is to exclude from protection 'peripheral stations' where the headquarters are on one side of a frontier and the transmitter on another.[686]

If the technical equipment in a Contracting State is owned by the postal administration but what is fed into the transmitter is prepared and presented by organisations such as in the United Kingdom the BBC, the latter and not the postal administration is to be considered the broadcasting organisation.[687] Furthermore, if a given programme is sponsored by an advertiser, or prerecorded by an independent

---

[676] Article 16.1(a)(iii).
[677] Article 16.1(a)(iv).
[678] Kaminstein Report on Article 16.
[679] Article 16.1(a)(iv).
[680] WIPO Guide to the Rome Convention, (1981), 16.10.
[681] Article 17. This was effected by deposit of notification with the Secretary-General of the United Nations at the time of ratification of the Convention. See Table E of Appendix III.
[682] Article 6.1(a).
[683] Kaminstein Report on Article 6.
[684] Article 6.1(b).
[685] Article 6.2. In accordance with Article 6.2, this reservation is made by notification to the Secretary-General of the United Nations at the time of ratification, acceptance or accession to the Convention or at any time thereafter, and in the last case, becomes effective six months after it has been deposited. See Table E of Appendix III.
[686] WIPO Guide to the Rome Convention, (1981), 6.4.
[687] Kaminstein Report on Article 3.

producer and transmitted by organisation such as the BBC, the latter rather than the sponsor or the independent producer, is to be considered the broadcasting organisation.[688]

(2) Rights Protected

7.216. National treatment. A Contracting State must grant to broadcasting organisations in another Contracting State, the identical rights it gives to broadcasting organisations which have their headquarters on its territory or transmit from transmitters situated in its territory ie they must confer on them 'national treatment'.[689] This requirement is however, subject to the following minimum rights and limitations.[690]

7.217. Rebroadcasting. Broadcasting organisations have the right to authorise or prohibit the rebroadcasting of their broadcasts.[691] In interpreting this right it is first necessary to define the meaning of a broadcast and then go on to define what is meant by 'rebroadcasting'.

A broadcast (ie broadcasting) is defined as 'the transmission by wireless means for public reception of sounds or of images and sounds.'[692] Only transmission by hertzian waves or other wireless means constitutes 'broadcasting.'[693] This includes both radio or television transmissions,[694] but excludes wire diffusion ie cable transmissions[695] (a severe limitation of the Convention). The status of a satellite broadcast had been unclear: 'The question whether the transmission of a programme by means of a space satellite with a view to it being seen by the public constitutes "broadcasting" within that definition is a matter of controversy.'[696] It is submitted that it is now beyond doubt that a Direct Broadcast Satellite transmission is covered by the term 'broadcast'.[697] The Model Law inclines towards the view that 'the transmission of a signal, for the ultimate distribution to the public' constitutes broadcasting.[698]

'Rebroadcasting' (the act prohibited) is defined as the 'simultaneous broadcasting by one broadcasting organisation of the broadcast of another broadcasting organisation.'[699] All the criteria mentioned above concerning the meaning of a 'broadcast' are equally applicable to the concept of 'rebroadcasting', the most significant of which, is that retransmission by cable is not covered by the definition. It should be noted that because the rebroadcast must be 'simultaneous', a deferred rebroadcast made from a fixation is not covered.[700] However, if a Contracting State exploits the

---

[688] *Ibid.*
[689] Article 6. But see §7.215 above concerning the possible reservation under Article 6.2.
[690] Article 2.2.
[691] Article 13(a).
[692] Article 3(f).
[693] Kaminstein Report on Article 3.
[694] WIPO Guide to the Rome Convention, (1981), 3.16.
[695] *Ibid.*
[696] *Ibid.* 3.17.
[697] It probably also includes a transmission made by distribution satellite where these can be received by members of the public. See 8.003 below for a discussion of these concepts.
[698] Model Law, commentary on Section 6, stating that four of six members of the Intergovernmental Committee of the Rome Convention came to that view in 1971.
[699] Article 3(g).
[700] Kaminstein Report on Article 3.

optional exception to allow ephemeral recordings, a rebroadcast of a broadcast which has itself been made from an ephemeral fixation, still retains the characteristic of simultaneity and is thus caught by the Convention.[701]

7.218. Fixation and reproduction of a fixation. Broadcasting organisations have the right to authorise or prohibit the fixation of their broadcasts.[702] This will include a part of a broadcast but it is not certain whether a single still photograph taken from a screen constitutes such a part and this is left for national courts to decide.[703] Broadcasting organisations also have the right to authorise or prohibit the reproduction of fixations of their broadcasts. This is permitted in two circumstances: the first is where the fixations have been made without their consent;[704] and the second is where fixations have been made as permitted by the Convention[705] ie for the purpose of private use, reporting current events, teaching or scientific research and the reproduction is then used for different purposes.[706]

7.219. Communication in a public place. Broadcasting organisations have the right to authorise or prohibit the communication to the public of their television broadcasts if such a communication is made in a place accessible to the public and in return for payment of an entrance fee.[707] A charge for meals and drinks does not amount to such a payment.[708] Since 'broadcasting' is defined as 'the transmission by wireless means for public reception of sounds or images and sounds,'[709] a communication to the public of a cable transmission is excluded. DBS broadcasts are probably covered, whilst 'point to point' transmissions may not be.[710]

It is matter for the domestic law of the State where the protection of this right is claimed to determine the conditions under which it may be exercised.[711] Furthermore, Contracting States are, given the right, at any time, to deny protection against this form of exploitation of a broadcast.[712] In this case the other Contracting State can deny this same protection to broadcasting organisations whose headquarters are in the former Contracting State.[713]

(3) Duration of Protection

7.220. Under the principle of 'national treatment,' the duration of protection is governed by the law in which protection is claimed.[714] However, the Convention

---

[701] WIPO Guide to the Rome Convention, (1981), 3.19.

[702] Article 13(b).

[703] Kaminstein Report on Article 13. The WIPO Guide to the Rome Convention, (1981), 13.3 notes that: 'Omission of the right to control the taking of still photographs can be damaging to the broadcasters, particularly in the news field. Leaving the press, who are in a sense competitors, free to take and publish photographs of news events or the winning goal in the World Cup competition from the TV screen does not make for good relations between them.'

[704] Article 13(c)(i).

[705] ie under Article 15.

[706] Article 13(c)(ii).

[707] Article 13(d).

[708] WIPO Guide to the Rome Convention, (1981), 13.6.

[709] Article 3(f).

[710] See §8.005 below for a discussion of these issues.

[711] Article 13(d).

[712] Article 16.1(b).

[713] Article 16.1(b). See Table E of Appendix III.

[714] Article 2. See WIPO Guide to the Rome Convention, (1981), 14.3.

determines that protection must last at least until the end of a period of twenty years which is computed from the end of the year in which the broadcast took place.[715] No Contracting State is, bound to apply the provisions of the Convention to broadcasts which took place before the date of coming into force of the Convention for that State.[716]

6. Exceptions to Protection — Fair Use

7.221. General principles. Contracting States are allowed to provide exceptions to the protection granted by the Convention to performers, producers of phonograms and broadcasting organisations. But, if the particular Contracting State does not provide for them expressly, they do not apply. Four exceptions are permitted: first, where the material is used for private use;[717] secondly, where short excerpts of the material is used in connection with the reporting of current events;[718] thirdly, where an ephemeral fixation is made by a broadcasting organisation by means of its own facilities for its own broadcasts[719] and fourthly, where the material is used solely for the purposes of teaching or scientific research.[720]

7.222. Power to align protection to that of copyright owners. Irrespective of the above, Contracting States are given the right to limit the protection of performers, producers of phonograms and broadcasting organisations to the same kind of protection they provide under their domestic law in respect of copyright in literary and artistic works: ie they may enlarge the exceptions.[721] This is merely an option given to Contracting States, intended as a hint that they should in principle consider treating copyright and neighbouring rights equally.[722] It is subject to the proviso that compulsory licences may only be imposed where they do not contravene the Convention.[723] This might include, for example, a compulsory licence allowing free quotation for the purposes of criticism or free use for charitable purposes.[724]

7. General Provisions

7.223. Commencement and parties. The Convention came into force on 18 May 1964.[725] It was open until 30 June 1962 for signature and subsequent ratification or

---

[715] Article 14(c).
[716] Article 20.2.
[717] Article 15.1(a).
[718] Article 15.1(b).
[719] Article 15.1(c). The purpose of this exception is to give broadcasting organisations which are entitled to make a 'broadcast' under the Convention, the flexibility necessary to make fixations for practical reasons such as the need for delayed broadcasting or the use of more efficient transmitting apparatus.
[720] Article 15.1(d).
[721] Article 15.2.
[722] WIPO Guide to the Rome Convention, (1981), 15.9.
[723] Article 15.2.
[724] Kaminstein Report on Article 15. The Model Law permits compulsory licences only for the reproduction of phonograms used for teaching purposes and they are subject to stringent rules (Model Law, commentary on Section 7).
[725] in accordance with Article 25.1.

acceptance, by any State that had been invited to the Diplomatic Conference on the International Protection of Performers, Producers of Phonograms and Broadcasting Organisations.[726] It is currently open for accession by any State Member of the United Nations.[727] Each Contracting State undertakes to adopt, in accordance with its Constitution, the measures necessary to ensure the application of the Convention[728] and at the time of deposit of its instruments of ratification, acceptance or to give effect to the terms of the Convention.[729] Any Contracting State may denounce the Convention, on its own behalf or on behalf of all or any of its territories,[730] although not before the expiry of a period of five years from the date on which it came into force there.[731]

In order to accede to the Convention, States must be a party to the Universal Copyright Convention or alternatively, a member of the International Union for the Protection of Literary and Artistic Works (the Berne Union).[732] This is required because it is considered inequitable to have the performers, producers of phonograms, and broadcasting organisations of a particular country enjoy international protection when the literary and artistic works they use might be denied protection in that country because it is not a party to at least one of the copyright conventions.[733] Thus a Contracting State ceases to be a party to the Convention from the time that it is neither a party to the Universal Copyright Convention nor the International Union for the Protection of Literary and Artistic Works.[734]

7.224. Non-retroactivity (pre-existing rights and performances). The Convention does not prejudice any rights acquired in a Contracting State before the date in came into force there.[735] However, no Contracting State is bound to apply the provisions of the Convention to performances or broadcasts which took place, or to phonograms which were fixed before the date of coming into force of the Convention in that State.[736] But it may do so if it wishes.

7.225. Reservations. The Convention provides for a number of reservations all of which (save for that contained in Article 17) may be made at any time and not just at the time the instruments of ratification, acceptance or accession are deposited. This is intended to allow countries to introduce a reservation after they have adhered to the Convention, if changes in their domestic law make this desirable.[737] However, no reservation other than that provided for in the Convention may be made by a Contracting State.[738] Any State which has made a reservation under the Convention, may reduce its scope or withdraw it.[739]

---

[726] Article 23 and Article 25.1.
[727] Article 24.2.
[728] Article 26.1.
[729] Article 26.2.
[730] Article 28.1.
[731] Article 28.3.
[732] Article 24.2 and Article 28.4. In accordance with Article 23, this was required of the signatory States.
[733] WIPO Guide to the Rome Convention (1981), 23.7.
[734] Article 28.4.
[735] Article 20.1.
[736] Article 20.2.
[737] Kaminstein Report.
[738] Article 31.
[739] Article 18. This is effected by deposit of notice with the Secretary-General of the United Nations.

7.226. Relationship of Convention to copyright. The protection granted under the Convention leaves intact the protection of copyright in literary and artistic works.[740] Thus whenever copyright law requires the author's consent for the reproduction or other use of his work, such a requirement is not affected by the Convention.[741] Conversely, when by virtue of the Convention, the consent of the performer, recorder or broadcaster is necessary, the need for his consent does not disappear because authorization by the author is also necessary.[742]

7.227. Relationship of Convention to other protection of neighbouring rights. The Convention is without prejudice to any protection otherwise given to performers, producers of phonograms or broadcasting organisations,[743] ie in national or international law. Furthermore, the Contracting States reserve the right to enter into special agreements amongst themselves which grant more extensive rights to performers, producers of phonograms or broadcasting organisations or which contain other provisions not contrary to the Convention.[744] In using the term 'agreements amongst themselves', the Convention makes clear that this provision deals only with special arrangements limited to countries who are parties to this (the Rome) Convention.[745]

7.228. Settlement of disputes. Disputes which arise between two or more Contracting States concerning the interpretation or application of the Convention and which are not settled by negotiation may be referred at the request of only one of the parties to the International Court of Justice, for decision, unless they agree to another mode of settlement.[746]

7.229. Extension of protection to territories. Any Contracting State may at any time extend protection to any territories for whose international relations it is responsible, provided that the Universal Copyright Convention or the Berne Convention for the Protection of Literary and Artistic Works applies to those territories.[747] Any reservations may be extended to cover all or any of those territories.[748]

VII. CONVENTION FOR THE PROTECTION OF PRODUCERS OF PHONOGRAMS AGAINST UNAUTHORISED DUPLICATION OF THEIR PHONOGRAMS OF 29 OCTOBER 1971

1. Introduction

7.230. History. During the 1960s, piracy spiralled to hitherto unimagined heights, due to both the growth of the record and tape cassette industry and the advance of

---

[740] Article 1.
[741] Kaminstein Report on Article 1.
[742] *Ibid.*
[743] Article 21.
[744] Article 22.
[745] WIPO Guide to the Rome Convention, (1981), 22.5.
[746] Article 30.
[747] Article 21.1. Notification is addressed to the Secretary General of the United Nations. See Table E of Appendix III.
[748] Article 27.2.

duplicating technology. Illicit recordings could be divided essentially into two categories.[749] Into the first category fell the pirating of legitimate tapes and records. Into the second category fell 'off the air' recording of both live performances (known as 'bootlegging') as well as prerecorded performances (ie performances on record).

Phonogram producers found it difficult to combat the pirates with existing treaties: they were denied rights under the Copyright Conventions since they were not authors of works.[750] And whilst the Rome Convention was enacted specifically to safeguard the interests of, amongst others, phonogram producers, it is limited in scope: it enshrines only exclusive rights of reproduction and does not prohibit the importation and distribution of illicit recordings. Furthermore, membership is limited to Contracting States who are a party to the Berne and Universal Conventions. Many countries belong to neither.

By 1970, the scale of piracy was so immense that immediate action was required. The phonogram industry voiced its anxieties to a committee of experts convened for the preparation of a revision of the Berne and Universal Conventions. The result was the rapid enactment of The Convention for the Protection of Producers of Phonograms Against Unauthorized Duplication of Their Phonograms (the 'Convention'). As the WIPO guide notes, less than eighteen months passed between the conception of the Convention and its adoption.

7.231. Scope of the Convention. The Convention protects producers of phonograms against the making and importation of illicit phonograms and the distribution of illicit phonograms. It does not afford protection against secondary uses of phonograms ie acts of public performance and broadcasting.[751] The Convention is solely concerned with protecting the rights of producers of phonograms, although it does sanction Contracting States to provide for the protection of performers whose performances are fixed on those phonograms.

7.232. Regime of protection. Unlike the Berne, Universal and Rome Conventions, this Convention does not provide for 'national treatment'. Instead it sets up the acceptance of specific mutual obligations,[752] and it leaves member countries free to choose, from as it were, a menu, the legal means by which to meet their obligations to other member countries.[753]

7.233. Interpretation of the Convention. The Intergovernmental Report compiled by Ekidi Samnik,[754] the Rapporteur-General (the 'Samnik Report') adopted by the Committee which approved the final draft of the Convention, may be used as an interpretative guide to the Convention and reference is made to it below.

The World Intellectual Property Organisation has written a 'Guide to the Phonograms Convention',[755] an invaluable tool in the analysis of the Convention. However, as the Guide itself makes clear, it is not to be regarded as an authentic interpretation of the Convention but rather has the aim of presenting 'an account

---

[749] WIPO Guide to the Phonograms Convention, (1981), Introduction para. VI.
[750] although it was possible for an author to assign to a phonogram producer the former's exclusive right of reproduction enshrined in those Conventions.
[751] Samnik Report, para. 58.
[752] WIPO Guide to the Phonograms Convention, (1981), 3.7.
[753] *Ibid*, 3.1.
[754] Copyright [1971] Issue 12, 240.
[755] The Guide has been written by Mr. Glaude Masouyé and Mr. William Wallace.

of the origins, aims, nature and scope of the provisions concerned'.[756] Its purpose is thus to aid in the implementation of the Convention. Ultimately, therefore, it is for the authorities (ie national courts and legislative bodies) to form their own opinions about the interpretation of the Convention.[757]

2. Who and What is Protected

7.234. Producers protected. The general rule is that protection is granted to producers of phonograms who are nationals of other Contracting States.[758] The 'producer of phonograms' means 'the person who, or the legal entity which, first fixes the sounds of a performance or other sounds'.[759] This may be an individual or a corporation. In the case of a corporation, nationality is determined by the place of its registered office.[760] The Convention applies to a successor in title who is merely substituted for the original owner of the rights.[761] Any Contracting State which, on 29 october 1971, afforded protection to producers of phonograms solely on the basis of the place of first fixation, may declare that it will apply this criterion instead of the criteria of nationality.[762]

7.235. Phonograms protected. A 'phonogram' is defined as 'any exclusively aural fixation of sounds of a performance or of other sounds'.[763] It thus excludes video cassettes or CD Rom discs. But it includes an ephemeral recording made by a broadcasting organisation.[764]

7.236. Protection of film or television soundtrack. It is unclear whether the definition of 'phonogram' includes the soundtrack of a cinematographic film or other audiovisual creation. Two theories have traditionally been posited. The first theory states that 'when a disc is made from the soundtrack of a film, the soundtrack constitutes the raw material for the recording, so that, when an exclusively aural fixation of the soundtrack is made, the resulting recording is a phonogram within the meaning of the Convention'.[765] Under the second theory it is said that 'the sounds embodied in the recording produced from the soundtrack, having been first fixed in the form of an audiovisual work, do not have a separate character as an exclusively aural fixation and that the recording cannot qualify as a phonogram under the Convention, but rather would be part of the original audiovisual work'.[766]

---

[756] WIPO Guide to the Phonograms Convention, (1981), Preface.
[757] *Ibid.*
[758] Article 2.
[759] Article 1(b).
[760] Guide to the Phongrams Convention (1981), 1.8.
[761] Samnik Report, para. 48.
[762] Article 7(4). In accordance with Article 7(4), declaration is made by notice deposited with the Director-General of the WIPO. See Table F of Appendix III.
[763] Article 1(a).
[764] Samnik Report, para. 39.
[765] Samnik Report, para. 36. The Report notes (para. 36) that this view is reinforced by the fact that the soundtrack is often edited or altered so that a new exclusively aural version is created.
[766] Samnik Report, para. 37.

3. Rights Protected

7.237. Making and importation. Each Contracting State must protect producers of phonograms of other Contracting States against the making of duplicates without the consent of the producer and the importation of these duplicates provided that either of these acts is for the purpose of distribution to the public.[767]

The Convention aims to frustrate unlawful commercial exploitation and prohibits only phonograms which are imported for the purpose of distribution to the public: thus immunity is given to individual illicit discs crossing a frontier.[768] As the WIPO Guide notes: 'The acquisition as souvenirs by a foreign tourist of the odd disc or cassette does not make him a pirate. The importation of a large number to make a profit would be a different matter'.[769]

7.238. Distribution. Each Contracting State must also protect producers of phonograms of other Contracting States against the distribution to the public of duplicates made without their consent.[770] There is no 'importation' requirement here and the duplicates nay thus have been made in the country of distribution.[771]

7.239. Meaning of 'duplicate'. A 'duplicate' is defined as 'an article which contains sounds taken directly or indirectly from a phonogram and which embodies all or a substantial part of the sounds fixed in that phonogram'.[772] The expression 'directly or indirectly' means that a copy of a copy is included ie it catches two successive pirates, one copying from the other.[773] It also includes duplicates made 'off the air' from broadcasts of phonograms.[774] The definition encompasses a 'substantial part' of a phonogram because the methods used in the field of recording offer all sorts of possibilities to take, superimpose and combine extracts of phonograms.[775] In this context, the word 'substantial' has a qualitative as well as a quantitative evaluation.[776] Thus a small part may amount to 'substantial'.[777] But the imitation or simulation of sounds of the original works does not fall within the definition of a 'duplicate'.[778]

7.240. Who may give consent. 'Consent' may, under the domestic law of a Contracting State, be given by the original producer or by his successor in title or by his exclusive licensee.[779]

7.241. Meaning of 'distribution'. A 'distribution to the public' means 'any act by which duplicates of a phonogram are offered, directly or indirectly, to the general public or any section thereof'.[780] This would include, for example, the supply of

---

[767] Article 2.
[768] WIPO Guide to the Phonograms Convention, (1981), 2.6.
[769] *Ibid.*
[770] Article 2.
[771] WIPO Guide to the Phonograms Convention, (1981), 2.7.
[772] Article 1(c).
[773] WIPO Guide to the Phonograms Convention, (1981), 1.9.
[774] Samnik Report para. 40.
[775] WIPO Guide to the Phonograms Convention, (1981), 1.10.
[776] Samnik Report, para 41.
[777] *Ibid.*
[778] *Ibid.*
[779] Samnik Report, para. 48.
[780] Article 1(d).

duplicates to a wholesaler for the purpose of sale to the public.[781] The duplicates need only be offered to the public by means of advertisements, and need not have actually changed hands.[782] Furthermore, the definition of 'offering' is probably wide enough to cover the hiring and not just the sale of illicit phonograms.[783] Offering copies to a 'section' of the public would, for example, cover offering them to members of a record or book club.[784] Whether or not the person making the phonograms can be traced, Contracting States must give a power to act against the distributor.[785]

4. Means of Protection

7.242. Introduction. Although the means by which the Convention is to be implemented is a matter for the domestic law of each Contracting States, it must include one or more of the three following regimes: the grant of a copyright or other specific right;[786] and/or protection by means of the law of unfair competition;[787] and/or protection by means of penal sanctions. [788]

7.243. Grant of a copyright or other specific right. The 'grant of copyright' treats the recording as the product of skill and labour and thus the maker is entitled to the same or virtually the same rights as the creator of the work.[789] A 'specific right' means a right in the nature of copyright but known by the different name of a 'neighbouring right'.[790] To meet the obligations of the Convention, the producer must be able to prevent all the prohibited acts.

7.244. By means of the law of unfair competition. As far as unfair competition is concerned, the acts prohibited by this Convention fall generally within the definition of that law found in Article 10bis of the Paris Convention for the Protection of Industrial Property (the 'Paris Convention').[791] According to the Paris Convention, 'unfair competition' amounts to 'any act of competition contrary to honest practices in industrial or commercial matters'.[792]

7.245. By means of penal sanctions. In a Contracting State which meets its obligations by means of penal sanctions, it must be a criminal offence to do any of the prohibited acts, punishable by fines and/or imprisonment. As Stewart points out,[793] 'the burden of proof on the prosecution is heavier than that on the plaintiff in civil cases and particularly the proof of a negative, ie that there was no consent,

---

[781] Samnik Report, para. 43.
[782] WIPO Guide to the Phonograms Convention, (1981), 1.13.
[783] Stewart, *op. cit.*, 9.04.
[784] *Ibid.*
[785] WIPO Guide to the Phonograms Convention, 1981, 2.7.
[786] Article 3.
[787] *Ibid.*
[788] *Ibid.*
[789] WIPO Guide to the Phonograms Convention, (1981), 3.2.
[790] *Ibid*, 3.3.
[791] *Ibid*, 3.4.
[792] See WIPO Guide to the Phonograms Convention, (1981), 3.4. As to whether the law of unfair competition is an adequate foundation for the rights enshrined in the Convention, see Stewart, *op. cit.*, 9.10.
[793] Stewart, *op. cit.*, 9.11.

may be difficult in cases of importation. So may be proof that the defendant knew that the phonograms were illicitly made'.

5. Duration of Protection

7.246. General principles. The duration of protection is a matter for the domestic law of each Contracting State.[794] However, if that law prescribes a specific duration, it must not be less than twenty years from the end either of the year in which the sounds embodied in the phonograms were first fixed or alternatively, the year in which the phonogram was first published.[795] In a country which chooses to meet its obligations by means of the law of unfair competition, there is often no duration laid down in the civil law. However, it is assumed that in this case protection should not in principle end before twenty years from the first fixation or first publication as provided for in the Convention.[796]

7.247. Affixation of a notice. If, as a condition of protecting the producers of phonograms, a Contracting State, under its domestic laws, requires compliance with certain formalities, the Convention dictates the circumstances under which these shall be deemed to have been fulfilled. Thus protection is secured if all the authorised duplicates of the phonogram distributed to the public, or their containers, bear a notice consisting of the symbol ℗ accompanied by the year date of first publication, placed in such manner as to give reasonable notice of a claim of protection;[797] and, if the duplicates or their containers do not identify the producer, his successor in title or exclusive licensee (by carrying his name, trademark or other appropriate designation), the notice must also include the name of the producer, his successor in title or the exclusive licensee.[798] The term 'exclusive licensee' means the person or legal entity who controls all rights in a phonogram for the entire Contracting State in question.[799] It is important to note that no State need prescribe any formalities at all.[800]

6. Exceptions to Protection

7.248. Fair use. The convention allows Contracting States who afford protection by means of copyright or other specific right (ie neighbouring right) or by penal sanctions, to impose the same kind of limitations against protection as are permitted in the case of the protection of authors of literary and artistic works.[801] Although this is a Convention which may be ratified or acceded to by a country which is not a member of either the Berne Convention for the Protection of Literary and Artistic Works or the Universal Copyright Convention, it is intended

---

[794] Article 4.
[795] *Ibid.*
[796] Samnik Report, para. 51.
[797] Article 5.
[798] *Ibid.*
[799] Samnik Report, para. 53.
[800] WIPO Guide to the Phonograms Convention, (1981), 5.2.
[801] Article 6.

that the principles enshrined in those conventions should apply in this context.[802] However, as the WIPO Guide notes, nothing in the Convention gives protection against public performance or broadcasting.[803]

7.249. Compulsory licences. Where, limitations against protection are guaranteed by the grant of compulsory licences, three conditions must be fulfilled. These are that: the duplication must be used solely for the purpose of teaching or scientific research;[804] the licence must be valid for duplication only within the territory of the Contracting State whose competent authority has granted the licence and it must not extend to the export of the duplicates;[805] and the duplication made under the licence must give rise to an equitable remuneration fixed by the competent authority taking into account, inter alia, the number of duplicates which will be made.[806]

7.250. Unfair competition. When an action alleging unfair competition is brought, the only question that the Court need address, is whether the conduct of the defendant amounts to competition, and if so whether or not it is unfair. Exceptions do not fall to be considered separately but form part of the consideration of this question.[807]

7. General Provisions

7.251. Commencement and parties. The Convention came into force on 18 April 1973.[808] It was open until 30 April 1972, for signature and subsequent ratification or acceptance by any State that was a member of the United Nations, any of the Specialised Agencies brought into relationship with the United Nations or the International Atomic Energy Agency, or was a party to the Statute of the International Court of Justice.[809] Any State which is a member of the United Nations, any of the Specialised Agencies brought into relationship with the United Nations or the International Atomic Energy Agency, or is a party to the Statute of the International Court of Justice may accede to the Convention.[810] It is understood that, at the time that a State becomes bound by the Convention, it will be in a position in accordance with its domestic law to give effect to the provisions of the Convention.[811] A Contracting State may denounce the Convention, on its own behalf or on behalf of any territories to which it has been extended.[812]

7.252. Non-retroactivity. No Contracting State is required to apply the provisions of the Convention to any phonogram fixed before the Convention entered into

---

[802] Samnik Report, para. 61.
[803] WIPO Guide to the Phonograms Convention, (1981), 6.5.
[804] Article 6(a).
[805] Article 6(b). However, this provision may be invalid within the European Community, see §1.019 above.
[806] Article 6(c).
[807] Samnik Report, para. 63.
[808] In accordance with Article 11(1).
[809] Article 9(1) and Article 9(2). See Table F of Appendix III.
[810] *Ibid.*
[811] Article 9(4).
[812] Article 12(1).

force in that State.[813] But they may do so if they wish. If Contracting States follow the non-retroactive principle, the effect of the Convention is weakened since pirated copies of a phonogram fixed earlier than the aforementioned date, may continue to circulate.[814]

7.253. Reservations. No reservations are permitted under the Convention.[815]

7.254. Relationship of Convention to other rights. The Convention may not be interpreted to limit or prejudice the protection otherwise secured to authors, to performers, to producers of phonograms or to broadcasting organisations under any domestic law or international agreement.[816] The relevant international agreements are the Berne Convention for the Protection of Literary and Artistic Works and Universal Copyright Convention as concerns copyright, the Rome Convention as concerns neighbouring rights and the Paris Convention for the Protection of Industrial Property as concerns unfair competition.[817] If a country is a member of both the Rome Convention and this (the Phonograms) Convention, 'it follows that if there is an overlap the convention which gives the greater protection applies, giving effect to Article 22 of the Rome Convention'.[818]

7.255. Rights of performers. It is a matter for the domestic law of each Contracting State to determine the extent, if any, to which performers whose performances are fixed in a phonogram are entitled to enjoy protection and the conditions for enjoying any such protection.[819] The WIPO Guide explains that this provision was inserted to show that the framers of the Convention had not ignored the damage which record piracy may cause not only to the industry but to performers as well, and to remind the Contracting States of the latter's needs.[820] Whether or not performers are given the right to take direct action against a pirate is decided by the terms of the contract between the phonogram producer and the performer but the framers of the Convention stated that it was desirable that performers should have the right to take action against the infringer.[821]

7.256. Extension to territories. Any State may declare that it will apply the Convention to all or any one of the territories for whose international affairs it is responsible.[822]

---

[813] Article 7(3) and Samnik Report, para. 26.
[814] WIPO Guide to the Phonograms Convention (1981), 7.10.
[815] Article 10.
[816] Article 7(1).
[817] WIPO Guide to the Phonograms Convention (1981), 7.3.
[818] Stewart, *op. cit.*, 9.15.
[819] Article 7(2).
[820] WIPO Guide to the Phonograms Convention (1981), 7.7.
[821] Samnik Report, para. 65.
[822] Article 11(3). Notice is addressed to the Secretary-General of the United Nations. See Table F of Appendix III. In accordance with Article 11(4), such an extension may in no way be understood as implying the recognition or tacit acceptance by a Contracting State of the factual situation concerning a territory to which this Convention is made applicable by another Contracting State.

VIII. CONVENTION RELATING TO THE DISTRIBUTION OF PROGRAMME-CARRYING SIGNALS TRANSMITTED BY SATELLITE OF 21 MAY 1974

1. Introduction

7.257. History. Almost from the moment that satellites were first orbiting the earth, there were fears that their signals would be pirated. Those fears were compounded by the refusal of international law to acknowledge that a transmission by satellite constituted a 'broadcast'. The transmission was considered to be merely transporting a signal between pieces of technology. Thus, under existing Conventions, right holders were not protected even at the point where an unauthorised cable operator distributed the signals. In fact, during the nascence of satellite technology, concerns about satellite piracy were slight, for the first satellites to come into being, so called 'point-to-point' satellites, were of low power. They were designed to relay signals solely between two fixed points on the globe and only receiving stations of immense sophistication (and expense) could receive and exploit the signals such satellites transmitted. But with the incessant onward march of technology, 'point-to-point' satellites were soon replaced by 'distribution satellites'. They were far more powerful than their predecessors, able to transmit signals to a large number of receiving stations and it was relatively easy for a pirate to tap into the signals they carried.

Of course, progress did not cease there and eventually an entirely new breed of satellite came into being: the Direct Broadcast Satellite. But by its mere invention, the Direct Broadcast Satellite presented a solution to the dangers of piracy of its signals. For it was able to transmit signals directly to dish aerials owned by the everyday subscriber. Thus international law soon came to recognise that a Direct Broadcast Satellite was 'broadcasting' material in much the same way as ordinary terrestrial transmitters. And therefore, authors and the owners of neighbouring rights were fully protected under the traditional conventions. Meanwhile, signals 'transported' by Fixed Service Satellite remained vulnerable.

In the late sixties, UNESCO and WIPO's predecessor (the International Bureaux for the Protection of Intellectual Property) began discussions aimed at bringing into force a convention which would protect material distributed by Fixed Service Satellite. The negotiations proved to be turbulent from the start, for there was disagreement as to who and what ought to be protected. Broadcasting organisations fought for protection of their broadcasts, whilst authors, performers and other artists argued that the Convention should enshrine rights in favour of those persons whose material composed the broadcast. The impasse was eventually resolved by a dramatic manoeuvre. The long held notion that the Convention ought to enshrine express rights either in favour of individuals or organisations was entirely swept away. Instead, it was agreed that the Convention would simply dictate that participating States were themselves to ensure by whatever means, that signals originating in another State were protected by the law. Thus the Convention was lifted out of the domain of private law inhabited by copyright and neighbouring rights and into the realm of public international law with its grand accords between Contracting States. As the Ringer Report prosaically puts it, it is the container (ie the signals) and not the content (the broadcast or the material of which it is composed) which is protected.[823]

7.258. Interpretation of the Convention. The final form of the Convention was negotiated and adopted at a conference in Brussels in 1974. The report of the conference, compiled by Barbara Ringer (the 'Ringer Report'), contains many interpretive points agreed upon by the delegates[824] and is referred to below in the analysis of the Convention.

7.259. Scope of the Convention. The Convention aims to prevent programme-carrying signals which are being relayed via a Fixed Service Satellite from being distributed by a pirate before they have been distributed by a distributor for whom they were intended. The Convention applies exclusively to international situations and none of its provisions can have any sort of effect on the law governing exclusively domestic situations in a Contracting State.[825]

7.260. Regime of protection. The Convention does not enshrine any particular rights in favour of individuals or bodies and this regime is reinforced by the Convention's neutral title.[826] It simply places a general duty on Contracting States to implement protection in any way they deem fit. Thus whilst this obligation might be undertaken within the framework of intellectual property laws granting protection to signals under copyright or neighbouring right laws, a Contracting State can just as appropriately adopt administrative measures, penal sanctions, or telecommunication laws or regulations.[827] The result of this freedom is of course the existence of a disparity of rights amongst the Contracting States.

7.261. Model regimes of protection. In fact, a Committee of Governmental Experts has settled on two models to aid Contracting States in their implementation of the Convention.[828] Under Model 1, national law would grant an originating organisation (ie broadcasting organisation), an express right (ie a neighbouring right) to authorise a distribution.[829] Any infringement of the rights established under this model would give rise to the same remedies and to the same sanctions as those provided for in the case of infringement of intellectual property rights.[830] Under Model 2, national law would make it an offence for a distributor to distribute a programme over which it has not acquired rights by contract from the originating organisation.[831] However, the absence of a contract would not result in the distribution being prohibited where the distributor establishes that the originating organisation does not object to the free distribution of its programmes.[832]

---

[823] B Ringer, *Report of the Brussels Diplomatic Conference on the Distribution of Programme Carrying Signals Transmitted by Satellites, (the 'Ringer Report') Copyright* [1974] Issue 11, para. 64.
[824] *Ibid.* para. 267 et seq.
[825] *Ibid.* para. 111.
[826] *Ibid.* para. 55.
[827] *Ibid.* para. 79.
[828] Report of Committee of Governmental Experts on the Implementation of the Satellites Convention, Paris June 11-14, 1979, Copyright [1979] Issue 9, 219 et seq. The model provisions serve only as guidelines for national legislators who are free to adopt any other approach (see para. 15. of the Report).
[829] Model Provisions Granting Specific Protection to Broadcasting Organisations under the Convention, Article 2.
[830] *Ibid*, Article 7.
[831] *Ibid*, Article 3(1) and Article 7.
[832] Article 3(2).

7.262. Exclusion of signals emitted by Direct Broadcast Satellites. The Convention excludes from protection signals which are being emitted by a direct broadcasting satellite on behalf of an originating organisation[833] ie, there is no redress under the Convention against a pirate who distributes DBS signals. This is because a DBS satellite is considered to be the originating broadcasting organisation's extended transmitter in space. Thus the signal coming from it is deemed to have already been 'distributed' by an intended distributor. However, the Convention does prohibit a 'pirate' distributor using a DBS system to distribute a signal which is being relayed via a Fixed Satellite Service and which has not already been distributed to the general public by an authorised distributor.[834]

2. Rights Protected

7.263. Protected signals. Each Contracting State undertakes to 'take adequate measures' to prevent, either on or from its territory, the unintended distribution of a programme-carrying signal[835] which is being emitted to or passing through a satellite and which originates from an organisation which is a national of another Contracting State.[836] Contracting States whose law so provided on 21 May, 1974 were permitted to extend protection to signals which did not necessarily originate, but were emitted from the territory of another Contracting State.[837]   The Convention applies not only to poaching at the end of the 'down-leg' of a transmission, but at any point during the 'up-leg' or 'down-leg' or from the storage unit of the satellite itself.[838] Furthermore, the phrase 'on or from its territory' means that Contracting States have an obligation to prevent a pirate transmitting from a sending station located on its territory, even where the members of the public for whom the pirated transmission is intended are entirely outside its territory.[839]

7.264. Unprotected signals. Contracting States have no obligation to prevent the distribution of signals which, before they are unlawfully distributed, have been distributed by a distributor for whom they were intended.[840] Thus where an unintended distributor distributes signals tapped from another terrestrial distributor at the end of a chain of terrestrial distributions, and at least one of the distributors further up the chain was intended to receive the signals, the fact that the signals were emitted through a satellite would not make the Convention applicable. The act of such a distributor would in any case constitute 'rebroadcasting' which is fully covered by the Rome Convention.[841] However, if none of the distributors up the

---

[833] Article 3. This wording follows the definition of a DBS Satellite service as defined then in Number 84AP Spa2 of the ITU Radio Regulations, as amended in 1971. In accordance with those regulations, the term 'direct reception' encompassed both individual and community reception (See Ringer Report, para. 106.).

[834] Ringer Report, para. 105.

[835] in the form of a 'derived signal' (see §7.269 below).

[836] Article 2(1).

[837] Article 8(2). Notification is deposited with the Secretary General of the United Nations. See Table G of Appendix III.

[838] Ringer Report, para. 83.

[839] Ibid. para. 82.

[840] Article 2(3). This is because the Convention is intended to deal primarily with space communications and not cover situations that are essentially terrestrial (see ibid. para. 100).

[841] Ibid. para. 100. See §7.217 above. Similarly if the unauthorised distribution is made by a cable operator, it would be a 'communication to the public' under the Berne Convention. See §7.052 above.

chain were intended to receive the signals emitted to or through the satellite, the Convention would apply.[842]

3. Definitions

7.265. Programme. A programme is defined as 'a body of live or recorded material consisting of images, sounds or both, embodied in signals emitted for the purpose of ultimate distribution'.[843] The concept of programme includes material such as privately made films or tapes not initially intended for public consumption, but excludes scientific and technical data, military intelligence, private communications, and other masses of material being transmitted by satellite for specialised uses.[844]

7.266. Signal. A signal is defined 'an electronically generated carrier capable of transmitting programmes'.[845] As long as a signal has the potential capacity of transmitting programmes, it makes no difference what the electronic means or combination of means, including radio waves of all sorts and laser beams, are used to generate or regenerate it.[846]

7.267. Satellite. A satellite is defined as 'any device in extraterrestrial space capable of transmitting signals'.[847] This implies a man made object for transmitting signals located in orbit around the earth or on a celestial body.[848] It includes both an active satellite which transmits or retransmits signals, and a passive satellite which is intended for transmission by reflection.[849] The word 'extraterrestrial' means that, at least during part of its orbit, the satellite must be located outside the earth and its atmosphere.[850] However, this does not exclude satellites in elliptical orbit ie those which pass through the earth's atmosphere during part only of their orbital path.[851]

7.268. Originating organisation. An originating organisation is defined as 'the person or legal entity that decides what programme the emitted signal will carry'.[852] It is intended to exclude telecommunication authorities and common carriers who exercise no control over what programmes the signals carry.[853] It is also intended to exclude the creators and producers of programmes as such, since their control is over the content of the programmes, not signals.[854] Thus, the originating organisa-

---

[842] *Ibid.* para. 101.
[843] Article 1(ii). In accordance with Article 1(iv), a 'signal emitted' is any programme-carrying signal that goes to or passes through a satellite.
[844] *Ibid.* para. 64.
[845] Article 1(i).
[846] Ringer Report, para. 63.
[847] Article 1(iii).
[848] Ringer Report, para. 66.
[849] *Ibid.*
[850] *Ibid.*
[851] *Ibid.*
[852] Article 1(vi).
[853] Ringer Report, para. 71.
[854] *Ibid.* para. 72.

tion is that body which possesses the ultimate power of decision. So, in the case of States[855] where an official public broadcasting authority owns rights in programmes but delegates production authority to contractors in various regions, the former is considered the originating organisation.[856]

7.269. The meaning of a 'distribution' of a satellite signal. 'Distribution' has a precise technical meaning. This is vital since any rights granted under the Convention turn upon whether or not a signal has been lawfully distributed. 'Distribution' is defined as 'the operation by which a distributor transmits derived signals to the general public or any section thereof'.[857] A signal is deemed to have been 'derived' only if its technical characteristics have been modified such that it is transformed into viewable images.[858] It is irrelevant whether or not there have been one or more intervening fixations.[859]

The phrase 'the general public or any section thereof', means any part of the public in any place on earth. This definition of a 'distribution' means that acts consisting merely of reception or fixation of signals are not prohibited. This is particularly important as testing and technical and experimental reception or fixation may be necessary by authorised parties from time to time in order to check the reception equipment as well as the orbital position of the satellite.[860] If such acts amounted to a distribution, they would terminate protection of those particular signals under the Convention.

A transmission constitutes a 'distribution' whether it is made simultaneously with the original emission to the satellite or from a fixation.[861] But the word 'transmits' does not include the marketing or supply of fixations such as phonograms or video tapes.[862] However, the definition is broad enough to cover any present or future telecommunications methods for transmitting signals, including not only traditional forms of broadcasting, but also transmission by cable or other fixed communications channels, laser transmission and transmission by direct broadcasting satellites.[863] Thus although the Convention excludes from protection the retransmission of signals taken from direct broadcast satellites, it does not affect the obligation of a Contracting State to prevent the unauthorised distribution by means of a direct broadcasting satellite, of signals received from a Fixed Satellite Service (ie 'point-to-point' or 'distribution' satellite).[864]

7.270. Meaning of 'distributor'. A distributor is defined as a 'person or legal entity that decides that the transmission of the derived signals to the general public or any section thereof should take place'.[865]

4. Duration of Protection

7.271. The Convention does not set out a maximum period of protection, but

---

[855] eg the United Kingdom ITV network.
[856] Ringer Report, para. 72.
[857] Article 1(viii).
[858] Article 1(v).
[859] *Ibid.*
[860] Ringer Report, para. 75.
[861] *Ibid.* para. 76.
[862] *Ibid.*
[863] *Ibid.*
[864] *Ibid.* paras. 103 and 105.
[865] Article 1(vii).

it permits Contracting States to limit the duration of protection in which case it must be specified under domestic law.[866] However, it is generally considered that a period of twenty years constitutes a reasonable period of protection.[867]

5. Exceptions to Unauthorised Distribution—Fair Use and Distribution by Cable

7.272. Fair use. The Convention permits Contracting States to deny protection against unintended distribution where the signal: carries short excerpts of a programme consisting of reports of current events, but only to the extent justified by the informatory purpose of such excerpts;[868] or carries, as quotations, short excerpts of a programme, provided that such quotations are compatible with fair practice and are justified by the informatory purpose of such quotations;[869] or is carried by a territory regarded as a developing country[870] and the distribution is used solely for the purpose of teaching (including teaching in the framework of adult education) or scientific research.[871] These exceptions do not supersede the obligations of a Contracting State under another Treaty, such as the copyright conventions, the Rome Convention or the ITU Convention.[872]

7.273. Distribution by cable. The domestic law of a few Contracting States provides that the retransmission of broadcasts to subscribers by wire or cable systems are outside the control of copyright owners.[873] Accordingly, the Convention states that Contracting States whose law so provided on 21 May, 1974, were permitted to continue limiting or denying protection against the unintended distribution of a programme carrying signal by wires, cable or other similar communications channels to subscribing members of the public, to the extent that and for so long as its domestic law limits or denies such protection.[874] However, a cable system should not pick up and distribute signals from a satellite before these signals have been terrestrially distributed in an area where the cable system can receive the terrestrial broadcast.[875]

---

[866] Article 2(2). The Secretary-General of the United Nations must be notified within 6 months of the entry into force or modification of this restriction. See Table G of Appendix III.

[867] Ringer Report, para. 98.

[868] Article 4(i): 'the programming must be done as part of a report of general news of the day and would therefore, as a rule, have to be transmitted on the basis of fixation' (*ibid.* para. 109).

[869] Article 4(ii).

[870] In accordance with Article 4(iii), in conformity with the established practice of the General Assembly of the United Nations.

[871] Article 4(iii). Any kind of instructional teaching is envisaged by this provision (Ringer Report, para. 110).

[872] Ringer Report, para. 111.

[873] *Ibid.* para. 127.

[874] Article 8(3)(a). In accordance with Article 8(3)(a), notification of this must be deposited with the Director-General of the United Nations. Furthermore, in accordance with Article 8(3)(b), States which have exploited this reservation must notify the Secretary-General of the United Nations within six months of the coming into force of any modification of this reservation under their domestic law. See Table G of Appendix III.

[875] Ringer Report, para. 129.

6. General Provisions

7.274. Commencement and parties. The Convention was enacted on 21 May, 1974 and came into force on 25 August, 1979.[876] It was open for signature until 31 March, 1975[877] and subsequent ratification or acceptance,[878] by any State that was a member of the United Nations, any of the Specialised Agencies brought into relationship with the United Nations, the International Atomic Energy Agency or was a party to the Statute of the International Court of Justice. The Convention is currently open for accession by any State referred to in the aforementioned States.[879] A State must, when it becomes bound by the Convention, be in a position to give effect to its terms in accordance with its domestic laws.[880] Any Contracting State may denounce the Convention[881] and denunciation takes effect twelve months after the date of reception of the notice.[882]

7.275. Non-retroactivity. Unless a Contracting State chooses to provide otherwise it need not apply the Convention to any signal emitted before the Convention entered into force in that State.[883]

7.276. Reservations. No reservations other than the two expressly provided for, are allowed.[884]

7.277. Relationship of Convention to law providing for the protection of copyright and neighbouring rights. The Convention does not in any way limit or prejudice the protection secured to authors, performers, producers of phonograms, or broadcasting organisations, under any domestic law or international agreement.[885] Stewart cites three examples of interaction between the rights conferred by this Convention and those accorded by the Berne and Universal Conventions.[886] The first is where the author consents but the broadcasting organisation does not consent to a piratical transmission. The second is the reverse. In both cases the interaction of the conventions produce a conflict of rights. In the third example, neither the author nor the broadcasting organisation consents to the transmission. In this case there is no conflict, the author asserting the Universal and Berne Conventions and the broadcasting organisation invoking this Convention.

7.278. Prevention of abuses of monopoly. The Convention does not in any way limit the right of any Contracting State to apply its domestic law in order to prevent abuses of monopoly.[887] This means that a distributor not designated by the originating organisation may be authorised by the competent authorities to distribute programme-carrying signals.[888] This type of measure cannot, however, be justified by the simple fact that the originating organisation is asking a price

---

[876] In accordance with Article 10(1).
[877] Article 9(1). See Table G of Appendix III.
[878] Article 9(2).
[879] *Ibid.*
[880] Article 9(4).
[881] Article 11(1).
[882] Article 11(2).
[883] Article 5.
[884] Article 8(1). See above at §§7.271 and 7.273.
[885] Article 6.
[886] Stewart, *op. cit.*, 10.16.
[887] Article 7.
[888] Ringer Report, para. 122.

considered too high, if it has not been determined that this price is not justified by the production and transport costs of the signal.[889] It has suggested that what these cumbersome phrases mean is 'that if a government "determines" that the price is too high it can expropriate the signal on anti-trust grounds'.[890]

In addition, a measure may not be applied when the originating organisation does not possess the rights to distribute the signal on the territory of the State in issue,[891] ie a broadcasting organisation which has not acquired all the rights to distribute a signal on the territory in issue cannot have that signal expropriated on the above grounds.

7.279. Extension to territories. To avoid any hint of colonialism, the Convention does not specify that a Contracting State may accede on behalf of its dependant countries.[892] However, the absence of this 'territorial dependency clause' does not prevent a Contracting State with dependant territories from acceding in respect of those territories. Thus it may find the practical means necessary to deal with the problem of making the Convention applicable in dependant territories.[893]

IX. EUROPEAN CONVENTION ON TRANSFRONTIER TELEVISION

1. Introduction

7.280. History. As long ago as 1981, the new satellite technologies were enabling broadcasting organisations to penetrate the furthest reaches of foreign territories. At that time the Parliamentary Assembly of the Council of Europe expressed its concern that this proliferation might endanger the diversity of media structures found in the Contracting States thus undermining each State's cultural heritage. As the years progressed the Council of Europe greeted each new threat posed by the new technology with a series of Recommendations and the European Convention on Transfrontier Television (the 'Convention') is, in essence, a synthesis of three of those instruments.

The first Recommendation[894] sought to regulate advertising material, stipulating that it should respect human rights giving particular attention to the moral values which form the basis of every democratic society, preserve the integrity of programmes and conform to minimum standards of honesty, truth and decency. Utmost attention, it said, should be paid to the harmful consequences of advertising concerning tobacco, alcohol and certain other products and the vulnerabilities of children ought to be of particular concern. A second Recommendation[895] in the same year set out guidelines which would determine State responsibility for broadcasts made by satellite. Clarification was needed because a broadcast was not

---

[889] *Ibid.*
[890] Stewart, *op. cit.*, 10.14.
[891] Ringer Report, para. 122.
[892] *Ibid.* para. 132.
[893] *Ibid.*
[894] Recommendation No. R(84)3 of 23 February, 1984 on principles on television advertising.
[895] Recommendation No R(84)22 of 7 December 1984, on the use of satellite capacity for television and sound radio.

always transmitted in the State where the broadcasting organisation was situated. The third Recommendation[896] was a product of European Cultural insecurity; its purpose being to nurture a European television production market. European States were fearful that the invasion of third country programmes would dilute the European content of broadcasting programmes and threaten the diversity of European culture.

But what galvanised the Council of Europe into enacting a Convention to bring together and rework these principles, was a concern that the European Community's then forthcoming Directive, 'Television Without Frontiers',[897] would partition televisual Europe into two camps: one consisting of those States belonging to the Community governed by one set of rules, and the other containing the remaining Contracting States of the Council of Europe, each bound by a different set of rules.

In fact, both institutions reached a consensus which favoured the Council of Europe. For it was agreed that the Council of Europe would finalise the terms of the Convention (with the participation of the Community delegation) and the Community's Directive would then be brought into line with the Convention.

It is worth noting a source of potential conflict between the aspirations of the Community and those of the Council of Europe.[898] The Community's task is to create a 'Common Market' comprising its Member States by erasing barriers to trade. It thus saw the proliferation of satellite technology (in particular DBS) as a powerful instrument to help secure a 'common market' in broadcasting services. On the other hand, it was precisely these possibilities offered by DBS which caused the Council of Europe concern—a body which takes for granted the existence of frontiers between States. The focus of the Covention is thus to preserve the integrity of national media structures.[899]

7.281. Interpretation of the Convention. The Steering Committee on the Mass Media which drafted the Convention has prepared an 'Explanatory Report on the European Convention' (the 'Explanatory Report') to aid its interpretation. Reference is made to that Report below.

7.282. Scope of the Convention. The Convention is concerned with programme services embodied in transmissions.[900] Its purpose is to facilitate the transfrontier transmission and retransmissions of television 'programme services' among the Contracting States.[901] The Convention applies to any programme service[902] which is transmitted or retransmitted by entities or by technical means within the jurisdiction of a Party, whether by cable, terrestrial transmitter or satellite, and which can be received, directly or indirectly, in one or more other Parties.[903] This includes regional and local programme services.[904]

---

[896] Recommendation No R(86)3 of 14 February 1986, on the promotion of audiovisual production in Europe.

[897] See §§2.018 and 6.056 et seq. above.

[898] F W Hondius, *Regulating Transfrontier Television—The Strasbourg Option* Yearbook of European Law (1988), p. 141.

[899] See Explanatory Report, para. 24.

[900] Article 1.

[901] *Ibid.*

[902] In accordance with Article 2.d, a programme service means 'all the items within a single service provided by a given broadcaster'.

[903] Article 3. Any form of overspill of a transmission made from one Party into the territory of another Party, whether or not intentional is to be taken into account in determining whether this definition is satisfied (Explanatory Report, para 77).

[904] Explanatory Report, para. 78.

The Convention is applicable to subscription television services or teletext services but excludes those services designed for a closed group ie members of one particular profession.[905] And it does not govern communication services operating on individual demand.[906] Therefore, signals employed in video conferencing, videotex, telefacsimile services, electronic data banks, interactive and similar communication services are excluded.[907] Also excluded are communications (ie transmissions of programmes) solely between broadcasters.[908]

2. Freedom of Reception and Retransmission

7.283. General principles. Parties must ensure freedom of expression and information in accordance with Article 10 of the European Convention for the Protection of Human Rights and Fundamental Freedoms ('ECHR').[909] This Convention thus dispels any doubt that broadcasting and cinema are covered by Article 10 of the ECHR.[910]

7.284. Specific rules. Parties must guarantee freedom of reception and retransmission in their territories of programme services which comply with the terms of the Convention.[911] Retransmission is defined as 'receiving and simultaneously transmitting, irrespective of the technical means employed,[912] complete and unchanged television programme services, or important parts of such services, transmitted by broadcasters for reception by the general public'.[913] Necessary delays of a few seconds for technical reasons will not deny the transmission the quality of simultaneity.[914] And the authorised decoding of an encrypted service would be covered.[915] Although the retransmission solely of individual programme items are within the scope of these terms, the integrity of the programme from which they are culled must be retained and the broadcaster's consent must be acquired.[916] As far as satellites are concerned, the Convention does not distinguish between a Fixed Service Satellite and a Direct Broadcast Satellite, both of whose signals are deemed to be embraced by the term 'retransmission'.[917] Finally, the obligation to retransmit

---

[905] *Ibid.* para. 48.

[906] Article 2.a.

[907] Explanatory Report, para. 47.

[908] *Ibid.* para. 49.

[909] For the text of Article 10 of the Convention for the Protection of Human Rights and Fundamental Freedoms, see §5.016 above.

[910] Hondius, *op. cit.* As Hondius explains, it has been argued that the effect of the third sentence of paragraph 1 of Article 10 of the ECHR is to exclude broadcasting and cinema enterprises from the protection offered (as well as the obligations imposed) by Article 10 of the ECHR.

[911] Article 4.

[912] At the time of drafting of the Convention, DBS and FSS technology were in existence but the drafters were conscious of the possibility of development of new technology and so their draft encompasses any as yet unknown mode of retransmission. See Hondius, *op. cit.*

[913] Article 2.b.

[914] Explanatory Report, para. 52.

[915] *Ibid.* para. 54.

[916] *Ibid.* para. 53.

[917] *Ibid.* para. 46. The Report states that '. . . as far as transmissions by satellite are concerned, the distinction prevailing in the Radio Regulations of the International Telecommunications Union (ITU) between a broadcasting satellite service (DBS) and a fixed satellite service (FSS) has not been retained'.

services does not concern situations where a Party is unable to guarantee retransmission because of limitations in technical capacity.[918]

7.285. Reservation—advertisements for alcoholic beverages. The obligation to retransmit broadcasts, is circumscribed by a reservation which may be made by the Parties. Thus Contracting States are entitled to impede the retransmission on their territory of programme services which do not conform with their domestic legislation and which contain advertisements for alcoholic beverages.[919]

3. Obligations of Transmitting Parties

7.286. General principles. The Convention places a duty on 'transmitting Parties' to ensure by appropriate means, that all programme services transmitted by entities or by technical means within its jurisdiction, comply with the terms of the Convention.[920] Transmission means[921] the 'initial emission by terrestrial transmitter, by cable, or by satellite of whatever nature, in encoded or unencoded form, of television programme services for reception by the general public'.[922] The identity of the transmitting Party is determined by whether the transmission is a terrestrial transmission or a transmission by satellite.

7.287. Terrestrial and cable transmissions. In the case of terrestrial transmissions, the transmitting Party (that Party responsible for ensuring compliance with the Convention) is the Party in which the initial emission is effected.[923] In the case of cable transmissions, the transmitting Party will usually be the Party in which the cable head-end is situated.[924]

7.288. Transmissions by satellite. In the case of transmissions by satellite, the responsible party is either: the Party in which the satellite uplink is situated;[925] or the Party which grants the use of the frequency or a satellite capacity when the uplink is situated in a State which is not a Party to the Convention;[926] or the Party in which the broadcaster has its seat when responsibility under the preceding principles cannot be established.[927]

7.289. Programme services transmitted from States not Parties to the Convention. When programme services transmitted from States which are not Parties to the Convention are retransmitted by entities or by technical means (ie by cable, terrestrial transmitter or satellite) within the jurisdiction of a Party and these services can be received directly or indirectly in one or more other Parties, the Convention gives to that Party the responsibility to ensure by appropriate means and through its competent organs, compliance with the terms of the Convention ie it is deemed to be the Transmitting Party.[928]

---

[918] Explanatory Report, para. 83. The Report states (para. 84), that 'It is not intended to inhibit Parties in the exercise of their general spectrum policies in ways authorised under other international agreements'.

[919] See under 'reservations', §7.340 below.

[920] Article 5.

[921] And therefore 'programme services transmitted' refers to.

[922] Article 2.a.

[923] Article 5.2.a.

[924] Explanatory Report, para. 43.

[925] Article 5.2.b.i.

[926] Article 5.2.b.ii.

[927] Article 5.2.b.iii.

[928] Article 5.3 and Article 3.

4. The Provision of Information

7.290. Duty to define broadcasters' responsibilities. The Convention stipulates that the responsibilities of the broadcaster must be clearly and adequately specified in the authorization issued by, or contract concluded with the competent authority of each Party, or by any other legal measure.[929] This refers to obligations under a contract or franchise, as well as civil and criminal liability.[930]

7.291. Definition of a 'broadcaster'. A broadcaster is defined as 'the natural or legal person who composes television programme services for reception by the general public and transmits them or has them transmitted, complete and unchanged, by a third party'.[931]

7.292. Obligation to provide information on broadcaster. Information about a broadcaster must be made available upon request to the competent authority of the Transmitting Party.[932] Such information must include, as a minimum, the name or denomination, seat and status of the broadcaster, the name of the legal representative, the composition of its capital and the nature, purpose and mode of financing the programme service the broadcaster is providing or intends providing.[933] Rules on data protection, professional secrecy and commercial secrets must, however, be respected.[934]

5. Responsibilities of the Broadcaster

7.293. General principles. All items contained in programme services must, as concerns both their presentation and content, respect the dignity of the human being and the fundamental rights of others.[935] Specifically, they must not be indecent and, in particular, must not contain pornography.[936] Neither must they give undue prominence to violence[937] or be likely to incite racial hatred.[938] In respect of the latter, it is the prominence of such material which is prohibited. Thus violence and hatred which exists in society may be portrayed.[939] Each of the aforementioned standards apply to programmes, advertisements, trailers, public announcement or any other programme item.[940] They are inspired by the European

---

[929] Article 6.1.
[930] Explanatory Report, para. 107.
[931] Article 2.c.
[932] Article 6.2. It is not, however, necessary for information to be published (see Explanatory Report, para. 109.)
[933] Article 6.2. The Explanatory Report notes (para. 56) that a single broadcasting service is involved when two or more organisations supply different parts of a single channel (ie one body controlling advertising and another controlling programming) providing that it is clear to viewers that together they constitute an integrated single service. However, where a given broadcaster offers two or more channels, they are considered as separate services under the Convention (Explanatory Report, para. 58).
[934] Explanatory Report, para. 111.
[935] Article 7.1.
[936] Article 7.1.a.
[937] Article 7.1.b.
[938] *Ibid.*
[939] Explanatory Report, para. 121.
[940] *Ibid.* para. 116.

Convention on Human Rights (especially Article 10 of that Convention) and should be interpreted in the light of the case law of its organs.[941]

7.294. Minors. All items of programme services which are likely to impair the physical, mental or moral development of children and adolescents may not be scheduled when, because of the time of transmission and reception, they are likely to watch them.[942] It is not, however, necessary that such transmissions contain a warning (either optical or acoustic), for this is considered to be an incentive for young persons to watch a broadcast.[943] The Convention thus relies upon parents exercising control over the viewing habits of their children.

7.295. News programmes. Broadcasters must ensure that news programmes fairly present facts and events and encourage the free formation of opinions.[944] The reference to 'free formation of opinion' indicates that the Convention respects domestic rules concerning electoral or political campaigns, provided that freedom of expression is not prejudiced.[945]

6. Right of Reply

7.296. General principles. Each Transmitting Party must ensure that every natural or legal person, regardless of nationality or place of residence, has the opportunity to exercise a right of reply or to seek other comparable legal or administrative remedies relating to programmes transmitted or retransmitted by entities or by technical means within its jurisdiction.[946] The right must give persons the opportunity to correct inaccurate facts or information, or to make known their view on such facts, in cases where such facts or information concern them, or constitute an attack on their dignity honour or reputation—or in the case of natural persons—an intrusion into their private life.[947] The right of reply must be exercisable even by persons who are neither nationals nor residents of a Party to the Convention.[948]

7.297. Effective exercise of right of reply. Parties are under an obligation to ensure that the effective timing and other arrangements for the exercise of the right of reply are such that the right can be effectively exercised.[949] The effective exercise of the right or other comparable legal or administrative remedies must be ensured both as regards the timing and modalities.[950] This means that 'the context in which

---

[941] *Ibid.* para. 117. The Explanatory Report (para. 118) notes that they also reflect the Preamble of the Universal Declaration Of Human Rights (1948). The notion of indecency in particular should be interpreted in accordance with the Handyside case (judgment of 7 December 1976) and the Müller case (judgment of 24 May 1988) (see Explanatory Report, para. 120.). See §§5.121 and 5.123 above.

[942] Article 7.2. For these purposes the time differences in the transmitting and receiving Parties must be taken into account (see Explanatory Report, para. 124).

[943] Explanatory Report, para. 125.

[944] Article 7.3.

[945] Explanatory Report, para. 128.

[946] Article 8.1.

[947] Explanatory Report, para. 135.

[948] *Ibid.* para. 131.

[949] Article 8.1.

[950] *Ibid.*

a right of reply is exercised should be comparable to that in which the incriminating statement was made'.[951]

7.298. Identification of broadcaster. The name of the broadcaster responsible for the programme service must be identified thereon at regular intervals by appropriate means.[952] This might for example consist of the presentation of a discreet logo at certain points during a broadcast or at advertising breaks.

7. Access of the Public to Major Works

7.299. The right to information is a principle focus of the Convention. Accordingly Parties are obliged to examine the legal measures necessary to avoid the right of the public to information being undermined due to the exercise by a broadcaster of exclusive rights for the transmission or retransmission[953] of an event of high public interest which has the effect of depriving a large part of the public in one or more other Parties of the opportunity to follow that event on television.[954] This could be a political, social, cultural or sports event which is of general interest.[955] It should be noted that the Convention's focus is on the right of the public to information and not competition law. Therefore, where exclusive rights have been granted for an event of high public interest, it is not intended that another broadcaster should have the right to transmit the entire event.[956] The Explanatory Report concedes, however, that the requirement may not be fulfilled simply by allowing another broadcaster to transmit small excerpts of the exclusive broadcast but may require the sublicensing of the broadcast for deferred retransmission.[957]

8. Cultural Objectives of the Convention

(1) The Production of Programmes

7.300. Reservation for European works. Each transmitting Party must ensure, where practicable and by appropriate means, that broadcasters reserve for European works, a majority proportion of their transmission time, excluding time appointed to news, sports events, games, advertising and teletext services.[958] This proportion should be achieved progressively on the basis of suitable criteria, having regard to the broadcaster's informational, educational, cultural and entertainment responsibilities to its viewing public.[959] There is no precise meaning of European audiovisual works. They are defined simply as 'creative works, the production or coproduction of which is controlled by European natural of legal persons'.[960] This means control over the content of the work, the production process and the end

---

[951] Explanatory Report, para. 133.
[952] Article 8.2.
[953] Within the meaning of Article 3.
[954] Article 9.
[955] Explanatory Report, para. 139.
[956] *Ibid.*, para. 140.
[957] *Ibid.*, para. 141.
[958] Article 10.1.
[959] *Ibid.*
[960] Article 2.e.
[961] Explanatory Report, para 60.

product.[961] Thus works may be financed by non-European sources, provided that the artistic and technical production control remains in the hands of European natural and legal persons.[962] The aforementioned provisions are without prejudice to the possibility for a transmitting Party to introduce stricter or more detailed rules for broadcasters of programme services transmitted by entities or by technical means within its jurisdiction.[963]

Parties to the Convention undertake to look together for the most appropriate instruments and procedures to support, without discrimination between broadcasters, the activity and development of European production, particularly in countries with a low audiovisual production capacity or restricted language area.[964] The words 'without discrimination between broadcasters' are designed to avoid discrimination between different types of broadcaster ie public service and private broadcasters.[965]

7.301. Disagreement between transmitting and receiving Party. In the case of disagreement between a receiving Party and a transmitting Party on the application of the aforementioned provisions, recourse may be had, at the request of one of the Parties, to the Standing Committee with a view to its formulating an advisory opinion on the subject. However, such a disagreement may not be submitted to the arbitration procedure provided for in the Convention.[966]

(2) Protection of Pluralism of the Press and of the Cinema Industry

7.302. General principles. Parties are obliged, 'in the spirit of co-operation and mutual assistance', which underlies the Convention, to endeavour to avoid that programme services transmitted or retransmitted within their jurisdiction,[967] endanger the pluralism of the press and the development of the cinema industries.[968]

7.303. Protection of pluralism of the press. The impetus for this objective was Germany. There was a vast decline in the number of newspapers during the 1970s and early 1980s which occurred as a result of the explosive growth of the broadcasting media diverting income from the press. Several States sought to stem the loss by allowing press groups to operate television companies. But at the same time they had to ensure that these enlarged media groups did not suffocate diversity of opinion.[969] Accordingly they implemented legislation to guard against this danger and the Convention endorses the legitimacy of such laws.

7.304. Protection of development of the cinema industries. To help protect the cinematographic industry, the Convention institutes a regime of 'windows' between the exhibition of a work in the cinema and its broadcast on television. Accordingly, no cinematographic work may be transmitted in a programme service, unless otherwise agreed between its rights holders and the broadcaster, until two years have elapsed since the work was first shown in cinemas; in the case of cinematographic works co-produced by the broadcaster, the minimum period is one

---

[962] *Ibid.*
[963] In accordance with Article 28. (See Explanatory Report, para. 150.)
[964] Article 10.3.
[965] Explanatory Report, para. 154.
[966] Article 10.2. Article 26 contains the arbitration procedure. See §7.331 below.
[967] within the meaning of Article 3. See §7.282 above.
[968] Article 10.4.
[969] Hondius, *op. cit.*, p. 141.

year.[970] In calculating this period, it is appropriate to consider the first showing of the cinematographic work whether in a State a Party to the Convention or not.[971]

9. Advertising

(1) Introduction

7.305. Aspects regulated. The Convention divides the rules concerning advertising into six categories, namely: general standards; duration; form and presentation; insertion of advertisements; advertising of particular products and advertising directed specifically at a single party.

7.306. Definition of 'advertisement'. An advertisement is defined as 'any public announcement intended to promote the sale, purchase or rental of a product or service, to advance a cause or idea or to bring about some other effect desired by the advertiser, for which transmission time has been given to the advertiser for remuneration or similar consideration'.[972] This covers both traditional spot advertisements as well as new forms of advertising such as teleshopping.[973] An announcement which aims to promote a body but not necessarily bring about a purchase or rental is covered by the definition of 'advertisement'.[974] But promotional material (eg a panel) at sports and similar events which is incidently and unavoidably transmitted on to viewers' screens, is excluded. It follows that such material will constitute 'advertisements' where it is presented permanently, repeatedly or prominently due to transmission techniques.[975]

Trailers and other publicity for television programmes, 'public interest' announcements (ie those made by political parties, religious organisations or in the course of health campaigns), is not advertising provided that no remuneration or similar consideration is received in respect of them.[976] This is subject to the proviso, that where the broadcaster is obliged to grant transmission time for public announcements, such announcements will not constitute advertisements even where remuneration is involved.[977] Finally, the featuring of cultural products within an information programme or critique does not amount to an advertisement.[978]

(2) General Standards

7.307. Advertisements must be fair and honest.[979] So they should not unfairly discredit the products or services of competitors.[980] Furthermore, they may not be

---

[970] Article 10.4.
[971] Explanatory Report, para. 156. The Report notes (para. 56) that therefore it could be that a film is transmitted in a transfrontier programme services at the same time as it is shown in the cinema in the transmitting Party.
[972] Article 2.f.
[973] Explanatory Report, para. 67.
[974] *Ibid.* para. 62.
[975] *Ibid.* para. 63.
[976] *Ibid.* para. 64. The Report makes it clear that even those advertisements not directly covered by the Convention should be guided by the terms of Article 11, Article 7.1, and 7.2, will always apply.
[977] *Ibid.* para. 65.
[978] *Ibid.* para. 66.
[979] Article 11.1.
[980] Explanatory Report, para. 160.

misleading and may not prejudice the interests of consumers,[981] ie they must not take advantage of the trust or lack of knowledge of consumers.[982] In particular, advertisements addressed to or using children must avoid anything which is likely to harm their interests and they must have regard to their special susceptibilities.[983] The advertiser may not exercise any editorial influence over the content of programmes.[984] Advertisements must comply with the general standards laid out in the Convention.[985] All of these rules are without prejudice to the civil or criminal law rules of unfair competition pertaining in a Contracting Party.[986]

(3) Duration

7.308. General principles. The amount of advertising may not exceed 15% of the daily transmission time.[987] However, this percentage may be increased to 20% to include forms of advertisements such as direct offers to the public for the sale, purchase or rental of products or for the provision of services, provided that the amount of spot advertising does not exceed 15%.[988]

7.309. Spot advertising etc. The amount of spot advertising within a given one-hour period may not exceed 20%.[989] This is designed to prevent an excessive concentration of spot advertising during prime time.[990] Forms of advertisements such as direct offers to the public for the sale, purchase or rental of products or for the provision of services may not exceed one hour per day.[991] The latter type of advertisement is not subject to maximum percentage in any hour period because it is accepted that they are generally more time consuming than spot advertisements.[992]

(4) Form and Presentation

7.310. Advertisements must be distinguishable. Advertisements must be clearly distinguishable as such and be kept recognisably separate from the other items of the programme service by either optical or acoustic means.[993] In principle, they must be transmitted in blocks.[994] Normally these will comprise two or more separate spots. But it is accepted that a single long block may be necessary to broadcast a long advertisement, or where because of the nature of the programme (ie those transmitting sports events such as boxing) the breaks will be too short to permit any advertisement or even where the broadcaster has insufficient advertising to justify more than one break.[995]

---

[981] Article 11.2.
[982] Explanatory Report, para. 161.
[983] Article 11.3.
[984] Article 11.4.
[985] ie those contained in Article 7.1 and 7.2. (See Explanatory Report, para. 159.)
[986] Explanatory Report, para. 162.
[987] Article 12.1.
[988] *Ibid.* The Explanatory Report (para. 170) states that 'a given programme service could transmit 15% spot advertising and 5% teleshopping, or 10% spot advertisements and 10% teleshopping, or even 20% teleshopping and no spot advertisements'.
[989] Article 12.2.
[990] Explanatory Report, para. 167.
[991] Article 12.3.
[992] Explanatory Report, para. 174.
[993] Article 13.1.
[994] *Ibid.*
[995] Explanatory Report, para. 177.

7.311. Subliminal and surreptitious advertisements. Subliminal advertising is absolutely prohibited.[996] Surreptitious advertisements, that is, advertisements which present products or services in programmes with the purpose of serving advertising purposes, are prohibited.[997] This prohibits forms of presentation which 'attach a value judgment to a product or service . . .',[998] but allows a presentation which refers to the characteristic features of a product or service for information purposes.[999]

7.312. Use of public figures. Advertisements must not feature, either visually or orally (ie in voice-overs), persons who regularly present news and current affairs programmes.[1000]

(5) Insertion of Advertisements

7.313. General principles. Advertisements may be inserted both between programmes and during programmes.[1001] However, advertisements may only be inserted during programmes in such a way that the integrity and value of the programme and the rights of the rights holders are not prejudiced.[1002] The Convention establishes a set of principles, (dealt with below), to ensure that this is the case. It should be noted that providing these principles are adhered to, the broadcaster is free to determine at which precise point the interruption should occur.[1003]

7.314. Programmes consisting of autonomous parts. In programmes consisting of autonomous parts, or in sports programmes and similarly structured events and performances comprising intervals, advertisements may only be inserted between the parts or in the intervals.[1004] Such programmes would include, amongst others, game shows with rounds, magazine programmes, plays, musical concerts or lectures.

7.315. Audiovisual programmes. The transmission of audiovisual works such as feature films and films made for television (excluding series, light entertainment programmes and in general documentaries) may be interrupted once for each complete period of 45 minutes provided that their scheduled duration is more than 45 minutes.[1005] A further interruption is allowed if their duration is at least twenty minutes longer than two or more complete periods of forty-five minutes.[1006] Documentaries having a degree of artistic merit are to be assimilated to the category 'audiovisual programmes' because they are similar to the latter in their content and the audience which they reach.[1007]

---

[996] Article 13.2.
[997] Article 13.3.
[998] Explanatory Report, para. 181.
[999] *Ibid.*, para. 182. Examples are descriptions of prizes in game shows, announcements for films in programmes devoted to the cinema etc.
[1000] Article 13.4.
[1001] Article 14.1.
[1002] *Ibid.*
[1003] Explanatory Report, para. 192.
[1004] Article 14.2.
[1005] Article 14.3.
[1006] *Ibid.*
[1007] Explanatory Report, para. 191. As for those lacking such artistic merit, see §7.317 below.

7.316. Light entertainment (ie series or serials). A period of at least twenty minutes must elapse between each successive advertising break within light entertainment programmes.[1008]

7.317. News and current affairs programmes, documentaries, religious programmes and children's programmes. Advertisements may not be inserted in news and current affairs programmes, documentaries, religious programmes, and children's programmes of less than thirty minutes' duration.[1009] Provided that such programmes are of thirty minutes' duration or longer, they may be interrupted by advertisements but a period of at least twenty minutes must elapse between each successive advertising break within such programmes.[1010]

7.318. Religious services. Advertisements may not be inserted in any broadcast of a religious service.[1011]

(6) Advertising of Particular Products

7.319. Tobacco. The Convention prohibits any advertisements for tobacco products.[1012] This includes: cigarettes, cigars, pipe tobacco or cigarette tobacco, chewing tobacco, snuff or any other tobacco-based product.[1013]

7.320. Alcohol. Advertisements for alcoholic beverages of all varieties must comply with the following five principles. They may not: be addressed particularly to minors and no one associated with the consumption of alcoholic beverages in advertisements should seem to be a minor;[1014] link the consumption of alcohol to physical performance or to driving;[1015] claim that alcohol has therapeutic qualities or that it is a stimulant, a sedative or a means of resolving personal problems;[1016] encourage immoderate consumption of alcohol or present abstinence or moderation in a negative light;[1017] place undue emphasis on the alcoholic content of beverages.[1018] This would exclude an advertisement from boasting not only the high, but also the low alcoholic content of a beverage.[1019]

7.321. Medicine. Advertisements for medicines and medical treatment which are available only on medical prescription in the transmitting Party are prohibited.[1020] Advertisements for other medicines and medical treatment are allowed provided that they are clearly distinguishable as such, honest, truthful and subject to verification and comply with the requirement of protection of the individual from harm.[1021] Thus they should not exaggerate the capabilities of a medicine, suggest that good health will be endangered if it is not used, suggest that its efficacy or

---

[1008] Article 14.4.
[1009] Article 14.5.
[1010] *Ibid.* and Article 14.4.
[1011] Article 14.5.
[1012] Article 15.1.
[1013] Explanatory Report, para. 197.
[1014] Article 15.2.a.
[1015] Article 15.2.b.
[1016] Article 15.2.c.
[1017] Article 15.2.d.
[1018] Article 15.2.e.
[1019] Explanatory Report, para. 201.
[1020] Article 15.3.
[1021] Article 15.4. Those advertisements which are available with or without prescription fall into this category (Explanatory Report, para. 205).

safety is due to the fact that it is natural, or offer a diagnosis or treatment by correspondence.[1022]

(7) Advertising Directed Specifically at a Single Party

7.322. Grounds for restricting transmission. In order to avoid distortions in competition and endangering the television system of a Party, advertisements which are specifically and with some frequency directed to audiences in a single Party other than the transmitting Party may not circumvent the television advertising rules in that particular Party.[1023] This is intended to prevent a broadcaster making a cross-border broadcast (and thus relying on the Convention's guarantee of freedom of reception) merely to circumvent the rules operating in the targeted territory. Intention is a crucial element, and in its absence, this provision of the Convention cannot be invoked.[1024] The Explanatory Report notes[1025] that elements which might indicate targeted advertising include: the name of the advertised product or service; the currency used in the advertisement; the selling points mentioned and the language used (whether speech and/or subtitles). It does not however, prohibit the targeting of a particular audience other than that of the transmitting Party.[1026]

7.323. Circumstances in which the prohibition cannot operate. This prohibition does not however apply where either: the rules in the targeted territory establish a discrimination between advertisements transmitted by entities or by technical means within the jurisdiction of that Party and advertisements transmitted by entities or by technical means within the jurisdiction of another Party;[1027] or the Parties concerned have concluded bilateral or multilateral agreements in this area.[1028]

Failure to observe rules of an ambiguous, obscure or imprecise character would not qualify as circumvention.[1029] Furthermore, where different rules apply to public and private broadcasting organisations in the targeted Party, the most favourable regime should be applied.[1030] The burden of proof will be on the Party in which the audience is targeted.[1031]

[1022] Explanatory Report, para. 206.
[1023] Article 16.1. The Netherlands provided the impetus for this provision. As a country with a widespread cable network, it has been an easy target for commercial advertising broadcast from neighbouring territories. It considered that this activity posed a threat to its non-commercial and pluralistic television channels which are funded by an independent organisation which collects revenue from television advertising broadcast on the national television networks. Consequently it imposed a ban on the retransmission of foreign advertising. The ban, however, has been declared void by the European Court of Justice in Case 352/85 *Bond Van Adverteerders v. The State* (Netherlands) [1988] ECR 2085, [1989] 3 CMLR 113 and the Netherlands is bound by the European Community Council Directive 89/552/EEC: 'Television Without Frontiers' which prohibits any such restrictions on advertising and which overrides the provisions of the Convention on Transfrontier Television. (See §2.036 et seq. above). Note however that it might be otherwise in the case of an abuse of the EEC Treaty. See §2.026 above.
[1024] Explanatory Report, para. 212.
[1025] *Ibid.* para. 213.
[1026] *Ibid.* para. 209.
[1027] Article 16.2.a. The Explanatory Report (para. 210) gives by way of example, laws which prohibit transmissions from another Party advertising a particular product, whilst no such prohibition exists in respect of domestic transmissions.
[1028] Article 16.2.b.
[1029] Explanatory Report, para. 215. The Report notes (in para. 215) that principles of legal certainty, accessibility and proportionality should be applied.
[1030] *Ibid.* para. 216.
[1031] *Ibid.* para. 217.

10.   Sponsorship

7.324. Definition of 'sponsorship'. The Convention defines sponsorship as 'the participation of a natural or legal person, who is not engaged in broadcasting activities or in the production of audiovisual works, in the direct or indirect financing of a programme with a view to promoting the name, trademark or image of that person'.[1032] Participation by providing material and goods for the production, or prizes for game shows etc, is included.[1033] But a sponsored event (where the sponsor does not sponsor the programme carrying it) which is transmitted or retransmitted in programme services falls outside the ambit of the Convention because the broadcaster receives no benefit.[1034]

7.325. Obligations. Sponsorship (whether in whole or part) of a programme or series of programmes must be clearly identified as such by appropriate credits at the beginning and/or end of the programme.[1035] This will be the name, trademark, logo or other denomination of the sponsor. In this context, the term 'logo' means the sign habitually used by the sponsor to refer to his name or trademark and not the representation of any of his products or services, or their symbol, which has an advertising effect.[1036] In the case of game shows in which the prizes comprise the products or services of the sponsor, one single oral or visual reference to the name or logo of the sponsor or the same product or service, is allowed as information for the public.[1037]

7.326. Restrictions. Sponsored programmes may not encourage the sale, purchase or rental of the products or services of the sponsor or a third party, in particular by making special promotional references to those products or services in such programmes.[1038] The content and scheduling of sponsored programmes may in no circumstances be influenced by the sponsor in such a way so as to affect the responsibility and editorial independence of the broadcaster in respect of programmes.[1039] Programmes may not be sponsored by natural or legal persons whose principal activity is the manufacture or sale of products or the provision of services prohibited under the Convention's advertising rules.[1040] These are, tobacco products, or medicines or medical treatment which is available only on prescription.[1041] To determine whether the activity in issue is the principal activity, it is relevant to consider: the share of the revenue drawn from the activity in relation to the global revenue of the natural or legal person; the activity for which the person is mainly known to the public and the nature of the connected activities.[1042]

[1032] Article 2.g. The words 'who is not engaged in broadcasting activities or in the production of audiovisual events' is designed to prevent coproductions between broadcasting organisations or independent producers from being considered a form of a sponsorship. (Explanatory Report, para. 73.)
[1033] Explanatory Report, para. 69. The Report says that 'Such participation will be established by an agreement or contract between the sponsor and the broadcaster concerned.'
[1034] *Ibid.* para. 72.
[1035] Article 17.1. This is to be the broadcaster's choice (Explanatory Report, para. 223).
[1036] Explanatory Report, para. 222.
[1037] *Ibid.* para. 227.
[1038] Article 17.3.
[1039] Article 17.2.
[1040] Article 18.1.
[1041] Article 15.
[1042] Explanatory Report, para. 229.

Sponsorship of news and current affairs programmes is prohibited.[1043] The term 'current affairs' means strictly news-related programmes such as commentaries on news, analysis of news developments and political positions on events in the news.[1044]

11. Obligation to Render Mutual Assistance

7.327. General principles. Generally, Parties are placed under an obligation to render mutual assistance in order to implement the Convention.[1045] They must in particular, designate one or more authority, the name and address of each of which is to be communicated to the Secretary General of the Council of Europe.[1046] Each Contracting State which has designated more than one authority must specify in the aforementioned communication, the competence of each authority.[1047]

7.328. Furnishing of information etc. A designated authority must: furnish information concerning the broadcaster required under the Convention;[1048] furnish information at the request of an authority designated by another Party on the domestic law and practices in the fields covered by the Convention;[1049] co-operate with the authorities designated by the other Parties whenever useful, and notably where this would enhance the effectiveness of measures taken in implementation of the Convention;[1050] and consider any difficulty arising from the application of the Convention which is brought to its attention by an authority designated by another Party.[1051]

12. Violations of the Convention

(1) Procedure for Settlement of Disputes

7.329. General principles. When a Party finds a violation of the Convention,[1052] it must communicate the alleged violation to the transmitting Party and the two Parties must endeavour to overcome the difficulty on the basis of the spirit of co-operation underlying the Convention[1053] and the conciliation[1054] and, if necessary arbitration procedure.[1055]

[1043] Article 18.2.
[1044] Explanatory Report, para. 232.
[1045] Article 19.1.
[1046] Article 19.2.a. In accordance with Article 19.2.a, this notice is to be given at the time of deposit of a Contracting State's instrument of ratification, acceptance, approval or accession.
[1047] Article 19.2.b.
[1048] Article 19.3.a. ie the information required to be provided under Article 6.2.
[1049] Article 19.3.b.
[1050] Article 19.3.c.
[1051] Article 19.3.d.
[1052] In accordance with Article 24.1.
[1053] Outlined in Article 19.
[1054] Contained in Article 25.
[1055] Contained in Article 26.

7.330. Conciliation. In the case of difficulty arising from the application of the Convention, parties concerned must endeavour to achieve a friendly settlement.[1056] Unless one of the Parties concerned objects, the Standing Committee may examine the question, by placing itself at the disposal of the parties concerned in order to reach a satisfactory solution as rapidly as possible and, where appropriate, formulate an advisory opinion on the subject.[1057] Each Party undertakes to accord the Standing Committee, without delay, all information and facilities necessary for the discharge of these functions.[1058]

7.331. Arbitration. If the parties concerned cannot reach a friendly settlement of the dispute in accordance with the conciliation procedure, they may, by common agreement, submit the dispute to arbitration (an arbitration procedure is provided for in the appendix).[1059] In the absence of such an agreement within six months following the first request to open the conciliation procedure, the dispute may be submitted to arbitration at the request of one only of the Parties.[1060] Any Party may, at any time, declare that it recognises as compulsory ipso facto and without special agreement with any other Party accepting the same obligation, the application of the arbitration procedure provided for in the Convention.[1061]

(2) Suspension of Retransmission

7.332. Introduction. The Convention permits a receiving Party provisionally to suspend the retransmission of a broadcast which contravenes certain of its Articles. Rights of suspension are determined by both the nature of the term breached and the gravity of the violation.

7.333. Grave breaches. Thus, if a broadcast contains either:

Programmes. Programme items that do not respect the dignity of the human being and the fundamental rights of others[1062] and in particular are indecent and contain pornography,[1063] give undue prominence to violence or are likely to incite racial hatred,[1064] or are likely to impair the physical, mental or moral development of children and adolescents and are transmitted at a time when children are likely to watch them;[1065] or

Advertising. Advertising which exceeds the daily permitted volume,[1066] is not kept clearly distinguishable as such and recognisably separate from the other items of the programme service,[1067] breaches the rules on timing,[1068] advertises tobacco products[1069] or medicines and medical treatment available only on prescription;[1070]

[1056] Article 25.1.
[1057] Article 25.2.
[1058] Article 25.3.
[1059] Article 26.1.
[1060] *Ibid.*
[1061] Article 26.2.
[1062] Article 24.2 and Article 7.1.
[1063] Article 24.2 and Article 7.1.a.
[1064] Article 24.2 and Article 7.1.b.
[1065] Article 24 and Article 7.2.
[1066] Article 24.2 and Article 12.
[1067] Article 24.2 and Article 13.1, first sentence.
[1068] Article 24.2 and Article 14.
[1069] Article 24.2 and Article 15.1.
[1070] Article 24.2 and Article 15.3.

and the breach is of a manifest, serious and grave nature which raises important public issues, then the receiving Party may provisionally suspend the broadcast if it is not terminated within two weeks of communication to the transmitting Party of notice of the alleged violation.[1071] The use of the phrase 'manifest, serious and grave' indicates that in considering whether a suspension is warranted, the Parties should have due regard to the principle of proportionality.[1072]

7.334. Non-grave breaches. If the broadcast breaches the above provisions but is not of a manifest, serious and grave nature or if the broadcast breaches other rules in the Convention (save for the exceptions mentioned below), then the receiving Party may provisionally suspend the broadcast only if it is not terminated within eight months of communication to the transmitting Party on notice of the alleged violation.[1073]

7.335. Prohibition of suspension of retransmission. A receiving Party may not provisionally suspend a retransmission of a broadcast which breaches certain terms of the Convention. Broadcasts which benefit from this immunity are those which: do not ensure that news fairly presents facts and events and does not encourage the free formation of opinions;[1074] fail to give the right of reply guaranteed by the Convention;[1075] feature an event of high public interest and because of the broadcaster's exclusive rights of transmission will deprive a large part of the public in one or more other Parties of the opportunity to follow the event on television;[1076] or fail to meet the cultural objectives of the Convention in that they do not contain a sufficient proportion of European works or endanger the cinema industry in a Party by broadcasting a film before the set period stipulated by the Convention has elapsed since its exhibition in the cinema.[1077]

In the case of such a broadcast, the receiving Party has no option other than to permit retransmission unless and until the dispute is resolved in its favour by the conciliation or if necessary arbitration procedure.

12. General Provisions

7.336. Commencement and parties. The Convention was adopted on 5 May 1989 and came into force on 1 May, 1993. [1078] It was open to signature and subsequent ratification, acceptance or approval by the Member States of the Council of Europe, other States party to the European Cultural Convention and also by the States party to the European Economic Community.[1079] Any other State may be invited to accede to the Convention by a decision of the Committee of Ministers of the Council of Europe and subject to certain other formal procedures.[1080] Any Party may, at any time, denounce the Convention.[1081]

[1071] Article 24.2.
[1072] Explanatory Report, para. 262.
[1073] Article 24.3.
[1074] Article 24.4 and Article 7.3.
[1075] Article 24.4 and Article 8.
[1076] Article 24.4 and Article 9.
[1077] Article 24.4 and Article 10.
[1078] In accordance with Article 29.2.
[1079] Article 29.1. See Table H of Appendix III.
[1080] Article 30.1.
[1081] Article 33.1. Notification is addressed to the Secretary General of the Council of Europe.

7.337. Relations of Convention to Parties who are Member States of the European Community. The Convention stipulates that Parties which are members of the European Economic Community, are to apply the Community rules (ie in general those formulated by the Directive of 3 October 1989[1082] and other Directives) and not the rules arising from the Convention unless there is no Community rule governing the particular subject concerned in which case the Convention may be invoked.[1083] The Convention will be of most use in enforcing rights against territories which are not Member States of the European Community.

7.338. Relations of Convention to other international agreements. Nothing in the Convention prevents the Parties from concluding international agreements completing or developing its provisions or extending their field of application.[1084] The Convention does not alter the rights and obligations of Parties which arise from other bilateral agreements and which do not affect the enjoyment of other Parties of their rights or the performance of their obligations under the Convention.[1085] In respect of authors' rights, recourse should be had, inter alia, to the Berne Convention for the Protection of Literary and Artistic Works as well as the various agreements enacted under the auspices of the Council of Europe. In respect of neighbouring rights recourse should be had to the Rome and Phonogram Conventions.

7.339. Relations between the Convention and internal law. Nothing in the Convention prevents the Parties from applying stricter or more detailed rules than those provided for in the Convention to programme services transmitted by entities or by technical means[1086] within their jurisdiction.[1087]

7.340. Reservations. The Convention provides for two reservations, and no other reservations may be made.[1088] Thus any State may declare that it reserves the right to restrict the retransmission on its territory, solely to the extent that it does not comply with its domestic legislation, of programme services containing advertisements for alcoholic beverages which have otherwise satisfied[1089] the terms of the Convention.[1090] A reservation made in accordance with the preceding provision may not be the subject of an objection.[1091] Any Contracting State which has made this reservation may wholly or partly withdraw it.[1092] A Party which has made the reservation may not claim the application of that provision by any other Party. It may, however, if its reservation is partial or conditional, claim the application of that provision in so far as it has itself accepted it.[1093]

[1082] Council Directive 89/552/EEC. See §6.056 et seq. above.
[1083] Article 27.1.
[1084] Article 27.2.
[1085] Article 27.3.
[1086] Within the meaning of Article 3.
[1087] Article 28.
[1088] Article 32.1.
[1089] In accordance with Article 15.2.
[1090] Article 32.1.a.
[1091] Article 32.2.
[1092] Article 32.3. In accordance with Article 32.3, notification is addressed to the Secretary General of the Council of Europe. The withdrawal takes effect on the date of receipt of the notification by the Secretary General.
[1093] Article 32.4.

The Convention provided that the United Kingdom could declare that it reserved the right not to fulfil the obligation[1094] to prohibit advertisements for tobacco products, in respect of advertisements for cigars and pipe tobacco broadcast by the Independent Broadcasting Authority by terrestrial means on its territory.[1095] Since the United Kingdom is bound by the EEC Directive 'Television Without Frontiers',[1096] and this prohibits any form of tobacco associated advertising, the United Kingdom cannot avail itself of the reservation specifically tailored for it in the Convention.

7.341. Standing Committee. The Convention sets up a Standing Committee.[1097] This body has several functions. It is responsible for making recommendations concerning the application of the Convention[1098] and suggesting necessary modifications,[1099] examining, at the request of one or more Parties, questions concerning the interpretation of the Convention,[1100] as well as using its best endeavours to secure a friendly settlement of any difficulty referred under the arbitration procedure.[1101] Finally, it can make recommendations to the Committee of Ministers, that States other than members of the European Economic Community, Council of Europe and European Cultural Convention be invited to accede to the Convention.[1102]

7.342. Extension to territories. Any State may at the time of signature or when depositing its instrument of ratification, acceptance, approval or accession, specify the territory or territories to which the Convention is to apply.[1103] Any State may, at a later date, extend the application of the Convention to any other territory specified in the declaration.[1104] Any declaration made in accordance with the preceding provisions, may be withdrawn.[1105] It was agreed that it would be against the philosophy of the Convention for any Party to exclude from the application of the Convention, parts of its main territory.[1106]

[1094] Set out in Article 15.1.

[1095] Article 32.1.b.

[1096] Council Directive 89/552/EEC of 3 October 1989. See §6.056 et seq. above.

[1097] Article 20.1. Article 20 sets out the governing rules applying to the Standing Committee.

[1098] Article 21.a.

[1099] Article 21.b. Article 23 contains the procedure for the proposal and enactment of amendments.

[1100] Article 21.c.

[1101] Article 21.d.

[1102] Article 21.e and Article 29.

[1103] Article 31.1.

[1104] Article 31.2. In accordance with Article 31.2, the declaration is addressed to the Secretary General of the Council of Europe.

[1105] Article 31.3.

[1106] Explanatory Report, para. 291.

CHAPTER EIGHT

Enforcing Rights in Broadcast and Cable Transmissions

I. INTRODUCTION

1. Legal Authorities

8.001. This section calls upon a series of authoritative principles (albeit non-binding). They are: the Annotated Principles of Protection of Authors, Performers, Producers of Phonograms and Broadcasting Organisations in Connection with Distribution of Programmes by Cable (the 'Annotated Principles'),[1] the Council of Europe Recommendations on Principles Relating to Copyright Law Questions in the Field of Television by Satellite and Cable (the 'COE Copyright Principles');[2] the Synthesis of Principles on Various Categories of Works (the 'Synthesis of Principles')[3] and the International Telecommunication Union Radio Regulations (the 'ITU Radio Regulations').[4]

Cable transmissions grew in abundance during the 1950s and 1960s but by the 1970s there was still little consensus either amongst legislators or the courts, of the precise contours of an author or performer's right to consent to the transmission of his work by cable. Perceiving the gravity of the problem, WIPO and Unesco gathered together a group of experts including those from the International Labour Office, to formulate general principles which could offer guidance. The outcome was the Annotated Principles. Their gestation period lasted for many years, and they contain the combined wisdom of many persons, organisations and State representatives.

The COE Copyright Principles are a series of principles forged by the Council of Europe for the guidance of its Member States when considering questions of

---

[1] Copyright Bulletin, Vol XVIII, No 2, [1984], 5.
[2] Recommendation No R(86)2 of 14 February 1986
[3] Copyright [1988], Issue 10, 364 et seq. Issue 11, 445 et seq. and Issue 12, 506 et seq.
[4] Edition 1990, ITU Geneva.

copyright and neighbouring rights in relation to transmissions by satellite and cable.

The Synthesis of Principles is, like the Annotated Principles, the work of WIPO and Unesco.[5] It gives guidance on the legal implications flowing from the exploitation of works by satellite and cable transmissions.

The ITU Radio Regulations form the legal foundation of telecommunications law. Their definitions are often borrowed by lawyers legislating in the field of copyright and neighbouring rights. However, it should be emphasised that because they are not focused on intellectual property, their validity as a source of reference in this domain is becoming increasingly challenged.

2. Terminology

8.002. The two basic terms. Virtually all the international agreements[6] which govern copyright and neighbouring rights employ two concepts in enshrining rights in the sphere of radio and television transmissions. They are the concept of:

(1) the broadcast and
(2) the communication to the public.

The threshold question for any rightholder wishing to enforce rights or any broadcaster wishing to acquire rights, is, whether a particular act qualifies either as a 'broadcast' or a 'communication to the public' for which consent is required or alternatively payment must be made.

8.003. Usage—general principle. The sections that follow, consider which activities come within the aforementioned terms. Before embarking on that analysis, the following general principle should be borne in mind: the term 'broadcast' applies solely to a transmission made without an artificial guide. An artificial guide would be, for example, a cable. The term 'communication to the public' applies to both transmissions made with and those made without an artificial guide.

II. TERRESTRIAL TRANSMISSIONS

8.004. A terrestrial broadcast or transmission is in literal transliteration, a transmission made over the earth. In less formal parlance it is referred to as an 'over the air' broadcast or transmission. The ITU Radio Regulations define a terrestrial transmission as:

---

[5] It was presaged by a report of a meeting of a Committee of Governmental Experts on Audiovisual Works and Phonograms convened by WIPO and UNESCO in Paris in 1986, Copyright [1986], 218 (the 'Audiovisual Works Experts Report').

[6] The Berne Convention for the Protection of Literary and Artistic Works, Articles 2bis, 10bis, 11, 11bis, 11ter, 14, 14bis (see §7.004 et seq. above); the Universal Copyright Convention, Article IVbis, only using the term 'broadcast' (see §7.102 et seq. above) and the International Convention for the Protection of Performers, Producers of Phonograms and Broadcasting Organisations, Articles 7, 12 and 13. (see §7.188 et seq. above). The principal exception is the Convention Relating to the Distribution of Programme-Carrying Signals Transmitted by Satellite, which does not enshrine specific rights. (see §7.257 et seq. above).

... a radiocommunication service in which the transmissions are intended for direct reception by the general public. This service may include sound transmissions, television transmissions or other types of transmissions.[7]

It is thus generally agreed that to qualify as a 'broadcast' or a 'communication to the public', a terrestrial transmission must simply have been intended for direct reception by the general public.[8] Since intention is the crucial element, it is irrelevant whether or not such a transmission is, in fact, received by the public.[9] Terrestrial transmissions which do not satisfy these criteria include, in particular, amateur radio and telephone communications, for they are not 'intended for reception by the general public'.[10]

III. SATELLITE TRANSMISSIONS

1. The Technology

8.005. Introduction. Law and technology are no more inextricably bound up together than in the case of satellite transmissions. Because the technology is constantly moving on and each new advance is shadowed by an adjustment in the law, it is necessary to have a little understanding of the hardware. This section therefore begins with a brief account of the different forms of satellite technology.

8.006. Direct Broadcast Satellite. A Direct Broadcast Satellite Service (also known as a 'DBS' service) requires no receiving station on earth. Subscribers to a DBS television channel are able to receive the satellite's signals directly via a personal small dish aerial and decode them into viewable images with the use of decoding equipment supplied by the broadcasting organisation. Under the ITU Radio Regulations, a Direct Broadcast Satellite Service is defined as:

... a radiocommunication service in which signals transmitted or retransmitted by spacestations are intended for direct reception by the general public.[11]

Under the ITU Radio Regulations, the term 'direct reception' is said to include both 'individual reception' and 'community reception'.[12] The latter refers to the case where, for example, all the occupants of a block of flats are supplied with a signal from a single antennae located on the roof.

8.007. Fixed Service Satellite. A Fixed Service Satellite (also known as 'FSS') is a satellite principally used to transmit signals between stations. There are two types of Fixed Service Satellite: 'point-to-point' satellites and 'distribution' satellites. The former, as their name suggests, are designed to send a signal from one station to

---

[7] Article 1.3.17.
[8] See e.g. WIPO Guide to the Berne Convention, (1978), 11bis.6.
[9] *Ibid.* 11bis.3.
[10] *Ibid.* 11bis.6.
[11] Article 1.3.18.
[12] *Ibid.*

another. The received signals are then converted into normal terrestrial or cable transmissions and relayed to individual receivers. Distribution satellites are more powerful and emit signals which are receivable by many ground stations spread over a large area. In some cases, their signals are capable of direct reception by members of the public using ordinary satellite receiving equipment. Under the ITU Radio Regulations, a Fixed Service Satellite is defined as:

> ... a radiocommunication service between earth stations at given positions when one or more satellites are used.[13]

2. The Key Issues in Acquiring Rights

8.008. There are two key issues which a broadcaster must address in the process of acquiring rights to make a satellite transmission and they are:

- whether a particular transmission (whether made from a Direct Broadcast Satellite or Fixed Service Satellite) is a 'broadcast' or a 'communication to the public' within the meaning of the international agreements;
- if a transmission can be considered to be a 'broadcast' or 'communication to the public', where are those acts deemed to occur ie in which States does the broadcaster need to acquire rights?

These questions are considered in turn by the following two sections.

3. Triggering Liability through Satellite Transmissions

8.009. Direct Broadcast Satellite. There is international consensus that a transmission by Direct Broadcast Satellite qualifies as both a 'broadcast' and a 'communication to the public'. In the words of one authority, this is because 'the satellite is only a relay, the technical means, through which—without need of diffusion by a terrestrial station—the signals emitted by the originating organisation can be intercepted by the public with ordinary receiving sets'.[14] In other words, a DBS satellite is treated like an earth transmitter, save that it is located in space. In 1985, a group of experts convened to discuss this issue . . . 'agreed that direct broadcasting of works by means of satellite (broadcasting satellite service) was broadcasting in the sense of both the Berne and Universal Copyright Conventions.'[15] The COE Copyright Principles also dictate that:

> The transmission of protected works and other contributions by means of a direct broadcasting satellite shall be governed by the provisions relating to the broadcasting or communication to the public of such contributions.[16]

This has been endorsed lately by the Synthesis of Principles, which state that:

---

[13] Article 1.3.3.

[14] G Ulmer, 'Protection of authors in relation to the tranmission via satellite of broadcast programmes' RIDA [1977] LXXXXIII, 3. Although this principle is firmly rooted, arguments against the view that a DBS transmission is a 'broadcast' have been expressed. See e.g. J Von Ungern-Sternberg, 'The transmission of broadcast emissions via satellites and copyright' RIDA [1973] LXXV, 3.

[15] Report of the Group of Experts on the Copyright Aspects of Direct Broadcasting by Satellite, (meeting held in Paris, 18–22 March, 1985), Copyright Bulletin, Vol XIX, No 3 [1985], 50 ('DBS Group of Experts Report'), para. 52.

[16] Principle 3.

Broadcasting by direct broadcasting satellite is broadcasting under the Berne Convention, the Universal Copyright Convention and the Rome Convention. Consequently, where audiovisual works are broadcast by such satellites, the owners of copyright in such works, as well as performers, phonogram producers and broadcasting organisations whose rights may be concerned should enjoy the same rights as in the case of traditional broadcasting (by earth stations).[17]

8.010. Fixed Service Satellite. There was little doubt that signals sent by 'point-to-point' satellites (the first type of FSS) were neither 'broadcast' nor 'communicated to the public' within the meaning of the international treaties because no member of the public could receive them directly.[18] The signals were simply 'transported' between pieces of technology and no copyright or neighbouring right liability could follow from that activity. The fundamental point was that they awaited some further decision on the part of the receiving station to transport them on to subscribers. But the picture has blurred with the arrival of 'distribution satellites'. For it is possible for members of the public to receive their signals either directly with the use of a dish aerial or with the intervention of cable relays. So the chief question now, is whether a transmission by Fixed Service Satellite which allows this immediate reception, qualifies as a 'broadcast' or 'communication to the public' and thus triggers copyright and neighbouring rights liability?

The DBS Copyright Experts Report chose (in 1985) to maintain the distinction between DBS and FSS transmissions whilst accepting the narrowing of the technical difference between the two technologies.[19] But by 1989, the convergence of technologies had led to the view that an FSS transmission was capable of constituting a 'broadcast'.[20] The Synthesis of Principles represent the current wisdom, which is that provided a transmission by Fixed Service Satellite requires no further decision to transport it to the consumer's set, it constitutes a 'broadcast':

> In the case of fixed service satellites, the entire process of transmission of programme-carrying signals (emission, 'up-leg,' 'down-leg,' transmission from the earth station further to the public) should be considered as one act of broadcasting composed of different phases, provided that the entire process is definitely decided and scheduled at the time of emission of the signals towards the satellite... If audiovisual works are broadcast through fixed service satellite in this way, the owners of copyright in such works as well as performers, phonogram producers and broadcasting organisations whose rights may be concerned should enjoy the same rights as in the case of traditional broadcasting (by earth stations).[21]
>
> If the transmission of the programme-carrying signals from the earth station further to the public is still conditional on decisions to be taken later, either by the originating broadcasting organisation or by the broadcasting organisation transmitting the programme from the earth station further to the public, such transmission of signals should not be considered broadcasting (but a mere technical transmission of signals).[22]

8.011. Summary of principles. A Direct Broadcast Satellite transmission is a broadcast (and communication to the public). A Fixed Service Satellite

---

[17] Principle AW11. See also Principle PH14. This principle was first declared in the Audiovisual Works Experts Report, Principle AW11.

[18] G. Hermann, 'Border-crossing Radio and Television Programmes in the Common Market', EBU Review, Vol XXXVI No 1 [1985] 27, 34. See §8.007 above (explanation of technologies).

[19] DBS Group of Experts Report, para. 19.

[20] S M Stewart, *International Copyright and Neighbouring Rights* (2nd Edn, 1989), 10.03.

[21] Principle AW15(1). See also Principle PH18(1).

[22] Principle AW15(2). See also Principle PH18(2).

transmission is a broadcast (and communication to the public) where it requires no further decision on the part of the body at the receiving station before the signals are sent on to the public or where the signals can be received by members of the public without the intervention of a cable operator.

4. Establishing the Territory of the Broadcast or Communication to the Public

8.012. Introduction. Where a transmission is deemed to be a 'broadcast' (and hence a 'communication to the public'), the essential matter for the broadcaster who has to acquire rights, is to determine the territory in which this 'broadcast' or 'communication to the public occurs.' Over the years, international law has evolved three models or theories which Courts may call upon to resolve this question.[23] One theory considers the signal to be governed only by the laws applicable in the country of emission of the signal towards the satellite. Another theory holds that the country of emission is irrelevant, the signal being governed by rights which prevail in all the countries of reception. The third theory considers that the signal is protected by rights in both the country of emission and reception. These are now explained in depth.

8.013. Model 1—'emission theory'. The first model to have evolved relies upon the definition of satellite broadcasting found in the ITU Radio Regulations which at one time stated that broadcasting was 'a (microwave) emission intended to be directly received by the public'.[24] Hence a broadcast only occurs where signals are emitted by the broadcasting organisation. And that can only be at one point on the globe. In one sense therefore, the emission theory likens a satellite to a terrestrial transmitter, but instead of being fixed into a building, the 'transmitter' (ie the satellite) is extended into outer space, hovering above the planet. The implication of this perspective is that the broadcaster need only acquire the copyright   or neighbouring right holder's authority to broadcast his work in the country of emission.[25] Consent then journeys with the signal to the furthest reaches of the satellite's footprint, however many territories this may encompass. Legally speaking, there is simply a 'reception' in each country within the satellite's footprint and a reception of broadcast signals never triggers copyright or neighbouring right liability.[26]

8.014. Model 2—'early communication theory'. The Berne Convention for the Protection of Literary and Artistic Works, gives to authors the exclusive right to authorise 'the broadcasting of their works or the communication thereof to the

---

[23] For literature on this subject, see the articles referred to by H Cohen Jehoram, 'Legal Issues of satellite television in Europe' RIDA [1984] 122, 147.

[24] ITU Radio Regulations, Article 28A.

[25] Opinions on where this occurs are divided. According to Kerever, there are five possibilities: the place from which the signals are emitted towards the satellite; the location of the broadcaster's final control centre; the location of the broadcaster's headquarters where decisions to include protected works in the programme are taken; the country authorised to use the satellite by the ITU and finally, the country where exploitation actually takes place (ie headquarters of the advertising corporation, or country of origin of the exploited products). See A Kerever, 'Satellite broadcasting and copyright' Copyright Bulletin Vol XXIV, No 3, [1990], 6.

[26] Kerever is a principal exponent of this theory. See Kerever, 'Copyright and space satellites' RIDA [1984], 121, 27 and recently: 'Satellite broadcasting and copyright', Copyright Bulletin Vol XXIV, No 3, [1990], 6.

public by any other means of wireless diffusion of signs, sounds or images.'[27] This phraseology has provided the source for one model, the so called communication theory. This goes as follows.[28] The Berne Convention uses the term 'communication thereof to the public'. Therefore, the notion of a 'communication to the public' is key and the concept of 'emission' being narrower and not found in the Berne Convention, must be cast aside. Consequently 'broadcasting takes place where the wireless diffusion takes place as a communication to the public.'[29] The transmission via the up-link to the satellite cannot be a broadcast because the transmission is made to outer space which is not occupied by people ie there is no 'communication to the public'. Neither can the act of sending the signal from the satellite be a broadcast because it occurs in outer space which is not governed by any copyright and neighbouring right treaties.[30] A broadcast only occurs when the signal pierces the atmosphere and enters a territory because it is only then that a 'communication to the public' is made. It follows that the broadcaster is obliged to scan the arc of the satellite's beam and gather rights for each country which falls within the satellite's footprint because in each country, a separate broadcast or 'communication to the public' occurs.[31] This is subject to the proviso that where the satellites footprint covers only a part of a country, under de minimus principles, that country can be ignored.[32]

If this model is accepted, collecting rights becomes a burdensome occupation. However, the responsibility is laid at the door of the person who makes the order to broadcast by satellite. No other entity has any other responsibility. In particular no person who receives the broadcast in any country has any responsibility, needs no authorisation from, and need not pay anything to, the owner of the copyright (or neighbouring right) in the broadcast work.[33]

8.015. Model 3—'later communication theory'. The third model to have evolved is essentially a development and refinement of the second model.[34] It provides that each successive phase of transmission via the up-leg and down-leg of the satellite is part of a single communication to the public and broadcast. Broadcasting (and hence a communication to the public) occurs both in the country where the signal is sent (emitted) to the satellite and in all the countries

---

[27] Article 11bis(1)(i). See §7.051 above.

[28] This is the view championed by Arpad Bogsch, Director General of WIPO. It can be found in the DBS Group of Experts Report, para. 12(i) et seq. See also G. Schricker, 'Grenzüberschreitende Fernseh-und Hörfunksendungen im Gemeinsamen Markt' [1984] GRUR Int, No 10, 592. For arguments in support as well as against this theory, see M J Freegard, Direct Broadcasting by Satellite (DBS): the implications for copyright, RIDA [1988], 136, 63.

[29] DBS Group of Experts Report, para. 12(ii).

[30] Outer space is governed by international treaties, the most important of which is The 1967 Treaty on Principles Governing the Activities of States in the Exploration and Use of Outer Space, including the Moon and Other Celestial Bodies.

[31] Because the Berne Convention centres on the concept of 'national treatment', the laws of each country must be separately considered, 'Otherwise, a communication to the public in one country would be governed by the national law of another country, a result contrary to the principle of national treatment.' (See DBS Group of Experts Report, para. 12(iii).)

[32] DBS Group of Experts Report, para. 12(iv).

[33] Ibid. para. 12(v).

[34] This model was advanced for discussion in the Audiovisual Works Experts Report. See also G Ulmer, 'Protection of authors in relation to the transmission via satellite of broadcast programmes' RIDA [1977] LXXXXIII, 3.

which are covered by the footprint.[35] The national laws of both the country where the programme-carrying signals are originated and that of each country covered by the 'footprint' of the satellite are applicable.[36] If the national laws involved do not grant the same kind or degree of protection, the highest level of protection should be applied.[37] However, it is always the broadcasting organisation emitting the signals which is responsible to the rightholders.[38]

In a case where an FSS transmits signals receivable by the general public in the same manner as DBS signals, the aforementioned regime applies.[39] In a case where the signals sent by an FSS are fed by cable, the broadcast (and hence communication to the public) occurs both in the country where the signal is sent (emitted) to the satellite and in all the countries in which the signal is sent to subscribers by cable operators.[40] A similar balancing exercise should be made in determining the level of protection as in the case of DBS transmissions.[41]

8.016. Model adopted by European Community. The communication theories came into being because of the possibility of there existing lesser protection for rightholders in the country of emission than in the countries covered by the footprint. The European Community, however, is harmonising its copyright and neighbouring right law so that the same level of protection will be offered in each Member State. The European Community therefore proposes to adopt Model 1 in forthcoming legislation.[42] Moreover, the emission theory is attractive because it eases rights negotiation. According to the proposed Directive, 'communication to the public by satellite' means:

> . . . the act of introducing, under the control and responsibility of the broadcasting organisation, the programme-carrying signals intended for reception by the public into an uninterrupted chain of communication leading to the satellite and down 'towards earth'.[43]
>
> The act of communication to the public occurs solely in the Member State where under the control and responsibility of the broadcasting organisation the programme-carrying signals are introduced into an uninterrupted chain of communication leading to the satellite and down towards the earth.[44]

IV. TRANSMISSIONS BY CABLE

1. Introduction

8.017. The basic concepts. Although television signals may be distributed by cable in many forms, experts have settled on just two categories in which to place them. Material distributed by cable may thus be either:

---

[35] Audiovisual Works Experts Report, Principle AW13. This view has been endorsed by the Synthesis of Principles, Principle AW13.

[36] *Ibid.* Principle AW14.

[37] *Ibid.*

[38] *Ibid.* Principle AW12.

[39] *Ibid.* Principle AW19.

[40] *Ibid.* Principle AW17.

[41] *Ibid.* Principle AW18.

[42] Amended proposal for a Council Directive on the co-ordination of certain rules concerning copyright and rights related to copyright applicable to satellite broadcasting and cable retransmission, COM (92) 526 final.

[43] Article 1(2).

[44] Article 1(2)(a).

- the distribution by cable of a broadcast, or
- the distribution of a cable originated programme.

8.018. Meaning of the term 'distribution by cable of a broadcast'. The Annotated Principles define a 'distribution by cable of a broadcast' as:

> . . . the distribution by cable of a broadcast programme item simultaneously with the broadcast of that programme item and without any change therein.[45]

For a cable retransmission to qualify as a 'distribution by cable of a broadcast', it is vital that the integrity of the initial broadcast is maintained, hence the concept of the 'programme item'.[46] 'Programme item' means a 'unit of the programme, continuous in time and of a given content, such as presentations of works, performances by artists, cultural or sports events, reports in words or both on current events, interviews, travelogues, lectures, group discussions and quiz shows'.[47]

Thus it is not necessary 'to require that the entirety of the broadcast programme of a broadcaster—that is each and all the programme items of that programme—be distributed by cable in order to qualify as distribution by cable of a broadcast...'[48]

8.019. Meaning of the term 'cable originated programme'. The Annotated Principles define a 'cable originated programme' as:

> . . . a programme or a programme item that is distributed by cable and where the programme or the programme item is not originating from a broadcast or where, although it originates from a broadcast, the distribution by cable is not simultaneous with the broadcast or, even where it is simultaneous with the broadcast, sounds or images or both not contained in the broadcast are superimposed on the broadcast when it is distributed by cable.[49]

Thus the distribution by cable, in a changed manner, of any broadcast sounds, or of any broadcast sounds and images, should be regarded as a 'cable originated programme', even where the sounds or sounds and images utilised (but amended) are distributed simultaneously with the broadcast.[50] What is meant is the case in which a broadcast is used by the distributor as background for his cable originated programme or, conversely, where background music or text, cable originated, is being superimposed on the broadcast.[51] Examples are the superimposition of spoken commentary on the broadcast of a sports event or on an opera performed in a foreign language.[52] It would also include 'live dubbing' ie the replacement of the original spoken words by words pronounced in translation by a speaker in the cable distribution.[53] As a practical matter, the subtitling of a particular broadcast is only generally possible where the distribution of that broadcast is deferred and thus the retransmitted subtitled programme would necessarily be a 'cable originated programme'.[54] However,

---

[45] Annotated Principles, para. 50(viii).
[46] *Ibid.* para. 40.
[47] *Ibid*, para. 50(vii). A 'programme' is defined as 'the sequence of sounds, or images, or both sounds and images, offered to the public by the broadcaster or by the cable distributor, through broadcast or distribution by cable, for hearing or viewing by the general public or a segment thereof, as the case may be' (see Annotated Principles, para. 50(vi)).
[48] *Ibid*, para. 40.
[49] *Ibid.* para. 50(ix).
[50] *Ibid.* para. 37.
[51] *Ibid.*
[52] *Ibid.*
[53] *Ibid.*
[54] *Ibid.*

in general, the 'blacking out' of advertisements or incidental passages of the broadcast programme, the communication of which is prohibited under law regulating the public order of the country where the distribution by cable takes place, will not change the 'distribution by cable of a broadcast' into that of a 'cable originated programme'.[55] Finally, a programme which is made by the cable organisation is a 'cable originated programme'.

8.020. Meaning of the term 'cable'. The Annotated Principles provide that the term 'cable' means:

> ... a wire, beam or any other conducting device through which electronically generated programme-carrying signals are guided over a distance.[56]

So, for example, as well as 'wire,' and 'co-axial cable', the term 'cable' can include 'optical fibres'.[57] But, it is not necessary for the conductor used to be something tangible.[58] What matters is whether the signals are artificially guided or not.[59] On this basis, guided transmission of programmes by laser beam will qualify as transmission by cable. This would include, amongst other technologies, laser guided 'point-to-point' satellite transmissions of electromagnetic waves.[60]

8.021. Meaning of the term 'broadcast'. The Annotated Principles define a 'broadcast' as:

> ... the transmission of sounds or images, or both sounds and images, by electromagnetic waves propagated in space without artificial guide for the purpose of enabling reception of the so transmitted sounds, images or both by the general public.[61]

This definition is wide enough to encompass terrestrial broadcasts, broadcasts by Direct Broadcast Satellite, and, where they are considered to be 'broadcasts',[62] transmissions by Fixed Service Satellite.

2. Acts Invoking Copyright

(1) Distribution by Cable of a Broadcast

8.022. The Annotated Principles state that:

> The author or other owner of the copyright has the exclusive right of authorizing any distribution by cable of the broadcast of his work protected by copyright.[63]

This makes it clear that the 'distribution of a work by cable' is to be considered, under the law of copyright, a restricted act of its own which requires the express authorization of the author.[64] This is the case whether what is so communicated to

---

[55] para. 38. The Annotated Principles, (para. 38) explain that this is justified on the grounds that the Berne Convention for the Protection of Literary and Artistic Works, Article 17 (see §7.096 above) permits such control. However, blacking out may not be exercised so as to prejudice the moral rights of the author which are guaranteed under Article 6bis of the Convention (see §7.075 above).
[56] *Ibid.* para. 50(ii).
[57] *Ibid.* para. 32.
[58] *Ibid.*
[59] *Ibid.* para. 33.
[60] *Ibid.* para. 32.
[61] *Ibid.* para. 50(i).
[62] See §8.010 above.
[63] Annotated Principles, Principle 1; endorsed by Synthesis of Principles, Principle AW20.
[64] *Ibid.* para. 54.

the public are works, performances, phonograms, broadcasts or other visual and audiovisual material.[65] As far as the meaning of 'the public' is concerned, it is the possibility of having access to the works that triggers copyright liability, irrespective of whether, and to what extent, the communicated work is actually received. Accordingly, the circle of recipients has to be regarded as consisting not only of actual, but also of all the potential listeners or viewers of the sounds, images or both transmitted by means of cable distribution, that is, those persons who may have access to the distribution service, if they so wish.[66] But cable technology does not make everybody a potential listener or viewer. So, the aforementioned is qualified inasmuch as 'the public' are only persons whom the cable technology allows to be reached.[67]

(2) Examples of a Distribution by Cable of a Broadcast

8.023. The following acts are generally considered to be a 'distribution by cable of a broadcast':

Simultaneous, complete and unchanged cable retransmission of a terrestrial broadcast. This is the most common form of cable transmission qualifying as a 'distribution by cable of a broadcast.'[68]

Simultaneous, complete and unchanged cable retransmission of a broadcast made by a Direct Broadcast Satellite. In this case, the cable operator picks up the broadcast made by Direct Broadcast Satellite and relays it to its subscribers. The COE Principles state that this act is to be regarded as 'a distribution by cable of a broadcast, if it is simultaneous, complete and unchanged.'[69] Likewise, the Annotated Principles state that if 'the distributor picks up, and distributes by cable, simultaneously and without any change, sounds, images or both, transmitted via direct broadcast satellite for public reception, this operation should be regarded as distribution by cable of a broadcast'.[70]

Simultaneous, complete and unchanged cable retransmission of 'broadcasts' made by means of Fixed Service Satellite. Where the transmission made by Fixed Service Satellite is not simply regarded as transporting signals between pieces of technology,[71] but can actually be received by members of the public by receiving equipment normally used, then, the subsequent transmission by cable of those signals to the public is a 'distribution by cable of a broadcast' providing that the distribution is simultaneous, complete and unchanged.[72]

(3) Distribution by Cable of a Cable Originated Programme

8.024. The Annotated Principles state that:

> The author or other owner of the copyright has the exclusive right of authorising the distribution of his work protected by copyright in the framework of a cable originated programme.[73]

---

[65] *Ibid.* para. 14.
[66] *Ibid.* para. 31. ie the number of actual subscribers is not in point.
[67] See also para. 50(x) of the Annotated Principles.
[68] *Ibid.* para. 50(viii).
[69] Principle 5.a.
[70] Annotated Principles, para. 45. However, if a cable operator, transmits a programme at the same time as that programme is transmitted by Direct Broadcast satellite, but independently, then such a programme is deemed to be 'cable originated' (see Annotated Principles, para. 46).
[71] COE Copyright Principles, Principle 6.a.
[72] *Ibid.* Principle 6.b.
[73] Annotated Principles, Principle 9; endorsed by Synthesis of Principles, Principle AW27.

The basic and unquestioned legal fact in connection with the use of works in the framework of cable originated programmes is that such a use is always subject to the author's exclusive right of authorization, be it deferred distribution of an earlier broadcast,[74] or the distribution of a live or already fixed performance or recitation of a protected work.[75]

(4) Examples of a Cable Originated Programme

8.025. The following programmes are generally regarded as 'cable originated programmes':

Simultaneous and changed cable retransmission of a terrestrial or Direct Broadcast Satellite transmission. In this situation, the cable operator may superimpose sounds or images or both on to the broadcast it distributes thus creating a 'cable-originated programme'.[76]

Non-simultaneous cable retransmission of a terrestrial or Direct Broadcast Satellite transmission. The broadcast received by the cable operator is recorded for later distribution. The cable operator may or may not make any change to the programme when it is distributed. Whether or not changes are made, the fact that the retransmission is delayed makes it a 'cable-originated programme'.[77]

Simultaneous and unchanged cable retransmission of a Fixed Service Satellite 'transmission'. In the case where a Fixed Service Satellite is deemed merely to transport signals between pieces of technology and cable retransmission is then employed to relay to the public, a programme transmitted by such a Fixed Service Satellite, such a programme is to be regarded as 'cable-originated'.[78]

Cable initiated transmission. The cable operator is a proper broadcasting organisation. It may make its own programmes or it may license tapes from distributors. The programmes it transmits are 'cable-originated programme'.[79]

(5) Reason for the Distinction between a 'Distribution by Cable of a Broadcast' and a 'Cable Originated Programme'

8.026. Since both a 'distribution by cable of a broadcast' and a 'cable originated programme' both attract copyright liability ie both constitute a 'communication to the public', the question that arises is, why the need for the distinction? The answer is to found in Article 11bis of the Berne Convention for the Protection of Literary and Artistic Works.

When cable operations first began, broadcasting technology was in its infancy. Video tape had not yet been invented and thus cable operators could do little more than simultaneously retransmit a terrestrial broadcast without making any changes thereto. The 1948 revision of Berne took into account the burgeoning of simultaneous cable retransmissions, by giving an author the right to authorise the communication of his work to the public by cable in such circumstances.[80] However, it also

---

[74] where the necessary fixation must be authorised.

[75] 'be it deferred distribution of an earlier broadcast, where also the necessary fixation of that broadcast has to be authorized, or the distribution of a live or already fixed performance or recitation of a protected work.' See Annotated Principles, para. 99.

[76] Annotated Principles, para. 50(ix). See also COE Copyright Principles, Principle 5.b.

[77] *Ibid.* para. 50(ix).

[78] COE Copyright Principles, Principle 6.a and Synthesis of Principles, Principle AW35 and Principle PH43.

[79] Annotated Principles, para. 50(ix).

[80] ie if operated by an organisation other than the organisation which made the terrestrial broadcast. (Article II bis (i)(ii)). See §7.052 above.

enacted the proviso that Contracting States could impose compulsory licences for such cable retransmissions if they so wished.[81] The framers of Berne believed that an author would not be prejudiced by having his work exploited in this way, provided his right to remuneration was protected. But with the incessant march forward of technology, it soon became possible for cable operators to relay a broadcast in altered form. To permit cable operators to shield themselves behind compulsory licences (where their own country had taken that option) would do grave harm to authors. Thus it was felt amongst the experts, that the time had come to make a distinction between the simultaneous 'distribution by cable of a broadcast' and the distribution of what became known as a 'cable originated programme'.[82]

As illustrated above, the Annotated Principles hammer home the notion that each type of transmission is 'a communication to the public' for copyright purposes but by maintaining the distinction, allows the compulsory licence for the 'distribution by cable of a broadcast'.

(6) Limitations of Protection

8.027. Cable originated programme. Although, a 'distribution by cable of a cable originated programme' can never benefit from compulsory licensing under the Berne Convention,[83] nevertheless, the normal fair use exceptions will always apply. As the Annotated Principles state:

> Limitations of copyright, except any kind of non-voluntary licensing, admitted under international conventions and applicable national law with regards to the broadcast of a work may be extended by national legislation to the distribution by cable of cable-originated programmes.[84]

Therefore, the fair use of the work by way of illustration for teaching purposes, the use of publicly accessible works as background or incidental to the essential matters represented, communication of articles published in the press on current economic, political or religious topics, all without reservation of the right to further uses, would for example, be justified in the case of cable-originated programmes.[85]

8.028. Distribution by cable of a broadcast. The aforementioned exceptions will also apply where countries do not permit even 'the distribution by cable of a broadcast' under compulsory licence as sanctioned by the Berne Convention.

---

[81] Those provisions have been maintained in the latest version of the Convention (the Paris Act) which in Article 11bis(1)(ii) states that 'Authors of literary and artistic works shall enjoy the exclusive right of authorizing . . . any communication to the public by wire or by rebroadcasting of the broadcast of the work, when this communication is made by an organisation other than the original one'.

[82] See Annotated Principles, para. 105, where it is stated that 'Although the requirement that the (cable) distribution of the broadcast must be simultaneous with the broadcast is not spelled out in . . . [Article 11bis(2)] (which simply refers to communication by wire of the broadcast) it is clear that the countries of the Berne Union are not entitled to introduce non-voluntary licensing for non-simultaneous, that is deferred, communications by wire (or cable) of the broadcast, since any deferred communication makes the fixation of the broadcast unavoidable and the possibility of making—not any fixation but—[an] ephemeral recording of the work broadcast is admitted under paragraph (3) of Article 11bis only for [the] purposes of broadcasts, and not for, or also for, the purposes of wire (cable) distribution.'

[83] See §8.026 fn 82 above.

[84] Principle 10: endorsed by Synthesis of Principles, Principle AW28.

[85] Annotated Principles, para. 104. See reservations permitted by the Berne Convention, §7.050 fn 154 above.

3. Acts Invoking Neighbouring Rights

(1) Rights of Performers

8.029. Distribution by cable of a broadcast containing a performance. The Annotated Principles make it clear that the distribution by cable of a broadcast of a performance is considered to be a distinct use of the performance. A performance is understood to be any kind of action by a performer for listeners or spectators, such as acting, impersonating, singing, delivering, declaiming, miming or playing.[86] Because it is a separate act, it is a 'communication to the public' to which a neighbouring right liability attaches.[87]

8.030. Distribution by cable of a cable originated programme containing a performance. The Annotated Principles dictate that the use of a performance in a cable originated programme is a distinct use of the performance and a separate act, ie it is a 'communication to the public' to which a neighbouring right liability is attached.[88] Similar exceptions should be made for a cable-originated programme containing a performance as are made for copyright works ie the usual fair use exceptions.[89]

(2) Rights of Producers of Phonograms

8.031. Distribution by cable of a broadcast containing a phonogram recording. The Annotated Principles recognise that the distribution by cable of a broadcast of material taken from a phonogram is a distinct use of that phonogram and therefore a separate restricted act[90] ie it is a 'communication to the public'.[91]

8.032. Distribution by cable of a cable originated programme containing a phonogram recording. The Annotated Principles state that the distribution by cable of a cable originated programme containing material taken from a phonogram is a distinct use of that phonogram and a separate restricted act, ie it is a 'communication to the public'.[92] Similar exceptions should be made for a cable-

---

[86] *Ibid.* para. 110.

[87] *Ibid.* para. 114. Principle 11 of the Annotated Principles confers a right to remuneration but not a right to authorize or prohibit the distribution of performances; Principle 21 Option (d) however, confers an exclusive right to authorise a performance. Principles AW29 and PH35 of the Synthesis of Principles confer a right to equitable remuneration.

[88] Principle 17 of the Annotated Principles gives performers an exclusive right to authorize the use of a live performance and an equitable right to remuneration if the performance is taken from a lawful fixation; alternatively, cable originated performances are treated in exactly the same way as the Rome Convention treats them when broadcast (Principle 22 Option (a)), or they are granted the absolute right to control any use of their performance, whether live or recorded (Principle 22 Option (b)). The Synthesis of Principles, Principle AW31 gives performers a right to equitable remuneration if the performance is contained in an audiovisual work.

[89] Annotated Principles, Principle 27 (these exceptions should be based on the Rome Convention, see §7.221 above); endorsed by Synthesis of Principles, Principle AW32.

[90] *Ibid.* para. 230.

[91] Principle 28 of the Annotated Principles confers on the producer a right to equitable remuneration; endorsed by Synthesis of Principles, Principle PH37.

[92] Principle 32 of the Annotated Principles gives the phonogram producer the same rights as he has under the Rome Convention, in respect of the broadcast of material taken from his phonogram ie the right to 'equitable remuneration'; as an alternative, he is granted the absolute right to authorize or prohibit the distribution by cable of his phonogram in a cable originated programme (Principle 34 Option (b)).

originated programme containing a phonogram recording as are made for copyright works, ie the usual fair use exceptions.[93]

(3) Rights of Broadcasting Organisations

8.033. Distribution by cable of a broadcast. The Annotated Principles recognise that the distribution by cable of a broadcast is a distinct use of that broadcast ie it is a separate act and thus a 'communication to the public' for which the broadcaster's authority is required.[94] A broadcaster is defined as 'the natural person who, or the legal entity which, decides that a broadcast should take place and who or which determines the programme and the day and hour of the broadcast'.[95] It should be noted, that the Annotated Principles underline that there is no justification for imposing compulsory licences for the distribution by cable of a broadcasting organisation's broadcast, since the cable operators can isolate the holder of the rights (ie the broadcasting organisation) well in advance of the transmission, something that cannot practically be done with the myriad holders of rights (ie performers, producers of phonograms etc) in material comprising a broadcast.[96]

8.034. Distribution by cable of a cable-originated programme containing a broadcast. The Annotated Principles dictate that the use of a broadcast in a cable-originated programme is a distinct act for which the right owner's consent is required.[97] Similar exceptions should be made for a cable-originated programme containing a broadcast as are made for copyright works ie the usual fair use exceptions.[98]

4. Special Considerations for the Distribution by Cable of a Broadcast within the Service Area of the Broadcast

(1) Introduction

8.035. A 'distribution by cable of a broadcast' may be made within the 'service area' of the broadcast, that is, within the area which the broadcast was intended to, or in fact covers. One commonplace example is the 'common aerial' fixed on a block of flats. It picks up a broadcast and distributes it to the dwellings sometimes amplifying it in the process. But many commercial cable operators also pick up and

---

[93] Annotated Principles, Principles 33 and 35 (exceptions should be along the lines of those contained in the Rome and Phonograms Conventions, see §§7.221 and 7.248 respectively above); endorsed by Synthesis of Principles, Principle PH40.

[94] Principle 36 of the Annotated Principles confers on broadcasters, the exclusive right to authorize simultaneous and unchanged distribution by cable of their broadcasts; endorsed by the Synthesis of Principles, Principle AW33.

[95] Annotated Principles, para. 50(iv).

[96] *Ibid.* para. 252. Principle 36 of the Annotated Principles gives the broadcaster an exclusive right to authorise the distribution by cable of its broadcast; endorsed by Synthesis of Principles, Principle PH41.

[97] Principle 36 of the Annotated Principles gives the broadcaster the exclusive right to authorise the distribution of its broadcasts in a cable originated programme; endorsed by the Synthesis of Principles, Principles AW33 and PH41.

[98] Annotated Principles, Principle 37(ii); endorsed by the Synthesis of Principles, Principle AW34(2) and Principle PH42(2).

retransmit a broadcast within that broadcast's service area. The issue for owners of copyright (and neighbouring rights) and the cable operators, is, whether either of these activities amounts to a 'communication to the public', thus triggering liability under the international conventions.

(2) Relays by a Commercial Cable Operator

(i) Copyright

8.036. Introduction. There are several arguments which come to the aid of the cable operator and an equal number which champion the cause of the copyright owner.[99] Those arguments can be broken down into three categories: the mere reception facility argument, arguments which analyse geographic zones and finally the argument based on the Berne Convention.[100]

8.037. Mere reception facility argument. One perspective is that the cable operator is merely providing a technical facility thus obviating the need for the subscribers it serves to install receiving antennae. It is argued that since this technical operation is merely aiding reception, it cannot be a 'communication to the public' and thus cannot produce copyright liability.[101] However, the opposing view is that any modification of broadcast signals involves a new kind of distribution and the fact that such a process might be necessary indicates that a new service is being offered inducing liability.[102]

8.038. Geographic zones argument. Geographic zones can be broadly divided into two categories: on the one hand shadow zones and on the other direct reception zones and public service zones. A shadow zone is the area supposed to be covered by the broadcast but which cannot be satisfactorily reached because of physical obstructions such as, for example, tall buildings, mountains or trees.[103] It is argued that the author should not be able to make a profit out of the elimination of hindrances.[104] The argument is opposed on the ground that the cable operator ekes out his living precisely because the broadcast cannot reach, or at least does not adequately reach the subscribers he serves. If it did, there would be no need for him. Besides, it is not possible to determine exactly those parts of a territory which are 'shadow zones'.[105]

A direct reception zone is the area in which the broadcast is, in fact, perfectly receivable and the public service zone that area which the broadcaster is obliged to cover. It is argued that by authorizing the broadcast of his work, the rights owner has consented to its distribution by whatever means (over the air or by cable) in the area in which it can or ought to be received.[106] Furthermore, the author is supposed to have authorised all sorts of receptions of his work against the remuneration agreed upon.[107] He would have had the audience in mind when he negotiated the remuneration in his contract with the broadcasting organisation. It would be unjust

---

[99] See generally *Ibid.* paras 54 to 69 for a discussion of the various conceptual arguments.
[100] There is a great wealth of literature on this subject cited by Pichler in *Copyright Problems of Satellite and Cable Television in Europe* (Utrecht Studies in Air and Space Law, 1987).
[101] Annotated Principles, para. 57.
[102] *Ibid.*
[103] *Ibid.* para. 58.
[104] *Ibid.* para. 59.
[105] *Ibid.*
[106] *Ibid.* para. 60(i).
[107] *Ibid.* para. 60(ii).

for the author to be twice remunerated for the use of his work, ie once for the broadcast and once for the distribution by cable.[108] Against this 'double remuneration' argument, it is said, amongst other things, that an absolute definition of the so called 'direct reception zone' is not possible.[109] Furthermore, there is can be no double remuneration because there are two separate services.[110]

8.039. Berne Convention argument. The 1948 revision of the Berne Convention gave authors protection against the exploitation of their work by cable retransmission. The revision conference in Brussels canvassed all the arguments which were to be taken into account in deciding whether to curtail the author's right to authorise this use of his work in the service area of the broadcast.[111] After much deliberation, the conference settled on wording which would give the author the absolute right to authorise or prohibit any communication to the public of his work, save for one exception; no authority was needed if the communication by cable was made by the same broadcasting organisation which made the initial broadcast. And that is the form, the Convention takes. It makes no difference that the cable retransmission occurs in the service area.[112] As the Annotated Principles note:

> Neither the wording of the relevant provisions of the Berne Convention nor the respective conference documents offer any basis for the restriction of the scope of that special right of communication to the public according to particular criteria such as geographical or technological considerations or 'must carry' obligation under public law.[113]

8.040. Conclusion—'Statement of Group of Experts'. In 1980, a group of independent experts were convened to give their judgment on the issues concerning the distribution of a broadcast in the broadcast's service area. Their conclusion is authoritative and emphatic. They stated that:

> The distribution by cable of broadcast (radio or television) programmes is effected for a public different from (although possibly partially overlapping with) the public which the broadcast can reach or can reach only with diminished quality or at a higher cost; otherwise, there would be no need for distribution by cable.
>
> Due to the said difference in the public and since broadcasting and distribution by cable are two different acts, the latter is a 'communication to the public' within the meaning this term has in the law of copyright. Consequently, the exclusive right of authorization of the owner of copyright generally recognised in connection with communication to the public should be clearly recognised where the communication to the public is effected by distribution by cable of broadcast programmes consisting of or including works protected by copyright.[114]

---

[108] *Ibid.*

[109] *Ibid.* para. 61.

[110] *Ibid.* para. 62(vi).

[111] See *Ibid.* para. 63 et seq.

[112] See Article 11bis(1)(ii). See §7.052 above.

[113] Annotated Principles, para. 68. The Annotated Principles also consider the same conclusion to be justified on consideration of Article IVbis(1) of the Universal Copyright Convention (see §7.122 above).

[114] Statement of Group of Independent Experts on the Impact of Cable Television in the Sphere of Copyright (Geneva, Switzerland, 10-14 March 1980), Annotated Principles, Annex 1, Copyright Bulletin, Vol XVIII, No 2, [1984], 75. See also the Court of Justice decision in Case 62/79 *Compagnie Générale pour la Diffusion de la Télévision, Coditel SA v. Ciné Vog Films SA* [1980] ECR 881, [1981] 2 CMLR 362, per Advocate General Warner, who reached the same conclusion.

(ii) Neighbouring rights

8.041. The considerations which pertain to owners of copyright apply equally to the owners of neighbouring rights where their works are distributed in the service area of the broadcast. Thus performances, material taken from phonograms and the works of broadcasters are 'communicated to the public' where distributed within the service area of a broadcast. As the Annotated Principles note:

> There is no basis for restricting performers' rights within the service area of the broadcast according to technological or geographical considerations.[115]

They should thus be treated in much the same way as copyright owners.

(3) Relays by a Common Aerial

(i) Copyright

8.042. The most common form of cable retransmission takes place in apartment blocks where 'community aerials' relay signals to the myriad tenants. There is general consensus that signals fed by community aerials, is exempted from copyright liability. The Annotated Principles state that:

> It does not amount to distribution by cable of the broadcast of the work where the broadcast received by an aerial larger than generally used for individual reception, is transmitted by cable to individual receiving sets within a limited area consisting of one and the same building or a group of neighbouring buildings, provided that the cable transmission originates in that area and is made without gainful intent.[116]

It follows that, 'authorization by the author would be required even in such cases if gainful intent was involved in operating the system of transmission of the broadcast within the community.'[117] The Annotated Principles emphasise that it is not considerations of technical characteristics of the aerial equipment used (ie whether it effects reception rather than retransmission) that justifies the limitation of the author's rights. What matters is the concept of the neighbourhood,[118] ie a cluster of apartment blocks closely situated to each other would qualify.

(ii) Neighbouring Rights

8.043. In keeping with general principles, neighbouring right liability is not triggered, where any performances,[119] phonogram recordings[120] and works of broadcasting organisations[121] are retransmitted by a community aerial.

---

[115] para. 114. See also *ibid.*, Annex 1.
[116] Annotated Principles, Principle 8, where it is explained that the concept of neighbourhood was defined by borrowing elements of the definition found in the then current ITU Regulations according to which community reception is the reception of emissions 'by receiving equipment which in some cases may be complex and have antennae larger than those used for individual reception, and intended for use by a group of the general public at one location, or through a distribution system covering a limited area' (Rule 84 APB). The concept of neighbourhood has been endorsed by the Synthesis of Principles, Principle AW26. For an analysis of a series of French cases on this subject, see H Desbois and A Francon, Copyright and the dissemination by wire of radio and television programmes, RIDA [1975], LXXXVI, 3.
[117] *Ibid.* para. 96.
[118] *Ibid.* para. 97.
[119] *Ibid.* Principle 16; endorsed by Synthesis of Principles, Principle AW30.
[120] *Ibid.* Principle 31; endorsed by Synthesis of Principles, Principle PH38.
[121] *Ibid.* Principle 37(i); endorsed by Synthesis of Principles, Principle AW34(1) and Principle PH42(1).

CHAPTER NINE

European Audiovisual Programmes

I. EUROPEAN COMMUNITY AUDIOVISUAL PROGRAMME

1. Introduction

9.001. The European Community's audiovisual programme has three interwoven strands. They have been prosaically described by the Commission as 'the triptych' and they are:[1]

(1) the rules of the game;
(2) the new technologies;
(3) the programme industries.

2. The Rules of the Game

9.002. The 'rules of the game' are essentially the legal mechanisms which are necessary for nurturing the audiovisual sector. The Commission has thus concentrated on:

(1) eradicating obstacles on the freedom of reception and retransmission of television programmes, by harmonising laws concerning advertising, sponsorship, the right of reply and the protection of minors;[2]
(2) ensuring that owners of copyright and neighbouring rights are fully protected;[3]

---

[1] Communication from the Commission to the Council and Parliament on audiovisual policy, COM (90) 78 final, Introduction.
[2] Guaranteed by Council Directive 89/552/EEC of 3 October 1989 'Television Without Frontiers', Chapters II, IV, V and VI. See §6.056 et seq. above.
[3] See §1.054 et seq. above: Harmonisation of Copyright and Neighbouring Rights.

(3) promoting independent production;[4]
(4) promoting distribution networks;[5]
(5) ensuring that the competition rules are not breached ie Articles 85, 86 and 90.[6]

3. The New Technologies

9.003. Introduction. The Commission wishes to encourage the exploitation of new television technologies. It has focused its attention on two innovations in particular, namely, the new generation of satellites and high definition television ('HDTV').

9.004. New standards for satellite broadcasts. Steps had been taken towards the standardisation of Direct Broadcast Satellite transmissions through the adoption of the MAC-Packet Directive.[7] That Directive obliged Member States to use technical systems derived from the MAC-packet family of European standards, then consisting of C-MAC (transmitting high-quality pictures on a single channel allowing eight channels for sound), D-MAC (a version of C-MAC adapted for cable transmissions, also having one picture channel and eight sound channels) and D2-MAC (four channels for sound and one for vision). A further Directive has been adopted which will oblige Member States to take appropriate measures to use the HD-MAC standard for completely digital high-definition television transmissions and the D2-MAC standard for other not completely digital transmission in the 16:9 aspect ratio format.[8]

9.005. 'High Definition' television. On 27 April 1989,[9] the Council adopted a decision outlining a strategy for the introduction of HDTV in Europe. That decision contained five proposed lines of action: the development of the technology components and equipment required for the launch of HDTV;[10] the adoption of a single standard (1250 lines) for the origination and exchange of HDTV programme material;[11] promotion of the HDTV throughout the world;[12] promotion of HDTV services in Europe;[13] and the introduction of HDTV programmes in Europe and the building-up of expertise in programme production.[14]

---

[4] Guaranteed by Council Directive 89/552/EEC of 3 October 1989 'Television Without Frontiers', Chapter III. See §6.091 et seq. above.
[5] *Ibid.*. See §6.091 et seq. above. See also the MEDIA programme, See 9.035 et seq. below.
[6] See §§4.003 et seq., 4.114 et seq. and 4.171 et seq. above.
[7] Council Directive 86/529/EEC of 3 November 1986 on the adoption of common technical specifications of the MAC/packet family of standards for direct satellite television broadcasting OJ No L 311, 06.11.86, p.28.
[8] Council Directive 92/38/EEC of 11 May 1992 on the adoption of standards for satellite broadcasting of television signals, OJ No L 137, 20.05.92, p.17.
[9] Council Decision 89/337/EEC of 27 April 1989 on high-definition television OJ No L 142, 25.05.89, p.1.
[10] Article 1, Objective 1.
[11] *Ibid.* Objective 2.
[12] *Ibid.* Objective 3.
[13] *Ibid.* Objective 4.
[14] *Ibid.* Objective 5.

4. The Failings of the Programme Industries

9.006. Instituting a legal framework to ensure the circulation of programmes and investing in technology to improve the quality of broadcasts will be of no value if the material they are designed to benefit, is lacking. The European Community is woefully short of programming: in short, demand far outstretches supply. There are many reasons for this state of affairs. Among them, the Commission has highlighted the following:[15] there are inadequate circuits for the distribution and broadcasting of audiovisual works (it has been the case that nearly 90% of all products have never gone beyond the frontiers of their country of origin); productions capacities are fragile; Europe has hitherto been unable to develop a 'second market' for its products ie there is little possibility of rebroadcasting works mainly because of the problems of royalty management. Finally, the audiovisual market is regarded as a high risk sector by the financial world.

5. The European Community 'MEDIA' Programme

(1) Introduction

9.007. History. MEDIA, which stands for 'Measures to Encourage the Development of the Audiovisual Industry' was set up to try to provide economic support for the European television and cinema industries. The impetus for MEDIA came in a Commission communication to the Council when it called for practical experimental projects in the areas of production and distribution.[16] Concrete steps were first taken in 1987 with in-depth consultations with the relevant industries. This resulted in the establishment of ten projects which were monitored during a pilot stage lasting from 1988 to 1990. By its close, the pilot stage had begun to bear fruit and in 1990, following a positive appraisal by a group of experts,[17] MEDIA was turned into a full scale programme.[18] The experts had concluded that:

> Film and television are where culture and economics cross. At present the European industry is strong in creative talent and professional skills, but is relatively weak economically. Strengthening the media in Europe will strengthen both European culture and European economies; both will suffer if some strengthening is not implemented.

9.008. Areas covered by MEDIA. MEDIA offers support in six fields, namely:

(1) training the professionals;
(2) improvement of production conditions;
(3) distribution mechanisms;

---

[15] An Action Programme to Promote the Development of the European Audiovisual Industry, MEDIA 92, 1991–1995, COM (90) 132 final.
[16] Communication to the EC Council on an Action Programme for the European Audiovisual Media Products Industry, COM (86) 255 final.
[17] Encouraging Europe's Media Industry—a Review of MEDIA 92, COM (90) 132 final.
[18] Council Decision 90/685/EEC of 21 December 1990 concerning the implementation of an action programme to promote the development of the European audiovisual industry (MEDIA) (1991 to 1995) OJ No L 380, 31.12.90, p.37. See also Communication from the Commission to the Council and Parliament on audiovisual policy, COM (90) 78 final.

(4) cinema production;
(5) contribution to the establishment of a 'second market';
(6) stimulating financial investment.

Each of the programmes of support offered by MEDIA is explained below.

(2) Training the Professionals

(i) European Audiovisual Entrepreneurs ('EAVE')

9.009. Objective. EAVE's objective is to train television producers in economics and marketing thus creating a pan-European network for producers which will nurture European co-productions.[19] It is aimed principally at European independent producers with projects in the development phase in any genre or format and intended for any audiovisual medium. But it is also open to candidates without projects but who have 'creative potential' ie writers, distributors, directors and even lawyers. EAVE has given birth to the European Producers Network, an international association designed both to improve the exchange of information and to develop contacts.

9.010. Programme details. Participation in EAVE entails three intensive 8-day workshops over one year, concerning respectively, project development, pre-production and marketing.[20] Each workshop takes place in a different European country. During the course, 25 production projects are simultaneously developed, analyzed and followed up by experts in the fields of scriptwriting, budgeting, marketing, contract negotiation, financing and packaging. EAVE aims to focus its expertise on, in particular, the needs of small countries and regions in Europe.

(ii) Media Business School ('MBS')

9.011. Objective. The purpose of MBS is to help the European Audiovisual sector take advantage of the opportunities offered by the single European market.[21]

9.012. Programme details. MBS initiates projects itself or supports those initiated by outsiders on financial, commercial, legal and technical aspects of the audiovisual industry which target different sections of the profession in the areas of film, television and video. The school will organise workshops, supervise the implementation of projects and channel output into the industry. The activities of the Media Business School may be located in any EC country willing to host them.

9.013. Eligibility. Any individual or entity involved in any aspect of the audiovisual industry can submit a project which can involve any training, research or development activity designed to strengthen the European audiovisual product on the world market.[22]

9.014. Financial arrangements. MBS will provide up to 50% of the funding for selected projects. The balance of the approved budget must then be raised by the project's initiators from public and private funds.[23]

---

[19] MEDIA GUIDE, p. 13.
[20] EAVE Guidelines, MEDIA GUIDE, p. 15.
[21] MBS Guidelines, Article 1, MEDIA GUIDE, p. 26.
[22] *Ibid.* Article 3, MEDIA GUIDE, p. 27.
[23] *Ibid.* Article 4, MEDIA GUIDE, p. 27.

(3) Improvement of Production Conditions

(i) European Script Fund ('SCRIPT')

9.015. Objective. Acknowledging that raising development finance for fiction projects is the most difficult stage of production, SCRIPT lends money to producers and writers in the European Community, Switzerland and Austria for the development of film and television fiction.[24]

9.016. Eligibility and application. SCRIPT will consider any form of fictional or drama documentary material which tells a story expressed in any language of a Member State of the Community and which is intended for production and distribution in any audio-visual medium.[25] Essentially, SCRIPT looks for strong stories that will travel across one or more European borders. Preference is given to projects with interest from co-development partners in countries other than those from which a project is submitted. Furthermore special consideration is given to countries with a small audio-visual industry but there are no quotas per country.[26] Applications should be made either from a writer or a team of individuals including a writer, (the others may include a producer, director, etc) who are engaged in developing a project.[27] All of these persons should normally be nationals of the Community, although an exception can be made in the case of a member of a team who is not the writer.[28] In the case of an application by a team, the script must respect and should not violate the laws and standards applying in the country of the writer's nationality as regards obscenity, violence, defamation, privacy, copyright and moral rights.[29] It must be delivered within nine months of payment by SCRIPT of the first instalment of the award and the applicants may not dispose of any rights to third parties without the permission of SCRIPT.[30] Criteria applying to an application by an individual writer are determined individually in each case.[31]

9.017. Financial arrangements. An award will not normally exceed 37,500 ECU, the applicant usually providing not less than 50% (and certainly no less than 20%) of the total development cost of the project. The award is paid in instalments, the first half on signature of the contract and the remaining half on delivery of the completed development package.[32] Second stage funding (normally limited to 50%) is possible after delivery of a script if it is likely to contribute decisively to the project going into production.[33] An applicant whose developed script goes into production, must ensure that repayment of the award and a commission for SCRIPT's services, is made to SCRIPT not later than the first day of principal photography. The commission must not be less than 5% per annum on the amount of the loan outstanding from time to time (although it should not exceed 20% of the award). However, other forms of commission such as gifting a share in profits may be negotiated instead.[34]

---

[24] MEDIA GUIDE, p. 37.
[25] SCRIPT Guidelines, Article 1, MEDIA GUIDE, p. 39.
[26] MEDIA GUIDE, p. 37.
[27] SCRIPT Guidelines, Article 2, MEDIA GUIDE, p. 39.
[28] *Ibid.* Article 2, MEDIA GUIDE, p. 39.
[29] *Ibid.*
[30] *Ibid.*
[31] *Ibid.* Article 2, MEDIA GUIDE, p. 40.
[32] *Ibid.*
[33] *Ibid.* Article 6, MEDIA GUIDE, p. 41.
[34] *Ibid.*

SCRIPT also provides 'Incentive Funding' to European Production Companies developing film and or television projects. Loans of between 30% and 50% of the development costs of a project are awarded to projects which SCRIPT agrees to support.[35] A proportion of the loan is repayable on the first day of principal photography and a commission is payable which should not exceed 20% of the loan (even, for example if the loan were outstanding for over 4 years).[36] Responsibility for selection of the projects is devolved on to the production companies themselves but SCRIPT will monitor the projects selected.[37]

SCRIPT may make awards (normally not more than 2,500 ECU) for attendance of individuals at training courses and may make awards (normally not more than 5,000 ECU) to a small number of selected events or courses, if such an award is essential for the proper functioning of the training.[38]

(ii)   Documentary ('DOCU')

9.018. Objective. DOCUMENTARY aims to strengthen this particular genre by awarding loans to European Independent Producers for the development of documentaries and for the promotion and packaging of a documentary.[39]

9.019. Eligibility and application. DOCUMENTARY is open only to independent television and film producers in the European Community, 'independent' meaning that producers and directors must be unconnected with television companies.[40] A 'documentary' means an original work on a subject drawn from reality. It thus excludes: corporate image productions meant to promote or show the corporation, news programming and current affairs, programmes where an image is not the essential element and didactic films and programmes.[41] It is necessary for the documentary to appeal to a wide audience and original and creative treatment has priority over subject matter.[42] Loans are given for either project development or project promotion. In the case of the former, the producer must have produced a documentary either as a co-production with at least one other EC country or had it sold to a foreign country in the present or previous calendar year (two years in the case of small countries).[43] In the case of an application for project promotion, the film or programme must have been completed in the previous calendar year or be presently under completion and the producer must have retained the right to exploit the work in at least European territories.[44] If financial assistance is granted, DOCUMENTARY must be mentioned in the promotion package and the film/programme.[45]

9.020. Financial arrangements. Loans of up to ECU 10,000 (maximum of 50% of the budget) are given for project development. Seventy five per cent of the loan is paid on signature of the contract with DOCUMENTARY, the remaining 25% on

---

[35] Ibid.
[36] Ibid.
[37] Ibid.
[38] Ibid.
[39] DOCUMENTARY Guidelines, MEDIA GUIDE, p. 57.
[40] Ibid. p. 59.
[41] Ibid.
[42] Ibid.
[43] Ibid.
[44] Ibid.
[45] Ibid. p. 60.

submission of the developed script, production plans and accounts. The loan is repayable without interest from the first day of principal photography.[46] Loans of up to ECU 5,000 (maximum of 50% of the budget) are given for project promotion. Seventy five per cent of the loan is paid on signature of the contract and the remaining 25% on submission of the promotion package and a financial and sales report of the film/programme. The loan is repayable without interest from the first sales income after the producer has recouped his or her investment in the promotion budget.[47]

(iii) Cartoon ('CARTOON')

9.021. Objective. CARTOON provides support to the European animated film industry with the purpose of developing the production capacities for cartoons in Europe. Its net is cast wide offering assistance to all the professions in the industry ie authors, directors, producers, technicians, studio-directors and even television stations.[48] CARTOON offers pre-production aids, financial aid for studio grouping and training, a forum to bring together European producers, and a database accessible to all containing information on studios, production companies, on-going projects, television channels, industry professionals, festivals and associations etc.[49]

(a) Pre-production aid

9.022. Eligibility. Pre-production aid is available to provide assistance for pre-production of animated film projects of a minimum of 50 minutes' duration. They can be a long or short series, feature length films or TV specials. The aid consists of support for: graphics research, writing and adaptation and the development of pilots.[50] Support may be requested by any author, director or producer who is a national of one of the CARTOON member countries and who can guarantee that pre-production is feasible in one of those countries. A minimum of 75% of CARTOON'S pre-production budget is allocated to independent producers.[51] Support is granted on condition that the applicant provides evidence of a third party contribution of a minimum of 50% of the budget and applicants may only receive one type of aid per project submitted (beneficiaries for graphic research may however request aid for the pilot film).[52]

9.023. Financial arrangements. Aid will not exceed the following amounts: 35,000 ECU per project being no more than 5,000 ECU for graphic research (80% paid on signature of the contract and 20% on submission of the dossier), 20,000 ECU for writing or adaptation (50% paid on signature of the contract and 20% on submission of a copy of at least 50 minutes of script or storyboard, with dialogue) and 35,000 for a pilot film (50% on signature of the contract, 30% at the end of line tests and 20% on submission of a video copy of the pilot film).[53] If the project comes to fruition, repayment of 100% must be made plus 5% per calendar year commencing on signature of the contract, until the start of production of the project

---

[46] Ibid. 59.
[47] Ibid. 60.
[48] MEDIA GUIDE, p. 73.
[49] Ibid.
[50] Pre-production Regulations, Article 1, MEDIA GUIDE, p. 75.
[51] Ibid. Article 2, MEDIA GUIDE, p. 75.
[52] Pre-production Aid Regulations, Article 3, MEDIA GUIDE, p. 75.
[53] Ibid. Articles 4 & 5, MEDIA GUIDE, p. 75.

with a ceiling of 120% of the amount of the aid. Repayment is made as soon as the beneficiary receives the first gross operating receipts.[54]

(b) Aid for studio groupings

9.024. Eligibility. CARTOON gives seed capital to studios wishing to group together to make large scale European productions. Aid is available to any studios belonging to CARTOON and who submit a European programme.[55] The grouping must consist of a minimum of three animation film studios from at least three member countries of CARTOON with a majority of European Community Member States.[56] The grouping must be able to provide evidence of a contribution of at least 50% of its budget from third parties.[57]

9.025. Financial arrangements. Awards will be made of either 600,000 ECU, 450,000 ECU or 300,000 ECU over three years. Payment is made annually: 30% on signature of the contract in the first year, and after approval of certain accounts, 50% in the second year after proof of full use of the first instalment and 20% in the third year after proof of full use of the second instalment.[58]

(c) Cartoon Forum

9.026. CARTOON operates a Forum to set up a synergy between television channels and between channels and producers to speed up financial arrangements and to increase co-productions. In order to be admitted to the Forum, animation projects must be submitted by one or more European producers who are members of CARTOON and who have their registered offices in a CARTOON member country.[59] The production phase of the project must meet a minimum quota of 8 points out of a possible 12 as follows:[60]

European director: 2 points
European scriptwriter 1: point
European storyboard 1: point
European layout and background: 1 point
50% of animation in Europe: 3 points
50% of painting/tracing in Europe: 2 points
European rostrum operator: 1 point
Post-production in Europe: 1 point

The project must be a product of a European co-operation arrangement between at least two countries in the case of projects for films between 26 and 120 minutes and at least three countries for films lasting over 120 minutes. 'Co-operation' is meant in the full meaning of the word and can involve authors, directors, producers and studios established in a CARTOON member country.[61] Each project must be submitted with a written statement of interest from a European television channel,

---

[54] *Ibid.* Articles 6, MEDIA GUIDE, p. 75.
[55] Studio Grouping Aid Regulations, Article 2, MEDIA GUIDE, p. 78.
[56] *Ibid.* Article 3, MEDIA GUIDE, p. 78.
[57] *Ibid.*
[58] *Ibid.* Article 4, MEDIA GUIDE, p. 78.
[59] Forum Regulations, Article 2, MEDIA GUIDE, p. 82.
[60] *Ibid.*
[61] *Ibid.*

although in the last resort, CARTOON may itself sponsor the project. Priority is in this case granted to projects from studio groupings, those that have benefited from pre-production assistance and projects from the smallest countries.[62]

(d) Mediabase Cartoon

9.027. The CARTOON Media Base is a working tool for the animation industry. It holds data on a multiplicity of subjects such as the availability of professionals, studio production capacity, technical innovations and aid systems, all on a country by country analysis. In fact, the database offers details on anything relating to the animation industry 'from Festivals to TV buyers, from aids to creative works to series currently under way'.[63]

(iv) Media Investment Club ('CLUB')

9.028. Objective. The CLUB was created in October 1988 and today has twelve members which include manufacturers and broadcasting companies. The CLUB exists to exploit advanced technologies, in three areas in particular. They are: applications in the audio-visual field of digital and computer techniques (ie computer graphics and special effects); the production of programmes in European Standard High Definition Video and the production of interactive multimedia programmes (ie CD-1 and CD-ROM linked to a computer).[64]

9.029. Support provided. The CLUB intervenes in two ways. Either it allocates financial support for projects which are presented to it. This support varies according to the project but usually amounts to a direct co-production investment with a return on the investment.[65] Alternatively, the CLUB itself proposes priority action. Thus for example, 'CD92' calls for European projects for the production of interactive multimedia programmes whilst another project 'HD MEDIA' calls for projects for the high definition video production of programmes in the European Standard. Preference is given to projects which promote innovative technologies. Each production project must have received the commitment of a broadcaster, a publisher and/or a distributor by the date of signature of the contract.[66]

(a) HD MEDIA

9.030. The CLUB invites audio-visual producers, authors and directors associated with a producer, television company programme directors (within the EC and in association with an EC company) to present projects for the production of programmes (fiction, creative documentaries, special programmes) in European High Definition Video Standard intended for commercial distribution. If the project is accepted, the CLUB offers to intervene financially as co-producer of the project or through a repayable loan which may represent a majority share of the additional high-definition production costs. The criteria of selection include: marketing perspectives; creative use of HDTV; possibility of extending programme into a series; programmes life-span and the cost of making the programme.[67]

---

[62] *Ibid.*
[63] CARTOON Mediabase, MEDIA GUIDE, p. 88.
[64] CLUB Guidelines, MEDIA GUIDE, p. 100.
[65] *Ibid.*
[66] *Ibid.*
[67] HD MEDIA Guidelines, MEDIA GUIDE, p. 105.

(b) CD-92

9.031. The CLUB invites publishers of books, discs and software, as well as authors and audio-visual producers to present projects for the production and/or financing and marketing of interactive programmes.[68] These programmes should be intended for large scale publishing and aimed at the international market. They should be conceived for one of the interactive optical multimedia CD-1 system, or a combination of CD-ROM with computers and should be adaptable according to the state of the market. Should the project be accepted, there are three planned stages: the design, production and publishing phase. The promoter and the CLUB decide together to produce a programme for which the producer is associate producer. The criteria of selection include: marketing perspectives; creative use of an old subject; the possibility of extending the subject into a series or collection and the programmes life-span and its cost.[69]

(v) Small Countries Improve their Audiovisual Level in Europe ('SCALE')

9.032. Objective. SCALE was created to encourage the development potential of those European Community countries with small audio-visual production capacities or those with a limited geographical and linguistic area.[70]

9.033. Eligibility. Support is provided to existing European audio-visual programmes or new initiatives or in limited cases, production companies or groups of companies which propose to introduce programmes of action which will benefit the audio-visual output of small countries.[71] Organisations applying should have a board composed of nationals of European countries, be funded from European sources and have the development of European audio-visual industry and culture as an integral part of their raison d'être.[72] Programmes or initiatives should be focused on solving the problems of audiovisual production in small countries with lesser audio-visual capacity and/or limited geographical or linguistic area, and they should be additional to existing programmes.[73]

9.034. Financial arrangements. SCALE may provide up to 50% of the costs of supported projects. (Where the applying organisation is funded already by the MEDIA programme, the combined contribution by the MEDIA programme or its projects cannot exceed 50% of the costs.)[74]

(4) Improving Distribution Mechanisms

(i) European Film Distribution Office ('EFDO')

9.035. Objective. Eighty per cent of European films do not cross the border of their country of origin. EFDO's aim is to improve this statistic by financially assisting the distribution of European theatrical films from all European Community Member States as well as Austria and Switzerland.[75]

---

[68] CD—92 Guidelines, MEDIA GUIDE, p. 107.
[69] Ibid.
[70] SCALE Guidelines, MEDIA GUIDE, p. 119.
[71] Ibid.
[72] Ibid.
[73] Ibid.
[74] Ibid.
[75] MEDIA GUIDE, p. 127.

9.036. Eligibility and applications. Films with production costs of up to 4.5 million ECUs qualify. Aid is available for the distribution of feature documentary and animation films with a minimum length of 60 minutes and whose production companies are based in a country of the European Communities or in a country with which a co-operation contracts exists and whose directors belong to the European cultural sphere.[76] In the case of international co-productions, the co-production partners from EC countries or from countries with which a co-operation contract exists must have participated to the amount of at least 51% of the total production costs.[77] Films that are clearly advertising mediums or pornographic or glorify violence are not eligible for distribution aid.[78] Aid is available only for theatrical distributors who have not transferred the rights of exploitation to a sub-distributor or do not intend to do so.[79] The applicant must guarantee that he himself will act as theatrical distributor and that he himself bears the distribution pre-costs accounted for to EFDO.[80] In addition, the following requirements must be met.[81] At least three different distributors form at least three different EC countries or from countries with which co-operation contracts exist must agree to exhibit a film theatrically in their countries. The application must be submitted by all the distributors concerned at the same application deadline. The start must be guaranteed within one year of receiving notice that the distribution aid has been granted. Distributors from countries in which the film has already been released before the respective application deadline are not eligible for support. The distributors submitting the application are required to include a signed distribution pre-contract with the film's producer or the holder of the rights. The pre-contract must state that the distributor ensures that he will release the film theatrically in his country as agreed in the contract, if the distribution aid is granted. Distributors must submit their applications to the EFDO office by the deadlines of 1 April and 1 November.

The EFDO operates a priority system.[82] First in line are films that bring together the greatest number of distributors ie that guarantee theatrical distribution in the most countries. Next are projects from 'difficult' film export countries. All countries other than France, Germany and Great Britain fall into the category of 'difficult film' export countries. In the case of projects of equal standing in accordance with the aforementioned priorities, preference is given to films from countries from which no film or only a few have yet received aid. If further criteria are needed, projects which due to their distribution concept show promise of mounting a more successful theatrical release will be given priority.

Twenty per cent of the EFDO's distribution budget is to be allocated for the distribution of films with production costs of up to 750,000 ECU, 60% are to be made available to distributors of films costing between 750,000 ECU and 2,250,000 ECU. The remaining 20% of the funds are allocated to distributors of films with production costs of between 2,250,000 and 4,500,000 ECU. A fixed amount is reserved for the support of the distribution of films for children and is known as

---

[76] EFDO Guidelines, Article B.II, MEDIA GUIDE, p. 129.
[77] *Ibid.*
[78] *Ibid.*
[79] *Ibid.* Article B.III.1, MEDIA GUIDE, p. 128.
[80] *Ibid.*
[81] *Ibid.*
[82] *Ibid.* Article B.VI.1, MEDIA GUIDE, p. 130.

'EFDO junior'. The EFDO may also conclude co-operation contracts with institutions of European countries with the aim of disseminating European films as widely as possible.[83]

9.037. Financial arrangements. Support for distribution amounts to up to 50% (in fact normally 50%) of the pre-costs calculated for theatrical release by the distributors for their own countries. The distributors are required to match at least this amount from their own resources.[84] The aid, which is granted in the form of a conditionally repayable interest free loan amounts to a maximum of 100,000 ECU per film and per distribution country.[85] Distributors receive the first instalment, being up to a maximum of 50% of the loan, after presentation of the licensing agreement and supporting documentation. The second instalment is paid immediately after the cinematic release of the film and presentation of supporting documentation. Claims must be made for each instalment: within 12 months after award of the loan for the first instalment and within 12 months after payment of the first instalment for the second instalment.[86]

Distributors that are granted distribution aid for a film from other national or international film funds are also eligible to receive a loan from EFDO for that film. However, the distributor's own share of the total distribution pre-costs must amount to at least 50%.[87] National subsidies that guarantee to cover possible losses of the distributor will be taken into account and deducted from the aid sum in the equivalent amount. Additional copies that are paid for by national subsidies will also be regarded as a subsidy and a corresponding amount will be deducted.[88]

The repayment of the loan is conditional on the distributor's expenditures and revenues and the distributor retains all of the returns until his share of the original pre-costs as well as the overhead share have been recouped.[89]

(ii) Espace Video European ('EVE')

9.038. Objective. The MEDIA programme gave birth to EVE to encourage the publication and distribution of European audio-visual works on formats used mainly in the domestic environment ie video cassette and video disc.[90] EVE provides two different types of schemes of assistance, although it will consider other proposals which would contribute significantly to improve the production and distribution of European audio-visual production on video cassette. The first scheme involves the granting of loans for the publication and distribution of feature length films and documentaries. The second scheme provides financial assistance for economic interest groupings of video publishers and distributors.

(a) Loans for feature length film

9.039. Eligibility. EVE gives conditionally repayable loans to publishers of contemporary European feature length films on video to an amount of 40% of the

---

[83] *Ibid.* Article B.ii, MEDIA GUIDE, p. 129.
[84] *Ibid.* Article IV.1, MEDIA GUIDE, p. 129.
[85] *Ibid.* Article IV.2-4, MEDIA GUIDE, p. 129.
[86] *Ibid.* Article IV.6, MEDIA GUIDE, p. 129.
[87] *Ibid.* Article IV.5, MEDIA GUIDE, p. 129.
[88] *Ibid.*
[89] *Ibid.* Article V, MEDIA GUIDE, p. 129.
[90] EVE Guidelines, Article 1, MEDIA GUIDE, p. 149.

publication cost (excluding only the cost of rights acquisition).[91] 'Contemporary' means a film which has been released within ten years preceding the application (although priority is given to more recent films). 'Feature length' means a minimum running time of 60 minutes. Films which are advertising, pornographic, racist or which glorify violence will not be eligible.[92] The film production companies must be incorporated in a Member State of the European Community and their Directors must belong to the European cultural sphere.[93] Any international co-productions must involve co-production partners from European Community countries which have participated to the amount of at least 51% of the total production costs.[94] The publication and distribution of the film must take place in at least three member States of the European Community in which the film has not already been distributed on video (which can include the country of origin) and involve at least three publishers. The applicants must prove that they have or will have all rights if the loan is granted.[95] Distribution of the video must be guaranteed to take place within one year of the aid being made available if legally possible.[96] A film which is supported by EVE in at least three countries at one of its deadlines is eligible for future resubmission providing that the resubmission involves at least three EC Member States which have not previously applied and in which the film has not already been distributed on video.[97]

Factors which are taken into account in assessing applications are: the involvement in the publication of the largest number of member countries of the European Community; proposals to publish and distribute films in the smaller European countries or those that originate in those countries; proposals for new routes or methods of distribution of video products and proposals to reduce costs by undertaking economies of scale with other applicants.[98]

9.040. Financial arrangements. Financial assistance comprises of a conditionally repayable loan of up to 40% of the publication costs of the film on video up to a maximum of 25,000 ECU per film per country. The loan is interest-free, however, a success contribution will be paid to EVE as soon as a profit is realised.[99] The publisher is required to invest at least 60% of the publication costs from his own resources.[100] If a publisher is granted aid for the publication of the film from any source other than his own resources, assistance from EVE is dependent on the publisher investing 60% of the remaining publication costs.[101] The loan is paid in two instalments, the first (being a maximum of 50% of the loan) on signature of the contract and evidence of rights ownership and the second immediately after publication of the film.[102] Publishers granted loans who invest more than originally calculated do so at their own risk. The publisher recovers from his revenues all of his own investment before repaying EVE.[103]

---

[91] *Ibid.* Article 3, MEDIA GUIDE, p. 149.
[92] *Ibid.*
[93] *Ibid.*
[94] *Ibid.*
[95] *Ibid.*
[96] *Ibid.*
[97] *Ibid.*
[98] *Ibid.* p. 150.
[99] *Ibid.* p. 149.
[100] *Ibid.*
[101] *Ibid.*
[102] *Ibid.*
[103] *Ibid.*

(b) Loans for documentaries

9.041. Eligibility. EVE grants loans specifically for the distribution of document-aries.[104] A 'documentary' means a subject drawn from reality but being an original work in the sense of the writing, research and analysis of the subject. Excluded are: corporate image productions meant to promote or show the corporation itself, its actions or products; programmes where the image is not essential (ie talk shows) and instructional films and programmes. Documentaries which are pornographic, racist or which glorify violence are not eligible.[105] The European publisher or distributor must be incorporated in an EC Member State, (although this concept will be broadened if agreements are made with other countries).[106] International co-productions must involve co-production partners from European Community countries who have participated to the amount of at least 51% of the total production costs.[107] For video publishers of documentaries to avail themselves of the scheme, the company applying must have a majority shareholding; the publication and distribution of the film must take place in at least three EC Member States (although, if the documentary has already been released on video in at least one of the EC Member States, a minimum of two applicants will suffice); the applicants must prove that they have or will have the necessary rights if aid is granted; the distribution of the video must be guaranteed to take place within one year of contract signature.[108] A documentary which has been supported by EVE is eligible for future resubmission if it involves at least two Member States who have not previously applied.[109]

9.042. Financial arrangements. Assistance takes the form of a conditionally repayable loan of up to 40% of the publication costs of the documentary on video, to a maximum of 15,000 ECU, the publisher being expected to invest at least 60% of the publication costs from his own resources.[110] In the event that the film is part of a series or collection (a 'series or collection' meaning five or more titles forming a unified concept) the maximum per series or collection and per country will be 30,000 ECU.[111] The loan is interest free, however, a success contribution must be paid to EVE as soon as a profit is realised.[112] The loan is paid in two instalments: the first instalment, being a maximum of 50% of the loan, is paid on signature of the contract and evidence of rights ownership; the second instalment is paid immediately after publication of the film.[113]

(c) Financial assistance for economic groupings

9.043. Eligibility. EVE provides financial assistance to publishers who are estab-lishing economic interest groupings in video publication and distribution with colleagues in other European countries.[114] Those eligible for assistance are organisa-

---

[104] *Ibid.* p. 152.
[105] *Ibid.*
[106] *Ibid.*
[107] *Ibid.*
[108] *Ibid.*
[109] *Ibid.*
[110] *Ibid.* p. 153.
[111] *Ibid.*
[112] *Ibid.*
[113] *Ibid.*
[114] *Ibid.* p. 160.

tions having their head office and business in one or several countries of the European Community and each grouping must involve at least three European companies in at least three Member States of the European Community.[115] The project of the grouping must primarily relate to programmes published and/or distributed on video. The groupings must be aimed at the implementation of projects to stimulate European co-operation, and in particular the creation of joint purchasing tools for publication and to the organisation of integrated distribution networks.[116] The joint projects must be realised primarily in Europe and must be for the benefit of the European audiovisual industry and yield additional economic and cultural worth to the business of each partner.[117] Economic groupings exclusively concerned with the publication of films for the purposes of advertising and/or industry and/or tourism are not available for financial assistance.[118] Neither are economic groupings which include in their proposed publications films that are pornographic, racist or which glorify violence.[119]

9.044. Financial assistance. Two kinds of financial assistance are available. The first is limited to 50% of the budget required to research and establish the economic grouping and has a ceiling of 7,000 ECU per profit. The second is more extensive and flexible taking into account the specific operating costs of the groupings.[120]

(iii) Groupement Européen pour la Circulation des O'Euvres ('GRECO')

9.045. Objective. GRECO was initiated by Coordination Europeenne des Producteurs Independent. Its fundamental purpose is to nurture a strong independent television production sector in Europe thus helping broadcasters fulfil their obligations towards independent production as required by Article 5 of the EC Directive 'Television Without Frontiers' as well as Article 10.3 of the Council of Europe's European Convention on Transfrontier Television.[121]

GRECO is to develop in two stages. The first is a pilot stage which started in July 1992 and will run for approximately 18 months. Thereafter the programme is to be fully operational. Fifty million ECUs have been made available for GRECO, sufficient to cover about 400 hours of high quality fiction.[122]

9.046. Eligibility. The GRECO system is open exclusively to television fiction projects to be made by independent production companies established in an EC Member State or a co-opting country. Such works must comply with the definition of European works as laid out under Article 6 of the Directive 'Television Without Frontiers'.[123] Special consideration will be given to applications from smaller Member States.[124]

To be considered for GRECO support, a producer must fulfil three conditions.[125] He must guarantee the completion of the production or reimburse GRECO if

---

[115] Ibid.
[116] Ibid.
[117] Ibid.
[118] Ibid.
[119] Ibid.
[120] Ibid.
[121] GRECO Guidelines, Article 1, MEDIA GUIDE, p. 175.
[122] Ibid., Article 2, MEDIA GUIDE, p. 175.
[123] Ibid., Article 4, MEDIA GUIDE, p. 175.
[124] Ibid.
[125] Ibid.

principal photography has not started within 12 months from the time of approval of the submission. He must submit a fiction project, together with guarantees of at least 75% of the project's budget. The budget must include contributions from at least three European broadcasters. GRECO contributes 50% of the remaining balance (subject to a maximum of 2.5 million ECU per project), provided that the other 50% is guaranteed directly by the applicant or by a distributor. Finally, the producer must have negotiated a position whereby he/she retains the rights in the programme once the initial rights assigned to the participating broadcasters have been exhausted or alternatively, a position whereby he/she will retain programme rights to the territories outside those of the participating broadcasters.

In order to qualify for support, producers must pass an 'independence' test.[126] This will generally be satisfied where: the production company submitting the project is not controlled directly by a broadcaster and the production company submitting the project does not control directly a broadcaster. However, a producer can apply jointly with a broadcaster involved in a project where the idea for the project is initiated by the broadcaster.

In addition, the projects must acquire 11 points in accordance with the following criteria:[127]

European director: 2 points
European author of the scenario: 2 points
50% or more of the other
wage earners are European: 2 points
One of the two best paid
actors is European: 1 point
European director of photography: 1 point
European art director: 1 point
European composer: 1 point
European editor: 1 point
Presentation of a European and
international marketing plan: 2 points
Support from SCRIPT: 1 point
Total: 14 points

Excluded from the GRECO system are: any programme which has already benefited from a specific national cinema subsidy in any EC country; non-fiction work; series exceeding 10 hours and programmes shorter than the full commercial hour.[128]

9.047. Financial arrangements. GRECO contributes 12.5% of the budget subject to a maximum of 2.5 million ECU per project.[129] Reimbursement of GRECO occurs with a reimbursement scheme starting with the first income and which percentage is determined for each application.[130] However, this percentage cannot be less than 5% and on top of this reimbursement there is a 5% bonus to ensure minimum replenishment of the GRECO fund.[131]

---

[126] Ibid.
[127] Ibid.
[128] Article 5, MEDIA GUIDE, p. 176.
[129] Ibid., Article 6, MEDIA GUIDE, p. 176.
[130] Ibid.
[131] Ibid.

(iv) European Association for a European Audiovisual Independent Market ('EURO AIM')

9.048. Objective. EURO AIM is a service and support structure for the promotion and marketing of European independent production. It ensures the presence of independent companies at major markets such as MIP-TV and MIPCOM as well as creating new marketing initiatives. It also offers a range of information databases and consultancy services which facilitate contacts between the buyers and sellers of European independent production.[132]

9.049. EURO AIM 'Umbrella' at MIP-TV and MIPCOM. EURO AIM organises forums at the international TV markets of MIP-TV and MIPCOM and welcomes applicants under its 'umbrella'. Applicants to join EURO AIM's 'umbrella' may come from any EC country and from Switzerland. Although no strict quota is organised, particular interest is shown in Italy, Portugal, Greece and Denmark. A limited number of places are available from European, non-EC countries.[133]

Applicants must have as their primary business, the production or distribution of European Independent films or programmes.[134] Priority is given to companies who have completed programmes to sell and those who are new to the markets. In the latter case, applicants should not have attended MIP-TV or MIPCOM before. Attendance at festivals or infrequent attendance at other types of markets will not disallow their application, but priority will be given to companies less experienced in promotion and marketing. There is a maximum of two delegates per company.

9.050. EURO AIM SCREENINGS. EURO AIM also organises its own four-day annual event, EURO AIM SCREENINGS which brings together over 250 recent European television productions (both fiction and documentary) to 100 invited international buyers. In order to enter productions, they must be made by European independent producers.[135] They must be 26 minutes or longer, being either one complete programme or an episode of a series. Productions may be in any genre, documentary or fiction (eg feature films, children's programmes, natural history, light entertainment etc). It is preferable that they have not been widely presented elsewhere and productions entered for previous EURO AIM screenings are not eligible. Productions may be in any European language but the programmes selected for the channels will be screened in English (whether original version, subtitled or dubbed).

EURO AIM is regularly present at other markets, namely: Monte Carlo International TV market (February), Berlin Film Market (February), Cannes Film Festival (May), Sunny Side of Doc/Marseilles (June), Medianet/Munich (July), Rendez-vous/Munich (September)

9.051. EURO AIM Rendez-vous. Rendez-vous is an itinerant market organised by EURO AIM with the function of bringing together co-producers and financiers. In order to qualify for entry to the market, a project must originate from a European independent producer, who must be, at the stage of submission, the executive

---

[132] EURO AIM Guidelines, Article 1, MEDIA GUIDE, p. 190.
[133] *Ibid.*
[134] *Ibid.*
[135] *Ibid.*, MEDIA GUIDE, p. 191.

producer of the project.[136] The project's financing requirements may represent 'classic' co-productions where production partners are sought to be involved as equity investors, 'financial' co-production where the finance is exchanged for distribution rights, 'technical' co-production where the sought for investment would be in terms of production/post production facilities or 'executive' co-production where the creative and management input of other partners is sought or any mix of the foregoing.[137]

The project must be a fiction feature film or TV movie with a completed script. Each producer/production company may enter only one project. Co-producers already involved in the project should be European, but minority co-producers from countries outside Europe will be allowed.[138]

If the project is a feature film, the minimum budget must be 1.5 million ECU. There are two categories of projects which are acceptable, those with at least 30% of the financing in place and those with already at least 60% of the financing in place. For the former, a distinction is made between productions according to whether the major producer comes from a 'large' country (France, Germany, Italy, Spain and the UK) or a 'small' country. For 'large' countries, the project must be accompanied either by a distribution agreement, or an agreement with a broadcaster interested in purchasing or co-producing or an agreement with a financial coproducer. For small countries, the producer need only prove that he has secured 30% of the budget. For projects which already have at least 60% of the financing in place, the producer must provide a detailed estimate of what sales potential is still available and what recoupment position is offered to financiers.[139]

If the project is a TV movie, the minimum budget must be 0.75 million ECU. Only projects which have already brought together 70% of the financing can be considered.[140]

9.052. Other EURO AIM services. EURO Aim provides three services for European independent producers/distributors and independent buyers.[141] Two are computerised databases entitled The Production Mediabase and The Producers Mediabase and the third is a consultancy service named Marketing/Distribution Consultants. The Production Mediabase is an information resource designed to aid buyers and distributors in their search for programming. It gives access free of charge to more than 5,500 titles. Only completed productions can be entered, the production's country of origin must be European, and the Executive/main producer must be independent. For each title, the sales contacts are given and interested buyers can make contact directly with the appropriate seller. The Producers Mediabase provides professional profiles of over 750 European independent production companies and is intended to help companies find suitable partners or coproducers in other European countries. Only European independent production companies are entered on the database. The Marketing/Distribution Consultants consist of a team of specialists who can answer questions submitted by independent producers. The specialists deal only with promotion, sales or marketing issues.

---

[136] *Ibid.*, MEDIA GUIDE, p. 192.
[137] *Ibid.*
[138] *Ibid.*
[139] *Ibid.*
[140] *Ibid.*
[141] *Ibid.*

(v) Broadcasting Across the Barriers of European Language ('BABEL')

9.053. Objective. The aim of BABEL is to provide financial support for dubbing, subtitling and voice-over of television programmes thus fostering cultural exchanges and helping countries with a low audiovisual output. It will also conduct training operations in those activities and collaborate in research into multilingual production techniques.[142] BABEL's priorities are works of fiction (notably those aimed at young viewers), animation, pilots for series and original documentaries.[143]

9.054. Subsidies for dubbing or subtitling. BABEL will contribute a maximum of 50% for the cost of dubbing or subtitling transfrontier and multilingual magazine and information programmes which promote European co-operation.[144] The same contribution may be made for training courses and promotion.[145] These grants would not be subject to any reimbursement from the beneficiary with the exception of launching of general-interest multilingual channels and transfrontier magazines which are sold to TV channels as opposed to being exchanged.[146] Grants for research will be treated on a case by case basis. However, they will normally be made under terms that the grant will be reimbursed together with an agreed percentage if the research results in a commercial application.[147]

9.055. Advances on returns for dubbing, subtitling or voice-overs. BABEL will provide an advance on returns for the dubbing, subtitling or voice-over of programmes produced by independent producers or TV channels with a view to their promotion among broadcasters and their eventual transmission.[148] These could be, for example, fiction programmes, original documentaries and animation films. However, in the case of a series, an advance on returns will be granted solely for the pilot programme.[149]

Advances cannot exceed the total investment previously made by the producer for sound post-production (ie detection, translation/adaption, music and special effects track, recording, synchronization, mixing and laboratory work).[150] Assistance will not be granted until production of the programme—or the pilot in the case of a series—has been completed.[151] Reimbursement of advances granted by BABEL will amount to 10% of the value of the rights for each transmission and/or commercialisation as negotiated by the producer to be paid six monthly.[152]

Every production supported by BABEL must mention this assistance, preferably in the credits, in the following way:[153]

With the assistance of:

BABEL (Broadcasting Across the Barriers of European language)
EBU (European Broadcasting Union)

---

[142] BABEL Guidelines, Article 2, MEDIA GUIDE, p. 217.
[143] *Ibid.*, Article 3, MEDIA GUIDE, p. 217.
[144] *Ibid.*, Article 4.1, MEDIA GUIDE, p. 217.
[145] *Ibid.*
[146] *Ibid.*
[147] *Ibid.*
[148] *Ibid.*, Article 4.2, MEDIA GUIDE, p. 217.
[149] *Ibid.*
[150] *Ibid.*
[151] *Ibid.*, Article 4.3, MEDIA GUIDE, p. 217.
[152] *Ibid.*, Article 5, MEDIA GUIDE, p. 218.
[153] *Ibid.*, Article 5, MEDIA GUIDE, p. 218.

MEDIA (Commission of the European Communities)
EATC (European Alliance for Television and Culture)

(5) Cinema Exhibition

(i) Media Salles ('SALLES')

9.056. Objective. SALLES aims to improve the distribution of films in the cinema. Any professional cinema exhibitors and associations, and national and international organisations pursuing these objectives may become members of SALLES.[154]

SALLES has already established several projects including: the promotion of European films in the cinema, the training of cinema exhibitors, the constitution of a network of cinema theatres and support for pilot films. MEDIA SALLES is open to any proposition likely to achieve its objectives.[155]

(ii) European Film Academy ('EFA')

9.057. Objective. EFA was founded in Berlin on 30 November 1991 to 'provide a meeting-place and a haven for reflection, to improve and extend knowledge and awareness of European cinema and to communicate experience'.[156]

The EFA is a non-profit making organisation. New members can only join by invitation and membership is only offered to recognised film professionals.[157]

EFA has taken over responsibility for the European Film Awards held annually in Berlin. The aims of the Awards are: to celebrate the quality and diversity of European cinema; to attract new audiences to European film; to emphasise to the public that European films are not only for specialist tastes but can also appeal to wider audiences and to draw attention to new, as yet undiscovered talent. The EFA organises screenings of the awarded films in European cities.[158]

Beginning in 1992 EFA has established an annual European Masterschool lasting for five days. The Masterschool will cater for young professionals such as producers, directors, screen-writers, production designers, actors etc who can apply to participate. The results of the Masterschools will be documented and made available to European Film Schools and to the media. At the end of each Masterschool, the Academy will present an international symposium. This will provide a public forum for reflection about European cinema.[159]

(6) Contribution to the Establishment of a 'Second Market'

(i) Memory—Archives—Programmes TV ('MAP-TV')

9.058. Objective. MAP-TV's aim is to enhance the value of the European audiovisual archives by helping to set up co-productions of archive based creative

---

[154] MEDIA GUIDE, p. 225.
[155] *Ibid.*
[156] EFA Guidelines, Article 1, MEDIA GUIDE, p. 232.
[157] *Ibid.* Article 2, MEDIA GUIDE, p. 232.
[158] *Ibid.* Article 3.1, MEDIA GUIDE, p. 232.
[159] *Ibid.* Article 3.2, MEDIA GUIDE, p. 232.

programmes.[160] It understands that this type of programme is research intensive and without investment in the development aspect of production, such programmes are likely to remain nationally focused.

9.059. Eligibility. Eligible for support are any project for a television programme in an existing or original genre which is composed of a minimum of 20% of audiovisual archives and which is 'in keeping with the hope of bringing together the peoples of Europe in the long term; as well as with a European view of world events and culture'.[161] Any European independent producer may apply provided that he/she has received an agreement in principle for his/her project from 2 potential co-producers coming from 2 countries other than his/her own and from at least one broadcast or distributor of video tapes. Also, 51% of producers' contributions to development must come from European Communities countries.[162] The development budget, which must not exceed 15% of the total production budget, must have the written commitment of co-financiers to cover at least 50% of the estimate with the executive producer financing at least 20% of this.[163] Projects will be selected for the perceived need of development, their creativity, originality of the archives used and the programmes' broadcasting prospects.

9.060. Financial arrangements The total of repayable loans provided by MAP-TV will not exceed 50% of the development budget, that is 75% of the total production budget with a ceiling fixed at 40,000 ECU.[164] The payment of the grant is subject to an agreement between the executive producer and MAP-TV. Payments are made in three instalments: 40% on signature of the agreement, 40% on justification of the first instalment and the balance on deposit of the developed project and finance plan accompanied by a firm commitment on the part of co-producers from 3 different countries as well as from one broadcaster.[165] The grant is without interest if the producer undertakes to repay it in one sum no later than one year after the signing of the contract.[166] In the case of a staggered repayment, the executive producer must repay MAP-TV the amount of the grant plus 5% interest starting from the date of signature of the agreement. Under no circumstances, may repayment be postponed to more than two years after signature of the agreement.[167]

(ii) Lumiere Project Association ('LUMIERE')

9.061. Objective. LUMIERE was launched by the leading European film archives to invest in the permanent preservation of films whose survival is in danger.[168]

9.062. Eligibility. Only projects aimed at the physical preservation and restoration of archive films will be considered and provided that the films or film materials are relevant to the European film heritage.[169] Two or more film archives in two or more

---

[160] MAP-TV Guidelines, Article 1, MEDIA GUIDE, p. 240.
[161] *Ibid.*, Article 2, MEDIA GUIDE, p. 240.
[162] *Ibid.*
[163] *Ibid.*
[164] *Ibid.*, Article 4, MEDIA GUIDE, p. 240.
[165] *Ibid.*
[166] *Ibid.*
[167] *Ibid.*
[168] LUMIERE Guidelines, MEDIA GUIDE, p. 251.
[169] *Ibid.*

countries must be jointly involved in the project in either: acquisition and/or re-assembly of film materials; technical co-operation; or research leading to restoration.[170]

9.063. Financial arrangements. LUMIERE will grant loans to finance up to a maximum of 50% of the extra costs brought about by the co-operation between film archives in order to carry out common projects. During the pilot phase of LUMIERE, the maximum amount for any one project is 25,000 ECU.[171]

(7) Stimulation of Financial Investments

(i) Euro Media Guarantees ('EMG')

9.064. Objective. EMG was founded to offer European financial institutions with a way to share the risks inherent in financing the European film and television productions sector. It will provide guarantees for a portion of loans that are advanced to cash flow European television and film productions.[172]

9.065. Eligibility. An application to EMG must be made by the majority co-producer.[173] The film or television project must have European nationality and have a minimum of 3 co-producers: the majority co-producer must be from an EC Member State.[174] Each co-producer must contribute a minimum of 20% of the budget and prior to application, distribution of the project must have been arranged in the respective countries of all 3 co-producers.[175]

EMG is primarily interested in larger budget films and television programme series, but will consider smaller projects which show the requisite commercial and artistic ambitions. Priority is given to projects which have already received funding from other MEDIA initiatives.[176] EMG does not require any particular quota of artists, technicians etc, or even that productions be shot in an EC country, although projects which seem to be specifically European may be given preference.[177] EMG's assessment of applications will include an evaluation of: the applicant producers professional qualifications and financial status; the professional qualifications and financial status of any and all co-producers; the recoupment position negotiated with the relevant financial institution(s) and the budget, finance plan and all other elements normal to the evaluation of film and television projects.[178]

9.066. Financial arrangements. EMG's funding comes from both public and private sectors (the former consisting of 1 million ECU half of which comes from the MEDIA 95 PROGRAMME and half of which has been provided by the French government through EUREKA AUDIOVISUEL and the latter provided by banks).[179]

---

[170] *Ibid.*
[171] *Ibid.*
[172] EMG Guidelines, Article 3, MEDIA GUIDE, p. 260.
[173] *Ibid.*, Article 4.a, MEDIA GUIDE, p. 260.
[174] *Ibid.*
[175] *Ibid.*
[176] *Ibid.* Article 4.b, MEDIA GUIDE, p. 260.
[177] *Ibid.*
[178] *Ibid.*
[179] *Ibid.*, Article 4.c, MEDIA GUIDE, p. 260.

EMG will be able to offer guarantees to a total value of 5 times the funds raised. It will guarantee a maximum of 70% of loans advanced by financial institutions to applicant productions.[180]

II. THE COUNCIL OF EUROPE MEDIA PROGRAMME

1. Introduction

9.067. The Council of Europe, which is composed of twenty nine European countries, has been focusing on the problems facing the media for over thirty years. Indeed, it provided the impetus for the conclusion of four international agreements concerning the audio and audio-visual sectors; namely, The European Agreement concerning Programme Exchanges by means of Television Films;[181] The European Agreement on the Protection of Television Broadcasts,[182] The European Agreement for the Prevention of Broadcasts transmitted from Stations outside National Territories and the European Convention on Transfrontier Television.[183]

9.068. Steering Committee. In 1976, the Council of Ministers established an intergovernmental work programme to concentrate on matters concerning the mass media. This programme has been entrusted to the 'Steering Committee on the Mass Media' (CDMM), an august body of experts plucked from the Member States of the Council of Europe. It is assisted by numerous subcommittees and working parties.

2. Measures to Improve Audiovisual Production

(1) Introduction

9.069. The Council of Europe has been concerned with promoting audio-visual production in Europe since 1986. For in that year, it adopted a Recommendation[184] the aim of which was to implement concrete measures of a financial and fiscal nature, amongst others, to encourage audio-visual creation and the development of programme industries. Like the European Commission, it is has expressed its concern that unless steps are taken to improve the volume of European material, there is every danger that the vacuum will be filled by what is described in neutral terms as 'extra-European' programmes. In particular, the Council of Europe has established a Europe Support Fund for the co-production and Distribution of Creative Cinematographic and Audiovisual Works known as 'EURIMAGES' and this is dealt with below.

---

[180] *Ibid.*
[181] See §7.155 above.
[182] See §7.164 above.
[183] See §7.280 above.
[184] Recommendation No. R (86) 3 (14 February 1986).

(2) Eurimages

9.070. Objective. Eurimages is a fund set up to support the co-production and distribution of creative cinematographic and audiovisual works.[185]

9.071. Eligibility. Aid may be granted for the co-production, distribution, broadcasting and/or promotion of films or audiovisual works originating in a member state of the fund.[186] Applicants must be natural or legal persons governed by the legislation of one of the funds member states, which produce or distribute or broadcast films and/or audiovisual works.[187] In reaching its decision on whether to grant aid the Eurimages board of management must take into account the quality of the work and must ascertain whether it is apt to reflect and to promote the contribution of the diverse national components to Europe's cultural identity.[188]

Co-production aid may be granted for schemes including at least three co-producers from the fund's member states. Such aid may also be granted for co-productions also involving co-producers from non-member states of the fund, provided that the latters' contribution does not exceed 30% of the cost of producing the co-production.[189] The contribution from public or private sources of each of the co-producers from fund member states may not exceed 60% of the production costs.[190]

Aid for the co-production of films and audiovisual works is granted in respect of co-productions of works primarily intended for cinema showing and of co-productions of works primarily intended for broadcasting by television or cable distribution, where such work is produced by producers independent of the broadcasting agencies.[191]

9.072. Financial arrangements. Aid for distribution, broadcasting and promotion is granted to cover expenditure specified in the application for the manufacture of copies, subtitling and/or dubbing and recourse to various means of promotion.[192] Such aid may not, however, exceed 50% of such expenditure.[193] The aid is allocated in the form of grants or loans at a preferential rate.[194]

III. MISCELLANEOUS PROGRAMMES

1. Audiovisual Eureka

9.073. Objective. In 1989, at an audiovisual conference held in Paris, the Council of Europe, the European Community and a number of East European countries as well as the then existing USSR, set up 'Audiovisual Eureka' with the purpose of

---

[185] Resolution (88) 15 Setting up a European support fund for the co-production and distribution of creative cinematographic and audiovisual works ('Eurimages'), Article 1.1.
[186] Article 5.1.
[187] Article 5.2.
[188] Article 5.3.
[189] Article 5.4.
[190] *Ibid.*
[191] Article 5.5.
[192] Article 5.6.
[193] *Ibid.*
[194] Article 5.7.

strengthening the audiovisual industry in Europe. Audiovisual Eureka's objectives are:[195]

(1) to foster the emergence of a transparent, dynamic European-scale market;
(2) the strengthening of the capacity of European enterprises;
(3) the achievement of the widest possible distribution of European programmes;
(4) the multiplication of European exchanges;
(5) the increasing of Europe's share of the world market;
(6) the development of the widest possible diffusion of production from countries with limited capacity;
(7) the promotion of European technologies.

9.074. Eligibility. Audiovisual Eureka projects must fulfil one of a number of qualifications. They must either:

(1) encourage the exchange and distribution of European Works on cinema, television or video cassette; or
(2) create the necessary preconditions for financing of production and coproduction; or
(3) foster contacts between professionals ensuring the clarity and proper distribution of information; or
(4) adapt training to the new job requirements of the audiovisual industry; or
(5) enhance the competitiveness of European firms; or
(6) encourage the development and expansion of the audiovisual sector in countries with a low production capacity and limited linguistic coverage; or
(7) promote new technologies.

In addition, projects must be implemented within the framework of co-operation agreements applying to enterprises of two European countries, and three European countries where possible. They must present identifiable positive features arising from co-operation on a European scale. They must also contain adequate financial commitments on the part of the participants.

---

[195] As stated in the Joint Declaration of 2 October 1989.

APPENDIX 1

European Community Directives

COUNCIL DIRECTIVE

of 15 October 1963

implementing in respect of the film industry the provisions of the General Programme for the abolition of restrictions on freedom to provide services

(63/607/EEC)

THE COUNCIL OF THE EUROPEAN ECONOMIC COMMUNITY,

Having regard to the Treaty establishing the European Economic Community, and in particular Article 63 (2) thereof;

Having regard to the General Programme for the abolition of restrictions on freedom to provide services,[1] and in particular Title V C (c) thereof;

Having regard to the proposal from the Commission;

Having regard to the Opinion of the European Parliament[2];

Having regard to the Opinion of the Economic and Social Committee[3];

Whereas the movement of films among Member States comes, as regards distribution and commercial exploitation, within the provisions of the General Programme for the abolition of restrictions on freedom to provide services;

Whereas the achievement of the common market in the film industry presents a number of problems which must be solved progressively during the transitional period; whereas the abolition of restrictions on the importation of films represents only one aspect of the overall problem posed by the film industry;

Whereas the second subparagraph of Title V C (c) of the General Programme provides, in respect of the film industry, that bilateral quotas existing between Member States at the time of the entry into force of the Treaty shall be increased by one-third in those States where the importation of exposed and developed films for distribution and commercial exploitation is restricted;

Whereas, in order to ensure that this Directive is correctly applied, it is necessary to define the term 'film' and to lay down common ciriteria for recognition of the nationality of films of Member States;

Whereas it is necessary to consolidate such liberalisation as has already been achieved with regard to distribution, commercial exploitation and trade in respect of films other than those subject to bilateral quotas;

HAS ADOPTED THIS DIRECTIVE:

Article 1

Persons entitled to the benefit of the measures adopted in pursuance of this Directive shall be those covered by Title I of the General Programme for the abolition of restrictions on freedom to provide services.

---

[1] OJ No 2, 15.1.1962, p. 32/62.
[2] OJ No 33, 4.3.1963, p. 476/63.
[3] OJ No 159, 2.11.1963, p. 2667/63.

This Directive shall apply to films which satisfy the provisions of Article 2 and which, under Articles 3 and 4, are to be regarded as having the nationality of a Member State.

Article 2

For the purposes of this Directive, 'film' means any copy which conforms to the master copy of a completed cinematographic work intended for public or for private exhibition and in which subsist all rights of commercial exploitation arising under international conventions or under other international arrangements.

Films shall be classified as follows:

(a) full-length films: 35-mm films equal to or exceeding 1600 m in length;
(b) short films: 35-mm films less than 1600 m in length;
(c) newsreel films: 35-mm films equal to or exceeding 200 m in average length the purpose of which is to provide regular reports and filmed accounts of current affairs and events; newsreel films in colour may be less than 200 m in length.

Lengths for films of other widths shall be such that their running times correspond to those of the films defined in (a), (b) and (c).

Article 3

For the purposes of this Directive, a film shall be regarded as having the nationality of a Member State where it satisfies the following conditions:

(a) the film must be produced by an undertaking which satisfies the provisions of Title I of the General Programme for the abolition of restrictions on freedom to provide services;
(b) studio-filming must take place in studios situated in Community territory; if the subject of the film requires the filming of outdoor scenes in a third country, up to 30% of the studio-filmed scenes may be shot in the territory of that third country;
(c) the original version must be recorded in the language, or in one of the languages, of the Member State in question, except for any parts of the dialogue which the screenplay requires to be in another language; where the film is recorded in more than one version, one of those versions must be in the language, or in one of the languages, of the Member State in question;
(d) the screenplay, adaptation, dialogue and, if specially composed for the film in question, musical score must be written or composed by persons who are nationals of the Member State in question or who come within its cultural domain;
(e) the director must be a national of the Member State in question or a person who comes within its cultural domain;
(f) the majority of the executants, that is to say of the following—principal players, executive producer, director of photography, sound engineer, editor, art director and wardrobe chief—must be nationals of the Member State in question or persons who come within its cultural domain.

Participation in the activities referred to in (d), (e) and (f) by nationals of other Member States, or by persons who come within the cultural domain of any such State, shall not preclude recognition of the nationality of a film where the Member State in question accords its nationality to that film. Neither shall participation in the activities referred to in (d) and (f) by nationals of third countries who are not persons coming within the cultural domain of a Member State preclude recognition of the nationality of a film where the Member State in question accords its nationality to that film provided that such nationals do not constitute more than two-fifths of the total of the persons participating in such activities. The same shall apply if the person referred to in (e) is a national of a third country who is not a person coming within the cultural domain of a Member State, provided that all the activities referred to in (d) and not less than four-fifths of the functions referred to in (f) are performed by nationals of Member States.

Article 4

By way of derogation from the provisions of Article 3, films shall be regarded has having the nationality of a Member State if they are made by producers from Member States as co-productions or in co-operation, with producers from third countries.

Films shall be regarded as being co-productions where they are made under the terms of reciprocal international agreements.

Films shall be regarded as being in co-operation with producers from one or more third countries where they are made with such producers by producers from one or more Member States in conformity with national laws.

In the case both of co-productions and of productions made in co-operation with other producers the artistic and technical contribution of the Member State or States shall be not less than 30%.

Films covered by this Article shall be allowed to circulate freely for the purposes of distribution and commercial exploitation among all Member States.

Article 5

Member States shall not restrict in any way the importation, distribution and commercial exploitation of:

(a) short films;
(b) newsreel films, subject to the right to maintain until the end of the transitional period any existing restrictions with regard to the distribution and commercial exploitation of newsreels containing items not intended for exhibition in more than one country;
(c) full-length films of documentary value, such as films of cultural, scientific, technical or industrial subjects, or instructional or educational films for young people, or films promoting the Community ideal.

Article 6

There shall be no restriction on the importation into, distribution in or commercial exploitation in, a Member State of full-length films having the nationality of another Member State and being for exhibition in the original version, with or without sub-titles in the language or one of the languages of the State in which they are to be exhibited.

Article 7

1. Where there are quota arrangements between Member States, such Member States shall allow the importation into, distribution in and commercial exploitation in, their territories of one another's films dubbed in the language of the State in which they are to be shown on the basis of existing quotas. Such quotas shall, from the date of implementation of this Directive, amount to not less than seventy films per film year.

2. The commercial exploitation of reissued films shall be subject to agreement between the competent authorities of the Member States concerned.

3. No Member State may introduce quotas for films, irrespective of their category, from other Member States in relation to which there are no existing quota restrictions.

Article 8

Authorisations granted in accordance with the provisions of the preceding Articles shall carry with them the right to import without restriction prints, dupes and advertising material.

Article 9

Nothing in this Directive shall affect the operation of rules applicable in a Member State to the exhibition of its own films or of films treated as such.

Article 10

No tax or measure having equivalent effect the application of or exemption from which might result in discrimination shall be imposed in respect of the granting of any authorisation for the importation, distribution or commercial exploitation of any film having the nationality of a Member State.

Article 11

Nothing in this Directive shall require the authorities of importing Member States to issue authorisations for the importation into and commercial exploitation in their territories of any film which is not accompanied by a certificate issued by the exporting Member State attesting to the nationality of that film, as determined in accordance with the provisions of Articles 3 and 4.

Article 12

Member States shall adopt the measures necessary to comply with this Directive within six months of its notification and shall forthwith inform the Commission thereof.

Article 13

This Directive is addressed to the Member States.

Done at Brussels, 15 October 1963.

For the Council
The President
L. de BLOCK

SECOND COUNCIL DIRECTIVE

of 13 May 1965

implementing in respect of the film industry the provisions of the General Programmes for the abolition of restrictions on freedom of establishment and freedom to provide services

(65/264/EEC)

THE COUNCIL OF THE EUROPEAN ECONOMIC COMMUNITY,

Having regard to the Treaty establishing the European Economic Community, and in particular Articles 54 (2) and (3) and 63 (2) thereof;

Having regard to the General Programme for the abolition of restrictions on freedom of establishment,[1] and in particular Title IV A thereof;

Having regard to the General Programme for the abolition of restrictions on freedom to provide services,[2] and in particular Title V C (c) thereof;

Having regard to the first Directive[3] concerning the film industry, adopted by the Council on 15 October 1963;

Having regard to the proposal from the Commission;

Having regard to the Opinion of the European Parliament[4];

Having regard to the Opinion of the Economic and Social Committee[5];

Whereas, in accordance with Title IV A of the General Programme for the abolition of restrictions on freedom of establishment, restrictions on the opening of cinemas specialising exclusively in the exhibition of foreign films in the language of their country of origin must be abolished by the end of the second year of the second stage of the transitional period;

Whereas, in accordance with Title V C (c) of the General Programme for the abolition of restrictions on freedom to provide services, the problems presented by the achievement of a common market in the film industry must be solved progressively before the end of the transitional period; whereas, with a view to the achievement of such a common market, and taking into account that part of the transitional period which has already elapsed, it is desirable that certain restrictions still remaining after adoption of the Council Directive of 15 October 1963 be abolished; whereas, of these restrictions, those relating to the importation and to the exhibition of films considerably restrict movement of films within the Community; whereas, since these restrictions are alike in their effects on such movement, they should be abolished simultaneously;

Whereas the dubbing of films can be carried out satisfactorily in the exporting country and whereas therefore the requirement that films having the nationality of a Member State must be dubbed in the country of exhibition is no longer justified;

---

[1] OJ No 2, 15.1.1962, p. 36/62.
[2] OJ No 2, 15.1.1962, p. 32/62.
[3] OJ No 159, 2.11.1963, p. 2661/63.
[4] OJ No 20, 6.2.1965, p. 265/65.
[5] OJ No 194, 27.11.1964, p. 3243/64.

Whereas the conditions of establishment must not be distorted by aids granted by the Member State of origin of any beneficiary under this Directive;

HAS ADOPTED THIS DIRECTIVE:

Article 1

Member States shall abolish, in respect of the natural persons and companies or firms covered by Title I of the General Programmes for the abolition of restrictions on freedom of establishment and freedom to provide services (hereinafter called 'beneficiaries'), the restrictions referred to in Title III of those Programmes affecting the film industry and relating to:

(a) the opening of cinemas specialising exclusively in the exhibition of foreign films in the language of their country of origin, with or without sub-titles;
(b) import quotas and screen quotas;
(c) the dubbing of films.

Article 2

For the purpose of this Directive, a film shall be regarded as having the nationality of one or more Member States where it satisfies the provisions of Articles 3 and 4 of the first Directive concerning the film industry, adopted by the Council on 15 October 1963.

Article 3

Article 1 (a) shall not apply in Member States in which films are usually shown in the language of their country of origin.

Article 4

The opening of a specialist cinema in a Member State shall not entitle any other Member State to grant any direct or indirect aid, whether financial or other, which would have the effect of distorting the conditions of establishment.

In particular, no such aid shall be granted for:

–the construction, reconstruction or modernisation of any cinema;
–the execution of work in connection with safety, hygiene or technical improvements;
–the purchasing of equipment;
–the renting of full-length films;
–the covering of risks or trading losses.

Any and every kind of aid available in the Member State in question for the opening of a specialist cinema shall be available without discrimination to operators who are nationals of other Member States of the Community.

Beneficiaries from Member States shall in no instance be treated less favourably than natural persons or companies or firms from third countries.

Article 5

A Member State which, on the day of notification of this Directive, requires cinemas to set aside a minimum number of days per calendar year for the exhibition of domestic films (screen quota) shall, by 31 December 1966 at the latest, allow films having the nationality of one or more Member States to be included in the quota under the same conditions as those applicable to domestic films. That Member State may increase the number of days comprising its screen quota so as to allow for the inclusion of films from other countries.

Member States which, on the day of notification of this Directive, do not impose screen quotas, may introduce such quotas provided that they are also applicable to films having the nationality of other Member States.

Screen quotas shall not be applied to the specialist cinemas referred to in Article 1 (a).

Article 6

The Council, acting on a proposal from the Commission and at the request of a Member State, may, by a qualified majority, authorise that State to impose limits on the exhibition, whether in specialist or in non-specialist cinemas, of foreign films in the language of their country of origin where such language is that of the region in which the cinema is situated.

Article 7

Import quotas for films having the nationality of one or more Member States shall be abolished by 31 December 1966 at the latest.

The Federal Republic of Germany shall, however, during the transitional period, retain the power to limit the importation of films having the nationality of one or more Member States and in respect of which the national censorship authority has granted a certificate more than four years before the date on which the application to import is submitted to the competent authorities.

Abolition of import quotas gives the right to import prints, dupes and advertising material without restriction.

Article 8

Provisions requiring that the dubbing of films must take place in the importing country shall, by 31 December 1966 at the latest, be repealed in respect of films having the nationality of one or more Member States.

Article 9

Member States shall adopt the measures necessary to comply with this Directive within six months of its notification and shall forthwith inform the Commission thereof.

Article 10

This Directive is addressed to the Member States.

Done at Brussels, 13 May 1965.

For the Council
The President
M. COUVE DE MURVILLE

COUNCIL DIRECTIVE

of 15 October 1968

concerning the attainment of freedom of establishment in respect of activities of self-employed persons in film distribution

(68/369/EEC)

THE COUNCIL OF THE EUROPEAN COMMUNITIES,

Having regard to the Treaty establishing the European Economic Community, and in particular Articles 54 (2) and (3) thereof;

Having regard to the General Programme for the abolition of restrictions on freedom of establishment,[1] and in particular Title IV thereof;

Having regard to the Council Directive of 15 October 1963[2] implementing in respect of the film industry the provisions of the General Programme for the abolition of restrictions on freedom to provide services, and to the Second Council Directive of 13 May 1965[3] implementing in respect of the film industry the provisions of the General Programmes for the abolition of restrictions on freedom of establishment and freedom to provide services;

Having regard to the proposal from the Commission;

Having regard to the Opinion of the European Parliament[4];

Having regard to the Opinion of the Economic and Social Committee[5];

Whereas Title IV E of the General Programme for the abolition of restrictions on freedom of establishment provides that the common market in the film industry must be achieved before the end of the transitional period;

Whereas, with a view to the progressive attainment of freedom of establishment in the film industry, the two Directives already adopted by the Council should be followed by a further Directive, relating to activities of self-employed persons in film distribution;

Whereas, in order to ensure that this Directive is correctly applied, it is necessary to define its scope by specifying what is meant by activities of self-employed persons in film distribution;

Whereas, as regards the provision of services, the Directive of 15 October 1963, while abolishing rules restricting the importation of films, did not abolish restrictions on the provision of services by distributors; whereas the attainment of freedom to provide services poses certain economic problems in the Member States; whereas, with a view to the solution of such problems, studies are in progress on the co-ordination of provisions relating to safeguards for creditors by setting up film registers; whereas, therefore, liberalisation as regards the provision of services should be postponed for the present and the scope of this

---

[1] OJ No 2, 15.1.1962, p. 36/62.
[2] OJ No 159, 2.11.1963, p. 2661/63.
[3] OJ No 85, 19.5.1965, p. 1437/65.
[4] OJ No 307, 18.12.1967, p. 27.
[5] OJ No 302, 13.12.1967, p. 10.

Directive should be confined to the attainment of freedom of establishment in respect of the activities in question;

Whereas the General Programme for the abolition of restrictions on freedom of establishment provides that restrictions on the right to join professional or trade organisations must be abolished where the professional activities of the person concerned necessarily involve the exercise of this right;

Whereas separate Directives, applicable to all activities of self-employed persons, concerning provisions relating to the movement and residence of beneficiaries, and where necessary Directives on the co-ordination of the safeguards required by Member States of companies or firms for the protection of the interests of members and of others, have been or will be adopted;

HAS ADOPTED THIS DIRECTIVE:

Article 1

Member States shall abolish, in respect of the natural persons and companies or firms covered by Title I of the General Programmes for the abolition of restrictions on freedom of establishment and freedom to provide services (hereinafter called 'beneficiaries'), the restrictions referred to in Title III of those General Programmes affecting the right to take up and pursue the activities specified in Article 2 of this Directive.

Article 2

1. The provisions of this Directive shall apply to activities of self-employed persons in film distribution, as referred to in Annex IV to the General Programme for the abolition of restrictions on freedom of establishment, ex Group 841, ex Major Group 84.

Distribution shall be taken to include the renting of films.

2. The distribution and renting of films shall be regarded as comprising any activity involving the making over of the rights of commercial exploitation of a film with a view to its being distributed on a commercial basis in a specific market and the temporary transfer of the right of public exhibition to any person who directly organises the exhibition of films in the host country.

Article 3

1. Member States shall in particular abolish the following restrictions:

(a) those which prevent beneficiaries from establishing themselves or providing services in the host country under the same conditions and with the same rights as nationals of that country;
(b) those existing by reason of administrative practices which result in treatment being applied to beneficiaries that is discriminatory by comparison with that applied to nationals.

2. The restrictions to be abolished shall include in particular those arising out of measures which prevent or limit establishment or provision of services by beneficiaries by the following means:

(a) *in Belgium*
   –the obligation to hold a *carte professionelle* (Article 1 of the Law of 19 February 1965);
(b) *in France*
   –the obligation to hold a *carte d'identité d'étranger commerçant* (*Décret-loi* of 12 November 1938, *Décret* of 2 February 1939, Law of 8 October 1940, Law of 14 April 1954, *Décret* No 59–852 of 9 July 1959);

(c) *in Luxembourg*
   –the limited period of validity of authorisations granted to foreign nationals (Article 21 of the Law of 2 June 62).

Article 4

1. Where a host Member State requires of its own nationals wishing to take up any activity referred to in Article 2 proof of good repute and proof that they have not previously been declared bankrupt, or proof of either one of these, that State shall accept as sufficient evidence, in respect of nationals of other Member States, the production of an extract from the 'judicial record' or, failing this, of an equivalent document issued by a competent judical or administrative authority in the country of origin or the country whence the foreign national comes showing that these requirements have been met.

Where the country of origin or the country whence the foreign national comes does not issue such documentary proof of no previous bankruptcy, such proof may be replaced by a declaration on oath made by the person concerned before a judicial or administrative authority, a notary, or a competent professsional or trade body, in the country of origin or in the country whence that person comes.

2. Documents issued in accordance with paragraph 1 may not be produced more than three months after their date of issue.

3. Member States shall, within the time limit laid down in Article 7, designate the authorities and bodies competent to issue these documents and shall forthwith inform the other Member states and the Commission thereof.

4. Where in the host Member State proof of financial standing is required, that State shall regard certificates issued by banks in the country of origin or in the country whence the foreign national comes as equivalent to certificates issued in its own territory.

Article 5

1. Member States shall ensure that beneficiaries have the right to join professional or trade organisations under the same conditions and with the same rights and obligations as their own nationals.

2. The right to join professional or trade organisations shall entail eligibility for election or appointment to high office in such organisations. However, such posts may be reserved for nationals where, in pursuance of any provision laid down by law or regulation, the organisation concerned is connected with the exercise of official authority.

3. In the Grand Duchy of Luxembourg, membership of the *Chambre de commerce* or of the *Chambre des métiers* shall not give beneficiaries the right to take part in the election of the administrative organs of those Chambers.

Article 6

No Member State shall grant to any of its nationals who go to another Member State for the purpose of pursuing any activitiy referred to in Article 2 any aid liable to distort the conditions of establishment.

Article 7

Member States shall adopt the measures necessary to comply with this Directive within six months of its notification and shall forthwith inform the Commission thereof.

Article 8

This Directive is addressed to the Member States.

Done at Luxembourg, 15 October 1968.

For the Council
The President
G. SEDATI

COUNCIL DIRECTIVE

of 29 September 1970

concerning the attainment of freedom of establishment and freedom to provide services in respect of activities of self-employed persons in film production

(70/451/EEC)

THE COUNCIL OF THE EUROPEAN COMMUNITIES,

Having regard to the Treaty establishing the European Economic Community, and in particular Articles 54 (2) and (3) and 63 (2) and (3) thereof;

Having regard to the General Programme for the abolition of restrictions on freedom of establishment,[1] and in particular Titles III and IV thereof;

Having regard to the General Programme for the abolition of restrictions on freedom to provide services,[2] and in particular Titles III and IV thereof;

Having regard to the proposal from the Commission;

Having regard to the Opinion of the European Parliament[3];

Having regard to the Opinion of the Economic and Social Committee[4];

Whereas this Directive covers activities of self-employed persons in film production, as listed under ISIC Group 841; whereas the activities of film studios or undertakings whose services are available to a producer and the activities of the persons directly involved with the producer in the making of a film are governed by special laws; such activities are therefore dealt with in separate Directives;

Whereas, in accordance with Article 54 (3) (h), the conditions of establishment must not be distorted by aids granted by the Member State of origin of any beneficiary under this Directive;

Whereas the General Programme for the abolition of restrictions on freedom of establishment provides that restrictions on the right to join a professional or trade organisations must be abolished where the professional activities of the person concerned necessarily involve the exercise of this right;

HAS ADOPTED THIS DIRECTIVE:

Article 1

Member States shall abolish, in respect of the natural persons and companies or firms covered by Title I of the General Programmes for the abolition of restrictions on freedom of establishment and freedom to provide services (hereinafter called 'beneficiaries'), the

---

[1] OJ No 2, 15.1.1962, p. 36/62
[2] OJ No 2, 15.1.1962, p. 32/62.
[3] OJ No C 65, 5.6.1970, p. 11.
[4] OJ No C 28, 9.3.1970, p. 5.

restrictions referred to in Title III of those General Programmes affecting the right to take up and pursue the activities specified in Article 2 of this Directive.

Article 2

The provisions of this Directive shall apply to activities of self-employed persons in film production as referred to in Annex IV to the General Programme for the abolition of restrictions on freedom of establishment (ex Group 841, ex Major Group 84).

They shall not apply to the activities of the persons directly involved with the producer in the making of a film.

Article 3

1. Member States shall in particular abolish the following restrictions:

(a) those which prevent beneficiaries from establishing themselves or providing services in the host country under the same conditions and with the same rights as nationals of that country;

(b) those existing by reason of administrative practices which result in treatment being applied to beneficiaries that is discriminatory in comparison with that applied to nationals.

2. The restrictions to be abolished shall include in particular those arising out of measures which prevent or limit establishment or provision of services by beneficiaries by the following means:

(a) *in Belgium*
    – the obligation to hold a *carte professionelle* (Article 1 of the Law of 19 February 1965);
    – the requirement that film producers, whether natural or legal persons, be of Belgian nationality or that there be reciprocal arrangements (*Arrêté royal* of 23 October 1963, Article 3 (1) (a)) and the requirement that producers of newsreel films, whether natural or legal persons, be of Belgian nationality (*Arrêté royal* of 23 October 1963, Article 3 (2) (a));

(b) *in France*
    – the obligation to hold a *carte d'identité d'étranger commercant* (*Décret-loi* of 12 November 1938, Law of 8 October 1940, Law of 14 April 1954, *Décret* No 59-852 of 9 July 1959);
    – the requirement that a person wishing to receive financial aid towards production shall be of French nationality (Article 14 of *Décret* No 59-1512 of 30 December 1959);
    – exclusion from the right to renew commercial leases (Article 38 of *Décret* of 30 September 1953);

(c) *in Italy*
    – the requirement that producers, whether natural or legal persons, be of Italian nationality (Law No 1213 of 4 November 1965);

(d) *in Luxembourg*
    – the limited period of validity of authorisations granted to foreign nationals (Article 21 of the Law of 2 June 1962).

Article 4

No Member State shall grant to any of its nationals who go to another Member State for the purpose of pursuing any activity referred to in Article 2 any aid liable to distort the conditions of establishment.

Article 5

1. Member States shall ensure that beneficiaries have the right to join professional or trade organisations under the same conditions and with the same rights and obligations as their own nationals.

2. In the case of establishment, the right to join professional or trade organisations shall entail eligibility for election or appointment to high office in such organisations. However, such posts may be reserved for nationals where, in pursuance of any provision laid down by law or regulation, the organisation concerned is connected with the exercise of official authority.

3. In the Grand Duchy of Luxembourg, membership of the *Chambre de commerce* or of the *Chambre des métiers* shall not give beneficiaries the right to take part in the election of the administrative organs of those chambers.

Article 6

1. Where a host Member State requires of its own nationals wishing to take up or pursue any activity referred to in Article 2 proof of good repute and proof that they have not been previously been declared bankrupt, or proof of either one of these, that State shall accept as sufficient evidence, in respect of nationals of other Member States, the production of an extract from the 'judicial record', or, failing this, of an equivalent document issued by a competent judicial or administrative authority in the country of origin or the country whence the foreign national comes, showing that these requirements have been met.

Where the country of origin or the country whence the foreign national comes does not issue such documentary proof of no previous bankruptcy, such proof may be replaced by a declaration on oath made by the person concerned before a judicial or administrative authority, a notary, or a competent professional or trade body, in the country of origin or in the country whence that person comes.

2. Documents issued in accordance with paragraph 1 may not be produced more than three months after their date of issue.

3. Member States shall, within the time limit laid down in Article 7, designate the authorities and bodies competent to issue these documents and shall forthwith inform the other Member States and the Commission thereof.

4. Where in the host Member State proof of financial standing is required, that State shall regard certificates issued by banks in the country of origin or in the country whence the foreign national comes as equivalent to certificates issued in its own territory.

Article 7

Member States shall adopt the measures necessary to comply with this Directive within six months of its notification and shall forthwith inform the Commission thereof.

Article 8

This Directive is addressed to the Member States.

Done at Brussels, 29 September 1970.

For the Council
The President
S. von BRAUN

COUNCIL DIRECTIVE

of 10 September 1984

relating to the approximation of the laws, regulations and administrative provisions of the Member States concerning misleading advertising

(84/450/EEC)

THE COUNCIL OF THE EUROPEAN COMMUNITIES,

Having regard to the Treaty establishing the European Economic Community, and in particular Article 100 thereof;

Having regard to the proposal from the Commission[1],

Having regard to the opinion of the European Parliament[2],

Having regard to the opinion of the Economic and Social Committee[3],

Whereas the laws against misleading advertising now in force in the Member States differ widely; whereas, since advertising reaches beyond the frontiers of individual Member States, it has a direct effect on the establishment and the functioning of the common market;

Whereas misleading advertising can lead to distortion of competition within the common market;

Whereas advertising, whether or not it induces a contract, affects the economic welfare of consumers;

Whereas misleading advertising may cause a consumer to take decisions prejudicial to him when acquiring goods or other property, or using services, and the differences between the laws of the Member States not only lead, in many cases, to inadequate levels of consumer protection, but also hinder the execution of advertising campaigns beyond national boundaries and thus affect the free circulation of goods and provision of services;

Whereas the second programme of the European Economic Community for a consumer protection and information policy[4] provides for appropriate action for the protection of consumers against misleading and unfair advertising;

Whereas it is in the interest of the public in general, as well as that of consumers and all those who, in competition with one another, carry on a trade, business, craft or profession, in the common market, to harmonize in the first instance national provisions against misleading advertising and that, at a second stage, unfair advertising and, as far as necessary, comparative advertising should be dealt with, on the basis of appropriate Commission proposals;

Whereas minimum and objective criteria for determining whether advertising is misleading should be established for this purpose;

Whereas the laws to be adopted by Member States against misleading advertising must be adequate and effective;

---

[1] OJ No C 70, 21. 3.1978, p. 4
[2] OJ No C 140, 5. 6. 1979, p. 23.
[3] OJ No C 171, 9. 7. 1979, p. 43.
[4] OJ No C 133, 3. 6. 1981, p. 1.

Whereas persons or organizations regarded under national law as having a legitimate interest in the matter must have facilities for initiating proceedings against misleading advertising, either before a court or before an administrative authority which is competent to decide upon complaints or to initiate appropriate legal proceedings;

Whereas it should be for each Member State to decide whether to enable the courts or administrative authorities to require prior recourse to other established means of dealing with the complaint;

Whereas the courts or administrative authorities must have powers enabling them to order or obtain the cessation of misleading advertising;

Whereas in certain cases it may be desirable to prohibit misleading advertising even before it is published; whereas, however, this in no way implies that Member States are under an obligation to introduce rules requiring the systematic prior vetting of advertising;

Whereas provision should be made for accelerated procedures under which measures with interim or definitive effect can be taken;

Whereas it may be desirable to order the publication of decisions made by courts or administrative authorities or of corrective statements in order to eliminate any continuing effects of misleading advertising;

Whereas administrative authorities must be impartial and the exercise of their powers must be subject to judicial review;

Whereas the voluntary control exercised by self-regulatory bodies to eliminate misleading advertising may avoid recourse to administrative or judicial action and ought therefore to be encouraged;

Whereas the advertiser should be able to prove, by appropriate means, the material accuracy of the factual claims he makes in his advertising, and may in appropriate cases be required to do so by the court or administrative authority.

Whereas this Directive must not preclude Member States from retaining or adopting provisions with a view to ensuring more extensive protection of consumers, persons carrying on a trade, business, craft or profession, and the general public,

HAS ADOPTED THIS DIRECTIVE:

Article 1

The purpose of this Directive is to protect consumers, persons carrying on a trade or business or practising a craft or profession and the interests of the public in general against misleading advertising and the consequences thereof.

Article 2

For the purposes of this Directive:

1. 'advertising' means the making of a representation in any form in connection with a trade, business craft or profession in order to promote the supply of goods or services, including immovable property rights and obligations;

2. 'misleading advertising' means any advertising which in any way, including its presentation deceives or is likely to deceive the persons to whom it is addressed or whom it reaches and which, by reason of its deceptive nature, is likely to affect their economic behaviour or which, for those reasons, injures or is likely to injure a competitor;

3. 'person' means any natural or legal person.

Article 3

In determining whether advertising is misleading account shall be taken of all its features, and in particular of any information it contains concerning:

(a) the characteristics of goods or services, such as their availability, nature, execution, composition, method and date of manufacture or provision, fitness for purpose, uses, quantity, specification, geographical or commercial origin or the results to be expected from their use, or the results and material features of tests or checks carried out on the goods or services;

(b) the price or the manner in which the price is calculated, and the conditions on which the goods are supplied or the services provided;

(c) the nature, attributes and rights of the advertiser, such as his identity and assets, his qualifications and ownership of industrial, commercial or intellectual property rights or his awards and distinctions.

Article 4

1. Member States shall ensure that adequate and effective means exist for the control of misleading advertising in the interests of consumers as well as competitors and the general public. Such means shall include legal provisions under which persons or organizations regarded under national law as having a legitimate interest in prohibiting misleading advertising may:

(a) take legal action against such advertising; and/or

(b) bring such advertising before an administrative authority competent either to decide on complaints or to initiate appropriate legal proceedings.

It shall be for each Member State to decide which of these facilities shall be available and whether to enable the courts or administrative authorities to require prior recourse to other established means of dealing with complaints, including those referred to in Article 5.

2. Under the legal provisions referred to in paragraph 1, Member States shall confer upon the courts or administrative authorities powers enabling them, in cases where they deem such measures to be necessary taking into account all the interests involved and in particular the public interest:

– to order the cessation of, or to insitute appropriate legal proceedings for an order for the cessation of, misleading advertising, or

– if misleading advertising has not yet been published but publication is imminent, to order the prohibition of, or to institute appropriate legal proceedings for an order for the prohibition of, such publication,

even without proof of actual loss or damage or of intention or negligence on the part of the advertiser.

Member States shall also make provision for the measures referred to in the first subparagraph to be taken under an accelerated procedure:

– either with interim effect, or

– with definitive effect,

on the understanding that it is for each Member State to decide which of the two options to select.

Furthermore, Member States may confer upon the courts or administrative authorities powers enabling them, with a view to eliminating the continuing effects of misleading advertising the cessation of which has been ordered by a final decision:

– to require publication of that decision in full or in part and in such form as they deem adequate,

– to require in addition the publication of a corrective statement.

3. The administrative authorities referred to in paragraph 1 must:

(a) be composed so as not to cast doubt on their impartiality;

(b) have adequate powers, where they decide on complaints, to monitor and enforce the observance of their decisions effectively;

(c) normally give reasons for their decisions.

Where the powers referred to in paragraph 2 are exercised exclusively by an administrative authority, reasons for its decisions shall always be given. Furthermore in this case, provision must be made for procedures whereby improper or unreasonable exercise of its powers by the administrative authority or improper or unreasonable failure to exercise the said powers can be the subject of judicial review.

Article 5

This Directive does not exclude the voluntary control of misleading advertising by self-regulatory bodies and recourse to such bodies by the persons or organizations referred to in Article 4 if proceedings before such bodies are in addition to the court or administrative proceedings referred to in that Article.

Article 6

Member States shall confer upon the courts or administrative authorities powers enabling them in the civil or administrative proceedings provided for in Article 4:

(a) to require the advertiser to furnish evidence as to the accuracy of factual claims in advertising if, taking into account the legitimate interests of the advertiser and any other party to the proceedings, such a requirement appears appropriate on the basis of the circumstances of the particular case; and

(b) to consider factual claims as inaccurate if the evidence demanded in accordance with (a) is not furnished or is deemed insufficient by the court or administrative authority.

Article 7

This Directive shall not preclude Member States from retaining or adopting provisions with a view to ensuring more extensive protection for consumers, persons carrying on a trade business, craft or profession, and the general public.

Article 8

Member States shall bring into force the measures necessary to comply with this Directive by 1 October 1986 at the latest. They shall forthwith inform the Commission thereof.

Member States shall communicate to the Commission the text of all provisions of national law which they adopt in the field covered by this Directive.

Article 9

This Directive is addressed to the Member States.

Done at Brussels, 10 September 1984.

For the Council
The President
P. O'TOOLE

COUNCIL DIRECTIVE

of 3 October 1989

on the coordination of certain provisions laid down by law, regulation or administrative action in Member States concerning the pursuit of television broadcasting activities

(89/552/EEC)

THE COUNCIL OF THE EUROPEAN COMMUNITIES,

Having regard to the Treaty establishing the European Economic Community, and in particular Articles 57 (2) and 66 thereof,

Having regard to the proposal from the Commission[1],

In cooperation with the European Parliament[2],

Having regard to the opinion of the Economic and Social Committee[3],

Whereas the objectives of the Community as laid down in the Treaty include establishing an even closer union among the peoples of Europe, fostering closer relations between the States belonging to the Community, ensuring the economic and social progress of its countries by common action to eliminate the barriers which divide Europe, encouraging the constant improvement of the living conditions of its peoples as well as ensuring the preservation and strengthening of peace and liberty;

Whereas the Treaty provides for the establishment of a common market, including the abolition, as between Member States, of obstacles to freedom of movement for services, and the institution of a system ensuring that competition in the common market is not distorted;

Whereas broadcasts transmitted across frontiers by means of various technologies are one of the ways of pursuing the objectives of the Community; whereas measures should be adopted to permit and ensure the transition from national markets to a common programme production and distribution market and to establish conditions of fair competition without prejudice to the public interest role to be discharged by the television broadcasting services;

Whereas the Council of Europe has adopted the European Convention on Transfrontier Televison;

Whereas the Treaty provides for the issuing of directives for the coordination of provisions to facilitate the taking up of activities as self-employed persons;

Whereas television broadcasting constitutes, in normal circumstances, a service within the meaning of the Treaty;

Whereas the Treaty provides for free movement of all services normally provided against payment, without exclusion on grounds of their cultural or other content and without

---

[1] OJ No C 179, 17. 7. 1986, p. 4
[2] OJ No C 49, 22. 2. 1988, p. 53, and OJ No C 158, 26. 6. 1989.
[3] OJ No C 232, 31. 8. 1987, p. 29.

restriction of nationals of Member States established in a Community country other than that of the person for whom the services are intended;

Whereas this right as applied to the broadcasting and distribution of television services is also a specific manifestation in Community law of a more general principle, namely the freedom of expression as enshrined in Article 10 (1) of the Convention for the Protection of Human Rights and Fundamental Freedoms ratified by all Member States; whereas for this reason the issuing of directives on the broadcasting and distribution of television programmes must ensure their free movement in the light of the said Article and subject only to the limits set by paragraph 2 of that Article and by Article 56 (1) of the Treaty;

Whereas the laws, regulations and administrative measures in Member States concerning the pursuit of activities as television broadcasters and cable operators contain disparities, some of which may impede the free movement of broadcasts within the Community and may distort competition within the Common market;

Whereas all such restrictions on freedom to provide broadcasting services within the Community must be abolished under the Treaty;

Whereas such abolition must go hand in hand with coordination of the applicable laws; whereas this coordination must be aimed at facilitating the pursuit of the professional activities concerned and, more generally, the free movement of information and ideas within the Community;

Whereas it is consequently necessary and sufficient that all broadcasts comply with the law of the Member State from which they emanate;

Whereas this Directive lays down the minimum rules needed to guarantee freedom of transmission in broadcasting; whereas, therefore, it does not affect the responsibility of the Member States and their authorities with regard to the organization — including the systems of licensing, administrative authorization or taxation — financing and the content of programmes; whereas the independence of cultural devlopments in the Member States and the preservation of cultural diversity in the Community therefore remain unaffected;

Whereas it is necessary, in the common market, that all broadcasts emanating from and intended for reception within the Community and in particular those intended for reception in another Member State, should respect the law of the originating Member State applicable to broadcasts intended for reception by the public in that Member State and the provisions of this Directive;

Whereas the requirement that the originating Member State should verify that broadcasts comply with national law as coordinated by this Directive is sufficient under Community law to ensure free movement of broadcasts without secondary control on the same grounds in the receiving Member States; whereas, however, the receiving Member State may, exceptionally and under specific conditions provisionally suspend the retransmission of televised broadcasts;

Whereas it is essential for the Member States to ensure the prevention of any facts which may provide detrimental to freedom of movement and trade in television programmes or which may promote the creation of dominant positions which would lead to restrictions on pluralism and freedom of televised information and of the information sector as a whole;

Whereas this Directive, being confined specifically to television broadcasting rules, is without prejudice to existing or future Community acts of harmonization, in particular to satisfy mandatory requirements concerning the protection of consumers and the fairness of commercial transactions and competition;

Whereas co-ordination is nevertheless needed to make it easier for persons and industries producing programmes having a cultural objective to take up and pursue their activities;

Whereas minimum requirements in respect of all public or private Community television programmes for European audio-visual productions have been a means of promoting production, independent production and distribution in the abovementioned industries and are complementary to other instruments which are already or will be proposed to favour the same objective;

Whereas it is therefore necessary to promote markets of sufficient size for television productions in the Member States to recover necessary investments not only by establishing common rules opening up national markets but also by envisaging for European productions where practicable and by appropriate means a majority proportion in television programmes of all Member States; whereas, in order to allow the monitoring of the application of these rules and the pursuit of the objectives, Member States will provide the Commission with a report on the application of the proportions reserved for European works and independent productions in this Directive; whereas for the calculation of such proportions account should be taken of the specific situation of the Hellenic Republic and the Portuguese Republic; whereas the Commission must inform the other Member States of these reports accompanied, where appropriate by an opinion taking account of, in particular, progress achieved in relation to previous years, the share of first broadcasts in the programming, the particular circumstances of new television broadcasters and the specific situation of countries with a low audio-visual production capacity or restricted language area;

Whereas for these purposes 'European works' should be defined without prejudice to the possibility of Member States laying down a more detailed definition as regards television broadcasters under their jurisdiction in accordance with Article 3 (1) in compliance with Community law and account being taken of the objectives of this Directive;

Whereas it is important to seek appropriate instruments and procedures in accordance with Community law in order to promote the implementation of these objectives with a view to adopting suitable measures to encourage the activity and development of European audio-visual production and distribution, particularly in countries with a low production capacity or restricted language area;

Whereas national support schemes for the development of European production may be applied in so far as they comply with Community law;

Whereas a commitment, where practicable, to a certain proportion of broadcasts for independent productions, created by producers who are independent of broadcasters, will stimulate new sources of television production, especially the creation of small and medium-sized enterprises; whereas it will offer new opportunities and outlets to the marketing of creative talents of employment of cultural professions and employees in the cultural field; whereas the definition of the concept of independent producer by the Member States should take account of that objective by giving due consideration to small and medium-sized producers and making it possible to authorize financial participation by the coproduction subsidiaries of television organizations;

Whereas measures are necessary for Member States to ensure that a certain period elapses between the first cinema showing of a work and the first television showing;

Whereas in order to allow for an active policy in favour of a specific language, Member States remain free to lay down more detailed or stricter rules in particular on the basis of language criteria, as long as these rules are in conformity with Community law, and in particular are not applicable to the retransmission of broadcasts originating in other Member States;

Whereas in order to ensure that the interests of consumers as television viewers are fully and properly protected, it is essential for television advertising to be subject to a certain number of minimum rules and standards and that the Member States must maintain the right to set more detailed or stricter rules and in certain circumstances to lay down different conditions for television broadcasters under their jurisdiction;

Whereas Member States, with due regard to Community law and in relation to broadcasts intended solely for the national territory which may not be received, directly or indirectly, in one or more Member States, must be able to lay down different conditions for the insertion of advertising and different limits for the volume of advertising in order to facilitate these particular broadcasts;

Whereas it is necessary to prohibit all television advertising promoting cigarettes and other tobacco products including indirect forms of advertising which, whilst not directly mentioning the tobacco product, seek to circumvent the ban on advertising by using brand names, symbols or other distinctive features of tobacco products or of undertakings whose known or main activities include the production or sale of such products;

Whereas it is equally necessary to prohibit all television advertising for medicinal products and medical treatment available only on prescription in the Member State within whose jurisdiction the broadcaster falls and to introduce strict criteria relating to the television advertising of alcoholic products;

Whereas in view of the growing importance of sponsorship in the financing of programmes, appropriate rules should be laid down;

Whereas it is furthermore, necessary to introduce rules to protect the physical, mental and moral development of minors in programmes and in television advertising;

Whereas although television broadcasters are normally bound to ensure that programmes present facts and events fairly, it is nevertheless important that they should be subject to specific obligations with respect to the right of reply or equivalent remedies so that any person whose legitimate interests have been damaged by an assertion made in the course of a broadcast television programme may effectively exercise such right or remedy.

HAS ADOPTED THIS DIRECTIVE:

CHAPTER 1

DEFINITIONS

Article 1

For the purpose of this Directive:

(a) 'television broadcasting' means the initial transmission by wire or over the air, including that by satellite, in unencoded or encoded form, of television programmes intended for reception by the public. It includes the communication of programmes between undertakings with a view to their being relayed to the public. It does not include communication services providing items of information or other messages on individual demand such as telecopying, electronic data banks and other similar services;

(b) 'television advertising' means any form of announcement broadcast in return for payment or for similar consideration by a public or private undertaking in connection with a trade, business, craft or profession in order to promote the supply of goods or services, including immovable property, or rights and obligations, in return for payment. Except for the purposes of Article 18, this does not include direct offers to the public for the sale, purchase or rental of products or for the provision of services in return for payment;

(c) 'surreptitious advertising' means the representation in words or pictures of goods, services, the name, the trade mark or the activities of a producer of goods or a provider of services in programmes when such representation is intended by the broadcaster to serve advertising and might mislead the public as to its nature. Such representation is considered to be intentional in particular if it is done in return for payment or for similar consideration;

(d) 'sponsorship' means any contribution made by a public or private undertaking not engaged in television broadcasting activities or in the production of audio-visual works, to the financing of television programmes with a view to promoting its name, its trade mark, its image, its activities or its products.

CHAPTER II

GENERAL PROVISIONS

Article 2

1. Each Member State shall ensure that all television broadcasts transmitted
– by broadcasters under its jurisdiction, or
– by broadcasters who, while not being under the jurisdiction of any Member State, make use of a frequency or a satellite capacity granted by, or a satellite up-link situated in, that Member State,
comply with the law applicable to broadcasts intended for the public in that Member State.

2. Member States shall ensure freedom of reception and shall not restrict retransmission on their territory of television broadcasts from other Member States for reasons which fall within the fields coordinated by this Directive. Member States may provisionally suspend retransmissions of television broadcasts if the following conditions are fulfilled:

(a)   a television broadcast coming from another Member State manifestly, serously and gravely infringes Article 22;
(b)   during the previous 12 months, the broadcaster has infringed the same provision on at least two prior occasions;
(c)   the Member State concerned has notified the broadcaster and the Commission in writing of the alleged infringements and of its intention to restrict retransmission should any such infringement occur again;
(d)   consultations with the transmitting State and the Commission have not produced an amicable settlement within 15 days of the notification provided for in point (c), and the alleged infringement persists.

The Commission shall ensure that the suspension is compatible with Community law. It may ask the Member State concerned to put an end to a suspension which is contrary to Community law, as a matter of urgency. This provision is without prejudice to the application of any procedure, remedy or sanction to the infringements in question in the Member State which has jurisdiction over the broadcaster concerned.

3. This Directive shall not apply to broadcasts intended exclusively for reception in States other than Member States, and which are not received directly or indirectly in one or more Member States.

Article 3

1. Member States shall remain free to require television broadcasters under their juridiction to lay down more detailed or stricter rules in the areas covered by this Directive.

2. Member States shall, by appropriate means, ensure, within the framework of their legislation, that television broadcasters under their jurisdiction comply with the provisions of this Directive.

CHAPTER III

PROMOTION OF DISTRIBUTION AND PRODUCTION OF TELEVISION PROGRAMMES

Article 4

1. Member States shall ensure where practicable and by appropriate means, that broadcasters reserve for European works, within the meaning of Article 6, a majority proportion

of their transmission time, excluding the time appointed to news, sports events, games, advertising and teletext services. This proportion, having regard to the broadcaster's informational, educational, cultural and entertainment responsibilities to its viewing public, should be achieved progressively, on the basis of suitable criteria.

2. Where the proportion laid down in paragraph 1 cannot be attained, it must not be lower than the average for 1988 in the Member State concerned.

However, in respect of the Hellenic Republic and the Portuguese Republic, the year 1988 shall be replaced by the year 1990.

3. From 3 October 1991, the Member States shall provide the Commission every two years with a report on the application of this Article and Article 5.

That report shall in particular include a statistical statement on the achievement of the proportion referred to in this Article and Article 5 for each of the television programmes falling within the jurisdiction of the Member State concerned, the reasons, in each case, for the failure to attain that proportion and the measures adopted or envisaged in order to achieve it.

The Commission shall inform the other Member States and the European Parliament of the reports, which shall be accompanied, where appropriate, by an opinion. The Commission shall ensure the application of this Article and Article 5 in accordance with the provisions of the Treaty. The Commission may take account in its opinion, in particular, of progress achieved in relation to previous years, the share of first broadcast works in the programming, the particular circumstances of new television broadcasters and the specific situation of countries with a low audiovisual production capacity or restricted language area.

4. The Council shall review the implementation of this Article on the basis of a report from the Commission accompanied by any proposals for revision that it may deem appropriate no later than the end of the fifth year from the adoption of the Directive.

To that end, the Commission report shall, on the basis of the information provided by Member States under paragraph 3, take account in particular of developments in the Community market and of the international context.

Article 5

Member States shall ensure, where practicable and by appropriate means, that broadcasters reserve at least 10% of their transmission time, excluding the time appointed to news, sports events, games, advertising and teletext services, or alternately, at the discretion of the Member State, at least 10% of their programming budget, for European works created by producers who are independent of broadcasters. This proportion, having regard to broadcasters' informational, educational, cultural and entertainment responsibilities to its viewing public, should be achieved progressively, on the basis of suitable criteria; it must be achieved by earmarking an adequate proportion for recent works, that is to say works transmitted within five years of their production.

Article 6

1. Within the meaning of this chapter, 'European works' means the following:

(a) works originating from Member States of the Community and, as regards television broadcasters falling within the jurisdiction of the Federal Republic of Germany, works from German territories where the Basic Law does not apply and fulfilling the conditions of paragraph 2;

(b) works originating from European third States party to the European Convention on Transfrontier Television of the Council of Europe and fulfilling the conditions of paragraph 2;

(c) works originating from other European third countries and fulfilling the conditions of paragraph 3.

2. The works referred to in paragraph 1 (a) and (b) are works mainly made with authors and workers residing in one or more States referred to in paragraph 1(a) and (b) provided that they comply with one of the following three conditions:

(a)   they are made by one or more producers established in one or more of those States; or

(b)   production of the works is supervised and actually controlled by one or more producers established in one or more of those States; or

(c)   the contribution of co-producers of those States to the total co-production costs is preponderant and the co-production is not controlled by one or more producers established outside those States.

3. The works referred to in paragraph 1 (c) are works made exclusively or in co-production with producers established in one or more Member State by producers established in one or more European third countries with which the Community will conclude agreements in accordance with the procedures of the Treaty, if those works are mainly made with authors and workers residing in one or more European States.

4. Works which are not European works within the meaning of paragraph 1, but made mainly with authors and workers residing in one or more Member States, shall be considered to be European works to an extent corresponding to the proportion of the contribution of Community co-producers to the total production costs.

Article 7

Member States shall ensure that the television broadcasters under their jurisdiction do not broadcast any cinematographic work, unless otherwise agreed between its rights holders and the broadcaster, until two years have elapsed since the work was first shown in cinemas in one of the Member States of the Community; in the case of cinematographic works co-produced by the broadcaster, this period shall be one year.

Article 8

Where they consider it necessary for purposes of language policy, the Member States, whilst observing Community law, may as regards some or all programmes of television broadcasters under their jurisdiction, lay down more detailed or stricter rules in particular on the basis of language criteria.

Article 9

This chapter shall not apply to local television broadcasts not forming part of a national network.

CHAPTER IV

TELEVISION ADVERTISING AND SPONSORSHIP

Article 10

1. Television advertising shall be readily recognizable as such and kept quite separate from other parts of the programme service by optical and/or acoustic means.

2. Isolated advertising spots shall remain the exception.

3. Advertising shall not use subliminal techniques.

4. Surreptitious advertising shall be prohibited.

Article 11

1. Advertisements shall be inserted between programmes. Provided the conditions contained in paragraphs 2 to 5 of this Article are fulfilled, advertisements may also be inserted during programmes in such a way that the integrity and value of the programme, taking into account natural breaks in and the duration and nature of the programme, and the rights of the rights holders are not prejudiced.

2. In programmes consisting of autonomous parts, or in sports programmes and similarly structured events and performances comprising intervals, advertisements shall only be inserted between the parts or in the intervals.

3. The transmission of audiovisual works such as feature films and films made for television (excluding series, serials, light entertainment programmes and documentaries), provided their programmed duration is more than 45 minutes, may be interrupted once for each complete period of 45 minutes. A further interruption is allowed if their programmed duration is at least 20 minutes longer than two or more complete periods of 45 minutes.

4. Where programmes, other than those covered by paragraph 2, are interrupted by advertisements, a period of at least 20 minutes should elapse between each successive advertising break within the programme.

5. Advertisements shall not be inserted in any broadcast of a religious service. News and current affairs programmes, documentaries, religious programmes, and children's programmes, when their programmed duration is less than 30 minutes shall not be interrupted by advertisements. If their programmed duration is of 30 minutes or longer, the provisions of the previous paragraphs shall apply.

Article 12

Television advertising shall not:

(a) prejudice respect for human dignity:
(b) include any discrimination on grounds of race, sex or nationality;
(c) be offensive to religious or political beliefs;
(d) encourage behaviour prejudicial to health or to safety;
(e) encourage behaviour prejudicial to the protection of the environment.

Article 13

All forms of television advertising for cigarettes and other tobacco products shall be prohibited.

Article 14

Television advertising for medicinal products and medical treatment available only on prescription in the Member State within whose jurisdiction the broadcaster falls shall be prohibited.

Article 15

Television advertising for alcoholic beverages shall comply with the following criteria:

(a) it may not be aimed specifically at minors or, in particular, depict minors consuming these beverages;
(b) it shall not link the consumption of alcohol to enhanced physical performance or to driving;
(c) it shall not create the impression that the consumption of alcohol contributes towards social or sexual success;

(d) it shall not claim that alcohol has therapeutic qualities or that it is a stimulant, a sedative or a means of resolving personal conflicts;

(e) it shall not encourage immoderate consumption of alcohol or present abstinence or moderation in a negative light;

(f) it shall not place emphasis on high alcoholic content as being a positive quality of the beverages.

Article 16

Television advertising shall not cause moral or physical detriment to minors, and shall therefore comply with the following criteria for their protection:

(a) it shall not directly exhort minors to buy a product or a service by exploiting their inexperience or credulity;

(b) it shall not directly encourage minors to persuade their parents or others to purchase the goods or services being advertised;

(c) it shall not exploit the special trust minors place in parents, teachers or other persons;

(d) it shall not unreasonably show minors in dangerous situations.

Article 17

1. Sponsored television programmes shall meet the following requirements:

(a) the content and scheduling of sponsored programmes may in no circumstances be influenced by the sponsor in such a way as to affect the responsibility and editorial independence of the broadcaster in respect of programmes;

(b) they must be clearly identified as such by the name and/or logo of the sponsor at the beginning and/or the end of the programmes;

(c) they must not encourage the purchase or rental of the products or services of the sponsor or a third party, in particular by making special promotional references to those products or services.

2. Television programmes may not be sponsored by natural or legal persons whose principal activity is the manufacture or sale of products, or the provision of services, the advertising of which is prohibited by Artice 13 or 14.

3. News and current affairs programmes may not be sponsored.

Article 18

1. The amount of advertising shall not exceed 15% of the daily transmission time. However, this percentage may be increased to 20% to include forms or advertisments such as direct offers to the public for the sale, purchase or rental of products or for the provision of services, provided the amount of spot advertising does not exceed 15%.

2. The amount of spot advertising within a given one-hour period shall not exceed 20%.

3. Without prejudice to the provisions of paragraph 1, forms of advertisements such as direct offers to the public for the sale, purchase or rental of products or for the provision of services shall not exceed one hour per day.

Article 19

Member States may lay down stricter rules than those in Article 18 for programming time and the procedures for television broadcasting for television broadcasters under their jurisdiction, so as to reconcile demand for televised advertising with the public interest, taking account in particular of:

(a) the role of television in providing information, education, culture and entertainment;

(b) the protection of pluralism of information and of the media.

Article 20

Without prejudice to Article 3, Member States may, with due regard for Community law, lay down conditions other than those laid down in Article 11 (2) to (5) and in Article 18 in respect of broadcasts intended solely for the national territory which may not be received, directly or indirectly, in one or more other Member States.

Article 21

Member States shall, within the framework of their laws, ensure that in the case of television broadcasts that do not comply with the provisions of this chapter, appropriate measures are applied to secure compliance with these provisions.

CHAPTER V

PROTECTION OF MINORS

Article 22

Member States shall take appropriate measures to ensure that television broadcasts by broadcasters under their jurisdiction do not include programmes which might seriously impair the physical, mental or moral development of minors, in particular those that involve pornography or gratuitous violence. This provision shall extend to other programmes which are likely to impair the physical, mental or moral development of minors, except where it is ensured, by selecting the time of the broadcast or by any technical measure, that minors in the area of transmission will not normally hear or see such broadcasts.

Member States shall also ensure that broadcasts do not contain any incitement to hatred on grounds of race, sex, religion or nationality.

CHAPTER VI

RIGHT OF REPLY

Article 23

1. Without prejudice to other provisions adopted by the Member States under civil, administrative or criminal law, any natural or legal person, regardless of nationality, whose legitimate interests, in particular reputation and good name, have been damaged by an assertion of incorrect facts in a television programme must have a right of reply or equivalent remedies.

2. A right of reply or equivalent remedies shall exist in relation to all broadcasters under the jurisdiction of a Member State.

3. Member States shall adopt the measures needed to establish the right of reply or the equivalent remedies and shall determine the procedure to be followed for the exercise

thereof. In particular, they shall ensure that a sufficient time span is allowed and that the procedures are such that the right or equivalent remedies can be exercised appropriately by natural or legal persons resident or established in other Member States.

4. An application for exercise of the right of reply or the equivalent remedies may be rejected if such a reply is not justified according to the conditions laid down in paragraph 1, would involve a punishable act, would render the broadcaster liable to civil law proceedings or would transgress standards of public decency.

5. Provision shall be made for procedures whereby disputes as to the exercise of the right of reply or the equivalent remedies can be subject to judicial review.

CHAPTER VII

FINAL PROVISIONS

Article 24

In fields which this Directive does not coordinate, it shall not affect the rights and obligations of Member States resulting from existing conventions dealing with telecommunications or broadcasting.

Article 25

1. Member States shall bring into force the laws, regulations and administrative provisions necessary to comply with this Directive not later than 3 October 1991. They shall forthwith inform the Commission thereof.

2. Member States shall communicate to the Commission the text of the main provisions of national law which they adopt in the fields governed by this Directive.

Article 26

Not later than the end of the fifth year after the date of adoption of this Directive and every two years thereafter, the Commission shall submit to the European Parliament, the Council, and the Economic and Social Committee a report on the application of this Directive, and, if necessary, make further proposals to adapt it to developments in the field of television broadcasting.

Article 27

This Directive is addressed to the Member States.

Done at Luxembourg, 3 October 1989.

For the Council
The President
R. DUMAS

COUNCIL DIRECTIVE

of 14 May 1991
on the legal protection of computer programs

(91/250/EEC)

THE COUNCIL OF THE EUROPEAN COMMUNITIES,

Having regard to the Treaty establishing the European Economic Community and in particular Article 100a thereof,

Having regard to the proposal from the Commission[1],

In cooperation with the European Parliament[2],

Having regard to the opinion of the Economic and Social Committee[3],

Whereas computer programs are at present not clearly protected in all Member States by existing legislation and such protection, where it exists, has different attributes;

Whereas the development of computer programs requires the investment of considerable human, technical and financial resources while computer programs can be copied at a fraction of the cost needed to develop them independently;

Whereas computer programs are playing an increasingly important role in a broad range of industries and computer program technology can accordingly be considered as being of fundamental importance for the Community's industrial development;

Whereas certain differences in the legal protection computer programs offered by the laws of the Member States have direct and negative effects on the functions of the common market as regards computer programs as such differences could well become greater as Member States introduce new legislation on this subject;

Whereas existing differences having such effects need be be removed and new ones prevented from arising, where differences not adversely affecting the functioning of the common market to a substantial degree need not be removed or prevented from arising;

Whereas the Community's legal framework on the protection of computer programs can accordingly in the first instance be limited to establishing that Member States should accord protection to computer programs under copyright law as literary works and, further to establishing who and what should be protected, the exclusive rights on which protected persons should be able to rely in order to authorize or prohibit certain acts and for how long the protection should apply;

Whereas, for the purpose of this Directive, the term 'computer program' shall include programs in any form including those which are incorporated into hardware; whereas this term also includes preparatory design work leading to the development of a computer program provided that the nature of the preparatory work is such that a computer program can result from it at a later stage;

Whereas, in respect of the criteria to be applied in determining whether or not a computer program is an original work, no tests as to the qualitative or aesthetic merits of the program should be applied;

---

[1] OJ No C 91, 12. 4. 1989, p. 4; and OJ No C 320, 20. 12. 1990, p. 22.

[2] OJ No C 231, 17. 9. 1990, p. 78; and Decision of 17 April 1991, not yet published in the Official Journal).

[3] OJ No C 329, 30. 12. 1989, p. 4.

Whereas the Community is fully committed to the promotion of international standardization;

Whereas the function of a computer program is to communicate and work together with other components of a computer system and with users and, for this purpose, a logical and, where appropriate, physical interconnection and interaction is required to permit all elements of software and hardware to work with other software and hardware and with users in all the ways in which they are intended to function;

Whereas the parts of the program which provide for such interconnection and interaction between elements of software and hardware are generally known as interfaces;

Whereas this functional interconnection and interaction is generally known as 'interoperability'; whereas such interoperability can be defined as the ability to exchange information and mutually to use the information which has been exchanged;

Whereas, for the avoidance of doubt, it has to be made clear that only the expression of a computer program is protected and that ideas and principles which underlie any element of a program, including those which underlie its interfaces, are not protected by copyright under this Directive;

Whereas, in accordance with this principle of copyright, to the extent that logic, algorithms and programming languages comprise ideas and principles, those ideas and principles are not protected under this Directive;

Whereas, in accordance with the legislation and jurisprudence of the Member States and the international copyright conventions, the expression of those ideas and principles is to be protected by copyright;

Whereas, for the purposes of this Directive, the term 'rental' means the making available for use, for a limited period of time and for profit-making purposes, of a computer program or a copy thereof; whereas this term does not include public lending, which, accordingly, remains outside the scope of this Directive;

Whereas the exclusive rights of the author to prevent the unauthorised reproduction of his work have to be subject to a limited exception in the case of a computer program to allow the reproduction technically necessary for the use of that program by the lawful acquirer;

Whereas this means that the acts of loading and running necessary for the use of a copy of a program which has been lawfully acquired, and the act of correction of its errors, may not be prohibited by contract; whereas, in the absence of specific contractual provisions, including when a copy of the program has been sold, any other act necessary for the use of the copy of a program may be performed in accordance with its intended purpose by a lawful acquirer of that copy;

Whereas a person having a right to use a computer program should not be prevented from performing acts necessary to observe, study or test the functioning of the program, provided that these acts do not infringe the copyright in the program;

Whereas the unauthorised reproduction, translation, adaptation or transformation of the form of the code in which a copy of a computer program has been made available constitutes an infringement of the exclusive rights of the author;

Whereas, nevertheless, circumstances may exist when such a reproduction of the code and translation of its form within the meaning of Article 4 (a) and (b) are indispensable to obtain the necessary information to achieve the interoperability of an independently created program with other programs;

Whereas it has therefore to be considered that in these limited circumstances only, performance of the acts of reproduction and translation by or on behalf of a person having a right to use a copy of the program is legitimate and compatable with fair practice and must therefore be deemed not to require the authorization of the rightholder;

Whereas an objective of this exception is to make it possible to connect all components of a computer system, including those of different manufacturers, so that they can work together;

Whereas such an exception to the author's exclusive rights may not be used in a way which prejudices the legitimate interests of the rightholder or which conflicts with a normal exploitation of the program;

Whereas, in order to remain in accordance with the provisions of the Berne Convention for the Protection of Literary and Artistic Works, the term of protection should be the life of the author and fifty years from the first of January of the year following the year of his death or, in the case of an anonymous or pseudonymous work, 50 years from the first of January of the year following the year in which the work is first published;

Whereas protection of computer programs under copyright laws should be without prejudice to the application, in appropriate cases, of other forms of protection; whereas, however, any contractual provisions contrary to Article 6 or to the exceptions provided for in Article 5 (2) and (3) should be null and void;

Whereas the provisions of this Directive are without prejudice to the application of the competition rules under Articles 85 and 86 of the Treaty if a dominant supplier refuses to make information available which is necessary for interoperability as defined in this Directive;

Whereas the provisions of this Directive should be without prejudice to specific requirements of Community law already enacted in respect of the publication of interfaces in the telecommunications sector or Council Decisions relating to standardization in the field of information technology and telecommunication;

Whereas this Directive does not affect derogations provided for under national legislation in accordance with the Berne Convention on points not covered by this Directive,

HAS ADOPTED THIS DIRECTIVE:

Article 1

Object of protection

1. In accordance with the provisions of this Directive, Member States shall protect computer programs, by copyright, as literary works within the meaning of the Berne Convention for the Protection of Literary and Artistic Works. For the purposes of this Directive, the term 'computer programs' shall include their preparatory design material.

2. Protection in accordance with this Directive shall apply to the expression in any form of a computer program. Ideas and principles which underlie any element of a computer program, including those which underlie its interfaces, are not protected by copyright under this Directive.

3. A computer program shall be protected if it is original in the sense that it is the author's own intellectual creation. No other criteria shall be applied to determine its eligibility for protection.

Article 2

Authorship of computer programs

1. The author of a computer program shall be the natural person or group of natural persons who has created the program or, where the legislation of the Member State permits, the legal person designated as the rightholder by that legislation. Where collective works are recognized by the legislation of a Member State, the person considered by the legislation of the Member State to have created the work shall be deemed to be its author.

2. In respect of a computer program created by a group of natural persons jointly, the exclusive rights shall be owned jointly.

3. Where a computer program is created by an employee in the execution of his duties or following the instructions given by his employer, the employer exclusively shall be entitled to exercise all economic rights in the program so created, unless otherwise provided by contract.

Article 3

Beneficiaries of protection

Protection shall be granted to all natural or legal persons eligible under national copyright legislation as applied to literary works.

Article 4

Restricted Acts

Subject to the provisions of Articles 5 and 6, the exclusive rights of the rightholder within the meaning of Article 2, shall include the right to do or to authorize:

(a) the permanent or temporary reproduction of a computer program by any means and in any form, in part or in whole. Insofar as loading, displaying, running, transmission or storage of the computer program necessitate such reproduction, such acts shall be subject to authorization by the rightholder;

(b) the translation, adaptation, arrangement and any other alteration of a computer program and the reproduction of the results thereof, without prejudice to the rights of the person who alters the program;

(c) any form of distribution to the public, including the rental, of the original computer program or of copies thereof. The first sale in the Community of a copy of a program by the rightholder or with his consent shall exhaust the distribution right within the Community of that copy, with the exception of the right to control further rental of the program or a copy thereof.

Article 5

Exceptions to the restricled acts

1. In the absence of specific contractual provisions, the acts referred to in Article 4 (a) and (b) shall not require authorization by the rightholder where they are necessary for the use of the computer program by the lawful acquirer in accordance with its intended purpose, including for error correction.

2. The making of a back-up copy by a person having a right to use the computer program may not be prevented by contract insofar as it is necessary for that use.

3. The person having a right to use a copy of a computer program shall be entitled, without the authorization of the rightholder, to observe, study or test the functioning of the program in order to determine the ideas and principles which underlie any element of the program if he does so while performing any of the acts of loading, displaying, running, transmitting or storing the program which he is entitled to do.

Article 6

Decompilation

1. The authorization of the rightholder shall not be required where reproduction of the code and translation of its form within the meaning of Article 4 (a) and (b) are indispensable to obtain the information necessary to achieve the interoperability of an independently created computer program with other programs, provided that the following conditions are met:

(a) these acts are performed by the licensee or by another person having a right to use a copy of a program, or on their behalf by a person authorized to do so;

(b) the information necessary to achieve interoperability has not previously been readily available to the persons referred to in subparagraph (a); and

(c) these acts are confined to the parts of the original program which are necessary to achieve interoperability.

2. The provisions of paragraph 1 shall not permit the information obtained through its application:

(a) to be used for goals other than to achieve the interoperability of the independently created computer program;
(b) to be given to others, except when necessary for the interoperability of the independently created computer program; or
(c) to be used for the development, production or marketing of a computer program substantially similiar in its expression, or for any other act which infringes copyright.

3. In accordance with the provisions of the Berne Convention for the protection of Literary and Artistic Works, the provisions of this Article may not be interpreted in such a way as to allow its application to be used in a manner which unreasonably prejudices the rightholder's legitimate interests or conflicts with a normal exploitation of the computer program.

Article 7

Special measures of protection

1. Without prejudice to the provisions of Articles 4, 5 and 6, Member States shall provide, in accordance with their national legislation, appropriate remedies against a person committing any of the acts listed in subparagraphs (a), (b) and (c) below:

(a) any act of putting into circulation a copy of a computer program knowing, or having reason to believe, that it is an infringing copy;
(b) the possession, for commercial purposes, of a copy of a computer program knowing, or having reason to believe, that it is an infringing copy;
(c) any act of putting into circulation, or the possession for commercial purposes of, any means the sole intended purpose of which is to facilitate the unauthorized removal or circumvention of any technical device which may have been applied to protect a computer program.

2. Any infringing copy of a computer program shall be liable to seizure in accordance with the legislation of the Member State concerned.
3. Member States may provide for the seizure of any means referred to in paragraph 1 (c).

Article 8

Term of protection

1. Protection shall be granted for the life of the author and for fifty years after his death or after the death of the last surviving author; where the computer program is an anonymous or pseudonymous work, or where a legal person is designated as the author by national legislation in accordance with Article 2 (1), the term of protection shall be fifty years from the time that the computer program is first lawfully made available to the public. The term of protection shall be deemed to begin on the first of January of the year following the abovementioned events.
2. Member States which already have a term of protection longer than that provided for in paragraph 1 are allowed to maintain their present term until such time as the term of protection for copyright works is harmonized by Community law in a more general way.

Article 9

Continued application of other legal provisions

1. The provisions of this Directive shall be without prejudice to any other legal provisions such as those concerning patent rights, trade-marks, unfair competition, trade secrets, protection of semi-conductor products or the law of contract. Any contractual provisions contrary to Article 6 or to the exceptions provided for in Article 5 (2) and (3) shall be null and void.

2. The provisions of this Directive shall apply also to programs created before 1 January 1993 without prejudice to any acts concluded and rights acquired before that date.

Article 10

Final provisions

1. Member States shall bring into force the laws, regulations and administrative provisions necessary to comply with this Directive before 1 January 1993.

When Member States adopt these measures, the latter shall contain a reference to this Directive or shall be accompanied by such reference on the occasion of their official publication. The methods of making such a reference shall be laid down by the Member States.

2. Member States shall communicate to the Commission the provisions of national law which they adopt in the field governed by this Directive.

Article 11

This Directive is addressed to the Member States.

Done at Brussels, 14 May 1991.

For the Council
The President
J.F. POOS

COUNCIL DIRECTIVE

of 19 November 1992

on rental right and lending right and on certain rights related to copyright in the field of intellectual property

(92/100/EEC)

THE COUNCIL OF THE EUROPEAN COMMUNITIES,

Having regard to the Treaty establishing the European Economic Community, and in particular Articles 57 (2), 66 and 100a thereof,

Having regard to the proposal from the Commission[1],

In cooperation with the European Parliament[2],

Having regard to the opinion of the Economic and Social Committee[3],

Whereas differences exist in the legal protection provided by the laws and practices of the Member States for copyright works and subject matter of related rights protection as regards rental and lending; whereas such differences are sources of barriers to trade and distortions of competition which impede the achievement and proper functioning of the internal market;

Whereas such differences in legal protection could well become greater as Member States adopt new and different legislation or as national case-law interpreting such legislation develops differently;

Whereas such differences should therefore be eliminated in accordance with the objective of introducing an area without internal frontiers as set out in Article 8a of the Treaty so as to institute, pursuant to Article 3 (f) of the Treaty, a system ensuring that competition in the common market is not distorted;

Whereas rental and lending of copyright works and the subject matter of related rights protection is playing an increasingly important role in particular for authors, performers and producers of phonograms and films; whereas piracy is becoming an increasing threat;

Whereas the adequate protection of copyright works and subject matter of related rights protection by rental and lending rights as well as the protection of the subject matter of related rights protection by the fixation right, reproduction right, distribution right, right to broadcast and communication to the public can accordingly be considered as being of fundamental importance for the Community's economic and cultural development;

Whereas copyright and related rights protection must adapt to new economic developments such as new forms of exploitation;

Whereas the creative and artistic work of authors and performers necessitates an adequate income as a basis for further creative and artistic work, and the investments required particularly for the production of phonograms and films are especially high and risky; whereas the possibility for securing that income and recouping that investment can only effectively be guaranteed through adequate legal protection of the rightholders concerned;

---

[1] OJ No C 53, 28. 2. 1991, p. 35 and OJ No C 128, 20. 5. 1992, p. 8

[2] OJ No C 67, 16. 3. 1992, p. 92 and Decision of 28 October 1992 (not yet published in the Official Journal).

[3] OJ No C 269, 14. 10. 1991, p. 54.

Whereas these creative, artistic and entrepreneurial activities are, to a large extent, activities of self-employed persons; whereas the pursuit of such activities must be made easier by providing a harmonized legal protection within the Community;

Whereas, to the extent that these activities principally constitute services, their provision must equally be facilitated by the establishment in the Community of a harmonized legal framework;

Whereas the legislation of the Member States should be approximated in such a way so as not to conflict with the international conventions on which many Member States, copyright and related rights laws are based;

Whereas the Community's legal framework on the rental right and lending right and on certain rights related to copyright can be limited to establishing that Member States provide rights with respect to rental and lending for certain groups of rightholders and further to establishing the rights of fixation, reproduction, distribution, broadcasting and communication to the public for certain groups of rightholders in the field of related rights protection;

Whereas it is necessary to define the concepts of rental and lending for the purposes of this Directive;

Whereas it is desirable, with a view to clarity, to exclude from rental and lending within the meaning of this Directive certain forms of making available, as for instance making available phonograms or films (cinematographic or audiovisual works or moving images, whether or not accompanied by sound) for the purpose of public performance or broadcasting, making available for the purpose of exhibition, or making available for on-the-spot reference use; whereas lending within the meaning of this Directive does not include making available between establishments which are accessible to the public;

Whereas, where lending by an establishment accessible to the public gives rise to a payment the amount of which does not go beyond what is necessary to cover the operating costs of the establishment, there is no direct or indirect economic or commercial advantage within the meaning of this Directive;

Whereas it is necessary to introduce arrangements ensuring that an unwaivable equitable remuneration is obtained by authors and performers who must retain the possibility to entrust the administration of this right to collecting societies representing them;

Whereas the equitable remuneration may be paid on the basis of one or several payments at any time on or after the conclusion of the contract;

Whereas the equitable remuneration must take account of the importance of the contribution of the authors and performers concerned to the phonogram or film;

Whereas it is also necessary to protect the rights at least of authors as regards public lending by providing for specific arrangements; whereas, however, any measures based on Article 5 of this Directive have to comply with Community law, in particular with Article 7 of the Treaty;

Whereas the provisions of Chapter II do not prevent Member States from extending the presumption set out in Article 2 (5) to the exclusive rights included in that chapter; whereas furthermore the provisions of Chapter II do not prevent Member States from providing for a rebutable presumption of the authorization of exploitation in respect of the exclusive rights of performers provided for in those articles, in so far as such presumption is compatible with the International Convention for the Protection of Performers, Producers of Phonograms and Broadcasting Organizations (hereinafter referred to as the Rome Convention);

Whereas Member States may provide for more far-reaching protection for owners of rights related to copyright than that required by Article 8 of this Directive;

Whereas the harmonized rental and lending rights and the harmonized protection in the field of rights related to copyright should not be exercised in a way which constitutes a disguised restriction on trade between Member States or in a way which is contrary to the rule of media exploitation chronology, as recognized in the Judgment handed down in Société Cinéthèque v. FNCF[1],

HAS ADOPTED THIS DIRECTIVE:

---

[1] Cases 60/84 and 61/84, ECR 1985, p. 2605.

CHAPTER 1

RENTAL AND LENDING RIGHT

Article 1

Object of harmonization

1. In accordance with the provisions of this Chapter, Member States shall provide, subject to Article 5, a right to authorize or prohibit the rental and lending of originals and copies of copyright works, and other subject matter as set out in article 2 (1).

2. For the purposes of this Directive, 'rental' means making available for use, for a limited period of time and for direct or indirect economic or commercial advantage.

3. For the purposes of this Directive, 'lending' means making available for use, for a limited period of time and not for direct or indirect economic or commercial advantage, when it is made through establishments which are accessible to the public.

4. The rights referred to in paragraph 1 shall not be exhausted by any sale or other act of distribution of originals and copies of copyright works and other subject matter as set out in Article 2 (1).

Article 2

Rightholders and subject matter of rental and lending right

1. The exclusive right to authorize or prohibit rental and lending shall belong:
— to the author in respect of the original and copies of his work,
— to the performer in respect of fixations of his performance,
— to the phonogram producer in respect of his phonograms, and
— to the producer of the first fixation of a film in respect of the original and copies of his film. For the purposes of this Directive, the term 'film' shall designate a cinemato-graphic or audiovisual work or moving images, whether or not accompanied by sound.

2. For the purposes of this Directive the principal director of a cinematographic or audiovisual work shall be considered as its author or one of its authors. Member States may provide for others to be considered as its co-authors.

3. This Directive does not cover rental and lending rights in relation to buildings and to works of applied art.

4. The rights referred to in paragraph 1 may be transferred, assigned or subject to the granting of contractual licences.

5. Without prejudice to paragraph 7, when a contract concerning film production is concluded, individually or collectively, by performers with a film producer, the performer covered by this contract shall be presumed, subject to contractual clauses to the contrary, to have transferred his rental right, subject to Article 4.

6. Member States may provide for a similar presumption as set out in paragraph 5 with respect to authors.

7. Member States may provide that the signing of a contract concluded between a performer and a film producer concerning the production of a film has the effect of authorizing rental, provided that such contract provides for an equitable remuneration within the meaning of Article 4. Member States may also provide that this paragraph shall apply *mutatis mutandis* to the rights included in Chapter II.

Article 3

Rental of computer programs

This Directive shall be without prejudice to Article 4 (c) of Council Directive 91/250/EEC of 14 May 1991 on the legal protection of computer programs[1] .

---

[1] OJ No L 122, 5. 1991, p. 42.

Article 4

Unwaivable right to equitable remuneration

1. Where an author or performer has transferred or assigned his rental right concerning a phonogram or an original or copy of a film to a phonogram or film producer, that author or performer shall retain the right to obtain an equitable remuneration for the rental.

2. The right to obtain an equitable remuneration for rental cannot be waived by authors or performers.

3. The administration of this right to obtain an equitable remuneration may be entrusted to collecting societies representing authors or performers.

4. Member States may regulate whether and to what extent administration by collecting societies of the right to obtain an equitable remuneration may be imposed, as well as the question from whom this remuneration may be claimed or collected.

Article 5

Derogation from the exclusive public lending right

1. Member States may derogate from the exclusive right provided for in Article 1 in respect of public lending, provided that at least authors obtain a remuneration for such lending. Member States shall be free to determine this remuneration taking account of their cultural promotion objectives.

2. When Member States do not apply the exclusive lending right provided for in Article 1 as regards phonograms, films and computer programs, they shall introduce, at least for authors, a remuneration.

3. Member States may exempt certain categories of establishments from the payment of the remuneration referred to in paragraphs 1 and 2.

4. The Commission, in cooperation with the Member States, shall draw up before 1 July 1997 a report on public lending in the Community. It shall forward this report to the European Parliament and to the Council.

CHAPTER II

RIGHTS RELATED TO COPYRIGHT

Article 6

Fixation right

1. Member States shall provide for performers the exclusive right to authorize or prohibit the fixation of their performances.

2. Member States shall provide for broadcasting organizations the exclusive right to authorize or prohibit the fixation of their broadcasts, whether these broadcasts are transmitted by wire or over the air, including by cable or satellite.

3. A cable distributor shall not have the right provided for in paragraph 2 where it merely retransmits by cable the broadcasts of broadcasting organizations.

Article 7

Reproduction right

1. Member States shall provide the exclusive right to authorize or prohibit the direct or indirect reproduction:
— for performers, of fixations of their performances,

— for phonogram producers, of their phonograms,
— for producers of the first fixations of films, in respect of the original and copies of their films, and
— for broadcasting organizations, of fixations of their broadcasts, as set out in Article 6 (2).

2. The reproduction right referred to in paragraph 1 may be transferred, assigned or subject to the granting of contractual licences.

Article 8

Broadcasting and communication to the public

1. Member States shall provide for performers the exclusive right to authorize or prohibit the broadcasting by wireless means and the communication to the public of their performances, except where the performance is itself already a broadcast performance or is made from a fixation.

2. Member States shall provide a right in order to ensure that a single equitable remuneration is paid by the user, if a phonogram published for commercial purposes, or a reproduction of such phonogram, is used for broadcasting by wireless means or for any communication to the public, and to ensure that this remuneration is shared between the relevant performers and phonogram producers. Member States may, in the absence of agreement between the performers and phonogram producers, lay down the conditions as to the sharing of this remuneration between them.

3. Member States shall provide for broadcasting organizations the exclusive right to authorize or prohibit the rebroadcasting of their broadcasts by wireless means, as well as the communication to the public of their broadcasts if such communication is made in places accessible to the public against payment of an entrance fee.

Article 9

Distribution right

1. Member States shall provide
— for performers, in respect of fixations of their performances,
— for phonogram producers, in respect of their phonograms,
— for producers of the first fixations of films, in respect of the original and copies of their films,
— for broadcasting organizations, in respect of fixations of their broadcast as set out in Article 6 (2),

the exclusive right to make available these objects, including copies thereof, to the public by sale or otherwise, hereafter referred to as the 'distribution right'.

2. The distribution right shall not be exhausted within the Community in respect of an object as referred to in paragraph 1, except where the first sale in the Community of that object is made by the rightholder or with his consent.

3. The distribution right shall be without prejudice to the specific provisions of Chapter I, in particular Article 1 (4).

4. The distribution right may be transferred, assigned or subject to the granting of contractual licences.

Article 10

Limitations to rights

1. Member States may provide for limitations to the rights referred to in Chapter II in respect of:

(a) private use;

(b) use of short excerpts in connection with the reporting of current events;
(c) ephemeral fixation by a broadcasting organization by means of its own facilities and for its own broadcasts;
(d) use solely for the purposes of teaching or scientific research.

2. Irrespective of paragraph 1, any Member State may provide for the same kinds of limitations with regard to the protection of performers, producers of phonograms, broadcasting organizations and of producers of the first fixations of films, as it provides for in connection with the protection of copyright in literary and artistic works. However, compulsory licences may be provided for only to the extent to which they are compatible with the Rome Convention.

3. Paragraph 1 (a) shall be without prejudice to any existing or future legislation on remuneration for reproduction for private use.

CHAPTER III

DURATION

Article 11

Duration of authors' rights

Without prejudice to further harmonization, the authors' rights referred to in this Directive shall not expire before the end of the term provided by the Berne Convention for the Protection of Literary and Artistic Works.

Article 12

Duration of related rights

Without prejudice to further harmonization, the rights referred to in this Directive of performers, phonogram producers and broadcasting organizations shall not expire before the end of the respective terms provided by the Rome Convention. The rights referred to in this Directive for producers of the first fixations of films shall not expire before the end of a period of 20 years computed from the end of the year in which the fixation was made.

CHAPTER IV

COMMON PROVISIONS

Article 13

Application in time

1. This Directive shall apply in respect of all copyright works, performances, phonograms, broadcasts and first fixations of films referred to in this Directive which are, on 1 July 1994, still protected by the legislation of the Member States in the field of copyright and related rights or meet the criteria for protection under the provisions of this Directive on that date.

2. This Directive shall apply without prejudice to any act of exploitation performed before 1 July 1994.

3. Member States may provide that the rightholders are deemed to have given their authorization to the rental or lending of an object referred to in Article 2 (1) which is proven to have been made available to third parties for this purpose or to have been acquired before 1 July 1994. However, in particular where such an object is a digital recording, Member

States may provide that rightholders shall have a right to obtain an adequate remuneration for the rental or lending of that object.

4. Member States need not apply the provisions of Article 2 (2) to cinematographic or audiovisual works created before 1 July 1994.

5. Member States may determine the date as from which the Article 2 (2) shall apply, provided that that date is no later than 1 July 1997.

6. This Directive shall, without prejudice to paragraph 3 and subject to paragraphs 8 and 9, not affect any contracts concluded before the date of its adoption.

7. Member States may provide, subject to the provisions of paragraphs 8 and 9, that when rightholders who acquire new rights under the national provisions adopted in implementation of this Directive have, before 1 July 1994, given their consent for exploitation, they shall be presumed to have transferred the new exclusive rights.

8. Member States may determine the date as from which the unwaivable right to an equitable remuneration referred to in Article 4 exists, provided that that date is no later than 1 July 1997.

9. For contracts concluded before 1 July 1994, the unwaivable right to an equitable remuneration provided for in Article 4 shall apply only where authors or performers or those representing them have submitted a request to that effect before 1 January 1997. In the absence of agreement between rightholders concerning the level of remuneration, Member States may fix the level of equitable remuneration.

Article 14

Relation between copyright and related rights

Protection of copyright-related rights under this Directive shall leave intact and shall in no way affect the protection of copyright.

Article 15

Final provisions

1. Member States shall bring into force the laws, regulations and administrative provisions necessary to comply with this Directive not later than 1 July 1994. They shall forthwith inform the Commission thereof.

When Member States adopt these measures, they shall contain a reference to this Directive or shall be accompanied by such reference at the time of their official publication. The methods of making such a reference shall be laid down by the Member States.

2. Member States shall communicate to the Commission the main provisions of domestic law which they adopt in the field covered by this Directive.

Article 16

This Directive is addressed to the Member States.

Done at Brussels, 19 November 1992.

For the Council
The President
E. LEIGH

APPENDIX 2
International Treaties

BERNE CONVENTION FOR THE PROTECTION OF LITERARY AND ARTISTIC WORKS

of September 9, 1886, completed at PARIS on May 4, 1896, revised at BERLIN on November 13, 1908, completed at BERNE on March 20, 1914, revised at ROME on June 2, 1928, at BRUSSELS on June 26, 1948, at STOCKHOLM on July 14, 1967, and at PARIS on July 24, 1971, and amended on October 2, 1979

TABLE OF CONTENTS

---

*This Table of Contents is added for the convenience of the reader. It does not appear in the original (English) text of the Convention.

Appendix

Special Provisions Regarding Developing Countries

The countries of the Union, being equally animated by the desire to protect, in as effective and uniform a manner as possible, the rights of authors in their literary and artistic works,

Recognizing the importance of the work of the Revision Conference held at Stockholm in 1967,

Have resolved to revise the Act adopted by the Stockholm Conference, while maintaining without change Articles 1 to 20 and 22 to 26 of that Act.

Consequently, the undersigned Plenipotentiaries, having presented their full powers, recognized as in good and due form, have agreed as follows:

Article 1

Establishment of a Union[1]

The countries to which this Convention applies constitute a Union for the protection of the rights of authors in their literary and artistic works.

Article 2

Protected Works
[1. "Literary and artistic works"; 2. Possible requirement of fixation; 3. Derivative works;
4. Official texts; 5. Collections; 6. Obligation to protect; beneficiaries of protection;
7. Works of applied art and industrial designs; 8. News]

1. The expression "literary and artistic works" shall include every production in the literary, scientific and artistic domain, whatever may be the mode of form of its expression, such as books, pamphlets and other writings; lectures, addresses, sermons and other works of the same nature; dramatic or dramatico-musical works; choreographic works and entertainments in dumb show; musical compositions with or without words; cinematographic works to which are assimilated works expressed by a process analogous to cinematography; works of drawing, painting, architecture, sculpture, engraving and lithography; photographic works to which are assimilated works expressed by a process analogous to photography; works of applied art; illustrations, maps, plans, sketches and three-dimensional works relative to geography, topography, architecture or science.

2. It shall, however, be a matter for legislation in the countries of the Union to prescribe that works in general or any specified categories of works shall not be protected unless they have been fixed in some material form.

3. Translations, adaptations, arrangements of music and other alterations of a literary or artistic work shall be protected as original works without prejudice to the copyright in the original work.

4. It shall be a matter for legislation in the countries of the Union to determine the protection to be granted to official texts of a legislative, administrative and legal nature, and to official translations of such texts.

5. Collections of literary or artistic works such as encyclopaedias and anthologies which, by reason of the selection and arrangement of their contents, constitute intellectual creations shall be protected as such, without prejudice to the copyright in each of the works forming part of such collections.

6. The works mentioned in this Article shall enjoy protection in all countries of the Union. This protection shall operate for the benefit of the author and his successors in title.

7. Subject to the provisions of Article 7 (4) of this Convention, it shall be a matter for legislation in the countries of the Union to determine the extent of the application of their

---

[1] Each Article and the Appendix have been given titles to facilitate their identification. There are no titles in the signed (English) text.

laws to works of applied art and industrial designs and models, as well as the conditions under which such works, designs and models shall be protected. Works protected in the country of origin solely as designs and models shall be entitled in another country of the Union only to such special protection as is granted in that country to designs and models; however, if no such special protection is granted in that country, such works shall be protected as artistic works.

8. The protection of this Convention shall not apply to news of the day or to miscellaneous facts having the character of mere items of press information.

Article 2bis

Possible Limitation of Protection of Certain Works
[1. Certain speeches; 2. Certain uses of lectures and addresses; 3. Right to make collections of such works]

1. It shall be a matter for legislation in the countries of the Union to exclude, wholly or in part, from the protection provided by the preceding Article political speeches and speeches delivered in the course of legal proceedings.

2. It shall also be a matter for legislation in the countries of the Union to determine the conditions under which lectures, addresses and other works of the same nature which are delivered in public may be reproduced by the press, broadcast, communicated to the public by wire and made the subject of public communication as envisaged in Article 11bis (1) of this Convention, when such use is justified by the informatory purpose.

3. Nevertheless, the author shall enjoy the exclusive right of making a collection of his works mentioned in the preceding paragraphs.

Article 3

Criteria of Eligibility for Protection
[1. Nationality of author; place of publication of work; 2. Residence of author; 3. "Published" works; 4. "Simultaneously published" works]

1. The protection of this Convention shall apply to:

(a) authors who are nationals of one of the countries of the Union, for their works, whether published or not;
(b) authors who are not nationals of one of the countries of the Union, for their works first published in one of those countries, or simultaneously in a country outside the Union and in a country of the Union.

2. Authors who are not nationals of one of the countries of the Union but who have their habitual residence in one of them shall, for the purposes of this Convention, be assimilated to nationals of that country.

3. The expression "published works" means works published with the consent of their authors, whatever may be the means of manufacture of the copies, provided that the availability of such copies has been such as to satisfy the reasonable requirements of the public, having regard to the nature of the work. The performance of a dramatic, dramatico-musical, cinematographic or musical work, the public recitation of a literary work, the communication by wire or the broadcasting of literary or artistic works, the exhibition of a work of art and the construction of a work of architecture shall not constitute publication.

4. A work shall be considered as having been published simultaneously in several countries if it has been published in two or more countries within thirty days of its first publication.

Article 4

Criteria of Eligibility for Protection of Cinematographic Works, Works of Architecture and Certain Artistic Works

The protection of this Convention shall apply, even if the conditions of Article 3 are not fulfilled, to:

(a) authors of cinematographic works the maker of which has his headquarters or habitual residence in one of the countries of the Union;

(b) authors of works of architecture erected in a country of the Union or of other artistic works incorporated in a building or other structure located in a country of the Union.

Article 5

Rights Guaranteed
[1. and 2. Outside the country of origin; 3. In the country of origin; 4. "Country of origin"]

1. Authors shall enjoy, in respect of works for which they are protected under this Convention, in countries of the Union other than the country of origin, the rights which their respective laws do now or may hereafter grant to their nationals, as well as the rights specially granted by this Convention.

2. The enjoyment and the exercise of these rights shall not be subject to any formality; such enjoyment and such exercise shall be independent of the existence of protection in the country of origin of the work. Consequently, apart from the provisions of this Convention, the extent of protection, as well as the means of redress afforded to the author to protect his rights, shall be governed exclusively by the laws of the country where protection is claimed.

3. Protection in the country of origin is governed by domestic law. However, when the author is not a national of the country of origin of the work for which he is protected under this Convention, he shall enjoy in that country the same rights as national authors.

4. The country of origin shall be considered to be:

(a) in the case of works first published in a country of the Union, that country; in the case of works published simultaneously in several countries of the Union which grant different terms of protection, the country whose legislation grants the shortest term of protection;

(b) in the case of works published simultaneously in a country outside the Union and in a country of the Union, the latter country;

(c) in the case of unpublished works or of works first published in a country outside the Union, without simultaneous publication in a country of the Union, the country of the Union of which the author is a national, provided that:

   (i) when these are cinematographic works the maker of which has his headquarters or his habitual residence in a country of the Union, the country of origin shall be that country, and

   (ii) when these are works of architecture erected in a country of the Union or other artistic works incorporated in a building or other structure located in a country of the Union, the country of origin shall be that country.

Article 6

Possible Restriction of Protection In Respect of Certain Works of Nationals of Certain Countries Outside the Union
[1. In the country of the first publication and in other countries; 2. No retroactivity; 3. Notice]

1. Where any country outside the Union fails to protect in an adequate manner the works of authors who are nationals of one of the countries of the Union, the latter country may

restrict the protection given to the works of authors who are, at the date of the first publication thereof, nationals of the other country and are not habitually resident in one of the countries of the Union. If the country of first publication avails itself of this right, the other countries of the Union shall not be required to grant to works thus subjected to special treatment a wider protection than that granted to them in the country of first publication.

2. No restrictions introduced by virtue of the preceding paragraph shall affect the rights which an author may have acquired in respect of a work published in a country of the Union before such restrictions were put into force.

3. The countries of the Union which restrict the grant of copyright in accordance with this Article shall give notice thereof to the Director General of the World Intellectual Property Organization (hereinafter designated as "the Director General") by a written declaration specifying the countries in regard to which protection is restricted, and the restrictions to which rights of authors who are nationals of those countries are subjected. The Director General shall immediately communicate this declaration to all the countries of the Union.

Article 6bis

Moral Rights
[1. To claim authorship; to object to certain modifications and other derogatory actions; 2. After the author's death; 3. Means of redress]

1. Independently of the author's economic rights, and even after the transfer of the said rights, the author shall have the right to claim authorship of the work and to object to any distortion, mutilation or other modification of, or other derogatory action in relation to, the said work, which would be prejudicial to his honor or reputation.

2. The rights granted to the author in accordance with the preceding paragraph shall, after his death, be maintained, at least until the expiry of the economic rights, and shall be exercisable by the persons or institutions authorized by the legislation of the country where protection is claimed. However, those countries whose legislation, at the moment of their ratification of or accession to this Act, does not provide for the protection after the death of the author of all the rights set out in the preceding paragraph may provide that some of these rights may, after his death, cease to be maintained.

3. The means of redress for safeguarding the rights granted by this Article shall be governed by the legislation of the country where protection is claimed.

Article 7

Term of Protection
[1. Generally; 2. For cinematographic works; 3. For anonymous and pseudonymous works; 4. For photographic works and works of applied art; 5. Starting date of computation; 6. Longer terms; 7. Shorter terms; 8. Applicable law; "comparison" of terms]

1. The term of protection granted by this Convention shall be the life of the author and fifty years after his death.

2. However, in the case of cinematographic works, the countries of the Union may provide that the term of protection shall expire fifty years after the work has been made available to the public with the consent of the author, or, failing such an event within fifty years from the making of such a work, fifty years after the making.

3. In the case of anonymous or pseudonymous works, the term of protection granted by this Convention shall expire fifty years after the work has been lawfully made available to the public. However, when the pseudonym adopted by the author leaves no doubt as to his identity, the term of protection shall be that provided in paragraph (1). If the author of an anonymous or pseudonymous work discloses his identity during the above-mentioned period,

the term of protection applicable shall be that provided in paragraph (1). The countries of the Union shall not be required to protect anonymous or pseudonymous works in respect of which it is reasonable to presume that their author has been dead for fifty years.

4. It shall be a matter for legislation in the countries of the Union to determine the term of protection of photographic works and that of works of applied art in so far as they are protected as artistic works; however, this term shall last at least until the end of a period of twenty-five years from the making of such a work.

5. The term of protection subsequent to the death of the author and the terms provided by paragraphs (2), (3) and (4) shall run from the date of death or of the event referred to in those paragraphs, but such terms shall always be deemed to begin on the first of January of the year following the death or such event.

6. The countries of the Union may grant a term of protection in excess of those provided by the preceding paragraphs.

7. Those countries of the Union bound by the Rome Act of this Convention which grant, in their national legislation in force at the time of signature of the present Act, shorter terms of protection than those provided for in the preceding paragraphs shall have the right to maintain such terms when ratifying or acceding to the present Act.

8. In any case, the term shall be governed by the legislation of the country where protection is claimed; however, unless the legislation of that country otherwise provides, the term shall not exceed the term fixed in the country of origin of the work.

Article 7bis

Term of Protection for Works of Joint Authorship

The provisions of the preceding Article shall also apply in the case of a work of joint authorship, provided that the terms measured from the death of the author shall be calculated from the death of the last surviving author.

Article 8

Right of Translation

Authors of literary and artistic works protected by this Convention shall enjoy the exclusive right of making and of authorizing the translation of their works throughout the term of protection of their rights in the original works.

Article 9

Right of Reproduction
[1. Generally; 2. Possible exceptions; 3. Sound and visual recordings]

1. Authors of literary and artistic works protected by this Convention shall have the exclusive right of authorizing the reproduction of these works, in any manner or form.

2. It shall be a matter for legislation in the countries' of the Union to permit the reproduction of such works in certain special cases, provided that such reproduction does not conflict with a normal exploitation of the work and does not unreasonably prejudice the legitimate interests of the author.

3. Any sound or visual recording shall be considered as a reproduction for the purposes of this Convention.

Article 10

Certain Free Uses of Works
[1. Quotations; 2. Illustrations for teaching; 3. Indication of source and author]

1. It shall be permissible to make quotations from a work which has already been lawfully made available to the public, provided that their making is compatible with fair practice, and

their extent does not exceed that justified by the purpose, including quotations from newspaper articles and periodicals in the form of press summaries.

2. It shall be a matter for legislation in the countries of the Union, and for special agreements existing or to be concluded between them, to permit the utilization, to the extent justified by the purpose, of literary or artistic works by way of illustration in publications, broadcasts or sound or visual recordings for teaching, provided such utilization is compatible with fair practice.

3. Where use is made of works in accordance with the preceding paragraphs of this Article, mention shall be made of the source, and of the name of the author if it appears thereon.

Article 10*bis*

Further Possible Free Uses of Works
[1. Of certain articles and broadcast works; 2. Of works seen or heard in connection with current events]

1. It shall be a matter for legislation in the countries of the Union to permit the reproduction by the press, the broadcasting or the communication to the public by wire of articles published in newspapers or periodicals on current economic, political or religious topics, and of broadcast works of the same character, in cases in which the reproduction, broadcasting or such communication thereof is not expressly reserved. Nevertheless, the source must always be clearly indicated; the legal consequences of a breach of this obligation shall be determined by the legislation of the country where protection is claimed.

2. It shall also be a matter for legislation in the countries of the Union to determine the conditions under which, for the purpose of reporting current events by means of photography, cinematography, broadcasting or communication to the public by wire, literary or artistic works seen or heard in the course of the event may, to the extent justified by the informatory purpose, be reproduced and made available to the public.

Article 11

Certain Rights in Dramatic and Musical Works
[1. Right of public performance and of communication to the public of a performance; 2. In respect of translations]

1. Authors of dramatic, dramatico-musical and musical works shall enjoy the exclusive right of authorizing:

(i)   the public performance of their works, including such public performance by any means or process;
(ii) any communication to the public of the performance of their works.

2. Authors of dramatic or dramatico-musical works shall enjoy, during the full term of their rights in the original works, the same rights with respect to translations thereof.

Article 11*bis*

Broadcasting and Related Rights
[1. Broadcasting and other wireless communications, public communication of broadcast by wire or rebroadcast, public communication of broadcast by loudspeaker or analogous instruments; 2. Compulsory licenses; 3. Recording; ephemeral recordings]

1. Authors of literary and artistic works shall enjoy the exclusive right of authorizing:

(i)   the broadcasting of their works or the communication thereof to the public by any other means of wireless diffusion of signs, sounds or images;

(ii) any communication to the public by wire or by rebroadcasting of the broadcast of the work, when this communication is made by an organization other than the original one;

(iii) the public communication by loudspeaker or any other analogous instrument transmitting, by signs, sounds or images, the broadcast of the work.

2. It shall be a matter for legislation in the countries of the Union to determine the conditions under which the rights mentioned in the preceding paragraph may be exercised, but these conditions shall apply only in the countries where they have been prescribed. They shall not in any circumstances be prejudicial to the moral rights of the author, nor to his right to obtain equitable remuneration which, in the absence of agreement, shall be fixed by competent authority.

3. In the absence of any contrary stipulation, permission granted in accordance with paragraph (1) of this Article shall not imply permission to record, by means of instruments recording sounds or images, the work broadcast. It shall, however, be a matter for legislation in the countries of the Union to determine the regulations for ephemeral recordings made by a broadcasting organization by means of its own facilities and used for its own broadcasts. The preservation of these recordings in official archives may, on the ground of their exceptional documentary character, be authorized by such legislation.

Article 11ter

Certain Rights in Literary Works
[1. Right of public recitation and of communication to the public of a recitation;
2. In respect of translations]

1. Authors of literary works shall enjoy the exclusive right of authorizing:

(i) the public recitation of their works, including such public recitation by any means or process;

(ii) any communication to the public of the recitation of their works.

2. Authors of literary works shall enjoy, during the full term of their rights in the original works, the same rights with respect to translations thereof.

Article 12

Right of Adaptation, Arrangement and Other Alteration

Authors of literary or artistic works shall enjoy the exclusive right of authorizing adaptations, arrangements and other alterations of their works.

Article 13

Possible Limitation of the Right of Recording of Musical Works and Any Words Pertaining Thereto
[1. Compulsory licenses; 2. Transitory measures; 3. Seizure on importation of copies made without the author's permission]

1. Each country of the Union may impose for itself reservations and conditions on the exclusive right granted to the author of a musical work and to the author of any words, the recording of which together with the musical work has already been authorized by the latter, to authorize the sound recording of that musical work, together with such words, if any; but all such reservations and conditions shall apply only in the countries which have imposed them and shall not, in any circumstances, be prejudicial to the rights of these authors to obtain equitable remuneration which, in the absence of agreement, shall be fixed by competent authority.

2. Recordings of musical works made in a country of the Union in accordance with Article 13(3) of the Conventions signed at Rome on June 2, 1928, and at Brussels on June 26, 1948, may be reproduced in that country without the permission of the author of the musical work until a date two years after that country becomes bound by this Act.

3. Recordings made in accordance with paragraphs (1) and (2) of this Article and imported without permission from the parties concerned into a country where they are treated as infringing recordings shall be liable to seizure.

Article 14

Cinematographic and Related Rights

[1. Cinematographic adaptation and reproduction; distribution; public performance and public communication by wire of works thus adapted or reproduced; (2) Adaptation of cinematographic productions; 3. No compulsory licenses]

1. Authors of literary or artistic works shall have the exclusive right of authorizing;

- (i) the cinematographic adaptation and reproduction of these works, and the distribution of the works thus adapted or reproduced;
- (ii) the public performance and communication to the public by wire of the works thus adapted or reproduced.

2. The adaptation into any other artistic form of a cinematographic production derived from literary or artistic works shall, without prejudice to the authorization of the author of the cinematographic production, remain subject to the authorization of the authors of the original works.

3. The provisions of Article 13(1) shall not apply.

Article 14bis

Special Provisions Concerning Cinematographic Works

[1. Assimilation to "original" works; 2. Ownership; limitation of certain rights of certain contributors; 3. Certain other contributors]

1. Without prejudice to the copyright in any work which may have been adapted or reproduced, a cinematographic work shall be protected as an original work. The owner of copyright in a cinematographic work shall enjoy the same rights as the author of an original work, including the rights referred to in the preceding Article.

2. (a) Ownership of copyright in a cinematographic work shall be a matter for legislation in the country where protection is claimed.

   (b) However, in the countries of the Union which, by legislation, include among the owners of copyright in a cinematographic work authors who have brought contributions to the making of the work, such authors, if they have undertaken to bring such contributions, may not, in the absence of any contrary or special stipulation, object to the reproduction, distribution, public performance, communication to the public by wire, broadcasting or any other communication to the public, or to the subtitling or dubbing of texts, of the work.

   (c) The question whether or not the form of the undertaking referred to above should, for the application of the preceding subparagraph (b), be in a written agreement or a written act of the same effect shall be a matter for the legislation of the country where the maker of the cinematographic work has his headquarters or habitual residence. However, it shall be a matter for the legislation of the country of the Union where protection is claimed to provide that the said undertaking shall be in a written agreement or a written act of the same effect. The countries whose legislation so provides shall notify the Director General by means of a written declaration, which will be immediately communicated by him to all the other countries of the Union.

(d) By "contrary or special stipulation" is meant any restrictive condition which is relevant to the aforesaid undertaking.

3. Unless the national legislation provides to the contrary, the provisions of paragraph (2)(b) above shall not be applicable to authors of scenarios, dialogues and musical works created for the making of the cinematographic work, or to the principal director thereof. However, those countries of the Union whose legislation does not contain rules providing for the application of the said paragraph (2)(b) to such director shall notify the Director General by means of a written declaration, which will be immediately communicated by him to all the other countries of the Union.

Article 14ter

"Droit de suite" in Works of Art and Manuscripts
[1. Right to an interest in resales; 2. Applicable law; 3. Procedure]

1. The author, or after his death the persons or institutions authorized by national legislation shall, with respect to original works of art and original manuscripts of writers and composers, enjoy the inalienable right to an interest in any sale of the work subsequent to the first transfer by the author of the work.

2. The protection provided by the preceding paragraph may be claimed in a country of the Union only if legislation in the country to which the author belongs so permits, and to the extent permitted by the country where this protection is claimed.

3. The procedure for collection and the amounts shall be matters for determination by national legislation.

Article 15

Right to Enforce Protected Rights
[1. Where author's name is indicated or where pseudonym leaves no doubt as to author's identity; 2. In the case of cinematographic works; 3. In the case of anonymous and pseudonymous works; 4. In the case of certain unpublished works of unknown authorship]

1. In order that the author of a literary or artistic work protected by this Convention shall, in the absence of proof to the contrary, be regarded as such, and consequently be entitled to institute infringement proceedings in the countries of the Union, it shall be sufficient for his name to appear on the work in the usual manner. This paragraph shall be applicable even if this name is a pseudonym, where the pseudonym adopted by the author leaves no doubt as to his identity.

2. The person or body corporate whose name appears on a cinematographic work in the usual manner shall, in the absence of proof to the contrary, be presumed to be the maker of the said work.

3. In the case of anonymous and pseudonymous works, other than those referred to in paragraph (1) above, the publisher whose name appears on the work shall, in the absence of proof to the contrary, be deemed to represent the author, and in this capacity he shall be entitled to protect and enforce the author's rights. The provisions of this paragraph shall cease to apply when the author reveals his identity and establishes his claim to authorship of the work.

4. (a) In the case of unpublished works where the identity of the author is unknown, but where there is every ground to presume that he is a national of a country of the Union, it shall be a matter for legislation in that country to designate the competent authority which shall represent the author and shall be entitled to protect and enforce his rights in the countries of the Union.

(b) Countries of the Union which make such designation under the terms of this provision shall notify the Director General by means of a written declaration giving full information concerning the authority thus designated. The Director General shall at once communicate this declaration to all other countries of the Union.

Article 16

Infringing Copies
[1. Seizure; 2. Seizure on importation; 3. Applicable law]

1. Infringing copies of a work shall be liable to seizure in any country of the Union where the work enjoys legal protection.

2. The provisions of the preceding paragraph shall also apply to reproductions coming from a country where the work is not protected, or has ceased to be protected.

3. The seizure shall take place in accordance with the legislation of each country.

Article 17

Possibility of Control of Circulation, Presentation and Exhibition of Works

The provisions of this Convention cannot in any way affect the right of the Government of each country of the Union to permit, to control, or to prohibit, by legislation or regulation, the circulation, presentation, or exhibition of any work or production in regard to which the competent authority may find it necessary to exercise that right.

Article 18

Works Existing on Convention's Entry Into Force
[1. Protectable where protection not yet expired in country of origin; 2. Non-protectable where protection already expired in country where it is claimed; 3. Application of these principles; 4. Special cases]

1. This Convention shall apply to all works which, at the moment of its coming into force, have not yet fallen into the public domain in the country of origin through the expiry of the term of protection.

2. If, however, through the expiry of the term of protection which was previously granted, a work has fallen into the public domain of the country where protection is claimed, that work shall not be protected anew.

3. The application of this principle shall be subject to any provisions contained in special conventions to that effect existing or to be concluded between countries of the Union. In the absence of such provisions, the respective countries shall determine, each in so far as it is concerned, the conditions of application of this principle.

4. The preceding provisions shall also apply in the case of new accessions to the Union and to cases in which protection is extended by the application of Article 7 or by the abandonment of reservations.

Article 19

Protection Greater than Resulting from Convention

The provisions of this Convention shall not preclude the making of a claim to the benefit of any greater protection which may be granted by legislation in a country of the Union.

Article 20

Special Agreements Among Countries of the Union

The Governments of the countries of the Union reserve the right to enter into special agreements among themselves, in so far as such agreements grant to authors more extensive rights than those granted by the Convention, or contain other provisions not contrary to this Convention. The provisions of existing agreements which satisfy these conditions shall remain applicable.

Article 21

Special Provisions Regarding Developing Countries
[1. Reference to Appendix; 2. Appendix part of Act]

1. Special provisions regarding developing countries are included in the Appendix.

2. Subject to the provisions of Article 28(1)(b), the Appendix forms an integral part of this Act.

Article 22

Assembly
[1. Constitution and composition; 2. Tasks; 3. Quorum, voting, observers; 4. Convocation; 5. Rules of procedure]

1. (a) The Union shall have an Assembly consisting of those countries of the Union which are bound by Articles 22 to 26.
   (b) The Government of each country shall be represented by one delegate, who may be assisted by alternate delegates, advisors, and experts.
   (c) The expenses of each delegation shall be borne by the Government which has appointed it.

2. (a) The Assembly shall:
   (i) deal with all matters concerning the maintenance and development of the Union and the implementation of this Convention;
   (ii) give directions concerning the preparation for conferences of revision to the International Bureau of Intellectual Property (hereinafter designated as the "International Bureau") referred to in the Convention Establishing the World Intellectual Property Organization (hereinafter designated as "the Organization"), due account being taken of any comments made by those countries of the Union which are not bound by Articles 22 to 26;
   (iii) review and approve the reports and activities of the Director General of the Organization concerning the Union, and give him all necessary instructions concerning matters within the competence of the Union;
   (iv) elect the members of the Executive Committee of the Assembly;
   (v) review and approve the reports and activities of its Executive Committee, and give instructions to such Committee;
   (vi) determine the program and adopt the biennial budget of the Union, and approve its final accounts;
   (vii) adopt the financial regulations of the Union;
   (viii) establish such committees of experts and working groups as may be necessary for the work of the Union;
   (ix) determine which countries not members of the Union and which inter-governmental and international non-governmental organizations shall be admitted to its meetings as observers;
   (x) adopt amendments to Articles 22 to 26;
   (xi) take any other appropriate action designated to further the objectives of the Union;
   (xii) exercise such other functions as are appropriate under this Convention;
   (xiii) subject to its acceptance, exercise such rights as are given to it in the Convention establishing the Organization.
   (b) With respect to matters which are of interest also to other Unions administered by the Organization, the Assembly shall make its decisions after having heard the advice of the Coordination Committee of the Organization.

3. (a) Each country member of the Assembly shall have one vote.
   (b) One-half of the countries members of the Assembly shall constitute a quorum.

(c) Notwithstanding the provisions of subparagraph (b), if, in any session, the number of countries represented is less than one-half but equal to or more than one-third of the countries members of the Assembly, the Assembly may make decisions but, with the exception of decisions concerning its own procedure, all such decisions shall take effect only if the following conditions are fulfilled. The International Bureau shall communicate the said decisions to the countries members of the Assembly which were not represented and shall invite them to express in writing their vote or abstention within a period of three months from the date of the communication. If, at the expiration of this period, the number of countries having thus expressed their vote or abstention attains the number of countries which was lacking for attaining the quorum in the session itself, such decisions shall take effect provided that at the same time the required majority still obtains.

(d) Subject to the provisions of Article 26(2), the decisions of the Assembly shall require two-thirds of the votes cast.

(e) Abstentions shall not be considered as votes.

(f) A delegate may represent, and vote in the name of, one country only.

(g) Countries of the Union not members of the Assembly shall be admitted to its meetings as observers.

4. (a) The Assembly shall meet once in every second calendar year in ordinary session upon convocation by the Director General and, in the absence of exceptional circumstances, during the same period and at the same place as the General Assembly of the Organization.

(b) The Assembly shall meet in extraordinary session upon convocation by the Director General, at the request of the Executive Committee or at the request of one-fourth of the countries members of the Assembly.

5. The Assembly shall adopt its own rules of procedure.

Article 23

Executive Committee

[1. Constitution; 2. Composition; 3. Number of members; 4. Geographical distribution; special agreements; 5. Term, limits of re-eligibility, rules of election. 6. Tasks; 7. Convocation; 8. Quorum, voting; 9. Observers; 10. Rules of Procedure]

1. The Assembly shall have an Executive Committee.

2. (a) The Executive Committee shall consist of countries elected by the Assembly from among countries members of the Assembly. Furthermore, the country on whose territory the Organization has its headquarters shall, subject to the provisions of Article 25(7)(b), have an *ex officio* seat on the Committee.

(b) The Government of each country member of the Executive Committee shall be represented by one delegate, who may be assisted by alternate delegates, advisors, and experts.

(c) The expenses of each delegation shall be borne by the Government which has appointed it.

3. The number of countries members of the Executive Committee shall correspond to one-fourth of the number of countries members of the Assembly. In establishing the number of seats to be filled, remainders after division by four shall be disregarded.

4. In electing the members of the Executive Committee, the Assembly shall have due regard to an equitable geographical distribution and to the need for countries partly to the Special Agreements which might be established in relation with the Union to be among the countries constituting the Executive Committee.

5. (a) Each member of the Executive Committee shall serve from the close of the session of the Assembly which elected it to the close of the next ordinary session of the Assembly.

    (b) Members of the Executive Committee may be re-elected, but not more than two-thirds of them.

    (c) The Assembly shall establish the details of the rules governing the election and possible re-election of the members of the Executive Committee.

6. (a) The Executive Committee shall:
      (i)   prepare the draft agenda of the Assembly;
      (ii) submit proposals to the Assembly respecting the draft program and biennial budget of the Union prepared by the Director General;
      (iii) *[deleted]*
      (iv) submit, with appropriate comments, to the Assembly the periodical reports of the Director General and the yearly audit reports on the accounts;
      (v)   in accordance with the decisions of the Assembly and having regard to circumstances arising between two ordinary sessions of the Assembly, take all necessary measures to ensure the execution of the program of the Union by the Director General;
      (vi) perform such other functions as are allocated to it under this Convention.

    (b) With respect to matters which are of interest also to other Unions administered by the Organization, the Executive Committee shall make its decisions after having heard the advice of the Coordination Committee of the Organization.

7. (a) The Executive Committee shall meet once a year in ordinary session upon convocation by the Director General, preferably during the same period and at the same place as the Coordination Committee of the Organization.

    (b) The Executive Committee shall meet in extraordinary session upon convocation by the Director General, either on his own initiative, or at the request of its Chairman or one-fourth of its members.

8. (a) Each country member of the Executive Committee shall have one vote.

    (b) One-half of the members of the Executive Committee shall constitute a quorum.

    (c) Decisions shall be made by a simple majority of the votes cast.

    (d) Abstentions shall not be considered as votes.

    (e) A delegate may represent, and vote in the name of, one country only.

9. Countries of the Union not members of the Executive Committee shall be admitted to its meetings as observers.

10. The Executive Committee shall adopt its own rules of procedure.

Article 24

International Bureau

[1. Tasks in general, Director General; 2. General information; 3. Periodical; 4. Information to countries; 5. Studies and services; 6. Participation in meetings; 7. Conferences of revision; 8. Other tasks]

1. (a) The administrative tasks with respect to the Union shall be performed by the International Bureau, which is a continuation of the Bureau of the Union united with the Bureau of the Union established by the International Convention for the Protection of Industrial Property.

    (b) In particular, the International Bureau shall provide the secretariat of the various organs of the Union.

    (c) The Director General of the Organization shall be the chief executive of the Union and shall represent the Union.

2. The International Bureau shall assemble and publish information concerning the protection of copyright. Each country of the Union shall promptly communicate to the International Bureau all new laws and official texts concerning the protection of copyright.

3. The International Bureau shall assemble and publish a monthly periodical.

4. The International Bureau shall, on request, furnish information to any country of the Union on matters concerning the protection of copyright.

5. The International Bureau shall conduct studies, and shall provide services, designed to facilitate the protection of copyright.

6. The Director General and any staff member designated by him shall participate, without the right to vote, in all meetings of the Assembly, the Executive Committee and any other committee of experts or working group. The Director General, or a staff member designated by him, shall be *ex officio* secretary of those bodies.

7. (a) The International Bureau shall, in accordance with the directions of the Assembly and in cooperation with the Executive Committee, make the preparations for the conferences of revision of the provisions of the Convention other than Articles 22 to 26.

   (b) The International Bureau may consult with intergovernmental and international non-governmental organizations concerning preparations for conferences of revision.

   (c) The Director General and persons designated by him shall take part, without the right to vote, in the discussions at these conferences.

8. The International Bureau shall carry out any other tasks assigned to it.

Article 25

Finances

[1. Budget; 2. Coordination with other Unions; 3. Resources; 4. Contributions; possible extension of previous budget; 5. Fees and charges; 6. Working capital fund; 7. Advances by host Government; 8. Auditing of accounts]

1. (a) The Union shall have a budget.

   (b) The budget of the Union shall include the income and expenses proper to the Union, its contribution to the budget of expenses common to the Unions, and where applicable, the sum made available to the budget of the Conference of the Organization.

   (c) Expenses not attributable exclusively to the Union but also to one or more other Unions administered by the Organization shall be considered as expenses common to the Unions. The share of the Union in such common expenses shall be in proportion to the interest the Union has in them.

2. The budget of the Union shall be established with due regard to the requirements of coordination with the budgets of the other Unions administered by the Organization.

3. The budget of the Union shall be financed from the following sources:

(i) contributions of the countries of the Union;

(ii) fees and charges due for services performed by the International Bureau in relation to the Union;

(iii) sale of, or royalties on, the publications of the International Bureau concerning the Union;

(iv) gifts, bequests, and subventions;

(v) rents, interests, and other miscellaneous income.

4. (a) For the purpose of establishing its contribution towards the budget, each country of the Union shall belong to a class, and shall pay its annual contributions on the basis of a number of units fixed as follows:

> Class I 25
> Class II 20
> Class III 15
> Class IV 10

Class V 5
Class VI 3
Class VII ... 1

(b) Unless it has already done so, each country shall indicate, concurrently with depositing its instrument of ratification or accession, the class to which it wishes to belong. Any country may change class. If it chooses a lower class, the country must announce it to the Assembly at one of its ordinary sessions. Any such change shall take effect at the beginning of the calendar year following the session.

(c) The annual contribution of each country shall be an amount in the same proportion to the total sum to be contributed to the annual budget of the Union by all countries as the number of its units is to the total of the units of all contributing countries.

(d) Contributions shall become due on the first of January of each year.

(e) A country which is in arrears in the payment of its contributions shall have no vote in any of the organs of the Union of which it is a member if the amount of its arrears equals or exceeds the amount of the contributions due from it for the preceding two full years. However, any organ of the Union may allow such a country to continue to exercise its vote in that organ if, and as long as, it is satisfied that the delay in payment is due to exceptional and unavoidable circumstances.

(f) If the budget is not adopted before the beginning of a new financial period, it shall be at the same level as the budget of the previous year, in accordance with the financial regulations.

5. The amount of the fees and charges due for services rendered by the International Bureau in relation to the Union shall be established, and shall be reported to the Assembly and the Executive Committee, by the Director General.

6. (a) The Union shall have a working capital fund which shall be constituted by a single payment made by each country of the Union. If the fund becomes insufficient, an increase shall be decided by the Assembly.

(b) The amount of the initial payment of each country to the said fund or of its participation in the increase thereof shall be a proportion of the contribution of that country for the year in which the fund is established or the increase decided.

(c) The proportion and the terms of payment shall be fixed by the Assembly on the proposal of the Director General and after it has heard the advice of the Coordination Committee of the Organization.

7. (a) In the headquarters agreement concluded with the country on the territory of which the Organization has its headquarters, it shall be provided that, whenever the working capital fund is insufficient, such country shall grant advances. The amount of these advances and the conditions on which they are granted shall be the subject of separate agreements, in each case, between such country and the Organization. As long as it remains under the obligation to grant advances, such country shall have an *ex officio* seat on the Executive Committee.

(b) The country referred to in subparagraph (a) and the Organization shall each have the right to denounce the obligation to grant advances, by written notification. Denunciation shall take effect three years after the end of the year in which it has been notified.

8. The auditing of the accounts shall be effected by one or more of the countries of the Union or by external auditors, as provided in the financial regulations. They shall be designated, with their agreement, by the Assembly.

Article 26

Amendments
[1. Provisions susceptible of amendment by the Assembly; proposals; 2. Adoption;
3. Entry into force]

1. Proposals for the amendment of Articles 22, 23, 24, 25, and the present Article, may be initiated by any country member of the Assembly, by the Executive Committee, or by the Director General. Such proposals shall be communicated by the Director General to the member countries of the Assembly at least six months in advance of their consideration by the Assembly.

2. Amendments to the Articles referred to in paragraph (1) shall be adopted by the Assembly. Adoption shall require three-fourths of the votes cast, provided that any amendment of Article 22, and of the present paragraph, shall require four-fifths of the votes cast.

3. Any amendment to the Articles referred to in paragraph (1) shall enter into force one month after written notifications of acceptance, effected in accordance with their respective constitutional processes, have been received by the Director General from three-fourths of the countries members of the Assembly at the time it adopted the amendment. Any amendment to the said Articles thus accepted shall bind all the countries which are members of the Assembly at the time the amendment enters into force, or which become members thereof at a subsequent date, provided that any amendment increasing the financial obligations of countries of the Union shall bind only those countries which have notified their acceptance of such amendment.

Article 27

Revision
[1. Objective; 2. Conferences; 3. Adoption]

1. This Convention shall be submitted to revision with a view to the introduction of amendments designed to improve the system of the Union.

2. For this purpose, conferences shall be held successively in one of the countries of the Union among the delegates of the said countries.

3. Subject to the provisions of Article 26 which apply to the amendment of Articles 22 to 26, any revision of this Act, including the Appendix, shall require the unanimity of the votes cast.

Article 28

Acceptance and Entry Into Force of Act for Countries of the Union
[1. Ratification, accession; possibility of excluding certain provisions; withdrawal of
exclusion; 2. Entry into force of Articles 1 to 21 and Appendix; 3. Entry into force of
Articles 22 to 38]

1. (a) Any country of the Union which has signed this Act may ratify it, and, if it has not signed it, may accede to it. Instruments of ratification or accession shall be deposited with the Director General.
   (b) Any country of the Union may declare in its instrument of ratification or accession that its ratification or accession shall not apply to Articles 1 to 21 and the Appendix, provided that, if such country has previously made a declaration under Article VI(1) of the Appendix, then it may declare in the said instrument only that its ratification or accession shall not apply to Articles 1 to 20.
   (c) Any country of the Union which, in accordance with subparagraph (b), has excluded provisions therein referred to from the effects of its ratification or accession may at any later time declare that it extends the effects of its ratification

or accession to those provisions. Such declaration shall be deposited with the Director General.

2. (a) Articles 1 to 21 and the Appendix shall enter into force three months after both of the following two conditions are fulfilled:
   (i) at least five countries of the Union have ratified or acceded to this Act without making a declaration under paragraph (1)(b),
   (ii) France, Spain, the United Kingdom of Great Britain and Northern Ireland, and the United States of America, have become bound by the Universal Copyright Convention as revised at Paris on July 24, 1971.
   (b) The entry into force referred to in subparagraph (a) shall apply to those countries of the Union which, at least three months before the said entry into force, have deposited instruments of ratification or accession not containing a declaration under paragraph (1)(b).
   (c) With respect to any country of the Union not covered by subparagraph (b) and which ratifies or accedes to this Act without making a declaration under paragraph (1)(b). Articles 1 to 21 and the Appendix shall enter into force three months after the date on which the Director General has notified the deposit of the relevant instrument of ratification or accession, unless a subsequent date has been indicated in the instrument deposited. In the latter case, Articles 1 to 21 and the Appendix shall enter into force with respect to that country on the date thus indicated.
   (d) The provisions of subparagraphs (a) to (c) do not affect the application of Article VI of the Appendix.

3. With respect to any country of the Union which ratifies or accedes to this Act with or without a declaration made under paragraph (1)(b), Articles 22 to 38 shall enter into force three months after the date on which the Director General has notified the deposit of the relevant instrument of ratification or accession, unless a subsequent date has been indicated in the instrument deposited. In the latter case, Articles 22 to 38 shall enter into force with respect to that country on the date thus indicated.

Article 29

Acceptance and Entry Into Force for Countries Outside the Union
[1. Accession; 2. Entry into force]

1. Any country outside the Union may accede to this Act and thereby become party to this Convention and a member of the Union. Instruments of accession shall be deposited with the Director General.

2. (a) Subject to subparagraph (b), this Convention shall enter into force with respect to any country outside the Union three months after the date on which the Director General has notified the deposit of its instrument of accession, unless a subsequent date has been indicated in the instrument deposited. In the latter case, this Convention shall enter into force with respect to that country on the date thus indicated.
   (b) If the entry into force according to subparagraph (a) precedes the entry into force of Articles 1 to 21 and the Appendix according to Article 28(2)(a), the said country shall, in the meantime, be bound, instead of by Articles 1 to 21 and the Appendix, by Articles 1 to 20 of the Brussels Act of this convention.

Article 29bis

Effect of Acceptance of Act for the Purposes of Article 14(2) of the WIPO Convention

Ratification of or accession to this Act by any country not bound by Articles 22 to 38 of the Stockholm Act of this Convention shall, for the sole purposes of Article 14(2) of the

Convention establishing the Organization, amount to ratification of or accession to the said Stockholm Act with the limitation set forth in Article 28(1)(b)(i) thereof.

Article 30

Reservations
[1. Limits of possibility of making reservations; 2. Earlier reservations; reservation as to the right of translation; withdrawal of reservation]

1. Subject to the exceptions permitted by paragraph (2) of this Article, by Article 28(1)(b), by Article 33(2), and by the Appendix, ratification or accession shall automatically entail acceptance of all the provisions and admission to all the advantages of this Convention.

2. (a) Any country of the Union ratifying or acceding to this Act may, subject to Article V(2) of the Appendix, retain the benefit of the reservations it has previously formulated on condition that it makes a declaration to that effect at the time of the deposit of its instrument of ratification or accession.

    (b) Any country outside the Union may declare, in acceding to this Convention and subject to Article V(2) of the Appendix, that it intends to substitute, temporarily at least, for Article 8 of this Act concerning the right of translation, the provisions of Article 5 of the Union Convention of 1886, as completed at Paris in 1896, on the clear understanding that the said provisions are applicable only to translations into a language in general use in the said country. Subject to Article 1(6)(b) of the Appendix, any country has the right to apply, in relation to the right of translation of works whose country of origin is a country availing itself of such a reservation, a protection which is equivalent to the protection granted by the latter country.

    (c) Any country may withdraw such reservations at any time by notification addressed to the Director General.

Article 31

Applicability to Certain Territories
[1. Declaration; 2. Withdrawal of declaration; 3. Effective date; 4. Acceptance of factual situations not implied]

1. Any country may declare in its instrument of ratification or accession, or may inform the Director General by written notification at any time thereafter, that this Convention shall be applicable to all or part of those territories, designated in the declaration or notification, for the external relations of which it is responsible.

2. Any country which has made such a declaration or given such a notification may, at any time, notify the Director General that this Convention shall cease to be applicable to all or part of such territories.

3. (a) Any declaration made under paragraph (1) shall take effect on the same date as the ratification or accession in which it was included, and any notification given under that paragraph shall take effect three months after its notification by the Director General.

    (b) Any notification given under paragraph (2) shall take effect twelve months after its receipt by the Director General.

4. This Article shall in no way be understood as implying the recognition or tacit acceptance by a country of the Union of the factual situation concerning a territory to which this Convention is made applicable by another country of the Union by virtue of a declaration under paragraph (1).

Article 32

Applicability of this Act and of Earlier Acts

[1. As between countries already members of the Union; 2. As between a country becoming a member of the Union and other countries members of the Union; 3. Applicability of the Appendix in Certain Relations]

1. This Act shall, as regards relations between the countries of the Union, and to the extent that it applies, replace the Berne Convention of September 9, 1886, and the subsequent Acts of revision. The Acts previously in force shall continue to be applicable, in their entirety or to the extent that this Act does not replace them by virtue of the preceding sentence, in relations with countries of the Union which do not ratify or accede to this Act.

2. Countries outside the Union which become party to this Act shall, subject to paragraph (3), apply it with respect to any country of the Union not bound by this Act or which, although bound by this Act, has made a declaration pursuant to Article 28(1)(b). Such countries recognize that the said country of the Union, in its relation with them:

(i)   may apply the provisions of the most recent Act by which it is bound, and

(ii) subject to Article I(6) of the Appendix, has the right to adapt the protection to the level provided for by this Act.

3. Any country which has availed itself of any of the faculties provided for in the Appendix may apply the provisions of the Appendix relating to the faculty or faculties of which it has availed itself in its relations with any other country of the Union which is not bound by this Act, provided that the latter country has accepted the application of the said provisions.

Article 33

Disputes

[1. Jurisdiction of the International Court of Justice; 2. Reservation as to such jurisdiction; 3. Withdrawal of reservation]

1. Any dispute between two or more countries of the Union concerning the interpretation or application of this Convention, not settled by negotiation, may, by any one of the countries concerned, be brought before the International Court of Justice by application in conformity with the Statute of the Court, unless the countries concerned agree on some other method of settlement. The country bringing the dispute before the Court shall inform the International Bureau; the International Bureau shall bring the matter to the attention of the other countries of the Union.

2. Each country may, at the time it signs this Act or deposits its instrument of ratification or accession, declare that it does not consider itself bound by the provisions of paragraph (1). With regard to any dispute between such country and any other country of the Union, the provisions of paragraph (1) shall not apply.

3. Any country having made a declaration in accordance with the provisions of paragraph (2) may, at any time, withdraw its declaration by notification addressed to the Director General.

Article 34

Closing of Certain Earlier Provisions

[1. Of Earlier Acts; 2. Of the Protocol to the Stockholm Act]

1. Subject to Article 29[bis], no country may ratify or accede to earlier Acts of this Convention once Articles 1 to 21 and the Appendix have entered into force.

2. Once Articles 1 to 21 and the Appendix have entered into force, no country may make a declaration under Article 5 of the Protocol Regarding Developing Countries attached to the Stockholm Act.

Article 35

Duration of the Convention; Denunciation

[1. Unlimited duration; 2. Possibility of denunciation; 3. Effective date of denunciation; 4. Moratorium on denunciation]

1. This Convention shall remain in force without limitation as to time.

2. Any country may denounce this Act by notification addressed to the Director General. Such denunciation shall constitute also denunciation of all earlier Acts and shall affect only the country making it, the Convention remaining in full force and effect as regards the other countries of the Union.

3. Denunciation shall take effect one year after the day on which the Director General has received the notification.

4. The right of denunciation provided by this Article shall not be exercised by any country before the expiration of five years from the date upon which it becomes a member of the Union.

Article 36

Application of the Convention

[1. Obligation to adopt the necessary measures; 2. Time from which obligation exists]

1. Any country party to this Convention undertakes to adopt, in accordance with its constitution, the measures necessary to ensure the application of this Convention.

2. It is understood that, at the time a country becomes bound by this Convention, it will be in a position under its domestic law to give effect to the provisions of this Convention.

Article 37

Final Clauses

[1. Languages of the Act; 2. Signature; 3. Certified copies; 4. Registration; 5. Notifications]

1. (a) This Act shall be signed in a single copy in the French and English languages and, subject to paragraph (2), shall be deposited with the Director General.

   (b) Official texts shall be established by the Director General, after consultation with the interested Governments, in the Arabic, German, Italian, Portuguese and Spanish languages, and such other languages as the Assembly may designate.

   (c) In case of differences of opinion on the interpretation of the various texts, the French text shall prevail.

2. This Act shall remain open for signature until January 31, 1972. Until that date, the copy referred to in paragraph (1)(a) shall be deposited with the Government of the French Republic.

3. The Director General shall certify and transmit two copies of the signed text of this Act to the Governments of all countries of the Union and, on request, to the Government of any other country.

4. The Director General shall register this Act with the Secretariat of the United Nations.

5. The Director General shall notify the Governments of all countries of the Union of

signatures, deposits of instruments of ratification or accession and any declarations included in such instruments or made pursuant to Articles 28(1)(c), 30(2)(a) and (b), and 33(2), entry into force of any provisions of this Act, notifications of denunciation, and notifications pursuant to Articles 30(2)(c), 31(1) and (2), 33(3), and 38(1), as well as the Appendix.

Article 38

Transitory Provisions
[1. Exercise of the "five-year privilege"; 2. Bureau of the Union, Director of the Bureau; 3. Succession of Bureau of the Union]

1. Countries of the Union which have not ratified or acceded to this Act and which are not bound by Articles 22 to 26 of the Stockholm Act of this Convention may, until April 26, 1975, exercise, if they so desire, the rights provided under the said Articles as if they were bound by them. Any country desiring to exercise such rights shall give written notification to this effect to the Director General; this notification shall be effective on the date of its receipt. Such countries shall be deemed to be members of the Assembly until the said date.

2. As long as all the countries of the Union have not become Members of the Organization, the International Bureau of the Organization shall also function as the Bureau of the Union, and the Director General as the Director of the said Bureau.

3. Once all the countries of the Union have become Members of the Organization, the rights, obligations, and property, of the Bureau of the Union shall devolve on the International Bureau of the Organization.

APPENDIX

SPECIAL PROVISIONS REGARDING DEVELOPING COUNTRIES

Article I

Faculties Open to Developing Countries
[1. Availability of certain faculties; declaration; 2. Duration of effect of declaration; 3. Cessation of developing country status; 4. Existing stocks of copies; 5. Declarations concerning certain territories; 6. Limits of reciprocity]

1. Any country regarded as a developing country in conformity with the established practice of the General Assembly of the United Nations which ratifies or accedes to this Act, of which this Appendix forms an integral part, and which, having regard to its economic situation and its social or cultural needs, does not consider itself immediately in a position to make provision for the protection of all the rights as provided for in this Act, may, by a notification deposited with the Director General at the time of depositing its instrument of ratification or accession or, subject to Article V(1)(c), at any time thereafter, declare that it will avail itself of the faculty provided for in Article II, or of the faculty provided for in Article III, or of both of those faculties. It may, instead of availing itself of the faculty provided for in Article II, make a declaration according to Article V(1)(a).

2. (a) Any declaration under paragraph (1) notified before the expiration of the period of ten years from the entry into force of Articles 1 to 21 and this Appendix according to Article 28(2) shall be effective until the expiration of the said period. Any such declaration may be renewed in whole or in part for periods of ten years each by a notification deposited with the Director General not more than fifteen months and not less than three months before the expiration of the ten-year period then running.

(b) Any declaration under paragraph (1) notified after the expiration of the period of ten years from the entry into force of Articles 1 to 21 and this Appendix according to Article 28(2) shall be effective until the expiration of the ten-year period then running. Any such declaration may be renewed as provided for in the second sentence of subparagraph (a).

3. Any country of the Union which has ceased to be regarded as a developing country as referred to in paragraph (1) shall no longer be entitled to renew its declaration as provided in paragraph (2), and, whether or not it formally withdraws its declaration, such country shall be precluded from availing itself of the faculties referred to in paragraph (1) from the expiration of the ten-year period then running or from the expiration of a period of three years after it has ceased to be regarded as a developing country, whichever period expires later.

4. Where, at the time when the declaration made under paragraph (1) or (2) ceases to be effective, there are copies in stock which were made under a license granted by virtue of this Appendix, such copies may continue to be distributed until their stock is exhausted.

5. Any country which is bound by the provisions of this Act and which has deposited a declaration or a notification in accordance with Article 31(1) with respect to the application of this Act to a particular territory, the situation of which can be regarded as analogous to that of the countries referred to in paragraph (1), may, in respect of such territory, make the declaration referred to in paragraph (1) and the notification of renewal referred to in paragraph (2). As long as such declaration or notification remains in effect, the provisions of this Appendix shall be applicable to the territory in respect of which it was made.

6. (a) The fact that a country avails itself of any of the faculties referred to in paragraph (1) does not permit another country to give less protection to works of which the country of origin is the former country than it is obliged to grant under Articles 1 to 20.

(b) The right to apply reciprocal treatment provided for in Article 30(2)(b), second sentence, shall not, until the date on which the period applicable under Article I(3) expires, be exercised in respect of works the country of origin of which is a country which has made a declaration according to Article V(1)(a).

Article II

Limitations on the Right of Translation

[1. Licenses grantable by competent authority; 2. to 4. Conditions allowing the grant of such licenses; 5. Purposes for which licenses may be granted; 6. Termination of licenses; 7. Works composed mainly of illustrations; 8. Works withdrawn from circulation; 9. Licenses for broadcasting organizations]

1. Any country which has declared that it will avail itself of the faculty provided for in this Article shall be entitled, so far as works published in printed or analogous forms of reproduction are concerned, to substitute for the exclusive right of translation provided for in Article 8 a system of non-exclusive and non-transferable licenses, granted by the competent authority under the following conditions and subject to Article IV

2. (a) Subject to paragraph (3), if, after the expiration of a period of three years, or of any longer period determined by the national legislation of the said country, commencing on the date of the first publication of the work, a translation of such work has not been published in a language in general use in that country by the owner of the right of translation, or with his authorization, any national of such country may obtain a license to make a translation of the work in the said language and publish the translation in printed or analogous forms of reproduction.

(b) A license under the conditions provided for in this Article may also be granted if all the editions of the translation published in the language concerned are out of print.

3. (a) In the case of translations into a language which is not in general use in one or more developed countries which are members of the Union, a period of one year shall be substituted for the period of three years referred to in paragraph (2)(a).

   (b) Any country referred to in paragraph (1) may, with the unanimous agreement of the developed countries which are members of the Union and in which the same language is in general use, substitute, in the case of translations into that language, for the period of three years referred to in paragraph (2)(a) a shorter period as determined by such agreement but not less than one year. However, the provisions of the foregoing sentence shall not apply where the language in question is English, French or Spanish. The Director General shall be notified of any such agreement by the Governments which have concluded it.

4. (a) No license obtainable after three years shall be granted under this Article until a further period of six months has elapsed, and no license obtainable after one year shall be granted under this Article until a further period of nine months has elapsed

   (i) from the date on which the applicant complies with the requirements mentioned in Article IV(1), or

   (ii) where the identity or the address of the owner of the right of translation is unknown, from the date on which the applicant sends, as provided for in Article IV(2), copies of his application submitted to the authority competent to grant the license.

   (b) If, during the said period of six or nine months, a translation in the language in respect of which the application was made is published by the owner of the right of translation or with his authorization, no license under this Article shall be granted.

5. Any license under this Article shall be granted only for the purpose of teaching, scholarship or research.

6. If a translation of a work is published by the owner of the right of translation or with his authorization at a price reasonably related to that normally charged in the country for comparable works, any license granted under this Article shall terminate if such translation is in the same language and with substantially the same content as the translation published under the license. Any copies already made before the license terminates may continue to be distributed until their stock is exhausted.

7. For works which are composed mainly of illustrations, a license to make and publish a translation of the text and to reproduce and publish the illustrations may be granted only if the conditions of Article III are also fulfilled.

8. No license shall be granted under this Article when the author has withdrawn from circulation all copies of his work.

9. (a) A license to make a translation of a work which has been published in printed or analogous forms of reproduction may also be granted to any broadcasting organization having its headquarters in a country referred to in paragraph (1), upon an application made to the competent authority of that country by the said organization, provided that all of the following conditions are met:

   (i) the translation is made from a copy made and acquired in accordance with the laws of the said country;

   (ii) the translation is only for use in broadcasts intended exclusively for teaching or for the dissemination of the results of specialized technical or scientific research to experts in a particular profession;

   (iii) the translation is used exclusively for the purposes referred to in condition (ii) through broadcasts made lawfully and intended for recipients on the territory of the said country, including broadcasts made through the medium of sound or visual recordings lawfully and exclusively made for the purpose of such broadcasts;

   (iv) all uses made of the translation are without any commercial purpose.

(b) Sound or visual recordings of a translation which was made by a broadcasting organization under a license granted by virtue of this paragraph may, for the purposes and subject to the conditions referred to in subparagraph (a) and with the agreement of that organization, also be used by any other broadcasting organization having its headquarters in the country whose competent authority granted the license in question.

(c) Provided that all of the criteria and conditions set out in subparagraph (a) are met, a license may also be granted to a broadcasting orgasnization to translate any text incorporated in an audio-visual fixation where such fixation was itself prepared and published for the sole purpose of being used in connection with systematic instructional activities.

(d) Subject to subparagraphs (a) to (c), the provisions of the preceding paragraphs shall apply to the grant and exercise of any license granted under this paragraph.

Article III

Limitation on the Right of Reproduction

[1. Licenses grantable by competent authority; 2. to 5. Conditions allowing the grant of such licenses; 6. Termination of licenses; 7. Works to which this Article applies]

1. Any country which has declared that it will avail itself of the faculty provided for in this Article shall be entitled to substitute for the exclusive right of reproduction provided for in Article 9 a system of non-exclusive and non-transferable licenses, granted by the competent authority under the following conditions and subject to Article IV.

2. (a) If, in relation to a work to which this Article applies by virtue of paragraph (7), after the expiration of

  (i) the relevant period specified in paragraph (3), commencing on the date of first publication of a particular edition of the work, or

  (ii) any longer period determined by national legislation of the country referred to in paragraph (1), commencing on the same date, copies of such edition have not been distributed in that country to the general public or in connection with systematic instructional activities, by the owner of the right of reproduction or with his authorization, at a price reasonably related to that normally charged in the country for comparable works, any national of such country may obtain a license to reproduce and publish such edition at that or a lower price for use in connection with systematic instructional activities.

  (b) A license to reproduce and publish an edition which has been distributed as described in subparagraph (a) may also be granted under the conditions provided for in this Article if, after the expiration of the applicable period, no authorized copies of that edition have been on sale for a period of six months in the country concerned to the general public or in connection with systematic instructional activities at a price reasonably related to that normally charged in the country for comparable works.

3. The period referred to in paragraph (2)(a)(i) shall be five years, except that

  (i) for works of the natural and physical sciences, including mathematics, and of technology, the period shall be three years;

  (ii) for works of fiction, poetry, drama and music, and for art books, the period shall be seven years.

4. (a) No license obtainable after three years shall be granted under this Article until a period of six months has elapsed

  (i) from the date on which the applicant complies with the requirements mentioned in Article IV(1), or

(ii) where the identity or the address of the owner of the right of reproduction is unknown, from the date on which the applicant sends, as provided for in Article IV(2), copies of his application submitted to the authority competent to grant the license.

(b) Where licenses are obtainable after other periods and Article IV(2) is applicable, no license shall be granted until a period of three months has elapsed from the date of the dispatch of the copies of the application.

(c) If, during the period of six or three months referred to in subparagraphs (a) and (b), a distribution as described in paragraph (2)(a) has taken place, no license shall be granted under this Article.

(d) No license shall be granted if the author has withdrawn from circulation all copies of the edition for the reproduction and publication of which the license has been applied for.

5. A license to reproduce and publish a translation of a work shall not be granted under this Article in the following cases:

(i) where the translation was not published by the owner of the right of translation or with his authorization, or

(ii) where the translation is not in a language in general use in the country in which the license is applied for.

6. If copies of an edition of a work are distributed in the country referred to in paragraph (1) to the general public or in connection with systematic instructional activities, by the owner of the right of reproduction or with his authorization, at a price reasonably related to that normally charged in the country for comparable works, any license granted under this Article shall terminate if such edition is in the same language and with substantially the same content as the edition which was published under the said license. Any copies already made before the license terminates may continue to be distributed until their stock is exhausted.

7. (a) Subject to subparagraph (b), the works to which this Article applies shall be limited to works published in printed or analogous forms of reproduction.

(b) This Article shall also apply to the reproduction in audio-visual form of lawfully made audio-visual fixations including any protected works incorporated therein and to the translation of any incorporated text into a language in general use in the country in which the license is applied for, always provided that the audio-visual fixations in question were prepared and published for the sole purpose of being used in connection with systematic instructional activities.

Article IV

Provisions Common to Licenses Under Articles II and III
[1. and 2. Procedure; 3. Indication of author and title of work; 4. Exportation of copies; 5. Notice; 6. Compensation]

1. A license under Article II or Article III may be granted only if the applicant, in accordance with the procedure of the country concerned, establishes either that he has requested, and has been denied, authorization by the owner of the right to make and publish the translation or to reproduce and publish the edition, as the case may be, or that, after due diligence on his part, he was unable to find the owner of the right. At the same time as making the request, the applicant shall inform any national or international information center referred to in paragraph (2).

2. If the owner of the right cannot be found, the applicant for a license shall send, by registered airmail, copies of his application, submitted to the authority competent to grant the license, to the publisher whose name appears on the work and to any national or international information center which may have been designated, in a notification to that effect deposited with the Director General, by the Government of the country in which the publisher is believed to have his principal place of business.

3. The name of the author shall be indicated on all copies of the translation or reproduction published under a license granted under Article II or Article III. The title of the work shall appear on all such copies. In the case of a translation, the original title of the work shall appear in any case on all the said copies.

4. (a) No license granted under Article II or Article III shall extend to the export of copies, and any such license shall be valid only for publication of the translation or of the reproduction, as the case may be, in the territory of the country in which it has been applied for.

   (b) For the purposes of subparagraph (a), the notion of export shall include the sending of copies from any territory to the country which, in respect of that territory, has made a declaration under Article I(5).

   (c) Where a governmental or other public entity of a country which has granted a license to make a translation under Article II into a language other than English, French or Spanish sends copies of a translation published under such license to another country, such sending of copies shall not, for the purposes of subparagraph (a), be considered to constitute export if all of the following conditions are met:

       (i)   the recipients are individuals who are nationals of the country whose competent authority has granted the license, or organizations grouping such individuals;

       (ii) the copies are to be used only for the purpose of teaching, scholarship or research;

       (iii) the sending of copies and their subsequent distribution to recipients is without any commercial purpose; and

       (iv) the country to which the copies have been sent has agreed with the country whose competent authority has granted the license to allow the receipt, or distribution, or both, and the Director General has been notified of the agreement by the Government of the country in which the license has been granted.

5. All copies published under a license granted by virtue of Article II or Article III shall bear a notice in the appropriate language stating that the copies are available for distribution only in the country or territory to which the said license applies.

6. (a) Due provision shall be made at the national level to ensure

       (i)   that the license provides, in favour of the owner of the right of translation or of reproduction, as the case may be, for just compensation that is consistent with standards of royalties normally operating on licenses freely negotiated between persons in the two countries concerned, and

       (ii) payment and transmittal of the compensation: should national currency regulations intervene, the competent authority shall make all efforts, by the use of international machinery, to ensure transmittal in internationally convertible currency or its equivalent.

   (b) Due provision shall be made by national legislation to ensure a correct translation of the work, or an accurate reproduction of the particular edition, as the case may be.

Article V

Alternative Possibility for Limitation of the Right of Translation

[1. Regime provided for under the 1886 and 1896 Acts; 2. No possibility of change to regime under Article II; 3. Time limit for choosing the alternative possibility]

1. (a) Any country entitled to make a declaration that it will avail itself of the faculty provided for in Article II may, instead, at the time of ratifying or acceding to this Act:

  (i) if it is a country to which Article 30(2)(a) applies, make a declaration under that provision as far as the right of translation is concerned;
  (ii) if it is a country to which Article 30(2)(a) does not apply, and even if it is not a country outside the Union, make a declaration as provided for in Article 30(2)(b), first sentence.
(b) In the case of a country which ceases to be regarded as a developing country as referred to in Article I(1), a declaration made according to this paragraph shall be effective until the date on which the period applicable under Article I(3) expires.
(c) Any country which has made a declaration according to this paragraph may not subsequently avail itself on the faculty provided for in Article II even if it withdraws the said declaration.

2. Subject to paragraph (3), any country which has availed itself of the faculty provided for in Article II may not subsequently make a declaration according to paragraph (1).

3. Any country which has ceased to be regarded as a developing country as referred to in Article I(1) may, not later than two years prior to the expiration of the period applicable under Article I(3), make a declaration to the effect provided for in Article 30(2)(b), first sentence, notwithstanding the fact that it is not a country outside the Union. Such declaration shall take effect at the date on which the period applicable under Article I(3) expires.

Article VI

Possibilities of applying, or admitting the application of, certain provisions of the Appendix before becoming bound by it
[1. Declaration; 2. Depository and effective date of declaration]

1. Any country of the Union may declare, as from the date of this Act, and at any time before becoming bound by Articles 1 to 21 and this Appendix:

  (i) if it is a country which, were it bound by Articles 1 to 21 and this Appendix, would be entitled to avail itself of the faculties referred to in Article I(1), that it will apply the provisions of Article II or of Article III or of both to works whose country or origin is a country which, pursuant to (ii) below, admits the application of those Articles to such works, or which is bound by Articles 1 to 21 and this Appendix; such declaration may, instead of referring to Article II, refer to Article V;
  (ii) that it admits the application of this Appendix to works of which it is the country of origin by countries which have made a declaration under (i) above or a notification under Article I.

2. Any declaration made under paragraph (1) shall be in writing and shall be deposited with the Director General. The declaration shall become effective from the date of its deposit.

UNIVERSAL COPYRIGHT CONVENTION AS REVISED AT PARIS ON 24 JULY 1971

THE CONTRACTING STATES,

Moved by the desire to ensure in all countries copyright protection of literary, scientific and artistic works,

Convinced that a system of copyright protection appropriate to all nations of the world and expressed in a universal convention, additional to, and without impairing international systems already in force, will ensure respect for the rights of the individual and encourage the development of literature, the sciences and the arts,

Persuaded that such a universal copyright system will facilitate a wider dissemination of works of the human mind and increase international understanding,

Have resolved to revise the Universal Copyright Convention as signed at Geneva on 6 September 1952 (hereinafter called "the 1952 Convention"), and consequently,

HAVE AGREED AS FOLLOWS:

Article I

Each Contracting State undertakes to provide for the adequate and effective protection of the rights of authors and other copyright proprietors in literary, scientific and artistic works, including writings, musical, dramatic and cinematographic works, and paintings, engravings and sculpture.

Article II

1. Published works of nationals of any Contracting State and works first published in that State shall enjoy in each other Contracting State the same protection as that other State accords to works of its nationals first published in its own territory, as well as the protection specially granted by this Convention.

2. Unpublished works of nationals of each Contracting State shall enjoy in each other Contracting State the same protection as that other State accords to unpublished works of its own nationals, as well as the protection specially granted by this Convention.

3. For the purpose of this Convention any Contracting State may, by domestic legislation, assimilate to its own nationals any person domiciled in that State.

Article III

1. Any Contracting State which, under its domestic law, requires as a condition of copyright, compliance with formalities such as deposit, registration, notice, notarial certificates, payment of fees or manufacture or publication in that Contracting State, shall regard these requirements as satisfied with respect to all works protected in accordance with this Convention and first published outside its territory and the author of which is not one of its nationals, if from the time of the first publication all the copies of the work published with the authority of the author or other copyright proprietor bear the symbol © accompanied by

the name of the copyright proprietor and the year of first publication placed in such manner and location as to give reasonable notice of claim of copyright.

2. The provisions of paragraph 1 shall not preclude any Contracting State from requiring formalities or other conditions for the acquisition and enjoyment of copyright in respect of works first published in its territory or works of its nationals wherever published.

3. The provisions of paragraph 1 shall not preclude any Contracting State from providing that a person seeking judicial relief must, in bringing the action, comply with procedural requirements, such as that the complainant must appear through domestic counsel or that the complainant must deposit with the court or an administrative office, or both, a copy of the work involved in the litigation; provided that failure to comply with such requirements shall not affect the validity of the copyright, nor shall any such requirement be imposed upon a national of another Contracting State if such requirement is not imposed on nationals of the State in which protection is claimed.

4. In each Contracting State there shall be legal means of protecting without formalities the unpublished works of nationals of other Contracting States.

5. If a Contracting State grants protection for more than one term of copyright and the first term is for a period longer than one of the minimum periods prescribed in Article IV, such State shall not be required to comply with the provisions of paragraph 1 of this Article in respect of the second or any subsequent term of copyright.

Article IV

1. The duration of protection of a work shall be governed, in accordance with the provisions of Article II and this Article, by the law of the Contracting State in which protection is claimed.

2. (a) The term of protection for works protected under this Convention shall not be less than the life of the author and twenty-five years after his death. However, any Contracting State which, on the effective date of this Convention in that State, has limited this term for certain classes of works to a period computed from the first publication of the work, shall be entitled to maintain these exceptions and to extend them to other classes of works. For all these classes the term of protection shall not be less than twenty-five years from the date of first publication.

(b) Any Contracting State which, upon the effective date of this Convention in that State, does not compute the term of protection upon the basis of the life of the author, shall be entitled to compute the term of protection from the date of the first publication of the work or from its registration prior to publication, as the case may be, provided the term of protection shall not be less than twenty-five years from the date of first publication or from its registration prior to publication, as the case may be.

(c) If the legislation of a Contracting State grants two or more successive terms of protection, the duration of the first term shall not be less than one of the minimum periods specified in sub-paragraphs (a) and (b).

3. The provisions of paragraph 2 shall not apply to photographic works or to works of applied art; provided, however, that the term of protection in those Contracting States which protect photographic works, or works of applied art in so far as they are protected as artistic works, shall not be less than ten years for each of said classes of works.

4. (a) No Contracting State shall be obliged to grant protection to a work for a period longer than that fixed for the class of works to which the work in question belongs, in the case of unpublished works by the law of the Contracting State of which the author is a national, and in the case of published works by the law of the Contracting State in which the work has been first published.

(b) For the purposes of the application of sub-paragraph (a), if the law of any Contracting State grants two or more successive terms of protection, the period of protection of that State shall be considered to be the aggregate of those terms. However, if a specified work is not protected by such State during the second or any subsequent term for any reason, the other Contracting States shall not be obliged to protect it during the second or any subsequent term.

5. For the purposes of the application of paragraph 4, the work of a national of a Contracting State, first published in a non-Contracting State, shall be treated as though first published in the Contracting State of which the author is a national.

6. For the purposes of the application of paragraph 4, in case of simultaneous publication in two or more Contracting States, the work shall be treated as though first published in the State which affords the shortest term; any work published in two or more Contracting States within thirty days of its first publication shall be considered as having been published simultaneously in said Contracting States.

Article IVbis

1. The rights referred to in Article I shall include the basic rights ensuring the author's economic interests, including the exclusive right to authorize reproduction by any means, public performance and broadcasting. The provisions of this article shall extend to works protected under this Convention either in their original form or in any form recognizably derived from the original.

2. However, any Contracting State may, by its domestic legislation, make exceptions that do not conflict with the spirit and provisions of this Convention, to the rights mentioned in paragraph 1 of this Article. Any State whose legislation so provides, shall nevertheless accord a reasonable degree of effective protection to each of the rights to which exception has been made.

Article V

1. The rights referred to in Article I shall include the exclusive right of the author to make, publish and authorize the making and publication of translations of works protected under this Convention.

2. However, any Contracting State may, by its domestic legislation, restrict the right of translation of writings, but only subject to the following provisions:

(a) If after the expiration of a period of seven years from the date of the first publication of a writing, a translation of such writing has not been published in a language in general use in the Contracting State, by the owner of the right of translation or with his authorization, any national of such Contracting State may obtain a non-exclusive licence from the competent authority thereof to translate the work into that language and publish the work so translated.

(b) Such national shall in accordance with the procedure of the State concerned, establish either that he has requested, and been denied, authorization by the proprietor of the right to make and publish the translation, or that, after due diligence on his part, he was unable to find the owner of the right. A licence may also be granted on the same conditions if all previous editions of a translation in a language in general use in the Contracting State are out of print.

(c) If the owner of the right of translation cannot be found, then the applicant for a licence shall send copies of his application to the publisher whose name appears on the work and, if the nationality of the owner of the right of translation is known, to the diplomatic or consular representative of the State of which such owner is a national, or to the organization which may have been designated by the government of that State. The licence shall not be granted before the expiration of a period of two months from the date of the dispatch of the copies of the application.

(d) Due provision shall be made by domestic legislation to ensure to the owner of the right of translation a compensation which is just and conforms to international standards, to ensure payment and transmittal of such compensation, and to ensure a correct translation of the work.

(e) The original title and the name of the author of the work shall be printed on all copies of the published translation. The licence shall be valid only for publication of the translation in the territory of the Contracting State where it has been applied for. Copies so published may be imported and sold in another Contracting State if a language in general use in such other State is the same language as that into which the work has been so translated, and if the domestic law in such other State makes provision for such licences and does not prohibit such importation and sale. Where the foregoing conditions do not exist, the importation and sale of such copies in a Contracting State shall be governed by its domestic law and its agreements. The licence shall not be transferred by the licensee.

(f) The licence shall not be granted when the author has withdrawn from circulation all copies of the work.

Article Vbis

1. Any Contracting State regarded as a developing country in conformity with the established practice of the General Assembly of the United Nations may, by a notification deposited with the Director-General of the United Nations Educational, Scientific and Cultural Organization (hereinafter called "the Director-General") at the time of its ratification, acceptance or accession or thereafter, avail itself of any or all of the exceptions provided for in Articles Vter and Vquater.

2. Any such notification shall be effective for ten years from the date of coming into force of this Convention, or for such part of that ten-year period as remains at the date of deposit of the notification, and may be renewed in whole or in part for further periods of ten years each if, not more than fifteen or less than three months before the expiration of the relevant ten-year period, the Contracting State deposits a further notification with the Director-General. Initial notifications may also be made during these further periods of ten years in accordance with the provisions of this Article.

3. Notwithstanding the provisions of paragraph 2, a Contracting State that has ceased to be regarded as a developing country as referred to in pargraph 1 shall no longer be entitled to renew its notification made under the provisions of paragraph 1 or 2, and whether or not it formally withdraws the notification such State shall be precluded from availing itself of the exceptions provided for in Articles Vter and Vquater at the end of the current ten-year period, or at the end of three years after it has ceased to be regarded as a developing country, whichever period expires later.

4. Any copies of a work already made under the exceptions provided for in Articles Vter and Vquater may continue to be distributed after the expiration of the period for which notifications under this Article were effective until their stock is exhausted.

5. Any Contracting State that has deposited a notification in accordance with Article XIII with respect to the application of this Convention to a particular country or territory, the situation of which can be regarded as analogous to that of the States referred to in paragraph 1 of this Article, may also deposit notifications and renew them in accordance with the provisions of this Article with respect to any such country or territory. During the effective period of such notifications, the provisions of Articles Vter and Vquater may be applied with respect to such country or territory. The sending of copies from the country or territory to the Contracting State shall be considered as export within the meaning of Articles Vter and Vquater.

Article Vter

1. (a) Any Contracting State to which Article Vbis (1) applies may substitute for the period of seven years provided for in Article V (2) a period of three years or any longer period prescribed by its legislation. However, in the case of a translation into

a language not in general use in one or more developed countries that are party to this Convention or only the 1952 Convention, the period shall be one year instead of three.

(b) A Contracting State to which Article V*bis* (1) applies may, with the unanimous agreement of the developed countries party to this Convention or only the 1952 Convention and in which the same language is in general use, substitute, in the case of translation into that language, for the period of three years provided for in sub-paragraph (a) another period as determined by such agreement but not not shorter than one year. However, this sub-paragraph shall not apply where the language in question is English, French or Spanish. Notification of any such agreement shall be made to the Director-General.

(c) The licence may only be granted if the applicant, in accordance with the procedure of the State concerned, establishes either that he has requested, and been denied, authorization by the owner of the right of translation, or that, after due diligence on his part, he was unable to find the owner of the right. At the same time as he makes his request he shall inform either the International Copyright Information Centre established by the United Nations Educational, Scientific and Cultural Organization or any national or regional information centre which may have been designated in a notification to that effect deposited with the Director-General by the government of the State in which the publisher is believed to have his principal place of business.

(d) If the owner of the right of translation cannot be found, the applicant for a licence shall send, by registered airmail, copies of his application to the publisher whose name appears on the work and to any national or regional information centre as mentioned in sub-paragraph (c). If no such centre is notified he shall also send a copy to the international copyright information centre established by the United Nations Educational, Scientific and Cultural Organization.

2. (a) Licences obtainable after three years shall not be granted under this Article until a further period of six months has elapsed and licences obtainable after one year until a further period of nine months has elapsed. The further period shall begin either from the date of the request for permission to translate mentioned in paragraph 1 (c) or, if the identity or address of the owner of the right of translation is not known, from the date of dispatch of the copies of the application for a licence mentioned in paragraph 1 (d).

(b) Licences shall not be granted if a translation has been published by the owner of the right of translation or with his authorization during the said period of six or nine months.

3. Any licence under this Article shall be granted only for the purpose of teaching, scholarship or research.

4. (a) Any licence granted under this Article shall not extend to the export of copies and shall be valid only for publication in the territory of the Contracting State where it has been applied for.

(b) Any copy published in accordance with a licence granted under this Article shall bear a notice in the appropriate language stating that the copy is available for distribution only in the Contracting State granting the licence. If the writing bears the notice specified in Article III (1) the copies shall bear the same notice.

(c) The prohibition of export provided for in sub-paragraph (a) shall not apply where a governmental or other public entity of a State which has granted a licence under this Article to translate a work into a language other than English, French or Spanish sends copies of a translation prepared under such licence to another country if:

(i) the recipients are individuals who are nationals of the Contracting State granting the licence, or organizations grouping such individuals;

(ii) the copies are to be used only for the purpose of teaching, scholarship or research;

(iii) the sending of the copies and their subsequent distribution to recipients is without the object of commercial purpose; and

(iv) the country to which the copies have been sent has agreed with the Contracting State to allow the receipt, distribution or both and the Director-General has been notified of such agreement by any one of the governments which have concluded it.

5. Due provision shall be made at the national level to ensure:

(a) that the licence provides for just compensation that is consistent with standards of royalties normally operating in the case of licences freely negotiated between persons in the two countries concerned; and

(b) payment and transmittal of the compensation; however, should national currency regulations intervene, the competent authority shall make all efforts, by the use of international machinery, to ensure transmittal in internationally convertible currency or its equivalent.

6. Any licence granted by a Contracting State under this Article shall terminate if a translation of the work in the same language with subtantially the same content as the edition in respect of which the licence as granted is published in the said State by the owner of the right of translation or with his authorization, at a price reasonably related to that normally charged in the same State for comparable works. Any copies already made before the licence is terminated may continue to be distributed until their stock is exhausted.

7. For works which are composed mainly of illlustrations a licence to translate the text and to reproduce the illustrations may be granted only if the conditions of Article V*quater* are also fulfilled.

8. (a) A licence to translate a work protected under this Convention, published in printed or analogous forms of reproduction, may also be granted to a broadcasting organization having its headquarters in a Contracting State to which Article V*bis*(1) applies, upon an application made in that State by the said organization under the following conditions:

  (i) the translation is made from a copy made and acquired in accordance with the laws of the Contracting State;

  (ii) the translation is for use only in broadcasts intended exclusively for teaching or for the dissemination of the results of specialized technical or scientific research to experts in a particular profession;

  (iii) the translation is used exclusively for the purposes set out in condition (ii), through broadcasts lawfully made which are intended for recipients on the territory of the Contracting State, including broadcasts made through the medium of sound or visual recordings lawfully and exclusively made for the purpose of such broadcasts;

  (iv) sound or visual recordings of the translation may be exchanged only between broadcasting organizations having their headquarters in the Contracting State granting the licence; and

  (v) all uses made of the translation are without any commercial purpose.

(b) Provided all of the criteria and conditions set out in sub-paragraph (a) are met, a licence may also be granted to a broadcasting organization to translate any text incorporated in an audio-visual fixation which was itself prepared and published for the sole purpose of being used in connexion with systematic instructional activities.

(c) Subject to sub-paragraphs (a) and (b), the other provisions of this Article shall apply to the grant and exercise of the licence.

9. Subject to the provisions of this Article, any licence granted under this Article shall be governed by the provisions of Article V, and shall continue to be governed by the provisions of Article V and of this Article, even after the seven-year period provided for in Article V (2) has expired. However, after the said period has expired, the licensee shall be free to request that the said licence be replaced by a new licence governed exclusively by the provisions of Article V.

Article Vquater

1. Any Contracting State to which Article Vbis (1) applies may adopt the following provisions:

(a) If, after the expiration of (i) the relevant period specified in sub-paragraph (c) commencing from the date of first publication of a particular edition of a literary, scientific or artistic work referred to in paragraph 3, or (ii) any longer period determined by national legislation of the State, copies of such edition have not been distributed in that State to the general public or in connexion with systematic instructional activities at a price reasonably related to that normally charged in the State for comparable works, by the owner of the right of reproduction or with his authorization, any national of such State may obtain a non-exclusive licence from the competent authority to publish such edition at that or a lower price for use in connexion with systematic instructional activities. The licence may only be granted if such national, in accordance with the procedure of the State concerned establishes either that he has requested, and been denied, authorization by the proprietor of the right to publish such work, or that, after due diligence on his part he was unable to find the owner of the right. At the same time as he makes his request he shall inform either the international copyright information centre established by the United Nations Educational, Scientific and Cultural Organization or any national or regional information centre referred to in sub-paragraph (d).

(b) A licence may also be granted on the same conditions if, for a period of six months, no authorized copies of the edition in question have been on sale in the State concerned to the general public or in connexion with systematic instructional activities at a price reasonably related to that normally charged in the State for comparable works.

(c) The period referred to in sub-paragraph (a) shall be five years except that:
  (i) for works of the natural and physical sciences, including mathematics, and of technology, the period shall be three years;
  (ii) for works of fiction, poetry, drama and music, and for art books, the period shall be seven years.

(d) If the owner of the right of reproduction cannot be found, the applicant for a licence shall send, by registered air mail, copies of his application to the publisher whose name appears on the work and to any national or regional information centre identified as such in a notification deposited with the Director-General by the State in which the publisher is believed to have his principal place of business. In the absence of any such notification, he shall also send a copy to the international copyright information centre established by the United Nations Educational, Scientific and Cultural Organization. The licence shall not be granted before the expiration of a period of three months from the date of dispatch of the copies of the application.

(e) Licences obtainable after three years shall not be granted under this Article:
  (i) until a period of six months has elapsed from the date of the request for permission referred to in sub-paragraph (a) or, if the identity or address of the owner of the right of reproduction is unknown, from the date of the dispatch of the copies of the application for a licence referred to in sub-paragraph (d);

(ii) if any such distribution of copies of the edition as is mentioned in sub-paragraph (a) has taken place during that period.

(f) The name of the author and the title of the particular edition of the work shall be printed on all copies of the published reproduction. The licence shall not extend to the export of copies and shall be valid only for publication in the territory of the Contracting State where it has been applied for. The licence shall not be transferable by the licensee.

(g) Due provision shall be made by domestic legislation to ensure an accurate reproduction of the particular edition in question.

(h) A licence to reproduce and publish a translation of a work shall not be granted under this Article in the following cases:

(i) where the translation was not published by the owner of the right of translation or with his authorization:

(ii) where the translation is not in a language in general use in the State with power to grant the licence.

2. The exceptions provided for in paragraph 1 are subject to the following additional provisions:

(a) Any copy published in accordance with a licence granted under this Article shall bear a notice in the appropriate language stating that the copy is available for distribution only in the Contracting State to which the said licence applies. If the edition bears the notice specified in Article III (1), the copies shall bear the same notice.

(b) Due provision shall be made at the national level to ensure:

(i) that the licence provides for just compensation that is consistent with standards of royalties normally operating in the case of licences freely negotiated between persons in the two countries concerned; and

(ii) payment and transmittal of the compensation; however, should national currency regulations intervene, the competent authority shall make all efforts, by the use of international machinery, to ensure transmittal in internationally convertible currency or its equivalent.

(c) Whenever copies of an edition of a work are distributed in the Contracting State to the general public or in connexion with systematic instructional activities, by the owner of the right of reproduction or with his authorization, at a price reasonably related to that normally charged in the State for comparable works, any licence granted under this Article shall terminate if such edition is in the same language and is substantially the same in content as the edition published under the licence. Any copies already made before the licence is terminated may continue to be distributed until their stock is exhausted.

(d) No licence shall be granted when the author has withdrawn from circulation all copies of the edition in question.

3. (a) Subject to sub-paragraph (b) the literary, scientific or artistic works to which this Article applies shall be limited to works published in printed or analogous forms of reproduction.

(b) The provisions of this Article shall also apply to reproduction in audio-visual form of lawfully made audio-visual fixations including any protected works incorporated therein and to the translation of any incorporated text into a language in general use in the State with power to grant the licence; always provided that the audio-visual fixations in question were prepared and published for the sole purpose of being used in connexion with systematic instructional activities.

Article VI

"Publication", as used in this Convention, means the reproduction in tangible form and the general distribution to the public of copies of a work from which it can be read or otherwise visually perceived.

Article VII

This Convention shall not apply to works or rights in works which, at the effective date of this Convention in a Contracting State where protection is claimed, are permanently in the public domain in the said Contracting State.

Article VIII

1. This Convention, which shall bear the date of 24 July 1971, shall be deposited with the Director-General and shall remain open for signature by all States party to the 1952 Convention for a period of 120 days after the date of this Convention. It shall be subject to ratification or acceptance by the signatory States.

2. Any State which has not signed this Convention may accede thereto.

3. Ratification, acceptance or accession shall be effected by the deposit of an instrument to that effect with the Director-General.

Article IX

1. This Convention shall come into force three months after the deposit of twelve instruments of ratification, acceptance or accession.

2. Subsequently, this Convention shall come into force in respect of each State three months after that State has deposited its instrument of ratification, acceptance or accession.

3. Accession to this Convention by a State not party to the 1952 Convention shall also constitute accession to that Convention; however, if its instrument of accession is deposited before this Convention comes into force, such State may make its accession to the 1952 Convention conditional upon the coming into force of this Convention. After the coming into force of this Convention, no State may accede solely to the 1952 Convention.

4. Relations between States party to this Convention and States that are party only to the 1952 Convention, shall be governed by the 1952 Convention. However, any State party only to the 1952 Convention may, by a notification deposited with the Director-General, declare that it will admit the application of the 1971 Convention to works of its nationals or works first published in its territory by all States party to this Convention.

Article X

1. Each Contracting State undertakes to adopt, in accordance with its Constitution, such measures as are necessary to ensure the application of this Convention.

2. It is understood that at the date this Convention comes into force in respect of any State, that State must be in a position under its domestic law to give effect to the terms of this Convention.

Article XI

1. An Intergovernmental Committee is hereby established with the following duties:

(a) to study the problems concerning the application and operation of the Universal Copyright Convention;
(b) to make preparation for periodic revisions of this Convention;
(c) to study any other problems concerning the international protection of copyright, in co-operation with the various interested international organizations, such as the United Nations Educational, Scientific and Cultural Organization, the International Union for the Protection of Literary and Artistic Works and the Organization of American States;

(d)   to inform States party to the Universal Copyright Convention as to its activities.

2. The Committee shall consist of the representatives of eighteen States party to this Convention or only to the 1952 Convention.

3. The Committee shall be selected with due consideration to a fair balance of national interests on the basis of geographical location, population, languages and stage of development.

4. The Director-General of the United Nations Educational, Scientific and Cultural Organization, the Director-General of the World Intellectual Property Organization and the Secretary-General of the Organization of American States, or their representatives, may attend meetings of the Committee in an advisory capacity.

Article XII

The Intergovernmental Committee shall convene a conference for revision whenever it deems necessary, or at the request of at least ten States party to this Convention.

Article XIII

1. Any Contracting State may, at the time of deposit of its instrument of ratification, acceptance or accession, or at any time thereafter, declare by notification addressed to the Director-General that this Convention shall apply to all or any of the countries or territories for the international relations of which it is responsible and this Convention shall thereupon apply to the countries or territories named in such notification after the expiration of the term of three months provided for in Article IX. In the absence of such notification, this Convention shall not apply to any such country or territory.

2. However, nothing in this Article shall be understood as implying the recognition or tacit acceptance by a Contracting State of the factual situation concerning a country or territory to which this Convention is made applicable by another Contracting State in accordance with the provisions of this Article.

Article XIV

1. Any Contracting State may denounce this Convention in its own name or on behalf of all or any of the countries or territories with respect to which a notification has been given under Article XIII. The denunciation shall be made by notification addressed to the Director-General. Such denunciation shall also constitute denunciation of the 1952 Convention.

2. Such denunciation shall operate only in respect of the State or of the country or territory on whose behalf it was made and shall not take effect until twelve months after the date of receipt of the notification.

Article XV

A dispute between two or more Contracting States concerning the interpretation or application of this Convention, not settled by negotiation, shall, unless the States concerned agree on some other method of settlement, be brought before the International Court of Justice for determination by it.

Article XVI

1. This Convention shall be established in English, French and Spanish. The three texts shall be signed and shall be equally authoritative.

2. Official texts of this Convention shall be established by the Director-General, after consultation with the governments concerned, in Arabic, German, Italian and Portuguese.

3. Any Contracting State or group of Contracting States shall be entitled to have established by the Director-General other texts in the language of its choice by arrangement with the Director-General.

4. All such texts shall be annexed to the signed texts of this Convention.

Article XVII

1. This Convention shall not in any way affect the provisions of the Berne Convention for the Protection of Literary and Artistic Works or membership in the Union created by that Convention.

2. In application of the foregoing paragraph, a declaration has been annexed to the present Article. This declaration is an integral part of this Convention for the States bound by the Berne Convention on 1 January 1951, or which have or may become bound to it at a later date. The signature of this Convention by such States shall also constitute signature of the said declaration, and ratification, acceptance or accession by such States shall include the declaration, as well as this Convention.

Article XVIII

This Convention shall not abrogate multilateral or bilateral copyright conventions or arrangements that are or may be in effect exclusively between two or more American Republics. In the event of any difference either between the provisions of such existing conventions or arrangements and the provisions of this Convention, or between the provisions of this Convention and those of any new convention or arrangement which may be formulated between two or more American Republics after this Convention comes into force, the convention or arrangement most recently formulated shall prevail between the parties thereto. Rights in works acquired in any Contracting State under existing conventions or arrangements before the date this Convention comes into force in such State shall not be affected.

Article XIX

This Convention shall not abrogate multilateral or bilateral conventions or arrangements in effect between two or more Contracting States. In the event of any difference between the provisions of such existing conventions or arrangements and the provisions of this Convention, the provisions of this Convention shall prevail. Rights in works acquired in any Contracting State under existing conventions or arrangements before the date on which this Convention comes into force in such State shall not be affected. Nothing in this Article shall affect the provisions of Articles XVII and XVIII.

Article XX

Reservations to this Convention shall not be permitted.

Article XXI

1. The Director-General shall send duly certified copies of this Convention to the States interested and to the Secretary-General of the United Nations for registration by him.

2. He shall also inform all interested States of the ratifications, acceptances and accessions

which have been deposited, the date on which this Convention comes into force, the notifications under this Convention and denunciations under Article XIV.

APPENDIX DECLARATION RELATING TO ARTICLE XVII

The States which are members of the International Union for the Protection of Literary and Artistic Works (hereinafter called "the Berne Union") and which are signatories to this Convention,

Desiring to reinforce their mutual relations on the basis of the said Union and to avoid any conflict which might result from the co-existence of the Berne Convention and the Universal Copyright Convention,

Recognizing the temporary need of some States to adjust their level of copyright protection in accordance with their stage of cultural, social and economic development,

Have, by common agreement, accepted the terms of the following declaration:

(a) Except as provided by paragraph (b), works which, according to the Berne Convention, have as their country of origin a country which has withdrawn from the Berne Union after 1 January 1951, shall not be protected by the Universal Copyright Convention in the countries of the Berne Union;

(b) Where a Contracting State is regarded as a developing country in conformity with the established practice of the General Assembly of the United Nations, and has deposited with the Director-General of the United Nations Educational, Scientific and Cultural Organization, at the time of its withdrawal from the Berne Union, a notification to the effect that it regards itself as a developing country, the provisions of paragraph (a) shall not be applicable as long as such State may avail itself of the exceptions provided for by this Convention in accordance with Article V*bis*;

(c) The Universal Copyright Convention shall not be applicable to the relationships among countries of the Berne Union in so far as it relates to the protection of works having as their country of origin, within the meaning of the Berne Convention, a country of the Berne Union.

RESOLUTION CONCERNING ARTICLE XI

The Conference for Revision of the Universal Copyright Convention,

Having considered the problems relating to the intergovernmental Committee provided for in Article XI of this Convention, to which this resolution is annexed,

Resolves that:

1. At it inception, the Committee shall include representatives of the twelve States members of the Intergovernmental Committee established under Article XI of the 1952 Convention and the resolution annexed to it, and, in addition, representatives of the following States: Algeria, Australia, Japan, Mexico, Senegal and Yugoslavia.

2. Any States that are not party to the 1952 Convention and have not acceded to this Convention before the first ordinary session of the Committee following the entry into force of this Convention shall be replaced by other States to be selected by the Committee at its first ordinary session in conformity with the provisions of Article XI (2) and (3).

3. As soon as this Convention comes into force the Committee as provided for in paragraph 1 shall be deemed to be constituted in accordance with Article XI of this Convention.

4. A session of the Committee shall take place within one year after the coming into force of this Convention; thereafter the Committee shall meet in ordinary session at intervals of not more than two years.

5. The Committee shall elect its Chairman and two Vice-Chairmen. It shall establish its Rules of Procedure having regard to the following principles:

(a) The normal duration of the term of office of the members represented on the Committee shall be six years with one-third retiring every two years, it being however understood that, of the original terms of office, one-third shall expire at the end of the Committee's second ordinary session which will follow the entry into force of this Convention, a further third at the end of its third ordinary session, and the remaining third at the end of its fourth ordinary session.

(b) The rules governing the procedure whereby the Committee shall fill vacancies, the order in which terms of membership expire, eligibility for re-election, and election procedures, shall be based upon a balancing of the needs for continuity of membership and rotation of representation, as well as the considerations set out in Article XI (3).

Expresses the wish that the United Nations Educational, Scientific and Cultural Organization provide its Secretariat.

In faith whereof the undersigned, having deposited their respective full powers, have signed this Convention.

Done at Paris, this twenty-fourth day of July 1971, in a single copy.

Protocol 1

Annexed to the Universal Copyright Convention as revised at Paris on 24 July 1971 concerning the application of that Convention to works of Stateless persons and refugees

The States party hereto, being also party to the Universal Copyright Convention as revised at Paris on 24 July 1971 (hereinafter called "the 1971 Convention")

Have accepted the following provisions:

1. Stateless persons and refugees who have their habitual residence in a State party to this Protocol shall, for the purpose of the 1971 Convention, be assimilated to the nationals of that State.

2. (a) This Protocol shall be signed and shall be subject to ratification or acceptance, or may be acceded to, as if the provisions of Article VIII of the 1971 Convention applied hereto.

   (b) This Protocol shall enter into force in respect of each State, on the date of deposit of the instrument of ratification, acceptance or accession of the State concerned or on the date of entry into force of the 1971 Convention with respect to such State, whichever is the later.

   (c) On the entry into force of this Protocol in respect of a State not party to Protocol 1 annexed to the 1952 Convention, the latter Protocol shall be deemed to enter into force in respect of such State.

In faith whereof the undersigned, being duly authorized thereto, have signed this Protocol.

Done at Paris this twenty-fourth day of July 1971, in the English, French and Spanish languages, the three texts being equally authoritative, in a single copy which shall be deposited with the Director-General of the United Nations Educational, Scientific and Cultural Organization. The Director-General shall send certified copies to the signatory States, and to the Secretary-General of the United Nations for registration.

Protocol 2

Annexed to the Universal Copyright Convention as revised at Paris on 24 July 1971 concerning the application of that Convention to the works of certain international organizations

The States party hereto, being also party to the Universal Copyright Convention as revised at Paris on 24 July 1971 (hereinafter called "the 1971 Convention"),

Have accepted the following provisions:

1. (a) The protection provided for in Article II (1) of the 1971 Convention shall apply to works published for the first time by the United Nations, by the Specialized Agencies in relationship therewith, or by the Organization of American States.
   (b) Similarly, Article II (2) of the 1971 Convention shall apply to the said organization or agencies.

2. (a) This Protocol shall be signed and shall be subject to ratification or acceptance, or may be acceded to, as if the provisions of Article VIII of the 1971 Convention applied hereto.
   (b) This Protocol shall enter into force for each State on the date of deposit of the instrument of ratification, acceptance or accession of the State concerned or on the date of entry into force of the 1971 Convention with respect to such State, whichever is the later.

In faith whereof the undersigned, being duly authorized thereto, have signed this Protocol.

Done at Paris, this twenty-fourth day of July 1971, in the English, French and Spanish languages, the three texts being equally authoritative, in a single copy which shall be deposited with the Director-General of the United Nations Educational, Scientific and Cultural Organization. The Director-General shall send certified copies to the signatory States, and to the Secretary-General of the United Nations for registration.

EUROPEAN AGREEMENT CONCERNING PROGRAMME EXCHANGES BY MEANS OF TELEVISION FILMS

THE GOVERNMENTS SIGNATORY HERETO, BEING MEMBERS OF THE COUNCIL OF EUROPE,

Considering that the aim of the Council of Europe is to achieve a greater unity between its Members;

Considering that it is important in the interests of European cultural and economic unity that programmes may be exchanged by means of television films between the member countries of the Council of Europe as freely as possible;

Considering that national legislations allow different conclusions as regards the legal nature of television films and as regards the rights which they grant in respect of such films;

Considering that it is necessary to resolve the difficulties arising from this situation;

Having regard to Article 20 of the Berne Convention for the Protection of Literary and Artistic Works, by the terms of which the Governments of the countries of the Union reserve to themselves the right to enter into special arrangements which do not embody stipulations contrary to that Convention,

HAVE AGREED AS FOLLOWS:

Article I

In the absence of any contrary or special stipulation within the meaning of Article 4 of the present Agreement, a broadcasting organisation under the jurisdiction of a country which is a Party to this Agreement has the right to authorise in the other countries which are Parties thereto the exploitation for television of television films of which it is the maker.

Article 2

1. All visual or sound and visual recordings intended for television shall be deemed to be television films within the meaning of the present Agreement.

2. A broadcasting organisation shall be deemed to be the maker if it has taken the initiative in, and responsibility for, the making of a television film.

Article 3

1. If the television film has been made by a maker other than the one defined in Article 2, paragraph 2, the latter is entitled, in the absence of contrary or special stipulations within the meaning of Article 4, to transfer to a broadcasting organisation the right provided in Article I.

2. The provision contained in the preceding paragraph applies only if the maker and the broadcasting organisation are under the jurisdiction of countries which are Parties to the present Agreement.

Article 4

By "contrary or special stipulation" is meant any restrictive condition agreed between the maker and persons who contribute to the making of the television film.

Article 5

This Agreement shall not affect the following rights, which shall be entirely reserved:

(a) any moral right recognised in relation to films;
(b) the copyright in literary, dramatic or artistic works from which the television film is derived;
(c) the copyright in a musical work, with or without words, accompanying a television film;
(d) the copyright in films other than television films;
(e) the copyright in the exploitation of television films otherwise than on television.

Article 6

1. This Agreement shall be open to signature by the Members of the Council of Europe, who may accede to it either by:

(a) signature without reservation in respect of ratification; or
(b) signature with reservation in respect of ratification, followed by the deposit of an instrument of ratification.

2. Instruments of ratification shall be deposited with the Secretary-General of the Council of Europe.

Article 7

1. This Agreement shall enter into force thirty days after the date on which three Members of the Council shall, in accordance with Article 6 thereof, have signed it without reservation in respect of ratification or shall have ratified it.
2. In the case of any Member of the Council who shall subsequently sign the Agreement without reservation in respect of ratification or who shall ratify it, the Agreement shall enter into force thirty days after the date of such signature or deposit of the instrument of ratification.

Article 8

1. After this Agreement has come into force, any country which is not a Member of the Council of Europe may accede to it, subject to the prior approval of the Committee of Ministers of the Council of Europe.
2. Such accession shall be effected by the deposit of an instrument of accession with the Secretary-General of the Council of Europe, and shall take effect thirty days after the date of deposit.

Article 9

Signature without reservation in respect of ratification, ratification or accession shall imply full acceptance of all the provisions of this Agreement.

Article 10

The Secretary-General of the Council of Europe shall notify Members of the Council, the Governments of any countries which may have acceded to this Agreement and the Director of the Bureau of the International Union for the protection of literary and artistic works:

(a) of the date of entry into force of this Agreement and the names of any Members of the Council which have become Parties thereto;

(b) of the deposit of any instruments of accession in accordance with Article 8 of the present Agreement;

(c) of any declaration or notification received in accordance with Articles 11 and 12 thereof.

Article 11

1. This Agreement shall apply to the metropolitan territories of the Contracting Parties.

2. Any Contracting Party may, at the time of signature, ratification or accession, or at any later date, declare by notice addressed to the Secretary-General of the Council of Europe that this Agreement shall apply to any territory or territories mentioned in the said declaration and for whose international relations it is reponsible.

3. Any declaration made in accordance with the preceding paragraph may, in respect of any territory mentioned in such a declaration, be withdrawn under the conditions laid down in Article 12 of this Agreement.

Article 12

1. This Agreement shall remain in force for an unlimited period.

2. Any Contracting Party may denounce this Agreement at one year's notice by notification to this effect to the Secretary-General of the Council of Europe.

In witness whereof the undersigned, being duly authorised thereto, have signed this Agreement.

Done at Paris, this 15th day of December 1958, in English and French, both texts being equally authoritative, in a single copy, which shall remain in the archives of the Council of Europe and of which the Secretary General shall send certified copies to each of the signatory and acceding Governments and to the Director of the International Bureau for the Protection of Literary and Artistic Works.

EUROPEAN AGREEMENT ON THE PROTECTION OF TELEVISION BROADCASTS

of 22 June 1960,

PROTOCOL TO THE EUROPEAN AGREEMENT

of 22 January 1965,

ADDITIONAL PROTOCOL TO THE PROTOCOL TO THE EUROPEAN AGREEMENT

of 14 January 1974

EUROPEAN AGREEMENT ON THE PROTECTION OF TELEVISION BROADCASTS

THE GOVERNMENTS SIGNATORY HERETO, BEING MEMBERS OF THE COUNCIL OF EUROPE,

Considering that the object of the Council is to achieve a greater unity between its Members;

Considering that exchanges of television programmes between the countries of Europe are calculated to further the achievement of that object;

Considering that these exchanges are hampered by the fact that the majority of television organisations are at present powerless to restrain the re-broadcasting, fixation or public performance of their broadcasts, whereas the organisers of musical or dramatic performances or the like, and the promoters of sports meetings, make their consent to broadcasting to other countries conditional upon an undertaking that the relays will not be used for purposes other than private viewing;

Considering that the international protection of television broadcast will in no way affect any rights of third parties in these broadcasts;

Considering that the problem is one of some urgency, in view of the installations and links now being brought into service throughout Europe, which are such as to make it easy from the technical point of view for European television organisations to exchange their programmes;

Considering that, pending the conclusion of a potentially universal Convention on "neighbouring rights" at present in contemplation, it is fitting to conclude a regional Agreement restricted in scope to television broadcasts and of limited duration,

HAVE AGREED AS FOLLOWS:

Article 1

Broadcasting organisations constituted in the territory and under the laws of a Party to this Agreement or transmitting from such territory shall enjoy, in respect of all their television broadcasts:

1. In the territory of all Parties to this Agreement, the right to authorise or prohibit:

(a) the re-broadcasting of such broadcasts;
(b) the diffusion of such broadcasts to the public by wire;
(c) the communication of such broadcasts to the public by means of any instrument for the transmission of signs, sounds or images;
(d) any fixation of such broadcasts or still photographs thereof, and any reproduction of such a fixation; and
(e) re-broadcasting, wire diffusion or public performance with the aid of the fixations or reproductions referred to in sub-paragraph (d) of this paragraph, except where the organisation in which the right vests has authorised the sale of the said fixations or reproductions to the public.

2. In the territory of any other Party to this Agreement, the same protection as that other Party may extend to organisations constituted in its territory and under its laws or transmitting from its territory, where such protection is greater than that provided for in paragraph 1 above.

Article 2

1. Subject to paragraph 2 of Article 1, and Articles 13 and 14, the protection provided for in paragraph 1 of Article 1 shall continue until the end of the tenth calendar year following the year in which the first broadcast was made from the territory of a Party to this Agreement.
2. No Party to this Agreement shall be required, in pursuance of paragraph 2 of Article 1, to accord to the broadcasts of any broadcasting organisations constituted in the territory and under the laws of another Party to this Agreement or transmitting from the territory of another Party longer protection than that granted by the said other Party.

Article 3

1. Parties to this Agreement, by making a declaration as provided in Article 10, and in respect of their own territory, may:

(a) withhold the protection provided for in sub-paragraph 1(b) of Article 1;
(b) withhold the protection provided for in sub-paragraph 1(c) of Article 1, where the communication is not to a paying audience within the meaning of their domestic law;
(c) withhold the protection provided for in sub-paragraph 1(d) of Article 1, where the fixation or reproduction of the fixation is made for private use, or solely for educational purposes;
(d) withhold the protection provided for in sub-paragraphs 1(d) and (e) of Article 1, in respect of still photographs or reproductions of such photographs;
(e) withhold the protection provided for in this Agreement from television broadcasts by broadcasting organisations constituted in their territory and under their laws or transmitting from such territory, where such broadcasts enjoy protection under their domestic law;
(f) restrict the operation of this Agreement to broadcasting organisations constituted in the territory and under the laws of a Party to this Agreement and also transmitting from the territory of such Party.

2. It shall be open to the aforesaid Parties, in respect of their own territory, to provide exceptions to the protection of television broadcasts:

(a) for the purpose of reporting current events, in respect of the re-broadcasting, fixation or reproduction of the fixation, wire diffusion or public performance of short extracts from a broadcast which itself constitutes the whole or part of the event in question;

(b) in respect of the making of ephemeral fixations of television broadcasts by a broadcasting organisation by means of its own facilities and for its own broadcasts.

3. The aforesaid Parties may, in respect of their own territory, provide for a body with jurisdiction over cases where the right of communication to the public referred to in sub-paragraph 1(c) of Article 1 has been unreasonably refused, or granted on unreasonable terms, by the broadcasting organisation in which the said right vests.

Article 4

1. Fixations of a broadcast in which protection under this Agreement subsists, or still photographs thereof, as well as reproductions of such photographs, made in a territory to which this Agreement does not apply and imported into the territory of a Party to this Agreement where they would be unlawful without the consent of the broadcasting organisation in which the right vests, shall be liable to seizure in the latter territory.

2. The provisions of the last preceding paragraph shall apply to the importation into the territory of a Party to this Agreement of still photographs of a broadcast in which protection under this Agreement subsists and of reproductions of such photographs, where such photographs or reproductions are made in the territory of another Party to this Agreement by virtue of sub-paragraph 1(d) of Article 3.

3. Seizure shall be effected in accordance with the domestic law of each Party to this Agreement.

4. No Party to this Agreement shall be required to provide protection in respect of still photographs, or the reproduction of such photographs, of broadcasts made by a broadcasting organisation constituted in the territory and under the laws of another Party to this Agreement or transmitting from such territory, if the said other Party has availed itself of the reservation provided for in sub-paragraph 1(d) of Article 3.

Article 5

The protection afforded by this Agreement shall apply both in relation to the visual element and in relation to the sound element of a television broadcast. It shall not affect the sound element when broadcast separately.

Article 6

1. The protection provided for in Article 1 shall not affect any rights in respect of a television broadcast that may accrue to third parties, such as authors, performers, film makers, manufacturers of phonographic records or organisers of entertainments.

2. It shall likewise be without prejudice to any protection of television broadcasts that may be accorded apart from this Agreement.

Article 7

1. This Agreement shall be open to signature by the Members of the Council of Europe, who may become Parties to it either by

(a) signature without reservation in respect of ratification; or
(b) signature with reservation in respect of ratification, followed by the deposit of an instrument of ratification.

2. Instruments of ratification shall be deposited with the Secretary-General of the Council of Europe.

Article 8

1. This Agreement shall enter into force one month after the date on which three Members of the Council of Europe shall, in accordance with Article 7 thereof, have signed it without reservation in respect of ratification or shall have ratified it.

2. In the case of any Member of the Council of Europe who shall subsequently sign the Agreement without reservation in respect of ratification or who shall ratify it, the Agreement shall enter into force one month after the date of such signature or deposit of the instrument of ratification.

Article 9

1. After this Agreement has come into force, any European Government which is not a Member of the Council of Europe or any non-European Government having political ties with a Member of the Council of Europe may accede to it, subject to the prior approval of the Committee of Ministers of the Council of Europe.

2. Such accession shall be effected by the deposit of an instrument of accession with the Secretary-General of the Council of Europe and shall take effect one month after the date of deposit.

Article 10

Signature, ratification or accession shall imply full acceptance of all the provisions of this Agreement; provided always that any country may declare, at the time of signature or of deposit of its instrument of ratification or accession, that it intends to avail itself of one or more of the options in paragraph 1 of Article 3 above.

Article 11

The Secretary-General of the Council of Europe shall notify Members of the Council, the Governments of any countries which may have acceded to this Agreement and the Director of the Bureau of the International Union for the Protection of Literary and Artistic Works:

(a)   of any signatures, together with any reservations as to ratification, of the deposit of instruments of ratification and of the date of entry into force of this Agreement;

(b)   of the deposit of any instruments of accession in accordance with Article 9;

(c)   of any declaration or notification received in accordance with Articles 12, 13 or 14;

(d)   of any decision of the Committee of Ministers taken in pursuance of paragraph 2 of Article 12.

Article 12

1. This Agreement shall apply to the metropolitan territories of the Parties.

2. Any Party may, at the time of signature, of the deposit of its instrument of ratification or accession, or at any later date, declare by notice addressed to the Secretary-General of the Council of Europe that this Agreement shall extend to any or all of the territories for whose international relations it is responsible.

3. Any Government which has made a declaration under paragraph 2 of this Article extending this Agreement to any territory for whose international relations it is responsible

may denounce the Agreement separately in respect of that territory in accordance with Article 14 thereof.

Article 13

1. This Agreement shall cease to be effective, except in regard to fixations already made, at such time as a Convention on "neighbouring rights", including the protection of television broadcasts and open to European countries, amongst others, shall have entered into force for at least a majority of the Members of the Council of Europe that are themselves Parties to the Agreement.

2. The Committee of Ministers of the Council of Europe shall at the appropriate time declare that the conditions laid down in the preceding paragraph have been fulfilled, thereby entailing the termination of this Agreement.

Article 14

Any Contracting Party may denounce this Agreement by giving one year's notice to that effect to the Secretary-General of the Council of Europe.

In witness whereof, the undersigned being duly authorised thereto, have signed this Agreement.

Done at Strasbourg, this 22nd day of June, 1960, in English and French, both texts being equally authoritative, in a single copy, which shall remain in the archives of the Council of Europe and of which the Secretary-General shall send certified copies to each of the signatory and acceding Governments and to the Director of the Bureau of the International Union for the Protection of Literary and Artistic Works.

For the Government of the Republic of Austria:

For the Government of the Kingdom of Belgium: *with reservation in respect of ratification*, Strasbourg, 13 September 1960. Jean SALMON

For the Government of the Republic of Cyprus: *with reservation in respect of ratification*, Strasbourg, 23 September 1969. C.N. PILAVACHI

For the Government of the Kingdom of Denmark: *with reservation in respect of ratification*, V.U. HAMMERSHAIMB

For the Government of the French Republic: LECOMPTE BOINET

For the Government of the Federal Republic of Germany: *with reservation in respect of ratification*, Strasbourg, 11 July 1960. A. REIFFERSCHEIDT

For the Government of the Kingdom of Greece: *with reservation in respect of ratification*, N. CAMBALOURIS

For the Government of the Icelandic Republic:

For the Government of Ireland: *with reservation in respect of ratification*, T. WOODS

For the Government of the Italian Republic: *with reservation in respect of ratification*, BOMBASSEI DE VETTOR

For the Government of the Grand Duchy of Luxembourg: *with reservation in respect of ratification*, Strasbourg, 13 September 1960. Pierre WURTH

For the Government of the Kingdom of the Netherlands: *with reservation in respect of ratification*, Strasbourg, 7 October 1964. W.J.D. PHILIPSE

For the Government of the Kingdom of Norway: *with reservation in respect of ratification,* Strasbourg, 29 June 1965. Ole ÅLGÅRD

For the Government of the Kingdom of Sweden: *with reservation in respect of ratification,* Strasbourg, 3 August 1960. Sture PETREN

For the Government of the Turkish Republic: *with reservation in respect of ratification,* M. BOROVALI

For the Government of the United Kingdom of Great Britain and Northern Ireland: *with reservation in respect of ratification.* Her Majesty's Government understand the word "signature" in the first line of Article 10 to refer only to signature without reservation as to ratification. Strasbourg, 13 July 1960. John PECK

Accession in accordance with Article 9: Spain–22 September 1971

PROTOCOL TO THE EUROPEAN AGREEMENT ON THE PROTECTION
OF TELEVISION BROADCASTS

THE MEMBER STATES OF THE COUNCIL OF EUROPE, SIGNATORY HERETO,

Considering the desirability of amending the European Agreement on the Protection of Television Broadcasts, signed at Strasbourg on 22nd June 1960, hereinafter referred to as "the Agreement";

Considering that the International Convention for the Protection of Performers, Producers of Phonograms and Broadcasting Organisations, signed in Rome on 26th October 1961, entered into force on 18th May 1964,

HAVE AGREED AS FOLLOWS:

Article 1

1. Paragraph 1 of Article 2 of the Agreement shall be amended as follows:

"Subject to paragraph 2 of Article 1, and Articles 13 and 14, the protection provided for in paragraph 1 of Article 1 shall last not less than a period of twenty years from the end of the year in which the broadcast took place."

2. Paragraph 2 of Article 2 of the Agreement shall be deleted.

Article 2

1. Sub-paragraph 1 (a) of Article 3 of the Agreement shall be amended as follows:

"(a) withhold the protection provided for in sub-paragraph 1 (b) of Article 1 as regards broadcasting organisations constituted in their territory or transmitting from such territory, and restrict the exercise of such protection, as regards broadcasts by broadcasting organisations constituted in the territory of another Party to this Agreement or transmitting from such territory, to a percentage of the transmissions by such organisations, which shall not be less than 50% of the average weekly duration of the broadcasts of each of these organisations."

2. Sub-paragraph 1 (e) of Article 3 of the Agreement shall be amended as follows:

"(e) without prejudice to sub-paragraph 1 (a) of this Article, withhold all protection provided for in this Agreement from television broadcasts by broadcasting organisations constituted in their territory and under their laws or transmitting from such territory, which such broadcasts enjoy protection under their domestic law."

3. Paragraph 3 of Article 3 of the Agreement shall be amended as follows:

"3. The aforesaid Parties may, in respect of their own territory, provide for a body with jurisdiction over cases where the right of diffusion to the public by wire referred to in sub-paragraph 1 (b) of Article 1, or the right of communication to the public referred to in sub-paragraph 1 (c) of Article 1, has been unreasonably refused or granted on unreasonable terms by the broadcasting organisation in which the said right vests."

4. Any State which in accordance with Article 10 of the Agreement has, before the entry into force of this Protocol, availed itself of the option in sub-paragraph 1 (a) of Article 3 of the Agreement may, notwithstanding anything in paragraph 1 of the present Article, maintain the application of such option.

Article 3

Article 13 of the Agreement shall be deleted and replaced by the following:
"1. This Agreement shall remain in force indefinitely.

2. Nevertheless, as from 1st January 1985, no State may remain or become a Party to this Agreement unless it is also a Party to the International Convention for the Protection of Performers, Producers of Phonograms and Broadcasting Organisations signed in Rome on 26th October 1961."*

Article 4

1. The Governments signatory to the Agreement and the Governments having acceded thereto may become Parties to this Protocol by the procedure laid down in Article 7 or Article 9 of the Agreement, according to whether they are member States of the Council of Europe or not.

2. This Protocol shall enter into force one month after the date on which all the Parties to the Agreement have signed this Protocol without reservation in respect of ratification, or deposited their instrument of ratification or accession in accordance with the provisions of the preceding paragraph.

3. As from the date on which this Protocol enters into force, no State may become a Party to the Agreement without becoming also a Party to this Protocol.

Article 5

The Secretary-General of the Council of Europe shall notify member States of the Council, other States Parties to the Agreement, and the Director of the Bureau of the International Union for the Protection of Literary and Artistic Works of any signature of this Protocol, together with any reservations as to ratification, and of the deposit of any instrument of ratification of the Protocol or of accession to it, and of the date referred to in paragraph 2 of Article 4 of this Protocol.

In witness whereof the undersigned, being duly authorised thereto, have signed this Protocol.

Done at Strasbourg, this 22nd day of January 1965 in English and French, both texts being equally authoritative, in a single copy which shall remain deposited in the archives of the Council of Europe. The Secretary-General of the Council of Europe shall transmit certified copies to each of the signatory and acceding States.

For the Government of the Republic of Austria:

For the Government of the Kingdom of Belgium: *with reservation in respect of ratification or acceptance*, Strasbourg, 2 February. Louis COUVREUR

For the Government of the Republic of Cyprus: *with reservation in respect of ratification or acceptance*, Strasbourg, 23 September 1969. C.N. PILAVACHI

For the Government of the Kingdom of Denmark: Morgens WARBERG

For the Government of the French Republic: C.H. BONFILS

For the Government of the Federal Republic of Germany: *with reservation in respect of ratification or acceptance*, Felician PRILL

---

*Text amended according to the provisions of the Additional Protocol of the said Protocol, which entered into force on 31 December 1974.

For the Government of the Kingdom of Greece: *with reservation in respect of ratification or acceptance*, Strasbourg, 30 November 1965. Léon MACCAS

For the Government of the Icelandic Republic:

For the Government of Ireland:

For the Government of the Italian Republic:

For the Government of the Grand Duchy of Luxembourg: *with reservation in respect of ratification or acceptance*, Jean WAGNER

For the Government of the Kingdom of the Netherlands:

For the Government of the Kingdom of Norway: *with reservation in respect of ratification or acceptance*, Strasbourg, 29 June 1965. Ole ALGARD

For the Government of the Kingdom of Sweden: Sten LINDH

For the Government of the Swiss Confederation:

For the Government of the Turkish Republic: *with reservation in respect of ratification or acceptance*, Strasbourg, 24 May 1974. R. GÜMRÜKÇÜOGLU

For the Government of the United Kingdom of Great Britain and Northern Ireland: Strasbourg, 23 February 1965. I.F. PORTER

Accession in accordance with Article 4, paragraph 1: Spain–22 September 1971

ADDITIONAL PROTOCOL TO THE PROTOCOL TO THE EUROPEAN AGREEMENT ON THE PROTECTION OF TELEVISION BROADCASTS

THE MEMBER STATES OF THE COUNCIL OF EUROPE, SIGNATORY HERETO,

Considering the desirability of extending the duration of the European Agreement on the Protection of Television Broadcasts and the Protocol to this Agreement for the benefit of States which are not yet Parties to the International Convention for the Protection of Performer, Producers of Phonograms and Broadcasting Organisations, signed in Rome on 26 October 1961,

HAVE AGREED AS FOLLOWS:

Article 1

Paragraph 2 of Article 3 of the Protocol to the Agreement is substituted by the following:

"2. Nevertheless, as from 1 January 1985, no State may remain or become a Party to this Agreement unless it is also a Party to the International Convention for the Protection of Performers, Producers of Phonograms and Broadcasting Organisations, signed in Rome on 26 October 1961."

Article 2

1. The States signatory to the Agreement and the Protocol thereto may become Parties to this Additional Protocol in accordance with the procedure laid down in Article 7 of the Agreement.
2. The States having acceded to the Agreement and to the Protocol may become Parties to this Additional Protocol by the deposit of an instrument of accession with the Secretary General of the Council of Europe.

Article 3

1. This Additional Protocol shall enter into force one month after the date on which all the Parties to the Agreement and the Protocol have signed this Additional Protocol without reservation in respect of ratification, or have deposited their instrument of ratification or accession in conformity with the provisions of Article 2.
2. After the date of entry into force of this Additional Protocol, no State may become a Party to the Agreement and the Protocol without becoming also a Party to this Additional Protocol.

Article 4

The Secretary General of the Council of Europe shall notify member States of the Council, other contracting Parties to the Agreement and the Director General of the World Intellectual Property Organisation of any signature of this Additional Protocol, together with any reservations as to ratification, and of the deposit of any instrument of ratification of the Additional Protocol or of accession to it, and of the date referred to in paragraph 1 of Article 3 of this Additional Protocol.

In witness whereof the undersigned, being duly authorised thereto, have signed this Additional Protocol.

Done at Strasbourg, this 14th day of January 1974, in the English and French languages, both texts being equally authoritative, in a single copy which shall remain deposited in the archives of the Council of Europe. The Secretary General of the Council of Europe shall transmit certified copies to each of the signatory and acceding States.

For the Government of the Republic of Austria:

For the Government of the Kingdom of Belgium: *with reservation in respect of ratification or acceptance*, J. LODEWYCK

For the Government of the Republic of Cyprus: *with reservation in respect of ratification or acceptance*, Polys MODINOS

For the Government of the Kingdom of Denmark: Strasbourg, 19 September 1974. Frode L.G. SCHÖN

For the Government of the French Republic: Strasbourg, 17 June 1974. A. FÉQUANT

For the Government of the Federal Republic of Germany: *with reservations in respect of ratification or acceptance*, Ellinor von PUTTKAMER

For the Government of the Icelandic Republic:

For the Government of Ireland:

For the Government of the Italian Republic:

For the Government of the Grand Duchy of Luxembourg: *with reservations in respect of ratification or acceptance*, Strasbourg, 26 February 1974. P. MERTZ

For the Government of Malta:

For the Government of the Kingdom of the Netherlands:

For the Government of the Kingdom of Norway: Strasbourg, 19 September 1974. Kirsten OHM

For the Government of the Kingdom of Sweden: Strasbourg, 1 April 1974. Arne FÄLTHEIM

For the Government of the Swiss Confederation:

For the Government of the Turkish Republic: *with reservation in respect of ratification or acceptance*, Strasbourg, 24 May 1974. R. GÜMRÜKÇÜOGLU

For the Government of the United Kingdom of Great Britain and Northern Ireland: Strasbourg, 15 March 1974. D.J.B. ROBEY

Accession in accordance with Article 2, paragraph 2: Spain–2 August 1974

ROME CONVENTION, 1961

International Convention for the protection of performers, producers of phonograms and Broadcasting organisations

Done at Rome on October 26, 1961

TABLE OF CONTENTS*

---

*This Table of Contents is added for the convenience of the reader. It does not appear in the original text of the Convention.

Article 32:   *Integovernmental Committee*
Article 33:   *Languages*
Article 34:   *Notifications*

The Contracting States, moved by the desire to protect the rights of performers, producers of phonograms, and broadcasting organisations,

HAVE AGREED AS FOLLOWS:

Article 1

Safeguard of Copyright Proper*

Protection granted under this Convention shall leave intact and shall in no way affect the protection of copyright in literary and artistic works. Consequently, no provision of this Convention may be interpreted as prejudicing such protection.

Article 2

Protection given by the Convention
[Definition of National Treatment]

1. For the purposes of this Convention, national treatment shall mean the treatment accorded by the domestic law of the Contracting State in which protection is claimed:

(a)   to performers who are its nationals, as regards performances taking place, broadcast, or first fixed, on its territory;
(b)   to producers of phonograms who are its nationals, as regards phonograms first fixed or first published on its territory;
(c)   to broadcasting organisations which have their headquarters on its territory, as regards broadcasts transmitted from transmitters situated on its territory.

2. National treatment shall be subject to the protection specifically guaranteed, and the limitations specifically provided for, in this Convention.

Article 3

Definitions
[(a) Performers; (b) Phonogram; (c) Producers of Phonograms; (d) Publication; (e) Reproduction; (f) Broadcasting; (g) Rebroadcasting]

For the purposes of this Convention:

(a)   "performers" means actors, singers, musicians, dancers, and other persons who act, sing, deliver, declaim, play in, or otherwise perform literary or artistic works;
(b)   "phonogram" means any exclusively aural fixation of sounds of a performance or of other sounds;
(c)   "producer of phonograms" means the person who, or the legal entity which, first fixes the sounds of a performance or other sounds;
(d)   "publication" means the offering of copies of a phonogram to the public in reasonable quantity;
(e)   "reproduction" means the making of a copy or copies of a fixation;

---

*Articles have been given titles to facilitate their identification. There are no titles in the signed text.

(f)   "broadcasting" means the transmission by wireless means for public reception of sounds or of images and sounds;

(g)   "rebroadcasting" means the simultaneous broadcasting by one broadcasting organisation of the broadcast of another broadcasting organisation.

Article 4

Performances Protected
[Points of Attachment for Performers]

Each Contracting State shall grant national treatment to performers if any of the following conditions is met:

(a)   the performance takes place in another Contracting State;

(b)   the performance is incorporated in a phonogram which is protected under Article 5 of this Convention;

(c)   the performance, not being fixed on a phonogram, is carried by a broadcast which is protected by Article 6 of this Convention.

Article 5

Protected Phonograms
[1. Points of Attachment for Producers of Phonograms; 2. Simultaneous Publication; 3. Power to exclude certain Criteria]

1. Each Contracting State shall grant national treatment to producers of phonograms if any of the following conditions is met:

(a)   the producer of the phonogram is a national of another Contracting State (criterion of nationality);

(b)   the first fixation of the sound was made in another Contracting State (criterion of fixation);

(c)   the phonogram was first published in another Contracting State (criterion of publication).

2. If a phonogram was first published in a non-contracting State but if it was also published, within thirty days of its first publication, in a Contracting State (simultaneous publication), it shall be considered as first published in the Contracting State.

3. By means of a notification deposited with the Secretary-General of the United Nations, any Contracting State may declare that it will not apply the criterion of publication or, alternatively, the criterion of fixation. Such notification may be deposited at the time of ratification, acceptance or accession, or at any time thereafter; in the last case, it shall become effective six months after it has been deposited.

Article 6

Protected Broadcasts
[1. Points of Attachment for Broadcasting Organizations; 2. Power to Reserve]

1. Each Contracting State shall grant national treatment to broadcasting organisations if either of the following conditions is met:

(a)   the headquarters of the broadcasting organisation is situated in another Contracting State;

(b)   the broadcast was transmitted from a transmitter situated in another Contracting State.

2. By means of a notification deposited with the Secretary-General of the United Nations, any Contracting State may declare that it will protect broadcasts only if the headquarters of the broadcasting organisation is situated in another Contracting State and the broadcast was transmitted from a transmitter situated in the same Contracting State. Such notification may be deposited at the time of ratification, acceptance or accession, or at any time thereafter; in the last case, it shall become effective six months after it has been deposited.

Article 7

Minimum Protection for Performers
[1. Particular Rights; 2. Relations between Performers and Broadcasting Organizations]

1. The protection provided for performers by this Convention shall include the possibility of preventing:

    (a) the broadcasting and the communication to the public, without their consent, of their performance, except where the performance used in the broadcasting or the public communication is itself already a broadcast performance or is made from a fixation;

    (b) the fixation, without their consent, of their unfixed performance;

    (c) the reproduction, without their consent, of a fixation of their performance;

        (i)   if the original fixation itself was made without their consent;

        (ii)   if the reproduction is made for purposes different from those for which the performers gave their consent;

        (iii) if the original fixation was made in accordance with the provisions of Article 15, and the reproduction is made for purposes different from those referred to in those provisions.

2. (1) If broadcasting was consented to by the performers, it shall be a matter for the domestic law of the Contracting State where protection is claimed to regulate the protection against rebroadcasting, fixation for broadcasting purposes and the reproduction of such fixation for broadcasting purposes.

   (2) The terms and conditions governing the use of broadcasting organisations of fixations made for broadcasting purposes shall be determined in accordance with the domestic law of the Contracting State where protection is claimed.

   (3) However, the domestic law referred to in sub-paragraphs (1) and (2) of this paragraph shall not operate to deprive performers of the ability to control, by contract, their relations with broadcasting organisations.

Article 8

Performers acting jointly

Any Contracting State may, by its domestic laws and regulations, specify the manner in which performers will be represented in connexion with the exercise of their rights if several of them participate in the same performance.

Article 9

Variety and Circus Artists

Any Contracting State may, by its domestic laws and regulations, extend the protection provided for in this Convention to artists who do not perform literary or artistic works.

Article 10

Right of Reproduction for Phonogram Producers

Producers of phonograms shall enjoy the right to authorise or prohibit the direct or indirect reproduction of their phonograms.

Article 11

Formalities for Phonograms

If, as a condition of protecting the rights of producers of phonograms, or of performers, or both, in relation to phonograms, a Contracting State, under its domestic law, requires compliance with formalities, these shall be considered as fulfilled if all the copies in commerce of the published phonogram or their containers bear a notice consisting of the symbol℗, accompanied by the year date of the first publication, placed in such a manner as to give reasonable notice of claim of protection; and if the copies or their containers do not identify the producer or the licensee of the producer (by carrying his name, trade mark or other appropriate designation), the notice shall also include the name of the owner of the rights of the producer; and, furthermore, if the copies or their containers do not identify the principal performers, the notice shall also include the name of the person who, in the country in which the fixation was effected, owns the rights of such performers.

Article 12

Secondary Uses of Phonograms

If a phonogram published for commercial purposes, or a reproduction of such phonogram, is used directly for broadcasting or for any communication to the public, a single equitable remuneration shall be paid by the user to the performers, or to the producers of the phonograms, or to both. Domestic law may, in the absence of agreement between these parties, lay down the conditions as to the sharing of this remuneration.

Article 13

Minimum Rights for Broadcasting Organizations

Broadcasting organisations shall enjoy the right to authorise or prohibit:

(a) the rebroadcasting of their broadcasts;
(b) the fixation of their broadcasts;
(c) the reproduction;
  (i)   of fixations, made without their consent, of their broadcasts;
  (ii) of fixations, made in accordance with the provisions of Article 15, of their broadcasts, if the reproduction is made for purposes different from those referred to in those provisions;
(d) the communication to the public of the television broadcasts if such communication is made in places accessible to the public against payment of an entrance fee; it shall be a matter for the domestic law of the State where protection of this right is claimed to determine the conditions under which it may be exercised.

Article 14

Minimum Duration of Protection

The term of protection to be granted under this Convention shall last at least until the end of a period of twenty years computed from the end of the year in which:

(a) the fixation was made—for phonograms and for performances incorporated therein;
(b) the performance took place—for performances not incorporated in phonograms;
(c) the broadcast took place—for broadcasts.

Article 15

Permitted Exceptions
[1. Specific Limitations; 2. Equivalents with copyright]

1. Any Contracting State may, in its domestic laws and regulations, provide for exceptions to the protection guaranteed by this Convention as regards:

(a) private use;
(b) use of short excerpts in connexion with the reporting of current events;
(c) ephemeral fixation by a broadcasting organisation by means of its own facilities and for its own broadcasts;
(d) use solely for the purposes of teaching or scientific research.

2. Irrespective of paragraph 1 of this Article, any Contracting State may, in its domestic laws and regulations, provide for the same kinds of limitations with regard to the protection of performers, producers of phonograms and broadcasting organisations, as it provides for, in its domestic laws and regulations, in connexion with the protection of copyright in literary and artistic works. However, compulsory licences may be provided for only to the extent to which they are compatible with this Convention.

Article 16

Reservations

1. Any State, upon becoming party to this Convention, shall be bound by all the obligations and shall enjoy all the benefits thereof. However, a State may at any time, in a notification deposited with the Secretary-General of the United Nations, declare that:

(a) as regards Article 12:
  (i)   it will not apply the provisions of that Article;
  (ii)   it will not apply the provisions of that Article in respect of certain uses;
  (iii) as regards phonograms the producer of which is not a national of another Contracting State, it will not apply that Article;
  (iv) as regards phonograms the producer of which is a national of another Contracting State, it will limit the protection provided for by that Article to the extent to which, and to the term for which, the latter State grants protection to phonograms first fixed by a national of the State making the declaration; however, the fact that the Contracting State of which the producer is a national does not grant the protection to the same beneficiary or beneficiaries as the State making the declaration shall not be considered as a difference in the extent of the protection;
(b) as regards Article 13, it will not apply item (d) of that Article; if a Contracting State makes such a declaration, the other Contracting States shall not be obliged to grant the right referred to in Article 13, item (d), to broadcasting organisations whose headquarters are in that State.

2. If the notification referred to in paragraph 1 of this Article is made after the date of the deposit of the instrument of ratification, acceptance or accession, the declaration will become effective six months after it has been deposited.

Article 17

Certain countries applying only the "fixation" criterion

Any State which, on October 26, 1961, grants protection to producers of phonograms solely on the basis of the criterion of fixation may, by a notification deposited with the Secretary-General of the United Nations at the time of ratification, acceptance or accession, declare that it will apply, for the purposes of Article 5, the criterion of fixation alone and, for the purposes of paragraph 1(a)(iii) and (iv) of Article 16, the criterion of fixation instead of the criterion of nationality.

Article 18

Withdrawal of reservations

Any State which has deposited a notification under paragraph 3 of Article 5, paragraph 2 of Article 6, paragraph 1 of Article 16 or Article 17, may, by a further notification deposited with the Secretary-General of the United Nations, reduce its scope or withdraw it.

Article 19

Performers' Rights in Films

Notwithstanding anything in this Convention, once a performer has consented to the incorporation of his performance in a visual or audio-visual fixation, Article 7 shall have no further application.

Article 20

Non-retroactivity

1. This Convention shall not prejudice rights acquired in any Contracting State before the date of coming into force of this Convention for that State.

2. No Contracting State shall be bound to apply the provisions of this Convention to performances or broadcasts which took place, or to phonograms which were fixed, before the date of coming into force of this Convention for that State.

Article 21

Protection by other means

The protection provided for in this Convention shall not prejudice any protection otherwise secured to performers, producers of phonograms and broadcasting organisations.

Article 22

Special agreements

Contracting States reserve the right to enter into special agreements among themselves in so far as such agreements grant to performers, producers of phonograms or broadcasting organisations more extensive rights than those granted by this Convention or contain other provisions not contrary to this Convention.

Article 23

Signature and deposit

This Convention shall be deposited with the Secretary-General of the United Nations. It shall be open until June 30, 1962, for signature by any State invited to the Diplomatic

Conference on the International Protection of Performers, Producers of Phonograms and Broadcasting Organisations which is a party to the Universal Copyright Convention or a member of the International Union for the Protection of Literary and Artistic Works.

Article 24

Become Party to the Convention

1. This Convention shall be subject to ratification or acceptance by the signatory States.

2. This Convention shall be open for accession by any State invited to the Conference referred to in Article 23, and by any State Member of the United Nations, provided that in either case such State is a party to the Universal Copyright Convention or a member of the International Union for the Protection of Literary and Artistic Works.

3. Ratification, acceptance or accession shall be effected by the deposit of an instrument to that effect with the Secretary-General of the United Nations.

Article 25

Entry into force

1. This Convention shall come into force three months after the date of deposit of the sixth instrument of ratification, acceptance or accession.

2. Subsequently, this Convention shall come into force in respect of each State three months after the date of deposit of its instrument of ratification, acceptance or accession.

Article 26

Implementation of the Convention by the Provision of Domestic Law

1. Each Contracting State undertakes to adopt, in accordance with its Constitution, the measures necessary to ensure the application of this Convention.

2. At the time of deposit of its instrument of ratification, acceptance or accesssion, each State must be in a position under its domestic law to give effect to the terms of this Convention.

Article 27

Applicability of the Convention to Certain Territories

1. Any State may, at the time of ratification, acceptance or accession, or at any time thereafter, declare by notification addressed to the Secretary-General of the United Nations that this Convention shall extend to all or any of the territories for whose international relations it is responsible, provided that the Universal Copyright Convention or the International Convention for the Protection of Literary and Artistic Works applies to the territory or territories concerned. This notification shall take effect three months after the date of its receipt.

2. The notifications referred to in paragraph 3 of Article 5, paragraph 2 of Article 6, paragraph 1 of Article 16 and Articles 17 and 18, may be extended to cover all or any of the territories referred to in paragraph 1 of this Article.

Article 28

Denunciation of the Convention

1. Any Contracting State may denounce this Convention, on its own behalf or on behalf of all or any of the territories referred to in Article 27.

2. The denunciation shall be effected by a notification addressed to the Secretary-General of the United Nations and shall take effect twelve months after the date of receipt of the notification.

3. The right of denunciation shall not be exercised by a Contracting State before the expiry of a period of five years from the date on which the Convention came into force with respect to that State.

4. A Contracting State shall cease to be a party to this Convention from that time when it is neither a party to the Universal Copyright Convention nor a member of the International Union for the Protection of Literary and Artistic Works.

5. This Convention shall cease to apply to any territory referred to in Article 27 from that time when neither the Universal Copyright Convention nor the International Convention for the Protection of Literary and Artistic Works applies to that territory.

Article 29

Revision of the Convention

1. After this Convention has been in force for five years, any Contracting State may, by notification addressed to the Secretary-General of the United Nations, request that a conference be convened for the purpose of revising the Convention. The Secretary-General shall notify all Contracting States of this request. If, within a period of six months following the date of notification by the Secretary-General of the United Nations, not less than one half of the Contracting States notify him of their concurrence with the request, the Secretary-General shall inform the Director-General of the International Labour Office, the Director-General of the United Nations Educational, Scientific and Cultural Organization and the Director of the Bureau of the International Union for the Protection of Literary and Artistic Works, who shall convene a revision conference in co-operation with the Inter-governmental Committee provided for in Article 32.

2. The adoption of any revision of this Convention shall require an affirmative vote by two-thirds of the States attending the revision conference, provided that this majority includes two-thirds of the States which, at the time of the revision conference, are parties to the Convention.

3. In the event of adoption of a Convention revising this Convention in whole or in part, and unless the revising Convention provides otherwise:

(a) this Convention shall cease to be open to ratification, acceptance or accession as from the date of entry into force of the revising Convention;

(b) this Convention shall remain in force as regards relations between or with Contracting States which have not become parties to the revising Convention.

Article 30

Settlement of disputes

Any dispute which may arise between two or more Contracting States concerning the interpretation or application of this Convention and which is not settled by negotiation shall, at the request of any one of the parties to the dispute, be referred to the International Court of Justice for decision, unless they agree to another mode of settlement.

Article 31

Limits on Reservations

Without prejudice to the provisions of paragraph 3 of Article 5, paragraph 2 of Article 6, paragraph 1 of Article 16 and Article 17, no reservation may be made to this Convention.

Article 32

Intergovernmental Committee

1. An Intergovernmental Committee is hereby established with the following duties:

(a) to study questions concerning the application and operation of this Convention; and

(b) to collect proposals and to prepare documentation for possible revision of this Convention.

2. The Committee shall consist of representatives of the Contracting States, chosen with due regard to equitable geographical distribution. The number of members shall be six if there are twelve Contracting States or less, nine if there are thirteen to eighteen Contracting States and twelve if there are more than eighteen Contracting States.

3. The Committee shall be constituted twelve months after the Convention comes into force by an election organised among the Contracting States, each of which shall have one vote, by the Director-General of the International Labour Office, the Director-General of the United Nations Educational, Scientific and Cultural Organization and the Director of the Bureau of the International Union for the Protection of Literary and Artistic Works, in accordance with rules previously approved by a majority of all Contracting States.

4. The Committee shall elect its Chairman and officers. It shall establish its own rules of procedure. These rules shall in particular provide for the future operation of the Committee and for a method of selecting its members for the future in such a way as to ensure rotation among the various Contracting States.

5. Officials of the International Labour Office, the United Nations Educational, Scientific and Cultural Organization and the Bureau of the International Union for the Protection of Literary and Artistic Works, designated by the Directors-General and the Director thereof, shall constitute the Secretariat of the Committee.

6. Meetings of the Committee, which shall be convened whenever a majority of its members deems it necessary, shall be held successively at the headquarters of the International Labour Office, the United Nations Educational, Scientific and Cultural Organization and the Bureau of the International Union for the Protection of Literary and Artistic Works.

7. Expenses of members of the Committee shall be borne by their respective Governments.

Article 33

Languages

1. The present Convention is drawn up in English, French and Spanish, the three texts being equally authentic.

2. In addition, official texts of the present Convention shall be drawn up in German, Italian and Portuguese.

Article 34

Notifications

1. The Secretary-General of the United Nations shall notify the States invited to the Conference referred to in Article 23 and every State Member of the United Nations, as well as the Director-General of the International Labour Office, the Director-General of the United Nations Educational, Scientific and Cultural Organization and the Director of the Bureau of the International Union for the Protection of Literary and Artistic Works:

(a)   of the deposit of each instrument of ratification, acceptance or accession.

(b)   of the date of entry into force of the Convention;

(c)   of all notifications, declarations or communications provided for in this Convention;

(d)   if any of the situations referred to in paragraphs 4 and 5 of Article 28 arise.

2. The Secretary-General of the United Nations shall also notify the Director-General of the International Labour Office, the Director-General of the United Nations Educational, Scientific and Cultural Organization and the Director of the Bureau of the International Union for the Protection of Literary and Artistic Works of the requests communicated to him in accordance with Article 29, as well as of any communication received from the Contracting States concerning the revision of the Convention.

IN FAITH WHEREOF, the undersigned, being duly authorised thereto, have signed this Convention.

DONE at Rome, this twenty-sixth day of October 961, in a single copy in the English, French and Spanish languages. Certified true copies shall be delivered by the Secretary-General of the United Nations to all the States invited to the Conference referred to in Article 23 and to every State Member of the United Nations, as well as to the Director-General of the International Labour Office, the Director-General of the United Nations Educational, Scientific and Cultural Organization and the Director of the Bureau of the International Union for the Protection of Literary and Artistic Works.

CONVENTION FOR THE PROTECTION OF PRODUCERS OF PHONOGRAMS AGAINST UNAUTHORIZED DUPLICATION OF THEIR PHONOGRAMS

THE CONTRACTING STATES,

Concerned at the widespread and increasing unauthorized duplication of phonograms and the damage this is occasioning to the interests of authors, performers and producers of phonograms;

Convinced that the protection of producers of phonograms against such acts will also benefit the performers whose performances, and the authors whose works, are recorded on the said phonograms;

Recognizing the value of the work undertaken in this field by the United Nations Educational, Scientific and Cultural Organization and the World Intellectual Property Organization;

Anxious not to impair in any way international agreements already in force and in particular in no way to prejudice wider acceptance of the Rome Convention of October 26, 1961,[1] which afford protection to performers and to broadcasting organizations as well as to producers of phonograms;

HAVE AGREED AS FOLLOWS:

Article 1

For the purposes of this Convention:
(a) "phonogram" means any exclusively aural fixation of sounds of a performance or of other sounds;
(b) "producer of phonograms" means the person who, or the legal entity which, first fixes the sounds of a performance or other sounds;
(c) "duplicate" means an article which contains sounds taken directly or indirectly from a phonogram and which embodies all or a substantial part of the sounds fixed in that phonogram;
(d) "distribution to the public" means any act by which duplicates of a phonogram are offered, directly or indirectly, to the general public or any section thereof.

Article 2

Each Contracting State shall protect producers of phonograms who are nationals of other Contracting States against the making of duplicates without the consent of the producer and against the importation of such duplicates, provided that any such making or importation is for the purpose of distribution to the public, and against the distribution of such duplicates to the public.

Article 3

The means by which this Convention is implemented shall be a matter for the domestic law of each Contracting State and shall include one or more of the following: protection by

---

[1] Treaty Series No. 38 (1964), Cmnd. 2425.

means of the grant of a copyright or other specific right; protection by means of the law relating to unfair competition; protection by means of penal sanctions.

Article 4

The duration of the protection given shall be a matter for the domestic law of each Contracting State. However, if the domestic law prescribes a specific duration for the protection, that duration shall not be less than twenty years from the end either of the year in which the sounds embodied in the phonogram were first fixed or of the year in which the phonogram was first published.

Article 5

If, as a condition of protecting the producers of phonograms, a Contracting State, under its domestic law, requires compliance with formalities, these shall be considered as fulfilled if all the authorized duplicates of the phonogram distributed to the public or their containers bear a notice consisting of the symbol Ⓟ, accompanied by the year date of the first publication, placed in such a manner as to give reasonable notice of claim of protection; and, if the duplicates or their containers do not identify the producer, his successor in title or the exclusive licensee (by carrying his name, trademark or other appropriate designation), the notice shall also include the name of the producer, his successor in title or the exclusive licensee.

Article 6

Any Contracting State which affords protection by means of copyright or other specific right, or protection by means of penal sanctions, may in its domestic law provide, with regard to the protection of producers of phonograms, the same kinds of limitations as are permitted with respect to the protection of authors of literary and artistic works. However, no compulsory licenses may be permitted unless all of the following conditions are met:

(a) the duplication is for use solely for the purpose of teaching or scientific research;
(b) the license shall be valid for duplication only within the territory of the Contracting State whose competent authority has granted the license and shall not extend to the export of duplicates;
(c) the duplication made under the license gives rise to an equitable remuneration fixed by the said authority taking into account, *inter alia*, the number of duplicates which will be made.

Article 7

1. This Convention shall in no way be interpreted to limit or prejudice the protection otherwise secured to authors, to performers, to producers of phonograms or to broadcasting organizations under any domestic law or international agreement.

2. It shall be a matter for the domestic law of each Contracting State to determine the extent, if any, to which performers whose performances are fixed in a phonogram are entitled to enjoy protection and the conditions for enjoying any such protection.

3. No Contracting State shall be required to apply the provisions of this Convention to any phonogram fixed before this Convention entered into force with respect to that State.

4. Any Contracting State which, on October 29, 1971, affords protection to producers of phonograms solely on the basis of the place of first fixation may, by a notification deposited with the Director General of the World Intellectual Property Organization, declare that it will apply this criterion instead of the criterion of the nationality of the producer.

Article 8

1. The International Bureau of the World Intellectual Property Organization shall assemble and publish information concerning the protection of phonograms. Each Contracting State shall promptly communicate to the International Bureau all new laws and official texts on this subject.

2. The International Bureau shall, on request, furnish information to any Contracting State on matters concerning this Convention, and shall conduct studies and provide services designed to facilitate the protection provided for therein.

3. The International Bureau shall exercise the functions enumerated in paragraphs (1) and (2) above in co-operation, for matters within their respective competence, with the United Nations Educational, Scientific and Cultural Organization and the International Labour Organization.

Article 9

1. This Convention shall be deposited with the Secretary-General of the United Nations. It shall be open until April 30, 1972, for signature by any State that is a member of the United Nations, any of the Specialized Agencies brought into relationship with the United Nations, or the International Atomic Energy Agency, or is a party to the Statute of the International Court of Justice.[2]

2. This Convention shall be subject to ratification or acceptance by the signatory States. It shall be open for accession by any State referred to in paragraph (1) of this Article.

3. Instruments of ratification, acceptance or accession shall be deposited with the Secretary-General of the United Nations.

4. It is understood that, at the time a State becomes bound by this Convention, it will be in a position in accordance with its domestic law to give effect to the provisions of the Convention.

Article 10

No reservations to this Convention are permitted.

Article 11

1. This Convention shall enter into force three months after deposit of the fifth instrument of ratification, acceptance or accession.[3]

2. For each State ratifying, accepting or acceding to this Convention after the deposit of the fifth instrument of ratification, acceptance or accession, the Convention shall enter into force three months after the date on which the Director General of the World Intellectual Property Organization informs the States, in accordance with Article 13, paragraph (4), of the deposit of its instrument.

3. Any State may, at the time of ratification, acceptance or accession or at any later date, declare by notification addressed to the Secretary-General of the United Nations that this Convention shall apply to all or any one of the territories for whose international affairs it is responsible. This notification will take effect three months after the date on which it is received.

4. However, the preceding paragraph may in no way be understood as implying the recognition or tacit acceptance by a Contracting State of the factual situation concerning a territory to which this Convention is made applicable by another Contracting State by virtue of the said paragraph.

---

[2] Treaty Series No. 67 (1946), Cmd. 7015.
[3] The Convention entered into force on 18 April, 1973.

Article 12

1. Any Contracting State may denounce this Convention, on its own behalf or on behalf of any of the territories referred to in Article 11, paragraph (3), by written notification addressed to the Secretary-General of the United Nations.

2. Denunciation shall take effect twelve months after the date on which the Secretary-General of the United Nations has received the notification.

Article 13

1. This Convention shall be signed in a single copy in English, French, Russian and Spanish, the four texts being equally authentic.

2. Official texts shall be established by the Director General of the World Intellectual Property Organization, after consultation with the interested Governments, in the Arabic, Dutch, German, Italian and Portuguese languages.

3. The Secretary-General of the United Nations shall notify the Director General of the World Intellectual Property Organization, the Director-General of the United Nations Educational, Scientific and Cultural Organization and the Director-General of the International Labour Office of:

(a) signatures to this Convention;
(b) the deposit of instruments of ratification, acceptance or accession;
(c) the date of entry into force of this Convention;
(d) any declaration notified pursuant to Article 11, paragraph (3);
(e) the receipt of notifications of denunciation.

4. The Director General of the World Intellectual Property Organization shall inform the States referred to in Article 9, paragraph (1), of the notifications received pursuant to the preceding paragraph and of any declarations made under Article 7, paragraph (4). He shall also notify the Director-General of the United Nations Educational, Scientific and Cultural Organization and the Director-General of the International Labour Office of such declarations.

5. The Secretary-General of the United Nations shall transmit two certified copies of this Convention to the States referred to in Article 9, paragraph (1).

IN WITNESS WHEREOF, the undersigned, being duly authorized, have signed this Convention.

DONE at Geneva, this twenty-ninth day of October, 1971.

CONVENTION
RELATING TO THE DISTRIBUTION
OF PROGRAMME-CARRYING SIGNALS
TRANSMITTED BY SATELLITE

Done at Brussels on May 21, 1974

THE CONTRACTING STATES,

Aware that the use of satellites for the distribution of programme-carrying signals is rapidly growing both in volume and geographical coverage;

Concerned that there is no world-wide system to prevent distributors from distributing programme-carrying signals transmitted by satellite which were not intended for those distributors, and that this lack is likely to hamper the use of satellite communications;

Recognizing, in this respect, the importance of the interests of authors, performers, producers of phonograms and broadcasting organizations;

Convinced that an international system should be established under which measures would be provided to prevent distributors from distributing programme-carrying signals transmitted by satellite which were not intended for those distributors;

Conscious of the need not to impair in any way international agreements already in force, including the International Telecommunication Convention and the Radio Regulations annexed to that Convention, and in particular in no way to prejudice wider acceptance of the Rome Convention of October 26, 1961, which affords protection to performers, producers of phonograms and broadcasting organizations,

HAVE AGREED AS FOLLOWS:

Article 1

For the purpose of this Convention:

(i) "signal" is an electronically-generated carrier capable of transmitting programmes;

(ii) "programme" is a body of live or recorded material consisting of images, sounds or both, embodied in signals emitted for the purpose of ultimate distribution;

(iii) "satellite" is any device in extraterrestrial space capable of transmitting signals;

(iv) "emitted signal" or "signal emitted" is any programme-carrying signal that goes to or passes through a satellite;

(v) "derived signal" is a signal obtained by modifying the technical characteristics of the emitted signal, whether or not there have been one or more intervening fixations;

(vi) "originating organization" is the person or legal entity that decides what programme the emitted signals will carry;

(vii) "distributor" is the person or legal entity that decides that the transmission of the derived signals to the general public or any section thereof should take place;

(viii) "distribution" is the operation by which a distributor transmits derived signals to the general public or any section thereof.

Article 2

1. Each Contracting State undertakes to take adequate measures to prevent the distribution on or from its territory of any programme-carrying signal by any distributor for whom the

signal emitted to or passing through the satellite is not intended. This obligation shall apply where the originating organization is a national of another Contracting State and where the signal distributed is a derived signal.

2. In any Contracting State in which the application of the measures referred to in paragraph (1) is limited in time, the duration thereof shall be fixed by its domestic law. The Secretary-General of the United Nations shall be notified in writing of such duration at the time of ratification, acceptance or accession, or if the domestic law comes into force or is changed thereafter, within six months of the coming into force of that law or of its modification.

3. The obligation provided for in paragraph (1) shall not apply to the distribution of derived signals taken from signals which have already been distributed by a distributor for whom the emitted signals were intended.

Article 3

This Convention shall not apply where the signals emitted by or on behalf of the originating organization are intended for direct reception from the satellite by the general public.

Article 4

No Contracting State shall be required to apply the measures referred to in Article 2(1) where the signal distributed on its territory by a distributor for whom the emitted signal is not intended

  (i)   carries short excerpts of the programme carried by the emitted signal, consisting of reports of current events, but only to the extent justified by the informatory purpose of such excerpts, or
 (ii)   carries, as quotations, short excerpts of the programme carried by the emitted signal, provided that such quotations are compatible with fair practice and are justified by the informatory purpose of such quotations, or
(iii)   carries, where the said territory is that of a Contracting State regarded as a developing country in conformity with the established practice of the General Assembly of the United Nations, a programme carried by the emitted signal, provided that the distribution is solely for the purpose of teaching, including teaching in the framework of adult education, or scientific research.

Article 5

No Contracting State shall be required to apply this Convention with respect to any signal emitted before this Convention entered into force for that State.

Article 6

This Convention shall in no way be interpreted to limit or prejudice the protection secured to authors, performers, producers of phonograms, or broadcasting organizations, under any domestic law or international agreement.

Article 7

This Convention shall in no way be interpreted as limiting the right of any Contracting State to apply its domestic law in order to prevent abuses of monopoly.

Article 8

1. Subject to paragraphs (2) and (3), no reservation to this Convention shall be permitted.

2. Any Contracting State whose domestic law, on May 21, 1974, so provides may, by a written notification deposited with the Secretary-General of the United Nations, declare that, for its purposes, the words "where the originating organization is a national of another Contracting State" appearing in Article 2(1) shall be considered as if they were replaced by the words "where the signal is emitted from the territory of another Contracting State."

3. (a) Any Contracting State which, on May 21, 1974, limits or denies protection with respect to the distribution of programme-carrying signals by means of wires, cable or other similar communications channels to subscribing members of the public may, by a written notification deposited with the Secretary-General of the United Nations, declare that, to the extent that and as long as its domestic law limits or denies protection, it will not apply this Convention to such distributions.

   (b) Any State that has deposited a notification in accordance with subparagraph (a) shall notify the Secretary-General of the United Nations in writing, within six months of their coming into force, of any changes in its domestic law whereby the reservation under that subparagraph becomes inapplicable or more limited in scope.

Article 9

1. This Convention shall be deposited with the Secretary-General of the United Nations. It shall be open until March 31, 1975, for signature by any State that is a member of the United Nations, any of the Specialized Agencies brought into relationship with the United Nations, or the International Atomic Energy Agency, or is a party to the Statute of the International Court of Justice.

2. This Convention shall be subject to ratification or acceptance by the signatory States. It shall be open for accession by any State referred to in paragraph (1).

3. Instruments of ratification, acceptance or accession shall be deposited with the Secretary-General of the United Nations.

4. It is understood that, at the time a State becomes bound by this Convention, it will be in a position in accordance with its domestic law to give effect to the provisions of the Convention.

Article 10

1. This Convention shall enter into force three months after the deposit of the fifth instrument of ratification, acceptance or accession.

2. For each State ratifying, accepting or acceding to this Convention after the deposit of the fifth instrument of ratification, acceptance or accession, this Convention shall enter into force three months after the deposit of its instrument.

Article 11

1. Any Contracting State may denounce this Convention by written notification deposited with the Secretary-General of the United Nations.

2. Denunciation shall take effect twelve months after the date on which the notification referred to in paragraph (1) is received.

Article 12

1. This Convention shall be signed in a single copy in English, French, Russian and Spanish, the four texts being equally authentic.

2. Offical texts shall be established by the Director-General of the United Nations Educational, Scientific and Cultural Organization and the Director General of the World Intellectual Property Organization, after consultation with the interested Governments, in the Arabic, Dutch, German, Italian and Portuguese languages.

3. The Secretary-General of the United Nations shall notify the States referred to in Article 9(1), as well as the Director-General of the United Nations Educational, Scientific and Cultural Organization, the Director General of the World Intellectual Property Organization, the Director-General of the International Labour Office and the Secretary-General of the International Telecommunication Union, of

(i) signatures to this Convention;
(ii) the deposit of instruments of ratification, acceptance or accession;
(iii) the date of entry into force of this Convention under Article 10(1);
(iv) the deposit of any notification relating to Article 2(2) or Article 8(2) or (3), together with its text;
(v) the receipt of notifications of denunciation.

4. The Secretary-General of the United Nations shall transmit two certified copies of this Convention to all States referred to in Article 9(1).

EUROPEAN CONVENTION
ON TRANSFRONTIER TELEVISION

Strasbourg, 5.V.1989

PREAMBLE

The member States of the Council of Europe and the other States party to the European Cultural Convention, signatory hereto,

Considering that the aim of the Council of Europe is to achieve a greater unity between its members, for the purpose of safeguarding and realising the ideals and principles which are their common heritage;

Considering that the dignity and equal worth of every human being constitute fundamental elements of those principles;

Considering that the freedom of expression and information, as embodied in Article 10 of the Convention for the Protection of Human Rights and Fundamental Freedoms, constitutes one of the essential principles of a democratic society and one of the basic conditions for its progress and for the development of every human being;

Reaffirming their commitment to the principles of the free flow of information and ideas and the independence of broadcasters, which constitute and indispensable basis for their broadcasting policy;

Affirming the importance of broadcasting for the development of culture and the free formation of opinions in conditions safeguarding pluralism and equality of opportunity among all democratic groups and political parties;

Convinced that the continued development of information and communication technology should serve to further the right, regardless of frontiers, to express, to seek, to receive and to impart information and ideas whatever their source;

Being desirous to present an increasing range of choice of programme services for the public, thereby enhancing Europe's heritage and developing its audiovisual creation, and being determined to achieve this cultural objective through efforts to increase the production and circulation of high-quality programmes, thereby responding to the public's expectations in the political, educational and cultural fields;

Recognising the need to consolidate the common broad framework of regulation;

Bearing in mind Resolution No. 2 and Declaration of the 1st European Ministerial Conference on Mass Media Policy;

Being desirous to develop the principles embodied in the existing Council of Europe Recommendations on principles on television advertising, on equality between women and men in the media, on the use of satellite capacity for television and sound radio, and on the promotion of audiovisual production in Europe,

HAVE AGREED AS FOLLOWS:

CHAPTER 1

GENERAL PROVISIONS

Article 1

Object and purpose

This Convention is concerned with programme services embodied in transmissions. The purpose is to facilitate, among the Parties, the transfrontier transmission and the retransmission of television programme services.

Article 2

Terms employed

For the purposes of this Convention:

(a) "Transmission" means the initial emission by terrestrial transmitter, by cable, or by satellite of whatever nature, in encoded or unencoded form, of television programme services for reception by the general public. It does not include communication services operating on individual demand;

(b) "Retransmission" signifies the fact of receiving and simultaneously transmitting, irrespective of the technical means employed, complete and unchanged television programme services, or important parts of such services, transmitted by broadcasters for reception by the general public;

(c) "Broadcaster" means the natural or legal person who composes television programme services for reception by the general public and transmits them or has them transmitted, complete and unchanged, by a third party;

(d) "Programme service" means all the items within a single service provided by a given broadcaster within the meaning of the preceding paragraph;

(e) "European audiovisual works" means creative works, the production or co-production of which is controlled by European natural or legal persons;

(f) "Advertisement" means any public announcement intended to promote the sale, purchase or rental of a product or service, to advance a cause or idea or to bring about some other effect desired by the advertiser, for which transmission time has been given to the advertiser for remuneration or similar consideration;

(g) "Sponsorship" means the participation of a natural or legal person, who is not engaged in broadcasting activities or in the production of audiovisual works, in the direct or indirect financing of a programme with a view to promoting the name, trademark or image of that person.

Article 3

Field of application

This Convention shall apply to any programme service transmitted or retransmitted by entities or by technical means within the jurisdiction of a Party, whether by cable, terrestrial transmitter or satellite, and which can be received, directly or indirectly, in one or more other Parties.

Article 4

Freedom of reception and retransmission

The Parties shall ensure freedom of expression and information in accordance with Article 10 of the Convention for the Protection of Human Rights and Fundamental Freedoms and they shall guarantee freedom of reception and shall not restrict the retransmission on their territories of programme services which comply with the terms of this Convention.

Article 5

Duties of the transmitting Parties

1. Each transmitting Party shall ensure, by appropriate means and through its competent organs, that all programme services transmitted by entities or by technical means within its jurisdiction, within the meaning of Article 3. comply with the terms of this Convention.

2. For the purposes of this Convention, the transmitting Party shall be:

(a) in the case of terrestrial transmissions, the Party in which the initial emission is effected;
(b) in the case of satellite transmissions:
    i.   the Party in which the satellite up-link is situated;
    ii.   the Party which grants the use of the frequency or a satellite capacity when the up-link is situated in a State which is not a Party to this Convention;
    iii. the Party in which the broadcaster has its seat when responsibility under sub-paragraphs i and ii is not established.

3. When programme services transmitted from States which are not Parties to this Convention are retransmitted by entities or by technical means within the jurisdiction of a Party, within the meaning of Article 3, that Party, acting as transmitting Party, shall ensure, by appropriate means and through its competent organs, compliance with the terms of this Convention.

Article 6

Provision of information

1. The responsibilities of the broadcaster shall be clearly and adequately specified in the authorisation issued by, or contract concluded with, the competent authority of each Party, or by any other legal measure.

2. Information about the broadcaster shall be made available, upon request, by the competent authority of the transmitting Party. Such information shall include, as a minimum, the name or denomination, seat and status of the broadcaster, the name of the legal representative, the composition of the capital, the nature, purpose and mode of financing of the programme service the broadcaster is providing or intends providing.

CHAPTER II

PROGRAMMING MATTERS

Article 7

Responsibilities of the broadcaster

1. All items of programme services, as concerns their presentation and content, shall respect the dignity of the human being and the fundamental rights of others.

In particular, they shall not:

(a) be indecent and in particular contain pornography;
(b) give undue prominence to violence or be likely to incite to racial hatred.

2. All items of programme services which are likely to impair the physical, mental or moral development of children and adolescents shall not be scheduled when, because of the time of transmission and reception, they are likely to watch them.

3. The broadcaster shall ensure that news fairly present facts and events and encourage the free formation of opinions.

Article 8

Right of reply

1. Each transmitting Party shall ensure that every natural or legal person, regardless of nationality or place of residence, shall have the opportunity to exercise a right of reply or to seek other comparable legal or administrative remedies relating to programmes transmitted or retransmitted by entities or by technical means within its jurisdiction, within the meaning of Article 3. In particular, it shall ensure that timing and other arrangements for the exercise of the right of reply are such that this right can be effectively exercised. The effective exercise of this right or other comparable legal or administrative remedies shall be ensured both as regards the timing and the modalities.

2. For this purpose, the name of the broadcaster responsible for the programme service shall be identified therein at regular intervals by appropriate means.

Article 9

Access of the public to major events

Each Party shall examine the legal measures to avoid the right of the public to information being undermined due to the exercise by a broadcaster of exclusive rights for the transmission or retransmission, within the meaning of Article 3, of an event of high public interest and which has the effect of depriving a large part of the public in one or more other Parties of the opportunity to follow that event on television.

Article 10

Cultural objectives

1. Each transmitting Party shall ensure, where practicable and by appropriate means, that broadcasters reserve for European works a majority proportion of their transmission time, excluding the time appointed to news, sports events, games, advertising and teletext services. This proportion, having regard to the broadcaster's informational, educational, cultural and entertainment responsibilities to its viewing public, should be achieved progressively, on the basis of suitable criteria.

2. In case of disagreement between a receiving Party and a transmitting Party on the application of the preceding paragraph, recourse may be had, at the request of one of the Parties, to the Standing Committee with a view to its formulating an advisory opinion on the subject. Such a disagreement shall not be submitted to the arbitration procedure provided for in Article 26.

3. The Parties undertake to look together for the most appropriate instruments and procedures to support, without discrimination between broadcasters, the activity and development of European production, particularly in countries with a low audiovisual production capacity or restricted language area.

4. The Parties, in the spirit of co-operation and mutual assistance which underlies this Convention, shall endeavour to avoid that programme services transmitted or retransmitted by entities or by technical means within their jurisdiction, within the meaning of Article 3, endanger the pluralism of the presss and the development of the cinema industries. No cinematographic work shall accordingly be transmitted in such services, unless otherwise

agreed between its rights holders and the broadcaster, until two years have elapsed since the work was first shown in cinemas; in the case cinematographic works co-produced by the broadcaster, this period shall be one year.

CHAPTER III

ADVERTISING

Article 11

General standards

1. All advertisements shall be fair and honest.
2. Advertisements shall not be misleading and shall not prejudice the interests of consumers.
3. Advertisements addressed to or using children shall avoid anything likely to harm their interests and shall have regard to their special susceptibilities.
4. The advertiser shall not exercise any editorial influence over the content of programmes.

Article 12

Duration

1. The amount of advertising shall not exceed 15% of the daily transmission time. However, this percentage may be increased to 20% to include forms of advertisements such as direct offers to the public for the sale, purchase or rental of products or for the provision of services, provided the amount of spot advertising does not exceed 15%.
2. The amount of spot advertising within a given one-hour period shall not exceed 20%.
3. Forms of advertisements such as direct offers to the public for the sale, purchase or rental of products or for the provision of services shall not exceed one hour per day.

Article 13

Form and presentation

1. Advertisements shall be clearly distinguishable as such and recognisably separate from the other items of the programme service by optical or acoustic means. In principle, they shall be transmitted in blocks.
2. Subliminal advertisements shall not be allowed.
3. Surreptitious advertisements shall not be allowed, in particular the presentation of products or services in programmes when it serves advertising purposes.
4. Advertisements shall not feature, visually or orally, persons regularly presenting news and current affairs programmes.

Article 14

Insertion of advertisements

1. Advertisements shall be inserted between programmes. Provided the conditions contained in paragraphs 2 to 5 of this Article are fulfilled, advertisements may also be inserted during programmes in such a way that the integrity and value of the programme and the rights of the rights holders are not prejudiced.

2. In programmes consisting of autonomous parts, or in sports programmes and similarly structured events and performances comprising intervals, advertisements shall only be inserted between the parts or in the intervals.

3. The transmission of audiovisual works such as feature films and films made for television (excluding series, serials, light entertainment programmes and documentaries), provided their duration is more than forty-five minutes, may be interrupted once for each complete period of forty-five minutes. A further interruption is allowed if their duration is at least twenty minutes longer than two or more complete periods of forty-five minutes.

4. Where programmes, other than those covered by paragraph 2, are interrupted by advertisements, a period of at least twenty minutes should elapse between each successive advertising break within the programme.

5. Advertisements shall not be inserted in any broadcast of a religious service. News and current affairs programmes, documentaries, religious programmes, and children's programmes, when they are less than thirty minutes of duration, shall not be interrupted by advertisements. If they last for thirty minutes or longer, the provisions of the previous paragraphs shall apply.

Article 15

Advertising of particular products

1. Advertisements for tobacco products shall not be allowed.

2. Advertisements for alcoholic beverages of all varieties shall comply with the following rules:

(a) they shall not be addressed particularly to minors and no one associated with the consumption of alcoholic beverages in advertisements should seem to be a minor;
(b) they shall not link the consumption of alcohol to physical performance or driving;
(c) they shall not claim that alcohol has therapeutic qualities or that it is a stimulant, a sedative or a means of resolving personal problems;
(d) they shall not encourage immoderate consumption of alcohol or present abstinence or moderation in a negative light;
(e) they shall not place undue emphasis on the alcoholic content of beverages.

3. Advertisements for medicines and medical treatment which are only available on medical prescription in the transmitting Party shall not be allowed.

4. Advertisements for all other medicines and medical treatment shall be clearly distinguishable as such, honest, truthful and subject to verification and shall comply with the requirement of protection of the individual from harm.

Article 16

Advertising directed specifically at a single Party

1. In order to avoid distortions in competition and endangering the television system of a Party, advertisements which are specifically and with some frequency directed to audiences in a single Party other than the transmitting Party shall not circumvent the television advertising rules in that particular Party.

2. The provisions of the preceding paragraph shall not apply where:

(a) the rules concerned establish a discrimination between advertisements transmitted by entities or by technical means within the jurisdiction of that Party and advertisements transmitted by entities or by technical means within the jurisdiction of another Party, or
(b) the Parties concerned have concluded bilateral or multilateral agreements in this area.

CHAPTER IV

SPONSORSHIP

Article 17

General standards

1. When a programme or series of programmes is sponsored in whole or in part, it shall clearly be identified as such by appropriate credits at the beginning and/or end of the programme.

2. The content and scheduling of sponsored programmes may in no circumstances be influenced by the sponsor in such a way as to affect the responsibility and editorial independence of the broadcaster in respect of programmes.

3. Sponsored programmes shall not encourage the sale, purchase or rental of the products or services of the sponsor or a third party, in particular by making special promotional references to those products or services in such programmes.

Article 18

Prohibited sponsorship

1. Programmes may not be sponsored by natural or legal persons whose principal activity is the manufacture or sale of products, or the provision of services, the advertising of which is prohibited by virtue of Article 15.

2. Sponsorship of news and current affairs programmes shall not be allowed.

CHAPTER V

MUTUAL ASSISTANCE

Article 19

Co-operation between the Parties

1. The Parties undertake to render each other mutual assistance in order to implement this Convention.

2. For that purpose:

(a) each Contracting State shall designate one or more authorities, the name and address of each of which it shall communicate to the Secretary General of the Council of Europe at the time of deposit of its instrument of ratification, acceptance, approval or accession;

(b) each Contracting State which has designated more than one authority shall specify in its communication under sub-paragraph (a) the competence of each authority.

3. An authority designated by a Party shall:

(a) furnish the information foreseen under Article 6, paragraph 2, of this Convention;

(b) furnish information at the request of an authority designated by another Party on the domestic law and practices in the fields covered by this Convention;

(c) co-operate with the authorities designated by the other Parties whenever useful, and notably where this would enhance the effectiveness of measures taken in implementation of this Convention;

(d) consider any difficulty arising from the application of this Convention which is brought to its attention by an authority designated by another Party.

CHAPTER VI

STANDING COMMITTEE

Article 20

Standing Committee

1. For the purposes of this Convention, a Standing Committee shall be set up.

2. Each Party may be represented on the Standing Committee by one or more delegates. Each delegation shall have one vote. Within the areas of its competence, the European Economic Community shall exercise its right to vote with a number of votes equal to the number of its member States which are Parties to this Convention; the European Economic Community shall not exercise its right to vote in cases where the member States concerned exercise theirs, and conversely.

3. Any State referred to in Article 29, paragraph 1, which is not a Party to this Convention may be represented on the Standing Committee by an observer.

4. The Standing Committee may seek the advice of experts in order to discharge its functions. It may, on its own initiative or at the request of the body concerned, invite any international or national, governmental or non-governmental body technically qualified in the fields covered by this Convention to be represented by an observer at one or part of one of its meetings. The decision to invite such experts or bodies shall be taken by a majority of three-quarters of the members of the Standing Committee.

5. The Standing Committee shall be convened by the Secretary General of the Council of Europe. Its first meeting shall be held within six months of the date of entry into force of the Convention. It shall subsequently meet whenever one-third of the Parties or the Committee of Ministers of the Council of Europe so requests, or on the initiative of the Secretary General of the Council of Europe in accordance with the provisions of Article 23, paragraph 2, or at the request of one or more Parties in accordance with the provisions of Articles 21, sub-paragraph c, and 25, paragraph 2.

6. A majority of the Parties shall constitute a quorum for holding a meeting of the Standing Committee.

7. Subject to the provisions of paragraph 4 and Article 23, paragraph 3, the decisions of the Standing Committee shall be taken by a majority of three-quarters of the members present.

8. Subject to the provisions of this Convention, the Standing Committee shall draw up its own Rules of Procedure.

Article 21

Functions of the Standing Committee

The Standing Committee shall be responsible for following the application of this Convention. It may:

(a) make recommendations to the Parties concerning the application of the Convention;

(b) suggest any necessary modifications of the Convention and examine those proposed in accordance with the provisions of Article 23;

(c) examine, at the request of one or more Parties, questions concerning the interpretation of the Convention;

(d) use its best endeavours to secure a friendly settlement of any difficulty referred to it in accordance with the provisions of Article 25;

(e) make recommendations to the Committee of Ministers concerning States other than those referred to in Article 29, paragraph 1, to be invited to accede to this Convention.

Article 22

Reports of the Standing Committee

After each meeting, the Standing Committee shall forward to the Parties and the Committee of Ministers of the Council of Europe a report on its discussions and any decisions taken.

CHAPTER VII

AMENDMENTS

Article 23

Amendments

1. Any Party may propose amendments to this Convention.

2. Any proposal for amendment shall be notified to the Secretary General of the Council of Europe who shall communicate it to the member States of the Council of Europe, to the other States party to the European Cultural Convention, to the European Economic Community and to any non-member State which has acceded to, or has been invited to accede to this Convention in accordance with the provisions of Article 30. The Secretary General of the Council of Europe shall convene a meeting of the Standing Committee at the earliest two months following the communication of the proposal.

3. The Standing Committee shall examine any amendment proposed and shall submit the text adopted by a majority of three-quarters of the members of the Standing Committee to the Committee of Ministers for approval. After its approval, the text shall be forwarded to the Parties for acceptance.

4. Any amendment shall enter into force on the thirtieth day after all the Parties have informed the Secretary General of their acceptance thereof.

CHAPTER VIII

ALLEGED VIOLATIONS OF THIS CONVENTION

Article 24

Alleged violations of this Convention

1. When a Party finds a violation of this Convention, it shall communicate to the transmitting Party the alleged violation and the two Parties shall endeavour to overcome the difficulty on the basis of the provisions of Articles 19, 25 and 26.

2. If the alleged violation is of a manifest, serious and grave nature which raises important public issues and concerns Articles 7, paragraphs 1 or 2, 12, 13, paragraph 1, first sentence, 14 or 15, paragraphs 1 or 3, and if it persists within two weeks following the communication, the receiving Party may suspend provisionally the retransmission of the incriminated programme service.

3. In all other cases of alleged violation, with the exception of those provided for in paragraph 4, the receiving Party may suspend provisionally the retransmission of the incriminated programme service eight months following the communication, if the alleged violation persists.

4. The provisional suspension of retransmission shall not be allowed in the case of alleged violations of Articles 7, paragraph 3, 8, 9 or 10.

CHAPTER IX

SETTLEMENT OF DISPUTES

Article 25

Conciliation

1. In case of difficulty arising from the application of this Convention, the parties concerned shall endeavour to achieve a friendly settlement.

2. Unless one of the parties concerned objects, the Standing Committee may examine the question, by placing itself at the disposal of the parties concerned in order to reach a satisfactory solution as rapidly as possible and, where appropriate, to formulate an advisory opinion on the subject.

3. Each party concerned undertakes to accord the Standing Committee without delay all information and facilities necessary for the discharge of its functions under the preceding paragraph.

Article 26

Arbitration

1. If the parties concerned cannot settle the dispute in accordance with the provisions of Article 25, they may, by common agreement, submit it to arbitration, the procedure of which is provided for in the appendix to this Convention. In the absence of such an agreement within six months following the first request to open the procedure of conciliation, the dispute may be submitted to arbitration at the request of one of the parties.

2. Any Party may, at any time, declare that it recognises as compulsory *ipso facto* and without special agreement in respect of any other Party accepting the same obiligation the application of the arbitration procedure provided for in the appendix to this Convention.

CHAPTER X

OTHER INTERNATIONAL AGREEMENTS AND THE INTERNAL LAW OF THE PARTIES

Article 27

Other international agreements or arrangements

1. In their mutual relations, Parties which are members of the European Economic Community shall apply Community rules and shall not therefore apply the rules arising from this Convention except in so far as there is no Community rule governing the particular subject concerned.

2. Nothing in this Convention shall prevent the Parties from concluding international agreements completing or developing its provisions or extending their field of application.

3. In the case bilateral agreements, this Convention shall not alter the rights and obligations of Parties which arise from such agreements and which do not affect the enjoyment of other Parties of their rights or the performance of their obligations under this Convention.

Article 28

Relations between the Convention and the internal law of the Parties

Nothing in this Convention shall prevent the Parties from applying stricter or more detailed rules than those provided for in this Convention to programme services transmitted by entities or by technical means within their jurisdiction, within the meaning of Article 3.

CHAPTER XI

FINAL PROVISIONS

Article 29

Signature and entry into force

1. This Convention shall be open for signature by the member States of the Council of Europe and the other States party to the European Cultural Convention, and by the European Economic Community. It is subject to ratification, acceptance or approval. Instruments of ratification, acceptance or approval shall be deposited with the Secretary General of the Council of Europe.

2. This Convention shall enter into force on the first day of the month following the expiration of a period of three months after the date on which seven States, of which at least five member States of the Council of Europe, have expressed their consent to be bound by the Convention in accordance with the provisions of the preceding paragraph.

3. A State may, at the time of signature or at any later date prior to the entry into force of this Convention in respect of that State, declare that it shall apply the Convention provisionally.

4. In respect of any State referred to in paragraph 1, or the European Economic Community, which subsequently express their consent to be bound by it, this Convention shall enter into force on the first day of the month following the expiration of a period of three months after the date of deposit of the instrument of ratification, acceptance or approval.

Article 30

Accession by non-member States

1. After the entry into force of this Convention, the Committee of Ministers of the Council of Europe, after consulting the Contracting States may invite any other State to accede to this Convention by a decision taken by the majority provided for in Article 20.d of the Statute of the Council of Europe and by the unanimous vote of the representatives of the Contracting States entitled to sit on the Committee.

2. In respect of any acceding State, this Convention shall enter into force on the first day of the month following the expiration of a period of three months after the date of deposit of the instrument of accession with the Secretary General of the Council of Europe.

Article 31

Territorial application

1. Any State may, at the time of signature or when depositing its instrument of ratification, acceptance, approval or accession, specify the territory or territories to which this Convention shall apply.

2. Any State may, at any later date, by a declaration addressed to the Secretary General of the Council of Europe, extend the application of this Convention to any other territory specified in the declaration. In respect of such territory, the Convention shall enter into force on the first day of the month following the expiration of a period of three months after the date of receipt of such declaration by the Secretary General.

3. Any declaration made under the two preceding paragraphs may, in respect of any territory specified in such declaration, be withdrawn by a notification addressed to the Secretary General. The withdrawal shall become effective on the first day of the month following the expiration of a period of six months after the date of receipt of such notification by the Secretary General.

Article 32

Reservations

1. At the time of signature or when depositing its instrument of ratification, acceptance, approval or accession:

(a) any State may declare that it reserves the right to restrict the retransmission on its territory, solely to the extent that it does not comply with its domestic legislation, of programme services containing advertisements for alcoholic beverages according to the rules provided for in Article 15, paragraph 2, of this Convention;

(b) the United Kingdom may declare that it reserves the right not to fulfil the obligation, set out in Article 15, paragraph 1, to prohibit advertisements for tobacco products, in respect of advertisements for cigars and pipe tobacco broadcast by the Independent Broadcasting Authority by terrestrial means on its territory.

No other reservations may be made.

2. A reservation made in accordance with the preceding paragraph may not be the subject of an objection.

3. Any Contracting State which has made a reservation under paragraph 1 may wholly or partly withdraw it by means of a notification addressed to the Secretary General of the Council of Europe. The withdrawal shall take effect on the date of receipt of such notification by the Secretary General.

4. A Party which has made a reservation in respect of a provision of this Convention may not claim the application of that provision by any other Party; it may, however, if its reservation is partial or conditional, claim the application of that provision in so far as it has itself accepted it.

Article 33

Denunciation

1. Any Party may, at any time, denounce this Convention by means of a notification addressed to the Secretary General of the Council of Europe.

2. Such denunciation shall become effective on the first day of the month following the expiration of a period of six months after the date of receipt of the notification by the Secretary General.

Article 34

Notifications

The Sectretary General of the Council of Europe shall notify the member States of the Council, the other States party to the European Cultural Convention, the European Economic Community and any State which has acceded to, or has been invited to accede to this Convention of:

(a) any signature;
(b) the deposit of any instrument of ratification, acceptance, approval or accession;
(c) any date of entry into force of this Convention in accordance with the provisions of Articles 29, 30 and 31;
(d) any report established in accordance with the provisions of Article 22;
(e) any other act, declaration, notification or communication relating to this Convention.

In witness whereof the undersigned, being duly authorised thereto, have signed this Convention.

Done at Strasbourg, the 5th day of May 1989, in English and French, both texts being equally authentic, in a single copy which shall be deposited in the archives of the Council of Europe. The Secretary General of the Council of Europe shall transmit certified copies to each member State of the Council of Europe, to the other States party to the European Cultural Convention, to the European Economic Community and to any State invited to accede to this Convention.

APPENDIX

ARBITRATION

1. A request for arbitration shall be notified to the Secretary General of the Council of Europe. It shall include the name of the other party to the dispute and the subject matter of the dispute. The Secretary General shall communicate the information so received to all the Parties to this Convention.

2. In the event of a dispute between two Parties one of which is a member State of the European Economic Community, the latter itself being a Party, the request for arbitration shall be addressed both to the member State and to the Community, which jointly shall notify the Secretary General, within one month of receipt of the request, whether the member State or the Community, or the member State and the Community jointly, shall be party to the dispute. In the absence of such notification within the said time-limit, the member State and the Community shall be considered as being one and the same party to the dispute for the purposes of the application of the provisions governing the consitution and procedure of the arbitration tribunal. The same shall apply when the member State and the Community jointly present themselves as party to the dispute. In cases envisaged by this paragraph, the time-limit of one month foreseen in the first sentence of paragraph 4 hereafter shall be extended to two months.

3. The arbitration tribunal shall consist of three members: each of the parties to the dispute shall appoint one arbitrator; the two arbitrators so appointed shall designate by common agreement the third arbitrator who shall be the chairman of the tribunal. The latter shall not be a national of either of the parties to the dispute, nor have his usual place of residence in the territory of either of those parties, nor be employed by either of them, nor have dealt with the case in another capacity.

4. If one of the parties has not appointed an arbitrator within one month following the communication of the request by the Secretary General of the Council of Europe, he shall

be appointed at the request of the other party by the President of the European Court of Human Rights within a further one-month period. If the President of the Court is unable to act or is a national of one of the parties to the dispute, the appointment shall be made by the Vice-President of the Court or by the most senior judge to the Court who is available and is not a national of one of the parties to the dispute. The same procedure shall be observed if, within a period of one month following the appointment of the second arbitrator, the Chairman of the arbitration tribunal is not designated.

5. The provisions of paragraphs 3 and 4 shall apply, as the case may be, in order to fill any vacancy.

6. Two or more parties which determine by agreement that they are in the same interest shall appoint an arbitrator jointly.

7. The parties to the dispute and the Standing Committee shall provide the arbitration tribunal with all facilities necessary for the effective conduct of the proceedings.

8. The arbitration tribunal shall draw up its own Rules of Procedure. Its decisions shall be taken by majority vote of its members. Its award shall be final and binding.

9. The award of the arbitration tribunal shall be notified to the Secretary General of the Council of Europe who shall communicate it to all the Parties to this Convention.

10. Each party to the dispute shall bear the expenses of the arbitrator appointed by it; these parties shall share equally the expenses of the other arbitrator, as well as other costs entailed by the arbitration.

APPENDIX 3
Treaty Tables

TABLE A

Berne Convention for the Protection of Literary and Artistic Works

State	Date on which became a Party	Act to which State is a Party and Date of Entry into Force				Notifications and Reservations		
		Rome	Brussels	Stockholm	Paris	Article 6(3)	Article 14bis (2) (c)	Article 14bis (2) (d)
Argentina	10 Jun 1967		10 June 1967		Articles 22 to 38: 8 Oct 1980			
Australia	14 Apr 1928				1 Mar 1978			
Austria	1 Oct 1920				21 Aug 1982			
Bahamas	10 Jul 1973		10 Jul 1973		Articles 22 to 38: 8 Jan 1977			
Barbados	30 Jul 1983				30 Jul 1983			
Belgium	5 Dec 1887		1 Aug 1951	Articles 22 to 38: 12 Feb 1975				
Benin	3 Jan 1961[4]				12 Mar 1975			
Brazil	9 Feb 1922				20 Apr 1975			

Bulgaria	5 Dec 1921			4 Dec 1974
Burkina Faso	19 Aug 1963[5]			24 Jan 1976
Cameroon	21 Sep 1964[4]			Articles 1 to 21: 10 Oct 1974 Articles 22 to 38: 10 Nov 1973
Canada	10 Apr 1928	1 Aug 1931	Articles 22 to 38: 7 Jul 1970	
Central African Rep	3 Sep 1977			3 Sep 1977
Chad	25 Nov 1971	25 Nov 1971	Articles[1,2] 22 to 38: 25 Nov 1971	
Chile	5 June 1970			10 Jul 1975
China	15 Oct 1992			15 Oct 1992
Colombia	7 Mar 1988			7 Mar 1988
Congo	8 May 1962[4]			5 Dec 1975
Costa Rica	10 Jun 1978			10 Jun 1978

State	Date on which became a Party	Act to which State is a Party and Date of Entry into Force				Notifications and Reservations		
		Rome	Brussels	Stockholm	Paris	Article 6(3)	Article 14bis (2) (c)	Article 14bis (2) (d)
Côte d'Ivoire	1 Jan 1962				Articles 1 to 21: 10 Oct 1974 Articles 22 to 38: 4 May 1974			
Croatia	8 Oct 1991				8 Oct 1991			
Cyprus	24 Feb 1964[4]				27 Jul 1983			
Czech Republic	1 Jan 1993				1 Jan 1993			
Denmark	1 Jul 1903				30 Jun 1979			
Ecuador	9 Oct 1991				9 Oct 1991			
Egypt	7 Jun 1977				7 Jun 1977			
Fiji	1 Dec 1971[4]		1 Dec 1971	Articles 22 to 38: 15 Mar 1972				
Finland	1 Apr 1928				1 Nov 1986			

France	5 Dec 1887	Articles 1 to 21: 10 Oct 1974 Articles 22 to 38: 15 Dec 1972
Gabon	26 Mar 1962	10 Jun 1975
Gambia	7 Mar 1993	7 Mar 1993
Germany	5 Dec 1887	Articles[3] 1 to 21: 10 Oct 1974 Articles 22 to 38: 22 Jan 1974
Ghana	11 Oct 1991	11 Oct 1991
Greece	9 Nov 1920	8 Mar 1976
Guinea	20 Nov 1980	20 Nov 1980
Guinea-Bissau	22 Jul 1991	22 Jul 1991
Holy See	12 Sep 1935	24 Apr 1975
Honduras	25 Jan 1990	25 Jan 1990

State	Date on which became a Party	Act to which State is a Party and Date of Entry into Force				Notifications and Reservations		
		Rome	Brussels	Stockholm	Paris	Article 6(3)	Article 14bis (2) (c)	Article 14bis (2) (d)
Hungary	14 Feb 1922				Articles 1 to 21: 10 Oct 1974 Articles 22 to 38: 15 Dec 1972			
Iceland	7 Sep 1947	7 Sep 1947			Articles 22 to 38: 28 Dec 1984			
India	1 Apr 1928				Articles 1 to 21: 6 May 1984 Articles 22 to 38: 10 Jan 1975		See note[6]	
Ireland	5 Oct 1927		5 Jul 1959	Articles 22 to 38: 21 Dec 1970				
Israel	24 Mar 1950		1 Aug 1951	Articles 22 to 38: 29 Jan or 26 Feb 1970				

Italy	5 Dec 1887				14 Nov 1979
Japan	15 Jul 1899				24 Apr 1975
Kenya	11 Jun 1993				11 Jun 1993
Lebanon	30 Sep 1947	30 Sept 1947			
Lesotho	28 Sep 1989				28 Sep 1989
Liberia	8 Mar 1989				8 Mar 1989
Libya	28 Sep 1976				28 Sep 1976
Liechten-stein	30 Jul 1931		1 Aug 1951	Articles 22 to 38: 25 May 1972	
Luxembourg	20 Jun 1888				20 Apr 1975
Madagascar	1 Jan 1966		1 Jan 1966		
Malawi	12 Oct 1991				12 Oct 1991
Malaysia	1 Oct 1990				1 Oct 1990
Mali	19 Mar 1962[4]				5 Dec 1977
Malta	21 Sep 1964	21 Sep 1964			Articles 22 to 38: 12 Dec 1977

State	Date on which became a Party	Act to which State is a Party and Date of Entry into Force				Notifications and Reservations		
		Rome	Brussels	Stockholm	Paris	Article 6(3)	Article 14bis (2) (c)	Article 14bis (2) (d)
Mauritania	6 Feb 1973				21 Sep 1976			
Mauritius	10 May 1989				10 May 1989			
Mexico	11 Jun 1967				17 Dec 1974			
Monaco	30 May 1889				23 Nov 1974			
Morocco	16 Jun 1917				17 May 1987			
Netherlands	1 Nov 1912				Articles[7] 1 to 21: 30 Jan 1986 Articles[8] 22 to 38: 10 Jan 1975			
New Zealand	24 Apr 1928	4 Dec 1947						
Niger	2 May 1962[4]				21 May 1975			
Nigeria	14 Sep 1993		28 Jan 1963		14 Sep 1993			
Norway	13 Apr 1896				Articles[3] 22 to 38: 13 Jun 1974			

Pakistan	5 Jul 1948	5 Jul 1948	Articles[1] 22 to 38: 29 Jan or 26 Feb 1970		
Paraguay	2 Jan 1992			2 Jan 1992	
Peru	20 Aug 1988			20 Aug 1988	
Philippines	1 Aug 1951	1 Aug 1951		Articles 22 to 38: 16 Jul 1980	
Poland	28 Jan 1920	21 Nov 1935		Articles 22 to 38: 4 Aug 1990	
Portugal	29 Mar 1911			12 Jan 1979	Yes
Romania	1 Jan 1927	6 Aug 1936	Articles[1] 22 to 38: 29 Jan or 26 Feb 1970		
Rwanda	1 Mar 1984			1 Mar 1984	
Saint Lucia	24 Aug 1993			24 Aug 1993	
Senegal	25 Aug 1962			12 Aug 1975	
Slovakia	1 Jan 1993			1 Jan 1993	

State	Act to which State is a Party and Date of Entry into Force					Notifications and Reservations		
	Date on which became a Party	Rome	Brussels	Stockholm	Paris	Article 6(3)	Article 14bis (2) (c)	Article 14bis (2) (d)
Slovenia	25 Jun 1991				25 Jun 1991			
South Africa	3 Oct 1928		1 Aug 1951		Articles 22 to 38: 24 Mar 1975			
Spain	5 Dec 1887				Articles 1 to 21: 10 Oct 1974 Articles 22 to 38: 19 Feb 1974			
Sri Lanka	20 Jul 1959*	20 Jul 1959			Articles 22 to 38: 23 Sep 1978			
Surinam	23 Feb 1977				23 Feb 1977			
Sweden	1 Aug 1904				Articles 1 to 21: 10 Oct 1974 Articles 22 to 38: 20 Sep 1973			

Switzerland	5 Dec 1887	2 Jan 1956		
Thailand	17 Jul 1931		Articles 22 to 38: 4 May 1970	Articles[9] 22 to 38: 29 Dec 1980
Togo	30 Apr 1975			30 Apr 1975
Trinidad and Tobago	16 Aug 1988			16 Aug 1988
Tunisia	5 Dec 1887			16 Aug 1975
Turkey	1 Jan 1952	1 Jan 1952		
United Kingdom	5 Dec 1887			2 Jan 1990
USA	1 Mar 1989			1 Mar 1989
Uruguay	10 Jul 1967			28 Dec 1979
Venezuela	30 Dec 1982			30 Dec 1982
Zaire	8 Oct 1963[4]			31 Jan 1975
Zambia	2 Jan 1992			2 Jan 1992
Zimbabwe	18 Apr 1980	18 Apr 1980		Articles 22 to 38: 30 Dec 1981

State	Notifications and Reservations						Territorial Application	
	Article 15(4)b	Article 30(2)b	Article 33(2)	Appendix Art II	Appendix Art III	Appendix Art V	Date of receipt of notification	Extension to
Argentina								
Australia								
Austria								
Bahamas			Yes					
Barbados								
Belgium								
Benin								
Brazil								
Bulgaria			Yes					
Burkina Faso								
Cameroon								
Canada								

Central African Rep				
Chad				
Chile				
China			Yes	Yes
Colombia				
Congo				
Costa Rica		Yes		
Côte d'Ivoire				
Croatia	Yes			
Cryprus	Yes	Yes		
Czech Republic				
Denmark				
Ecuador				
Egypt		Yes	Yes	Yes
Fiji				

| State | Notifications and Reservations | | | | | | Territorial Application | |
	Article 15(4)b	Article 30(2)b	Article 33(2)	Appendix Art II	Appendix Art III	Appendix Art V	Date of receipt of notification	Extension to
Finland								
France								
Gabon								
Gambia								
Germany								
Ghana								
Greece								
Guinea								
Guinea-Bissau								
Holy See								
Honduras								
Hungary								
Iceland	Yes							

India	Yes			
Ireland				
Israel				
Italy				
Japan				
Kenya				
Lebanon				
Lesotho		Yes	Yes	Yes
Liberia		Yes	Yes	Yes
Libya		Yes		
Liechtenstein			Yes	Yes
Luxembourg				
Madagascar				
Malawi				
Malaysia			Yes	Yes
Mali				

State	Notifications and Reservations						Territorial Application	
	Article 15(4)b	Article 30(2)b	Article 33(2)	Appendix Art II	Appendix Art III	Appendix Art V	Date of receipt of notification	Extension to
Malta			Yes					
Mauritania								
Mauritius			Yes	Yes	Yes			
Mexico				Yes	Yes			
Monaco								
Morocco								
Netherlands								
New Zealand								
Niger								
Nigeria								
Norway								
Pakistan								
Paraguay								

Peru		
Philippines		
Poland		
Portugal		
Romania	Yes	
Rwanda		
Saint Lucia	Yes	
Senegal		
Slovakia		Yes
Slovenia	Yes	
South Africa	Yes	
Spain		
Sri Lanka		
Surinam		
Sweden		
Switzerland		

State	Notifications and Reservations						Territorial Application	
	Article 15(4)b	Article 30(2)b	Article 33(2)	Appendix Art II	Appendix Art III	Appendix Art V	Date of receipt of notification	Extension to
Thailand			Yes					
Togo								
Trinidad and Tobago								
Tunisia			Yes					
Turkey		Yes						
United Kingdom								
USA								
Uruguay								
Venezuela			Yes					
Zaire								
Zambia								
Zimbabwe								

Notes

1 This State deposited its instrument of ratification of (or of accession to) the Stockholm Act in its entirety; however, Articles 1 to 21 (substantive clauses) of the Stockholm Act have not entered into force.

2 In accordance with the provision of Article 29 of the Stockholm Act applicable to the States outside the Union which accede to the said Act, this State is bound by Articles 1 to 20 of the Brussels Act.

3 This State has declared that it admits the application of the Appendix of the Paris Act to works of which it is the State of origin by States which have made a declaration under Article VI(1) (i) of the Appendix or a notification under Article I of the Appendix. The declarations took effect on 18 October 1973 for Germany and on 8 March 1974 for Norway.

4 Date on which the declaration of continued adherence was sent, after the accession of the State to independence.

5 Burkina Faso, which had acceded to the Berne Convention (Brussels Act) as from 19 August 1963, denounced the said Convention as from 20 September 1970. Later on, Burkina Faso acceded again to the Berne Convention (Paris Act); this accession took effect on 24 January 1976.

6 This State declared that its ratification shall not apply to the provisions of Article 14bis (2) (b) of the Paris Act (presumption of legitimation for some authors who have brought contributions to the making of the cinematographic work).

7 Ratification for the Kingdom in Europe.

8 Ratification for the Kingdom in Europe. Articles 22 to 38 of the Paris Act also apply to the Netherlands Antilles and Aruba.

9 Thailand continues to be a Party to the Berlin Act. Accession was subject to reservations concerning works of applied art, conditions and formalities required for protection, the right of translation, the right of reproduction of articles published in newspapers or periodicals, the right of performance, and the application of the Convention to works not yet in the public domain at the date of its coming into force.

TABLE B

Universal Copyright Convention of 1952 and annexed Protocols 1, 2 and 3

I. Entry into Force

Text	Initial Entry into Force	Subsequent Entry into Force
Universal Copyright Convention	16 September 1955 in accordance with Article IX, paragraph 1	Three months after deposit of the instrument of ratification, acceptance or accession in accordance with Article IX, paragraph 2
Annexed Protocol No. 1 concerning the application of that Convention to the works of stateless persons and refugees	16 September 1955 in accordance with paragraph 2(b)	Date of deposit of the instrument of ratification, acceptance or accession, subject to the concerned State being a party to the Convention (paragraph 2(b))
Annexed Protocol No. 2 concerning the application of that Convention to the works of certain international organisations	16 September 1955 in accordance with paragraph 2(b)	Date of deposit of the instrument of ratification, acceptance or accession, subject to the concerned State being a party to the Convention (paragraph 2(b))
Annexed Protocol No. 3 concerning the effective date of instruments of ratification or acceptance of, or accession to, that Convention	19 August 1954 in accordance with paragraph 6(b)	Date of deposit of the instrument of ratification, acceptance or accession (paragraph 6(b))

II. Ratifications, Acceptances and Accessions

| State | Date of Deposit of Instrument | | | | Territorial Application | |
	Convention	Protocol 1	Protocol 2	Protocol 3	Date of receipt of notification	Extension to
Algeria[1]	28 May 1973					
Andorra[2]	31 Dec 1952 22 Jan 1953	22 Jan 1953	31 Dec 1952 22 Jan 1953	31 Dec 1952 22 Jan 1953		
Argentina	13 Nov 1957	13 Nov 1957	13 Nov 1957			
Australia	1 Feb 1969	24 Jul 1969	24 Jul 1969	24 Jul 1969		
Austria	2 Apr 1957	2 Apr 1957	2 Apr 1957	2 Apr 1957		
Bahamas **D**	13 Jul 1976					
Bangladesh[3]	5 May 1975	5 May 1975				
Barbados[4]	18 Mar 1983					
Belgium	31 May 1960	31 May 1960	31 May 1960	31 May 1960	24 Jan 1961	Ruanda-Urundi
Belize[5] **D**	1 Dec 1982					
Bolivia[6]	22 Dec 1989	22 Dec 1989	22 Dec 1989	22 Dec 1989		
Brazil	13 Oct 1959	13 Oct 1959	13 Oct 1959	13 Oct 1959		
Bulgaria[7]	7 Mar 1975					

State	Date of Deposit of Instrument				Territorial Application	
	Convention	Protocol 1	Protocol 2	Protocol 3	Date of receipt of notification	Extension to
Cambodia	3 Aug 1953	3 Aug 1953	3 Aug 1953	3 Aug 1953		
Cameroon[8]	1 Feb 1973					
Canada	10 May 1962			10 May 1962		
Chile	18 Jan 1955		18 Jan 1955			
China	30 Jul 1992					
Colombia[9]	18 Mar 1976					
Costa Rica	7 Dec 1954	7 Dec 1954	7 Dec 1954	7 Dec 1954		
Croatia	11 Feb 1966	11 Feb 1966	11 Feb 1966	11 Feb 1966		
Cuba	18 Mar 1957	18 Mar 1957	18 Mar 1957			
Cyprus[10]	19 Sep 1990	19 Sep 1990				
Czech Republic	6 Oct 1959		6 Oct 1959	6 Oct 1959		
Denmark	9 Nov 1961	9 Nov 1961	9 Nov 1961	9 Nov 1961		
Dominican Republic[11]	8 Feb 1983					
Ecuador	5 Mar 1957	5 Mar 1957	5 Mar 1957			

El Salvador[12]	29 Dec 1978	29 Dec 1978			
Fiji D	13 Dec 1971				
Finland	16 Jan 1963	16 Jan 1963	16 Jan 1963		
France	14 Oct 1955	14 Oct 1955	14 Oct 1955	16 Nov 1955	Departments of Algeria, Guadeloupe, Martinique, Guiana, Réunion
Germany[13]	3 Jun 1955	3 Jun 1955	3 Jun 1955		
Ghana	22 May 1962	22 May 1962	22 May 1962		
Greece	24 May 1963	24 May 1963	24 May 1963		
Guatemala	28 Jul 1964	28 Jul 1964	28 Jul 1964		
Guinea[14]	13 Aug 1981	13 Aug 1981			
Haiti	1 Sep 1954	1 Sep 1954	1 Sep 1954		
Holy See	5 Jul 1955	5 Jul 1955	5 Jul 1955		
Hungary[15]	23 Oct 1970	23 Oct 1970			
Iceland	18 Sep 1956				
India	21 Oct 1957	21 Oct 1957	21 Oct 1957	21 Oct 1957	

| State | Date of Deposit of Instrument | | | | Territorial Application | |
	Convention	Protocol 1	Protocol 2	Protocol 3	Date of receipt of notification	Extension to
Ireland	20 Oct 1958	20 Oct 1958	20 Oct 1958	20 Oct 1958		
Israel	6 Apr 1955	6 Apr 1955	6 Apr 1955	6 Apr 1955		
Italy	24 Oct 1956	19 Dec 1966	24 Oct 1956	24 Oct 1956		
Japan	28 Jan 1956	28 Jan 1956	28 Jan 1956	28 Jan 1956		
Kazakhstan	27 Feb 1973					
Kenya	7 Jun 1966	7 Jun 1966	7 Jun 1966	7 Jun 1966		
Laos	19 Aug 1954	19 Aug 1954	19 Aug 1954	19 Aug 1954		
Lebanon	17 Jul 1959	17 Jul 1959	17 Jul 1959	17 Jul 1959		
Liberia	27 Apr 1956	27 Apr 1956	27 Apr 1956			
Liechtenstein	22 Oct 1958	22 Oct 1958	22 Oct 1958			
Luxembourg	15 Jul 1955	15 Jul 1955	15 Jul 1955	15 Jul 1955		
Malawi	26 Jul 1965					
Malta	19 Aug 1968					
Mauritius[16] D	20 Aug 1970	20 Aug 1970	20 Aug 1970	20 Aug 1970		

TABLE B

Country					Territories
Mexico	12 Feb 1957	12 Feb 1957	12 Feb 1957	12 Feb 1957	
Monaco	16 Jun 1955	16 Jun 1955	16 Jun 1955	16 Jun 1955	
Morocco	8 Feb 1972	8 Feb 1972	8 Feb 1972	8 Feb 1972	
Netherlands	22 Mar 1967	22 Mar 1967	22 Mar 1967	22 Mar 1967	
New Zealand	11 Jun 1964	11 Jun 1964	11 Jun 1964	11 Jun 1964	11 Jun 1964 — Cook Islands (including Niue), Tokelau Islands
Nicaragua	16 May 1961	16 May 1961	16 May 1961	16 May 1961	
Niger[17]	15 Feb 1989	15 Feb 1989			
Nigeria	14 Nov 1961				
Norway	23 Oct 1962	23 Oct 1962	23 Oct 1962	23 Oct 1962	
Pakistan	28 Apr 1954	28 Apr 1954	28 Apr 1954	28 Apr 1954	
Panama	17 Jul 1962	17 Jul 1962	17 Jul 1962	17 Jul 1962	
Paraguay	11 Dec 1961	11 Dec 1961	11 Dec 1961	11 Dec 1961	
Peru	16 Jul 1963	22 Apr 1985			
Philippines[18]	19 Aug 1955	19 Aug 1955	19 Aug 1955	19 Aug 1955	
Poland[19]	9 Dec 1976	9 Dec 1976			
Portugal	25 Sep 1956	25 Sep 1956	25 Sep 1956	25 Sep 1956	

State	Date of Deposit of Instrument				Territorial Application	
	Convention	Protocol 1	Protocol 2	Protocol 3	Date of receipt of notification	Extension to
Republic of Korea[20]						
Russian Federation[21]	27 Feb 1973					
Rwanda[22]	10 Aug 1989	10 Aug 1989				
Saint Vincent and the Grenadines[23] **D**	22 Jan 1985					
Senegal[24]	9 Apr 1974	9 Apr 1974				
Slovak Republic	6 Oct 1959		6 Oct 1959	6 Oct 1959		
Slovenia	11 Feb 1966	11 Feb 1966	11 Feb 1966	11 Feb 1966		
Spain	27 Oct 1954	27 Oct 1954[25]	27 Oct 1954	27 Oct 1954[25]		
Sri Lanka[26]	25 Oct 1983	27 Jul 1988	27 Jul 1988	27 Jul 1988		
Sweden	1 Apr 1961	1 Apr 1961	1 Apr 1961	1 Apr 1961		
Switzerland	30 Dec 1955	30 Dec 1955	30 Dec 1955			

Tadfikistan	27 Feb 1973				
Trinidad and Tobago[27]	19 May 1988				
Tunisia	19 Mar 1969	19 Mar 1969	19 Mar 1969	19 Mar 1969	
United Kingdom	27 Jun 1957	27 Jun 1957	27 Jun 1957	27 Jun 1957	

United Kingdom territories:

Territory	Date
Isle of Man, Fiji, Gibraltar, Sarawak	29 Nov 1961
Zanzibar, Bermuda, North Borneo[28]	4 Feb 1963
Bahamas, Virgin Islands	26 Apr 1963
Falkland Islands,[29] Kenya, Saint Helena, Seychelles	29 Oct 1963
Mauritius	6 Oct 1964
Bechuanaland, Montserrat, Saint Lucia	8 Feb 1966
Grenada	15 Feb 1966
Cayman Islands	11 Mar 1966
British Guiana	15 Mar 1966
British Honduras[30]	19 Jul 1966
Saint Vincent	10 Aug 1967
Hong Kong	2 May 1973

State	Date of Deposit of Instrument				Territorial Application	
	Convention	Protocol 1	Protocol 2	Protocol 3	Date of receipt of notification	Extension to
United States of America	6 Dec 1954	6 Dec 1954	6 Dec 1954	6 Dec 1954	6 Dec 1954 17 May 1957	Alaska, Hawaii, Panama Canal Zone,[31] Puerto Rico, Virgin Islands Guam
Uruguay	12 Jan 1993	12 Jan 1993	12 Jan 1993	12 Jan 1993		
Venezuela	30 Jun 1966	30 Jun 1966	30 Jun 1966	30 Jun 1966		
Zambia	1 Mar 1965					

Notes

Symbol "D". The symbol "D" denotes a declaration by a State recognising itself bound, as from the date of its independence, by the Convention and/or annexed Protocols 1, 2 and 3, the application of which had been extended to its territory by a State then responsible for the conduct of its foreign relations. The date shown is the date of receipt by the Director-General of UNESCO.

[1] The instrument of accession by Algeria to the Universal Copyright Convention as revised at Paris on 24 July 1971 was deposited with the Director-General of UNESCO on 28 May 1973. Article IX(3) of the revised Convention provides: "Accession to this Convention by a State not party to the 1952 Convention shall also constitute accession to that Convention; however, if its instrument of accession is deposited before this Convention comes into force, such State may make its accession to the 1952 Convention conditional upon the coming into force of this Convention. . .". Since Algeria's accession was not made conditional upon the coming into force of the revised Convention, its accession to the 1952 Convention came into force on 28 August 1973.

[2] The Director-General of UNESCO received from the French Ministry of Foreign Affairs, in the name of the President of the French Republic, co-Prince of Andorra, a communication dated 17 January 1953 and from His Excellency the Bishop of Urgel, co-Prince of Andorra, a communication dated 10 March 1953, regarding the instrument of ratification deposited on 31 December 1952. These two communications were transmitted to the States concerned by letter CL/806 of 25 July 1953.

3 The instrument of accession by Bangladesh to the Universal Copyright Convention as revised at Paris on 24 July 1971 and annexed Protocols 1 and 2 was deposited with the Director-General of UNESCO on 5 May 1975. Article IX(3) of the revised Convention provides: "Accession to this Convention by a State not party to the 1952 Convention shall also constitute accession to that Convention; . . .". Consequently, in respect of Bangladesh, the 1952 Convention came into force on 5 August 1975. Paragraph 2(c) of Protocol 1 annexed to the Universal Copyright Convention as revised at Paris on 24 July 1971 provides: "On the entry into force of this Protocol in respect of a State not party to Protocol 1 annexed to the 1952 Convention, the latter Protocol shall be deemed to enter into force in respect of such State." Consequently, in respect of Bangladesh, Protocol 1 annexed to the 1952 Convention entered into force on 5 August 1975.

4 The instrument of accession by Barbados to the Universal Copyright Convention as revised at Paris on 24 July 1971 was deposited with the Director-General of UNESCO on 18 March 1983. Article IX(3) of the revised Convention provides: "Accession to this Convention by a State not party to the 1952 Convention shall also constitute accession to that Convention; . . .". Consequently, in respect of Barbados, the 1952 Convention came into force on 18 June 1983.

5 On 1 December 1982, the Director-General of UNESCO received from the Government of Belize a communication notifying him that it had decided to apply provisionally, and on the basis of reciprocity, the Convention, the application of which had been extended to its territory before the attainment of independence.

6 On 22 December 1989, Bolivia deposited also with the Director-General of UNESCO its instrument of accession to the Universal Copyright Convention as revised at Paris on 24 July 1971.

7 The instrument of accession by Bulgaria to the Universal Copyright Convention as revised at Paris on 24 July 1971 was deposited with the Director-General of UNESCO on 7 March 1975. Article IX(3) of the revised Convention provides: "Accession to this Convention by a State not party to the 1952 Convention shall also constitute accession to that Convention; . . .". Consequently, in respect of Bulgaria, the 1952 Convention entered into force on 7 June 1975. The instrument of accession contained a declaration with respect to Article XIII (see below, note 4 of the Table containing details of States party to the Universal Copyright Convention as revised at Paris on 24 July 1971).

8 Cameroon deposited its instrument of accession to the Universal Copyright Convention as revised at Paris on 24 July 1971 with the Director-General of UNESCO on 1 February 1973. Article IX(3) of the revised Convention provides: "Accession to this Convention by a State not party to the 1952 Convention shall also constitute accession to that Convention; however, if its instrument of accession is deposited before this Convention comes into force, such State may make its accession to the 1952 Convention conditional upon the coming into force of this Convention. . .". Since Cameroon's accession was not made conditional upon the coming into force of the revised Convention, its accession to the 1952 Convention came into force on 1 May 1973.

9 The instrument of accession by Colombia to the Universal Copyright Convention as revised at Paris on 24 July 1971 was deposited with the Director-General of UNESCO on 18 March 1976. Article IX(3) of the revised Convention provides: "Accession to this Convention by a State not party to the 1952 Convention shall also constitute accession to that Convention; . . .". Consequently, in respect of Colombia, the 1952 Convention came into force on 18 June 1976.

10 The instrument of accession by Cyprus to the Universal Copyright Convention as revised at Paris on 24 July 1971 and annexed Protocols 1 and 2 was deposited with the Director-General of UNESCO on 19 September 1990. Article IX(3) of the revised Convention provides: "Accession to this Convention by a State not party to the 1952 Convention shall also constitute accession to that Convention; . . .". Consequently, in respect of Cyprus, the 1952 Convention came into force on 19 December 1990. Paragraph 2(c) of Protocol 1 annexed to the Universal Copyright Convention as revised at Paris on 24 July 1971 provides: "On the entry into force of this Protocol in respect of a State not party to Protocol 1 annexed to the 1952 Convention, the latter Protocol shall be deemed to enter into force in respect of such State." Consequently, in respect of Cyprus, Protocol 1 annexed to the 1952 Convention entered into force on 19 December 1990.

11 The instrument of accession by the Dominican Republic to the Universal Copyright Convention as revised at Paris on 24 July 1971 was deposited with the Director-General of UNESCO on 8 February 1983. Article IX(3) of the revised Convention provides: "Accession to this Convention by a State not party to the 1952 Convention shall also constitute accession to that Convention; . . .". Consequently, in respect of the Dominican Republic, the 1952 Convention came into force on 8 May 1983.

[12] The instrument of accession by El Salvador to the Universal Copyright Convention as revised at Paris on 24 July 1971 and annexed Protocols 1 and 2 was deposited with the Director-General of UNESCO on 29 December 1978. Article IX(3) of the revised Convention provides: "Accession to this Convention by a State not party to the 1952 Convention shall also constitute accession to that Convention; ...". Consequently, in respect of El Salvador, the 1952 Convention came into force on 29 March 1979. Paragraph 2(c) of Protocol 1 annexed to the Universal Copyright Convention as revised at Paris on 24 July 1971 provides: "On the entry into force of this Protocol in respect of a State not party to Protocol 1 annexed to the 1952 Convention, the latter Protocol shall be deemed to enter into force in respect of such State." Consequently, in respect of El Salvador, Protocol 1 annexed to the 1952 Convention entered into force on 29 March 1979.

[13] The Director-General of UNESCO received from the Permanent Delegate of the Federal Republic of Germany a letter dated 3 October 1990 informing him that "through the accession of the German Democratic Republic to the Federal Republic of Germany with effect from 3 October 1990, the two German States have united to form one sovereign State". This letter was accompanied by a verbal note dated 3 October 1990, informing UNESCO that "with regard to the continued application of treaties of the Federal Republic of Germany and the treatment of treaties of the German Democratic Republic following its accession to the Federal Republic of Germany with effect from 3 October 1990, the Treaty of 31 August 1990 between the Federal Republic of Germany and the German Democratic Republic on the establishment of German unity (Unification Treaty) contains the following relevant provisions:

1. Article II
Treaties of the Federal Republic of Germany
The contracting parties proceed on the understanding that international treaties and agreements to which the Federal Republic of Germany is a contracting party... shall retain their validity and that the rights and obligations arising therefrom shall also relate to the territory specified in Article 3 of this Treaty". (Länder of Brandenburg, Mecklenburg-Western Pomerania, Saxe, Saxe-Anhalt and Thuringia as well as the sector of the Land of Berlin where the Fundamental Law of the Federal Republic of Germany was not applicable.)

[14] The instrument of accession by Guinea to the Universal Copyright Convention as revised at Paris on 24 July 1971 and annexed Protocols 1 and 2 was deposited with the Director-General of UNESCO on 13 August 1981. Article IX(3) of the revised Convention provides: "Accession to this Convention by a State not party to the 1952 Convention shall also constitute accession to that Convention; ...". Consequently, in respect of Guinea, the 1952 Convention came into force on 13 November 1981. Paragraph 2(c) of Protocol 1 annexed to the Universal Copyright Convention as revised at Paris on 24 July 1971 provides: "On the entry into force of this Protocol in respect of a State not party to Protocol 1 annexed to the 1952 Convention, the latter Protocol shall be deemed to enter into force in respect of such State." Consequently, in respect of Guinea, Protocol 1 annexed to the 1952 Convention entered into force on 13 November 1981.

[15] The deposit of the instrument of accession by Hungary was effected under cover of a verbal note (No. U/43/1970), dated 22 October 1970, containing the following declaration: "... the Hungarian Permanent Delegation declares on behalf of the Presidential Council of the Hungarian People's Republic that the provisions of Article XIII of the said Convention are contrary to the fundamental principle of international law concerning the self-determination of peoples which the United Nations General Assembly also wrote into its resolution 1514(XV) on the granting of independence to colonial countries and peoples...".

[16] On 20 August 1970, the Director-General of UNESCO received from the Government of Mauritius a communication notifying that it considers itself bound, as from 12 March 1968, by the Universal Copyright Convention and annexed Protocols 1, 2 and 3, the application of which had been extended to its territory before the attainment of independence.

17 The instrument of accession by Niger to the Universal Copyright Convention as revised at Paris on 24 July 1971 and annexed Protocols 1 and 2 was deposited with the Director-General of UNESCO on 15 February 1989. Article IX(3) of the revised Convention provides: "Accession to this Convention by a State not party to the 1952 Convention shall also constitute accession to that Convention; . . .". Consequently, in respect of Niger, the 1952 Convention came into force on 15 May 1989. Paragraph 2(c) of Protocol 1 annexed to the Universal Copyright Convention as revised at Paris on 24 July 1971 provides: "On the entry into force of this Protocol in respect of a State not party to Protocol 1 annexed to the 1952 Convention, the latter Protocol shall be deemed to enter into force in respect of such State." Consequently, in respect of Niger, Protocol 1 annexed to the 1952 Convention entered into force on 15 May 1989.

18 On 16 November 1955, the Director-General of UNESCO received from the Government of the Republic of the Philippines a communication dated 14 November 1955 informing him that " . . His Excellency the President of the Republic of the Philippines has directed the withdrawal of the instrument of accession of the Republic of the Philippines to the Universal Copyright Convention prior to the date of 19 November 1955, at which the Convention would become effective in respect of the Philippines". The text of this communication was transmitted to the States concerned by letter ODG/SJ/569/973 of 11 January 1956. Observations received from governments were communicated to the Government of the Philippines and to the other States concerned by letter ODG/SJ/666.278 of 16 April 1957.

19 The instrument of accession by Poland to the Universal Copyright Convention as revised in Paris on 24 July 1971 and annexed Protocols 1 and 2 was deposited with the Director-General of UNESCO on 9 December 1976. Article IX(3) of the revised Convention provides: "Accession to this Convention by a State not party to the 1952 Convention shall also constitute accession to that Convention; . . .". Consequently, in respect of Poland, the 1952 Convention came into force on 9 March 1977. Paragraph 2(c) of Protocol 1 annexed to the Universal Copyright Convention as revised on 24 July 1971 provides: "On the entry into force of this Protocol in respect of a State not party to Protocol 1 annexed to the 1952 Convention, the latter Protocol shall be deemed to enter into force in respect of such State." Consequently, in respect of Poland, Protocol 1 annexed to the 1952 Convention entered into force on 9 March 1977.

20 The instrument of accession by the Republic of Korea to the Universal Copyright Convention as revised at Paris on 24 July 1971 and annexed Protocols 1 and 2 was deposited with the Director-General of UNESCO on 1 July 1987. Article IX(3) of the revised Convention provides: "Accession to this Convention by a State not party to the 1952 Convention shall also constitute accession to that Convention; . . .". Consequently, in respect of the Republic of Korea, the 1952 Convention came into force on 1 October 1987. Paragraph 2(c) of Protocol 1 annexed to the Universal Copyright Convention as revised at Paris on 24 July 1971 provides: "On the entry into force of this Protocol in respect of a State not party to Protocol 1 annexed to the 1952 Convention, the latter Protocol shall be deemed to enter into force in respect of such State." Consequently, in respect of the Republic of Korea, Protocol 1 annexed to the 1952 Convention entered into force on 1 October 1987.

21 On 26 December 1991, the Permanent Delegate of the Russian Federation transmitted to the Director-General of UNESCO a verbal note from the Ministry of Foreign Affairs of his country, the terms of which are as follows: "The Ministry of Foreign Affairs of the Russian Federation . . . has the honour to inform you that the participation of the Union of Soviet Socialist Republics. . . in all the conventions, agreements and other instruments of international law concluded therein or under its auspices is continued by the Russian Federation (RF) and that, to that end, the title 'Union of Soviet Socialist Republics' should be replaced within UNESCO by 'Russian Federation'. . .". Consequently, the Russian Federation is bound by the Universal Copyright Convention adopted at Geneva in 1952 since 27 May 1973, the date on which this instrument came into force for the Union of Soviet Socialist Republics.

The instrument of accession of the Union of Soviet Socialist Republics contained the following; "In acceding to the Universal (Geneva) Copyright Convention 1952, the Union of Soviet Socialist Republics declares that the provisions of Article XII of the Convention are outdated and are contrary to the Declaration of the General Assembly of the United Nations on the granting of independence to colonial countries and peoples (Resolution 1514(XV), 14 December 1960), which proclaims the necessity of bringing to a speedy and unconditional end colonialism in all its forms and manifestations."

22 The instrument of accession by Rwanda to the Universal Copyright Convention as revised at Paris on 24 July 1971 and annexed Protocols 1 and 2 was deposited with the Director-General of UNESCO on 10 August 1989. Article IX(3) of the revised Convention provides: "Accession to this Convention by a State not party to the 1952 Convention shall also constitute accession to that Convention; . . ." Consequently, in respect of Rwanda, the 1952 Convention came into force on 10 November 1989. Paragraph 2(c) of Protocol 1 annexed to the Universal Copyright Conventions as revised at Paris on 24 July 1971 provides: "On the entry into force of this Protocol in respect of a State not party to Protocol 1 annexed to the 1952 Convention, the latter Protocol shall be deemed to enter into force in respect of such State." Consequently, in respect of Rwanda, Protocol 1 annexed to the 1952 Convention entered into force on 10 November 1989.

23 The Director-General of UNESCO received on 22 January 1985 from the Government of Saint Vincent and the Grenadines a communication notifying him that that Government has decided to apply provisionally, and on the basis of reciprocity, multilateral treaties extended to the former British Associated State of Saint Vincent and the Grenadines, and, in particular, the Universal Copyright Convention adopted at Geneva in 1952.

24 The instrument of accession by Senegal to the Universal Copyright Convention as revised at Paris on 24 July 1971 and annexed Protocols 1 and 2 was deposited with the Director-General of UNESCO on 9 April 1974. Article IX(3) of the revised Convention provides: "Accession to this Convention by a State not party to the 1952 Convention shall also constitute accession to that Convention; however, if its instrument of accession is deposited before this Convention comes into force, such State may make its accession to the 1952 Convention conditional upon the coming into force of this Convention. . .". Since Senegal's accession was not made conditional upon the coming into force of the revised Convention, its accession to the 1952 Convention came into force on 9 July 1974. Paragraph 2(c) of Protocol 1 annexed to the Universal Copyright Convention as revised at Paris on 24 July 1971 provides: "On the entry into force of this Protocol in respect of a State not party to Protocol 1 annexed to the 1952 Convention, the latter Protocol shall be deemed to enter into force in respect of such State." Consequently, in respect of Senegal, Protocol 1 annexed to the 1952 Convention entered into force on 10 July 1974.

25 The instrument of ratification deposited on behalf of Spain on 27 October 1954 referred to the Convention and the three Protocols annexed thereto. Since Protocols 1 and 3 had not been signed on behalf of Spain, the Director-General of UNESCO, by letter of 12 November 1954, drew the attention of the Government of Spain to this fact. In reply, the Director-General received on 27 January 1955 from the Spanish Government a communication stating that ". . . the Spanish ratification of the Universal Copyright Convention applies solely to the documents in fact signed, viz. the Convention and Protocol No. 2". This communication was transmitted to the States concerned by letter CL/1030 of 25 March 1955.

26 The instrument of accession by Sri Lanka to the Universal Copyright Convention as revised at Paris on 24 July 1971 was deposited with the Director-General of UNESCO on 25 October 1983. Article IX(3) of the revised Convention provides: "Accession to this Convention by a State not party to the 1952 Convention shall also constitute accession to that Convention; . . .". Consequently, in respect of Trinidad and Tobago, the 1952 Convention came into force on 19 August 1988.

27 The instrument of accession by Trinidad and Tobago to the Universal Copyright Convention as revised at Paris on 24 July 1971 was deposited with the Director-General of UNESCO on 19 May 1988. Article IX(3) of the revised convention provides: "Accession to this Convention by a State not party to the 1952 Convention shall also constitute accession to that Convention . . .". Consequently, in respect of Trinidad and Tobago, the 1952 Convention came into force on 19 August 1988.

28 On 3 May 1963, the Director-General of UNESCO received from the Government of the Republic of the Philippines a communication dated 16 April 1963 informing him that the Philippines Government does not recognise the declaration of the Government of the United Kingdom concerning the application of the provisions of the Universal Copyright Convention to North Borneo. The Government of the United Kingdom informed the Director-General of UNESCO by a communication dated 29 August 1963 that: ". . . Her Majesty's Government have no doubt of the validity of the declaration made by the United Kingdom whereby the Convention applies to North Borneo, a territory over which the United Kingdom has full Sovereignty". These communications were transmitted to the States concerned respectively by letter CL/1652 of 27 May 1963 and letter CL/1678 of 25 September 1963.

29 On 28 January 1964, the Director-General of UNESCO received from the Government of Argentina a communication dated 28 January 1964 informing him that the Government of Argentina does not recognise the declaration of the Government of the United Kingdom concerning the application of the Convention to the Falkland Islands, South Georgia and the South Sandwich Islands. The Government of the United Kingdom informed the Director-General of UNESCO by a communication dated 12 March 1964 that: "... Her Majesty's Government ... have no doubts as to their sovereignty over the Falkland Islands, South Georgia and the South Sandwich Islands and they reserve their rights in this matter...". These communications were transmitted to the States concerned respectively by letter CL/1704 of 2 March 1964 and letter CL/1718 of 20 April 1964.

30 On 27 September 1966, the Director-General of UNESCO received from the Government of Guatemala a communication dated 19 September 1966 informing him that this Government contests the inclusion of the territory of Belize within the English colonies and they reserve their rights on this Guatemalan territory. The Government of the United Kingdom informed the Director-General of UNESCO by a communication dated 17 February 1967 that: "... Her Majesty's Government ... have no doubts as to their Sovereignty over the territory of British Honduras and they reserve their rights in this matter...". These communications were transmitted to the States concerned respectively by letter CL/1855 of 22 November 1966 and letter CL/1872 of 11 April 1967.

31 On 9 December 1957, the Director-General of UNESCO received from the Government of Panama a communication dated 21 November 1957 contesting the right of the Government of the United States of America to extend the application of the Convention to the Panama Canal Zone. The Government of the United States of America informed the Director-General of UNESCO, by a communication dated 28 February 1958, that such extension was proper under Article 3 of its 1903 treaty with Panama. The communications were transmitted to the States concerned respectively by letter CL/1263 of 13 February 1958 and letter CL/1284 of 22 April 1958.

Universal Copyright Convention as revised at Paris on 24 July 1971 with annexed Protocols 1 and 2

I. Entry into Force

Text	Initial Entry into Force	Subsequent Entry into Force
Universal Copyright Convention as revised at Paris on 24 July 1971	10 July 1974 in accordance with Article IX, paragraph 1	Three months after deposit of the instrument of ratification, acceptance or accession, in accordance with Article IX, paragraph 2
Annexed Protocol No. 1 concerning the application of that Convention to the works of stateless persons and refugees	10 July 1974 in accordance with paragraph 2(b)	Date of deposit of the instrument of ratification, acceptance or accession, subject to the concerned State being a party to the Convention (paragraph 2(b))
Annexed Protocol No. 2 concerning the application of that Convention to the works of certain international organisations	10 July 1974 in accordance with paragraph 2(b)	Date of deposit of the instrument of ratification, acceptance or accession, subject to the concerned State being a party to the Convention (paragraph 2(b))

II. Ratifications, Acceptances and Accessions

| State | Date of Deposit of Instrument | | | Territorial Application | |
	Convention	Protocol 1	Protocol 2	Date of receipt of notification	Extension to
Algeria[1]	28 May 1973				
Australia	29 Nov 1977	29 Nov 1977	29 Nov 1977		
Austria	14 May 1982	14 May 1982	14 May 1982		
Bahamas	27 Sep 1976				
Bangladesh[2]	5 May 1975	5 May 1975	5 May 1975		
Barbados	18 Mar 1983				
Bolivia[3]	22 Dec 1989				
Brazil	11 Sep 1975	11 Sep 1975	11 Sep 1975		
Bulgaria[4]	7 Mar 1975				
Cameroon	1 Feb 1973				
China	30 Jul 1992				
Colombia	18 Mar 1976				

II. Ratifications, Acceptances and Accessions

| State | Date of Deposit of Instrument | | | Territorial Application | |
	Convention	Protocol 1	Protocol 2	Date of receipt of notification	Extension to
Costa Rica	7 Dec 1979				
Croatia **D**	3 Jul 1973				
Cyprus	19 Sep 1990	19 Sep 1990	19 Sep 1990		
Czech Republic[5] **D**	17 Jan 1980		17 Jan 1980		
Denmark	11 Apr 1979	11 Apr 1979	11 Apr 1979		
Dominican Republic	8 Feb 1983				
Ecuador	6 Jun 1991	6 Jun 1991	6 Jun 1991		
El Salvador	29 Dec 1978	29 Dec 1978	29 Dec 1978		
Finland	1 Aug 1986				
France	11 Sep 1972	11 Sep 1972	11 Sep 1972		
Germany[6]	18 Oct 1973	18 Oct 1973	18 Oct 1973		
Guinea	13 Aug 1981	13 Aug 1981	13 Aug 1981		

Holy See	6 Feb 1980	6 Feb 1980	6 Feb 1980
Hungary[7]	15 Sep 1972		15 Sep 1972
India	7 Jan 1988	7 Jan 1988	7 Jan 1988
Italy[8]	25 Oct 1979	25 Oct 1979	25 Oct 1979
Japan	21 Jul 1977	21 Jul 1977	21 Jul 1977
Kenya	4 Jan 1974	4 Jan 1974	4 Jan 1974
Mexico[9]	31 Jul 1975		
Monaco	13 Sep 1974	13 Sep 1974	13 Sep 1974
Morocco	28 Oct 1975	28 Oct 1975	28 Oct 1975
Netherlands	30 Aug 1985	30 Aug 1985	30 Aug 1985
Niger	15 Feb 1989	15 Feb 1989	15 Feb 1989
Norway	7 May 1974	13 Aug 1974	13 Aug 1974
Panama	3 Jun 1980		
Peru	22 Apr 1985	22 Apr 1985	22 Apr 1985
Poland	9 Dec 1976	9 Dec 1976	9 Dec 1976
Portugal	30 Apr 1981	30 Apr 1981	30 Apr 1981

II. Ratifications, Acceptances and Accessions

State	Date of Deposit of Instrument			Territorial Application	
	Convention	*Protocol 1*	*Protocol 2*	*Date of receipt of notification*	*Extension to*
Republic of Korea[10]	1 Jul 1987	1 Jul 1987	1 Jul 1987		
Rwanda	10 Aug 1989	10 Aug 1989	10 Aug 1989		
Saint Vincent and the Grendadines[11]	22 Jan 1985	22 Jan 1985	22 Jan 1985		
Senegal	9 Apr 1974	9 Apr 1974	9 Apr 1974		
Slovak Republic **D**	17 Jan 1980		17 Jan 1980		
Slovenia **D**	3 Jul 1973	16 Dec 1992	16 Dec 1992		
Spain	10 Apr 1974	16 Oct 1974[12]	10 Apr 1974		
Sri Lanka	25 Oct 1983	27 Jul 1988	27 Jul 1988		
Sweden	27 Jun 1973	27 Jun 1973	27 Jun 1973		
Switzerland	21 Jun 1993	21 Jun 1993	21 Jun 1993		
Trinidad and Tobago	19 May 1988				

Tunisia[13]	10 Mar 1975	10 Mar 1975	10 Mar 1975	10 Mar 1975	
United Kingdom	19 May 1972	19 May 1972	19 May 1972	19 May 1972	2 May 1973 6 Sep 1973	Hong Kong British Virgin Islands, Gibraltar, Grendada, Isle of Man, Saint Helena, Saint Lucia, Saint Vincent, Seychelles
United States of America	18 Sep 1972	18 Sep 1972	18 Sep 1972	18 Sep 1972	18 Sep 1972	Gaum, Panama Canal Zone, Puerto Rico, Virgin Islands

Application of the Convention to the works of authors of the Russian Federation

On 4 April 1978, the Government of the Union of the Soviet Socialist Republics communicated to the Director-General of UNESCO in accordance with Article IX(4) of the Universal Copyright Convention as revised at Paris on 24 July 1971, the following declaration: "Desirous of helping to create favourable conditions for the use of the works of Soviet authors by the developing countries for educational purposes, the Union of Soviet Socialist Republics agrees to the application of the aforementioned Convention to the works of Soviet authors.

"On the occasion of this declaration, the Union of Soviet Socialist Republics notes that the provisions of Article XIII of the Convention are obsolete and contravene the Declaration of the United Nations General Assembly on the granting of independence to colonial countries and peoples (Resolution 1514(XV) of 14 December 1960), which proclaimed the necessity of bringing to a speedy and unconditional end colonialism in all its forms and manifestations."

This declaration remains in force with regard to the application of the Universal Copyright Convention as revised at Paris on 24 July 1971 to the works of authors of the Russian Federation, in accordance with the terms of the verbal note of the Ministry of Foreign Affairs of that country, the text of which was transmitted to the Director-General of UNESCO on 26 December 1991. (See above, note 21 of the Table containing details of States party to the Universal Copyright Convention of 1951.)

Notes

Symbol "D". The symbol "D" denotes a declaration by a State recognising itself bound, as from the date of its independence, by the Convention and/or annexed Protocols 1, 2 and 3, the application of which had been extended to its territory by a State then responsible for the conduct of its foreign relations. The date shown is the date of receipt by the Director-General of UNESCO.

[1] On 11 June 1976, the Government of Algeria deposited with the Director-General of UNESCO a notification by which, in accordance with Article Vbis(1) of the Universal Copyright Convention as revised at Paris on 24 July 1971, it declared to avail itself "of all the exceptions which are provided for in Articles Vter and Vquater of the Convention and which were drafted for the benefit of developing countries, referring to the right to translate and reproduce literary, artistic and scientific works protected by copyright and introducing compulsory provisions in respect of the granting of licences in favour of such countries".

On 5 August 1983, the Government of Algeria deposited a new notification with the Director-General of UNESCO, in conformity with Article Vbis of the Convention "in order to avail itself for a second period of ten years of all the exceptions provided for in Articles Vter and Vquater of the Convention, which were drafted for the benefit of developing countries, referring to the right to translate and reproduce literary, artistic and scientific works protected by copyright and introducing compulsory provisions in respect of the granting of licences in favour of such countries".

[2] On 4 December 1979, the Government of Bangladesh deposited with the Director-General of UNESCO a notification by which in accordance with Article Vbis(1) of this Convention, it declared that "being a developing country, the Government of the People's Republic of Bangladesh, having considered all the provisions of Article Vbis, Vter and Vquater of the aforesaid Convention, do hereby notify in terms of Article Vbis(1) that the Government of Bangladesh shall avail itself of all the exceptions provided in the provisos of the above articles and undertake faithfully to carry out the stipulations therein contained".

On 3 April 1984, the Government of Bangladesh deposited with the Director-General of UNESCO a further notification, in accordance with Article Vbis of the Convention, renewing the previous notification for a second ten-year period as from 10 July 1984.

[3] The instrument of accession contained the following declaration: "In accordance with Article Vbis of the Convention revised in 1971, I would like to inform you that Bolivia wishes to be considered as a developing country for the purposes of the application of the provisions relating to those countries."

[4] The instrument of accession contained the following declaration: "The People's Republic of Bulgaria considers that the provisions of Article XIII of the Universal Copyright Convention as revised at Paris on 24 July 1971 are at variance with the Declaration of the United Nations General Assembly on the granting of independence to colonial countries and peoples adopted by Resolution 1514(XV) of 14 December 1960, which proclaimed the necessity of bringing to a speedy and unconditional end colonialism in all its forms and manifestations."

[5] The instrument of accession contained the following declaration: "Acceding to the Convention we declare that the provisions of its Article XIII is contrary to the Declaration of the United Nations General Assembly on Granting Independence to Colonial Countries and Peoples and that the provisions of its Article XV on the obligatory jurisdiction of the International Court is contradictory to the principle of the international law on free selection of means for the settlement of disputes between States."

On 14 May 1991, the Director-General of UNESCO received from the Permanent Delegate of Czechoslovakia a letter, dated 2 May 1991, notifying him of the withdrawal by the Government of Czechoslovakia of the reservation concerning Article XV of the Convention.

6 The Director-General of UNESCO received from the Permanent Delegate of the Federal Republic of Germany a letter dated 3 October 1990 informing him that "through the accession of the German Democratic Republic to the Federal Republic of Germany with effect from 3 October 1990, the two German States have united to form one sovereign State". This letter was accompanied by a verbal note dated 3 October 1990 informing UNESCO that "with regard to the continued application of treaties of the Federal Republic of Germany and the treatment of treaties of the German Democratic Republic following its accession to the Federal Republic of Germany with effect from 3 October 1990, the Treaty of 31 August 1990, between the Federal Republic of Germany and the German Democratic Republic on the establishment of German unity (Unification Treaty) contains the following relevant provisions:

1. Article 11

Treaties of the Federal Republic of Germany

The contracting parties proceed on the understanding that international treaties and agreements to which the Federal Republic of Germany is a contracting party. . . shall retain their validity and that the rights and obligations arising therefrom. . . shall also relate to the territory specified in Article 3 of this Treaty". (Länder of Brandenburg, Mecklenburg-Western Pomerania, Saxe, Saxe-Anhalt and Thuringia as well as the sector of the Land of Berlin where the Fundamental Law of the Federal Republic of Germany was not applicable.)

7 In depositing the instrument of ratification, the Permanent Delegation of Hungary to UNESCO made the following declaration on behalf of the Presidential Council of the Hungarian People's Republic: "The Hungarian People's Republic declares that the provisions of Article XIII, paragraph 1, of the Universal Copyright Convention signed at Geneva on 6 September 1952 and revised at Paris on 24 July 1971 run counter to the Declaration on the granting of independence to colonial countries and peoples contained in Resolution 1514(XV) which was adopted on 14 December 1960 by the General Assembly of the United Nations."

8 The deposit of the instrument of ratification by Italy was effected under cover of a letter dated 19 October 1979, containing the following declaration: "With reference to Article IV, paragraph 4, of the Universal Copyright Convention as revised at Paris on 24 July 1971, the Italian Government declares that within the Italian Republic protection to a work shall not be granted for a period longer than that fixed for the class of works to which the work belongs, in the case of unpublished works, by the law of the Contracting State of which the author is a national, and, in the case of published works, by the law of the Contracting State in which the work has been first published."

"If the law of any Contracting State grants two or more terms of protection, and a specified work is not protected by such State during the second or any subsequent term for any reason, that work shall not be granted protection within the Italian Republic during the second or any subsequent term."

9 On 21 November 1975, the Government of Mexico deposited with the Director-General of UNESCO a notification by which, in accordance with Article Vbis(1) of the Universal Copyright Convention as revised at Paris on 24 July 1971, it declared that it wished Mexico "to be regarded as a developing country for the purpose of the provisions which refer to such countries". On 19 August 1985, the Director-General of UNESCO received from the Government of Mexico a communication dated 14 August 1985 informing him that the Government intended to renew, for a second ten-year period, its previous notification under Article Vbis of the aforementioned Convention by which it had availed itself of the exceptions provided for in Articles Vter and Vquater of the Convention. The Mexican authorities were informed by UNESCO that their notification had not been presented within the time-limit prescribed by Article Vbis, paragraph 2, of the Convention. Subsequently, the Mexican authorities placed the matter before the Intergovernmental Copyright Committee, which discussed it during its seventh ordinary session (June 1987). The Committee agreed: (a) that the question raised by Mexico was within the Committee's competence under Article XI of the Universal Copyright Convention which provides that the Committee may study the problems concerning the application and operation of the Convention; (b) that Mexico was and is a developing country within the meaning of the Convention as far as the advantages established for the benefit of developing countries were concerned; (c) that it was up to each State party to the Universal Copyright Convention to determine for itself, in the final analysis, the question of the timeliness and consequences, if any, of Mexico's notice of renewal under Article Vbis(2) of the Convention. Pursuant to the request of the Committee, the text of the notification of the Government of Mexico was transmitted to the States concerned by letter LA/STD/87/100 of 20 October 1987.

10 On 5 November 1987, the Government of the Republic of Korea deposited with the Director-General of UNESCO a notification by which, in accordance with Article Vbis of the Convention, it declares that it shall avail itself of all the exceptions provided for in Articles Vter and Vquater of the said Convention.

11 The Director-General of UNESCO received on 22 January 1985 from the Government of Saint Vincent and the Grenadines a communication notifying him that that Government has decided to apply provisionally, and on the basis of reciprocity, multilateral treaties extended to the former British Associated State of Saint Vincent and the Grenadines, and, in particular, the Universal Copyright Convention as revised at Paris on 24 July 1971 and the annexed Protocols 1 and 2.

12 The instrument of ratification contained the following declaration: "Ratification by Spain of this Protocol shall in no way signify acceptance of the definition of refugee established in the IRO Constitution and maintained in Article 1, paragraph A.1, of the Convention relating to the status of refugees, of 28 July 1951, and Article 1 of the New York Protocol of 31 January 1967."

13 The instrument of ratification contained the following notification: "Considering that Article Vbis of the said Convention permits any Contracting State regarded as a developing country in conformity with the established practice of the General Assembly of the United Nations, by a notification deposited with the Director-General of the United Nations Educational, Scientific and Cultural Organisation, to avail itself, at the time of its ratification, of any or all of the exceptions provided for in Articles Vter and Vquater;

    . . . .
    Notifies as well, in accordance with Article Vbis of the Convention, that Tunisia intends to avail itself of all the exceptions provided for in Articles Vter and Vquater."
    On 18 January 1984, the Government of Tunisia deposited a new notification with the Director-General of UNESCO, in conformity with Article Vbis of the Convention, "in order to avail itself for a second period of ten years of all the exceptions provided for in Articles Vter and Vquater of the Convention, which were drafted for the benefit of developing countries".

TABLE C   575

TABLE C

European Agreement concerning Programme exchanges by means of Television Films

State	Date of Entry into Force	Declaration Art 11(2)
Belgium	8 Apr 1962	
Cyprus	20 Feb 1970	
Denmark	25 Nov 1961	
France	1 Jul 1961	
Greece	9 Feb 1962	
Ireland	4 Apr 1965	
Israel	15 Feb 1978	
Italy	signed only	
Luxembourg	31 Oct 1963	
Netherlands	5 Mar 1967	Yes
Norway	15 Mar 1963	
Spain	4 Jan 1974	
Tunisia	22 Feb 1969	
Sweden	1 Jul 1961	
Turkey	28 Mar 1964	
United Kingdom	1 Jul 1961	

TABLE D

European Agreement for the Protection of Television Broadcasts

State	Date of Entry into Force					Notifications and Reservations		
	Original Agreement	Protocol	First Additional Protocol	Second Additional Protocol	Third Additional Protocol	Article 3.1(a)	Article 3.1(a) Protocol	Article 3.1(b)
Belgium[1,2]	8 Mar 1968	8 Mar 1968	31 Dec 1974	1 Jan 1985	signed only	Yes		Yes
Cyprus[1]	22 Feb 1970	22 Feb 1970	31 Dec 1974	1 Jan 1985				
Denmark	27 Nov 1961	24 Mar 1965	31 Dec 1974	1 Jan 1985	signed only			
France	1 Jul 1961	24 Mar 1965	31 Dec 1974	1 Jan 1985	signed only			
Germany[3]	9 Oct 1967	9 Oct 1967	31 Dec 1974	1 Jan 1985	signed only			Yes
Greece	signed only							
Ireland	signed only							
Italy	signed only							
Luxembourg	signed only							
Netherlands[4]	signed only					Yes		Yes
Norway	10 Aug 1968	10 Aug 1968	31 Dec 1974	1 Jan 1985	signed only			Yes
Spain[1]	23 Oct 1971	24 Oct 1971	31 Dec 1974	1 Jan 1985				
Sweden[5]	1 Jul 1961	24 Mar 1965	31 Dec 1974	1 Jan 1985	signed only			Yes
Turkey[1]	20 Jan 1976	20 Jan 1976	20 Jan 1976	1 Jan 1985	signed only			
United Kingdom	1 Jul 1961	24 Mar 1965	31 Dec 1974	1 Jan 1985	signed only	Yes		Yes

State	Notifications and Reservations			
	Article 3.1(c)	Article 3.1(d)	Article 3.1(e)	Article 3.1(f)
Belgium[1]				
Cyprus[1]	Yes			
Denmark		Yes		Yes
France	Yes			
Germany	Yes		Yes	
Greece				
Ireland				
Italy				
Luxembourg				
Netherlands	Yes			
Norway	Yes			
Spain[1]				
Sweden	Yes			
Turkey[1]				
United Kingdom	Yes[7,8]	Yes[8]		Yes

Notes

[1] Insofar as the Third Additional Protocol did not enter into force on 1 January 1990, this State ceased to be a Party to the Agreement on this date, in application of the provisions contained in Article 13, paragraph 2 of the Agreement.

[2] On ratification, the Belgium Government in respect of Belgium territory, made an exception to the protection of television broadcasts for the purpose of reporting current events, in respect of the re-broadcasting, fixation or reproduction of the fixation, wire diffusion or public performance of short extracts from a broadcast which itself constitutes the whole or part of the event in question.

[3] The European Agreement on the Protection of Television Broadcasts and Protocol to the said Agreement shall also apply to the Land Berlin with effect from the date on which they enter into force in respect of Germany.

[4] The Government of the Kingdom of the Netherlands interprets the word "signature" in the first line of Article 10 as meaning only the signature, without any reservation in respect of ratification.
In their application to the Kingdom of the Netherlands, the words "metropolitan territories" in Article 12, paragraph 1 of the Agreement no longer have their original sense but shall be deemed to signify "European Territory" in view of the equality existing in public law between the Netherlands, Surinam and the Netherlands West Indies.

[5] When ratifying the Agreement, Sweden also made the reservation provided for under Article 3.1(f). However, Sweden subsequently withdrew this reservation with effect from 1 July 1986.

[6] The Government of Turkey, while ratifying the Protocol to the European Agreement on the Protection of Television Broadcasts, declared that '. . . it does not consider itself bound to carry out the provision of the said Protocol in relation to the Greek Cypriot Administration, which is not constitutionally entitled to represent alone the Republic of Cyprus'.

[7] The Government of the United Kingdom of Great Britain and Northern Ireland withhold the protection provided for in Article 1.1(d) of the Agreement, where the fixation or reproduction of the fixation is made for private use or solely for educational purposes.

[8] The Government of the United Kingdom of Great Britain and Northern Ireland withhold the protection provided for in Article 1.1(d) and (e) of the Agreement, in respect of still photographs or reproductions of such photographs.

TABLE E

International Convention for the Protection of Performers, Producers of Phonograms and Broadcasting Organisations

State	Date of Entry into Force	Notifications and Reservations					
		Article 5.3	Article 6.2	Article 16.1(a)(i)	Article 16.1(a)(ii)	Article 16.1(a)(iii)	Article 16.1(a)(iv)
Argentina	2 Mar 1922						
Australia	30 Sep 1992	Yes, criterion of first publication excluded	Yes	Yes			
Austria	9 June 1973					Yes	Yes
Barbados	18 Sep 1983						
Brazil	29 Sep 1965						
Burkina Faso	14 Jan 1988						
Chile	5 Sep 1974						
Colombia	17 Sep 1976						
Congo	18 May 1964	Yes, criterion of first publication excluded			Yes		

State	Date of Entry into Force	Notifications and Reservations					
		Article 5.3	Article 6.2	Article 16.1(a)(i)	Article 16.1(a)(ii)	Article 16.1(a)(iii)	Article 16.1(a)(iv)
Costa Rica	9 Sep 1971						
Czech Republic[1]						Yes	Yes
Denmark	23 Sep 1965		Yes		Yes[2]		Yes
Dominican Republic	27 Jan 1987						
Ecuador	18 May 1964						
El Salvador	29 Jun 1979						
Fiji	11 Apr 1972	Yes, criterion of first publication excluded	Yes	Yes	See note[3]	See note[4]	See note[5]
Finland	21 Oct 1983		Yes	Yes[6]	Yes[7]		Yes
France	3 Jul 1987	Yes, criterion of first publication excluded				Yes	Yes
Germany[9]	21 Oct 1966	Yes, criterion of first publication excluded					Yes
Greece	6 Jan 1963						

Country	Date						
Guatemala	14 Jan 1977						
Honduras	16 Feb 1990						
Ireland	19 Sep 1979	Yes, criterion of first publication excluded	Yes		Yes[10]		
Italy	8 Apr 1975		Yes		Yes[11]	Yes	Yes
Japan	26 Oct 1989	Yes, criterion of first publication excluded			Yes[12]		Yes
Lesotho	26 Jan 1990[13]					Yes[14]	
Luxembourg	25 Feb 1976	Yes, criterion of first publication excluded		Yes			
Mexico	18 May 1964						
Monaco	6 Dec 1985	Yes, criterion of first publication excluded		Yes			
Niger	18 May 1964	Yes, criterion of first publication excluded		Yes			
Norway	10 Jul 1978		Yes		Yes[15]	Yes	

State	Date of Entry into Force	Notifications and Reservations					
		Article 5.3	Article 6.2	Article 16.1(a) (i)	Article 16.1(a) (ii)	Article 16.1(a) (iii)	Article 16.1(a) (iv)
Panama	2 Sep 1983						
Paraguay	26 Feb 1970						
Peru	7 Aug 1985						
Philippines	25 Sep 1984						
Slovak Rep	1 Jan 1993						
Spain	14 Nov 1991	Yes, criterion of first publication excluded	Yes			Yes	Yes
Sweden	18 May 1964		See note[16]		Yes[17]		Yes
United Kingdom	18 May 1964	Yes, criterion of first publication excluded	Yes		Yes[20]	Yes	Yes
Uruguay	4 Jul 1977						

State	Notifications and Reservations		Territorial Application	
	Article 16.1(b)	Article 17	Date of receipt of notification	Extension to
Argentina				
Australia	Yes			
Austria	Yes			
Barbados				
Brazil				
Burkina Faso				
Chile				
Colombia				
Congo				
Costa Rica				
Czech Republic[1]				
Denmark		Yes		
Dominican Republic				
Ecuador				
El Salvador				
Fiji				
Finland	Yes[8]	Yes		
France				
Germany				
Greece				
Guatemala				
Honduras				
Ireland				

State	Notifications and Reservations		Territorial Application	
	Article 16.1(b)	Article 17	Date of receipt of notification	Extension to
Italy	Yes	Yes		
Japan				
Lesotho	Yes			
Luxembourg	Yes			
Mexico				
Monaco	Yes			
Niger				
Norway				
Panama				
Paraguay				
Peru				
Philippines				
Slovak Republic				
Spain				
Sweden	Yes[18]	See note[19]		
United Kingdom			20 Dec 1966 10 Mar 1970	Gibraltar[21] Bermuda[21]
Uruguay				

Notes

[1] The situation of this State in respect of this Convention is under examination.

[2] The provisions of Article 12 will be applied solely with respect to use for broadcasting or for any other communication to the public for commercial purposes.

[3] In its instrument of accession, deposited by the Government of Fiji on 11 January 1972, Fiji declared that it would not apply the provisions of Article 12 in respect of:
   (i) the causing of a phonogram to be heard in public at any premises where persons reside or sleep, as part of the amenities provided exclusively or mainly for residents or inmates therein except where a special charge is made for admission to the part of the premises where the phonogram is to be heard;

(ii) the causing of a phonogram to be heard in public as part of the activities of, or for the benefit of, a club, society or other organisation which is not established or conducted for profit and whose main objects are charitable or are otherwise concerned with the advancement of religion, education or social welfare, except where a charge is made for admission to the place where the phonogram is to be heard, and any of the proceeds of the charge are applied otherwise than for the purpose of the organisation.

On 12 June 1972, the Secretary-General of the United Nations received a communication according to which the Government of Fiji declared: ". . . the Government of Fiji, having reconsidered the said Convention, hereby withdraws its declaration in respect of certain provisions of Article 12 and in substitution thereof declares in accordance with Article 16(1) of the said Convention that Fiji will not apply the provisions of Article 12."

[4] In its instrument of accession, deposited by the Government of Fiji on 11 January 1972, Fiji declared that in respect of Article 12, as regards phonograms the producer of which is not a national of another Contracting State, Fiji would not grant protection unless the phonogram had been first published in a Contracting State.

On 12 June 1972, the Secretary-General of the United Nations received a communication according to which the Government of Fiji declared: ". . . the Government of Fiji, having reconsidered the said Convention, hereby withdraws its declaration in respect of certain provisions of Article 12 and in substitution thereof declares in accordance with Article 16(1) of the said Convention that Fiji will not apply the provisions of Article 12."

[5] In its instrument of accession, deposited by the Government of Fiji on 11 January 1972, Fiji declared that in respect of Article 12, as regards phonograms the producer of which is a national of a Contracting State which has made a declaration under Article 16(1)(a)(i) stating that it would not apply the provisions of Article 12, Fiji would not grant protection provided for by Article 12 unless the phonogram had been first published in a Contracting State which had made no such declaration.

On 12 June 1972, the Secretary-General of the United Nations received a communication according to which the Government of Fiji declared: "... the Government of Fiji, having reconsidered the said Convention, hereby withdraws its declaration in respect of certain provisions of Article 12 and in substitution thereof declares in accordance with Article 16(1) of the said Convention that Fiji will not apply the provisions of Article 12."

[6] The provisions of Article 12 will be applied with respect to phonograms acquired by a broadcasting organisation before 1 September 1961.

[7] The provisions of Article 12 will be applied solely with respect to use for broadcasting.

[8] The provisions of Article 13(d) will be applied only to the communication to the public of television broadcasts in a cinema or other similar place.

[9] With the accession of the German Democratic Republic to the Federal Republic of Germany with effect from 3 October 1990, the two German States have united to form one sovereign State. With regard to the continued application of treaties of the Federal Republic of Germany and the treatment of treaties of the German Democratic Republic following its accession to the Federal Republic of Germany with effect from 3 October 1990, the Treaty of 31 August 1990 between the Federal Republic of Germany and the German Democratic Republic on the establishment of German unity (Unification Treaty) contains the following relevant provisions:
"1. Article II
Treaties of the Federal Republic of Germany
The contracting parties proceed on the understanding that international treaties and agreements to which the Federal Republic of Germany is a contracting party . . . shall retain their validity and that the rights and obligations arising therefrom . . . shall also relate to the territory specified in Article 3 of this Treaty". (Länder of Brandenburg, Mecklenburg-Western Pomerania, Saxe, Saxe-Anhalt and Thuringia as well as the sector of the Land of Berlin where the Fundamental Law of the Federal Republic of Germany was not applicable.)

[10] Protection will not be given to broadcasts heard in public (a) at any premises where persons reside or sleep, as part of the amenities provided exclusively or mainly for residents or inmates therein unless a special charge is made for admission to the part of the premises where the recording is to be heard or (b) as part of the activities of, or for the benefit of, a club, society or other organisation which is not established or conducted for profit and whose main objects are charitable or are otherwise concerned with the advancement of religion, education or social welfare, unless a charge is made for admission to the part of the premises where the recording is to be heard and any of the proceeds of the charge are applied otherwise than for the purposes of the organisation.

[11] The provisions of Article 12 will be applied with the exception of cinematography.

[12] The provisions of Article 12 will be applied only in respect of uses for broadcasting or for wire diffusion.

[13] The Government of the Kingdom of Lesotho has declared that it does not consider itself bound by the provisions of Article 13(d).

[14] The provisions of Article 12 will not be applied in respect of broadcasts made for non-profit-making purposes or where communication to the public in public places is not the result of a purely commercial activity.

[15] In its instrument of accession, the Government of Norway declared that the provisions of Article 12 would not be applied in respect of use other than for the purpose of economic gain. Upon depositing the instrument of accession, the Government of Norway made the following declaration:

The Norwegian Act of 14 December 1956 concerning a Levy on the Public Presentation of Recordings of Artists' Performances, etc., establishes rules for the disbursement of that levy to producers and performers of phonograms.

A proportion of the annual revenue from this levy devolves, as of right, to producers of phonograms as a group, without distinction as to nationality, in remuneration for the public use of phonograms.

Under the terms of the Act, contributions from the levy may be made to Norwegian performing artists and their survivors on the basis of individual needs. This benevolent arrangement falls entirely outside the scope of the Convention.

The regime established by the said Act, being fully consistent with requirements of the Convention will be maintained.

In a communication received on 30 June 1989, the Government of Norway notified the Secretary-General of the United Nations that "Pursuant to Article 16, paragraph 1, item (a)(ii), reservation is made to the effect that Article 12 shall not apply in respect of use other than use of phonograms in broadcast transmissions."

[16] On ratification, the Government of Sweden made a notification in respect of Article 6.2. On 27 June 1986, the Secretary-General of the United Nations received from the Government of Sweden, notification that the declaration in respect of Article 6.2 was withdrawn with effect from 1 July 1986.

[17] On ratification, the Government of Sweden declared that the provisions of Article 12 would be applied only with respect to use for broadcasting. On 27 June 1986, the Secretary-General of the United Nations received from the Government of Sweden, notification that it will reduce the scope of this declaration to the effect that Sweden will apply Article 12 to broadcasting and to such communication to the public which is carried out for commercial purposes with effect from 1 July 1986.

[18] The provisions of Article 13(d) will be applied only with respect to the communication to the public of television broadcasts in a cinema or similar place.

[19] On ratification, the Government of Sweden declared a reservation in respect of Article 17. On 27 June 1986, the Secretary-General of the United Nations received from the Government of Sweden, notification that this notification was withdrawn with effect from 1 July 1986.

[20] The provisions of Article 12 will not be applied in respect of (i) the causing of a phonogram to be heard in public at any premises where persons reside or sleep, as part of the amenities provided exclusively or mainly for residents or inmates therein except where a special charge is made for admission to the part of the premises where the phonogram is to be heard and (ii) the causing of a phonogram to be heard in public as part of the activities of, or for the benefit of, a club, society or other organisation which is not established or conducted for profit and whose main objects are charitable or are otherwise concerned with the advancement of religion, education or social welfare, except where a charge is made for admission to the place where the phonogram is to be heard, and any of the proceeds of the charge are applied otherwise than for the purposes of the organisation.

[21] The identical notifications made by the United Kingdom in respect of the domestic territory were extended to these territories.

TABLE F

Convention for the Protection of Producers of
Phonograms Against Unauthorised Duplication of Their Phonograms

State	Date of Entry into Force	Reservation Article 7(4)	Territorial Application (Article 11(3))	
			Date on which notification takes effect	Extention to
Argentina	30 Jun 1973			
Australia	22 Jun 1974			
Austria	21 Aug 1982			
Barbados	29 Jul 1983			
Brazil	28 Nov 1975			
Burkino Faso	30 Jan 1988			
Chile	24 Mar 1977			
China	30 Apr 1993			
Costa Rica	17 Jun 1982			
Czech Republic[1]				
Cyprus	30 Sep 1993			
Denmark	24 Mar 1977			
Ecuador	14 Sep 1974			
Egypt[2]	23 Apr 1978			
El Salvador	9 Feb 1979			
Fiji	18 Apr 1973			
Finland	18 Apr 1973	Yes		
France	18 Apr 1973			
Germany[3]	18 May 1974			
Guatemala	1 Feb 1977			

State	Date of Entry into Force	Reservation Article 7(4)	Territorial Application (Article 11(3))	
			Date on which notification takes effect	Extention to
Holy See	18 Jul 1977			
Honduras	6 Mar 1990			
Hungary[4]	28 May 1975			
India	12 Feb 1975			
Israel	1 May 1978			
Italy	24 Mar 1977	Yes		
Japan	14 Oct 1978			
Kenya	21 Apr 1976			
Luxembourg	8 Mar 1976			
Mexico	21 Dec 1974			
Monaco	2 Dec 1974			
New Zealand	13 Aug 1976			
Norway	1 Aug 1978			
Panama	29 Jun 1974			
Paraguay	13 Feb 1979			
Peru	24 Aug 1985			
Republic of Korea	10 Oct 1987			
Slovakia	1 Jan 1993			
Spain	24 Aug 1974			
Sweden	18 Apr 1973	See note[5]		
Switzerland	30 Sep 1993			
Trinidad and Tobago	1 Oct 1988			

State	Date of Entry into Force	Reservation Article 7(4)	Territorial Application (Article 11(3))	
			Date on which notification takes effect	Extention to
United Kingdom	18 Apr 1973		4 Mar 1975	Bermuda, British Virgin Islands, Cayman Islands, Gibraltar, Isle of Man, Hong Kong, Montserrat, Saint Lucia, Seychelles
USA	10 Mar 1974			
Uruguay	18 Jan 1983			
Venezuela	18 Nov 1982			
Zaire	29 Nov 1977			

Notes

[1] The situation of this State in respect of this Convention is under review.

[2] The instrument of accession contained the declaration that the accession of the Arab Republic of Egypt "does not imply any recognition of Israel, or entering into any relationship with Israel governed by the provisions of the Convention".

[3] By a letter dated 3 October 1990, the Federal Republic of Germany has declared that "through the accession of the German Democratic Republic to the Federal Republic of Germany with effect from 3 October 1990, the two German States have united to form one sovereign State". This letter was accompanied by a verbal note dated 3 October 1990 informing WIPO that "with regard to the continued application of treaties of the Federal Republic of Germany and the treatment of treaties of the German Democratic Republic following its accession to the Federal Republic of Germany with effect from 3 October 1990, the Treaty of 31 August 1990 between the Federal Republic of Germany and the German Democratic Republic on the establishment of German unity (Unification Treaty) contains the following relevant provisions:
1. Article II
Treaties of the Federal Republic of Germany
The contracting parties proceed on the understanding the international treaties and agreements to which the Federal Republic of Germany is a contracting party . . . shall retain their validity and that the rights and obligations arising therefrom . . . shall also relate to the territory specified in Article 3 of this Treaty". (Länder of Brandenburg, Mecklenburg-Western Pomerania, Saxe, Saxe-Anhalt and Thuringia as well as the sector of the Land of Berlin where the Fundamental Law of the Federal Republic of Germany was not applicable.)

[4] At the time of the deposit of the instrument of accession with the Secretary-General of the United Nations, the Hungarian Government made the following declarations: "In the opinion of the Hungarian People's Republic, Article 9, paragraphs (1) and (2) of the Convention have a discriminatory character. The Convention is a general, multilateral one and therefore every State has the right to be a party to it, in accordance with the basic principles of international law."

"The Hungarian People's Republic declares that the provisions of Article 11, paragraph (3), of the Convention are inconsistent with the principles of the independence of colonial countries and peoples, formulated, inter alia, also in Resolution No. 1514(XV) of the United Nations General Assembly."

[5] On 11 January 1973, the Government of Sweden deposited with the Director-General of the World Intellectual Property Organisation a notification dated 28 December 1972 declaring that, in accordance with Article 7(4) of the Convention for the Protection of Producers of Phonograms against Unauthorised Duplication of their Phonograms, adopted at Geneva on 29 October 1971, it will apply the criterion according to which it affords protection to producers of phonograms solely on the basis of the place of first fixation instead of the criterion of the nationality of the producer.

According to a notification dated 30 June 1986, the Government of Sweden declared that, with effect on 1 July 1986, it withdraws its declaration, made at the time of deposit of its instrument of ratification of the Convention for the Protection of Producers of Phonograms against Unauthorised Duplication of their Phonograms, that it will apply the criterion according to which it affords protection to producers of phonograms solely on the basis of the place of first fixation instead of the criterion of the nationality of the producer.

TABLE G

Convention Relating to the Distribution of Programme-Carrying Signals Transmitted by Satellite

State	Date of Entry into Force	Notifications and Reservations		
		Article 2(2)	Article 8(2)	Article 8(3)(a)
Australia	26 Oct 1990			
Austria	6 Aug 1982			
Germany[1]	25 Aug 1979	Yes, 25 yrs		
Greece	22 Oct 1991			
Italy	7 Jul 1981	Yes, 25 yrs		
Kenya	25 Aug 1979			
Mexico	25 Aug 1979			
Morocco	30 Jun 1983			
Nicaragua	25 Aug 1979			
Panama	25 Sep 1985			
Peru	7 Aug 1985			
Russian Federation[2]	25 Dec 1991			
Slovenia	25 Jun 1991			
Switzerland	24 Sep 1993			
USA	7 Mar 1985			
Yugoslavia	25 Aug 1979			

Notes

[1] The Federal Republic of Germany has declared that through the accession of the German Democratic Republic to the Federal Republic of Germany with effect from 3 October 1990, the two German States have united to form one sovereign State. With regard to the continued application of treaties of the Federal Republic of Germany and the treatment of treaties of the German Democratic Republic following its accession to the Federal Republic of Germany with effect from 3 October 1990, the Treaty of 31 August 1990 between the Federal Republic of Germany and the German Democratic Republic on the establishment of German unity (Unification Treaty) contains the following relevant provisions:
"1. Article 11
Treaties of the Federal Republic of Germany
The contracting parties proceed on the understanding the international treaties and agreements to which the Federal Republic of Germany is a contracting party . . . shall retain their validity and that the rights and obligations arising therefrom . . . shall also relate to the territory specified in Article 3 of this Treaty". (Länder of Brandenburg, Mecklenburg-Western Pomerania, Saxe, Saxe-Anhalt and Thuringia as well as the sector of the Land of Berlin where the Fundamental Law of the Federal Republic of Germany was not applicable.)

[2] The Russian Federation has declared that the participation of the Union of Soviet Socialist Republics in all the conventions, agreements and other instruments of international law concluded therein or under its auspices is continued by the Russian Federation and that to that end, the title 'Union of Soviet Socialist Republics' should be replaced by 'Russian Federation'. Consequently, the Russian Federation is bound by the convention relating to the Distribution of Programme-carrying Signals Transmitted by Satellite since 20 January 1989, the date on which this instrument came into force for the Union of Soviet Socialist Republics.

TABLE H

European Convention on Transfrontier Televison

States	Date of Entry into Force	Notifications and Reservations			
		Article 26.2	Article 31.1	Article 32.1.a	Article 32.1.b
Austria	signed only				
Cyprus	1 May 1993				
Finland	signed only				
France[1]	signed only				
Germany[2]	signed only				
Greece	signed only				
Holy See	1 May 1993				
Hungary	signed only				
Italy	1 May 1993				
Liechten-stein	signed only				
Luxembourg	signed only				
Malta	1 May 1993				
Netherlands	signed only				
Norway	signed only			Yes	
Poland	1 May 1993				
Portugal	signed only				
San Marino	1 May 1993				
Spain	signed only				
Sweden	signed only				
Switzerland	1 May 1993			Yes	
Turkey	signed only				
United Kingdom	1 May 1993				

Notes

[1] France made the following declaration on signature of the Convention on 12 February 1991:

In the same spirit as at the time of the adoption of the Community's "Television Without Frontiers" Directive in October 1989, France has decided to sign the Council of Europe's Convention on Transfrontier Television with a view to promoting the freedom of information as well as the exchange and production of audio-visual programmes in Europe.

Now that the Audio-visual Eureka project is beginning to bear fruit, France intends to make every endeavour to ensure that the Convention contributes in a wider geographical framework to the promotion of European programmes and the emergence of a structured and competitive continental market.

This Convention was not designed, and should not be used, to justify projects whose sole purpose is to circumvent national and Community regulations intended to encourage European programming and production.

In committing itself, therefore, France is sure that all the signatory countries to the Convention share the same concerns, as any interpretation or measure contrary to such principles would constitute a serious undermining of the very foundation of the policy of European audio-visual co-operation.

[2] The Federal Republic declared that "... it would like to make it clear that its signing of the Convention does not at the same time prejudice its consent to the European Communities' accession to the Convention".

Index